PREACHING GOD'S TRANSFORMING JUSTICE

A Lectionary Commentary, Year A

Edited by
Ronald J. Allen
Dale P. Andrews
Dawn Ottoni-Wilhelm

WESTMINSTER
JOHN KNOX PRESS
LOUISVILLE · KENTUCKY

First edition
Published by Westminster John Knox Press
Louisville, Kentucky

13 14 15 16 17 18 19 20 21 22—10 9 8 7 6 5 4 3 2 1

Book design by Sharon Adams
Cover design by Eric Walljasper, Minneapolis, MN
Cover artwork by Carlos Cazares titled The Fish, *www.carloscazares.com.*

Library of Congress Cataloging-in-Publication Data

Preaching god's transforming justice : a lectionary commentary, year A / Edited by Ronald J. Allen, Dale P. Andrews, Dawn Ottoni-Wilhelm. — First edition
    pages cm
    Includes index.
    ISBN 978-0-664-23453-9 (alk. paper)
    1. Social justice—Sermons. 2. Social justice—Biblical teaching. 3. Church year sermons. 4. Common lectionary (1992). Year A. I. Allen, Ronald J. (Ronald James), 1949– II. Andrews, Dale P., 1961– III. Wilhelm, Dawn Ottoni.
    BS680.J8P744 2013
    251'.6—dc23

2012047999

Contents

Preface

The editors are grateful to the members of our households—spouses and children—not only for love and understanding during the preparation of these volumes but also for conversation, child care, and running to the store for necessary supplies of chocolate, coffee, and other things important to editorial work. We recognize our presidents, deans, and colleagues for encouragement, questions, and suggestions. The editors particularly thank the ninety persons who wrote for this series. To their already overflowing lives as activists, ministers, and scholars, they added responsibility for preparing the articles for these volumes. We honor Jon Berquist for his formative role in this project and for multiple forms of support. The editors express appreciation to J. B. Blue and Song Bok Jon, graduate students at Boston University School of Theology, who sacrificed time from their own academic responsibilities to engage in research on the Holy Days for Justice. The editors and contributors are responsible for limitations that result from not following the suggestions of these learned colleagues.

We send this book forward with the prayer that God will use it to help recreate the world as a community of love, peace, freedom, mutuality, respect, security, and abundance. May it be a resource for preaching that, under the influence of the Holy Spirit, empowers social transformation.

Introduction

Many people today yearn to live in a world of love, peace, freedom, mutuality, respect, security, and abundance for all. The Bible calls this combination of qualities justice. The best of the Bible and Christian tradition envision the heart of God's own mission as re-creating the world as a realm of love and justice. Joining God in this mission is at the heart of the calling of the preacher and the congregation. The aim of this three-volume series is to empower sermons as active agents in God's mission.

Ninety preachers and scholars contribute to this work. These writers are known for their insight into social dimensions of the divine purposes as well as for their capacity to interpret the social vision boldly and sensitively. Approximately half of the writers are women and half are men; about 40 percent of them African American, Hispanic, Asian American, or Native American.

Preaching for Justice: A World of Love, Peace, Freedom, Mutuality, Respect, Security, and Abundance

This commentary is a resource for preaching for a world of justice from the deepest theological convictions of biblical texts. *Preaching God's Transforming Justice* is distinctive in two ways. First, while other aids for preaching from the lectionary sometimes discuss matters of social justice, this series is the first commentary on the Revised Common Lectionary to highlight God's life-giving intentions for the social world from start to finish.[1] *Preaching God's Transforming Justice* is not simply a mirror of other lectionary commentaries (such as the impressive *Feasting on the Word: Preaching the Revised Common Lectionary*) but concentrates on how the lectionary readings can help the preacher identify and reflect theologically and ethically on the social implications of the biblical readings. Second, this series introduces twenty-two Holy Days for Justice. Explained further below, these days are intended to enlarge the church's awareness of the depth and insistence of God's call for justice and of the many ways that call comes to the church and world today.

The comments on the biblical texts are intended to be more than notes on contemporary social issues. The comments are designed to help preachers and congregations develop a deep and broad theological vision out of which to interpret the social world. Furthermore, this book aims to provide practical guidance for living more justly as individuals and communities.

Special Feature: Twenty-Two Holy Days for Justice

This commentary augments the traditional liturgical calendar by providing resources for twenty-two special Holy Days for Justice. The title for these noteworthy days, suggested by Professor Amy-Jill Levine of Vanderbilt University, requires explanation. God's mission for justice is holy. Consequently, the church's commitment to justice is holy. Some of the events, however, that call forth these special days are not holy. Indeed, some days—such as Yom haShoah (which remembers the murder of six million Jewish people by the Nazis)—are occasions for mourning. However, at the same time these days also call the church to take bold and powerful actions to join the holy work

---

1. The Revised Common Lectionary (RCL) was developed by the Consultation on Common Texts, an ecumenical consultation of liturgical scholars and denominational representatives from the United States and Canada. The RCL provides a collection of readings from Scripture to be used during worship in a schedule that follows the seasons of the church year: Advent, Christmas, Epiphany Day, Lent, Easter, Day of Pentecost, Ordinary Time. In addition, the RCL provides for a uniform set of readings to be used across denominations or other church bodies.

The RCL provides a reading from the Hebrew Bible, a Psalm response to that reading, a Gospel, and an Epistle for each preaching occasion of the year. It is presented in a three-year cycle, with each year centered around one of the Synoptic Gospels. Year A largely follows the Gospel of Matthew, Year B largely follows Mark, and Year C largely follows Luke. Selections from John are also read each year, especially during Advent, Lent, and Easter.

The RCL offers two tracks of Hebrew Bible texts for the Season after Pentecost or Ordinary Time: a semicontinuous track, which moves through stories and characters in the Hebrew Bible, and a complementary track, which ties the Hebrew Bible texts to the theme of the Gospel texts for that day. Both tracks are included in this volume.

For more information about the Revised Common Lectionary, visit the official RCL Web site at http://lectionary.library.vanderbilt.edu/ or see *The Revised Common Lectionary: The Consultation on Common Texts* (Nashville: Abingdon Press, 1992).

of God in attempting to transform the circumstances that led to lamentation. We can never undo pain and suffering, but we can try to reshape the world to minimize the danger of such things recurring, and to encourage possibilities for people and nature to live together in justice.

Each Holy Day for Justice derives from either a person or an event that helps the contemporary community become aware of arenas in the world that cry for justice. These Holy Days bridge significant phenomena in our history and present culture that do not receive adequate attention in the church's liturgical calendar or may not otherwise be noted in the congregation. They draw our attention to circumstances in need of social transformation.

Each Holy Day for Justice has a different focus. In *Preaching God's Transforming Justice* these days are placed close to the Sunday on which they occur in the Christian year and the ordinary calendar. When reaching a Holy Day for Justice in the lectionary, the preacher can choose whether to follow the readings from the Revised Common Lectionary or to work instead with the readings and themes of the Holy Day for Justice.[2] The concerns highlighted in these special days may also inspire preachers to bring those concerns to the fore in sermons prepared in conversation with the traditional lectionary readings.

In the list of Holy Days for Justice below, the editors place in parentheses a date or season when the congregation might naturally observe a Holy Day for Justice. The dates for many of the Holy Days for Justice are already widely accepted, such as the dates for World AIDS Day, the Universal Declaration of Human Rights, Martin Luther King Jr. Day, Salt March, Earth Day, Yom haShoah, and the Fourth of July. The editors assigned the dates for other Holy Days for Justice in conversation with scholars who work closely with the concerns of those days and with communities closely related to the origin of the person or concern at the center of the day. Of course, preachers and worship planners are free to observe the Holy Days for Justice on other dates that fit more naturally into the congregation's local calendar.

The Holy Days for Justice are:

1. World AIDS Day (December 1)
2. Universal Declaration of Human Rights (December 10)
3. Martin Luther King Jr. Day (January 15)
4. Asian American Heritage Day (February 19)
5. International Women's Day (March 8)

---

2. In addition, the Revised Common Lectionary already sets aside possible readings for All Saints' Day and Thanksgiving. The specific dates of some of the Holy Days for Justice change from year to year. These days are placed in the commentary in the season of the lectionary year when they typically occur.

6. Salt March Day: Marching with the Poor (March 12)
7. Oscar Romero of the Americas Day (March 24)
8. César Chávez Day (March 31)
9. Earth Day (April 22)
10. Holocaust Remembrance Day: Yom haShoah (27th of Nissan, usually from early April to early May)
11. Peace in the Home: Shalom Bayit (second Sunday in May)
12. Juneteenth: Let Freedom Ring (June 19)
13. Gifts of Sexuality and Gender (June 29)
14. Fourth of July: Seeking Liberty and Justice for All
15. Sojourner Truth Day (August 18)
16. Simchat Torah: Joy of the Torah (mid-September to early October)
17. International Day of Prayer and Witness for Peace (September 21)
18. Peoples Native to the Americas Day (fourth Friday in September)
19. World Communion Sunday (first Sunday in October)
20. Night of Power (27th Night of Ramadan: From 2011 through 2020 the date moves from September to August, July, June, May, and April)
21. World Food Day (October 16)
22. Children's Sabbaths (third weekend in October or another date that works for the congregation)

The discussions of these days in the commentary are distinctive in three ways. (1) In the case of almost every special day (with the exception of Simchat Torah: Joy of the Torah), the editors selected four biblical texts that relate to these special emphases, including a reading from the Torah, Prophets, and Writings, a reading from a Psalm, a reading from a Gospel, and another from an Epistle. The editors chose the texts for each day in the hope that the passages can become good conversation partners in helping the congregation reflect on how the day enlarges the congregation's vision and practice of justice. Most of the texts were chosen because they support potential emphases in the day, but some were chosen because they give the preacher the opportunity to enter into critical dialogue with the text or with the way the biblical text has been used in the church or the culture. While a few of the biblical texts for the Holy Days for Justice duplicate passages in the Revised Common Lectionary, most of the texts for the Holy Days for Justice are not found in the lectionary. (2) Each day is introduced by a brief paragraph offering a perspective on why that day is included. We repeat the same introductory paragraph in all three volumes. (3) Each day also includes a quote from a figure or document in the past or the present that voices a provocative perspective on the concerns represented by that day. For example, in Year A on Martin Luther King Jr. Day, the preacher is presented with an excerpt from *Strength to Love*.

Some readers may initially be put off by some of these selections, especially days that also appear in the civic calendar in the United States, such as "Fourth of July: Seeking Liberty and Justice for All." These days are not intended to promote uncritical celebration of present culture. On the contrary, the appearance of these days can become the occasion for the preacher to reflect critically with the congregation on the themes of those days. Some of the motifs associated in popular culture with the Fourth of July, for instance, run against the grain of God's best hopes for the human family. In the name of being faithful, some preachers studiously avoid speaking about days suggested by the civic calendar. However, the congregation may too easily construe such silence as the preacher's consent to the culture's prevailing mind-set. The sermon can attempt to redress the prevailing cultural mind-set that either neglects attention to questions of justice or actively promotes injustice.

The Holy Days for Justice address the criticism that the Revised Common Lectionary does not adequately represent biblical texts that deal with matters of justice as fully as those texts are represented in the Bible. Such special days might also enlarge the vision of the preacher and the congregation while offering preachers a venue for addressing matters that are sometimes hard to reach when following the lectionary. For the congregation that may be hesitant to consider such matters, the appearance of these emphases in a formal lectionary commentary might add to the preacher's authority for speaking about them.

God's Vision for the Social World

The purposes of this commentary series are rooted in the core of God's vision for the social world. To be sure, the Bible is a diverse document in the sense that its parts were written at different times and places, in different cultural settings, and from different theological and ethical points of view—for example, Priestly, Deuteronomic, Wisdom, and apocalyptic. Nevertheless, the different materials in the Bible share the common perspective that God intends for all individuals and communities (including the world of nature) to live together in justice.

The Priestly theologians begin the Bible with the vision in Genesis 1 by picturing God creating a world in which each and every entity has a particular place and purpose and in which all entities—the ecosphere, animals, and human beings—live together in covenantal community. The role of the human being is to help the different entities live together in the mutual support that God envisions. The aim of the Ten Commandments and Israel's other laws is to create a social community that embodies how God wants people to live together in blessing. The Priestly theologians show special concern for ensuring that the poor and marginalized experience providence through care practiced by the community. Israel is to model how God wants all peoples to live together in blessing (Gen. 12:1–3). Israel is to be a light to the nations in these regards (Isa. 42:6). The church later understands its message to be grafted onto that of Israel (e.g., the church shares in the mission of being a light in the world, Matt. 5:13–14).

The Deuteronomic thinkers envisioned Israel as a community not only in covenant with God, but also as a community whose members were in covenant with one another so that all could live in love, peace, and security. Deuteronomy 15:7–8 epitomizes this attitude. "If there is among you anyone in need . . . do not be hard-hearted or tight-fisted toward your needy neighbor. You should rather open your hand, willingly lending enough to meet the need, whatever it may be." The Deuteronomic monarch is to rule with a copy of the Torah present at all times and is not to be "above other members of the community nor turning aside from the commandment" (Deut. 17:19–20). The monarch is responsible to God and to the community for seeing that justice is enacted in all aspects of Jewish life. The covenant includes nature such that when the people are faithful, nature blesses them, but when they are unfaithful, nature itself curses them (Deut. 28:1–45).

The Wisdom literature encourages practices that not only provide for individual and household prosperity but also build up the community. The wise life shows respect for the poor as full members of the community (Sir. 4:1–10). The Wisdom literature cautions the prosperous not to become self-absorbed by their possessions but to use their resources to strengthen the community. Indeed, the wise are to "speak out for those who cannot speak, for the rights of all the destitute . . . [to] defend the rights of the poor and needy" (Prov. 31:8–9). Moreover, the sages thought that God charged the natural order with wisdom so that by paying attention to the way in which the elements of nature work together, human beings can learn how God wants human beings to live as individuals and in community, as we can see in the case of the ant modeling wisdom (Prov. 6:6).

The apocalyptic theologians believed that the present world—both the social sphere and nature—is so broken, unjust, and violent that God must replace it with a new world, often called the realm of God. The apocalyptic book of 4 Ezra (2 Esdras) vividly expresses this hope:

> It is for you that Paradise is opened, the tree of life is planted, the age to come is revealed, plenty is provided, a city is built, rest is appointed, goodness is established and wisdom perfected beforehand. The root of evil is sealed up from you, illness is banished from you, and death is hidden; hell has fled and corruption has been forgotten; sorrows

have passed away, and in the end the treasure of immortality is made manifest.[3] (4 Ezra 8:52–56)

In this new world all relationships and situations manifest God's purpose. Those who defy God's desires through idolatry, exploitation of the poor, and violence are condemned.

Paul, Mark, Matthew, Luke, and most other early Christian writers share this general viewpoint (e.g., Rom. 8:18–25; Mark 13:24–27). These first-century theologians believed that the life, ministry, death, and resurrection of Jesus signaled that the final and complete manifestation of the realm of God had begun in a limited way in the ministry of Jesus and would come in its fullness with the return of Jesus. The ministry of Jesus both points to that realm and embodies it. Jesus' disciples are to alert others to the presence and coming of the realm and to live in the present as if the realm is fully here. The church is to embody the transformed world.

From the perspective of the Bible, God's vision for the interrelated communities of humankind and nature is, through and through, a social vision. It involves the intertwining relationships of God with humankind and nature, of human communities with one another, and of human communities with nature. Marjorie Suchocki, a major contemporary theologian, uses the evocative phrase "inclusive well-being" to sum up God's desire for every created entity to live in love, peace, justice, dignity, freedom, and abundance in a framework of mutually supportive community.[4] Anything that threatens the well-being of any entity in the created world goes against the purposes of God.

Individual Bible Readings and Implications for Social Justice and Transformation

Every passage in the Bible has social implications. In connection with each text in the lectionary, the commentators in this series help the congregation envision God's purposes for human community. Some texts are quite direct in this way. For example, Amos exhorts, "Let justice roll down like waters, and righteousness like an ever-flowing stream" (Amos 5:24). The prophet wants the people to practice justice. Other texts are less direct but are still potent in their implications. According to the book of Acts, Priscilla was a teacher of the gospel alongside her spouse, Aquila (Acts 18:24–28). From this and many

3. "The Fourth Book of Ezra," trans. Bruce M. Metzger, in *The Old Testament Pseudepigrapha: Apocalyptic Literature and Testaments*, ed. James H. Charlesworth (Garden City, NY: Doubleday & Co., 1983), 1:544. Fourth Ezra was written in the late first century CE and is sometimes known as 2 Esdras.

4. Marjorie Suchocki, *The Fall to Violence: Original Sin in Relational Theology* (New York: Continuum, 1994), 66.

other texts, we glimpse the vital role of women in the leadership of the earliest churches (e.g., Mark 16:8; Luke 8:1–3; Acts 9:36–42; 16:11–15; Rom. 16:1–3, 6, 7, 12; 1 Cor. 1:11; Phil. 4:2–4).

The contributors to these volumes articulate what the biblical writers hoped would happen in the social world of those who heard these texts in their original settings and point to ways in which interaction with the biblical texts helps today's congregations more fully embrace and enact God's intent for all to experience inclusive well-being. The following are among the questions the writers consider:

- What are God's life-giving intentions in each text?
- What does a particular text (in the context of its larger theological world) envision as a community that embodies God's social vision, a vision in which all live in inclusive well-being?
- What are the benefits of that vision for humankind and (as appropriate) nature?
- How do human beings and nature fall short of God's possibilities when they do not follow or sustain that vision?
- Do individuals or communities get hurt in the world of the text or in the way that text has been interpreted?
- What needs to happen for justice, healing, re-creation, and inclusive well-being?

At the same time, writers sometimes criticize aspects of the occasional biblical text whose social vision does not measure up to the fullness of God's intentions. For example, according to Ezekiel, God ordered marks placed on faithful people who lamented abominations that took place in Israel. God then commanded some of the faithful to murder the unfaithful. "Pass through the city . . . and kill; your eye shall not spare, and you shall show no pity. Cut down old men, young men and young women, little children and women, but touch no one who has the mark" (Ezek. 9:5–6). This passage invites the reader to believe that God commanded murder. The first letter of Peter asserts, "Slaves, accept the authority of your masters with all deference, not only those who are kind and gentle but also those who are harsh. For it is a credit to you if, being aware of God, you endure pain while suffering unjustly" (1 Pet. 2:18–19). This passage assumes the validity of slavery and encourages recipients to accept being abused.

Texts such as these do not measure up to the Bible's highest vision of God's desire for a just world; hence, many preachers cannot commend such barbed texts as positive guidance for today's community. Instead, such a preacher critiques the passage. However, even when the preacher cannot fully endorse what a text invites the congregation to believe and do, the appearance of theologically and ethically problematic texts in the lectionary can open an important door for a conversation among preacher and congregation regarding what they most truly believe concerning God's social vision. The text may not be directly instructive, but the congregation's encounter with the text can be an important occasion of theological and ethical reflection.

Naming and Confronting Systems That Frustrate God's Purposes

Individuals acting alone and with others can defy God's purposes for humankind and nature. But beyond individual and small-group actions, a key insight to emerge in recent generations is that systemic forces distort God's purposes for humankind and the larger created world. Ethicists often refer to such phenomena as systemic evil.

A system is a transpersonal network of attitudes, values, and behaviors that shape the lives of individuals and communities. Systemic evil creates force fields that push individuals and communities to distort God's purposes in the social world. Systems can affect communities as small as the Wednesday night prayer group and as large as nations and transnational associations. Examples of systemic evils that subvert God's life-giving purposes are racism, sexism, neocolonialism, ageism, nationalism, classism, heterosexism, and ecological destruction.

Preachers need to recognize and name systemic distortions of God's purposes for the social community. While this analysis is important, it sometimes leaves individuals and congregations feeling impotent in the face of massive structural forces. When possible, the writers in this series urge preachers to give these concerns a human face and to offer specific insights and stories that help congregations envision practical steps that they can take to join God in seeking to transform the social world. What attitudes and actions can individuals and congregations take to become agents of transformation? These writers want congregations to feel empowered to make a difference. We hope that each comment will offer a horizon of hope for the preacher and the congregation.

The Preacher Speaks from, to, and beyond the Local Context

The importance of taking account of the context of the congregation is a permeating emphasis today in preaching and more broadly in theological scholarship. The preacher is called to understand the congregation as a culture in its own right. The preacher should conduct an exegesis of the congregation that reveals the events, memories, values, practices, attitudes, feelings, patterns of relationship (especially power relationships), physical spaces, and larger systems that combine to make the congregation a distinct culture.

This commentary does not intend to provide the minister with prepackaged ideas for sermons but urges ministers to begin their approach to preaching on matters of justice from inside the culture of the congregation. The local pastor who has a thick understanding of the local community knows much better than a scholar in a far-off city how the life of that congregation needs to develop in order to witness more fully to God's purposes.

The preacher should typically speak *from* and *to* the local context. Rather than impose a social vision that the preacher has found in a book of theological ethics, on the Internet, or at the latest clergy network for peace and justice, the preacher can approach matters of social justice from inside the worldview of the congregation. Hence, one can usually identify points of contact between the world of the congregation and the need for transformation. The preacher can then use the base of identification and trust between the pulpit and the pew to speak *to* the congregation. To help the congregation participate more fully in God's transformative movement, the preacher will typically need to help the congregation think beyond itself.

From this point of view, the contributors to *Preaching God's Transforming Justice* intend to be conversation partners in helping preachers identify particular areas in which the congregation might reinforce patterns of thought and behavior that manifest their deepest theological convictions. We hope the book will help congregations to grow in the direction of God's social vision and to find steps they can take to become agents of justice.

Recent literature in preaching leads preachers to think of the congregation not just as a collection of individuals but as a *community*, the *body* of Christ. While sermons should help individuals imagine their particular social witnesses, sermons should also be addressed to the congregation as community and its corporate social witness.

Moreover, the congregation is itself a social world. While the larger goal of the book is to help preachers move the congregation toward reflection and mission in the larger social arena, some texts may lead the preacher to help the listeners reflect on how the internal life of the congregation can more fully witness to God's life-giving purposes.

Prophetic Preaching with a Pastoral Goal

In the broad sense, this book calls for prophetic preaching. We think of prophetic preaching in contrast to two popular notions. From one popular perspective, prophetic preaching predicts specific future events, especially those that point to the return of Jesus. This way of thinking does not catch the fullness of prophetic preaching in the Bible itself. A second popular viewpoint associates prophetic preaching with condemnation. This prophetic preacher identifies what the text is against and what is wrong in the social world, sometimes denouncing the congregation and others. These sermons can chastise the congregation without providing a word of grace and empowerment. This perspective is also incomplete.

The editors of *Preaching God's Transforming Justice* regard the purpose of all preaching as helping the congregation and others interpret the world from the standpoint of God's life-giving purposes. Preaching seeks to build up the congregation as a community of witness and to help the world embody the divine realm. The goal of all preaching is pastoral in the root sense of building up the flock so that the congregation can fulfill God's purposes. The word "pastoral" derives from the world of flocks and shepherds in which the shepherd (the pastor) did whatever was necessary to maintain the health of the flock.

From the perspective of the Bible, the prophet is a kind of ombudsperson who compares the actual behavior of the community with God's purposes of inclusive blessing. The special call of the prophet is to help the community recognize where it falls short of those purposes and what the community needs to do to return to them. On the one hand, a prophet such as Amos concentrated on how the community had departed from God's purposes by exploiting the poor and, consequently, faced judgment. On the other hand, a prophet such as Second Isaiah called attention to the fact that the community in exile did not trust in the promise of God to return them to their homeland. In both cases, the community is not living up to the fullness of God's purposes. While the prophet may need to confront the congregation, the prophet's goal is to prompt the congregation to take steps toward transformation. Prophetic preaching ultimately aims at helping the congregation to identify what needs transformation and how to take part.

Representative Social Phenomena

Preaching God's Transforming Justice urges preachers and communities toward conscious and critical theological reflection on things that are happening in the contemporary social world from the perspective of God's purpose to re-create the world as a realm of love, peace, freedom, mutuality, abundance, and respect for all. Nevertheless, some preachers refer to a limited number of social phenomena in their sermons. A preacher's hermeneutical imagination is sometimes enlarged by pondering a panorama of representative social phenomena that call for theological and ethical interpretation, such as the following:

Abortion
Absent fathers
Addictions
Affirmative action
Aging
Animal rights
Anti-Semitism
Arms sales
Church and nation
Civil religion
Classism
Colonialism
Consumerism
Death penalty
Disability perspectives
Diversity
Domestic violence
Drugs
Ecological issues
Economic exploitation
Education
Empire
Energy
Eurocentrism
Exclusivism
Flight to the suburbs
Foster care
Gambling

Gender orientation
LGBTQA
Geneva Convention
Genocide
Gentrification
Glass ceiling
Greed
Gun control
Health care
Homelessness
Housing
Human rights
Hunger
Idols (contemporary)
Immigration
Islam and Christianity
Islamophobia
Judaism and
    Christianity
Language (inclusive,
    repressive)
Margins of society
Militarism
Multiculturalism
Nationalism
Native American rights
Neocolonialism
Peace movements
Pluralism

Police brutality
Pollution
Pornography
Postcolonialism
Poverty
Prisons
Public schools/private
    schools
Racism
Repression
Reproductive rights
Sexism
Socialism
Stranger
Systemic perspectives
Terrorism
Torture
Transnational
    corporations
Tribalism
Unemployment
Uninsured people
U.S. having no single
    racial/ethnic major-
    ity by 2040
Violence
White privilege
Xenophobia

This catalog is not suggested as a checklist of social issues that a preacher should cover in a given preaching cycle. Returning to an earlier theme, the minister who is in touch with the local culture can have a sense of where God's vision for justice interacts with particular social phenomena. Nonetheless, such a list may help some ministers think more broadly about possible points of contact between the core theological convictions of the church and the social world.[5]

5. A preacher might find it useful to review regularly the social forces that are current in the sphere of the congregation and in the larger world. Preachers can easily slip into thinking about social perspectives from limited and dated points of view. Preachers may find it helpful

Index of Passages in the Order of Books of the Bible

For preachers who do not regularly preach from the lectionary, and for preachers who want to look up a particular passage but do not know where it is in the lectionary, an index of passages discussed in the commentary is at the end of the volume. This index lists biblical texts in the order in which they are found in the Bible.

The contributors typically discuss the biblical texts in the following order: first lesson(s) from the Torah, Prophets, and Writings; the Psalm(s); the Epistle; and the Gospel. However, a writer will occasionally take up the texts in a different sequence as part of his or her interpretive strategy for the day.

Inclusive Language, Expansive Language

This series uses inclusive language when referring to humankind. In other words, when contributors refer to people in general, they use language that includes all of their intended audience (e.g., humankind, humanity, people). When a writer refers to a particular gender (female or male), the gender-specific referent is used.

We seek to use expansive language when referring to God. In other words, the contributors draw on various names, attributes, and images of God known to us in Scripture and in our individual and corporate encounter of God in worship. We avoid using exclusively masculine references to God. When a Scripture passage repeatedly uses language for God that is male, we have sought more gender-inclusive emendations that are consistent with the intent of the original. Readers searching for an entire inclusive-language translation might try *The Inclusive Bible: The First Egalitarian Translation*.[6]

The Bible and Christian tradition use the term "Lord" to speak of both God and Jesus. The word "lord" is masculine. The English word "Lord" derives from a time when much of the European social world was hierarchical, with the lord and lady at the top and with human beings arranged in a pyramid of descending social power with the upper classes at the top and with males having authority over women. People in the upper reaches of the pyramid are authorized to dominate those below them. While we try to minimize the occurrence of the title "Lord," occasional writers in this book use "Lord" for God to call attention to God's absolute sovereignty; these writers do not

---

to interview members of the congregation regarding the social phenomena that are most in the consciousness of the congregation.

6. Priests for Equality, *The Inclusive Bible: The First Egalitarian Translation* (Lanham, MD: Rowman & Littlefield, 2007).

intend for the use of the expression "Lord" to authorize masculine superiority or the detailed social pyramid implied in the history of the word. Indeed, this book sees the purposes of God pointing toward a human community in which hierarchical domination is dismantled and power is shared.

Although the historical Jesus was a male, he announced the coming of the realm of God, a social world that is egalitarian with respect to gender and social power. In the hope of evoking these latter associations (and minimizing the pyramidal associations with "Lord"), we have shifted the designations of some historic days in the Christian Year that highlight aspects of the ministry of Jesus from lordship language to the language of "Jesus" and "Christ": Nativity of Jesus, Baptism of Jesus, Resurrection of Jesus, and Reign of Christ (in place of Nativity of the Lord, Baptism of the Lord, Resurrection of the Lord, and Christ the King).

We have also tried to speak expansively of the realm of God (NRSV: kingdom of God) by using terms such as "realm," "reign," "rule," "dominion," "kin-dom," and "holy commonwealth." The word "kingdom" appears where the author has specifically requested it.

Language for the Parts of the Bible

The contemporary world is a time of experimentation and critical reflection regarding how to refer to the parts of the Bible that many Christian generations referred to as the Old and New Testaments. The discussion arises because in much contemporary usage, the word "old" suggests worn-out and outdated, while "new" often implies "better" and "improved." Many Christians believe that the unexplained use of the phrases Old Testament and New Testament can contribute to supersessionism: the conviction that new and improved Christianity has taken the place of old and outdated Judaism. The old covenant is no longer in force, but has been replaced by the new covenant. When used without interpretation, this way of speaking contributes to injustice by supporting anti-Judaism and anti-Semitism. In an attempt to use language that is more just, many people today are exploring several ways forward.

As a part of the contemporary exploration, the writers in this series use a variety of expressions for these parts of the Bible. There is no fully satisfactory way of speaking. We note now the most common expressions in this series and invite the reader to remember the strengths and weaknesses of each approach.

Some leaders think that today's community can use the expressions Old and New Testaments if the church explains what that language does and does not mean.[7] In antiquity old things were often valued and honored. Moreover, the words "old" and "new" can imply nothing more than chronology: The literature of the Old Testament is older than that of the New. The church would then use the terms Old and New Testaments without casting aspersion on Judaism and without suggesting that God has made Christianity a much purer and truer religion. Occasional writers in the series use the phrases Old Testament and New Testament in this way. However, a growing number of speakers and writers think that the words Old Testament and New Testament are so deeply associated with negative pictures of Jewish people, writings, institutions, and practices that, even when carefully defined, the language feeds negative perceptions.

"Hebrew Bible" and "Hebrew Scriptures" are popular ways of referring to the first part of the Bible. These titles came about because English versions are not based primarily on the Septuagint (the translation of the Hebrew Scriptures into Greek in the third and second centuries BCE) but are translated from Hebrew (and Aramaic) manuscripts in consultation with the Septuagint. However, the designation "Hebrew Bible" raises the question of what to call the twenty-seven books that make up the other part of the Bible. We cannot call the other books the "Greek Scriptures" or the "Greek Bible" because the Septuagint is also in Greek. We cannot call them the "Christian Scriptures" or the "Christian Bible" since the church honors the entire Bible.

Occasionally Christians refer to the Old Testament as the "Jewish Bible." This nomenclature is unsatisfactory because people could understand it to mean that the first part of the Bible belongs only to the Jewish community and is not constitutive for the church. Furthermore, the Christian version differs from the Jewish Tanakh in the way that some of the books are ordered, named, and divided.

The designations "First and Second Testaments" are increasingly popular because many people see them as setting out a chronological relationship between the two bodies of literature—the First Testament came prior to the Second. However, in competitive North American culture, especially in the United States, "first" can imply first in value while "second" can imply something not as good as the first. The winner receives first place. Second place is often a disappointment. Moreover, "second" can imply second best or secondhand.

Seeking a way of referring to the Bible that respects its diversity but suggests its continuities, and that promotes respect for Judaism, writers in this

---

7. On this discussion, see further Ronald J. Allen, "Torah, Prophets, Writings, Gospels, Letters: A New Name for the Old Book," *Encounter* 68 (2007): 53–63.

series sometimes refer to the parts of the Bible as Torah, Prophets, Writings, Gospels, and Letters. This latter practice adapts a Jewish way of speaking of the Scriptures as TANAKH, an acronym derived from the Hebrew for Torah, Prophets, and Writings (*torah*, *neviim*, *ketuviim*), and adds the categories of Gospels and Letters.[8] To be sure, the books in Tanakh are divided and arranged differently than in the Christian Bible. Furthermore, while some may object that the books of Acts, Hebrews, and Revelation do not fall into these categories, we note that Acts is less a separate genre and more a continuation of the Gospel of Luke. In the strict sense, Revelation has the form of a letter. Although scholars today recognize that Hebrews is an early Christian sermon, it likely circulated much like a letter.

All designations for the parts of the Bible are vexed by the fact that different churches include different books. We should really speak of a Roman Catholic canon, several Orthodox canons, and a Protestant canon. As a concession to our inability to distinguish every permutation, we ask the reader to receive these designations with a generous but critical elasticity of mind and usage.

The designation "son of man" is challenging in a different way, especially when it is used of or by Jesus. Interpreters disagree as to whether the phrase "son of man" is simply a way of saying "child of a human being" or "son of humanity" (or, more colloquially, simply "human being") or whether the phrase has a specialized theological content, such as "apocalyptic redeemer" (as in Dan. 7:13–14). Since individual contributors interpret this phrase in different ways, we sometimes leave the expression "son of man" in the text of the commentary, with individual contributors explaining how they use it.

Diverse Points of View in the Commentary

The many writers in this commentary series are diverse not only in gender, race, and ethnicity, but also in exegetical, theological, and ethical viewpoints. Turning the page from one entry to the next, the reader may encounter a liberation theologian, a neo-orthodox thinker, an ethnic theologian, a process thinker, a socialist, or a postliberal. Moreover, the writers are often individually creative in the ways in which they see the forward movement of their texts in calling for social transformation today. While all authors share the deep conviction that God is even now seeking to lead the world toward more inclusive, just community, the nuances with which they approach the biblical material and even the social world can be quite different.

---

8. For further discussion, see Allen, "Torah, Prophets, Writings, Gospels, Letters."

Rather than enforce a party line with respect to matters of exegesis, theology, and ethical vision, the individual writers bring their own voices to clear expression. The editors' hope is that each week the preacher can have a significant conversation with a writer who is an other and that the preacher's social vision will be broadened and deepened by such exposure.

Diversity also characterizes the process by which this book came into being. The editorial team itself is diverse, as it includes an African American man in the AME Zion Church, a woman of European origin from the Church of the Brethren, a historic peace church, and a man of European origin from the Christian Church (Disciples of Christ). While the editors share many convictions, their vision has been impacted deeply by insights from preachers and scholars from many other churches, movements, communities, and cultures. Dawn took the lead in editing Year A, Ron for Year B, and Dale for Year C. While the editors regarded one of their core tasks as helping the individual writers bring out their own voices forcefully, each has inevitably edited in light of her or his theological and ethical commitments.

Ultimately the goal of *Preaching God's Transforming Justice* is not simply to give preachers resources for talking about social issues, but to empower congregations to develop a theological life perspective that issues in practices of justice and to participate with God in working toward a time when all created entities—every human being and every animal and plant and element of nature—can live together as a community of love through mutual support with abundance for all.

First Sunday of Advent

Leonora Tubbs Tisdale

ISAIAH 2:1–5
PSALM 122
ROMANS 13:11–14
MATTHEW 24:36–44

While Advent is often seen to be a season of preparation and expectation, it is not often viewed as a season for peacemaking. Yet as the lectionary texts for this day remind us, what better time to be reminded of God's call to work for justice and peace than in this season when we await the coming of the Prince of Peace.

The prophet Isaiah sounds that call most clearly in those familiar words about beating our swords into plowshares and spears into pruning hooks. Indeed, if we view the other lectionary texts through the lens of the prophet (rather than starting with the Gospel text and working backward), we hear in them a strong call to awake from our slumber and complacency, and to be about the work of Christ while we also await the new peaceable reality God will inaugurate in and through Christ. Taken altogether these texts shake us out of our slumber and complacency, and challenge us to "put on . . . Christ" (Rom. 13:14a) rather than adopt the ways of our warring world.

Isaiah 2:1–5

In a sense, the entire trajectory of the book of Isaiah is foreshadowed in its first two chapters. Just as the book as a whole moves from judgment to the promise of redemption and restoration, so the first chapter of Isaiah proclaims judgment on Judah and Jerusalem, while the second holds forth the vision of a new peaceable reign of God to come.

What are the sins of Judah and Jerusalem? They are sins not uncommon in our own day: sins of greed, self-interest, corruption in high places, and religion gone awry. Instead of seeking the welfare of the orphan, the widow, and the oppressed, as the Torah had commanded, the people of God are seeking

1

to cushion their own bank accounts and pension funds, and to insure their own health benefits. They still practice their religious rituals, but they do not practice the justice of their God. Consequently there is no peace within or without the land.

Thus God's first words to them through the prophet Isaiah are words of judgment.

> Your new moons and your appointed festivals
>   my soul hates;
> they have become a burden to me,
>   I am weary of bearing them.
> When you stretch out your hands,
>   I will hide my eyes from you;
> even though you make many prayers,
>   I will not listen;
>   your hands are full of blood.
>   (Isa. 1:14–15)

But in chapter 2, the tone changes. The language of criticizing turns to the language of energizing as the prophet recounts a vision he has seen concerning Judah and Jerusalem. It is a vision in which all the peoples of the earth gather on the holy mountain of Jerusalem and worship the same God together; a vision in which God, operating like a great cosmic and highly effective United Nations, judges fairly and equitably among the nations of the world; a vision in which the nations—because of their common devotion to God and because they have also received justice at God's hand—cease their warring ways, and instead turn their weapons into farming tools. In other words, the resources that were once used for guns are now used for bread and butter.

Surely there is much here that is preachable for our day. The people of God still fall prey to the sins of greed, self-interest, and religion gone awry. Nations still wage wars because they do not receive the justice they seek. And our costly wars continue to use precious resources that could be directed toward feeding the hungry.

But remember: the prophet's words not only criticize; they also energize. In a manner that is reminiscent of Martin Luther King Jr.'s "I Have a Dream" speech, Isaiah here paints a vision of a new world to come. And through that vision, the prophet not only invites us to turn from our bloodthirsty ways; he also models how to call people to live into a new reality.

Psalm 122

Psalm 122 both echoes and expands on Isaiah's focus on Jerusalem as the dwelling place of God and God's justice. The psalm is one that pilgrims sang

[handwritten margin note: destruction → creation / chaos → creation]

as they approached the Jerusalem temple on festival days, and its language bespeaks both the deep love the Israelites have for their holy city and their adoration for the God who sits enthroned in its midst.

> I was glad when they said to me,
>   "Let us go to the house of the LORD!"
> Our feet are standing
>   within your gates, O Jerusalem.
>   (vv. 1–2)

Once again, peace and justice are closely linked in this passage, as the worshipers both give thanks for the "thrones for judgment" that are in the Holy City (v. 5) and pray for the peace and security of the city (vv. 6–7). And once again we see that only in the presence of justice—a commitment to the well-being of all people—can peace be achieved.

Surely Jerusalem is as much in need of prayer for its peace today as it was several thousand years ago. And the interrelations of justice and peace in that land are complex. What would a peace look like that also ensured justice for all those who would worship in that land: Jews, Christians, and Muslims? What would a peace look like that also ensured justice for all those who desire to live in that land: Israelis and Palestinians alike?

Sometimes we are prone to despair that peace will ever come to Jerusalem. But this psalm calls us to pray fervently and without ceasing for the peace of this holy land. Somehow, the peace of Jerusalem and the peace of the earth are linked. If people who worship the same God cannot live in harmony, then what hope is there for the rest of our warring world?

Romans 13:11–14

While our texts from the Hebrew Scriptures for this first Sunday in Advent call us to embrace and work toward God's vision of peace with justice, our lections from Paul's Letter to the Romans and the Gospel of Matthew press upon us the urgency of doing so. "Awake from your sleep!" says Paul to the Romans. "For salvation is near!" (v. 11, paraphrased).

The ethical injunctions in Romans 13 come after twelve chapters in which Paul emphasizes that we are justified by grace through faith, and that our salvation is not our own work, but that of God in Christ Jesus. We do good works, according to the apostle, not in order to secure our place with God, but as a grateful response to a God who has first reached out to us with grace. Indeed, now the law becomes our friend and guide for how to live ethically in Christ.

And so Paul, in the verses that immediately precede our text for the day, urges us to follow the commandments that are summed up in the word "love"

(vv. 9–10). Then he presses upon us the urgency of doing so (vv. 11–14), calling us to lay aside our old ways and instead to "put on the Lord Jesus Christ" (v. 14), which may well be an allusion to baptism.

Two things strike me about this text when we focus on its implications for preaching and teaching about social transformation. The first is that what is often needed for Christians today is a wake-up call regarding the social evils of our day and our ethical injunction as Christians to respond to them. Often people are not so much intentionally evil as they are complacent and slumbering. Paul's call to us to move out of the darkness of our sleeplike state and to move into the light of Christ's work in the world is a needed one. Second, this text (given its locus in the book of Romans) reminds us that we do not do good works to earn our salvation. Rather, we do them out of gratitude to God and as a way of living into our baptismal callings in Christ.

Matthew 24:36–44

The Gospel text for this Sunday—one that focuses on the unexpected advent of the Son of Man—has often evoked fear in the hearts of its hearers. And for good reasons! Visions of the rapture, in which one person is unexpectedly taken away while another is left behind, and scenes of the flood that wiped out everyone but Noah and his family, or of a thief who breaks in and steals everything you own while you are sleeping, are not for the fainthearted! Is it any wonder that whole series of books have been written about these graphic images, and whole theologies of the second coming have developed around them?

But if we take a second look, we see that this text, like our Epistle lesson, is really about urgency. And watchfulness. About waking from our slumbering state and being ready for the unexpected inbreaking of Christ.

What is clear here is that no one knows the day or the hour when the Son of Man will return, so trying to read the signs and the symbols to figure it out is not an occupation with which we should whittle away our days. Instead, we are called to be about the works Christ calls us to undertake in his name—works named in our Hebrew Bible texts as peacemaking and justice seeking—so that when Christ comes, we will be found alert and awake and ready for his advent.

The figures of Noah and the householder are set forth to show us what we should *not* be doing. We should not be listening to those around us who tell us (as they told Noah) that there is no flood coming and that we are causing much ado about nothing. Instead we should be about the work of creating and securing arks of safety for those who are most likely to be affected by the storms of life (both literal and metaphorical).

Nor should we be slumbering under the false security that all is well in our world house when, in reality, thieves are breaking in and stealing things of value from people God loves. Instead, we should be alert, awake, aware of the evil that is lurking in the shadows, and doing all in our power to confront and contain it.

But we are called to do more than to stay awake and to confront evil here. We are also called to be on the lookout for God and goodness to break into our world at any minute! Christ will come again one day. And when Christ comes, that great vision of a world united in God, where peace and justice reign, will be realized. Of that promise, we can be sure!

In the meantime, we are called to live in eager expectation of that inbreaking here and now. Whenever justice breaks out unexpectedly, God is in our midst! Whenever people make peace instead of war, God is in our midst! Whenever people of faith break through their doctrinal dividing lines to worship the same God, God is in our midst. For those small signs of goodness we see in our daily life are but a foretaste of the goodness we will taste in fullness when Christ comes again in glory.

So stay awake! Keep alert. Because whatever happens, you don't want to miss the presence of the God who comes not only to judge but also to redeem us.

World AIDS Day (December 1)

Chris Glaser

JEREMIAH 17:14–18
PSALM 6
JAMES 4:11–12
LUKE 16:19–31

World AIDS Day began in 1988 to heighten awareness of the ways the HIV/
AIDS pandemic ravages the human family and to take steps to deal with this disease.[1] This day opens the door for the preacher to help the congregation learn
how many people are affected by this disease and to provide reliable information
about the disease in order to reduce the mystery and fear that still surround it in
some corners. The preacher can help the congregation claim what they can do
to end HIV/AIDS and to ease the suffering of those directly afflicted by HIV/
AIDS and their families and friends.

    I am Lazarus.
Can you see me, sores and all?
Can you hear me, callin' at all?
Can you be with me, beggin' and all?
    I am Lazarus. I live with HIV/AIDS.
I am not invisible.
I am not unapproachable.
    I am Lazarus. I live with HIV/AIDS.
I am loveable.
I am acceptable.
    I am Lazarus.
I am possible.
I am available.
I am reachable.
    I am Lazarus.
I can see you now.

1. Visit www.worldaidsday.org for the theme of World AIDS Day for the current year.

6

I can hear you now.
I can be with you now.
　I am Lazarus.
I live with HIV/AIDS.
　　Kelvin Sauls[2]

The AIDS pandemic began for me in the early 1980s in the gay community of the United States, but now it has been recognized worldwide among people of every nationality, ethnicity, hue, and sexual and gender identity. Just as we began to discern that "the church has AIDS," so we understand that "the world has AIDS." It is not only an affliction of individuals or specific communities but one that affects almost every woman, child, and man on the planet, directly or indirectly. This confirms the biblical theme that one person's experience helps shape the community and its destiny: from the Hebrew concept that a whole community may be delivered or held accountable by God for an individual's actions or circumstances, to the Christian metaphor of the spiritual community as the body of Christ consisting of many members who are part of one another.

World AIDS Day is an opportunity to recognize our solidarity in our efforts to control HIV and confront its devastation during a Holy Day for Justice. Observing World AIDS Day in the church is additionally an opportunity to commemorate those we have lost to AIDS, and especially to remember that they were often members of communities considered dispensable by the majority culture: at first, gay men, Haitians, intravenous drug users, hemophiliacs; and now, more widespread, heterosexuals, women, children, people in developing nations, and the poor. Traditionally a feast day in the Christian calendar is the first full day of a saint in paradise, often a martyr to the cause of Christianity. Our contemporary AIDS saints are those who have gone before us in this crisis, warning us, exhorting us, many of them martyrs to our sin of xenophobia. "Silence = Death" was the slogan, the mantra, of those who boldly and courageously chained themselves to church pillars and organized sit-ins at government, health, and pharmaceutical facilities. They scandalized "decent" society by their abrasive, demanding, and uncompromising candor about the need for HIV/AIDS education, safer sex, a Manhattan-style Project[3] for finding a cure and a vaccine, humane treatment of those living with HIV and AIDS, and research into more effective treatments for HIV and its

---

2. "I am Lazarus" by the Rev. Kelvin Sauls (United Methodist), used with permission from The General Board of Discipleship, The United Methodist Church.
3. The Manhattan Project brought together U.S. scientists to do intensive research to produce the first atomic bomb during World War II. The idea of doing the same to find a cure or treatment for HIV/AIDS had been proposed.

opportunistic infections. At the same time, they had to beat back those who would quarantine them, "out" them, or otherwise punish them.

With some notable and noble exceptions, the church largely came late to serving those living with HIV and AIDS—so much so that when the San Francisco Bay area, an epicenter of the crisis, commissioned its first religious leaders as ministers in the AIDS crisis, those leaders asked community activists to give them their blessing, effectively laying hands on them in a service of worship. Just as a feast day contains a remembrance of a saint's often painful history of rejection, persecution, or martyrdom, World AIDS Day observed as a Holy Day for Justice cannot ignore the initial resistance of the church and the culture toward serving those early AIDS martyrs. But the purpose in both instances is to recognize the good done in the face of evil and ignorance, to serve as a model for what the church and the world might become. World AIDS Day may serve not only as a reminder that the world is still suffering AIDS, but as a memorial of—in the words of Albert Camus in *The Plague*— "what had to be done, and what assuredly would have to be done again in the never ending fight against terror and its relentless onslaughts, despite their personal afflictions, by all who, while unable to be saints but refusing to bow down to pestilences, strive their utmost to be healers."[4]

Jeremiah 17:14–18

The word "jeremiad" suggests a woeful lament characteristic of the prophet and priest Jeremiah and captures the woeful experience and expressions of individuals, couples, families, and communities first hit by HIV. Written around the turn of the sixth century BCE, Jeremiah's laments contain thoughtful and questioning critiques of his religious and political context. Although any of these could prove insightful for understanding the religious and political dimensions of AIDS today, 17:14–18 is one of Jeremiah's six *personal* laments.[5]

Many affected or infected with HIV wonder if AIDS is some kind of punishment from God. This interpretation is not far removed from the condemning attitudes of their childhood churches. Thus they may echo Jeremiah's plea to God, "Do not become a terror to me" (v. 17a). Even though we now know there are other ways to transmit HIV (birth, breast milk, blood, blood products), diseases that are also sexually transmitted may feel tainted in our own eyes and the eyes of others because of our erotophobia, our fear and disdain of sexuality.

---

4. Albert Camus, *The Plague* (New York: Vintage Books, 1972), 287.
5. See Jer. 11:18–12:6; 15:10–21; 18:18–23; 20:7–13; 20:14–18.

Jeremiah's illness is more emotional than physical, for he has been prophesying a day of judgment that never seems to come. Although he is not interested in hurrying it along, he would nonetheless like to be vindicated. Like Jeremiah, the early AIDS activists also came to be known as doomsayers for their repeated and dramatic warnings, and similarly despaired that their prophecies of a worldwide pandemic affecting generations to come were being ignored. As one example, one church refused to have a safer-sex seminar for their youth because, I was told, "Our young people are not having sex." The sensitive political position of the emerging gay rights movement also sometimes caused it to censor or tone down dire scenarios, a phenomenon documented in Randy Shilts's book *And the Band Played On: Politics, People, and the AIDS Epidemic.*[6] Jeremiah would have understood the frustration of early AIDS activists who repeatedly beat their heads against walls of resistance, envisioning what was to come and yet hoping against hope it would not happen: "But I have not run away from being a shepherd in your service, nor have I desired the fatal day" (v. 16).

Psalm 6

The fear evident in Psalm 6 leaps off the pages of the Bible for those who remember what it was like to live in the days before AIDS had a name or even a simple diagnosis. An unexplained fever, an otherwise ordinary bout of intestinal or respiratory flu, a skin blemish that looked like Kaposi's sarcoma—all could strike terror in the heart. Add to that the terrifying reports in the media—though initially rare in mainstream publications—and personal knowledge of people dying, untreatably, of "the gay cancer" or "GRID: Gay Related Immune Deficiency," as it was first called, and we surely knew the terror of the psalmist:

> O LORD, heal me, for my bones are shaking with terror.
> My soul also is struck with terror,
> while you, O LORD—how long?
>
> (6:2b–3)

The psalms famously contain uncensored feelings, sometimes politically incorrect, represented as dramatically as they are poetically worded. They capture something genuine, something heartfelt in the human condition, whether praising or lamenting, condemning or contemplative. Here the psalmist prays desperately for healing from a life-threatening illness, "for I

---

6. Randy Shilts, *And the Band Played On: Politics, People, and the AIDS Epidemic* (New York: St. Martin's Press, 1987).

am languishing" (v. 2). In the face of death there is bargaining with God (v. 5): "For in death there is no remembrance of you; in Sheol who can give you praise?" Though it is tears that drench the psalmist's bed (v. 6), the symptomatic night sweats effectively are the body's tears fighting AIDS.

What is also striking about this text is the parallel experience of its writer and that of many people living with AIDS of being judged by others, based on an ancient belief that illness is somehow God's punishment or the contemporary belief that AIDS is a consequence of a person's "lifestyle." The psalmist seems to begin there, praying, "O LORD, do not rebuke me in your anger, or discipline me in your wrath," but concludes that the prayer will be answered and "all my enemies shall be ashamed." A seminarian once told me that she had no idea what the psalmist meant by "enemies" until she came out as a lesbian in the church, an experience shared by many with AIDS.

Luke 16:19–31

The Gospel writer Luke is often concerned about practical applications of faith. The "poor in spirit" in Matthew's Beatitudes become simply "the poor" in Luke. Luke's Good Samaritan fulfills the religious obligation to love the neighbor by ministering to a roadside mugging victim even as the priest and lay priest remain ritually undefiled by passing by on their way to the temple. In this parable, Jesus tells of a rich man who did not share his wealth with the beggar Lazarus, losing his privilege in the next life, in which Lazarus finally receives comfort in the bosom of Abraham. The image of Lazarus (vv. 20–21) "covered with sores, who longed to satisfy his hunger," brings to mind people living with AIDS covered by Kaposi's sarcoma lesions, unable to eat because of thrush or tubes in the throat, or appetites suppressed by medications. The image of the rich man brings to mind governmental, religious, and even medical authorities who ignored far too long the plight of people infected with HIV.

The contrast here is not simply between wellness and illness, but between rich and poor. The inequities of health-care systems and the marginalization of "dispensable" populations became ever more evident as AIDS ravaged those whom society and the church chose to ignore, at best, and often condemned and rejected, at worst. In the gay community, it also served as a wake-up call for those of us who, as white men, previously enjoyed medical and media attention not afforded nonwhites and women.

The rich man asks Abraham to send Lazarus from the dead to warn his brothers of the consequences of ignoring the poor. Abraham refuses, saying that it would not help if they had not listened to Moses and the prophets, indicating that their religious tradition should be enough to help them do the right thing. The church benefits from the teachings of Moses and the prophets, as well as having its central teacher, Jesus, return from the dead. We not only have a religious foundation to guide us; we also have a great cloud of witnesses to cheer us from the other side to do the right thing in the face of AIDS.

James 4:11–12

James is a collection of wisdom sayings that grows out of our command to love as Christians. Preceded by a passage on humility, this text serves as the perfect response to those who torment the prophet Jeremiah and the writer of Psalm 6 with their judgment. Only God can judge ("there is one lawgiver and judge," v. 12), and for the spiritual community to "speak evil against another" or judge another is an affront to the Law itself. Not only does this echo Jesus, this could be said to be a central teaching of the fourth-century Christian monastic movement, "Do not judge."[7]

During the funeral of a gay man who died of AIDS, the pastor stunned the family by declaring that he died for the sin of homosexuality and was now in hell. But before we too readily judge the pastor, better that we look at all the ways, large and small, that we judge any person with HIV.

Thus Jeremiah prays for healing of the grief caused by his adversaries, those who will not heed his cries of coming destruction. The psalmist prays for God's deliverance from life-threatening illness and the terror it brings. Luke presents Jesus' parable of the Rich Man and the Poor Beggar, demonstrating contrasts not just of health and illness, but of those who are privileged and underprivileged. And James reminds us to hold our tongues and our hearts, refraining from judgment as we practice humility and love. On this Holy Day for Justice, World AIDS Day, we may offer thanks for those who prayed and prophesied, those who were ignored and judged, those who, from God's bosom, urge us to repent and bring healing and hope to those still with us.

---

7. See Thomas Merton's discussion of the Desert Abbots' refusal to judge in his book *The Wisdom of the Desert: Sayings from the Desert Fathers of the Fourth Century* (New York: New Directions, 1960), 19.

Second Sunday of Advent

Marvin A. McMickle

Isaiah 11:1–10
Psalm 72:1–7, 18–19
Romans 15:4–13
Matthew 3:1–12

In Advent the church prepares for the coming of Jesus, God's representative who inaugurates the realm of God. This realm includes peace, a traditional focus for the second Sunday of Advent. The texts today promise the coming of the realm of peace (Isa. 11) and stress the importance of governments creating a just and peaceful social world (Ps. 72). This divine realm brings together Jewish and Gentile peoples in a community of mutual support (Rom. 15). Repentance is the means of becoming a part of the community of God's realm (Matt. 3).

Isaiah 11:1–10

The eleventh chapter of Isaiah follows God's promise in the tenth chapter that a remnant of Israel will be restored and returned to the promised land following the horrific destruction of the northern nation of Israel by the Assyrians in 722 BCE. The nation sinned, in large measure as a result of the corruption of the nation's leaders. In 10:1–2 the prophet decries those who "make unjust laws, . . . issue oppressive decrees, . . . deprive the poor of their rights and withhold justice from the oppressed" (NIV, for this and all other quotations in this essay). Isaiah 11 is a vision of what will happen when a new ruler, emerging from the line of David, establishes a world in which the wolf and the goat as well as the lion and the lamb lie down together (Isa. 11:1–3, 6–9). At the same time, God will hold all people and nations accountable for the ways they treat the poorest and neediest among them (Isa. 11:4–5). It is all too easy for a nation to say that it is "faithful to God." However, when its treatment of the poor contradicts its self-described religious values, there will be consequences from the God who, as liberation theology reminds us, is on the side of the oppressed.

Isaiah 11 points to the opportunity for renewal that arises when those who govern will judge the needy with righteousness and "will give decisions for the poor of the earth" (NIV, v. 4a). Peace does not come with more and bigger weapons but with governments that seek justice and display mercy and compassion for all people, especially the poor. Today, we hope for a time when all wars will cease, and when Republicans and Democrats, the "1 percent" and the "99 percent," may live and work together toward fulfilling the needs of our nation and neighbors. More than a distant hope, Isaiah gives voice to our present needs and longings.

Psalm 72:1–7, 18–19

Psalm 72 describes the compassionate and strong goals of a godly king: the power and willingness to do justice, judge with righteousness, defend the afflicted, protect the poor, and be especially sensitive to the needs of children.

This prayer calls to mind the "last words of David" found in 2 Samuel 23:3–4. In this touching scene David gives counsel to his son and successor on the virtues that make for an effective ruler. Similarly, Psalm 72:6 describes the effect of a good and godly ruler: "like rain that falls on the mown grass, like showers that water the earth." Someone who governs with justice and righteousness will be a blessing to the people, and their lives will flourish.

However, in verses 8–11 David asks something quite different from God. David wants God to grant victory over enemies and preeminence among nations. In the mind of David, the ideal ruler is loved by the people because the ruler is just and is feared by enemies because he or she is powerful. This was the ideal rule in the days of David and Saul: justice for everyone within the borders of Israel and power to discourage, dissuade, or defeat any nation that threatened Israel.

 In light of this, several challenges arise when we consider current political policies and practices. Does the United States place the highest premium on using the government as an instrument that protects and safeguards the rights and lives of the poor and the oppressed, especially children? In a country where political power is too often financed by wealthy donors and rich corporate interests, the values of the ideal ruler in Psalm 72 seem both unimaginable and unachievable. Big donors clearly want to shape the policies and programs of their government so that they work in favor of the wealthy. Leaders who fail to tear down forms of oppression and corruption today can quickly and easily find themselves entangled in the very web of corruption that Psalm 72 would have them oppose.

David may not have had to take money away from caring for the poor and needy members of his own nation to keep his army strong enough to defend his own country and to expand its influence beyond Israel. However, that has been the direct consequence of U.S. foreign and domestic policies for the last seventy-five years.

During the Great Depression, there was great resistance from the wealthy to the programs of President Franklin Roosevelt's New Deal, even though most of those programs were designed to help people who had been hardest hit by the poverty and suffering that covered the country like a blanket. However, with World War II, many who opposed spending government money during the New Deal favored receiving government money to build tanks and planes and munitions. Sadly, wealthy industrialists in the United States were not willing to hire African Americans to work in their plants except among the janitorial staff. It took an executive order by President Roosevelt, who seemed to understand the implications of Psalm 72, to end segregation in war-related industries that received money from the federal government.

In 1965 President Lyndon Johnson declared a war on poverty, suggesting that poverty throughout the United States could be eliminated once and for all. However, at the same time that funding was needed to begin a war on poverty, funding for the war in Vietnam was escalating. The war in Vietnam consumed $15 million per month, and funding for the poor, the needy, and the most vulnerable in society was diverted into military spending as the body count in Vietnam rose to more than 58,000 American fatalities.

Those who govern must give serious thought to how Psalm 72 speaks about their responsibilities. More importantly, preachers must not remain silent when they see injustice occurring while those who govern turn away and refuse to address what is taking place. Martin Luther King Jr. may well have had his finest hour when he staunchly opposed President Johnson's diversion of funds from the war on poverty to the war in Vietnam. We have now gone from spending $15 million per month in Vietnam to $15 billion per month in 2011 in Afghanistan and Iraq. We who preach to those who govern as well as the people they govern must not be afraid to point to this text.

Advent is a season of hope and expectation. The preacher can encourage us to help fulfill Advent expectations by urging our governments and political leaders to act with justice, compassion, and concern for all people, especially those whose needs are greatest.

Romans 15:4–13

In Romans 15:4–13 Paul tackles an area of conflict for the early Christian community: how to relate to those perceived to be outsiders. Paul's special

ministry was not only to preach to the Gentiles, but also to persuade Jewish
Christians to receive Gentile converts as brothers and sisters in Christ. Galatians 3:28 also speaks to Paul's challenge as he tried to tear down three great
social barriers in the ancient world: "no longer Jew or Greek, . . . slave or free,
. . . male and female." However, for Paul to say this was one thing; but for
Christians in Rome and elsewhere to embrace that vision is another matter.

To strengthen his argument Paul employs a vision that no Jewish Christian could easily ignore, the messianic vision in Isaiah 11 in which "the root
of Jesse shall come, the one who rises to rule the Gentiles; in him the Gentiles shall hope" (Rom. 15:12). In Romans 15:5 Paul appeals for unity among
those who follow Christ. In verses 7–9 he reminds Jewish Christians of God's
covenant with Abram in Genesis 12:2–3, in which God says, "In you all the
families of the earth shall be blessed." With that in mind, Paul writes, "Christ
has become a servant of the circumcised on behalf of the truth of God in order
that he might confirm the promises given to the patriarchs, and in order that
the Gentiles might glorify God for [God's] mercy" (Rom. 15:8–9).

What a challenging word this is for today's church, which still practices
the patterns of the 1960s: Sunday morning is still the most segregated time
in America, despite Paul's admonition to welcome one another as Christ has
welcomed us (v. 7). What a challenging word this is for those of us in the
twenty-first century church who oppose women in ministry despite Paul's
urging us to glorify God together with one voice (v. 6). What a challenging
word this is for a nation still driven by the belief in American exceptionalism
while Paul teaches us that God in Christ has accepted all people. Whether
our segregation, sexism, and nationalism are self-imposed or inherited, Paul
calls us to believe and hope in the Spirit's power to transform these as we live
toward the fulfillment of God's vision of unity and peace among people.

Matthew 3:1–12

Matthew 3:1–12 lifts up a word that one seldom hears from the pulpits of
America these days: repent. Too many preachers seem fascinated with prosperity theology and the idea that all God wants is to bless people, and the only
form that blessing takes is "health and wealth." What would happen to the
preacher today who joins John the Baptist in calling for repentance and for
bearing fruit that shows the sincerity of our repentance?

There are a great many things for which people and nations need to
repent. We need to repent for centuries of racism and sexism. We need to
repent for saying "in God we trust" when we really trust in the money on
which those words are stamped. Too many preachers are more interested in
being affirmed by their congregations than they are in being fully faithful to

God and to the message of Scripture, which Paul refers to in Acts 20:27 as "the whole purpose of God." Some preachers will not use the words "sin" or "repent" because their people do not want to hear about such things. These preachers prefer to satisfy "itching ears" and tell people what they want to hear (2 Tim. 4:3). John reminds us that God is able to turn stones into children of Abraham. Thus, the church must remember that repentance and entry into the baptismal waters is not enough: God issues a prophetic call to live in ways that reveal our loyalties, commitment, and faith. During the season of Advent when we are tempted to worry more about buying Christmas presents than reaching out to strangers, enemies, and persons in need, preachers need to declare what was at the heart of John's message: "Produce fruit in keeping with repentance." In Mark 1:4 and 15 John the Baptist and Jesus make repentance the theme of their first sermons. Preachers would do well to keep that theme alive in their preaching, perhaps especially when we are tempted to ignore it.

Universal Declaration of Human Rights (December 10)

Christine Marie Smith

Exodus 23:1–9
Psalm 102:12–22
Mark 12:28–34
Romans 12:9–13

In the shadow of World War II, the United Nations set forth the Universal Declaration of Human Rights on December 10, 1948. This document asserts that all human beings are free, equal, and entitled to dignity, safety, peace, and security regardless of nationality, gender, race, ethnicity, or religion. It prohibits actions that deny these values (such as slavery, torture, or discrimination). Commemorating it in Advent, the preacher may help the congregation to repent of violations of these rights and to recognize that living by them can be an important component in preparing for the Advent of Christ.

Recognition of the inherent dignity and of the equal and inalienable rights of all members of the human family is the foundation of freedom, justice, and peace in the world (Preamble). Everyone has the right to life, liberty, and security of person (Article 3). No one shall be held in slavery or servitude; slavery and the slave trade shall be prohibited in all their forms (Article 4). No one shall be subjected to torture or to cruel, inhuman or degrading tension or punishment (Article 5).

United Nations Universal Declaration of Human Rights

There are many creative and important ways to integrate the social and theological themes of Advent with the challenge and vision of the Universal Declaration of Human Rights. Preachers can help members of privileged congregations recognize in new ways our own complicity in the lack of human rights that so many of our sisters and brothers experience around the globe.

This is surely a disgrace worthy of our repentance. Preachers could also help the congregations they serve to acknowledge and name in specific ways the multitude of human beings who still are waiting for the equity and justice of this Universal Declaration of Human Rights to become realities in their communities and nations. Repentance and waiting intersect in Advent as we embrace the courage and commitment to speak about the privileges many of us enjoy, while so many of God's people seem to be forever waiting. In this Advent season we are not just waiting for the advent of Christ's transformative power in our own lives and the lives of our churches and our communities, we are awaiting the advent of Christ's transformative power for the entire globe. We await the realm of God for all creation, and speak in this season about all the justice work that can and must be done while all creation moans in waiting. We wait for the Advent of Christ during this holy season, but we know that Christ comes with power, with grace, and with justice often while too many of us are waiting.

A different approach for preachers concerning the Universal Declaration of Human Rights would be to turn our attention to individuals and communities who are rising up and taking the issue of human rights into their own hands because the privileged and powerful have failed to bring justice and failed to secure basic human rights for all people. Maybe this Advent season it is time for preachers to honor some of our sisters and brothers who are too often seen only as victims rather than as agents and creators of their own human history. Focusing on the lives of people who are struggling for their own human rights in the midst of horrible forms of repression and death is often shocking and painful. Perhaps preachers are hesitant to honor those who are struggling against systems of oppression because this is when we are likely to be criticized and accused that our preaching has become "political." We need to help each other as preachers remember that the Universal Declaration of Human Rights was an economic, social, and political act when it was adopted in 1948, and that if we are to lift up and honor those who are working for greater human rights for all of God's people, our preaching will always be social and political as surely as it will be religious, spiritual, and theological.

As these words are being written in early March 2011, the world's people have been watching for weeks as our sisters and brothers in Egypt and Libya struggle mightily for basic human rights within their countries. Many people have placed their bodies in the streets and in public places where they have been killed. They have been showing the world just how heinous it can be when people of power control, limit, and repress the people of an entire country, and how people of power can fundamentally deny and violate people's basic human rights without accountability. This basic struggle for human rights goes on all of the time in our world; we only have to look around us this

Advent season to see individuals and communities who deserve our words and actions of solidarity and support. Where is the church in the face of repression throughout the ages? The children of South Africa protested in townships and city streets the enslaving nature of apartheid, as they showed the world what it looked like to risk one's life for basic human rights. The Zapatistas, the poor yet organized indigenous Mayan people of Chiapas, Mexico, cried "¡Basta ya!" (enough) and took to the streets the morning after the North American Free Trade Agreement (NAFTA) took effect in 1994 to show the world that torture, cruelty, and servitude are daily realities for the Mayan people in Chiapas.[1] With their resistance they proclaimed to the world that it is intolerable to live without basic human rights and that economic agreements that privilege a few while the masses of people in a state or country are starving are criminal.

It is time for preachers to do our social, economic, political, and theological homework so that we can speak with prophetic voices about the people who are teaching the world what the Universal Declaration of Human Rights is all about, so that all of God's people will have some form of the many rights this declaration points to and promises for all.

Exodus 23:1–9

If we focus this day on people who are struggling for basic human rights, lifting up their stories and their lives as faithful examples of those trying to embody the Universal Declaration of Human Rights, this passage will guide us in a clear and demanding way. This text calls for just, humane treatment not only for all people, even our enemies, but for our enemy's animals. It instructs us about being just in judicial matters and legal matters, but it challenges us to see with absolute certainty that treating all people in a just and humane way acknowledges that all people have rights. Not only are we to not "join hands with the wicked," which is demanding in itself for people of privilege, but we are to join our hands and lives with those who are tirelessly working for their own human rights and the rights of others. This might mean this Advent that we find our hands outstretched in solidarity to the Zapatistas in Chiapas, Mexico. This might just mean that this Advent we find our hands outstretched in solidarity with all of the "resident aliens" in our land, insisting that no human person is illegal! There is certainly work to do to mend a broken immigration system, but God would have us never lose sight of the humanity and the human rights of all our neighbors. This passage

1. John Ross, *The War Against Oblivion: The Zapatista Chronicles* (Monroe & Philadelphia: Common Courage Press, 2000), 20.

commands us not to "side with the majority so as to pervert justice," but to side with people everywhere who are working for what is just for everyone, not only a privileged few.

Psalm 102:12–22

Proclaiming a psalm that lifts up God's restorative power for the people in the midst of their experience of exile is an act of radical faith. This psalm asks if we are listening to the groans of the prisoners all around us. Are we among those who set free persons who are sentenced to die? Psalm 102 provides a powerful reminder of God's eternal care for creation and assures the people that they will never be abandoned. Perhaps the preacher this Advent Sunday could focus on those who are struggling in the midst of their own contemporary "exile" and on how our religious communities can be a presence to others so that people struggling for justice do not feel abandoned or literally doomed to die.

When we stand in solidarity with those who are struggling for their own and others' human rights, we embody God's holy promise that those who are in exile will never be alone or forsaken. To take this psalm into our hearts and lives, we must we willing to look at peoples and nations who are in exile and see their realities as ones we cannot ignore or turn away from, and we must believe that God does not abandon anyone. We must be living witnesses to that truth in places we have not wanted to go or cannot imagine. We must come down from the protected and privileged places in which we live and become psalms of eternal hope.

Mark 12:28–34

In carefully reading this passage from Mark, something curious becomes clear. When the scribe repeats what Jesus says, he turns loving God "with all your mind" into loving with all your "understanding," and he does not even mention loving God "with all your soul." This may seem a small oversight, but omitting how we love with our "souls" leaves out the core of who we are, what we are, and how we fundamentally understand ourselves in relation to the rest of creation. It would be very powerful to hear preachers talk about what kind of "understandings" we must have as human beings in order to realize the Universal Declaration of Human Rights, and what is missing in many of us that enables us to allow ourselves to live prosperous and secure lives while most of God's people live miserable lives of suffering throughout the world.

Even more critical to who we are is the condition of our souls. What happens to our souls when we live abundant lives alongside so many of God's people who will only know various kinds of servitude their entire lives? Instead of focusing in a more general way on these two great commandments of loving God and loving neighbor, as we have heard so many sermons do, why not challenge ourselves as preachers to talk about the true sickness of our souls and the diminishment of our very humanity when we live in denial, fear, entitlement, and privilege, alongside the very ones we have been commanded to love as we genuinely love ourselves.

When we examine our souls and speak aloud our denial, fear, entitlement, and privilege, Jesus might say to us, "You have glimpsed the kingdom of God." When we understand what we must do to respond to the suffering in this world, Jesus might say to us, "You are not far from the kingdom of God." Finally, when we move our hearts, our souls, our minds, and all the strength of our bodies into direct action to alleviate some of the suffering in this world, Jesus might say, "You are now part of the kingdom of God unfolding in our world."

Romans 12:9–13

This is one of those biblical texts that is direct in its mandates, clear in naming the ethics of just human behavior, and forever inspiring because the writers believe that human beings can embody so much generosity, commitment, and spiritual power. It would be a worthy project for preachers to try to rewrite this short text with basic human rights as the solitary focus. It might start with something like this: "Let the global community be constant and genuine in its struggle for the dignity and equitable rights of all people; resist all forces that give rights to some at the expense of rights for all; love one another as if all people were your sisters and brothers, and do not allow the slavery, servitude, torture, or cruelty of another human being to become acceptable for any reason; honor every single person God has created by working tirelessly until each one has a home, health care, work, enough food, and other necessary resources to sustain life." Turning these biblical mandates into a smaller, but no less powerful, declaration of human rights could lead to a very challenging sermon.

Third Sunday of Advent

Monica A. Coleman

ISAIAH 35:1–10
PSALM 146:5–10
LUKE 1:46B–55
JAMES 5:7–10
MATTHEW 11:2–11

This week's lectionary readings remind us of the saying that "good things come to those who wait." While these readings focus on the deliverance of God's promises after a long season of waiting, they also remind us to be open in our expectations about how God is manifest among us. Isaiah's prediction of restoration, the psalmist's celebration of justice, Mary's song of praise during pregnancy, the admonition to practice patience in James, and John the Baptist's quest for the messiah—all of these remind us that God seeks deliverance for God's people, but it may not come in the time and form that we expect. God is faithful to God's promises, but we are often surprised by how and when God fulfills them. Amid the seemingly eternal wait for justice to be manifest among us, these texts encourage us to be prepared to wait and to be surprised by what comes our way.

Isaiah 35:1–10

Isaiah 35 seems to lead us to the hopeful promises of Deutero-Isaiah in chapters 40–55. After chapters pronouncing destruction and judgment on Judah, the prophet concludes with encouraging words about the restoration of Israel. This promised restoration serves as a bridge between the previous condemnation of Israel and the upcoming passages about the Suffering Servant.

The prophet speaks about restoration in holistic ways, including both humanity and the created world. The chapter begins with the personification of the land, whose fertility is understood as praise to God. The wilderness, desert, and flowers rejoice and sing. The land that has been taken from them—Lebanon, Carmel, and Sharon—will be returned. There is an end of human sickness: the blind see, the deaf hear, the lame leap, the speechless will sing. The exiles will return through a holy way, in safety, to their holy city. Israel—the people and the land—will experience all of this with joyfulness.

This passage reminds us of the beauty of God's justice. When people are working hard for justice, small victories can be overlooked. It is easy to move on to the next project or cause that demands our attention. These verses remind us of the joy of seeing God working for justice in the world. They remind us to celebrate and sing when we experience the fulfillment of God's promises. When new public policies extend health care to persons who cannot afford private insurance, praise God! When a house is refinanced so that a family can remain in their home, praise God!

This passage also focuses on the fertility of the land and reminds us that we are intimately connected to the places where we live. The connections between environmental abuse and human depravity are disturbing. We must remember to fight to secure fair treatment and use of the created world while we struggle for human dignity and equality. As justice is restored, how amazing it is to imagine the earth rejoicing as it flourishes around us.

Psalm 146:5–10

This psalm echoes Isaiah's theme of rejoicing for justice that has been restored, but it gives even more attention to the connection between hope and faith in God and a just outcome. It implies that God's role in promoting justice is cause for our trust in God. The same God who undergirds our faith also grants justice for the oppressed. Psalm 146 offers clear portraits of God's care for the disenfranchised: the prisoners, the blind, strangers, orphans, and widows. This passage reminds us to remain faithful in our efforts to seek justice for today's correlative populations: those treated unfairly in the prison-industrial complex, immigrants, individuals living with disabilities in a society that is less than accommodating, single mothers, children in the foster care system. Our care for these populations is a sign both of our faith and of God's justice in the world.

Finally, this is one of the "Hallelujah" psalms (written as "Praise the LORD" in some translations) that close out the Psalter. It reminds us that the appropriate response to our care for the oppressed is praise to God.

Luke 1:46b–55

This passage in Luke is one of the best-known praises in the Bible. Echoing Miriam's praise in Exodus for the deliverance of the Hebrews from their oppressors the Egyptians, Mary praises God for using her to deliver God's promises to future generations.

At her cousin Elizabeth's home, Mary celebrates Elizabeth's pregnancy and God's ability to effect the seemingly impossible through her, as God did with Sarah in Genesis. Having been told by the messenger Gabriel that she will bear "the Son of God," Mary thanks God in this praise poem known as the Magnificat.

The most significant justice-related implication of this passage is that we should not overlook anyone as a possible embodiment or conveyor of God's activity among us. Mary is the equivalent of today's single mother. Those whom society ordinarily judges and ostracizes, God looks upon with favor. Mary recognizes that she is considered "lowly" by those around her, but she is confident that God is working through her to fulfill God's promises. Mary asserts that her role in creating God's vision for the world may not be immediately recognized. Yet later, others will call her blessed. She knows that God's vision for the world is larger than she, but Mary is sure that she plays a part in it. This passage is a support to those of us who work with disenfranchised communities. We must encourage individuals to see themselves not as the wider world may see them, but rather through God's eyes. Mary reminds us to look for God all around us—especially among those whom we least expect to bear God's promise of newness of life. As Mary praises God, contemporary readers are reminded that when God brings justice to the world, it may come in unexpected ways, through individuals and communities whom most of our society eschews.

Matthew 11:2–11

Like the Magnificat, this passage in Matthew's Gospel asks us to adjust our expectations about how God works in the world.

While John the Baptist is imprisoned, he sends his disciples to ask Jesus if he is "the one." Although John clearly wants to know whether Jesus is the messiah, Jesus' response reminds us to focus our attention less on the Savior and more on the just and loving presence of God in the world. His words point toward the movement and work of God around us. When we see God's active presence in the healing of persons who are blind, lame, leprous, and deaf; when the dead are raised and the poor receive good news; we will know that God is present to bring about greater justice and mercy in the world. Jesus tells John's disciples that they are witnesses of the same signs that are predicted in this week's readings in Isaiah and Psalms.

Jesus' admonition to John's disciples also serves as an admonition to contemporary Christians. We often have expectations about how God's vision for justice will be fulfilled. Some communities believe it will happen through prosperity or political changes. While this may well happen, the Gospel urges us to seek evidence of God's empowering work among the disenfranchised and marginalized; that is, among immigrant and undocumented children in our schools who receive helpful counsel and support from teachers and community leaders, and among persons who cannot find jobs yet receive weekly encouragement from neighbors, friends, and church members who ask how they are doing and offer help as they are able.

Also, Matthew's Jewish audience would have recognized Jesus' reference to Malachi in verse 10, a reference that seems to relate John the Baptist to Elijah. Jesus points away from his own personage earlier in this chapter and chooses to emphasize instead others who work for justice and prepare the way for God's new work among us. His words remind us that we should not undervalue the role that we and others play in bringing God's justice to the world.

James 5:7–10

The text from James echoes the lessons from the Gospels: be careful about what you expect and do not be surprised by how God chooses to fulfill God's promises. The early Christians expected Jesus to return almost immediately. As this failed to happen, James encouraged them to be patient.

The justice-related implication is found in James's encouragement to be patient in our work for a more just and equitable world. As the farmer waits for the harvest, the work of social justice involves planting, nourishing, tending, and waiting patiently for what arises around us. Impatience can breed greater division and conflict. With patience, however, we can trust that God will fulfill the promises spoken of in the other Scripture texts for this day. While God's justice may not come when and how we expect it, we need to trust that we will see the fruit of God's justice around us. Like the prophets before us, we must not become weary of speaking and acting on behalf of others but should build one another up in ministries that anticipate the fruit of our good labor. This passage reminds us to pay attention to even the smallest signs of God's care for the oppressed, for the early and late rains that will sustain our efforts to continue supporting our community's human rights commission and food banks. It reminds us of Martin Luther King Jr.'s teaching that "the arc of the moral universe is long but it bends toward justice."[1]

---

1. Martin Luther King Jr., "Where Do We Go from Here?" in *A Testament of Hope: The Essential Writings of Martin Luther King, Jr.*, ed. James Melvin Washington (San Francisco: Harper & Row, 1986), 252.

Fourth Sunday of Advent

John M. Buchanan

ISAIAH 7:10–16
PSALM 80:1–7, 17–19
ROMANS 1:1–7
MATTHEW 1:18–25

Among the most important, radical, and transformative words are these: " 'and they shall name him Emmanuel,' which means, 'God is with us' " (Matt. 1:23). It is the word the preacher must find a way to say on this Sunday, at the very moment the noise of the cultural holiday celebration reaches its crescendo. It is a word anticipated for centuries by people in slavery, on a dangerous journey through the wilderness, in exile, and living under the hand of brutal political oppression. It is a word longed for by suffering, lonely, marginalized people in every age. It is a quiet word, spoken by prophets and poets and angels appearing in the dreams of frightened and perplexed people. "Emmanuel . . . God is with us." In the midst of all the noisy holiday clamor, the lovely customs and traditions that touch our hearts, the preacher must find a way to say "God is with us."

God, who, it was generally believed in antiquity, is holy and powerful and righteous, is also merciful and kind and ready to act in ways that are liberating and just on behalf of God's people. Ancient prophets in Israel proposed that the power of God, which everybody who ever shuddered at the raw power of a thunderstorm understands, is equally expressed in compassion and justice, perhaps more so. The idea has implications, both personal and political.

The texts for today are gathered around the theme of God's liberating activity, which is often obscured by fear, anxiety, and deadly despair.

Isaiah 7:10–16

Study of this traditional Advent pericope must begin with the preceding nine verses, Isaiah 7:1–9, which describe the all-important context. Ahaz, king of

Judah, is frightened, and all his subjects with him. Two neighboring states have teamed up to attack Jerusalem, and "the heart of his people shook as trees of the forest shake before the wind" (7:2b). The Lord sends Isaiah to Ahaz to assure him that all will be well: "Be quiet, do not fear. . . . If you do not stand firm in faith, you shall not stand at all" (7:4, 9b).

The assigned text begins in the middle of this familiar human drama of paralyzing fear. Ahaz is too frightened to trust the promise transmitted by the prophet. So the Lord speaks directly to Ahaz and invites the anxious monarch to ask God for a sign to seal the promise. Ahaz is too paralyzed by fear even to take God up on the offer. Exasperated, Isaiah takes Ahaz by the hand and points to the sign that has already been given. "Look, the young woman is with child and shall bear a son." Ahaz would have preferred something a little more substantial, a division or two of battle-ready soldiers, for instance, to repel the expected invasion. A pregnant young woman? An infant son? This infant son, however, is Emmanuel, and in him and his name will be power to give courage and stiffen the resolve and hope of a frightened king and his people, and all frightened people, under all sorts of threatening and oppressive circumstances—including those in which people in our own congregations find themselves during Advent. One thinks of economic uncertainty, shrinking savings and assets, loss of the job that was expected to sustain until retirement, the threat of aging and illness, the prospect of a future without a beloved partner. There are always, the preacher must remember, frightened people in every congregation.

Psalm 80:1–7, 17–19

The lectionary edits out of this psalm the historic grounding that inspired it. Verses 8–16 move from hopeful abstraction to bitter, tragic reality. The people eat the bread of tears, drink a full measure of tears, and are the laughingstock of their neighbors, because tragic, historic calamity has happened. The once vibrant, luxurious vine of the nation lies in waste, ravaged by wild boars, its fruit plucked indiscriminately by all who pass by.

The psalm expresses the timeless human longing for God to come and put things right in the world. The late Walter Bouman, a Lutheran theologian, used to say that psalms like this one are like a child's prayer: "Dear God: You better come down and do something quick!"

The beginning and ending plea sets the tone: "Restore us . . . ; let your face shine, that we may be saved." The psalm is reminiscent of Isaiah 7:14. God is at work in even the most frightening, tragic, and oppressive circumstances, and God's people have heard the promise in exile and prison, bound by structures of injustice, slavery, racism, poverty, and political oppression.

Some of the most profoundly meaningful incidents in Christian memory happen amid dreadful circumstances. The timeless power of *Letters and Papers from Prison* resides in the oppressive hopelessness of the author's circumstance.[1] Somehow Dietrich Bonhoeffer could be strong, thoughtfully faithful, affectionate, and even whimsical as his situation worsened and he was beset with doubts and depression. When it became clear that the Nazis would never release him and that he would be executed, Bonhoeffer continued to write with grace, courage, and amazing serenity. Martin Luther King Jr.'s sojourn in the Birmingham jail and the appeal of white Birmingham clergy to soften his demand for equal rights resulted in one of the most eloquent and hopeful documents in contemporary Christian literature, the "Letter from Birmingham City Jail."[2] Nelson Mandela, victim and prisoner of the oppressive apartheid regime in South Africa, forged a resolve to forgive his oppressors rather than retaliate, which resulted in a miraculous and peaceful transition from tyranny to freedom.

Heroic examples of God's redeeming activity in difficult circumstances remind the preacher and congregation of ways God continues to work redemptively in society and also in the lives of ordinary people facing extraordinary challenges.

Romans 1:1–7

It is helpful to remember that Paul was in a tenuous situation when he wrote his Letter to the Romans. Not long after composing this epistle he was in Rome, a political prisoner, on his way to trial and execution. The believers who first read the letter were a tiny minority in the capital city of the mightiest empire the world had known, a brutal political and military juggernaut that had executed the one the believers knew as Christ and would, in the near future, turn its full force against them. It is this background that makes verse 7 of Paul's salutation, "To all God's beloved in Rome . . . grace to you and peace," leap from the page and pierce the heart.

Paul sets out major themes in this salutation: "called to be an apostle, . . . the gospel . . . promised beforehand, . . . his Son . . . descended from David . . . [and] Son of God . . . by resurrection from the dead, Jesus Christ our Lord." It is tempting to read it as so much theological boilerplate and miss the startling centerpiece of his vocation as an apostle: "Jesus Christ our Lord, through

---

1. Dietrich Bonhoeffer, *Letters and Papers from Prison*, ed. Eberhard Bethge (New York: Macmillan, 1971).

2. See "Letter from Birmingham City Jail (1963)," in *A Testament of Hope: The Essential Writings of Martin Luther King, Jr.*, ed. James Melvin Washington (San Francisco: Harper & Row, 1986), 289–302.

whom we have received grace and apostleship to bring about the obedience of faith among *all the Gentiles*" (emphasis added). Paul's unmistakable inclusivity is there in the salutation. Surely he was remembering that remarkable day when he was summoned to Jerusalem, with Barnabas, to give an account of their preaching to the Gentiles and their conclusion that God's love and grace, that is, the Good News, transcended even the distinctive and precious traditions of their religion, such as circumcision. Surely he was remembering how Peter himself had stood with him that day and testified that God made no distinction between Jew and Gentile, and how the Jerusalem council that day struck down a racial and religious barrier in the name of the inclusive love of God (see Acts 15).

The church has continued to challenge barriers that exclude and oppress people in our day, even among its own members. Under the mandate of the grace and inclusive love of God, the church has reexamined, changed its mind, and undone exclusive and oppressive policies, rules, standards, and structures in matters of race and gender. Today the whole church is challenged to rethink time-honored traditions and exclusivist structures in regard to sexual orientation.

In this brief but brilliant salutation, Paul anticipates issues that are relevant in every age because of God's unconditional love in Jesus Christ for all people. Religious exclusivism will never be the same.

Matthew 1:18–25

The people in the congregation have heard this reading before. Many of them know it by heart, which means the words live deeply in their hearts. On this Sunday the preacher needs to be careful not to get in the way of the words.

There was a time when many of us assumed that thoughtful Christians ought to grapple with the doctrine of incarnation, even to learn a little bit about the fourth-century incarnation controversies: was Jesus the same essence as God, or the same substance? We learned and were eager to impart the information that there is only a letter or two of difference in the Greek words. About the same time many of us concluded that the way Christmas is celebrated in our culture is an abomination, so commercial and glitzy and vulgar that it is an impediment to the real business of the season, which is thinking about incarnation. A particularly egregious example of the cultural captivity of "our" Christmas is the annual Christmas pageant in which the children of the congregation act out the nativity, combining Matthew and Luke so that the center aisle and chancel of the church are crowded with sheep, cattle, donkeys, shepherds, angels, wise men, and finally Mary and Joseph and a baby Jesus represented by someone's favorite, gender-neutral doll. Occasionally, according to local custom, Santa even appears at the end of the evening to distribute small gifts, and the process of syncretism, we think, is complete.

Minds change, thankfully. It is not merely that one's children and grand-children begin to appear in the pageant. Theological clarity also arises over the years. The children get it right. It was an unplanned, messy, chaotic, totally human occasion, a birth in a cow stall, with all the noise and stench. The characters could not be more marginal, more unlikely than the little ones who portray them in their bathrobes, processing down the aisle of the church: a badly frightened teenager, unmarried and nine months pregnant, missing her mother when she most needed her, accompanied by a man she barely knew, twice her age, the target of crude jokes when she began to show and everyone knew she was engaged but still single. Joseph is underrecognized— an embarrassed man whose fiancée turns up pregnant and he knows he isn't the father, a good man who declines to prosecute and punish, a courageous man who does the most unlikely thing: trusts an angel, marries his pregnant fiancé, becomes father to the baby he knows is not his.

Emmanuel—God with us, in these unlikely marginal characters, poor, scorned, homeless. God knows what it is like to be weary and discouraged and caught up in political structures over which one has no control. God knows what it is like to be pushed to the sidelines, overlooked when important deci-sions are made. Emmanuel—God cares about how life is lived in this world. God—this story intimates—cares a lot more about compassion and justice in the public sphere than about theological orthodoxy in the private. God cares about human suffering in the Middle East and the cities of America and in the lives of respectable but quietly desperate and anxious people.

The most important, radical, and hopeful words in human history include these: "'and they shall name him Emmanuel,' which means, 'God is with us.'"

Christmas Day

Elizabeth Conde-Frazier

ISAIAH 9:2–7
PSALM 96
TITUS 2:11–14
LUKE 2:1–14 (15–20)

The Scriptures for Christmas Day acclaim God as righteous king who moves us from the darkness of oppression to the light and promise of a righteous reign. They challenge us to righteous living and to thinking carefully about how Christ is incarnated in our personal and congregational lives.

Isaiah 9:2–7

The writer of First Isaiah (chaps. 1–39) was active during the second half of the eighth century BCE, during the rise and fall of Near Eastern kingdoms. He was a prophet with access to Judah's most powerful institutions and kings.

Before the death of King Uzziah of Judah (between 742 and 733 BCE), Tiglath-pileser III came to power in Assyria (745 BCE) and began to expand his empire across Syria and Palestine. Kings after him continued his military expansion and political policies. Thus, the context of Isaiah's life was one in which Judah lived under the constant threat of Assyrian domination. Isaiah's theological interpretation of these realities asserted that God was using the Assyrians as a "rod of anger" (10:5), punishing the unfaithfulness of God's people.

According to Gene Tucker, these chapters also reflect two theological themes that dominate all of First Isaiah: the chosen king and the chosen city. The chosen king ensured the continuation of the Davidic dynasty through the divine promise that one of David's heirs would occupy the throne. Promised by God, the Davidic dynasty was considered a manifestation of divine grace and a means of divine protection. However, when kings were not faithful to God, then the people's security was no longer assured, and they turned instead to messianic hope for their survival.[1]

The dramatic change from the gloom and darkness of chapter 8 to the promise and light of chapter 9 has to do with God's assurance of justice under a righteous king. Most scholars consider Isaiah 9:2–7 to be a hymn of celebration for the birth of a new prince, a descendant of David through whom God's deliverance is assured. This birth offers hope amid the threat of military conquest and Assyrian rule.[2]

The first verses of the passage (vv. 2–3) speak of trouble and salvation, whereas verses 4–7 offer praise to God for the inevitable fulfillment of divine promises, including release from military and political danger. God is now the one who has broken "the rod of their oppressor" so that there can be an end to oppression and war. The fullness of Isaiah's hope is evident in the destruction of military garments and gear and in the birth of one who embodies the coming reign of divine justice, righteousness, and peace.

Gloom and darkness continue to cast their shadow over us today as people suffer political and economic upheaval. When there is neither political nor economic security, people experience oppression and violence in many ways. We regularly hear of poverty and community upheaval in the news, such as the occupation of the 99 percent, the mortgage crisis that has led to homelessness for families, political unrest in the Middle East, and the European debt crisis. The effects of poverty on individual and communal life make poverty itself a form of violence. The light of hope comes to us through education, jobs, integrity in government and business practices, affordable housing, and safety. It takes the form not only of jobs but also of meaningful employment. This is connected to one's call or vocation. Vocation leads us to productive connections with others. It gives purpose to what we do beyond ourselves. These connections multiply and contribute to the edification of an entire nation that may more positively influence global relations.

Luke 2:1–14 (15–20)

The themes of hope and joy in Isaiah 9 are echoed in Luke 2:1–14 (15–20). This passage follows a long chapter announcing the births of John and Jesus.

Luke sets the historical context of Jesus' birth during the census that was taken when Quirinius was governor of Syria. However, scholars disagree as to whether Quirinius was governor when the census reported in Luke 2 was taken. (There is evidence of another census taken in 6 CE, when there was

---

1. Gene M. Tucker, "The Book of Isaiah 1–39," in *The New Interpreter's Bible*, ed. Leander Keck et al., vol. 9 (Nashville: Abingdon Press, 2001), 38.
2. Ibid., 121 and 123.

a revolt by a group of Galilean patriots against taxation.) It is also confusing that Joseph and Mary travel together for the census in Bethlehem, because tax laws did not require all family members to accompany the head of the household to the census. Craig Keener posits that "Joseph may have simply wished not to leave Mary alone at this point in her pregnancy, especially if the circumstances of her pregnancy had deprived her of other friends."[3]

It is Luke who describes the indignity of Jesus' birth, of God coming as a helpless child who had only a feeding trough for his crib. This is a very different version of a king's birth and points therefore to the different nature of this king's reign.

In this birth, God identifies with those who live in the indignity and humiliation of poverty and oppression. The birth of this king ushers in a new world order where shepherds, not magi (as in Matthew's Gospel), receive the announcement of God's favor. In first-century Palestine, shepherds were often despised by others and assumed to be dishonest and lazy, allowing their sheep to graze on others' land. Tensions often existed between them and wealthier landowners. Their occupation also kept them from regularly participating in the religious life of their communities. We can almost hear the angry words, insults, and accusations they endured. In contrast to these, Luke depicts the angelic chorus ringing in their ears: "Glory to God in the highest heaven, and on earth peace among those whom God favors!" (v. 14). These words no doubt brought relief and joy to the outcast shepherds.

Who are the shepherds of today? What does God's favor look like for those who are despised, oppressed, or outcast? These may include persons of different ethnicities, races, or sexual orientation, the homeless, or the differently abled. Are our charitable efforts during this season an adequate representation of God's favor toward others? If the angels are announcing a reign to come, how can we give expression to this reign throughout the year so that our charitable efforts during Advent may represent the inauguration of the kingdom of God?

Psalm 96

While in the Lukan passage it is the angels who sing, the psalmist urges *us* to sing "a new song" (v. 1). Psalm 96 acclaims God as creator and ruler. It is part of a collection of hymns known as Enthronement Psalms that proclaim God's reign (including Pss. 93, 95–99). Some scholars believe that it was sung as part of the autumnal festival that included the tradition of singing about God's reign. Similar themes also appear in 1 Chronicles 16:23–33 on the occasion

3. Craig S. Keener, *The IVP Bible Background Commentary: New Testament* (Downers Grove, IL: InterVarsity Press, 1993), 193.

of bringing the ark of the covenant to Jerusalem. Other scholars suggest that the psalms proclaim God's reign not as part of an autumnal festival but as a response to the crisis of exile. During exile, the people of Israel no longer had an earthly monarch, but they trusted and celebrated the good news that God was still sovereign. The psalmist imagines God's sovereignty over all nations (v. 10) as well as the entire creation (vv. 11–12).

However, God's sovereignty is characterized not by the superiority of God or of Israel, but by divine justice. Justice differentiates YHWH from all other gods. These gods and idols are condemned to death because they are not righteous and they practice injustice, showing partiality to some at the expense of others. God, however, comes to establish justice on earth by transforming the chaos of unjust rulers and policies. The God of Israel is feared by idols.

In our time also, there are idols that create false hope and/or chaos among us. Where do they dwell? What are their powers among us? In defiance of them, we may participate in elections, budget meetings of school boards, PTA meetings in our school districts, and meetings in local churches to promote diversity and help sing a new song of God's just and loving purposes among us.

Titus 2:11–14

One of the most prominent features of this short letter is the theological rationale that underlies its ethical code. Chapter 2 begins with rules for good household management. To be sure, the admonition for slaves to be submissive to their masters is thoroughly disturbing, especially when we consider the exploitation of children and women through slave labor practices that continue today. Paul is addressing persons who are not in a position of power, and he wants to ensure their safety. Those who are in power need to understand that this letter does not condone their oppressive practices. More helpful are the other detailed instructions for everyday routines and relationships. In Latino/a theology this is called *lo cotidiano*, everyday actions that are considered to be the locus of theology, where our lives meet God. Why is this valued by Paul as well as many of today's Latino/a theologians?

Right relationships or righteousness are the building blocks of justice. Households were the basic foundation of Greco-Roman society, and they were not disconnected from the political realm. The same is true today. While many of our songs narrowly define salvation as the relationship between an individual and God through Jesus, in reality this is only the starting place for salvation. The reconciliation of the person with God begins a domino effect in all of our relationships, including the institutional relationships we participate in. The influence we have as employers, citizens, and voting members of these institutions reflects our relationship with Jesus Christ as members of God's household.

How do we live so that God's presence through Jesus' birth is evident in our lives for all to see? Titus tells us that the grace of salvation empowers us to live godly lives (v. 11). God's grace empowers us to live counterculturally so that our lives might witness to a different set of values.

In a consumerist society such as ours, we have confused want with need, driving us to produce more goods more quickly and more cheaply. This creates a demand for cheap labor both here and abroad. The lack of just wages for workers abroad creates the need for them to immigrate. When they arrive we continue to exploit their labor, making them a permanent underclass without dignity in either their country of origin or their current place of residence.

What does self-control look like in a consumerist society? Avariciousness is to want something without regard for how much it might cost another person: "I want it even if it costs your livelihood." If chocolate is a product of child slave labor or a blouse is made by workers who are paid only 67 cents a week, should we be aware of this so that it might influence our personal habits and church mission? More often than not, I am not even aware of the sequence of events that is responsible for bringing goods to the mall where I shop. Should I not be aware if it is indeed costing someone's livelihood? Why am I not? How is this hidden from me? How might we bring this reality to light? What spiritual practices would help us to embody the virtues mentioned by Titus?

The arrival of God's grace in Jesus Christ brings salvation, right relationships, and justice, and makes it possible for us to live godly lives. Our godly living then brings salvation, livelihood, compassion, equity, healing, and *shalom* to others. When we tell the Christmas narrative about the arrival of God in Bethlehem, the oppressed people of today (like the shepherds of yesterday) hear and see the good news of God's salvation. May they find the Savior incarnated among us in godly living so that our witness might become the telling of the story, the reappearing of the glory of God today.

First Sunday after Christmas

Ruthanna B. Hooke

ISAIAH 63:7–9
PSALM 148
HEBREWS 2:10–18
MATTHEW 2:13–23

During the Christmas season, when preachers center their reflections on the incarnation of God in Jesus Christ, today's lessons focus our attention on the cost of this incarnation. Matthew 2:13–23 demands center stage among today's texts because of the serious theological implications and clear social justice issues it raises. The other texts for the day provide illuminating commentary on this reading and the call to justice that it implies. Hebrews 2 reminds us that God came among us in Jesus Christ to be with us and redeem our suffering, while Isaiah 63:7–9 calls us to act with justice toward the most vulnerable because of God's unconditional love for us. The summons to praise God in Psalm 148 reorients us to a deeper solidarity with the creation that God so deeply loves as to become incarnate within it.

Matthew 2:13–23

The horrific story of the massacre of the infants in Bethlehem recounted in this text cannot be glossed over; it cries out for our attention. Immediately following Christmas, this text comes as a severe jolt. The peace and joy of Christmas give way almost immediately to fear, impending danger, and horrific violence. In a perverse way, the very diligence and faithfulness of the magi contribute to unimaginable evil; as soon as they tell King Herod whom they are seeking, his jealous lust for power perceives a threat to his rule and he issues a decree for mass murder. The joy of the magi quickly becomes the anguish of Rachel weeping for her slaughtered children. Juxtaposing this text with those of the nativity jerks us out of the coziness and merriment of the season, and brings us face to face with the reality of evil and with the

36

danger and violence of this world in which we live and which the Son of God has entered. The forces that oppose God's way in the world are strong indeed.

From a social justice perspective, Matthew 2:13–23 compels us to speak out against forces of evil and violence that threaten the least powerful among us, especially children. However, even more uncomfortably, this text prods us to examine the ways in which our own lives are complicit in the suffering of children. Many thousands of children in the United States do not have access to clean, safe drinking water, in part because we do not raise an outcry against manufacturers that pollute our water sources with impunity. Many thousands of children in this country live below the poverty line, in part because we do not put sufficient pressure on the officials we have elected to take measures (such as raising taxes for the wealthiest Americans) to help close the widening gap between rich and poor people. Many thousands of children eat contaminated food, because we do not insist on regulations for food producers who cut corners of safety and cleanliness in order to maximize profits.

If we are appalled by Herod's murder of children, we need to change our own priorities and actions so that we protect the children in our midst from suffering and death. The first action we can take is that of Rachel, who "weeps for her children . . . because they are no more" (Matt. 2:18). In situations of injustice, lament is the first act of awakening our consciences and spurring our wills to action. To join Rachel's lament over injustice, violence, and murder is to take the first step toward rectifying these situations.

Hebrews 2:10–18

From a theological perspective, the massacre of the innocents raises the question of theodicy in a particularly sharp way: if God is good, why do the innocent suffer? But still more pressing, why does God provide for God's own Son to be saved, sending the angel to warn Joseph and Mary to flee, yet permit innocent babies to be killed? Indeed, God saves his own Son *at the expense of* these children. In response to these theological questions, Hebrews offers the picture of the suffering Christ. This answer works on a couple of levels. First, in terms of the Matthew story itself, it reminds us that the infant Jesus was spared death not so that he could go on to lead a life of safety and ease, but in order that ultimately he might die a cruel death, just as the children of Bethlehem did. He was spared death as a child so that his later death would be for the redemption and healing of the world from all such acts of violence. Second, the message of Hebrews is a reminder that God's answer to the theodicy question is not to explain *why* we suffer, but rather to promise divine accompaniment *in* our suffering.

In this way, we shift the focus away from questions about *God's* responsibility for suffering to questions about *our* responsibility for suffering. The question is no longer "Why did God not spare the children?" but rather "Why did Herod kill the children?" There have always been, and likely always will be, Herods who oppose God and what is good in the world because of their greed for power. We can think of such despots today, political leaders whose determination to protect their own position leads them to torture and murder their own people. Such abuse always falls most harshly on the vulnerable, especially children. This text calls us as Christians to speak out against such injustices wherever they may occur in the world. Finally, however, we must examine our own complicity in the suffering of others, so that ultimately the most pressing question is "Why do *we* keep killing the children?"

As we seek to transform our lives and those of others in accord with God's justice, Hebrews provides a word of encouragement. The author of Hebrews exhorts the community to endure persecution faithfully for the sake of Christ. If we challenge the powers that cause hardship to children, we may find ourselves facing persecution as well, but Hebrews reminds us that the suffering Christ is the pioneer who goes before us and redeems us in the midst of our struggles, especially the suffering we undergo in the cause of justice for the least of Christ's brothers and sisters.

Isaiah 63:7–9

At first glance, this passage sits awkwardly next to Matthew 2:13–23. The Isaiah text seems like a straightforward declaration of God's mighty intervention on behalf of God's people. This proclamation of God's saving power begs the question of where God's saving power was when the children of Bethlehem were murdered. However, if we examine Isaiah 63:7–9 in context, the text becomes more complicated and more helpful in relation to the other texts.

Isaiah 63:7–9 is part of Third Isaiah (chaps. 56–66). While Isaiah 1–39 (First Isaiah) is set in Judah prior to the Babylonian exile, and chapters 40–55 (Second Isaiah) address the people during exile, chapters 56–66 are set after the return from exile. While Second Isaiah promised a glorious return, according to Third Isaiah the return from exile was less glorious than had been expected, and those returning encountered many hardships in their homeland: the temple was still in ruins, many had returned to pagan practices, and the poor suffered economic oppression. In keeping with Third Isaiah's chastened tone, 63:7–9 is not a simple celebration of God's saving power, but rather the beginning of a communal lament in which the people bewail their unhappy circumstances and implore God to act on their behalf. As is common for the beginning of a communal lament, these verses recount God's mighty deeds of old, which become the ground for the present complaint: because God has saved our people in the past, we trust and demand that God will do so again. The passage begins by heaping up praise of God, extolling God's "gracious deeds," God's "praiseworthy acts," "all that the LORD has done," and the "great favor" God has shown. Verse 8 recalls the central fact of God's covenant with the people in which God vowed to save the people of Israel. In verse 9, God's love for the people is described in strikingly intimate terms: God saves them and carries them as a parent carries a child.

The implications for social justice become apparent when we consider the passage in light of the overall message of Third Isaiah. First Isaiah exhorted the people to practice righteousness or else be judged, and Second Isaiah proclaimed God's unconditional grace and power to save the people. Third Isaiah blends these two emphases into the proclamation that because God has elected the people, they are required to act righteously in order to fulfill their covenant with God, something they can do only by God's grace. There is an emphasis in these verses on ethical righteousness required of those who have returned from exile and want to rebuild Judah. This emphasis is found in passages in which God exhorts the people to "loose the bonds of injustice" (58:6) and "proclaim liberty to the captives" (61:1). In response to the community's lament in 63:7–64:11, God promises to answer their pleas, and will even go beyond what they are asking to create "new heavens and a new earth," a society in which the people shall "build houses and inhabit them" and will "plant vineyards and eat their fruit," where "they shall not hurt or destroy on all my holy mountain" (65:17, 21, 25).

To preach social justice from Isaiah 63:7–9 is to insist that, precisely *because* of God's unbreakable covenant with us, we are required to participate in God's work of creating a new society that manifests divine justice. The unjust suffering of children, as in Matthew 2:13–23, calls us to raise a lament to God, as Third Isaiah does, and yet the answer to this lament is God's call to participate in the divine work of doing justice. Just as God maternally cares for us, we are called to care tenderly for the most vulnerable in our midst, including children. The prevalence of economic injustice in Third Isaiah's time focuses our attention specifically on economic injustice among us and around the world, particularly as it hurts children most of all.

Psalm 148

This passage contains one of the most expansive and inclusive calls to praise God found anywhere in the Psalter. The psalmist calls for praise of God from sun, moon, stars, "highest heavens," and "the earth"—not only from humans, animals, and plants, but even from inanimate objects such as mountains and hills. Although the final line of the Psalter (Ps. 150:6) calls for "everything that breathes" to praise the Lord, Psalm 148 goes further, inviting praise of God from everything that exists, both animate and inanimate. In particular, Psalm 148 demands that kings and princes praise God. Those who rule over the earth are required to recognize the ultimate sovereignty of God, and to give God praise accordingly.

From a social justice perspective, this invocation of the sweep of God's creation calls us to see our partnership with creation. Since we are partners with animals, plants, mountains, and stars in giving praise to God, we also need to be partners with the entire created world by demonstrating our care for it. In this season of incarnation, Psalm 148 reminds us of God's blessing of creation, not only by creating it but also by becoming a fleshly participant in it through Jesus of Nazareth. God's solidarity with and love for creation spurs us on to show similar solidarity with all that exists and to see ourselves as profoundly connected to it. In relation to Matthew 2:13–23, the psalmist's call to praise God entails acting in accordance with God's ways. We cannot praise God with our lips while our actions are far from God. To praise God truly is to protect the littlest ones, so that no more massacres of the innocents take place ever again.

Holy Name of Jesus

Dianne Bergant, CSA

NUMBERS 6:22–27
PSALM 8
GALATIANS 4:4–7
LUKE 2:15–21

What is in a name? We may not appreciate the importance of this feast because in Western society the practice of naming does not hold the significance that it does in many other societies around the world, or that it did in ancient Israel or even early Christianity. While many people today do name their children after family members or good friends, some people choose names like Moon, Apple, or Blanket. Just what is in a name?

Traditional people believe that the name contains part of the essence of the person. That is why they sometimes name a child after a recent cosmic event or after memorable occasions in the family. Furthermore, individuals in such societies often possess at least three names: a public name that everyone may use, a name by which the person is addressed only within the group, and a private name known only to intimates. The importance of God's name is seen in each of the readings for today's feast.

Galatians 4:4–7

In this letter, Paul insists that the purpose of Christ's mission was the transformation of humanity for the Galatians; this meant that Christ sought to liberate them from being enslaved by the law and to elevate them to adoption as children of God. The apostle draws a contrast between being enslaved by the law and being free in Christ. Paul devises an analogy with a common practice of that time. In antiquity a legal guardian was appointed when a person was too young to manage an inheritance. The guardian supervised the inheritance until the heir became old enough to handle it. In this analogy, the members of the Galatian congregation are similar to minors who need a guardian until the fullness of time had come (4:4a). During their wait, their guardian was the law. With the coming of Christ, their circumstances changed. The Galatian believers were no longer minors but were now of age; they were no longer under the guardianship of the law. They have full standing as legal heirs since God has fully adopted them as children. Christ "redeemed those [previously] under the law."

To underscore the reliability of this claim, Paul points to evidence in the experience of the Galatian congregation: under the influence of the Spirit of Christ, they now address God by the term "Abba." This word is evidence of their new relationship with God. In the 1970s, Joachim Jeremias, a renowned biblical scholar, suggested that "Abba" meant "Daddy." Although challenged by scholars, this rendition of the word caught the imagination of believers and has continued to be so understood by many today. Actually, "Abba" is an Aramaic word for "Father," not "Daddy." It appears in three places in the New Testament: Mark 14:36; Romans 8:15; and here in Galatians. In each case, the word is followed by its translation, "Father." While "Abba" is not a formal title for God, it is a warm, trusting, and intimate term. The word "Abba" betokens such a relationship between God and believers.

The reading ends as it began, declaring that all of this is God's doing. God sent the Son to make sons and daughters of the rest of us. This is accomplished by means of the indwelling of the Spirit, which empowers us to call God Abba, tender Father.

Some people today resist using this male term for God. However, since it originated in a patriarchal (father-headed), androcentric (male-centered) society, one should not be surprised by its gender bias. In antiquity the emphasis was less on arbitrary male rule and more on the role of the father in an extended family to ensure the household had everything needed for a secure life and to help the members of the family live in covenant. The major importance of the term lies in its reference to an intimate relationship with God, not in its gender identification.

In the minds of the ancients, names often contain within them something of the essence of the one so named. If we call God "Abba, Father," we imply that we enjoy an intimate relationship with God, as did Jesus. How can mere human beings make such a bold claim? Paul clarifies this. In both Galatians and Romans he speaks of adoption. Christians are adopted children of God, thus legal heirs. Just what do they inherit? All of the privileges of belonging to the family of God.

Paul sets up a contrast between servitude under the law and freedom in Christ. Contrary to what some people might claim, Paul does not entertain a negative attitude toward the law. Like Jesus before him, Paul was an observant Jew. However, with the coming of Christ, a new relationship with God has been established and, therefore, a new relationship with the law. No longer are the people servants of the law. Instead, they now enjoy freedom as children of God and heirs of the reign of God. Once the Spirit takes hold of the believer, dependence on the law ends and freedom in the Spirit, the rightful inheritance of the children of God, begins.

The implications of this perspective are astounding. Believers have been transformed. They are no longer "minors," who need the restrictions of the law in order to know how to act. Instead, they are now mature heirs, directed by the Spirit to live lives that are genuinely faithful to the law. Furthermore, they recognize that the distinction of being a child of God who is invited to call God "Abba, Father," belongs to all believers, regardless of gender, race, nationality, economic status, and so forth. All genuine social justice is rooted in the realization of our common heritage as children of God. We are all being transformed from underage minors to legitimate heirs.

When we dare to use the designation "Abba, Father" (or some female equivalent), we are not simply turning to God as a child turns to "Daddy." We are acknowledging what is most fundamental to our own identity. We are children of God, heirs to the blessings of the reign of God. And this designation is intended to include all people.

Numbers 6:22–27

Many scholars believe this text is one of the oldest pieces of poetry in the Bible. The blessing that it contains is well known even by those not acquainted with the biblical book within which it is found. Moses transmits a blessing from God to Aaron and his sons (vv. 22–23), thus giving Aaron's leadership both divine and Mosaic legitimation.

There is some question about the actual use of this blessing by ancient Israel, since there is a strong tradition among Jews, standing to this day, that forbids the use of the personal name of God. (This is why some translations circumvent the use of the divine name by printing the consonants of the name, YHWH, while others substitute LORD for the personal name.) This reverence grew out of the belief that a name possesses some of the very identity of the person named (as mentioned above). To know someone's name was to have intimate knowledge of and some form of control over that person. Thus, to know and use God's personal name presumed this kind of intimacy and even control over God. The Israelites certainly would not make this latter claim.

When read with the passage from Galatians, this blessing reinforces the idea of intimacy with God. This becomes clear when we read that the priests are told to "put my name on the Israelites." To place God's name on the people implies that they belong to God in a very special way. This is a concrete way of understanding God's intimate relationship with the people. It is as if God were saying, "You are mine."

Psalm 8

This responsorial psalm is a hymn that praises the name of God because of the splendor of the world God created. The psalmist begins by pondering the night sky, captivated by its beauty and deeply moved by the place of human beings who share in exercising the dominion of God in the created world. The psalmist is moved not merely by the creation but by the name of God to which the creation points.

The first part of this ancient hymn compares the vastness of the heavens with the limited size of the human being. The bodies in the night heavens—moon and stars—are vast, radiant, and seemingly permanent. By comparison, a human being is small, insignificant, and transient. Despite their apparent insignificance, human beings exercise a unique role in creation and, therefore, they enjoy a special relationship with the creator.

While translators sometimes use the word "angels" in verse 5, the Hebrew here is really the plural for "gods" (*'elohim*), that is, members of God's heavenly court. The point is that God created humankind with only slightly less authority than the members of God's retinue in heaven, so that on the earth human beings are to exercise dominion in the same way that God does in Genesis 1:26–28. This imagery from the royal court depicts the human being as a member of royalty. The psalmist states that humankind is crowned with glory and honor, a reference to an ancient coronation ceremony when royalty were so crowned.

The other creatures are put under their feet, an image that sometimes implies conquest but here suggests the fealty that ancient subjects owed their rulers. This royal dignity does not belong to human beings by right. Nevertheless, while Psalm 8 acknowledges the profound dignity apportioned to the human being, it is utterly clear in proclaiming the name of God as responsible for the world and for the distinct and honored role of the human being. Indeed, the psalm begins and ends with the name of God.

Luke 2:15–21

This Gospel account is one of the most popular Christmas stories. The passage is made up of two sections: the shepherds going from the fields to the manger, and the traditional Jewish practice of circumcision along with the naming of Jesus.

The shepherds were considered irreligious because their occupation prevented them from actively participating in the worship of the community.

Because they typically needed to be physically present with the sheep, it was most unusual for the shepherds to leave them and make their way to the manger. If the flock belonged to the shepherds, they would lose income if something detrimental happened to the sheep during their absence. If the sheep belonged to someone else, the shepherds would be held legally responsible for any harm to the flock. Nevertheless, the shepherds show us how Luke wants all people to respond to the news about Jesus: they leave their fields and go to him.

Upon arriving at the manger, the shepherds grasp the angel's message. They believe that Jesus is the fulfillment of Israel's messianic hope and, in a sense, are among the first to preach this fulfillment. They take a huge risk by deserting the sheep and speaking in ways that could bring opprobrium on them.

As faithful Jews, Mary and Joseph have Jesus circumcised after eight days. They give him a name that was typical yet also dramatic in its implications. In the Aramaic language that was used in those days, "Jesus" is a form of "Joshua," a name given to many people at that time. Yet the meaning of "Joshua" is "the LORD delivers." In this way, the name "Jesus" interprets his identity and purpose: God will deliver, or save, through him.

This passage follows the account of the visit of the shepherds, people who lived on the margins of society, people who were despised by the self-righteous. Luke places these stories back to back to make a point. Throughout Luke's Gospel, God shows special interest in those who live on the margins. Certainly the name "Jesus" (the LORD delivers) sends a message of hope to them, as it does to all who are despised or oppressed today.

Second Sunday after Christmas

Alyce M. McKenzie

JEREMIAH 31:7–14
PSALM 147:12–20
EPHESIANS 1:3–14
JOHN 1:1–18

Every story has a main character who wants something and who acts to get it. What he or she wants is often called "the object of desire." There are obstacles to the character getting the object of desire that come from events or the actions of other characters. And, finally, there is the kind of life that results from obtaining that object of desire. These three components of main character's desire, object of desire, and life formed by getting that desire can be seen in biblical texts as well, whether they are narrative texts or other genres. There is always a story behind the text.

These four texts from John, Ephesians, Jeremiah, and the Psalter show up like old friends this second Sunday after Christmas in Years A, B, and C. Based on our three-part understanding of story, we are going to have a slightly different conversation with these texts each year. In Year A we focus on what God desires in each passage. We find that, in each case, God's desire is to give us a gift. In Year B we focus on the obstacles to God's conveying that gift to us. In Year C we talk about the kind of life that results when we accept the gift God offers to us.

John 1:1–18

The Gospel of John is addressed to a group of Christians near the end of the first century who have been put out of their synagogues. In the prologue (vv. 1–18), John takes the job description of Woman Wisdom (Sophia) from the book of Proverbs and ascribes it to the male-gendered Word (Logos) of God.[1]

---

1. The apocryphal book the Wisdom of Solomon and the Jewish philosopher Philo are his precedents for this connection.

Woman Wisdom in Proverbs helps God with creation (8:22–31), offers the path of life (3:5–8; 8:35–36), and offers light (13:9; 31:18b), nourishment (9:5, 6), and protection (4:5, 8, 9; 31:11–12).

The prologue tells us that Jesus emanates from God, exists before creation, and is an active agent in creation and in Israel's salvation history. The Johannine community has accepted him as the Word and Wisdom of God and is being persecuted as a result. Jesus' identity as Wisdom offers them the sustenance they need during their trials.

The Gospel elaborates and puts flesh on the identity and qualities of Jesus the Wisdom and Word of God to whom we are introduced in the prologue. John teaches us the identity of Jesus with seven "I am" sayings: Jesus is bread of life (6:35, 51), light of the world (8:12; 9:5), sheep gate (10:7, 9), good shepherd (10:11, 14), resurrection and life (11:25), way, truth, and life (14:6), and true vine (15:1, 5).

Sister Mary Lou Kownacki, in her book *A Monk in the Inner City*, tells the story of Sister Claire stopping by Tom's house to pick him up to help deliver a truckload of furniture.[2] She honked the horn and waited for him to come out. Tom for most of his life had been on Supplemental Security Income, poor, hungry, and often homeless. Determined to get off government assistance, he had recently started earning a little money by doing maintenance work at the food pantry and the art center. He came to the door and called to Sister Claire, "Come see my garden." In his small backyard he had a plot of zucchini, tomatoes, and peppers. He picked the ripest tomato and largest zucchini and handed them to her. "These are for the soup kitchen. The Bible says we are to offer our first fruits back to God."

We can tell people about our gardens or we can offer them its fruits. If we take the prologue's picture of Jesus to heart, we will extend the gifts that Jesus the Word and Wisdom of God came to earth to offer to us: light, nourishment, and guidance.

Ephesians 1:3–14

The Letter to the Ephesians is traditionally ascribed to Paul, writing from prison, probably in Rome in the early 60s. It may well have been written in the early second century to a multicultural congregation of Jews and Gentiles in Asia Minor. It is a dramatic call to unity in the church based on God's offer of salvation to the whole world "in Christ." You cannot read the letter and miss the emphasis on unity that pulses through each chapter. This points to a context in which there was a growing split between those who had been

2. Mary Lou Kownacki, *A Monk in the Inner City: The ABCs of a Spiritual Journey* (Maryknoll, NY: Orbis Books, 2008), 125.

Jewish and Gentile Christians. The author states clearly that God offers the gift of salvation to those "who were the first to set our hope on Christ" (v. 12) as well as those who later "heard the word of truth . . . and believed" (v. 13). Some say that Onesimus, the freed slave who is the subject of Philemon, wrote Ephesians. Others theorize that Tychicus, one of the seventy disciples and a companion of Paul mentioned in 6:21, wrote Ephesians. Whoever wrote Ephesians was on a mission to unify divided groups by reminding them that God's salvation is for everyone, not just a chosen few.

The letter expresses the saving activity of God "in Christ" in extravagantly joyful terms. The first several verses announce that God "in Christ" is blessing us "with every spiritual blessing in the heavenly places" (v. 3), choosing us "in Christ before the foundation of the world to be holy and blameless before him in love" (v. 4), and destining us "for adoption as his children through Jesus Christ" (v. 5). In the Corinthian correspondence the phrase "in Christ" refers primarily to the transformative effect of Christ's presence in the inner life of the believer. Here the phrase "in Christ" is more a description of how God works in bringing about our salvation. God works "in Christ" to effect a plan for the fullness of time that unites or sums up all things in Christ.[3]

To get this point across, the author, in the opening to the letter, speaks of God's choosing Jews and Gentiles alike in terms reminiscent of God's choosing Israel. God chose Israel simply because God loved them (Deut. 23:5). For that reason alone, not because of their number or righteousness, God made Israel God's child (Exod. 4:22; Jer. 31:20).[4] The same is true of us. God chose us. We did not choose God. As the author clearly says in chapter 2, through Christ both Jews and Gentiles "have access in one Spirit to the Father" (Eph. 2:18).

In Ephesians, God's gift is choosing us so that we can share God's gift of forgiving, uplifting love with a hurting world. The seal of the Holy Spirit is not a designer label that sets some above others, but a mark that we belong to God, who works "in Christ" to unify the whole world in God's saving embrace.

Jeremiah 31:7–14

Jeremiah (650–587) lived in a small town (Anathoth) in a vulnerable country (Judah) located in the crosshairs of two voracious superpowers, Assyria and Babylon. Judah's plight is similar to that reflected by the Korean proverb "When whales fight, the shrimp's back is broken," reflecting that larger, competing

---

3. G. H. P. Thompson, *The Letters of Paul to the Ephesians, to the Colossians and to Philemon*, Cambridge Bible Commentary (New York: Cambridge University Press, 1967), 24.
4. Walter F. Taylor Jr., *Ephesians*, Augsburg Commentary on the New Testament (Minneapolis: Augsburg, 1985), 26.

nations buffet smaller, more vulnerable ones.[5] Jeremiah's story is one of a thankless lifelong task of telling people what they do not want to hear. It was the message that Judah, because of its imitation of the worship of other gods and its moral decay, would go the way of Israel some seventy-five years earlier. Judah would fall to the Babylonians, as Israel had been overrun by the Assyrians.

The book of Jeremiah contains many oracles of doom and coming judgment. Yet our text from chapter 31 shows us Jeremiah as a prophet of hope, pointing forward to a time of divine restoration before the judgment has even struck. Our passage (31:7–14) comes from what is traditionally known as the Book of Consolations (chaps. 30–33). It provides a brief respite of sunshine between two torrential storms. Commentator R. E. O. White calls these chapters a "foregleam" of the restoration to come.[6]

What Jeremiah sees in his "foregleam" of the future is a vision of God's gathering the exiled peoples back home. He glimpses God's gift of a homecoming for the people and a time of flourishing back at home. This will be a time of abundance, joy, and satisfaction in relationship with God (31:12–14).

Homecoming is a deep yearning for exiled people. A couple of years ago I interviewed pastors serving in multicultural church settings. Said one pastor, "Whenever I talk about exile and return, bondage and freedom, people's faces light up with recognition. It's a redemptive connection from then to now." Biblical experiences of enslavement and freedom are existential bridges to the lives of contemporary people who experience abuse and oppression. They are prophetic eye-openers to the privileged who prefer to think such conditions belong to ancient Bible times simply because they are not part of their own relatively sanitized, comfortable lives. This text leaves us with questions: How can we as the church be the "foregleam" of God's full homecoming in a world of storm and shadows? How can we be "home" for the poor and the discouraged in our communities?

Psalm 147:12–20

Among the several types of psalms in the Psalter (e.g., praise, thanksgiving, individual and communal lament, wisdom, and royal), Psalm 147 is a hymn of praise to God.[7] The Psalter, read as a whole, moves from laments, concentrated in the first half of the Psalter, to hymns of praise. It ends with four

---

5. Joseph Raymond, "Tensions in Proverbs: More Light on International Understanding," in *Wisdom of Many: Essays on the Proverb*, ed. Wolfgang Mieder and Alan Dundes (Madison: University of Wisconsin Press, 1994), 301.

6. R. E. O. White, *The Indomitable Prophet: A Biographical Commentary on Jeremiah* (Grand Rapids: Eerdmans, 1992), 117.

7. For a categorization of psalms, see Lawrence Boadt, *Reading the Old Testament: An Introduction* (New York: Paulist Press, 1984), 282.

glorious psalms of praise. Psalm 147 refers to the return of the exiles from Babylon as well as to the construction of the second temple, probably the repairs carried out by Nehemiah (Neh. 12:27). It points to a postexilic date, perhaps around 500 BCE.[8]

The first eleven verses of Psalm 147 enjoin us to praise God because God is the Creator, and because God the Creator is compassionate. God's power in creation is linked with God's tender care for us in our weakness.[9] The last portion of the psalm (vv. 12–20) focuses on praise of God because God has chosen Israel and promised to keep it secure. The last few lines contain references to Torah ("statutes and ordinances," v. 19) and to God's choosing Israel (v. 20).

In times of confusion and crisis, hymns of praise provide a moment of clarity, reminding us of who and whose we are, God's provision for us, and our dependency on God. This moment of clarity holds two reminders.

The first reminder that praise psalms offer is that our faith is communal, not individualistic. Hymns of praise are communal acts of worship, not individualistic songs to God. In his helpful book *The Biblical Psalms in Christian Worship*, John D. Witvliet gathers testimony from people of faith past and present on the importance of the psalms for their faith. A common theme among their testimonies is gratitude to the psalms for showing them that prayer is a communal and not only a personal act. Says Eugene Peterson,

> The assumption that prayer is what we do when we are alone—the solitary soul before God—is an egregious, and distressingly persistent, error. We imagine a lonely shepherd on the hills composing lyrics to the glory of God. We imagine a beleaguered soul sinking into a swamp of trouble calling for help. But our imaginations betray us. We are part of something before we are anything, and never more so than when we pray. Prayer begins in community.[10]

A second reminder that praise psalms offer is that not everyone experiences life as good and ordered, as depicted in psalms of praise. Praise psalms nudge us to ask if our own praise embraces the pain of the world and its injustice or ignores it. Do we view those who are not secure and well-off as outside God's blessing of creation? Do we undergird structures of injustice with our status quo praise that keeps the powerless in line?[11]

---

8. Samuel Terrien, *The Psalms: Strophic Structure and Theological Commentary* (Grand Rapids: Eerdmans, 2003), 917.

9. Denise Dombkowski Hopkins, *Journey through the Psalms* (St. Louis: Chalice Press, 2002), 33.

10. Eugene Peterson, *Answering God: The Psalms as Tools for Prayer* (San Francisco: Harper & Row, 1989), 83–84. Quoted in John D. Witvliet, *The Biblical Psalms in Christian Worship: A Brief Introduction and Guide to Resources* (Grand Rapids: Eerdmans, 2007), 141.

11. Hopkins, *Journey*, 36.

Epiphany of Jesus

Terriel R. Byrd

Isaiah 60:1–6
Psalm 72:1–7, 10–14
Matthew 2:1–12
Ephesians 3:1–12

Just like the four seasons of the year, all of the texts for Epiphany Sunday reveal different manifestations of God's justice. Like the arresting chill of winter, the psalmist captures our attention with a prayer that reorders the entrenched social structure by giving the poor a voice in the king's court during a royal coronation. The Gospel of Matthew offers the promise of a refreshing spring-time breeze on a cold, clear night when a star shone brightly and three wise men were comforted and encouraged by the revelation of Jesus, the Messiah who is born amid humble surroundings. With the warmth of summer's penetrating rays, the prophet Isaiah points to a persistent prophetic message of redemption, hope, and abundant blessings. Finally, the apostle invites us to enjoy the revelation of the mysteries of God given to him, not unlike autumnal leaves that change color and fall from the trees, as he welcomes new, splendid, and variegated encounters with Jews and Gentiles in the united and diverse body of Jesus Christ. Let us celebrate the justice of God in all seasons and for all peoples!

Isaiah 60:1–6

The prophet envisions tangible restoration for all! "Arise, shine; for your light has come, and the glory of the Lord has risen upon you" (v. 1). The years of brokenness, battery, misfortune, and misgivings have come to an end under the light of God. Gone are vain rituals and empty offerings. "What to me is the multitude of your sacrifices? says the Lord; I have had enough of burnt offerings of rams and the fat of fed beasts; I do not delight in the blood of bulls, or of lambs, or of goats" (1:11) The light shines brightly upon truth

51

and justice. "Learn to do good; seek justice, rescue the oppressed, defend the orphan, plead for the widow" (1:17).

According to N. T. Wright, "God's passion for justice must become ours, too. When Christians use their belief in Jesus as a way of escaping from that demand and challenge, they are abandoning a central element in their own faith."[1] If God's passion for justice is not our passion, we become mere accessories to the turmoil and bewilderment of the human predicament. For instance, today the United States faces its toughest economic downturn since the Great Depression. The result is that 45 million Americans—an estimated half of them children—are now living at or below the poverty level. Much of the reason for this crisis is massive unemployment due to moral injustices committed by corrupt members of the financial sector. One would hope that the church might, or could, be the leading voice of righteous indignation and protest—to demand restitution and righteous change in a system that is capable of destroying American lives by pursuing unrestrained greed. Without such a voice, we fail to fully live out authentic Christian faith.

The glory of God's truth is powerful enough to dispel darkness. The darkness associated with creation manifested itself with chaos and confusion (Gen. 1:1–3). God spoke, then light shone forth, revealing the beauty of God's creation.

The prophet declares, "Nations shall come to your light, and kings to the brightness of your dawn" (Isa. 60:3). Nelson Mandela endured twenty-seven harsh years of imprisonment in a dark, dreary jail cell for speaking out against the brutal system of apartheid in South Africa, until finally his day of light came on February 11, 1990, when all nations of the world were able to behold the light of truth that conquered injustice. It is inspiring to witness the unity and support of nations working for the cause of human rights and social justice. Isaiah echoes this theme when he says, "Lift up your eyes and look around; they all gather together, they come to you; your sons shall come from far way, and your daughters shall be carried on their nurses' arms" (Isa. 60:4). The culmination of God's covenantal promise will not merely bring victory and bless Zion, but all the nations will shine in the radiant beauty of God's abundant blessings.

Psalm 72:1–7, 10–14

Imagine a world where the poor, the oppressed, and the socially outcast are highly esteemed and valued. Imagine a world where justice is not determined by the interests of the stronger party, such as that of the alliance between Wall

1. N. T. Wright, *Simply Christian* (New York: HarperCollins, 2006), 13.

Street and K Street in Washington, where wealthy corporate lobbyists pay for the bidding of the powerful and wealthy. We could witness a world where "justice [is] the line and righteousness the plummet" (Isa. 28:17). Such is the world for which the orator in Psalm 72 prays and hopes. "Give the king your justice, O God, and your righteousness to a king's son. May he judge your poor with righteousness, and your poor with justice" (Ps. 72:1–2). George A. F. Knight notes that "using the word *justice*, the RSV [Revised Standard Version of the Bible] hides the fact that the word is plural. Justice, of course, is an abstract idea only. But here at the enthronement festival of Israel's king an orator prays God to give the king the power to do *acts of justice*."[2]

The church must engage in acts of justice that are desperately needed today to eradicate poverty and other forms of social injustice. Not surprisingly, involvement among youth in local church communities contributes to a lower rate of crime among black youths. In a recent study, Byron Johnson found that "religious institutions such as churches, mosques, or synagogues are well suited to produce the relational networks of social and emotional support that help prevent at-risk youth from participating in negative behavioral outcomes such as crime."[3]

More than words, acts of justice include a shared vision and commitment to work for racial reconciliation, social justice, and human rights for everyone. According to the psalmist, the king is called to "defend the cause of the poor of the people, give deliverance to the needy, and crush the oppressor" (Ps. 72:4). Spiritual blessings follow as a result of remembering the poor. "Whoever is kind to the poor lends to the LORD, and will be repaid in full" (Prov. 19:17). As noted earlier, many are hurting because of the economic downturn. Many hardworking individuals find themselves unemployed or, worse yet, unemployable due to circumstances beyond their control. The psalmist declares: "He has pity on the weak and the needy, and saves the lives of the needy. From oppression and violence he redeems their life; and precious is their blood in his sight" (Ps. 72:13–14). The church must continue the king's work by confronting acts of injustice against the poor and challenging political policies that enable economic systems to leave so many people bereft of their most basic needs.

2. George A. F. Knight, *Psalms*, Daily Study Bible Series (Philadelphia: Westminster Press, 1982), 1:331.
3. Byron R. Johnson, "The Role of African American Churches in Reducing Crime among Black Youth" (University of Pennsylvania, Center for Research on Religion and Urban Civil Society, 2001). This research was reissued under the same title in 2008 as a Baylor Institute for Studies of Religion Report, available at www.baylorisr.org/wp-content/uploads/ISR_Role_African_American.pdf.

Matthew 2:1–12

Matthew begins this passage by saying, "In the time of King Herod, *after Jesus was born*" (emphasis added). Life would be forever transformed. God had provided a visible manifestation of divine incarnation on earth for all to behold, Jesus Christ. The child was born to Mary, a poor young maiden, amid humble surroundings. God is forever and always present with the poor! "'Look, the virgin shall conceive and bear a son, and they shall name him Emmanuel,' which means, 'God is with us'" (Matt. 1:23). Howard Thurman says, "The economic predicament with which he [Jesus] was identified in birth placed him initially with the great mass of persons on the earth. The masses of the people are poor."[4] Many of the masses come from small, lowly, insignificant places, such as Bethlehem. As of 2011, more than 1.5 million children in the United States live in families without a home and 42 percent of these are under the age of 6.[5] The poor are on the margins of society due to some form of disenfranchisement. However, all who are disenfranchised can find comfort in knowing that Jesus, their Savior, understands what it means to live with unmet needs, suffering, and alienation. The message of hope found in these Scriptures is the reality of God being with us. This living Word reminds us that even the Almighty King who came to liberate the oppressed could identify with the poor and outcast while also overcoming the powers of sin, evil, and death. What a profound assurance there is in knowing that victory is possible even in poverty and for those who come from the lowliest places, all because "God is with us!" "*After Jesus was born* in Bethlehem of Judea"—that fact makes all the difference!

Ephesians 3:1–12

Saul the persecutor of the newly founded Christian movement (Acts 9:1–15) becomes Paul the apostle who led that same movement to amazing heights. Paul is the embodiment of transformation (Eph. 3:7–8). His transformation and subsequent missionary work was of enormous significance and changed the face of Christianity forever. In Paul, the bully and the brute, the victim and the victimizer alike, can find hope that change is possible. Also those who have patiently sought ways to be reconciled with others who are ethnically, racially, and culturally different can find hope in Paul's narrative of change. In this lectionary reading, Paul is imprisoned in Rome, awaiting trial before the Roman emperor Nero (Acts 28:16–20). He acknowledges that he has been

4. Howard Thurman, *Jesus and the Disinherited* (Boston: Beacon Press, 1976), 17.
5. See Yumiko Aratani, "Homeless Children and Youth: Causes and Consequences," National Center for Children in Poverty, September 2009, Mailman School of Public Health Columbia University. http://nccp.org/publications/pdf/text_888.pdf (accessed February 12, 2013).

assigned the task of bringing forth a secret revelation from God, "for surely you have already heard of the commission of God's grace that was given me for you, and how the mystery was made known to me by revelation"(Eph. 3:2–3). The Spirit revealed the mystery that Gentiles have become joint heirs with their Jewish sisters and brothers in the body of Christ (vv. 5–6).

How interesting that Paul, who knew the intense strife that existed between Jews and Gentiles, placed such strong emphasis on unity within the church. Throughout this letter Paul offers different ways of communicating the theme of unity. In Ephesians 4, we are given the conditions for unity: "With all humility and gentleness, with patience, bearing with one another in love, making every effort to maintain the unity of the Spirit in the bond of peace" (4:2–3). The apostle then says, "From whom the whole body, joined and knit together by every ligament with which it is equipped, as each part is working properly, promotes the body's growth in building itself up in love" (4:16). This idea suggests collective interdependence. We were not created as isolated beings; we were created in and for community.

One of the most powerful expressions of unity is evident in Paul's admonition "Husbands, love your wives, just as Christ loved the church and gave himself up for her" (5:25). This is one of the purest illustrations of caring and commitment (5:29). When a bigot or racist becomes culturally sensitive and caring, the effects of God's redeeming love are manifested. When blacks and whites, Jews and Gentiles, Catholics, Protestants, and evangelicals sit down together at the table of sisterhood and brotherhood, we see the effects of God's love manifested. When the unforgiving person practices forgiveness, we see the effect of God's love manifested. As Paul's own life testifies, the best manifestation of God's love is a transformed life.

If the church truly and fully lived out the mystery of unity in the body of Christ, there would be no room for racism, classism, or entrenched forms of disenfranchisement. Paul preaches "the plan of the mystery hidden for ages in God who created all things; so that through the church the wisdom of God in its rich variety might now be made known to the rulers and authorities in the heavenly places" (3:9–10). Indeed, only God-inspired spiritual transformation can bring forth the radiant, splendid, beautiful, and beloved community. Reconciliation is possible, but it must be bathed in obedience, where it will encounter the soothing balm of God's truth, grace, mercy, and love.

First Sunday after the Epiphany (Baptism of Jesus)

Joseph Evans

ISAIAH 42:1–9
PSALM 29
ACTS 10:34–43
MATTHEW 3:13–17

For those of us who came to maturity during the 1960s civil rights and post–civil rights eras, it may come as a surprise to hear an account told by Taylor Branch about an authentic American global prophet, Martin Luther King Jr. I refer to the story as King's "kitchen table religion." After receiving a series of threatening phone calls, King was deeply disturbed and unsettled about his role in the Civil Rights Movement, in particular, his involvement in the Montgomery boycott. According to Branch, "King buried his face in his hands at the kitchen table. He admitted to himself that he was afraid, that he had nothing left, that the people would falter if they looked to him for strength."[1] During this time, King experienced something that he could only describe as the first transcendent religious experience in his life. According to Branch, for King, "The moment lacked the splendor of a vision or of a voice speaking out loud," but "the moment awakened and confirmed his belief that the essence of religion was not a grand metaphysical idea but something personal, grounded in experience—something that opened up mysteriously beyond the predicaments of human beings in their frailest and noblest moments."

Inherent in these crisis moments are calls to serve. The call to serve is a prominent theme in this week's texts for the season of Epiphany. They suggest that ecclesial baptism is an outward response to God's spiritual call to discipleship. I define discipleship as receiving a call from God (which is often abstract and mysterious) and then serving in some form of vocation wherever and however God chooses.

---

1. Taylor Branch, "The Montgomery Bus Boycott," in *Parting the Waters* (New York: Simon & Schuster, 1988), 162.

Isaiah 42:1–9

At a time of personal insecurity and desperation, King found courage from another source. King personalized his "otherwise" experience as the presence of God.[2] It is important to note that King does not describe his experience with God in Eurocentric theological terms and constructs such as evangelical or liberal Protestant categories. If read through a Eurocentric lens, King does not clearly explain whether he is experiencing a religious conversion or an epiphany of reassurance. Eurocentric terms and constructs are unable to fully describe what King felt.

John McClure's *Other-wise Preaching: A Postmodern Ethic for Homiletics* provides a point of departure for us to consider our "King-like" episodes with God. We may discover a relationship between postmodern theological ethics and biblical revelation that provides space for different categories of tradition and experience to coexist. Thus, in a postmodern context, it is ethical to accept King's self-described experience as revelation and a call from God which is often experienced as abstract and mysterious.[3] The prophet Isaiah writes about similar experiences. During periods of social unrest and injustice, the poet-prophet expresses the belief that God is personally involved in human affairs. According to Isaiah, God personally chooses servants for God's own mission. The chosen servants will bring justice to all nations (42:1).

According to some commentators, Isaiah is writing to exiled citizens of Israel (chaps. 40–55). These exiled Hebrew citizens had become socioeconomically comfortable, and the oldest members of the exiled Hebrew people were dead or dying. The younger, more prosperous Hebrews understood Israel only from distant stories and romantic memories of aging ancestors. In this context, Isaiah tells them that God had revealed they must return to Israel to confront declining circumstances and uncertain political conditions. As one commentator writes:

> The question is how do you get a group of people to move who are comfortable, settled, whose children are born in this new country, to move back to a wreck of a city taken over by people from the surrounding countries, Edom, Moab, Transjordan etc. You want to transport them back to a rocky and barren landscape; where there [were] no immediate opportunities for making a living. We have the experience of Kosovar refugees who were only in Australia a few

---

2. See John S. McClure, *Other-wise Preaching: A Postmodern Ethic for Homiletics* (St. Louis: Chalice Press, 2001).

3. McClure provides rhetorical and theological space to address King's conversion experience. Chapters 2 and 3, "Exiting the House of Tradition: Preaching and Countermemory" and "Exiting the House of Experience: Preaching and Fragmented Subjectivities," add to our understanding of call, response, and the call to service which underlie this essay.

months not 40 plus years and some of them had no desire to return to probable hardship and possible death [in their homeland].[4]

Similarly, the Hebrew people had finally made a place for themselves in exile when they were disturbed by Isaiah's prophecy, recalling them to Israel and commissioning them to establish equality and justice in their ancestral homeland. The enormity of God's call weighed heavily on their hearts. The exiled Hebrew people were asked to leave their adopted homelands and return to social unrest, upheaval, and economic and personal insecurity.

If we relate Isaiah's called-out servants to the experiences of Dr. King, we may discover some surprising similarities. King admits he was not capable of protecting or sustaining his family or himself against enemies and opponents. What is more, King's unusual encounter with God during his soul-searching experience at the kitchen table was overwhelming, but it affirmed that he was a chosen advocate for social change in the American South and, eventually, the world.

Branch's account reveals that King was not always certain about his calling. Most of us would be uncertain and unsettled to discover that we were called to lead social resistance movements. Nevertheless, to resist the call of God is to remain uncertain, unsettled, and without purpose and destiny. To move forward, King believed that he was compelled by a transcendent Spirit to stand up for social justice. This is consistent with Isaiah's God who called the chosen people to emancipate Jerusalem: "I have put my spirit upon [Israel]; [Israel] will bring forth justice to the nations" (Isa. 42:1).

Psalm 29

Those who are willing to accept the risks associated with God's calling will find that worshiping and serving God is central to experiencing God's presence, comfort, and assurance. Without these kinds of experiences, our callings will remain uncertain and life's missions unfulfilled. According to the psalmist, an authentic recognition of God's presence in storms or tempests is overwhelming and unmistakable in part because of its splendor and power (29:2), compelling worshipers to focus on God rather than themselves. Thus, praise and worship are appropriate responses. They affirm the personal meanings that we attribute to our experiences and motivate us to serve God outside of our comfort zones. Those who do not worship and praise God as the psalmist describes seem to remain frustrated, doubtful, and depressed.

4. Anna Grant-Henderson, relating the experiences of Kosovan refugees and immigrants to Australia to God's call to the exiles in Isa. 40-55. See "Purpose of Isaiah 40-55," http://otl.uniting church.org.au/index.php?page=saiah-55-1-9 (accessed 12 February 2013).

The psalmist describes worship as an overwhelming, all-encompassing experience. It is similar to the experience that King had while sitting at his kitchen table, which may also be considered worship. Like the psalmist, King experienced an overwhelming, all-encompassing presence of "otherness" that included a sense of divine presence, comfort, and assurance. In response, he accepted with faith the risks inherent in his call. King's call was nothing less than to become a new abolitionist: a prophet of social justice in the tradition of his abolitionist African American mothers and fathers.

For King, and for all of us who want to make sense out of our lives, the psalmist advises, "Give unto the Lord, O you mighty ones, Give unto the Lord glory and strength. Give unto the Lord the glory due to [God's] name; Worship the Lord in the beauty of holiness" (vv. 1–2 NKJV). According to John Trapp, "Give unto the Lord" is correctly translated and interpreted this way: "This showeth how unwilling such are usually to give God his right, or to suffer a word of exhortation to this purpose."[5] If Trapp is suggesting that it takes overwhelming events to inspire us to consider God, I believe he is correct. To overwhelm humanity with sudden storms and tempests may be a very effective way to get selfish humanity to ascribe glory, strength, and beauty to God. For those who need to overcome debts, doubts, and depression, we must have an overwhelming encounter with something larger than ourselves, something that moves us out of our narrow self-interests.

It is plain to see that the psalmist was describing the power of God during storms and tempests. We also are utterly amazed at sovereign power and authority written in the peals of thunder and glistening lightning. Like the psalmist, we may see the natural beauty of God on display in these events. However, they also make us keenly aware of our human vulnerability and helplessness. Through the power and beauty of nature, God breaches the safe shelters where we reside. God overcomes our defenses and communes with us. God's fellowship with us is in the realm of God's creation. It is not intended to defeat us but to help us overcome our debts, doubts, and depressions.

Acts 10:34–43

What have the world's societies made of Dr. King's closing words in his civic sermon "I Have a Dream"? He said, "When we allow freedom to ring . . . we will be able to speed up that day when all of God's children—black men and white men, Jews and Gentiles, Catholics and Protestants—will be able

5. Charles H. Spurgeon, *The Treasury of David*, vol. 1, *Psalms 1–57* (Peabody, MA: Hendrickson, 1876), 34.

to join hands and to sing . . . , 'Free at last.' "[6] One conclusion we can draw from King's message is that freedom is a global yearning, and another is that freedom is not for certain classes of people but for all people.

While in Joppa, the apostle Peter discovers in the home of Cornelius, a prominent centurion and Gentile worshiper of God, that equality is a first principle (Acts 10:1–16). Justice follows equality, and both are universally desired. As John Polhill writes, "Peter saw that God does not discriminate on the basis of race or ethnic background. . . . But God does discriminate between those whose behavior is acceptable and those whose attitude is not acceptable. Those who reverence God and practice what is right are acceptable to God (v. 35; cf. Luke 8:21)."[7] Polhill's insights offer us a further homiletical jewel: the Holy Spirit discloses to Peter and to us that God's baptismal calling comes to Peter first as a baptism without water and then as a spiritual baptism that empowers him to serve with unrelenting passion in a multiracial, multicultural coalition of Jesus' disciples who are called to continue Christ's ministry of preaching peace, bearing witness, and becoming an abolitionist people (vv. 34–39). Before King grappled with God at his kitchen table and before his "I Have a Dream" civic sermon was heard around the world, Peter had a similar kind of overwhelming encounter with the Holy Spirit's presence, as did the psalmist who experienced the storms and tempests described in Psalm 29.

Matthew 3:13–17

In this short passage, we encounter the themes identified in each of the other texts. In Matthew's narrative of Jesus' baptism, Jesus is an obedient servant who responds to God's call to fulfill his divine vocation. That is, Jesus is reverent toward God. He personifies God's beauty and holiness as described by the psalmist (Ps. 29:1–2) and the words that burst from heaven: "This is my Son, the Beloved, with whom I am well pleased" (Matt. 3:17).

Jesus' baptism also reveals his passion. Baptism itself is a passionate symbol for believers who enter willingly into a life of servitude. Believers must understand that a call to repentance, which accompanies baptism, is a call to see the world differently; that is, in their repentance believers develop a different level of spiritual consciousness (i.e., social, kingdom consciousness). Believers answer their call to confront social and global inequalities and injustices through baptism and following the way of Jesus Christ.

6. See "I Have a Dream," King's civic sermon delivered at the Lincoln Memorial in Washington, D.C., on August 28, 1963, as part of the March on Washington, in *A Testament of Hope: The Essential Writings and Speeches of Martin Luther King, Jr.*, ed. James M. Washington (San Francisco: HarperCollins, 1991), 220.

7. John B. Polhill, *Acts*, The New American Commentary (Nashville: Broadman, 1992), 260.

Thus, Jesus' baptism serves at least two purposes. First, although Jesus did not need baptism for the remission of sins, he enters the baptismal waters as an example of his devotion to God and for the sake of all who follow him, modeling what would become an ecclesial practice through the ages. It further means that Jesus' disciples are called to be obedient participants in two kinds of fellowship: fellowship with God and fellowship with the people of God. What is significant here is that Jesus' baptism is a symbol of a personal call to service and it emerges out of his faithful relationship with God (v. 17). Jesus walked by faith as a man, but also perfectly as God.

King also walked by faith—although not as perfectly as Jesus Christ did. He struggled with his religion at a kitchen table. His faith cannot be descriptively reduced to known constructs, but it is important to realize that King's experience was no less significant or meaningful. I would further suggest that King also experienced a kind of "spiritual baptism." Spiritual baptism forces an individual to totally immerse her or himself into the driving passion that is associated with a God-given vocation. Today's lectionary texts call us to full immersion into social justice, just as King's total immersion afforded him total peace with God in his vocation as an abolitionist. His all-encompassing passion for social justice allowed him to follow God in prophetic service; the fulfillment of our vocations will also allow us to discover divine peace and faithful service to God and others.

Second Sunday after the Epiphany

Lincoln E. Galloway

ISAIAH 49:1–7
PSALM 40:1–11
1 CORINTHIANS 1:1–9
JOHN 1:29–42

In today's readings, signs call our attention to the relationship between God and the individual messenger or witness, as well as between God and the faith community. These relationships have significant implications for understanding divine activity in the world.

Isaiah 49:1–7

The voice of God announces: "Here is my servant" (Isa. 42:1). This chosen servant in whom God delights and on whom God's spirit rests is charged with bringing forth "justice to the nations" and establishing "justice in the earth" (42:1, 3, 4). The coastlands wait for divine teaching. Here in Isaiah 49, it is now the voice of the servant that speaks directly to the coastlands and people far away (49:1; cf. 41:1). From this speech, we learn that the servant's activities are a response to God's call and commission, and that it is God's initiative and God's advance work that are displayed before the servant in ways that are both mysterious and intimate.

The servant testifies to the mysterious nature of God, who called the servant into service before birth (49:1) and, in a very intimate way, according to the servant, "named" and "formed me in the womb" (vv. 1, 5). This intimacy extends also to God's servant Israel, who is chosen by God and formed in the womb (44:2). God's intimate fashioning and forming "in the womb" applies to the servant as an individual as well as to Israel as a community. Today, our faith communities and each individual within them stand before God, called and commissioned as God's chosen servant.

We may also recognize similarities in the mission and the tasks that are articulated. Israel's purpose is focused on the nations. The servant's charge is to bring forth justice, walk in righteousness, and be "a light to the nations" (42:6). The promise is reiterated to both the individual and community: "I will give you as a light to the nations, that my salvation may reach to the end of the earth" (49:6). This universal mission of bearing light to others is established in works of justice, righteousness, and salvation.

Today's readers of Isaiah must consider how to be light to the nations. Can we bear witness to justice and righteousness when our rampant consumerism is linked to economic exploitation of less-developed countries? Can faith communities speak salvation and still be repositories for nationalistic protectionism and jingoistic policies? Are faith communities "light to the nations" in matters of racial understanding, standing up for the rights of marginalized and voiceless people? Are faith communities bearers of salvation to those who have been victimized by greed and have lost their homes, pensions, or access to health care?

As in the text of Isaiah, so also in our witness today: God calls individuals and communities to be light (i.e., justice, righteousness, and salvation) to the world. In the life and witness of Dr. Martin Luther King Jr. we see the challenge given to an individual servant who answered God's call when the nation was at risk and many faith communities had compromised their witness of God's justice for all people. The community needed to be reminded that "injustice anywhere is a threat to justice everywhere."[1] When communities fail in their mission, individuals must step forward to proclaim the God who takes the initiative, goes before us, names us, forms us in the womb, and calls us to be "light to the nations" so that God's "salvation may reach to the end of the earth" (49:6).

Psalm 40:1–11

The psalmist speaks of waiting for God as action that God recognizes and rewards. "May integrity and uprightness preserve me, for I wait for you" (Ps. 25:21). The act of waiting is encouraged elsewhere also: "Wait for the LORD; be strong, and let your heart take courage; wait for the LORD!" (Ps. 27:14; cf. 37:34). In today's text the psalmist testifies that waiting has been rewarded: "I waited patiently for the LORD; he inclined to me and heard my cry" (40:1). Yet waiting on God is not equated with doing nothing while injustice prevails.

---

1. Martin Luther King Jr., "Letter from Birmingham City Jail," in *A Testament of Hope: The Essential Writings and Speeches of Martin Luther King Jr.*, ed. James M. Washington (San Francisco: HarperCollins, 1991), 290.

Those involved in the Civil Rights Movement in the United States understood that the popular admonition to "wait" reflected people's fear of change and allowed further opportunities for injustice to prevail. They understood that "justice too long delayed is justice denied."[2]

The psalmist offers personal testimony of God who saves in time of trouble, God who establishes a firm and secure pathway, and God who puts a new song in the mouths of those who wait and "put their trust in the LORD" (vv. 2–3). In today's violent world, the images in the psalm (such as "desolate pit" and "secure steps") remind us of those who walk in enemy territory and whose lives are threatened by roadside bombs, land mines, and other dangerous and lethal weapons.

Two things must be noted at this point. First, personal testimony is for the edification of the larger community. It calls forth trust in God (vv. 3b, 4a). Second, personal testimony is contextualized within the larger story of the community. The God of the psalmist ("my God," v. 5a) is also "our God" (v. 3) who has multiplied "your wondrous deeds and your thoughts toward us" (v. 5). The psalmist determines that the right response to God is not located in sacrifice but rather in the ears that God has opened to him or her (v. 6). Out of waiting on the Lord come hearing, telling the glad news of deliverance, and not restraining the lips. Instead of concealing God's saving help, steadfast love (*hesed*), and faithfulness, we are to speak of God's faithfulness and salvation (vv. 9–10). All of this flows from strong conviction and assurance: "Happy are those who make the LORD their trust" (v. 4).

Like the servant in Isaiah 49, the psalmist is very sure that his or her voice and testimony are important for the good of the community so that "many will see and fear, and put their trust in the LORD" (v. 3). This testimony speaks of God's character, which is marked by faithfulness (vv. 10b, 11), salvation (vv. 9, 10), and steadfast love (vv. 10, 11). Even the psalmist's own story of trust, dependence, and deliverance is placed in continuity with God's historic and salvific activity on behalf of the community. Whether individually or as a community, we wait on God, we listen, and we speak the glad news of deliverance (v. 9), faithfulness, salvation, and love.

1 Corinthians 1:1–9

Paul's greeting goes beyond the formulaic to establish very clear theological understandings. Paul is called to be an apostle (v. 1); the Corinthians are called to be saints (v. 2); and together they stand in solidarity with Christians everywhere whose identity comes from Jesus Christ, "both their Lord and

---

2. Ibid., 292.

ours" (v. 2). In the term "called" we are reminded that God takes the initiative in the world, in creation, and in salvation. The Corinthians have responded to God's gracious invitation to be in the world as saints (holy, sanctified ones) set apart by God. Further, their relationship with God has implications for the rest of the world. Paul's greeting is framed in terms of grace and peace to a community that is in solidarity with others "who in every place call on the name of our Lord Jesus Christ, both their Lord and ours" (v. 2). The Christian message must continue to be grace and peace across national boundaries and oceans, across markers of ethnicity and social status. Grace is God's gift and is meant to be the ground of our faith and lives from the cradle to the grave. God's gift of grace makes possible our salvation, abundant living, compassionate and just communities, radical and transformative hope. Along with grace, Paul also knew of God's gift of *shalom*, which calls forth a new relationship with God and with people everywhere through the work of peace building. The goal is not, in the words of Dr. King, a "negative peace which is the absence of tension" but rather a "positive peace which is the presence of justice."[3]

Paul gives thanks that the Corinthians had been blessed with gifts for the work that God had called them to do. First, they had to recognize that these spiritual gifts (*charismata*) of speech and knowledge were to be used for the common good (1 Cor. 12:7–8, 11). One can suggest to faith communities in contemporary society that their proclamation, prayers, music, testimony, dance, petitions, advocacy, and acts of resistance must serve the common good. The gifts of God (grace, peace, *charismata*) are for the people of God and are not intended to support religious exclusivism, special groups, or individualistic piety.

Finally, this work is not our own. It is divine grace that makes possible our work in transforming lives and providing hope. God empowers and sustains our efforts at peace building and God grants a vision of the common good. Paul suggests that God will bring to completion what God has begun. His words of encouragement resonate with us today as he asserts that God "will also strengthen you to the end" (1:8). Those whom God has called dare not shrink from the task of building *shalom* and working for the common good. This is God's work, and "God is faithful" (v. 9).

John 1:29–42

In the reading from Isaiah, the servant testifies to God's promise to send God's chosen one(s) as a light to the nations. Isaiah anticipates the faithful

3. Ibid., 295.

witness of a faithful messenger. Similarly, John the Baptist is portrayed as a man sent from God. "He came as a witness to testify to the light" (John 1:6–9). John did not always have this knowledge (vv. 31a, 33a), and a faithful witness is called to testify to what one has seen or heard. In today's text, John speaks not only of what has been revealed to him but also of what must "be revealed to Israel" (v. 31). He testifies to what he has seen (vv. 29, 32, 34), what he has heard (v. 33), and what was revealed to him. John also declares the content of the revelation: "Here is the Lamb of God who takes away the sin of the world!" (v. 29). This is he "who ranks ahead of me because he was before me" (v. 30; cf. John 1:1–4, 10).

John ushers in the work of Jesus and models a ministry of truth telling for the first disciples. Now those disciples would begin their journey with Jesus with an invitation to discover truth for themselves (v. 39). They understood that faithful witnesses seek the truth and testify to the truth in a context of darkness which is "the sin of the world" (v. 29; see also 1:5; 3:19). Such faithful witness to the truth confronts evil deeds that shun the light, whether in individuals or groups. Dr. Martin Luther King Jr. took the position that "individuals may see the moral light and voluntarily give up their unjust posture; but . . . groups are more immoral than individuals."[4] Faithful witnesses confront the evil deeds of groups that tolerate bigotry and deny dignity and justice to others; the evil deeds of governments that use military or clandestine methods to destabilize other nations, invest in weaponry, and engage in brutal policing tactics that harm the poor and powerless who need food, health care, and education. People live in darkness when prison systems become good investments, when advocating for the right to own guns becomes more important than advocating for better schools for our children. People live in darkness when children are sexually abused or exploited for economic gain. Faithful witnesses will speak truthfully to those who live in darkness, both the oppressed and the oppressor, the abuser and abused, and announce the coming of light, new life, and salvation in the one who has come to work with them to take away the sin of the world.

4. Ibid., 292.

Martin Luther King Jr. Day (January 15)

Dale P. Andrews

AMOS 5:18–24
PSALM 33:16–22
GALATIANS 3:23–29
LUKE 6:27–36

Racism is the one of the most pernicious and permeating realities of life in North America. If left unchecked, racism will destroy both people of color and people of European origin. The gospel insists that the church be anti-racist and pro-reconciling. The birthday of Martin Luther King Jr. (1929–1968) offers to preachers the opportunity not only to honor the life of this prophetic leader, not only to name the abiding oppression of marginalized racial/ethnic communities and the duplicitous dominating effects on European communities, but also to help congregations recognize practical ways that the community can join the struggle for justice.

> The church must be reminded that it is not the master or the servant of the state, but rather the conscience of the state. It must be the guide and the critic of the state, and never its tool. . . . But if the church will free itself from the shackles of a deadening status quo, . . . it will rekindle the imagination of [humankind] and fire the souls of [all] imbuing them with a glowing and ardent love for truth, justice, and peace.
>
> *Martin Luther King Jr.*[1]

What can possibly unlock the "shackles" that bind us to the "deadening status quo" of which King spoke? For that matter, what is the status quo itself? Is it our racial climate, our trumping trust in military might, or the exclusivity of our faiths? It would be too narrow to choose among the possibilities. King's

---

1. Martin Luther King Jr., *Strength to Love* (Philadelphia: Fortress Press, 1963, 1981), 64.

appeal in the quote for this day hinges on the divine love that drives divine care and divine justice. The Scripture texts for today redefine our distortions of divine wrath, our vainglorious fear of God and one another, the rules of human engagement with enemies, and our twisted disciplines of justice. Our call, our strength, and our transformation are only in God's unrelenting love!

Amos 5:18–24

This passage was one of King's go-to scriptural references during the civil rights campaigns. King would herald verse 24, "Let justice roll down like waters, and righteousness like an ever-flowing stream," in sermons and public addresses alike.

The prophet King stood among an expansive community of prophets: Amos, Jeremiah, Hosea, Ezekiel, yes, . . . but also Ella Baker, Diane Nash, and Fannie Lou Hamer. King stood with prophets who would lift the Word of God in hymns of praise and proclamation; "we shall overcome, we shall overcome." King stood with moral and spiritual courage, calling us to be "maladjusted" in joining with him to lift the Word of God to the people of God and to a nation: "Let justice roll down like waters, and righteousness like an ever-flowing stream."[2]

It is hard sometimes to see hope and divine promise while standing in the shoes of prophets. The promise fades from our vision when we face dismissal or charges from insatiable anger, never mind physical threat or harm. The prophetic call feels like dispensing judgment without recourse. Mainstream America repeatedly wondered with resentment just how much reform would be enough for King and Black America! We must also wonder how to sustain a prophetic call or a prophetic community. Does the justice of Amos have a thriving, unending source? Does the righteousness of Amos bellow from life to give life? Do waterfalls run full of life? Do streams sweep us into life?

No, the prophet seems to speak only from impending doom! Amos does not receive a fanfare of life to speak in the name of God. No illusions in grand forums of national acclaim at the foot of the capital's memorials! No world peace prize to herald a ministry of justice, righteousness, and the love of God! Expulsion and exile are his threats. Even our nation could not bear to see a prophet called to speak from the frustrated wrath of God's love to give life, a frustrated wrath of God's love to sustain life, a frustrated wrath of love to live within God's covenant, to love the gift of life in the other. The nation would choose to see only doom! The nation would hear only gloom!

2. Martin Luther King Jr., "The American Dream," speech given February 5, 1964, at Drew University, Madison, NJ; available at http://depts.drew.edu/lib/archives/online_exhibits/King /speech/TheAmericanDream.pdf (accessed February 25, 2012).

Has our nation moved into the "promised land"? Does the promised land belong to the nation? We give God our honor and praise for our blessed inheritance. We commonly hear sermons proclaiming a covenant of divine favor and divine sanction upon blessings, upon the promise. We own prosperity; it is our divine election. We have because we are God's favored. Even within our gates we determine the faithful and favored by the haves and the hoarding. And when we have, we praise God from our hoarding. We preach, urging others to give so that God can further bless us. We preach that if we give, we cause God to unleash untold blessings for our faithfulness, because God is eager to bless our storehouses. It becomes a divine transfer of funds.

Will we preachers be able to take on the mantle of this passage? Like King in his age, how will we address a complacent society impressed with its own image? How do we open the gates to the storehouse? Frankly, the wrath of God's love demands justice for the other, righteousness demands care for the other, to seek their thriving, to seek out the other in the wilderness, to seek out the other in desert wandering from years of neglect, to seek out the other wandering from generations of withholding, to seek out the other wandering out from the desert.

Preachers take note of what King derived from this passage. The wrath of God is divine love driving justice and righteousness. The wrath of God's love rages against the gates of self-contentment. The wrath of God's love thrusts forth against the idolatry of craven self-images. The prophet Amos announces the wrath of God's love that will not abate.

The wrath of God's love is the paradox of this text. Injustice causes God's wrath. Our tolerance of others' suffering incites God's disgust. We pray for God's blessing and vindication, and yet we do not face or perhaps even perceive that God may look upon our spirituality with the wrath of God's love; God may look upon our righteousness and the worship we offer from claims of divine favor or election with the wrath of God's love.

Like prophets of any age, preachers will likely struggle with this text over how to find a word of hope. Where is the joy of salvation? The joy is in God's unrelenting love; the wrath of God's love is empowered by love that is never "done," never satiated or satisfied. The joy of the wrath of God's love is that justice ferrets out injustice. The joy of the wrath of God's love is that the righteousness of God's care stored up is a pressure cooker heaving and bursting. Divine wrath becomes judgment to be feared when we become content with our own image, when worship expresses only the desire to store more of God's blessings. We come under God's judgment when we seek and ordain our fortune more in privilege than mission, when we attempt to funnel God's grace into privilege before responsibility! We struggle to understand that God's wrath does not destroy relationship; in fact, divine wrath grieves how we have forsaken relationship!

The joy of the wrath of God is that God will not rest. The joy of the wrath of God's love is that God will not withdraw, nor relinquish justice. Let justice roll down like waters and righteousness like an ever-flowing stream.

Psalm 33:16–22

"The war horse is a vain hope" (v. 17). We place so much hope in the vindication of military might, and yet this psalm warns that the use of physical force simply cannot save us. In verses 10–12, the psalmist cautions us that God frustrates the plans of a people seeking their own sovereignty. A nation is secure only in God. God observes all of humanity and our vain efforts to rule outside of God's vision. That vision is not merely a physical sight, but it is theological also. What does God see in our making war? Does God perceive our claims of self-protection as we offer them? Does God focus on our claims of rooting out the evil other, as we have named them?

"The war horse is a vain hope for victory." Preachers might find it difficult to preach on war from such a hymn of praise as this. The temptation, of course, is to reassert claims of divine election as the hand of God working out righteousness in the world. Yet the claim of human faithfulness in divinely sanctioned war is not the message of this psalm. Our hope survives only because of God's steadfast love (v. 18). Perhaps the most difficult point to grasp from this psalm is the call to fear God as it is juxtaposed with God's steadfast love. Strangely, we fear losing power enough to make war and do not fear God enough to find another way! The psalm asks us to trust in God to be our help (vv. 20–21). Instead, we tend to trust executing might and calling it righteousness. As King's vision of God's steadfast love grew from the nonviolence of civil disobedience against injustice to a national campaign against war, he encountered great resistance. In all debates of just and unjust war, we must acknowledge that all war is humanity's failure and endemic sin. King's nonviolence was not a distorted passivity or disassociating pacifism. It was—is—trust in God's steadfast love to deliver us from ourselves.

Luke 6:27–36

Preachers will experience plenty of toil when constructing sermons on the principles of love. The fulcrum of this passage is the "golden" standard, "Do to others as you would have them do to you" (v. 31). This sermon is located on the plain, as opposed to its counterpart, in Matthew 5–7, on a mount. The implications of its location are profound. In Luke's account, Jesus seeks access and presence and is able to move from the mount of calling his twelve disciples to being directly present in people's lives. Verses 27 and 35 bracket the passage with the frank admonition to "love your enemies." To love one's enemies is not a sentimental vocation. We typically employ careful rules of engagement with enemies that we construct on rather sound ethics of protection. We extend ourselves with meted generosity measured on scales of mutual benefit. This passage, however, upends our understanding of mutual benefit. Jesus reverses the rules of engagement and measures of mutuality. The initial verses (vv. 27–30) redress how we engage those whom we avoid or seek to conquer—those who already hate us, abuse us, or deplete us. The later verses (vv. 32–34) address the distortions of our own favor toward those whom we find more appealing—those who love us and treat us well already. Jesus redefines the life of faithful love in God's reign—generosity, kindness, and mercy to the ungrateful and even the wicked (vv. 35–36).

King wrestled continuously with the ethics of this love on both social and personal scales of mutuality and protection. How does one balance respect and love for self with love for the other? King struggled with the painful spiritual crises of love, engagement with enemies, and self-protection.[3] The temptations to meet spiritual violence with spiritual violence are no less real than the encounter with physical violence; in fact the two temptations are seldom absent from one another. Would King raise the ethic of protection as a metaethic or way of life? This is the challenge Jesus raises in this sermon. Preachers will need to struggle with the metaethics of love in the rules of engagement with enemies and the perceived absence of mutual benefit.

Galatians 3:23–29

If we are tempted by the Gospel reading to catalog the reversals that a meta-ethic of love might delineate as the way of life, then this Galatians passage should flag the hazards or limitations of a "lawful" approach to love. Verse 24 depicts inherited law as our disciplinarian. As such, the law instructs us in the means and manner of a disciplined faith. The law is clearly a gift to humanity to decipher faithfulness in concrete terms of life. The law reflects on our worship lives, interpersonal relationships, and society. If worship is an expression of faithful love to God, and human relations express the love we seek from one another, then social justice becomes the navigation of God's love as divine gift to society. We often preach that God is just. However, we all had better pray that God is truly more than just.

---

3. *The Autobiography of Martin Luther King Jr.*, ed. Clayborne Carson (New York: Warner Books, 1998, 2001), 63–82.

Galatians teaches us that God desires to be more than our disciplinarian. Justice is God's gift to society as God's love is a gift to humanity. According to Paul, the law serves to protect us from ourselves before God and with one another (vv. 23–25). Paul is not arguing that the law is unneeded. Instead, we now understand it within the eschatological reign that the love of God in Christ assembles (vv. 26–29). This faith that Paul defines transforms how we live with one another, even how we regard one another. Relationships of domination and servitude are overturned; chasms of alienation are bridged.

Toward the latter years of King's ministry, he increasingly perceived that faith in Christ required deconstructing domination and constructing bridges as the very means of protecting us from ourselves. In his *Where Do We Go from Here: Chaos or Community?* King argued that it was a matter of faith that all of the world's faiths need to come together, as do the races, to commune in the "world house" of God, or else we shall destroy our household and human family.[4]

4. Martin Luther King Jr., *Where Do We Go from Here: Chaos or Community?* (Boston: Beacon Press, 1968, 1986), 177–202.

Third Sunday after the Epiphany

Melinda A. Quivik

ISAIAH 9:1–4
PSALM 27:1, 4–9
1 CORINTHIANS 1:10–18
MATTHEW 4:12–23

The power of these texts is in the juxtaposition of "repent" and "the kingdom of heaven has come near." The call to repentance is a command, pointing to the need for "amendment of life," as some of the older liturgical books put it. In contrast, announcing the presence of the reign of God offers an already-amended reality. Each reading for this day lays out strong contrasts between "need" and "gift." The texts also include important historical references. Both the Hebrew Bible and the Gospel readings name a land on the other side of the Jordan, "Galilee of the nations/Gentiles." The reference is to Judah, a land overrun in 732 BCE by Assyria, the superpower of its time, with more weapons and money than any other nation.

Isaiah 9:1–4

Even when this text is not laid out on the page in poetic form, it "sings" of liberation. Verses 2–4 (as well as 5–7) are an oracle, singing a promise: "there will be no gloom for those who were in anguish" (v. 1). The history of that anguish is recalled as the time when the people of Zebulun and Naphtali were oppressed during the rule of King Ahaz of Judah (735–715 BCE). The Assyrians held power over the region and extorted the people with heavy taxes. The rulers of Syria and Israel were allied against Assyria, but they could not enlist Ahaz's support. Instead, Ahaz sought ways to placate Assyria's greed, even handing over the temple treasures (2 Kgs. 16:8).

Following Ahaz's despotism was a period of greater stability and peace, but Isaiah insists that instead of attributing the improved living conditions to a wiser ruler, it was YHWH's power that broke the yoke and bar across

73

their shoulders (i.e., the taxes paid to the Assyrians) "as on the day of Midian" (referring to Judg. 7 when Gideon's army fought against their oppressors). Why is power attributed to YHWH? Why is "the day of Midian" presented as an image of liberation?

The image of Midian's defeat calls up sudden, unexpected, unthinkable, and impossible release. Midian, like Assyria, held the people to levels of taxation that put them in danger of starvation. In the face of that horror, YHWH calls Gideon to challenge the Midianites by destroying the altar to Baal (Judg. 6:25–27). Gideon knows well the consequences of challenging their oppressor and carries out the sabotage under cover of night. The Midianites are incensed by the desecration. Gideon's destruction strikes at the heart of what his people believe to be the primary cause of their suffering: the Midianites do not worship the true God.

Gideon's victory further defies their power because he defeats the enemy not with hordes of soldiers but with few (300 rather than 33,000; see Judg. 7:2–8) and with trumpets. YHWH has commanded this, and they are successful. Although the battle is not without bloodshed, there were fewer deaths than would have occurred under conventional methods of warfare. The odds always seem to favor those with the most weapons, but Gideon is victorious because of his faith in God's ultimate power.

We who are Assyrians or Midianites have a difficult time seeing past our perceptions of what it takes to make things right. This is the crux of the problem facing the developed and developing nations, the first- and the two-thirds worlds. Our visions run along completely different avenues. Even for Christians of both "worlds," the seductions of contemporary cultural values and societal pressures cloud our understanding. The church too easily associates power with outward signs of success, prestige, and might rather than with God's redemptive and life-giving purposes. Whenever the church believes that larger numbers of the faithful validate its ministry, it succumbs to Assyrian values. Whenever the church preaches a prosperity gospel (i.e., that faith will beget monetary riches), it falls down and worships the gods of Wall Street. The one true God then is not worshiped and Jesus is denied. The scales on the eyes of those who will not see this grow thicker, and the military budget grows fatter.

When Isaiah invokes Midian, the effect is to remind the people of Judah that God promises a stunning reversal, turning darkness to light. YHWH is responsible, cries Isaiah, for lifting the oppression of the Midianites from the shoulders of the people. So will it be again. This reference suggests that liberation will not be achieved in a manner most expected, but it is sure to come, because success and bounty are assured by God.

Psalm 27:1, 4–9

In response to Isaiah's insistence that the Lord is the one who increases our joy, the psalmist asserts that "the LORD is the stronghold of my life." There is nothing to fear. The Lord gives shelter, lifts up, and defends. The psalmist proclaims the desire of the faithful, "to live in the house of the LORD . . . to behold the beauty of the LORD" (v. 4). For those for whom social and political activism is the expected response to injustice and who may find themselves weary of the never-ending need to address wrongs, this passage offers a deep well of strength. For those who are afraid and lost in the morass of pain that so many people endure, the psalmist offers the respite that can be found in beauty, singing, music, and in gazing on the giver of all things. To "offer sacrifices with shouts of joy" (v. 6) is a desired and fruitful occupation. In it resides the grounding (i.e., dwelling in the house of the Lord) that makes all action worthwhile. When the assembly responds to the reading from Isaiah with this cry of assurance regarding God's shelter and salvation, worshipers assert the power of the Lord.

1 Corinthians 1:10–18

This is precisely why Jesus' power is so profound. It is not the power of armies but of stopping, resting, and dying for others. It is not triumphant but compassionate. According to this epistle, the power of God is foolishness: God dies on the cross. We are called to that cross, to the emptying of all pride, and to humility that arises out of our encounter with the incarnate and crucified Christ.

But this is not a popular truth. It does not seem as if the forces of evil can be turned back without matching the strength of evil's own means of combat. To what, then, are the Corinthians—are we—called to do? We are called to be of one mind, to regain unity among ourselves, to be restored. Significantly, the same word for "united" in verse 10b is used elsewhere for mending nets (Matt. 4:21; Mark 1:19). What is broken is to be made whole.

The people of God confront the oppression of unjust policies or damaging theologies by attending to the repair of our own schisms. What is required of us? Paul says it is to "proclaim the gospel, and not with eloquent wisdom," lest the cross be "emptied of its power" (1 Cor. 1:17). This may be a caution against preaching that is too slick, pays too much attention to the form of the message rather than its theological import, offers too much pride of showmanship, and sets too much store in attaining "success" and achieving "what works." The church's focus needs to be on the cross from which all power comes. Concerns for individual standing (e.g., who baptized us, whether we are "good enough," to whom we belong, and all manner of relatively small matters that divide the church today) are nothing. Because the cross is everything, preachers are not to concern themselves with eloquence but with humility, not to preach with gimmicks but with honesty, not to divide but to unite, not to avoid the foolishness of the hope we have in Christ Jesus but to assure us of its power.

Matthew 4:12–23

Those who yearn for justice in the sociopolitical and economic realms need to take notice of Jesus' reaction to the news that John the Baptist was arrested. All indications are that John had recently baptized Jesus. In the face of John's imprisonment, Jesus withdraws. Whether he goes to his hometown or from Nazareth to Capernaum, he is, at least, in Galilee, the region of Zebulun. At its heart are Nazareth and Naphtali whose people have known suffering. They fought the Midianites (Judg. 6–7) and endured deportation to Assyria (2 Kgs. 15:29). These are lands living in the darkness of rule by the Roman government, particularly Pontius Pilate (26–36 CE).

Matthew's narrative directs our attention to John's arrest, Jesus' withdrawal, the assertion of Galilee's yoke of oppression, and the accompanying proclamation of light coming into the darkness (quoting Isa. 9). Jesus' next move is to begin assembling his followers. In those days, disciples sought out their teacher; here, the teacher finds the disciples.[1] We might say that in response to the obvious political move against the Baptist who came preaching repentance and initiating the people into a new perspective, Jesus sets his energies toward deepening and expanding upon what John proclaimed. Jesus takes up John's cry: "Repent, for the kingdom of heaven has come near." The new reality, however, requires a community through whom the vision of justice can be announced. Jesus' role, therefore, is to pull people together and in their midst teach, proclaim, and heal. He is the one who makes the changes happen. He is the one who calls the followers into a new body.

There is nothing in the Gospel text to tell us what it was about Jesus that made these fishers drop their work and follow him into the future. The description is almost frighteningly brief: "Immediately they left their nets and followed him" (v. 20). Jesus is portrayed as a whirlwind of hope, turning those whom he called from their old ways to a new way with no promise of success, no mention of the overthrow of Rome, no army to free John the Baptist, no utopian scheme.

1. Daniel J. Harrington, SJ, *The Gospel of Matthew* (Collegeville, MN: Liturgical Press, 1991), 75.

When he learns of the unjust imprisonment of John, who had called people to repent and be baptized, Jesus' first response is to withdraw to Galilee. The withdrawal is a time of strengthening and coming to recognize what the true nature of his work will be. Jesus' withdrawal to the lands that are in darkness tells us that where there is darkness, Jesus has come there to be at home. The law of the gospel is to follow the reorientation offered to us by and in Christ Jesus. Oppression is obliterated by the reorientation of our lives toward the light of Christ present among those in need. What is that light? It is the foolishness of the cross that directly challenges the powers of darkness by giving hope to the poor rather than victory to armies.

In this Gospel story, the disciples are not called to lead but to follow. They are not called to be the best, but to be together. Following is the relationship between all Christians and Jesus. Even more to the point, according to biblical scholar Ulrich Luz, "following has its center in suffering."[2] The suffering may well have to do with the fact that following—according to Jesus—means taking on the work of inviting more people to follow. It is not about overcoming the monster, it is about building the community. This may be hard to hear. It is counterintuitive, whether you live with the mind-set of the conqueror or the conquered. One wants to keep power and expand it; the other, to destroy the powerful and create a paradise. Instead, Jesus' way is foolishness, the "power of God." This means that those who are called to follow Jesus may find themselves in a minority, advocating for unpopular movements, asking disquieting questions, objecting to the abuse of others, standing in the way of the bombastic and proud. God's way unites us through what is weak and foolish. This is not a theology of triumphal victory but of dying and rising to newness of life.

---

2. Ulrich Luz, *Matthew 1–7: A Commentary* (Minneapolis: Augsburg Fortress, 1989), 201.

Fourth Sunday after the Epiphany

Kenyatta R. Gilbert

MICAH 6:1–8
PSALM 15
1 CORINTHIANS 1:18–31
MATTHEW 5:1–12

Spanning diverse times and contexts, the texts for today all reflect a divine vision of holy living. Micah reminds us to honor the grace of God by critiquing the status quo and struggling against unjust social arrangements; the psalmist teaches us that a holy life yields eternal security; Paul's message offends our sensibilities and points believers to the cross's saving power; and Matthew proclaims that we be doers of God's will and not hearers alone.

Micah 6:1–8

The book of Micah is a policy critique. The book's leading light, Micah of Moresheth, speaks the hard, divine word in the name of God. Forbearance for recalcitrant Israel no more! Micah is commissioned by God to scold his kinspeople. Israel's economic boon under the reigns of Uzziah and Jotham secured their political clout in the region, but with the nation's increased prosperity came "a strong current of egotistic materialism" that coincided with maltreatment of the poor by the ruling elite.[1]

The open-eyed preacher quickly notices that preceding this sixth chapter, a verdict has been rendered: "I will execute vengeance on the disobedient." Israel's defiance against God's holiness code and failure to honor their fundamental obligation to practice justice is the marked offense. The political and religious gatekeepers ignored God's law and are therefore indicted for their wickedness.

Although Emancipation had represented slavery's demise on paper, for Black sharecroppers, America's democratic experiment failed miserably.

1. Juan I. Alfaro, OSB, *Justice and Loyalty: A Commentary on the Book of Micah*, International Theological Commentary (Grand Rapids: Eerdmans, 1989), 6.

78

Exploited for their labor and swindled out of their rightful property by the unjust economic practices of their former slaveholders, they found themselves victims within a nefarious social system, similar to certain dwellers in the foothills of Judah.

"Thou shalt not covet" is one law clearly broken. The land of the field workers was coveted and seized, householders sustained injury by oppressive taxation under the religious watch of Jerusalem's prophets who cried out "peace," and the social elite lived undisturbed by the plight of the weak and poor (2:2; 3:5). The verdict "guilty" is merited by unrepentant Israel.

In the sixth chapter, God challenges Israel. We are offered a stunning image of a divine magistrate exhausted of patience and fishing for an admission of guilt from wayward Israel. Micah's biting oracle takes the tack of the parental reprimand, "Now what do you have to say for yourself?" But one also hears the satiric chastisement of an exasperated Sovereign, "O my people, what have I done to you?" How have I failed you?

Despite the rhetorical dance between a loving yet disappointed God and God's willful people, only one voice speaks with authority from the text. "Is this how you repay me after all I have done for you? I thought we had a deal!" To find imaginative ways to think about God's intimate feelings toward us is to perceive something about our own lives lived before a lovingly patient God. A creative rereading might proceed along these lines: "I have put the mountains and hills on the witness stand and they testify of your moral laxity and abominable practices. The only requirement I have made of you is that you worship me wholeheartedly, 'to do justice, and to love kindness, and to walk humbly' with me" (vv. 1–8).

To preach this passage faithfully is to give witness to the justice and grace of God. To enthrone materialism over right worship and just practices is to break covenant. Unchecked authority may secure prosperity, but it carries with it the price of exploitation of the economically disenfranchised—the indigent human beings of society. This country's undocumented immigrant workers are hired to work in the suburbs and are paid menial wages to labor without guarantee of workers' rights. Few will plead the case for the undocumented person who performs tasks we would not.

In the end, the prophet Micah clearly sees that for Israel redemption will not come cheap. It will come at the cost of true religion and purity of heart. The avenue to redemption is good ethics and purity of heart. According to biblical scholar Juan Alfaro, "there is something worse than appearing before the Lord empty-handed . . . appearing before him dirty-handed and empty-hearted, without justice."[2] To practice justice is to exercise compassion (loving mercy) for the poor and marginalized.

2. Ibid., 67.

Psalm 15

This psalm makes an appeal for holy living. As in Jesus' beatitude, "Blessed are those who hunger and thirst for righteousness, for they will be filled" (Matt. 5:6), the psalmist offers direction for those who seek sanctuary in the presence of God. The dos and don'ts of God's holiness code are to "walk blamelessly," "speak the truth," avoid "slander," refrain from evil acts, honor God-fearers, keep promises, unburden the financially enslaved, and protect the innocent. To live thus is to earn the label "righteous one." The reward is a firm footing in the world and residence in the presence of God.

Hebrew Bible scholar James Luther Mays contends that to characterize this psalm as prescriptive in intent is to miss the point. The psalmist paints a picture of what life is like for those who conform their will to God's. Mays believes that the work of the believer is to envision, comprehend, and imagine one's personal identity reorganized based on holiness traits and divine admonitions. The key words here are envision, comprehend, and imagine. To have right ideals and uphold just practices is the pursuit of the holy hill (v. 1) and recognition of the sovereign workings of Almighty God. God is beyond the hills and "calls and commands, judges and redeems."[3]

This psalm is also an introspective prayer from a person who realizes that he has no inherent right to abide in the tent of the Lord. The psalmist has considered her or his own life in view of her or his ultimate hope. What does it mean to consider one's end with hope? In light of the gospel, preachers seeking to find a gracious and comforting message to deliver shoulder the obligation to be self-critical about their own professed consecration to live the holy life. Moreover, one must keep in mind that to obtain godly refuge is to fulfill moral and ethical requirements. The older saints of my childhood would say, "If you want to get to heaven, you've got to walk the walk, and talk the talk." In other words, one's character bespeaks one's ultimate hope.

For the preacher who seeks to instruct hearers on the merits and modes of spiritual and ethical conduct as a Christian disciple, the safeguards are abundant in Psalm 15. In this text for the Fourth Sunday after the Epiphany, one finds that to proclaim the gospel message in view of the psalmist's prayer is to encourage listeners, in their soul-cleansing treatment, to understand the opportunity to start anew, this time with the mirror of God's Word in hand.

---

3. James Luther Mays, *Psalms*, Interpretation series (Louisville, KY: John Knox Press, 1994), 84–86.

1 Corinthians 1:18–31

The question "What is the message of the gospel?" may elicit a number of responses. But few, if any, would claim that this message of love should be characterized using terms like "stumbling block" or "foolishness." "God's foolishness" and "human weakness" are the threads holding this passage together. Eloquence and human wisdom are worldly desires. The Greeks and Jews require these signs, Paul contends. However, God is unimpressed by eloquence and human wisdom because neither requires faith.

The cantankerous Corinthians are culturally and bitterly divided over the issue of what should be prized most—eloquent speech and knowledge or the cross of Christ. In this passage the apostle seeks to make clear that human wisdom pales in comparison to the wisdom of God. Paul records that for some the message about the cross is useless, but for those *being saved* it is power. "The world did not know God through wisdom, . . . God decided, through . . . foolishness . . . to save" (v. 21).

Paul is also pointing out that without faith it is illogical to think that Jesus Christ would literally die on behalf of sinners (Rom. 5:6; 1 Cor. 8:11; Gal. 1:4), "taking their place" on the cross, and receiving the judgment that sinners rightly deserve. If this is not a foolish act, what is? This is the subject and substance of preaching, is it not? Richard Lischer maintains that preaching is a message about how the cross becomes a hindrance because it "bears the impossible weight of its own message, which is God's willingness to be pushed out of the world and onto a cross."[4]

Preaching themes are plentiful. The preacher-interpreter who is alert to our postmodern situation may call attention to (1) what it means to hear the gospel among a collage of narratives, (2) the spiritual and social power of the cross, and (3) the importance of humility in a self-serving culture.

Matthew 5:1–12

Scripture tells us that Jesus drew the multitudes to himself because of the mighty acts he performed. Some arrived on the scene out of curiosity. Others had followed him along his path out of devotion despite the bewildering call to follow him. Still others, sprinkled throughout the crowd, were there to test and trap him. Each of these variously motivated people arrived at the foot of the mountain, where Jesus began to teach them what is commonly called the Beatitudes. There are nine. Each one provides insight into holy living, the

---

4. Richard Lischer, *The End of Words: The Language of Reconciliation in a Culture of Violence* (Grand Rapids: Eerdmans, 2005), 8.

best traditions of communal life, norms of citizenship in the kingdom of God, the raison d'être, and responsibilities of the church.[5] The careful preacher will struggle with this text to discover its layers of meaning.

The Beatitudes pair practical wisdom and spiritual blessing. They address and instruct flesh-and-blood human beings of the ancient world affected by oppressive political systems and unethical social arrangements, as surely as they address us today. Blessed are the

> poor in spirit—those persons left homeless after natural disaster—for the kingdom of God is their just inheritance;
> mourners—parents whose sons have been senselessly gunned down in mean inner-city streets—for they will be comforted;
> meek—nonviolent resisters of the 1950s and 1960s—for they will inherit the earth;
> ones who hunger and thirst for righteousness—new Christian converts committed to a spiritually and morally disciplined life—for they will be filled;
> mercy givers—the judge who pardons the first offense of a teenage boy caught in possession of an illicit drug—for they will receive mercy;
> pure hearted—pastors who hold the hands of the bereaved and pray—for they will see God;
> peacemakers—breakers of the gridlock stifling the nation's progress—for they will be called children of God;
> pursuers of righteous causes—the cast of World Vision—for theirs is the kingdom of heaven;
> ones who are reviled, persecuted, vilified, slandered for believing in Jesus— thick-skinned counterculturalists—for they will be greatly rewarded in heaven.

Homiletical possibilities abound. For example, the people who are "poor in spirit" are literally physically poor. Today, they are those who have nearly reached retirement at a previously stable company that has now downsized, leaving them without work; those whose homes and lives have been over-turned as a result of natural disaster or home foreclosures in a dismal economy. Who are they? They are persons who "can see no hope," who have "no control over their own destiny."[6] In spite of this the "blessed" are indeed blessed, if they have placed their hope in the giver of hope—Jesus Christ.

---

5. Thomas G. Long, *Matthew*, Westminster Bible Companion (Louisville, KY: Westminster John Knox Press, 1997), 46–47.

6. Warren Carter, *Matthew and the Margins: A Sociopolitical and Religious Reading* (Maryknoll, NY: Orbis, 2001), 131–32.

Fifth Sunday after the Epiphany

Chandra Taylor Smith

ISAIAH 58:1–9A (9B–12)
PSALM 112:1–9 (10)
1 CORINTHIANS 2:1–12 (13–16)
MATTHEW 5:13–20

This week's Scripture texts firmly nudge us to make sure that our work for social justice is motivated by the right reasons and intentions. The overarching message of each text vigorously reminds us that only righteous actions achieve the ends of social justice. In the book of Isaiah, God charges the Prince of Prophets to sternly warn the people in Zion about the difference between actions that radiate from a spiritually grounded humility and actions that are the results of hubristic ritual and/or personal gain. The psalmist reiterates the understanding that true happiness results from conducting our affairs justly, while the apostle Paul attests that the wisdom of his ministry and righteous actions are revealed through the Spirit of God. Finally, the Gospel text is a vivid reminder that our social justice actions must be held to and exceed the highest measures of righteousness in order to overturn the depths of social injustice and, as Matthew concludes, "enter the kingdom of heaven."

Isaiah 58:1–9a (9b–12)

A key threat to the achievement of social justice is practice disconnected from faith and the inspiration of God's Spirit. It is especially problematic when unjust actions are disguised in what appear to be righteous intentions. In other words, even when we purport to be just, the injustice in our actions is revealed in the contradictions inherent in our motivations and the internal agendas we hope to achieve through our external deeds. In Isaiah 58:1–5, wrongheaded motivations to achieve social justice are revealed in how God's people seek self-interested recognition for their virtuous acts. Accordingly, Isaiah's understanding of fasting is, in its most literal sense, the act of abstaining from

83

food, and in its more figurative meaning fasting represents an effort "to loose the bonds of injustice, to undo the thongs of the yoke, to let the oppressed go free, and to break every yoke" (v. 6). Moreover, it is right to observe the discipline of fasting as a way of intensifying or strengthening the sincerity of one's prayer. However, the righteousness of fasting is negated and becomes handily exploitative (v. 3b) when it is practiced to incite quarreling or fighting (v. 4a). Fasting literally or metaphorically to take advantage of others results in the repression of others and the degradation of God's just vision.

Similarly, acting with humility as a genuine gesture of modesty and without pride epitomizes the disposition of a righteous nature (58:5). However, humbling oneself simply to receive God's notice, kindness, and praise typifies a false show of piety and an insincere commitment to true justice. God requires more than the pretense of bowing. Hollow and insincere benevolence is further characteristic of our thoughtless selection of our old and unwanted canned goods given away to food drives from our bountiful pantries, dropping only our cast-off pennies in the homeless person's cup, or distribution of our out-of-season, unfashionable, or tattered clothing to a family recovering from a natural disaster. Outward acts of helping others must be inspired and carried out with an inner motivation by the righteousness of the act of benevolence in order to truly fulfill God's vision of justice.

Another way to talk about the vital message in this text is to focus on the work of social justice as a humble act and privilege that must be done in a socially just way. This means being consciously unpretentious in character and grateful for the opportunity to contribute toward a socially just society. Disingenuous actions committed under the guise of just actions are especially harmful when motivated by racist assumptions about the poor and oppressed. Misperceived notions of self-righteousness or superiority are at the heart of the intentions of those who want to be rewarded for putting on a Superman cape and swooping in to help the poor and needy. Such false humility is transparent and insults those who are already victims of injustice. Thus, Isaiah is adamant in verse 9b that to achieve genuine humility one must be free of the yoke or agency of oppressive actions such as "the pointing of the finger, the speaking of evil." Only an authentic humility advances just social relations and actions that are sensitive to the limitations of personal, cultural, racial/ethnic, and economic capital; maintains equitable expectations of every person's ability; and never assumes to play Superman. Then, as Isaiah explains, "your light shall rise in the darkness, and your gloom be like the noonday" (v. 10b).

Finally, a deeper, heartfelt, and communal measure of righteousness is held out in Isaiah's text that admonishes us to share bread with the hungry, bring the homeless poor into our houses, cover those who are naked, and not hide ourselves from our own kin (v. 7). While the reference to kin appears to be a reminder of communal accountability among the ancient Israelites, given the advances of technology that connect humanity across the planet today, a contemporary global vision of how we are all connected and must be accountable to one another worldwide is also clear. Moreover, unrighteous neglect and abuse of people, animals, and nature both locally and globally can have a devastating effect on God's entire creation.

Psalm 112:1–9 (10)

The psalmist highlights the need for social justice actions to focus on fulfilling God's vision rather than our self-centered human motivations and intentions. Our human ability to sustain a focus on the righteous revelation of God rests on our strategically being just as the baseline of our everyday living, for "it is well with those who deal generously and lend, who conduct their affairs with justice" (v. 5). Even more appealing is that living justly is pleasing and satisfying, as the psalmist accentuates in verses 2–4: those who are actively upright are happy and receive many forms of blessings, including physical and material wealth as well as righteous judgments from God forever. Thus, while conscientiously working on the long-term goal of establishing God's vision for a just society, we are also recipients of God's riches in our daily short-term efforts to live and act justly.

The practice of ardently acknowledging God through praise (v. 1a) as well as delighting in the fear of the Lord (v. 1b) anchors our human ability to sustain our social justice work as a principled lifestyle. For example, this is how freedom marchers during the Civil Rights Movements of the 1960s sustained their protests for social justice. They did not anchor their fear in the attack dogs, water hoses, or the other tangible and often brutal assaults to their efforts to end racism and poverty. On the contrary, they anchored their fear in the Lord, and "they [were] not afraid of evil tidings; their hearts [were] firm, secure in the LORD" (v. 7). Thus, for the long term, living in fear only of the Lord assures that our "hearts are steady," we are not afraid, and, in the end, we are able to "look in triumph on [the] foes" (v. 8). Furthermore, being God-fearing grounds and steadies our motivation and intention to overturn social injustices without being concerned that God notices our actions (cf. Isa. 58:3).

1 Corinthians 2:1–12 (13–16)

In this chapter of Paul's First Letter to the Corinthians, he offers a powerful testament to the wisdom of the Spirit of God that inspires the message of his ministry and further grounds righteous actions for social justice in Christian faith. Paul is fundamentally concerned about the divisions and confusion among the people of Corinth (1 Cor. 1:10–17), and the last thing he wants is for the Corinthians to misunderstand his proclamation concerning the mystery of God (ch. 2). He makes the fundamental point in this chapter that human wisdom lacks credibility (i.e., it is implausible) in contrast to the credibility of the power and wisdom of God. Human wisdom is limited, according to Paul, because it only knows the human spirit that is within (2:11a). Thus, no one knows "what is truly God's except the Spirit of God" (v. 11b).

The limitations placed on human knowledge and wisdom by the internal musings of the human spirit have implications for the implausibility and unrighteousness of our human motivations and intentions in our daily social relations and actions for justice. Quoting Isaiah 64, Paul reminds the church that God will reveal through the Spirit "what no eye has seen, nor ear heard, nor the human heart conceived, what God has prepared for those who love him." Thus credible and righteous motivations and intentions are revealed in the wisdom of the Spirit of God who searches everything, even the depths of God (1 Cor. 2:10). Paul assures the Corinthians that "we speak of these things in words not taught by human wisdom but taught by the Spirit, interpreting spiritual things to those who are spiritual" (v. 13). The wisdom of the Spirit can only come from the mind of Christ, "who has known the mind of the Lord" (v. 16), Paul concludes. Thus, the credibility and righteousness of our motivations and intentions to do social justice are derived from our faith in the wisdom of God through Jesus Christ.

Matthew 5:13–20

Matthew's metaphors of salt and light illuminate the powerful impact of those who are righteous and whose actions are socially just. The righteous characteristics of those described as the "salt of the earth" (v. 13) and "the light of the world" (v. 14) are outlined in Jesus' earlier teaching of the Beatitudes (5:1–12). They are blessed, which is another word for what the psalmist described as "happy" (Ps. 112:1). These righteous qualities include poverty of spirit (Matt. 5:3), mournfulness (v. 4), meekness (v. 5), and others that reflect the internal characteristics of people who have complete faith and trust in God. Thus the Beatitudes establish how social justice actions must be held to and exceed the highest measures of righteousness (v. 20) in order to overturn the depths of social injustice. This means that, according to Jesus, whoever breaks or falls short of the least of these qualities, "and teaches others to do the same, will be called least in the kingdom of heaven; but whoever does them and teaches them will be called great in the kingdom of heaven" (v. 19).

Matthew's vivid depiction of the fervor and commitment required to realize God's just society brings to mind the stirring a cappella voices of the African American women in the stylized vocal troupe Sweet Honey in the Rock singing a song by Bernice Johnson Reagon, "Ella's Song." This song demands that "We who believe in freedom cannot rest until it comes." Similarly, the import of the Gospel is that we cannot rest or hide the light of Christ until God's just society is accomplished. Indeed, it is Christ who shines forth among us to shed light on the world's injustices. He declares that "no one after lighting a lamp puts it under the bushel basket, but on the lampstand, and it gives light to all in the house" (v. 15). Thus in verse 16 Jesus urges us to "let your light shine before others, so that they may see your good works and give glory to your Father in heaven." Ultimately, the good works of social justice are the fulfillment of the law through Christ (v. 17).

In conclusion, those who maintain the qualities described in the Beatitudes are spiritually grounded in humility and reject the hubristic rituals and personal gain described by Isaiah (58:3). Thankfully, God's expectation for righteousness exceeds the human wisdom of scribes, Pharisees, and all other religious leaders today. Without God's vision and help, humanity will never be able to enter the kingdom of heaven (Matt. 5:20). We can only try to create God's heaven on earth through our just and righteous actions and our faithful belief in God's vision of social justice for the entire planet.

Asian American Heritage Day (February 19)

Fumitaka Matsuoka

1 Chronicles 29:10–19
Psalm 18:1–6, 16–20
2 Peter 1:3–11
John 15:12–17

This Day of Remembrance is honored on a Sunday near February 19, the day in 1942 on which Japanese American citizens and their families were locked into U.S. concentration camps for the duration of World War II. Asian American Heritage Day celebrates the distinctive qualities of Asian cultures and provides a venue for non-Asians to become more acquainted with those cultures. The preacher can lift up the contributions that people of Asia have made to North America and the world at large and call the congregation to repent of the injustices inflicted upon people of Asian origin in the United States (e.g., exploitation during the building of the first transcontinental railway, Japanese internment following the Pearl Harbor attack). Preachers may also celebrate Asian Pacific American Heritage Month in May, which was recognized by a congressional and presidential act in 1979.

> From the low seats of the Camaro, I looked out. . . . I thought, So this is what Chinatown looks like from inside those dark Greyhound buses; this slow view, these strange color combinations, these narrow streets, this is what tourists come to see. I felt a small lightening up inside, because I knew, no matter what people saw, no matter how close they looked, our inside story is something entirely different.[1]

The theme of justice appears in all four Scripture passages for this day. They speak of faith that is nomadic in character (1 Chr. 29), the abyss of love that is

---

1. Fae Ng, *Bone* (New York: Hyperion Press, 1993), 45.

stronger than the abyss of death (Ps. 18), God's Word not failing to produce virtue (John 15), and virtues as the expression of faith (2 Pet. 1). This theme is also woven throughout Asian American stories, as Asian Americans have shown great tenacity in overcoming various forms of injustice.

1 Chronicles 29:10–19

David's admission that Israelites are "aliens and transients" before God speaks of a particular kind of faith that is lived in the nomadic state. Faith and the nomadic and transient nature of life are intimately familiar to the Israelites. These words of David also speak to Asian Americans' cultural and religious identity. In spite of the popular perception of a "model minority" (i.e., highly successful immigrants), Asian Americans are "in-between" people, not really fitting into the prevailing norm of American society. Asian Americans are called "People on the Way" just as Israelites reminded themselves of their transient and nomadic identity long after the days of the Babylonian captivity were over.[2]

The books of Chronicles were written to highlight the sacredness of the Israelites' entire history. But the sacredness of these events is experienced in part within the context of their exilic identity. The Israelites knew that all that they had was given to them by God, and they were grateful because they had received these gifts as a transient people who longed for a place of residence and security, a place of worship and thanksgiving (v. 14b). Japanese Americans were reminded of their own exilic lives when they were placed behind barbed wires in desolate locations during World War II. A poem written in a concentration camp by a Japanese American woman speaks of this reality. "Four months have passed, and at last I learn to call this horse stall my family's home," says Yukari.[3] Japanese Americans were placed in "desert exile." Even today in a more peaceful time, "Asian Americans are often not at home in our own home, displaced in the very society we live."[4] This in-between experience has produced an exilic mentality.

The message of this biblical passage is that faith is about learning to value and appreciate richness and deep meaning amid the transience of life. Asian Americans have responded culturally to the American mandate to assimilate us into society's mainstream. When life is exilic, we cherish the trust, closeness, and honesty that arise out of building relationships with fellow nomads.

---

2. See David Ng, *People on the Way: Asian North Americans Discovering Christ, Culture, and Community* (Valley Forge, PA: Judson Press, 1996).

3. Yoshiko Yoshida, *Desert Exile: The Uprooting of a Japanese American Family* (Seattle: University of Washington Press, 1984), 83.

4. Fumitaka Matsuoka, *Learning to Speak a New Tongue: Imagining a Way That Holds People Together—An Asian American Conversation* (Eugene, QR: Pickwick Publications, 2011), 6.

As I have written elsewhere, Asian Americans' exilic racial identity "is fragile and its transmission to subsequent generations is by no means guaranteed." This exilic orientation helps us, just as it did the Israelites, to recognize that the life given to us is a gift from God that needs to be received in gratitude.[5]

Psalm 18:1–6, 16–20

This psalm testifies to a time when Israel's sufferings had been overcome. (See the comments on this entire psalm in Year B, Asian American Heritage Day, of this series.) These particular verses focus on David calling out to God amid severe persecution. It was only after he and his people had been delivered and their worst calamities were over that the psalmist could speak of God having heard their voices (v. 6b). However, when the Israelites were in the midst of their difficulties, the only thing David was able to do was cry to God "in my distress I called upon the Lord; to my God I cried for help" (v. 6a). In very specific terms, the psalmist names God's presence as "my strength," "rock," "fortress," "deliverer," "shield," "horn of salvation," and "stronghold." The power of these metaphors is matched by the severity of David's situation as he and his people are assailed by enemies, entangled in deathly snares, and threatened with physical and spiritual annihilation.

For Japanese Americans and Christians in U.S. concentration camps during World War II, faithfulness meant calling for God's help amid horrific conditions of wrongful confinement, deprivation, and the denial of due process of law (in violation of Amendment 5 of the U.S. Constitution). They inevitably questioned the incomprehensibleness of their situation and doubted God's deliverance. Why does the God of love and justice allow such injustices, suffering, and humiliation to happen to innocent people?

Anyone who continues in religious faith will sooner or later come to a point where all their pictures of God have been smashed because they are too tiny. By contrast, the psalmist offers numerous large and graphic images of God who acts with determination to save those who are oppressed. These metaphors describe God in the strongest possible terms (vv. 1–2). Whether or not Japanese Americans who were imprisoned in concentration camps could call forth such images during their cruel ordeal, David's "rock" and "deliverer" is the God who hears and responds to the plight of all who are unjustly punished. In verses 16–20, the psalmist bears witness to God's determination to overcome the people's enemies amid the worst possible circumstances. They are words to be sung when liberation comes to Asian Americans and all who are persecuted because of our fears and prejudices.

---

5. Ibid., 8.

Then we may also join the psalmist's song and say, "We love you, O LORD, my strength" (v.1).

John 15:12–17

The farewell discourse of Jesus found in John 14:1–17:26 reminds us of words that are attributed to Martin Luther: "God's Word cannot fail to produce virtue." For contemporary Christians who live in a religiously pluralistic world, assertions about the power of God's Word may sound archaic. Is it arrogant to make such assertions about the power of God's Word? And yet, John speaks powerfully of the meaning of Christian faith through these words of Jesus, spoken shortly after Christ had washed his disciples' feet (13:1–20).

An example of the power of God's Word at work among us occurred during a service of Love Feast, a worship service held in commemoration of Jesus' Last Supper. In 1946, the Oakland Church of the Brethren in California served as a transitional house for missionaries who had served in China and India during the war and had been incarcerated by the Japanese military. The church also extended hospitality to another family who experienced dire suffering during the war, in another context. Susumu "Sim" Togasaki and his family had been interned at the Poston concentration camp in the Arizona desert. After the war, the Togasaki family were relocated to Chicago and, with the aid of Brethren Service, were able to return to their home in Berkeley (near Oakland). Out of gratitude to the Church of the Brethren, they began attending the Oakland church.

On Maundy Thursday of 1946, the service of Love Feast was held at the Oakland church, including an opportunity for footwashing for members of the congregation. Sim Togasaki sat next to the missionary who had just returned from a concentration camp in China. After the Scripture was read from John's Gospel, Sim washed the feet of the missionary. Once the footwashing was done, they exchanged the kiss of peace and participated in sharing the bread and cup of Communion.

While the bitter and painful experiences of both Sim and the missionary during the war were still deeply etched in their memories, something new entered into their lives following the service of Love Feast. The living Word of God had been embodied in that moment of footwashing, and God's Word "produced virtue" in their lives. The new relationship between Sim and the missionary was not based on the pain of their past experiences, or suspicion and distrust of one another, but it became "fruit that will last," the fruit of God's love incarnated in the experience of the Love Feast. "God's Word cannot fail to produce virtue."

2 Peter 1:3–11

According to Peter, faith needs to be supported by a series of virtues (v. 5)—love (*agapē*) along with goodness, knowledge, self-control, and endurance. *Agapē* is love that originates with God, and because God is love, we are to love as people of God! *Agapē* manifests itself by seeking another person's highest good, even at a cost to oneself. It is not inconsistent with justice but tempers it by aiming at redemption and renewed relationships. These words of Peter suggest the means by which God's call may be exercised in one's life.

For Japanese Americans, one of the most powerful expressions of justice and love is illustrated by the 1944 Supreme Court case *Fred Korematsu v. the United States*. Korematsu challenged the constitutionality of Executive Order 9066, which detained and confined all persons of Japanese descent at the outbreak of World War II.[6] In a 6–3 decision, the court upheld the constitutionality of the government's decision, insisting that concerns about espionage outweighed the rights of Korematsu and other Americans of Japanese descent.[7]

Korematsu was not deterred by the court's decision. His belief in justice was motivated by his care and love for his own community. He challenged this decision even after the concentration camps were closed at the end of World War II and continued his work despite resistance and opposition from others. Finally, the U.S. District Court for the Northern District of California overturned his original conviction in 1983. Korematsu's case underscores the reality of racial discrimination in U.S. culture, society, and governance. It was not until the 1980s that the government offered its official apology for the internment of Japanese Americans during World War II, finally paying $1.2 billion in reparations. Fred Korematsu was awarded the Presidential Medal of Freedom by President Bill Clinton. However, Korematsu's work was not yet complete. In 2004, he filed an *amicus curiae* ("friend of the court") brief in the cases of *Khaled Odah v. United States*, *Shafiq Rasul v. George W. Bush*, and *Yasir Hamdi v. Donald Rumsfeld*, which challenged the detention of detainees in Guantanamo and in the United States during the George W. Bush administration. The brief argued that "the extreme nature of the . . . position in these cases is reminiscent of its positions in past episodes in which the United States too quickly sacrificed civil liberties in the rush to accommodate overbroad claims of military necessity."[8]

---

6. See http://usgovernmentandpolitics.com, discussion of "Landmark Supreme Court Cases," No. 94.
7. See *Korematsu v. U.S.*, 1944, WL 42849, Appellate Brief, p. 4.
8. See http://www-news.uchicago.edu/releases/03/031016.korematsu.shtml.

Korematsu died in 2005 at the age of 86 while still pursuing justice. In reflecting on his life's work, it is evident that justice is the most powerful expression of *agapē*. As Peter insisted, "you must make every effort to support your faith with goodness, and goodness with knowledge, and knowledge with self-control, and self-control with endurance, and endurance with godliness, and godliness with mutual affection, and mutual affection with love" (vv. 5–7).

Sixth Sunday after the Epiphany

Charles L. Campbell

DEUTERONOMY 30:15–20
PSALM 119:1–8
1 CORINTHIANS 3:1–9
MATTHEW 5:21–37

For Christians, social ethics begins in the community of faith. Our life together in the church is to be an embodiment of a social ethic that both exposes the injustices in the world and offers an alternative to the ways of death. As Stanley Hauerwas has repeatedly argued, "The church does not have a social ethic; the church is a social ethic."[1] That is, the Christian community embodies a particular social ethic in the midst of the world, and that embodied, communal ethic is more important than all the church's pronouncements about justice. As Hendrik Berkhof has written, with regard to the church's engagements with the "powers that be":

> All resistance and every attack against the gods of this age will be unfruitful, unless the church herself is resistance and attack, unless she demonstrates in her life and fellowship how [people] can live freed from the Powers. We can only preach the manifold wisdom of God to Mammon if our life displays that we are joyfully freed from its clutches. To reject nationalism we must begin by no longer recognizing in our own bosoms any difference between peoples. We shall only resist social injustice and the disintegration of community if justice and mercy prevail in our own life and social differences have lost their power to divide. Clairvoyant and warning words and deeds aimed at state or nation are meaningful only in so far as they spring from a church whose inner life is itself her proclamation of God's manifold wisdom to the "Powers in the air."[2]

1. See, for example, Stanley Hauerwas, "Reforming Christian Social Ethics (1981)," in *The Hauerwas Reader*, ed. John Berkman and Michael Cartwright (Durham, NC: Duke University Press, 2001), 111.
2. Hendrik Berkhof, *Christ and the Powers*, trans. John H. Yoder (Scottdale, PA: Herald Press, 1962), 51.

Hauerwas and Berkhof present an important challenge to the church: we must seek to embody in our life together the kind of social ethic we proclaim to the world.

The lections for this Sunday call the church to just such embodiment. While they may be applied to the society at large, they are first and foremost addressed to the people of God. Indeed, preachers need to be careful about rushing too quickly to address biblical texts to the larger society before exploring the word they speak more directly to God's people. The first step, as Berkhof notes, is always to build up the church as an odd people who enact in our life together the justice we call for in the world.

Deuteronomy 30:15–20 and Psalm 119:1–8

Moses' great sermon in Deuteronomy is a case in point. Moses preaches to Israel as they stand on the edge of the Jordan River, preparing to cross over into the promised land. He sets before Israel the communal life they are to embody when they cross the river and become a settled people, no longer wandering in the wilderness. In today's lection, toward the end of the sermon, Moses calls the people to choose whether they will obey the commands he has previously set before them. Their choice is a matter of blessing or curse, life or death. (Psalm 119 invites a similar choice with a similar promise of life for those who "walk in the law of the LORD"; v. 1.) Importantly, this decision is not simply for individuals; it is a decision placed before God's people about their life together.

The covenant commands in Deuteronomy, to which Moses refers, are extensive. They do not just concern the "religious" life, but also focus on matters of justice, which are critical to a people's healthy life together. In particular, many of these commands focus on care for the poor, the "outsider," the widow and the orphan:

> You shall not withhold the wages of poor and needy laborers, whether other Israelites or aliens who reside in your land in one of your towns. You shall pay them their wages daily before sunset, because they are poor and their livelihood depends on them; otherwise they might cry to the LORD against you, and you would incur guilt. (24:14–15)

> You shall not deprive a resident alien or an orphan of justice; you shall not take a widow's garment in pledge. Remember that you were a slave in Egypt and the LORD your God redeemed you from there; therefore I command you to do this. (24:17–18)

> When you reap your harvest in your field and forget a sheaf in the field, you shall not go back to get it; it shall be left for the alien,

the orphan, and the widow, so that the Lord your God may bless
you in all your undertakings. When you beat your olive trees, do not
strip what is left; it shall be for the alien, the orphan, and the widow.
(24:19–20)

In choosing to serve God, Israel chooses a life together shaped by these
kinds of commitments. And blessing and life (and "happiness" or "blessedness," as the psalmist puts it in Psalm 119) are inseparable from these commitments. All must have life together, or no one will have fullness of life at
all. Apart from the commitments called for in Deuteronomy the powers of
death rule, not only for the poor and alien and widow and orphan who literally suffer and die in their oppression, but also for the privileged, who suffer
the death of their conscience, their compassion, their spirit. Apart from these
practices of justice, the society as a whole becomes a place where death reigns.

Because Israel was a political entity as well as a religious one, the commitments the people make do have significant implications for the larger society.
But first and foremost, they challenge the people of God. How does our life
together welcome the alien—the "other"? How do our churches welcome
the poor into our midst and provide support for them? Who does the menial
work in our congregations, and are they paid a *living* (not a *deathly*) wage?
How do our congregations hoard endowments, rather than offering them
to be "gleaned" by those in need? How, that is, do our communities of faith
participate in the way of life, and how are we captive to the powers of death?
Before calling the society to justice, churches need to examine themselves.
Just as Israel's life together was to be a unique witness to the surrounding
nations, so the church offers its most important witness as we enact justice in
our life together. Moses thus calls the people of God to choose life—the life
that is inseparable from a justly ordered community.

Matthew 5:21–37

In the Sermon on the Mount, Jesus is similarly constituting a community—an
odd people whose life together will embody an alternative to the ways of a
rebellious world and the powers of death. Through a series of "buts" (often
the most important word in Scripture), he moves several traditional commands beneath outward actions to the deep places where life-giving relationships are grounded. Do not simply refrain from murder, Jesus announces, but
avoid anger and insult, and seek reconciliation with your enemy (vv. 21–26).
Do not just refrain from adultery, but treat others as persons of value, rather
than mere objects of lust (vv. 27–30). Do not make divorce a simple and
easy option for husbands, reinforcing patriarchal power and oppression, but
make divorce an option only in the most extreme circumstances, and hold

the husband ethically accountable for his behavior as well (vv. 31–32). Do not simply avoid false vows, but eschew vows altogether, for they "legalize" relationships, create distrust, and often lead to death (as Jephthah's vow led to the death of his daughter, and Herod's vow led to the beheading of John the Baptist). Instead, seek relationships based on simple honesty and mutual trust (vv. 33–37).

In all of these ways, Jesus seeks to build up a distinctive community grounded not simply in external actions, but in relationships that value and seek the good of others. Justice in the community of faith, Jesus suggests, will not ultimately be sustained by merely refraining from certain external deeds or following a particular set of rules. Rather, justice will flourish when it is internalized in a community shaped by mutuality and trust. Where such mutuality and trust is missing, laws and rules can be manipulated and used to benefit those with power and privilege. Remember the ways in which African Americans remained enslaved long after slavery was legally abolished.[3] Or the ways in which unions have been prohibited or busted long after workers were legally permitted to unionize. Or the ways in which even the church has, for example, found ways to justify killing enemies, despite the commandment "You shall not kill" (one of the commandments Moses holds before the people in Deut. 5:17) and Jesus' command to love our enemies (which follows today's text, in Matt. 5:44). In the midst of the powers that be, Jesus calls the church to embody a radical form of justice, one grounded in relationships of mutuality and trust. By living together in this way, the church will offer an alternative to a world that often "legalizes" relationships and then finds ways to skirt the requirements of the law.

1 Corinthians 3:1–9

In his Letter to the Corinthians, Paul also seeks to build up the church as an alternative community that will bear a distinctive witness in the midst of the world. On first reading, Paul's words to the Corinthians may seem to be narrowly addressed to the church. He criticizes the Corinthians' internal jealousy and quarreling as indications that they are "of the flesh," in rebellion against the way of God. However, on a deeper reading, the broader social implications of his words are clear. The church is divided because different members have become devotees of seemingly competing orators—Apollos and Paul. This kind of rhetorical competition, with different rhetoricians commanding the allegiance of faithful followers, was characteristic of Roman culture in that

---

3. See Doug Blackmon's Pulitzer Prize–winning work, *Slavery by Another Name: The Re-Enslavement of Black Americans from the Civil War to World War II* (New York: Anchor Books, 2008).

day. Rhetoric was one of the great competitive "sports," and people divided up according to their loyalty to different orators. Moreover, such divisions were further deepened by a culture that was profoundly shaped by notions of superior and inferior, insider and outsider, honored and shamed. Thus, by critiquing the church's division over which orator is superior and honorable, Paul is at a deeper level critiquing the church's accommodation to the values of the culture—just as he will do later with reference to the Lord's Supper (11:17–34).

Paul's words are socially radical. In calling for reconciliation within the church, he invites the community of faith to embody an alternative to the surrounding culture. He subverts the role of the orator, making both Apollos and himself mere servants (3:9), rather than people who seek personal honor from their speech (a valuable word for preachers!). Indeed, he reduces the orator to a mere gardener, a thoroughly subordinate laborer in God's vineyard: "So neither the one who plants nor the one who waters is anything, but only God who gives the growth" (v. 7). Moreover, Paul calls the church in Corinth to move beyond the social divisions of superior and inferior, honored and shamed. He reminds them that such categories have no place in the church, for the church is *God's* field, *God's* building (v. 9). The honor and gratitude due to God subvert all human competition and divisions within the community of faith. Paul's theological vision thus leads to radical Christian practices that embody an alternative to the surrounding culture. Rather than simply reflect the social divisions of the time, Paul declares, those who trust in God are called to subvert those divisions in their life together. In a church and society that are deeply divided today, Paul's words remain critical and challenging.

Seventh Sunday after the Epiphany

Stephen G. Ray Jr.

LEVITICUS 19:1–2, 9–18
PSALM 119:33–40
1 CORINTHIANS 3:10–11, 16–23
MATTHEW 5:38–48

Our texts for today weave around the common biblical theme of living in ways pleasing to God. More importantly, we are invited to contemplate the question of the character of our lives and of life's meaning in light of the Epiphany. If we take seriously Paul's admonitions in 1 Corinthians 3:10–11, the answer may not be clear, but at least the predicate of an answer becomes clearer: namely, that any fitting answer will necessarily have as its foundation Jesus Christ. So then, Jesus becomes the prism through which this commentary reads the other texts.

Before turning to these texts, I think it is important to note that I refer to Jesus as the prism and do not use the more common approach of a christological reading. This distinction is made because of my sense that too often the language of christological interpretation has had two untoward tendencies. The first has been to minimize the concrete and *material actions* of Jesus Christ; and the second has been to overlook Paul's clear assumption that while faith is the basis of the Christian life, attention to its material conduct is essential. Focusing on Jesus as the prism through which we view these texts in no way seeks to diminish the christological import of them. Rather it is a means of resisting the tendency to spiritualize the writings of Scripture, particularly when it comes to matters of justice and the material conduct of Christian ecclesial and individual life. Put another way, I want to resist the tendency to privilege a "Christology from above" because of my sense that Paul did not engage in such privileging.

Leviticus 19:1–2, 9–18

Chapter 19 specifically sets itself up as a text about the nature and expectations of holiness for the people of Israel. Immediately we notice that before any content is given to the word "holy," its significance is rooted in the relationship between God and the people Israel. Put another way, what follows the opening verses is not to be understood as propositional truth but as truth that is rooted in the people's relationship with God. They are to be holy because God is holy (v. 2). This establishes that the ways of holiness which follow in the chapter draw their gravity from being God's ways.

As we read the verses that importune the farmer and the vintner to always leave something for the poor and the alien (vv. 9–10), challenge all to deal fairly and truthfully with others (vv. 11–16), and admonish all to avoid those actions corrosive to the soul (namely, hateful and vengeful actions; see vv. 17–18), it is important to note that each indicative is given the same coda: *I am the* LORD *your God.* Thus, it becomes clear that the call to remember the poor, to deal justly, and to shun what are acidic inclinations to the heart are rooted not only in God's identity but also in Israel's identity as God's people. While we may place the emphasis on several places in the phrase "I am the LORD your God," it seems that the inescapable meaning of this phrase is grounded in our relationship with God. We do these things because it is the Lord who is our God who commands us to do them, not some other neighborhood deity. This is made clear when we recall that the book of Leviticus has as a primary goal the establishment of Israelite identity in the face of differing and competing Canaanite, Egyptian, and other religions. If indeed the Lord is our God, then there are particular ways of being and doing that form the core of both our personal and communal identities. These ways may be thought of as the materialization of our deepest convictions about God's Being in creation, a way of Being that exemplifies love and justice. In a word, grace.

Psalm 119:33–40

The psalmist here draws the contrast between what he understands to be God's ways and the psalmist's own tendencies to self-indulgence and vanity. Understanding that there are indeed two ways of being, the psalmist sets his heart on the precepts of God as the way to orient himself and his life. If we take seriously the point being made by the psalmist in light of the reading from Leviticus, then it becomes clear that it is only with God's help that we may live in the ways of righteousness. In light of this, it is also clear that while this plaintive plea may be uttered by an individual, it has further implications for communal accountability. For if God's ways are given voice in the Decalogue, then it is that to which our hearts ought to incline themselves. This particular text adds a significant dimension to today's readings: namely, the psalmist recognizes that our natural inclination is to form our lives in ways that are both pleasing and edifying to ourselves, with little concern for God's ways.

This tendency is named by Augustine and refined by much of the Christian tradition as pride. For much of the history of Christian biblical interpretation, the terms "pride" and "vanity" have been used interchangeably. While there is a significant correspondence between them and the ideas behind them, the psalmist provides a way to distinguish between these two words. While pride has traditionally been understood as self-assertion at the expense of adequate regard for God, vanity may be understood as preference for one's own image over the image cast by a life conformed to God's will. The first instance has to do with a malformed sense of one's significance in the scheme of things, and the second one finds beauty in the malformation.

While space does not permit a full explication of the significance of this, we can at least observe that this is precisely the way that evils such as racism and ethnocentrism work. They not only rely on a false sense of a group's significance in the scheme of things, but also go further to assert a false and illusory sense of what is beautiful, a sense that denies and annihilates the beauty of others. We see this in the historical reality that racial and ethnic oppression has never been confined to the mere working of material power. It has also been necessary to render those oppressed as being aesthetically repugnant to both the oppressor and God. The psalmist's clear admonition that vanity is one of the ways in which we separate ourselves from God's ways is a helpful reminder that although pride may be at the root of sin, it is vanity that allows pride to blossom and flourish.

1 Corinthians 3:10–11, 16–23

In this brief passage, Paul unashamedly talks about the foundations he laid for the Christian community in Corinth, going so far as to call his work that of a master builder. Throughout the epistle, Paul wryly points out that if anyone has a right to boast it is he, yet he does not. He lifts up a theme which runs throughout 1 Corinthians, that there is no place for boasting of one's work on behalf of Christ. Instead, he boasts of the good work that is done in the Christian community at Corinth as it reflects God's grace into the world. This is precisely what one may assume he understands the work of Jesus to have been and to be. Alternatively, he takes issue with those who assume that their work is worthy of praise.

This admonition from Paul, which forms the center of his letter to the Christian community at Corinth, is well to be remembered by Christian communities in the contemporary era. A temptation before any community is to look on its own works as laudable and to lose sight of the work of grace that they reflect into the world as they seek to conform their lives to that of Jesus. The difficulty is not only that the grace of God is obscured by a self-referential and self-congratulatory posture of Christian communities in the world; it is also that this posture obscures unhelpful and in some cases destructive ways of being in the world by Christian communities. This is borne out not only in the Christian missions of the last three centuries that participated in the destruction of indigenous peoples and cultures around the world, but also in the continuing conceit that enfeebles the witness of many communions within the church; namely, the belief that the most authentic expressions of the Christian faith are those that have particular lineages traced through the racial and ethnic lines of its missionaries.

Matthew 5:38–48

At the center of this Gospel text is a continuation of the idea that perfection is found in a disposition of life that reflects God's disposition toward creation. Of particular note is the way that Jesus frames this disposition. It is explicitly toward the well-being and flourishing of those normally cast outside of one's circle of care. Specifically, the text enjoins this felicitous disposition toward those who would normally be objects of our enmity. It is just here that I think we have the thread that binds our texts for today.

At its root, the declaration of one, or a group, as enemy is the profoundest form of objectification to corrupt human relationships. For who are our enemies but those whom we have reduced to the most objectionable qualities and identified as evil? This is nowhere more apparent than in the history of deadly oppression in which entire groups are rendered objectionable in their very being and correlatively considered worthy of our most lethal response. The Shoah and the genocide in Rwanda are perhaps the two most poignant examples of this dynamic in recent history. Thus when Jesus admonishes us to seek the well-being of our enemies, he is inviting us to once again see their humanity. It is only when this image, distorted by enmity, has been restored that we may hope to restore the ground of creative relationality with others. It is no wonder that Jesus establishes it as the human analogue to God's perfection.

If we take seriously the intimation by Jesus that an expression of God's perfection is the continual ability to see beyond the distortions of enmity, to see the creative possibilities in our relationships with "others," then perhaps we find a thread by which to weave together today's texts. In Jesus, Immanuel, God is about the work of reconciling Godself to us, even while the walls of enmity are raised. Turning to Leviticus, our reason for engaging this work is because it is this particular God, the God of reconciliation seen in Christ, who is our God. The psalmist evokes for us the difficulty of cultivating and maintaining this posture in life due to human inclinations to define our own sense of power and beauty through the imputation of repugnance to those over whom we hold power and those we call our enemies. As noted earlier, we see this power/aesthetic dynamic in virtually every case in which oppression becomes lethal. Paul's admonition against a boastful way of being in the world is precisely the point here. For is it not the case that wherever oppression is present, those in power manufacture regimes of knowledge and aesthetic cultural performances to legitimate that power? Do those who hold oppressive power over others ever attribute this relationship to simple avarice or raw covetousness? The passage from 1 Corinthians cautions us against the decidedly unholy inclination to ascribe to ourselves and our communities a power that is not our own. It is far better on Paul's account to ascribe to divine grace any power that our community might have. This ascription to grace is valid when we understand that whatever power we have is to be placed in the service of reconciliation and breaking down the walls of enmity that lead us to call anyone our enemy.

Eighth Sunday after the Epiphany

Jeffery L. Tribble Sr.

ISAIAH 49:8–16A
PSALM 131
1 CORINTHIANS 4:1–5
MATTHEW 6:24–34

In these readings, we encounter passages that feed our holy imagination for proclaiming and witnessing to the ministry and mission of Jesus Christ. The sensitive interplay of these texts, our self-awareness, and our ministry contexts yield innumerable possibilities for transformative ministry. Each of these texts speaks of concrete expressions of ministry in particular ancient times and places, and they also address specific situations of injustice today: battered women and battered cities, people needing to find calm as they seek to do justice in an anxious and bitterly divided public arena, persons jailed and sometimes executed by flawed human systems of criminal justice, and our struggle to single-mindedly seek God's "justice-righteousness" in an era of idolatrous materialism.

Isaiah 49:8–16a

Isaiah calls the people of God to prophetic proclamation of and participation in God's compassionate, timely, and just response to human suffering. It is crucial that we discern in a myriad of situations and contexts what Dr. Martin Luther King Jr. called "the fierce urgency of now." *Now* is "the accepted time" to respond with mother love (v. 15a) to the cries of those who are suffering.

The prophet writes to a deported community devastated by the triumph of Babylon over them. He encourages people who doubt their status and the worth of God's love for this city and its people. God reigns despite crippling circumstances and beckons desolate prisoners in darkness to "come out" and be free (v. 9a).

104

God's compassion will be seen in restorative deliverance, a glorious journey evoking joyful praise in heaven and on earth (v. 13). Like the first exodus, this deliverance will be characterized by God's gracious provision, protection, and guidance (vv. 9b–10). Prophetic imagination and foresight anticipate mountainous struggles on the arduous journey of freedom; but "the God who makes a way out of no way" transforms these mountains into roads of growth, development, and progress (v. 11). Creating new and effective complementary levels of ministry—ministries of charity and mercy, ministries of nurture and sustained support, ministries of human service delivery, ministries of justice, and ministries of comprehensive community transformation[1]—results in a wide-ranging impact even to those who come "from far away" (v. 12).

Susan Ackerman suggests that the feminine verb used of Zion (the Hebrew word *Watt-omer*), another name for Jerusalem, in conjunction with the maternal imagery of God in verse 15, evokes an image of the city as the anguished daughter of God. Zion is in pain because she believes that the Lord has forsaken her. Even though a human mother's compassion may wane, the compassion of the divine Mother, the Lord our God, will not fail.[2]

Who might you see as forsaken and forgotten because of protracted suffering and injustice in your time and place? In my holy imagination I see Zion as a woman battered by cycles of violence, isolation, and fear that sap her strength and self-esteem. I also see Zion as a city battered by cycles of economic policies and political practices that sap its strength and culture. Letty Russell asks, "In the face of those sexist, racist, and classist structures that batter women and city alike, what is the Spirit saying to the churches?"[3] We must help battered persons to "come out" of their situations and lead them to restoration of *shalom*. Likewise, through our ministries of charity and justice, battered cities filled with comprehensive social needs must be saved. The prophetic church enacts ministries of social justice and transformation and celebrates in worship: "Sing for joy, O heavens, and exult, O earth; break forth, O mountains, into singing! For the LORD has comforted his people, and will have compassion on his suffering ones" (v. 13).

---

1. Robert M. Franklin, preface to *Transforming the City: Reframing Education for Urban Ministry*, ed. Eldin Villafane, Bruce W. Jackson, Robert A. Evans, and Alice Frazer Evans (Grand Rapids: Eerdmans, 2002).
2. Susan Ackerman, commentary on Isaiah 49:14–15 in *The New Interpreter's Study Bible: New Revised Standard Version with the Apocrypha* (Nashville: Abingdon, 2003), 1025–26.
3. Letty Russell, "The City as a Battered Woman," in *Envisioning the New City: A Reader on Urban Ministry*, ed. Eleanor Scott Meyers (Louisville, KY: Westminster/John Knox Press, 1992), 152–55.

Psalm 131

This psalm is a song of quiet trust. A leader's individual prayer of trust and confidence (vv. 1–2) closes with a summons to the faith community to place hope and confidence in Israel's God now and forever (v. 3). In the presence of God, the psalmist experiences complete submission before God, an attitude of humility and contentment. The opposite of this disposition is a heart lifted up, eyes raised too high, and preoccupation with things beyond one's capacity to comprehend or control (v. 1). Instead of reacting instinctively to perplexing and anxiety-producing circumstances, the psalmist has learned to calm emotions and quiet swirling thoughts (v. 2a). As a child who no longer feeds on its mother's milk is freed from fretting for this milk, the mature believer who has been weaned from instinctively reacting to emotionally challenging events is freed to tap into a deep reservoir of trust in the triune God.

By tapping into this reservoir, we increase our capacity to be a nonanxious presence. This is crucial for the work of social justice in a partisan and acrimonious public arena. In his book *Congregational Leadership in Anxious Times*, Peter Steinke contrasts two key parts of the brain.[4] One part, the amygdala (uh-mig-da-la), regulates the "instinctual level" of our brain that is wired for human survival. Another part, the left prefrontal cortex, is crucial for all higher-order purposeful behavior. Steinke calls the latter part "holy tissue"— the part of our brain that he says is specially "set apart to lead the people of God." The strength of the amygdala is its quickness, not its accuracy. Sensing that you are in harm's way, it operates quickly before there is time to deliberate or mull over details. This "primitive" survival instinct operates in a "yes-or-no fashion." We automatically react: "Is this safe or dangerous?" We are limited to either–or thinking. The amygdala relies on generalizations and stereotypes to do its rapid and urgent work. Also, if a stimulus registers as fear early on in life, when that stimulus is registered later in life, the same reaction occurs.

This strikes me as a plausible explanation for the increasingly bitter and acrimonious partisan debates that rage in the public arenas of church and society. Unfortunately, too many people are willing to exploit people's lower instincts. These instincts, born of generalizations and stereotypes deeply embedded in our culturally conditioned scripts, are designed to protect us from perceived harm. It is easy to automatically react to perceived threats rather than respond thoughtfully. When our brain "takes the low road," we are not capable of thoughtful, imaginative responses to emotionally challenging events or people. As people of faith, we must learn to "take the high

---

4. Peter L. Steinke, *Congregational Leadership in Anxious Times: Being Calm and Courageous No Matter What* (Herndon, VA: Alban Institute, 2006), 49–64.

road"—to calm and quiet our soul. By doing so, we can step back from our anxious fears and thoughtfully engage others, trusting God who truly understands "things too great and marvelous" for our instincts.

1 Corinthians 4:1–5

Servants of Christ are stewards of God's mysteries and are entrusted with God's holy mission of justice. Human beings, both holy and sinful, are charged with administering justice. At their best, human judgments are partial and biased, for we are shaped by invisible and sometimes insidious social forces. Even our judgments about ourselves can be self-serving and self-protecting. Tragically, justice is unfairly administered. Yet in the face of injustice we must declare, "God's justice is sometimes delayed, but never denied."

In 1944, Lena Baker, an African American maid whose employer had imprisoned and threatened to shoot her if she attempted to escape, turned her employer's gun against him and killed him. She was condemned to death in 1945 as the only woman in the State of Georgia to have been executed by electrocution. In her defense, Baker is reported to have said, "What I done, I did in self-defense. I have nothing against anyone. I'm ready to meet my God." Years later, members of the Baker family petitioned the State of Georgia, and she was granted a full and unconditional pardon in 2005. The gross injustice of the original verdict was seen to reflect the racist attitudes of the state. Justice was served sixty years after her death.

Paul had firsthand experience in human courts of justice that dealt him the bitter blows of unjust sentencing and imprisonment. With painful insight he writes, "But with me it is a very small thing that I should be judged by you or by any human court. I do not even judge myself. I am not aware of anything against myself, but I am not thereby acquitted. It is the Lord who judges me" (vv. 3–4). In my holy imagination, this text inspires me to see people like Lena Baker who are the object of unjust laws and are treated unfairly in human courts of law. Like the early apostles, apostles of social movements were jailed or executed unjustly. In human courts, they were unfairly treated in their quest for freedom, justice, and equality. Embracing God's holy mission of justice sometimes involves the work of reforming human courts of justice.

Matthew 6:24–34

Perhaps one of the greatest needs of this age is sound (i.e., balanced) prophetic preaching and teaching about wealth and economics. Wealth can become master of a person's time and values, as well as bring harm to others. This prophetic warning about the love of money and the blessings of being content with enough is a missing message amid prosperity preaching today. Liberation theologians must provide descriptive as well as normative perspectives in their preaching. One prophetic preacher, describing the grip of American individualism on his middle-class African American congregation, declared insightfully, "No matter what, (some) black folk are going to drink, drive, and dress!" Prophetic preaching and teaching offers critique of harmful uses of wealth and guides disciples in learning to use wealth justly, mercifully, and wisely.

Wealth belongs in a relationship of trusting God, who provides for creation. Wealthy disciples have a communal responsibility to use a portion of their wealth to provide for the common good of creation. On the other end of the economic spectrum, there are many who, through poverty or prolonged unemployment amid massive shifts in the global economy, worry about the basic necessities of life. Disciples are not to worry about physical necessities. Worry is more likely to shorten life than prolong it. Stress, improperly managed, leads to chronic diseases. Ultimately, the length of our days is in God's hands.

Though worry is antithetical to faith, work is not. The point of this portion of Jesus' Sermon on the Mount is not that disciples need not work. God's provision for the birds is not accomplished by their simply waiting for food to drop into their beaks. They actively work to gather food. Prophetic preaching challenges the poor to embrace their personal responsibilities and accept "a hand up, not a handout." While stressing the dignity of work for the poor, we must also work to transform unethical economic systems that deny hardworking people a living wage. Disciples in all economic classes are called to single-mindedly seek God's justice-righteousness while daily trusting God through personal as well as communal trouble.

Ninth Sunday after the Epiphany

Sharon H. Ringe

DEUTERONOMY 11:18–21, 26–28
PSALM 31:1–5, 19–24
ROMANS 1:16–17; 3:22B–28 (29–31)
MATTHEW 7:21–29

Law and grace, faith and works: for millennia these apparent polarities have worried theologians and laypeople attempting to live their religion. Martin Luther drew on them to characterize his struggles with the Roman Catholic Church. Members of the "religious right" do not embrace Torah as the way of righteousness, but rather they point to a set of Christian rules, doctrines, and values as a litmus test that reveals true Christians. Christians of a liberationist stripe talk about the inclusiveness of God's grace and God's advocacy for those whom dominant cultures disvalue, but then they fret over whether they or anyone can do enough work for justice to deserve to be called a true follower of Christ.

This week's readings assigned near the end of the season of Epiphany lay out the tension between those approaches to Christian life so starkly that one might be tempted to select among them instead of reading all of them, but the point is that they belong together. Deuteronomy's celebration of the amazing gift of the words of the law stands beside the psalmist's prayer that God's righteousness continue to sustain us. Matthew's conclusion of the Sermon on the Mount with Jesus' admonition that we be doers of the word and not hearers only goes hand in hand with Paul's affirmation that our status before God—our "justification" or "righteousness" (both are translations of the Greek word *dikaiosyne*)—is granted on the basis of faith and grace, not works of the law. And all of these readings bid for our attention on this day.

Deuteronomy 11:18–21, 26–28

God's covenant with Israel was a gift from God. Its cause was God's grace, not any human meritorious behavior. To live so intimately connected to God is

109

wonderful and fearsome: how should we live in that relationship, and what do we need to do to make it work? It is important to remember that torah came at this moment of Israel's life, as a gift to reassure them about the first gift of the covenant.

If we approach torah with the Gospel writers' lenses in our glasses, we get it wrong. We hear their attribution to Jesus of accusations of self-righteousness and hypocrisy against the leaders of the Jewish community who especially oppress the poor among their people—those whose economic and social marginality make it impossible for them to follow the requirements of the law. The law tied onto one's wrist and forehead, and tucked into *mezzu-zoth* on the doorposts of one's home (vv. 18–21), seems more like a straitjacket than a cause for rejoicing.

The writer of Deuteronomy, however, sees the situation differently. The law was not given so that one could earn a blessing as a reward, but rather having the law as a guide to the way one should walk is itself the blessing (vv. 26–28). It is important to recall that the law should be viewed as a single entity, not a list of 613 individual rules with a scorecard to chart one's success-ful completion of them. The totality of the law functions both as a map for one's journey through life and as a companion on the way. In Jewish theology, torah is often personified as God's presence with God's people in the form of a guide who shares life with us and who helps us to know the way to travel.

Psalm 31:1–5, 19–24

The emphasis in Deuteronomy on actions, on walking in the way of torah, as a fitting response to God's grace is balanced by the psalmist's simple and total trust in God. Any who sing this psalm are led to praise and to count on God's utter reliability (a "rock of refuge," a "fortress"; vv. 2–4) for their own well-being. The first part of the reading (vv. 1–5) is a prayer of confidence that God can and will live into that identity. Luke's Gospel quotes verse 5 as Jesus' final triumphant cry at the moment of death.

So confident is the psalmist that God will remain true to God's nature and ways that an exuberant thanksgiving (vv. 19–24) can follow directly on the prayer for God to help, with no intervening narrative of how God has actu-ally accomplished what was prayed for. The thanksgiving can even include a sheepish admission of lapses of confidence along the way (v. 22).

Prayers like this come to the lips and the hearts of people in all generations who face their moments of reckoning while knowing that they are not alone. Through the centuries they have sustained many of God's faithful servants whose commitment to God's project of justice and peace has led them to put their very lives on the line. This psalm was literally the prayer of a group of pastors struggling to accompany people and communities in the cities and villages of Mexico in recent years in the wake of the economic collapse and the violence of the drug trade. They found strength to share the good news with their people in the rhythms of imploring God for relief from the violence and suffering they were enduring, and resting in secure confidence that God was, is, and always will be there to hold them in the palm of God's hand.

In the United States, whose recent history has been the locus of many struggles for justice and peace, the affirmations of this psalm have accompanied people in fasts, protests, and jail. Individual phrases from this psalm, and certainly its confident mood, have graced the freedom songs and spirituals of the Civil Rights Movement, the "war" to end poverty, and struggles for workers' rights. They translate readily into "We shall overcome!" and "¡Sí, se puede!"

Romans 1:16–17; 3:22b–28 (29–31)

The Hellenistic world, like the one in which we live, was a world of ethnic, cultural, and religious diversity. Nowhere was that more evident than in the city of Rome. The earliest Christian presence in Rome arose from conservative, law-observant Jewish origins. Their ties to the church in Jerusalem were strong, and in both places Paul's contention that Gentile believers did not have to take on the whole Jewish law as part of their Christian practice met opposition. In 49 CE, when Claudius expelled Jews (including Christian Jews) from Rome, the Gentiles who had not been among the leaders of the church suddenly found themselves providing the leadership. By the time Claudius died in 54 CE and the edict of expulsion lapsed, the culture, theology, and practices of the Roman church had changed under the Gentile leaders. When the former leaders returned and saw the changes, the arguments began.

Paul's letter to the communities that were not founded by him presents his effort to clarify the meaning and implications of the gospel as he understands it. Not only does the letter address the specific pastoral situation in Rome, but it also allows him to rehearse the arguments he will need to make to the church in Jerusalem, and to prepare a clear statement of the message he will share during a projected mission trip to Spain and other points in the west.

Romans 1:16–17 is Paul's thesis statement for the letter, emphasizing the parity of Jews and Gentiles before God. For everyone "the righteousness of God is revealed through faith for faith" (v. 17). So far, so good. After making clear that Jews and Gentiles stand before God on the same terms, and that no one has a head start on this relationship with God, or an alternate route (such as through obedience to the law), however, Paul gets into grammatical trouble. The Greek genitive case, "the faith of Jesus Christ" (*he pistis Iesou*

Christou), can mean both "faith *in* Jesus Christ" and "the faith that Jesus has." The church has generally understood the former as the meaning, but the rest of the passage that accents faith as God's gift and evidence of God's grace (3:22b–31) suggests that the latter meaning fits better with Paul's message. If it were a matter of our faith *in* Jesus, that faith could be a matter of our achievement: is it correct enough or sincere enough? The wonder and gift of Paul's proclamation is to remove such anxious self-concern and replace it with a new parity of status as "justified" or "set right" before God.

Confident of that relationship, we can be free to act with courage to "uphold the law" (3:31), which includes doing the deeds of justice the law mandates. It is important to remember that justice more than ritual purity or moral legalism is at the heart of torah. "Upholding the law" calls us to commitment on behalf of justice. Often in justice or advocacy work on behalf of people who are pushed to the margins by the dominant culture and economic institutions, we need to act before every bit of evidence is in. To wait for absolute certainty about the right course of action can collude in the harmful situation we are trying to address. As it is put in the quote attributed in various forms to Edmund Burke, "All that is needed for evil to triumph is for good people to do nothing." To know ourselves freed by God's grace from the need to be perfect can free us in turn to act with timely courage, trusting that God's grace continues to sustain and perfect what we have begun.

Matthew 7:21–29

This section of Matthew recalls the language of James 2:14–26, that faith must be expressed in action or else it is dead. Here it is doing the will of God, not verbal confession or praise, that enables one to participate in God's sovereign project of justice and peace (vv. 21–23). This is one of a number of places where Matthew's Gospel portrays Jesus as echoing the Jewish understanding of torah as instruction or guidance—we might even say a GPS—for our covenant walk with God. It's not a matter of faith or works, but of the recognition that the only suitable human response to God's gracious faithfulness requires the engagement of our entire lives. It really is all about faith! Current debates between the political left and political right really come down to the theological question of how to "do" faith in partnership with God.

Often Paul's celebration of faith and grace is set over against Matthew's and James's position. "Faith alone" was the great cry of the Reformation that is traced to Paul. The disagreement between Paul, on one hand, and Matthew and James, on the other, is a matter of language rather than substance, because for Paul "faith" is incarnate in our lives. It is not principally belief in a doctrine or bit of information, nor is it a warm feeling of trust in one's heart, although it can include both of these. Rather it is letting the whole weight of one's life be borne by God. We "do" faith, not with our heads or hearts, but with bodies—our hands and feet. The words attributed to Jesus in this Gospel reading seem to make the same point: words alone do not get the job done. Or in the cadence of African American preaching, you have to walk the walk, not just talk the talk of God's good news.

Transfiguration Sunday (Last Sunday after the Epiphany)

Ched Myers

EXODUS 24:12–18
PSALM 2
2 PETER 1:16–21
MATTHEW 17:1–9

> Without wildness, civilization could not survive. The converse does not hold.
>
> —*Evan Eisenberg*[1]

Transfiguration Sunday invites us to a mountaintop experience. While most churchly commentators focus on the *theology* of this episode, I will examine its *mythic geography*, in the hope that the preacher might see this morning's texts as an opportunity to pursue the urgent task of proclaiming ecojustice in a world on the verge of environmental collapse.[2]

Exodus 24:12–18 and Matthew 17:1–9

The book of Exodus narrates three great approaches by Moses to YHWH on Sinai. In the first, Israel camps at the foot of the mountain, where YHWH calls to Moses to prepare the people for an encounter (Exod. 19:3). Israel has *seen* what YHWH did to liberate them from imperial Egypt (v. 4); now they must *hear* YHWH's voice (vv. 5–19). YHWH "comes down" from the mountain to give Israel instructions on how to live after empire (v. 11), encapsulated in the Ten Commandments (20:1–17). This inaugural epiphany sets a dramatic tone for future encounters: thunder and lightning, smoke and fire, and a great cloud (19:16–19).

---

1. Evan Eisenberg, *The Ecology of Eden* (New York: Vintage, 1998), 106.
2. For the most succinct analysis of the ecological crisis, see James Gustave Speth, *The Bridge at the Edge of the World: Capitalism, the Environment, and Crossing from Crisis to Sustainability* (New Haven, CT: Yale University Press, 2008).

The same effects mark this morning's reading, in which Moses ascends the mountain a second time to receive the Decalogue on stone tablets. Matthew's Transfiguration account is clearly shaped by this vignette:

> Exodus 24:15–18: Then Moses went up on the mountain, and the cloud covered the mountain. The glory of the Lord settled on Mount Sinai, and the cloud covered it for six days; on the seventh day YHWH called to Moses out of the cloud. Now the appearance of the glory of the Lord was like a devouring fire on the top of the mountain in the sight of the people of Israel. Moses entered the cloud, and went up on the mountain.

> Matthew 17:1, 3, 5 RSV: And after six days Jesus took with him Peter and James and John his brother, and led them up a high mountain apart. . . . And behold, there appeared to them Moses and Elijah, talking with him. . . . He was still speaking, when lo, a bright cloud overshadowed them, and a voice from the cloud said . . .

Matthew also alludes to Moses' third encounter, in which the prophet again ascends the mountain for forty days, receives a second set of tablets reiterating the Covenant Code, and comes down with his face "aglow":

> Exodus 34:29: Moses did not know that the skin of his face shone because he had been talking with God.

> Matthew 17:2 RSV: And Jesus was transfigured before them, and his face shone like the sun, and his garments became white as light.[3]

Matthew, who is concerned to portray Jesus as the messianic renewer of Torah, means these Exodus allusions to focus our attention on Moses' appearance at the Mount of Transfiguration (he is named before Elijah, inverting Mark 9:4). Just as Moses mediated the covenant on Sinai, so now Jesus communicates the will of YHWH to the people: "Listen to *him!*" (Matt. 17:5; cf. Deut. 18:15).

But what is the significance of these mountain geographies? Evan Eisenberg writes in *The Ecology of Eden*: "The fact that Canaan . . . contains the lowest dry land on the planet (the shore of the Dead Sea) as well as deserts, coastal plains, and steppe only makes its great mountains the more imposing."[4] He goes on to explore the sacred mountain as a sort of environmental *axis mundi* in ancient Near Eastern mythology:

---

3. Though the RSV translates the verbs the same, Matthew uses *elampsen* (cf. Matt. 5:15), which differs from the Septuagint's *doxaz*. See my comment on Exod. 34:29–35 for Transfiguration Sunday, Year C.

4. Eisenberg, *Ecology of Eden*, 72.

The World Mountain is mythic shorthand for an ecological fact. There are certain places on earth that play a central role in the flow of energy and the cycling of water and nutrients, as well as in the maintenance of genetic diversity and its spread by means of gene flow. Such places provide many of the services that keep the ecosystems around them (and the biosphere as a whole) more or less healthy for humans and other life forms. They help control flooding and soil erosion. They provide fresh infusions of pollinating birds and insects. . . . They regulate the mix of oxygen, carbon dioxide, water vapor, and other ingredients in the air and keep its temperature within bounds. They are spigots for the circulation of wildness through places made hard and almost impermeable by long human use. All such places are more or less wild; many are forested . . . and from them great rivers flow.[5]

Because the mountains of Lebanon represented such an "ecological spigot" for Canaan, Eisenberg concludes, their "holiness" was grounded in a primal consciousness that these wild highlands represented the cradle of all life. Spiritual leaders thus ascended these heights not only to commune with the Divine, but to journey to the origins of all natural fertility, in order to bring blessing to their people.

To the cosmic mountain the biblical prophets, too, journey, to receive instruction on how the people should live (Moses) and assurance of divine accompaniment (Elijah).[6] In the transfiguration story, Moses and Elijah represent not only biblical archetypes of the law and the prophets. They are also feral visionaries who communed with the radically undomesticated YHWH on sacred peaks far from empire and its discontents. Jesus seeks to follow in their footsteps.

Ancient church tradition identifies the mount of transfiguration with Mount Tabor, a freestanding, hemispherical peak about five miles southeast of Nazareth that rises 1,843 feet above the Mediterranean Sea (see Ps. 89:12; Jer. 46:18; Hos. 5:1). Tabor was the staging area where the Hebrew guerrilla warriors Deborah and Barak and their vastly outnumbered forces defeated a heavily armored, professional Canaanite army.[7] In the Gospel story, however, Jesus ascends the mount in order to draw strength from his ancestors for his *nonviolent* march to Jerusalem to face down the powers.

---

5. Ibid., 75.
6. Elijah walks "forty days" to take refuge in a cave on "the mount of YHWH at Horeb" (1 Kgs. 19:8). Significantly, Horeb is identified by the Deuteronomist with Mount Sinai (Deut. 5:2; see also Exod. 3:1, 12; 17:6).
7. The biblical writer attributes this miraculous victory to the intervention of YHWH (see Judg. 4:6–14; 6:2–7:19). Not so fortunate were later Judean rebels, who according to Josephus took a last stand on Tabor before being slaughtered by Roman counterinsurgency forces.

Jesus' "transfiguration" (Gk. *metemorphōthē*, Matt. 17:2) provides two trajectories for homiletic reflection. On one hand, the mountaintop experiences of both Moses and Jesus cause them to "glow"—symbolizing a profound connection to the Source. The great wilderness prophets, from John the Baptist to John Muir to Jim Corbett, have attested to the transformative power of unshackled nature. Most of us have some experience, however partial, of feeling cleansed and renewed by time spent hiking or camping in the wild. The unmediated biosphere offers a very different energy than that generated (and venerated) by urban life, and we are both attracted to it and—as creatures domesticated by civilization—afraid of it. Yet the Bible, the Desert Mothers and Fathers, and countless poets all attest to the wilderness as the primal space of spiritual renewal.

A second trajectory is found in the metaphor of brilliant white light. This alludes to Daniel's apocalyptic visions (Dan. 7:9; 10:6), in which the Divine Judge vindicates the oppressed.[8] The literary tradition of biblical apocalyptic articulates a spirituality and politics of resistance to empire, which raises another aspect of the ancient "World Mountain" suggested by Eisenberg. The urban civilizations of Mesopotamia attempted to reproduce (and thus domesticate) the peaks "where the gods dwelled":

> At the heart of every Mesopotamian city was a sacred precinct, and at the heart of every sacred precinct was a ziggurat, a stepped pyramid of mud brick . . . [which] seem to have imitated mountains in a fairly literal way. . . . It is a sign of the Mesopotamians' pride that they drew the gods—and paradise itself—down from the mountains and into their own cities.[9]

From this artificially engineered mountain the rulers communed with gods who were the patrons of empire, looking down upon the realm with managerial authoritarianism. Eisenberg rightly sees in the tower of Babel story (Gen. 11) a biblical parody of this social and structural architecture of domination.

Given the archetypal opposition of mountain and tower in the Bible, it should not be surprising that the heroes named in the transfiguration story stand *with* the undomesticated YHWH on the shrouded wild crags in order to stand *against* urban fantasies of control and omnipotence. Moses is liberated from Pharaoh's Egypt and embraced by YHWH on Sinai. Elijah flees the royal threats of Ahab and Jezebel, taking refuge at Horeb in order to

---

8. Matthew also echoes Daniel's reassuring touch of the messenger's hand upon those frightened by the epiphany (Dan. 10:10 = Matt. 17:6–7). The transfigured countenance of the vindicated righteous is also echoed in the apocalyptic book of *1 Enoch*: "those who possess the earth will neither be rulers nor princes, they shall not be able to behold the faces of the holy ones, for the light of the Lord of the Spirits has shined upon the face of the holy" (*1 Enoch* 38:4).

9. Eisenberg, *Ecology of Eden*, 82–83.

gain strength to continue YHWH's freedom struggle. And Jesus goes to the misty Source to gather himself for the difficult journey to the capital city to confront yet another generation of imperial rulers. The prophetic wilderness experience of transcendence is not trying to *escape* the world, then; rather it fuels the struggle for true justice. It is to *both* these strands of ancient wisdom—the divine mountain as spiritual fount and as geopolitical counterpoint to empire—that the disciples (and we readers) are instructed to "pay attention" (Matt. 17:5c).

Psalm 2 and 2 Peter 1:16–21

At the culmination of Matthew's transfiguration story, the voice from heaven designates Jesus as "beloved Son, with whom I am well pleased" (Matt. 17:5 RSV). This pronouncement echoes the earlier moment of Jesus' baptism, another archetypal wilderness setting: the wild waters of the river Jordan, far from the domesticated ritual baths of the city (Matt. 3:16–17). The moniker alludes both to Isaiah 42:1 and to today's psalm: "You are my son; today I have begotten you" (Ps. 2:7).[10] Admittedly, Psalm 2's royal theology comes close to the idolatrous ziggurat cosmology noted above. But Brevard Childs rightly points out that "the mythopoetic setting of the older adoption formula . . . has long since been forgotten. Rather, the weight of the psalm falls on God's claim of the whole earth as his possession, and the warning of his coming wrath against the presumption of earthly rulers."[11]

In Psalm 2, YHWH derides the attempts of the "kings of the earth" to plot autonomy (vv. 1–4). Matthew's messianic appropriation of this psalm, in the context of both river and mountain, thus coheres with the wilderness tradition of resistance to empire: "Be warned, O rulers" (Ps. 2:10). As Warren Carter has shown, this perspective is articulated throughout Matthew in Jesus' anti-imperial proclamation of the kingdom of heaven.[12]

Second Peter was chosen as today's epistle because of its explicit appeal to the transfiguration event. Widely understood by scholars as a late New Testament pseudepigraphical "last will and testament," 2 Peter invokes apostolic authority to counter certain worrisome tendencies in the early Christian movement. Apparently some (third- or fourth-generation?) believers were dismissing the notion of Jesus' return in glory as a "cleverly devised myth," since it had not yet occurred (2 Pet. 1:16). The epistle cites Peter's experience on the mount of transfiguration as a foreshadowing of Christ's *parousia*, and

---

10. Psalm 99 is an alternative reading; I comment on it in Transfiguration Sunday, Year C.
11. Brevard S. Childs, *Introduction to the Old Testament as Scripture* (Philadelphia: Fortress, 1979), 516.
12. Warren Carter, *Matthew and the Margins: A Sociopolitical and Religious Reading* (Maryknoll, NY: Orbis, 2000).

insists that only this "prophetic promise" can sustain lives of resistance to the dominant culture of empire.

This represents a timely word to modern Christians living under a different imperial shadow, amid a culture that similarly ridicules any suggestion of a divine transfiguration of history. Faith in the transcendent, "mountaintop" Christ who haunts our past *and* our future may well be the only antidote strong enough to counter the delusions of modernity. In the gloom of our ecological endgame, we too should "be attentive" to the prophetic message "as to a lamp shining in a dark place, until the day dawns and the morning star rises in your hearts" (2 Pet. 1:19). Transfiguration Sunday invites us to recover old wisdom: a biblical cosmology that affirms the sacred mountain as an *axis mundi* connecting us to the divine and as a radically alternative space to empire. If the Creator mysteriously "inhabits" such wild places, then our relentless technological destruction of them—notably the current practice of mountaintop removal mining—is not just unsustainable, but *idolatrous*.[13] Our texts summon the preacher to proclaim Jesus' transfiguration in a way that challenges and empowers Christians to resist actively the disfiguration of creation.

13. See, for example, Shirley Stewart Burns, Mari-Lynn Evans, and Silas House, eds., *Coal Country: Rising Up against Mountaintop Removal Mining* (San Francisco: Sierra Club Books, 2009); http://mountainjustice.org.

Ash Wednesday

Peter J. Paris

Isaiah 58:1–12
Psalm 51:1–17
2 Corinthians 5:20b–6:10
Matthew 6:1–6, 16–21

The season of Lent is an appropriate time for Christians to follow Jesus' practice when he spent forty days in the wilderness preparing himself spiritually for the mission he was being called to undertake. In doing so it is altogether fitting to attend to the following Scriptures: the prophet Isaiah's admonitions (Isa. 58:1–12) about the importance of true worship expressing itself in acts of justice, mercy, and helpfulness toward those in need; the psalmist's prayer (Ps. 51: 1–17) of repentance and a plea for a new spirit and a new heart; Paul's teaching (2 Cor. 5:20b–6:10) to keep our eyes on the mission of being reconciled to God and wholly dedicated to the mission God has called us to undertake; and Jesus' warnings (Matt. 6:1–6, 16–21) about the dangers implicit in giving wide publicity to our spiritual disciplines.

Isaiah 58:1–12

In this text Second Isaiah focuses attention on the nation's call for the Lord's help in the midst of its suffering. The prophet summons the nation to proclaim publicly its unjust practices while seeking the Lord's protection. The prophet further reminds the people how they have served their own interest by fasting while they were oppressing their workers. Thus they are admonished that their worship can only be acceptable to the Lord if they take action "to loose the bonds of injustice, to undo the thongs of the yoke, to let the oppressed go free" (v. 6). Then and only then will they be able to experience the fruits of the new creation and be well protected by the glory of the Lord.

Reading this text in a predominantly African American congregation in the wake of Hurricane Katrina's massive destruction of the Ninth Ward in New

Orleans, listeners will be prompted to raise the question of God's justice. Had not the poor Black population of that city suffered enough for many generations? Why could God not have protected them from this undeserved catastrophe?

Such questions conceal the real cause of the disaster, which was the deliberate neglect of the city's poorest citizens by the governing forces who could have treated them more fairly. Most importantly, those governing forces were not confined to the city alone, but they also functioned in the state as well as the federal government. None of those governing systems dispensed justice to the Black citizens in the Ninth Ward. Consequently, other parts of the city fared better during the crisis because they were not as vulnerable as the predominantly Black population in the Ninth Ward. Thus, the entire governing system was guilty of the sin of deliberate neglect, which, in turn, rendered all their emergency endeavors little more than self-serving platitudes. Time and again, the Scriptures teach us that doing God's work is measured by the fairness with which we treat the least of God's people.

Psalm 51:1–17

This text represents one of the great Penitential Psalms in the Jewish and Christian traditions. From the days of antiquity up to the present time, this psalm has been associated with David's confession of his adultery with Bathsheba, which he came to see as a sin against God and not merely taking advantage of another man's wife, which in itself is reprehensible. In his plea for mercy, however, he manifested a humble spirit and a profound trust in God's steadfast love. Fully aware of God's justifiable judgment, he humbly sought divine forgiveness. Clearly, this prayer demonstrates the link between God's justice and God's mercy. Connecting these two ethical principles is significantly better than a mere emphasis on obedience to the letter of the law alone. David's repentance for breaking the law and God's forgiveness of him combine in anchoring the hope for a new beginning in which David promises to be a faithful witness to God's act of deliverance. David's forgiveness and his new relationship with God provide the groundwork for others in future generations who would link the faith and worship of Judaism with that of Christ's followers.

This text is often read in the midst of approaching danger, such as times when the certainty of death is near at hand. It applies to any occasion when people of faith are vividly aware of their dependency on God as their creator, sustainer, and savior. Such awareness of God also prompts one to remember one's own sin against God and, hence, one's unworthiness of divine deliverance. At all such times, however, the plea for mercy comes quickly to our lips and is never far away. Individually and collectively, those who are most vulnerable in society are likely to call on God's help more frequently because of their needs, uncertainties, dependencies, and wrongdoings. Accordingly, for many weeks following the 9/11 horror, numerous informal shrines kept emerging in locations throughout New York City, symbolizing human awareness of our need for and dependency on God as the ultimate source of security, since our human means of securing ourselves can be destroyed in a flash. One such shrine was at the fire station on Thirty-second Street, commemorating the hundreds of firefighters who lost their lives as they attempted to rescue people who were trapped in the twin towers.

2 Corinthians 5:20b–6:10

Paul wrote this second letter to the church he had founded at Corinth because he had heard about conflicts and rivalries in the congregation, some of which pertained to accusations made about him and his apostolic authority. Clearly, Paul had learned that the congregation was disturbed that he chose not to visit them a second time. Paul defends that decision in the early part of the letter (2:1–2). In this section of the text he reminds the church that he and they are ambassadors of Christ. Thus, God is making an appeal through them, which means that they must be reconciled to God. By such reconciliation they will take on the righteousness of God.

Churches frequently have conflicts with their pastors. In this letter, we see that Paul shares in these experiences. In his absence, much conflict has arisen. Paul's method of self-defense is to focus attention on his commitment to the mission of proclaiming Christ. Accordingly, he reminds the church that he and they are ambassadors of Christ and that God is working through them. Thus he admonishes them to become reconciled to God so that they might manifest the righteousness of God. Though we today might see Paul as pleading his own innocence in this congregational dispute, he is justified nonetheless in focusing attention on their common mission rather than the dispute itself. In doing so, he is quick to remind them that despite the many obstacles and sufferings he had experienced in his ministry, the grace of God enabled him to remain faithful.

It is important to note that there may be times when the wrongdoing of pastors results in the loss of their moral authority in the congregations they serve. The impact of that loss may signal the end of their effectiveness in those contexts. Though such pastors should repent of their wrongdoing and seek the forgiveness of those whom they have hurt, it may take a very long while for trust to be fully restored.

In the wider political realm, the Truth and Reconciliation Commission in South Africa made a valiant attempt to restore justice by inviting public confessions by the officials responsible for implementing the apartheid government's policies of racial oppression. Though the commission's work was a helpful and necessary part of that nation's healing process, the breadth and depth of the racial wounds will require careful attention for many generations to come. In short, our actions have enduring consequences that require repentance and forgiveness as the first steps toward reconciliation, restorative justice, and trust.

Matthew 6:1–6, 16–21

More than any other Gospel, Mathew presents Jesus as a master Jewish teacher. It begins with an account of Jesus' genealogy that traces it back to Abraham, the ancestral father of the Jewish people. This narrative speaks about Jesus being born to a family held in low social esteem, unlike most leaders. Yet his future greatness is foreseen as the story depicts the visit of wise men from the east coming to see the birth of this long-expected king. Throughout this Gospel, Mathew seeks to show the connections between Jesus and the covenants that God made with Abraham and Moses.

In the Sermon on the Mount, Jesus focuses his attention on three important religious practices of the Jewish people: almsgiving, fasting, and prayer. Clearly, each is a publicly visible act. Jesus warns the people, however, that they need to be careful in the public expression of their piety. If such acts are to be authentic, they must be done properly. Otherwise, they could have a contrary effect. For example, he tells them that their giving of alms should not be accompanied by fanfare but, rather, done in secret. They should expect their reward to come from God and not from the wider public. If their act of almsgiving is undertaken in the spirit of humility, God will see it and reward them accordingly. True worship seeks God's blessing rather than the praise of others. This message needs to be heard by those who are prone to making a public display of their piety rather than give a secret offering that comes from the inner depths of their hearts.

Time and again, we have witnessed political figures and televangelists boldly proclaiming their personal piety and family devotion and later being disgraced by the disclosure of their own moral hypocrisy. All too often, their personal and family virtues have been displayed publicly as they exercise moral superiority over such vulnerable peoples as undocumented immigrants, nonheterosexuals, and adult victims of rape and sexual harassment. Such acts of hypocrisy may be among the most heinous sins because of their total lack of spiritual or moral integrity.

Many people think of Lent as a time for reflecting on their own private relationship with God through the spiritual disciplines of prayer, meditation, fasting, benevolent offerings, and charity. The danger implicit in such an understanding is that these actions may be carried out without giving any attention whatsoever to the needy and the people unjustly treated in our midst: the homeless, the hungry, the unemployed, the sick, the lonely, the imprisoned, neglected children, strangers, and many others. The season of Lent should inspire us to allow the circumstances of our world to evoke from us the desire to bring wholeness to a broken world, just as Jesus did during his forty days of fasting in the wilderness, when he chose to consider others even as he was tempted to think only of himself and his own glory in isolation from the needs of the world. Jesus chose not to yield to the temptations of self-absorption and prepared himself for ministries of love, justice, and mercy in the world at large. May we do likewise.

First Sunday in Lent

Nicole L. Johnson

GENESIS 2:15–17; 3:1–7
PSALM 32
ROMANS 5:12–19
MATTHEW 4:1–11

The readings for the first Sunday in Lent present both challenges and promises for the Christian community. As we prepare to enter with Jesus into the dark and despair of the tomb, the Genesis reading asks us to wrestle with the very existence of evil and the social injustices that are part of it. We also have hints of the light and joy that the Easter event will bring when the psalmist points to the possibility, through confession of sin and genuine repentance, of overcoming injustice, and when Paul encourages us to understand the corporate nature of God's forgiveness and grace. As the Gospel reading suggests, it is through our imitation of Christ's radical obedience to God's will that the body of Christ exhibits God's call to justice, mercy, and compassion.

Genesis 2:15–17; 3:1–7

On this First Sunday in Lent, we come into contact with one of the most problematic biblical passages for Christian theology, for it begs the question of the origin of evil—a question that has been debated by theologians for centuries. Why would a good God create a good creation with the potential for evil within it? Answers proffered through the past two millennia leave us with some distasteful images of the Creator. At best, God creates and then some other force inflicts the presence of evil on the world, leaving a situation in which God seems not to have control of God's own creation; at worst, God creates, gives humans free will, and then sets up an impossible prohibition using the serpent (also part of the creation) as a foil, which makes God appear manipulative and sadistic.[1]

In this passage, or rather in centuries of interpreting it, women get a bad rap also. I still recall a "girls vs. boys" playground argument in which one of my fifth-grade male classmates stated matter-of-factly that a girl was responsible for bringing sin into the world, so boys must be "better and smarter" than girls. Centuries of patriarchy, misogyny, and other forms of gender injustice have some pretty solid foundations in a literal interpretation of the events in Eden.

In a women's Bible study in college (led by a theologically and socially conservative female campus minister), the whole story was reframed for me. Instead of a dim-witted or gullible woman, Eve became a sophisticated debater of things theological, able to hold her own in the first theological discussion with the "crafty" (3:1) serpent. In this reframed version, Eve is certainly no heroine, but at least she is willing to wrestle with the serpent over the issue of what humans may or may not do. Adam demonstrates no such gumption—Adam "who was with her" (3:6), not Adam who was far away in another part of the garden. Why the silence on Adam's part? If anything, the reframed version seems to paint Adam as the submissive one—silently watching and listening, neither confronting the serpent nor supporting Eve, and then blithely and without apparent hesitation eating the fruit that Eve hands to him. If he was "with her," we must surmise that he did indeed know from which tree the fruit came, and we must accord equal culpability to the woman *and* the man.

Regardless of whom we hold responsible, this text provides an explanation of how evil comes into the world—and with it, the existence of myriad forms of injustice. If justice and acting justly are attributes of God and the good, then injustice and acting unjustly are characteristics of the absence of God, or evil. It is ironic that the very biblical event that unleashes injustice into the world has been interpreted in such an unjust manner, resulting in the justification of gender injustice!

Finally, we would be remiss in not highlighting in this passage the early biblical grounds for an eco-friendly attitude toward God's good creation. While some scholarship has pointed to the acceptance of Judeo-Christian values and teachings as the basis for centuries of planet-pillaging,[2] the mandate to "till" and "keep" is rightly the basis for an increasing number of arguments for environmental justice and the responsible stewardship of creation. The

---

1. For a brief and accessible treatment of some of the traditional answers (and their problems), see Jay G. Williams, "Genesis 3," *Interpretation* 35 (1981): 274–79.
2. See, for example, Lynn White, "The Historical Roots of Our Ecological Crisis," *Science* 155, no. 3767 (1967): 1203–7.

attitude of *domination* of the earth must be replaced with one of *cultivation;* God does not tell the first couple to use up Eden's resources for their own benefit, but instead places them in the garden to "keep" it. It is not ours to destroy and deplete, but to cultivate and care for creation, presumably for future generations.

Psalm 32

This Penitential Psalm deals with a fundamental aspect of genuine justice in human relationships: authentic repentance made possible through confession of and forgiveness for the wrongs we commit. Sin, after all, is about broken relationships: with God, with others, and even with ourselves. Anyone who has attempted to live a lie for any period of time knows the internal schism and havoc such lack of integrity can wreak on one's psyche and one's relationships with others. The psalmist notes how spiritual illness leads to physical disorder: "While I kept silence" (choosing not to confess the wrongdoing), "my body wasted away" (v. 3). It is in confession (assuming true penitence on the part of the wrongdoer) and forgiveness that one finds health, solace, restored relationships—indeed, we might even say, *freedom.*

We should be careful not to confuse ill health (spiritual or physical) that arises from failure to confess sin and seek forgiveness with the very bad theology that asserts that all affliction experienced by humans is the result of God's punishment for some bad thing we did in the near or distant past. Such theology has been used by some in the Christian community to explain the devastation caused by tsunamis, hurricanes, and earthquakes in recent years. To suggest that God wipes out a quarter of a million people to "punish" them for existing in a predominantly Muslim culture or that God kills 3,000 people because of the acceptance of an openly gay lifestyle by some inhabitants of a particular city—and that God uses natural disasters to mete out such justice—is absurd. This is the same theology which asserts that poverty, violence, oppression, and marginalization are God's punishments for sin and, on the flip side, that wealth, health, and good fortune are God's blessings on particular individuals and nations. This same theology has contributed to feelings of national exceptionalism; racial, gender, and economic superiority; and a host of other unjust behaviors and attitudes.

When suffering and injustice are attributed to God's will or plan, it becomes far too easy to justify our apathy and our unwillingness to work toward the very things to which God calls us: compassion, mercy, kindness, and justice amid circumstances of human abuse, neglect, and prejudice. God is not somehow behind the affliction doled out by natural, economic, or political forces, but is instead present in the suffering and aftermath of such forces—when communities come together to grieve and comfort one another, when strangers provide tangible care for those in need, and when people come together to fight injustice. God is present in our faithfulness and in our willingness to praise God, who is the source of all good gifts and the power to overcome evil, even when we are stricken by poverty, violence, and oppression.

Romans 5:12–19

In a society plagued by individualism, this passage can be difficult for us to get our minds around, at least where the sin of Adam and the ensuing "condemnation for all" (v. 18) are concerned. In the United States and other Western nations, people do not easily take the blame for sins they commit themselves, let alone for the sins of their ancestors—if the long-overdue 2009 U.S. congressional apology for slavery is any indication. Of course, we are unlikely to find it difficult to participate in the "free gift" (v. 16) provided by Christ's "righteousness" that leads to "justification and life for all" (v. 18) since it is to our benefit to be so opportunistic!

As many others have treated the Adam-Christ theological analogy in this passage, the intention here is not to emphasize that very important aspect of today's Epistle reading but to note the broad theme of Paul's concern with corporate identity. According to one commentator, "for Paul there is also a real unity of humankind. . . . Paul is not so concerned with the origins of sin here as he is with corporate identity, even corporate personality as represented in Adam and in Christ. A new humanity emerges in Christ."[3]

Here we have the workings of a more inclusive ecclesiology and, perhaps, of a more inclusive humanity. When, through a sense of corporate identity, others are not perceived as terrifyingly "other," we find ourselves unable to oppress, violate, war against, and exploit them. Within the body of Christ, this "corporate identity" or "new humanity" is at the heart of a commitment to working for justice for all people and on all levels of society. If I can *truly* see another person as a part of my own being, how can I allow that person to be treated unjustly in any way? This is true for another member of the body of Christ, no matter if she is of another nationality, race, ethnicity, or social class. And if we believe that God's grace is available to *all* people, then this is also true for those outside the body of Christ; how can I allow a person to be treated unjustly who is created and loved by God in the same way that I am? This passage reminds us how closely connected we are to our brothers and sisters in Christ and to all human beings whom we may consider outside the body of Christ.

3. Alistair Drummond, "Romans 5:12–21," *Interpretation* 57 (2003): 68.

Matthew 4:1–11

In this week's reading from the Hebrew Scriptures, we followed the coming of sin and injustice into the world as a result of human failure to stand against evil. In the Gospel reading, we find a different story, one of moral courage and victory over and against temptation by Satan. In Jesus' example, the church finds its own courage to stand victorious against evil.

Matthew tells us that Jesus fasted forty days and nights "and afterwards he was famished" (v. 2). Satan then offered him the chance to prove his salt by turning stones into bread; Jesus refused, despite his hunger. Then Satan asked Jesus to verify his identity by flinging himself from the temple's pinnacle to see if angels would arrive to protect him; again, Jesus refused. Finally, Satan offered Jesus all the power and wealth he could imagine in exchange for his allegiance. Again, Jesus refused—and afterward, angels arrived to help him.

Looking at this lection through a social justice lens, the path of one who seeks to follow Christ very often begins with the third temptation. Before we can pick up the cross, we need to reject all that the cross is *not:* a symbol of prestige, wealth, or power. Jesus chooses obedience to the will of God over fame, fortune, and political power. His allegiance is clear and radical, and the allegiance of the community that claims to be his body in the world today must have a similarly clear and radical allegiance. When our allegiance to God becomes confused with loyalties to flags, political parties, economic systems, and other structures of power, we fail to reject what Jesus did in the desert. This is what Stanley Hauerwas and William Willimon are getting at when they suggest that Christians "have an opportunity to discover what has [been] and always is the case—that the church, those called out by God, embodies a social alternative that the world cannot on its own terms know."[4] If we want to follow Christ, we must do so radically by first saying no to all that the cross is not, and then saying yes to all that the cross is: justice, mercy, and compassion.

4. Stanley Hauerwas and William H. Willimon, *Resident Aliens: Life in the Christian Colony* (Nashville: Abingdon, 1989), 17–18.

Second Sunday in Lent

Alejandro F. Botta

GENESIS 12:1–4A
PSALM 121
ROMANS 4:1–5, 13–17
MATTHEW 17:1–9

The texts for the Second Sunday in Lent tell the story of our human journey to a better place, a better time, and our wariness of the uncertainties of such pilgrimages.

Genesis 12:1–4a

The Abraham cycle in Genesis encompasses chapters 11–25. The whole cycle is concentrically arranged around the expulsion and rescue of Hagar in 16:1–16. Chapter 12 finds Abram settled in Haran, where, for the first time, he is addressed by the Lord. The Lord commands Abram to leave his country and his family to go to a land that is not named. The Lord does not tell Abram to march to the land of Canaan, but we know that Canaan was the final destination of Terah's migration (11:31). The Torah, as a composite work, has an irreconcilable contradiction here. Haran is declared to be the birthplace of Abram in one tradition (Gen. 24:4, 10 = J) and Ur in another (Gen. 15:7 = R).[1]

This passage includes both a command and a promise. The command: "Go forth from your country and your kindred and your father's house to the land that I will show you" (v. 1). This is one of many uncertain journeys that the Jewish people have undertaken. From Haran/Ur to the land the Lord would show us; then fleeing from hunger in that land to Egypt; and later through the desert to a land that God promised but we had never seen. Exiled to Babylon and returned to Jerusalem, occupied and then expelled from our land to live

---

1. J refers to the Yahwist tradition and R to the final redactor of the Pentateuch.

in multiple diasporas, always looking forward to the land that the Lord has shown or will show us. More often than not, the journeys we pursue seek destinations we know precious little about.

> The goals we pursue are always veiled. A girl who longs for marriage longs for something she knows nothing about. The boy who hankers after fame has no idea what fame is. The thing that gives our every move its meaning is always totally unknown to us.[2]

The promise: According to Rashi's commentary, because the journey poses peril to the traveler in three areas (reproduction, money [the way Rashi interpreted this area], and reputation), God blesses Abram according to these three needs.[3]

There is general agreement among Hebrew Bible scholars that Genesis 12:1–4a belongs to the Yahwist tradition of the Pentateuch dated ca. 922–722 BCE.[4] It is essential, however, to understand the exilic context of the final production or redaction of this text in order to grasp its message in its final canonical form. The promise to Abram can be summarized in verse 2a: "I will make of you a great nation." The audience of this text includes those who were exiled in Babylon and the Jewish diaspora of the fifth century BCE. The purpose of this narrative is to bring hope to those who are in danger of ceasing to be a people and are at risk of losing their identity. Therefore, we can affirm that it is not the literary figure of Abram who needs to become a great nation, to be blessed and protected from the curses of other nations, but the exiles who, like Abram, are commanded by the Lord to return to the land of Israel. Again, to return to Eretz Israel (which is in ruin) meant leaving behind the stability achieved in Babylon. It was far from a safe bet, but a risk worth taking.

Similar to the slaves who left Egypt, the exiles who returned from Babylon, and God's dispersed people who returned to Eretz Israel, Martin Luther King Jr. could proclaim, "I've seen the promised land. I may not get there with you. But I want you to know tonight, that we, as a people, will get to the promised land."[5] To reach the promised land may take more than one generation, but it is our duty to begin the journey.

---

2. Milan Kundera, *The Unbearable Lightness of Being* (New York: Harper & Row, 1984), 122.
3. Rabbi Yisrael Isser Zvi Herczeg, *The Torah with Rashi's Commentary Translated, Annotated, and Elucidated* (New York: Mesorah, 1995), 116.
4. Richard Elliott Friedman, *Who Wrote the Bible?* (New York: HarperCollins, 1997), 87.
5. Martin Luther King Jr., "I've Been to the Mountaintop," speech given April 3, 1968, in Memphis, Tennessee, in Josh Gottheimer, *Ripples of Hope: Great American Civil Rights Speeches* (New York: Basic Civitas Books, 2003), 317.

Psalm 121

Psalm 121 is one of the Psalms of Ascent (Pss. 120–134), perhaps used by pilgrims while going up to Jerusalem. It is also a text about a journey. This psalm provides a window into the human soul and its deepest needs, the unfulfilled desire for safety and cover that are nowhere to be found except perhaps transcendently in the divine presence. Surrounded by uncertainty, the psalmist needs to lift eyes to the unknown, to the unreachable, looking for what is not otherwise available. God is the believer's guardian in every circumstance and against every danger.

Rabbinical commentaries were very aware of the problematic character of these statements. Ovadiah Sforno noted that it is actually in the "world to come" that this protection would be granted.[6] Psalm 121 is appropriately located in the lectionary alongside God's commandment to Abram to begin a journey with an unpredictable destiny that only God could control, a fundamentally unforeseeable and uncertain one. Our coming of age and leaving the image of God as a deus ex machina[7] who would solve the problems of our lives by intervening in human affairs has somehow left us orphans, still looking to our "father who is in heaven" while knowing that, as an Israeli children's song states, "that is just a cloud."[8]

Nevertheless, there is a hidden truth in the assurance provided by the psalmist: existential reassurance won't be provided by anything we can find around us, nothing we can acquire, nothing that could be materially obtained. To live in a state of constant vulnerability is an essential component of our lives, and to try to compensate for this with any kind of material security (e.g., personal, political, financial, or military power) will ultimately prove ineffective. Only when we lift our eyes to the transcendent aspect of life, only when we can feel that we are ultimately destined to live as defenseless creatures, and only when we embrace that "only life that opens itself to the other, life that risks being wounded or killed, contains promise,"[9] only then do we become fully human.

Every journey toward our promised land of freedom, justice, and peace has its risks. God calls us to begin walking.

---

6. Rabbi Avrohom Chaim Feuer, *Tehillim: A New Translation with a Commentary Anthologized from Talmudic, Midrashic, and Rabbinic Sources* (New York: Mesorah, 1995), 2:1513.

7. "Deus ex machina" is a Latin expression coined by Horace, one of the most significant Roman poets during the time of August, in his "The Art of Poetry" to denote an apparently insoluble plot crisis solved by the sudden intervention of a god. The expression was also used by Dietrich Bonhoeffer to denounce the church's image of God.

8. "Rivim qetanim" in Yehonathan Gefen, *Hakeves hashisha asar* (The Sixteenth Lamb) (Tel Aviv: Dvir, 1992), 44.

9. Dorothee Sölle, *The Window of Vulnerability* (Minneapolis: Fortress, 1990), 7.

Romans 4:1–5, 13–17

In this passage Paul grapples with the relationship between faith and works that had elicited controversy within the early church. As reflected in the Epistle of James,

> Was not our ancestor Abraham justified by works when he offered his son Isaac on the altar? You see that faith was active along with his works, and faith was brought to completion by the works. Thus the scripture was fulfilled that says, "Abraham believed God, and it was reckoned to him as righteousness," and he was called the friend of God. You see that a person is justified by works and not by faith alone. Likewise, was not Rahab the prostitute also justified by works when she welcomed the messengers and sent them out by another road? For just as the body without the spirit is dead, so faith without works is also dead. (2:21–26)

James goes on to condemn those who assert that it is enough only to believe that "God is one" (2:19; cf. the Shema, Deut. 6:4, recited in Jewish worship), without demonstrating proper ethical behavior. But is this really what Paul is arguing about in Romans?

A key for understanding Paul's thought may be found in some of the verses omitted by the lectionary. To illustrate his argument, Paul states, "So also David speaks of the blessedness of those to whom God reckons righteousness apart from works" (Rom. 4:6). Paul then quotes Psalm 32:1–2: "Blessed are those whose iniquities are forgiven, and whose sins are covered; blessed is the one against whom the Lord will not reckon sin." Rabbinic tradition sets this psalm in the context of David's transgression with Bathsheba and his subsequent repentance and forgiveness. The story in 2 Samuel 11:1–12:24 shows how David received God's forgiveness just by acknowledging his sin (2 Sam. 12:13) without the need of any "work." Perhaps it is the power of God's mercy given after the guilty person offers sincere repentance that is associated with being justified before the Lord. The faith that justifies is the one that believes it is only through God's mercy that we can be declared justified. As James insists, "Mercy triumphs over judgment" (Jas. 2:13).

It would be a mistake to understand Paul to be saying that Jews believed works bring about our justification before God. According to Pamela Eisenbaum, "The doctrine that one is saved by one's work is largely a Christian chimerical projection of what Jews in antiquity believed."[10] The issue that Paul is trying to address in his Letter to the Romans is how to articulate God's universal goal (the salvation of all humans) to the particularities of Israel's election and traditions. As Mark Nanos states, "For Paul, the pattern of

---

10. Pamela Eisenbaum, *Paul Was Not a Christian* (New York: HarperOne, 2009), 203.

salvation history has been, and always will be, even in the midst of confronting misguided exclusivity on the part of some of the children of Jacob, 'to the Jew *first* and *also* to the Greek.' "[11] It is through embracing the faith of Abraham (Rom. 4:16) that non-Jews, the wild olive shoot, are grafted onto the olive tree to share its rich root. The tragedy is that the wild olive shoot has become arrogant and forgotten that "it is not you that support the root, but the root that supports you" (11:17–18).

Matthew 17:1–9

The Gospel of Matthew is the product of one of several Jewish groups in the diaspora (perhaps in Antioch, the capital of Syria) that accepted Jesus of Nazareth as a messianic figure and proclaimed that the community of his followers was the true Israel.

To properly understand this passage we must remember that Jesus did not become a divine figure for the early Christian community until a few centuries later. The Jesus of Matthew's Gospel is not the incarnated preexisting Logos of the Gospel of John or the second person of the Trinity as postulated by the Nicene church fathers. The Gospel of Matthew, written during the first century CE, should be read in light of Jewish hopes for an anointed one who would be the leading figure in a restoration of justice and peace in Israel and throughout the world.

The central focus of this passage is God's declaration, "This is my Son, the Beloved; with him I am well pleased; listen to him!" (v. 5). This is the third time in Matthew that a voice from heaven speaks to certify Jesus' divine commission. The two previous statements (Matt. 3:17 and 12:18) differ slightly from this one. When Jesus is baptized by John the Baptist, Matthew 3:17 records, "And a voice from heaven said, 'This is my Son, the Beloved, with whom I am well pleased.'" According to Matthew 12:18, "'Here is my servant, whom I have chosen, my beloved, with whom my soul is well pleased.'" This last quote is introduced in the Gospel to declare Jesus' ministry as fulfilling Isaiah's oracle, and it holds the key for understanding our passage. According to Matthew 12:17–21,

> This was to fulfill what had been spoken through the prophet Isaiah:
> "Here is my servant, whom I have chosen, my beloved, with whom
> my soul is well pleased. I will put my Spirit upon him, and he will
> proclaim justice to the Gentiles. He will not wrangle or cry aloud, nor
> will anyone hear his voice in the streets. He will not break a bruised

---

11. Mark D. Nanos, *The Mystery of Romans: The Jewish Context of Paul's Letter* (Minneapolis: Fortress, 1996), 21.

reed or quench a smoldering wick until he brings justice to victory. And in his name the Gentiles will hope."

The original context of this passage, the first of the so-called Servant Songs of Deutero-Isaiah (Isa. 42:1–4), proclaims that Israel has been called to bring God's justice to the rest of the world. Not by means of coercion, powerful armies, or violent imposition (the way of world empires) but by being what you want the world to be. In the words of Thicht Nhat Hanh, "There is no way to peace; peace is the way. There is no way to enlightenment; enlightenment is the way. There is no way to liberation; liberation is the way."[12]

---

12. Thich Nhat Hanh and Fred Eppsteiner, *Interbeing: Fourteen Guidelines for Engaged Buddhism* (Berkeley: Parallax, 1998), 6.

International Women's Day (March 8)

Dawn Ottoni-Wilhelm

NUMBERS 27:1–11
PSALM 4
ROMANS 16:1–16
LUKE 24:1–11

This Holy Day for Justice recognizes the extraordinary acts of courage and determination by ordinary women around the world. In 1908, National Women's Day was established in honor of the garment workers' strike in New York. Thereafter, women in the United States and Europe held rallies to express solidarity with other activists and the Russian women's peace movement during World War I. International Women's Day was first celebrated by the United Nations in 1975 and has continued its global connections. In worship and daily living, Christians are called to greater support of women's rights and their full participation in political and economic arenas of life.

The world has never yet seen a truly great and virtuous nation, because in the degradation of women, the very fountains of life are poisoned at their source.

Attributed to Lucretia Mott, nineteenth-century Quaker suffragist and abolitionist[1]

The texts chosen to honor this holy day acknowledge not only women's individual efforts but also their collective wisdom and fortitude in confronting economic, social, political, and religious injustices. As women work together, they become a powerful force of God at work in the world: the daughters of Zelophehad step forward in sisterly solidarity to demand their rightful

1. Elizabeth Cady Stanton, "The First and Closing Paragraphs of Mrs. Stanton's Address, Delivered at Seneca Falls, New York, July 19, 20, 1848," in *American Feminism: Key Source Documents; Suffrage*, ed. Janet Beer, Anne-Marie Ford, and Katherine Joslin (London: Routledge, 2003), 14.

136

inheritance (Num. 27); the psalmist decries the undeserved suffering and shame of persons despised by others (Ps. 4); women at the empty tomb become vital witnesses to Christ's resurrection (Luke 24); and Paul commends several women leaders in the early church (Rom. 16). With these lessons for International Women's Day, we seek God's blessing and empowerment of women who work together to overcome forces of oppression, prejudice, and injustice.

Numbers 27:1–11

Throughout history, women have struggled for access to material resources, means of economic self-determination, and property rights. Even today, women produce half of the world's food but own approximately 1 percent of its farmland.[2]

In God's presence and among God's people, the five daughters of Zelophehad stake their claim and petition Israel's elders for land that was due to their family. They know, however, that powerful forces converge against them: the culture they inhabit is patriarchal (dominated by men), patrilocal (wives live with husbands' families), and patrilineal (land is inherited through male heirs).[3] Their father died during the forty years of wilderness wandering, and when a census was taken of men over the age of twenty (chap. 26), Zelophehad did not have male descendants to inherit the Manassite territories. However, his daughters, Mahlah, Noah, Hoglah, Milcah, and Tirzah, devise a plan to secure property rights and ensure the continuation of their father's name.

We cannot help but to admire their bravado. Before Moses, Eleazar the priest, the leaders, and the entire congregation, the five sisters take their stand at the entrance of the tent and argue their case. They seek a future for themselves and challenge the injustice of losing their father's inheritance. The women's plea challenges God's earlier decree, and they wait with the crowd for God's response. Moses returns with the divine verdict: "The daughters of Zelophehad are right." They will possess the land of Manasseh due to them (v. 7). It is an extraordinary moment as God recognizes, blesses, and supports the insights and initiative of these five women.

Even as we celebrate their remarkable accomplishments, however, we must also recognize the limitations imposed on them: God instructs Moses that it is only in the absence of sons that daughters may inherit their father's property, and if there are no sons or daughters, the land will be passed along to other kinsmen (vv. 8–11). No mention is made of the sisters' mother; they build

2. Phil Borges, *Women Empowered: Inspiring Change in the Emerging World* (New York: Rizzoli Books, 2007), 12–13.
3. Lisa Wilson Davison, *Preaching the Women of the Bible* (St. Louis: Chalice Press, 2006), 35.

their case solely around the need to perpetuate their father's name (vv. 3–4). Later in the narrative, when the tribesmen of Manasseh realize that the five sisters may choose to marry and have children outside the clan (resulting in the transfer of property to other tribes), they prohibit the women from doing so, thus limiting their choice of marriage partners (36:1–13). The advances attained by these sisters are real but incremental.

Another important facet of their story begs our attention. Although all five sisters are named, the text does not identify which one of them addresses the congregation, but presents their voices speaking as one. They come forward together (v. 1), and with one voice they address the powers that be (vv. 3–4). Women of different cultures know the power of joining together to effect change, not only for their own lives and families but for the sake of the wider community as well. For example, when the women of Wajir, Kenya, feared for the safety of their children during clan-based shootings in the early 1990s, several of them began meeting quietly. They soon devised a plan to secure the safety of the marketplace so that any woman of any clan background could sell or buy food for her family. Monitors watched what was happening and reported any infractions against another person because of her clan or geographic origin. When problems arose, a committee quickly responded to help resolve them. Before long, a zone of peace was established in the market, thanks to the newly formed Wajir Women's Association for Peace. Widening their circle of concern, the association helped promote cease-fires and develop commissions to aid the process of disarming the clan-based factions. Amid poverty, warfare, and social degradation, women of different clans joined together to create a better inheritance for themselves and their children.[4]

Psalm 4

This lament is often characterized by scholars as a prayer for deliverance from personal enemies. But I wonder if there is any such thing as an *im*personal enemy!

Many women know what it is to be humiliated or degraded by those who refuse to recognize their God-given call to ministry. We know of denominations that refuse to ordain women, of seminaries that will not hire women professors, of local churches who will not call us to pastoral service, and of people who leave worship when a woman rises to preach. I suspect that nearly every woman in ministry has heard someone say, "It's nothing personal, but I just don't believe women should be pastors, priests, or preachers." Yet there is

---

4. See John Paul Lederach, *The Moral Imagination: The Art and Soul of Building Peace* (New York: Oxford University Press, 2005), 10–13.

nothing more personal—that is, more intimately related to the person of the pastor, priest, or preacher—than his or her body.

This psalm is well suited for women who have suffered the shame and injustice of being rejected, demoralized, overlooked, belittled, and silenced because of their sexuality or gender. Both beyond the church and within it, the degradation of women is a long-standing problem perpetuated by lies (v. 2). We hear them spoken among us: *God does not want you to* . . . ; *How arrogant of you to think* . . . ; *You cannot possibly* . . . It is tempting to stay in bed and pull the covers over our heads. But the image of pondering one's sins silently in bed (v. 4) is not addressed, according to James Mays, to those who have been wronged, but to their detractors.[5] They are the ones who must not allow their anger and judgmental attitudes to get the better of them but must stand in awe before God (v. 5). Those who oppose women called by God to lead others do not understand how hypocritical it is to pray for the blessing of God's face to shine upon them while refusing to acknowledge the face of God in women who are blessed with divine gifts to lead, serve, preach, and teach (v. 6).

Thankfully, many women offer thoughtful, caring leadership in the church, and the light of God's countenance shines through them as they minister to others. But even when persons refuse to recognize our vocation, God makes room for us, giving inner assurance of our calling (v. 1). We are blessed by God to explore our vocation, pray with one another, seek supportive allies, and grow in divine gladness and peace (vv. 7–8).

Luke 24:1–11

Before they walked to the tomb to anoint Jesus' body, Mary Magdalene, Joanna, Mary the mother of James, and the other women had shared many experiences together. The previous day, they stood side by side and witnessed Jesus' crucifixion (23:49). In the long night that followed, they prepared spices and cloth, offered silent and spoken prayers, and perhaps sat beside Jesus's mother, holding one another's hands until dawn. We know from the comments of the two men at the tomb that the women had also been in Galilee together, listening to Jesus's teaching (24:6). They were his disciples and they remembered his words (v. 8).

Unfortunately, Luke tells us very little about each of these women. Mary Magdalene is no doubt the most familiar to us. She is one of several women who were exorcised of demons and followed Jesus (8:2–3). Some traditions favored by churches in the East portrayed Mary as disclosing special

5. James L. Mays, *Psalms*, Interpretation series (Louisville, KY: John Knox Press, 1994), 55.

revelations from Jesus (see the *Gospel of Philip* and the *Pistis Sophia*).[6] Churches in the West identified Mary as the woman who "was a sinner" and washed Jesus' feet with her tears, drying them with her hair (7:36–50). Her reputation became that of a reformed prostitute, despite no textual evidence to support this speculation. Two lists of women begin with Mary Magdalene (8:2–3; 24:10), thus signaling her role as leader and spokeswoman for the group. Joanna was likely also among the women who had been exorcised of demons. Her marriage to Chuza, Herod's steward, suggests that she may have been a woman with resources to provide a measure of independence and the means to provide sustenance for Jesus' followers. We know even less about Mary the mother of James, and the text says nothing about the other women who were with them.

But of this much we can be certain: they shared a common faith in Jesus Christ and an uncommon love for him. Although many persons might discount their words as nonsense (v. 11), their roles as disciples and witnesses to the gospel of Jesus Christ are indispensable to the church and world.

No doubt it is because women are often discounted or devalued that they have learned to create supportive communities among themselves. Through shared experiences of bearing children, caring for elders, laboring in fields or factories, passing along wisdom, lamenting losses, and helping their neighbors, women have forged networks of sisterly solidarity within the church and beyond. Look around your congregation and you will find women who follow Jesus by developing respectful, caring relationships with others, women who testify to his crucifixion by lamenting the hungers and violence of this world, and women who bear witness to God's resurrection power by creating ministries of compassion to the communities they love.

Romans 16:1–16

Paul closes his Letter to the Romans with a remarkable roll call of saints. Among them are ten women: Phoebe, Prisca, Mary, Junia, Tryphaena, Tryphosa, Persis, Rufus's mother, Julia, and the sister of Nereus. Two women are paired together (Tryphaena and Tryphosa), several are listed without partners (i.e., Phoebe, Mary, Persis, perhaps Rufus's mother, and Julia, who may or may not be paired with Philologus), and some are named with male companions (i.e., Prisca with Aquila, Junia with Andronicus, the sister of Nereus). Paul's brief comments about these women suggest two things: (1) they were vital leaders in the church, and (2) many of them developed cooperative alliances with other women and men in ministry.

---

6. Carolyn Osiek, "Mary 3," in *Women in Scripture: A Dictionary of Named and Unnamed Women*, ed. Carol Meyers (Grand Rapids: Eerdmans, 2000), 121–23.

According to Daisy Machado, "praxis" is what Latin American liberation theologians call the challenge of awakening to God's dreams and learning to live in solidarity with others.[7] Machado quotes Jon Sobrino, who insists, "Solidarity is the tenderness of peoples." We have glimpses of this kind of solidarity among the women Paul mentions.

Phoebe is very likely the bearer of his letter to Rome (v. 1). Paul introduces her as "our sister," suggesting that she, like Timothy (1 Thess. 3:2), was a coworker in Christ. As *diakonos* of the church at Cenchreae in eastern Corinth, her title is the same as that given to others in the church who engage in preaching and teaching ministries (1 Cor. 3:5; 2 Cor. 6:4; Phil. 1:1). She was the benefactor of many, a gifted leader, and a woman of means who was willing to share what she had in solidarity with those in need. Prisca and her husband Aquila not only served as overseers of one or more house churches, but also risked their necks for Paul's sake (v. 4). Paul commends Mary, Tryphaena, Tryphosa, and Persis for their hard work, a term Paul uses to describe his own apostolic labor (Phil. 2:16). Junia and Andronicus are relatives or compatriots who suffered imprisonment alongside Paul. The apostle is clear: this first generation of women leaders in the church stepped into their ministries with courage, resourcefulness, and perseverance.

7. Daisy L. Machado, "Awaken to God's Dream," in *Those Preaching Women*, ed. Ella Pearson Mitchell and Valerie Bridgeman Davis (Valley Forge, PA: Judson Press, 2008), 3–8.

Third Sunday in Lent

Nyasha Junior

Exodus 17:1–7
Psalm 95
Romans 5:1–11
John 4:5–42

When I was a teenager, my father operated a nonprofit organization that participated in the U.S. Department of Agriculture's commodity food distribution program. He invited me to volunteer at the distribution one Saturday. We arrived early to set up and to meet the delivery trucks. As we drove into the parking lot, I was shocked to see that people had formed a line around the building. It was already warm at 6:00 a.m., and the Florida sun would only shine brighter and hotter as the day went on. From my perspective, food was a matter of choice. My parents asked if I wanted steak or chicken, broccoli or green beans, fries or a baked potato. I could not believe that so many people needed a block of cheese and dry milk enough to stand in line for them. That day, I learned that not everyone had the same choices available to them. That day, I learned compassion. This week's lectionary texts invite us to be more self-aware in our readings of biblical texts and to cultivate compassion in our responses to others.

Exodus 17:1–7

In Exodus 17, the Israelites are camped at Rephidim (location unknown) following their dramatic crossing of the Red Sea (Sea of Reeds). They quarrel (Hebrew root: *ryb*) with Moses regarding their lack of water. This is not their first quarrel with Moses (cf. Num. 20:2–13). The Hebrew Bible includes other texts that describe the murmuring of the Israelites in the wilderness (e.g., Exod. 14:10–14; 15:22–26; 16; Num. 11:1–14; 21:4–9). According to Brevard Childs, these murmuring traditions include two major patterns. Pattern I involves genuine need and then complaint, while Pattern

142

II involves complaint without genuine need. Childs regards Exodus 17 as falling into Pattern I, since the text indicates that the people do not have water to drink.[1]

It may be too much to ask of any preacher not to read this passage without a self-satisfied smirk. It is too easy to draw parallels between Moses and the Israelites and a pastor and his or her obstreperous congregation. How often have pastors offered some variation of Moses' words in appealing to the Lord, "What shall I do with this people? They are almost ready to stone me" (Exod. 17:4). Many lectionary discussions of this text focus on the faithlessness of the Israelites. The commentators contend that although the Israelites have experienced the Lord's miraculous works in delivering them from the Egyptians, they still do not trust the Lord. Also, commentators point out that the place names, Massah and Meribah, play on the words "test" (Hebrew root: *nsh*) and "quarrel" (Hebrew root: *ryb*). These place names are used in other texts to indicate Israel's faithlessness (e.g., Deut. 6:16; 9:22; 33:8; Ps. 95:8).

Instead of pointing out Israel's faithlessness, I would like to highlight the need for compassionate understanding of the people's situation. The reader has the full canon available and knows of the covenant that will be made at Mount Sinai (Exod. 19) and that the Israelites will cross the Jordan River into the promised land (Josh. 3). Yet at this point in the text, the Israelites are just a band of runaway slaves in the wilderness. Yes, they heard the announcement that God is the God of their ancestors. Yes, they have seen the plagues in Egypt and the deliverance from the Egyptians. However, their need in this text is real. They do not have water to drink (Exod. 17:1).

African American painter Jacob Lawrence's work *Forward* (1967) depicts Harriet Tubman taking a group of slaves to freedom through the Underground Railroad. With her left hand she pushes forward an enslaved man, and she carries a gun in her right hand. Lawrence's depiction recalls stories that Tubman did not carry the gun for the slave patrols or "paddyrollers" but for those previously enslaved men and women who would turn back and put the escapees in danger. Certainly I am not promoting gun violence in churches. Nevertheless, Lawrence's work causes us to reflect on the difficulties and conflicting emotions involved in gaining freedom.

When you are in the wilderness, slavery in Egypt may seem preferable. The Israelites have been afraid for their lives (Exod. 14:10), hungry (16:3), and thirsty (15:23; 17:1). Moses is trying to lead the people, but Moses was never a slave in Egypt. Transformative change takes time and patience. When

---

1. On murmuring traditions, see Brevard Childs, "Introduction to Wilderness Wandering Traditions," in *The Book of Exodus: A Critical, Theological Commentary*, Old Testament Library (Philadelphia: Westminster Press, 1974), 254–64.

people are still concerned with basic needs, they require not a rebuke for lack of faithfulness, but compassion.

Psalm 95

Psalm 95 offers a call to worship that praises the Lord. God is distinguished as incomparable to other gods (v. 3), the creator of the world and all humanity, and worthy of praise. Furthermore, the Lord is shepherd to the people. Many hymns and contemporary praise songs are based on this psalm, but nearly all of them use only verses 1–7 and neglect the second half of the psalm.

In verse 8, the psalm changes abruptly in mood and speaker. Here, the psalm provides a rare instance of the Lord's perspective and thoughts. It quotes divine speech in which God recalls particular elements of the wilderness experience of the Israelites. God charges the people directly not to "harden [their] hearts" (Hebrew root: *qšh*) as they did at Meribah and Massah. Although hardening the heart is not mentioned in the Meribah and Massah texts, it is used to refer to the hardening of Pharaoh's heart (Exod. 7:3). The admonition in Psalm 95:8 refers to several texts that discuss the incidents at Meribah and Massah, including Exodus 17 and Deuteronomy 33:8. As well, Psalm 95:8 refers to the parallel account of the Meribah incident in Numbers 20:1–13, in which Moses is punished at Meribah for not trusting the Lord (v. 12). Psalm 95 continues with a reference to the forty years of wandering (Num. 14; 32:13).

Psalm 95 ends with the punishment of the wilderness generation, which is not allowed to enter Canaan. The Lord declares, "They shall not enter my rest" (Hebrew root: *nwh*). While Hebrews 3:11 and 4:3 quote Psalm 95:11, using the Greek term *katapausis* for "rest," Hebrews 4:9 interprets "rest" uniquely as a spiritual Sabbath rest (*sabbatismos*). Nevertheless, the "rest" in Psalm 95:11 is better translated as "resting place" (cf. Gen. 49:15; Deut. 12:9), especially given that the immediate context refers to the wilderness wandering. Thus the punishment involves not entering into the resting place of Canaan.

Romans 5:1–11

This lectionary text provides Paul's famous discussion of justification by faith. It is one of the texts used by Martin Luther and Protestant Reformers to support one of the five key points of the Protestant Reformation, *sola fide*, "by faith alone." Usually it is connected with this week's other lectionary texts through its emphasis on faith. Nevertheless, as an African American woman, I read this text as a text of terror. Phyllis Trible's *Texts of Terror: Literary-Feminist*

Readings of Biblical Narratives reinterpreted the stories of four women in the Hebrew Bible: Hagar (Gen. 16:1–16; 21:9–21), Tamar (2 Sam. 13:1–22), the unnamed concubine of the Levite (Judg. 19:1–30), and the unnamed daughter of Jephthah (Judg. 11:29–40).[2] Although Trible did not define "terror," scholars have used the phrase "texts of terror" to refer to texts that involve violence or are disturbing in some sense.

Romans 5 is a text of terror due to its glorification of suffering. According to Paul, we "boast in our sufferings [*thlipsis*]" (v. 3), which sets off a chain reaction that results in the reward of God's love. This text and its sentiments have been used against oppressed peoples, who are taught to regard themselves as deserving of suffering. For example, some battered wives see themselves as deserving of physical and psychological abuse. Also, some of those in poverty regard their poverty as a burden to be accepted and borne stoically.

In *Ain't I a Woman: Black Women and Feminism*, African American writer bell hooks explains, "Usually, when people talk about the 'strength' of black women they are referring to the way in which they perceive black women coping with oppression. They ignore the reality that to be strong in the face of oppression is not the same as overcoming oppression; endurance is not to be confused with transformation."[3] Despite the text's focus on faith, it can and has been used to support oppression, which is not in keeping with the abundant and transformative love that God promises.

John 4:5–42

This text describes the encounter between Jesus and the Samaritan woman at the well. It connects with the other liturgical texts this week due to its association with water and with baptism. In Oaxaca, Mexico, Dia de la Samaritana is celebrated during Lent by giving free flavored water to passersby to commemorate the Samaritan woman's gift of water to Jesus. In the Orthodox Church, the Samaritan woman is named St. Photini, "the Enlightened One," and she is regarded as an apostle and a martyr for the faith.

Often, commentators celebrate the ways in which Jesus crosses social boundaries in order to reach out to the Samaritan woman. As a Samaritan woman with a complex marital and relationship history, she is an outsider, which is underscored by her drawing water at noon (v. 6). Jesus' interaction with her is a breach of social convention. Also, commentators note favorably the faith of the Samaritan woman and her evangelism, since it is due to her witness that many Samaritans believed in Jesus (v. 39).

2. Phyllis Trible, *Texts of Terror: Literary-Feminist Readings of Biblical Narratives* (Philadelphia: Fortress Press, 1984).

3. bell hooks, *Ain't I a Woman: Black Women and Feminism* (Boston: South End Press, 1981), 6.

While the Samaritan woman put aside her immediate need by leaving her water jar to return to the city (v. 28), her need remains when she returns. Others have benefited from her words, but there is no change in her situation. The outsider is used for the benefit of others. The living water (*hudōr zōn*; v. 10) that Jesus provides does not replace her physical need.

During a time of increased obesity in the United States, we also have unprecedented food insecurity. While many in the United States purchase eco-friendly, BPA-free, stainless steel water bottles, many others in the world live without clean drinking water. We cannot refer to the metaphor of water without addressing people's concrete and basic need for food and water.

Lent is a time of preparation. For baptismal candidates, it is a time of preparation before beginning life as a new creation. For others, it is a time of preparation before the recommitment and renewal offered by Easter. For some, it is a time of giving up something as a symbolic fast. Still, giving up requires having something to give. We must consider the perspectives of those whose basic needs are not yet met. We must offer not only the living water of Jesus but the compassion of our hearts toward persons whose most basic needs of food and water await fulfillment.

Salt March Day: Marching with the Poor (March 12)

Rebecca Todd Peters

NEHEMIAH 5:1–13
PSALM 72:12–14
ROMANS 13:1–7
MARK 12:13–17

During their occupation of India, the British had a monopoly on the sale of salt and taxed its purchase. This arrangement burdened the poor. Moreover, Indians viewed the salt tax as a symbol of oppression. On March 12, 1930, Mohandas K. Gandhi (1869–1948) led a march to protest the tax and to call for Indian independence. Such nonviolent resistance in India inspired similar nonviolent civil disobedience in other places (including the Civil Rights Movement in the United States).

If my letter makes no appeal to your heart, on the eleventh day of this month I shall proceed with such co-workers of the Ashram as I can take, to disregard the provisions of the Salt Laws. I regard this tax to be the most iniquitous of all from the poor [person's] standpoint. As the Independence movement is essentially for the poorest in the land, the beginning will be made with this evil.
Mahatma Mohandas Karamchand Gandhi[1]

The British tax on salt during the colonial era was so high that it put the price of salt out of reach for many Indian peasants (it could tally up to as much as two weeks' wages for a poor Indian laborer with a family).[2] The excessive tax on a necessary staple of the human diet came to symbolize the

---

1. From Mahatma Gandhi's letter to the British viceroy protesting the British salt tax. The 240-mile march began March 12, 1930, and culminated in Gandhi's picking up a piece of salt at the seashore of Dandi, thus breaking British law. The letter is from Louis Fischer, *The Life of Gandhi* (New York: Harper & Row, 1983), 266.
2. Geoffrey Ashe, *Gandhi* (New York: Stein & Day, 1968), 285.

abuse of leadership and power by the ruling authorities in the British colonial empire. Our texts for today all touch on issues of leadership, authority, and empire, and raise critical questions about the relationship between political leaders and social justice. Nehemiah struggles with the implicit perpetuation of injustice that occurs when some members of the community gain wealth and power through the exploitation of their poorer neighbors. In philosophizing about the qualities of a just leader in Psalm 72, the writer highlights the responsibility of a just leader to champion the weak, the needy, and the poor. While the Mark and Romans passages are often read as endorsing a separation of religion and the state, they can also be read as the subversive call of colonized subjects to resist the abusive power of illegitimate political authorities.

Nehemiah 5:1–13 and Psalm 72:12–14

Nehemiah 5 is part of a larger story in the Ezra-Nehemiah cycle about the return from exile of many members of the Jewish community and the rebuilding of the city of Jerusalem. After the southern kingdom fell to the Babylonian Empire in 586 BCE, the conquerors followed an imperial strategy of dispersion and assimilation by sending everyone but the farmers into exile in Babylon.[3] With the urban center of Jerusalem decimated, the area necessarily transitioned to an agricultural and more rural lifestyle as the farmers maintained the productive value of the land and likely supported the Babylonian Empire economically through taxation.[4]

Meanwhile, given the fact that the conquerors had relocated the most skilled and elite members of the Jewish community to Babylon, many of the exiled successfully integrated into Babylonian culture. Some, like Nehemiah, even found positions of power and influence within the king's court. As the cupbearer to the king, Nehemiah was a trusted servant of the Persian Empire. After Cyrus's edict opened up the possibility of a return to Judah for the exiled Jewish community, the king commissioned Nehemiah to return to Jerusalem as its governor. The current text is set in the midst of the rebuilding of the city wall.

The work of rebuilding the wall was not only laborious, but also the threat of disruption from the leaders of the surrounding areas led to intensified work conditions that included round-the-clock armed guards watching over

3. Jacob M. Myers, *Ezra-Nehemiah*, Anchor Yale Bible Commentaries (New Haven, CT: Yale University Press, 1995), xx.
4. Jon L. Berquist, "Resistance and Accommodation in the Roman Empire," in *In the Shadow of the Empire: Reclaiming the Bible as a History of Faithful Resistance*, ed. Richard A. Horsley (Louisville, KY: Westminster John Knox Press, 2008), 42.

the construction, as well as a curfew requiring inhabitants of the city to stay within the walls until the defenses were secured. While the people were likely supportive of the efforts at rebuilding and fortification, the increased work requirements on the able-bodied males as well as the termination of the free movement of the city dwellers seem to have caused unrest among the general population who bore the economic brunt of such restrictive living conditions.

The working poor of the community cried out in response to the injustice of starvation and usury that resulted from the building campaign. Without knowing the exact circumstances, we can imagine debts coming due during a time of lost income or increases in the price of grain in a city cut off from trade with its neighbors. People needed to leave the city walls to tend their land and animals and to engage in trade with the surrounding communities. If the most able-bodied workers were tied up in construction, even for a short time, the daily needs of households could not be met. Indeed, as the most marginalized members of the community found themselves forced into mortgaging farms and houses or selling sons and daughters into indentured servitude, the wives and mothers of the community, in particular, cried out against their Jewish kin who were taking advantage of their desperation to turn a profit through a well-placed loan or the cheap purchase of the labor of their neighbors' children.

As we examine this text through a social justice lens, what is remarkable is that Nehemiah, who later becomes the champion of justice, is initially one of the perpetrators of injustice. The fact that Nehemiah, who is portrayed as a noble and venerable prophet and governor, engages in this behavior prior to the people's outcry indicates that he saw nothing wrong with lending with interest. It is only when he listens to the cry of injustice and begins to look at how this behavior is impacting the lives and well-being of his fellow citizens that he begins to understand the damage that this behavior has caused on the life of the community at large.

For those of us who live in the center of economic and political power in our contemporary world, Nehemiah's actions are instructive. It is often hard for us who are privileged to see the ways in which our behavior, in particular our business practices, affect other people. One of the most important things that Nehemiah does is to *listen* to the people's grievances. As we examine the injustices perpetrated by imperial powers throughout history, one of the recurring themes is the disempowerment and disregard of the perspectives and experiences of the poor and exploited people in society. As we consider what it means to "march with the poor" in our own context, we must remember that true solidarity requires mutuality, which, in turn, requires building relationships of trust. Nehemiah's actions embody the description of a good leader in Psalm 72, "he delivers the needy when they call, the poor and those who have no helper." Good leaders, be they in the political, economic, or social realms of society, must always remember to pay attention to who is at the table when decisions are being made, and they must ensure the broadest participation of people, including those most often overlooked.

Mark 12:13–17 and Romans 13:1–7

These two passages have a long history of interpretation and debate within Christian theology. On the one hand, they seem to imply that Jesus, Paul, and the early church supported the legitimacy of the Roman Empire by encouraging the payment of taxes and by encouraging the followers of Christ in Rome to submit themselves to the "governing authorities." In fact, this passage from Romans is one of the foundational texts used to promote the Christian theological position that political authorities are appointed and ordained by God to help provide order in society. On the other hand, these texts must be read within the larger context of their respective Gospel and Epistle as well as within the larger interpretive structure of what we know about Jesus' and Paul's ministries and their relation to the Roman Empire. If we read this Gospel story as a confrontation between Jesus as a political dissident and the Pharisees as the local collaborators and enforcers of Roman imperialism, the story opens up new questions about the nature of authority and agency in the midst of empire.

Jesus' relationship with the Roman Empire, throughout his ministry, was clearly marked by an attitude and behavior of independence and resistance to the domination of the Jewish people by the Romans. In fact, the threat that he posed to the Roman authorities is often cited as the reason he was crucified as a common criminal, a punishment so shameful and degrading it was usually reserved for thieves, slaves, and political troublemakers. Richard Horsley has argued that Jesus' use of the language of "realm of God" was not metaphorical, but, rather, an intentional choice of language that prophesied the imminent political enfranchisement of the Jewish people under the authority of YHWH, who was recognized as their Monarch.[5]

The Pharisees, who represented the priestly aristocracy and held the highest positions of honor and responsibility within the Jewish religious cult, were political as well as religious leaders. Their partnership with the Roman imperial state is evidenced by the collusion that occurred between the Pharisees and the imperial authorities in the events leading up to Jesus' trial and crucifixion (Mark 3:6; 15:1). The priests would have held some responsibility in collecting the temple or tribute tax, which is the tax referred to in verses

---

5. Richard Horsley, "Roman Imperial Theology," in *In the Shadow of Empire*, 86–89.

14–15. What we see in this text is an attempt to trick Jesus into either endorsing the Roman Empire and the tribute tax (which was as unpopular as the salt tax was in Gandhi's day) or advocating open revolt against the empire (which would have landed him quickly in prison).

Jesus, however, finds a third path, through which he is able to reframe the dilemma placed before him and model a new form of resistance and transgression against imperial power. William Herzog refers to Jesus' (and Paul's) actions as "dissembling," a term describing the subversive behavior of dominated or subordinated people who appear to support or endorse the authorities that oppress them while simultaneously working to undermine and subvert that authority.[6] While both Jesus and Paul employ language that appears to endorse the Roman authority, the listeners in their own time would have heard a very different message. The coins themselves were propaganda of the empire, and the denarius that Jesus requests had images of Emperor Tiberius and of his mother enthroned as the goddess of peace, along with an inscription confirming the emperor's divine status ("Tiberius Caesar, augustus, son of divine Augustus").[7] By holding up a denarius and asking "Whose head is this, and whose title?" and then rejecting it and encouraging the crowds to reject the Roman coins, Jesus is, in effect, encouraging them to reject the legitimacy of the empire itself along with its propaganda. Rather than encouraging the people to support the empire through the payment of the tribute tax, he is rejecting the very money itself as a symbol of the oppression of the empire *and* its tribute tax.

Reading these texts today challenges us to think carefully about how empires continue to shape our contemporary world. While we no longer have the overt political or colonizing empires of the ancient Near East, Rome, or Britain, our world is still shaped by the imperial attitudes and practices of economic, political, and military domination. As we consider the questions of empire and economic exploitation, it is important to listen to the voices of the marginalized. The Accra Confession from the World Alliance of Reformed Churches is a prophetic document for our age that reflects the perspective of many Christians in the global South when it states, "As seekers of truth and justice and looking through the eyes of powerless and suffering people, we see that the current world (dis)order is rooted in an extremely complex and immoral economic system defended by empire. In using the term 'empire' we mean the coming together of economic, cultural, political and military power that constitutes a system of domination led by powerful nations to protect and

---

6. William R. Herzog II, "Dissembling, A Weapon of the Weak: The Case of Christ and Caesar in Mark 12:13–17 and Romans 13:1–7," *Perspectives in Religious Studies* 21, no. 4 (Winter 1994): 339–60.

7. Ibid., 346.

defend their own interests."[8] The Accra Confession challenges first-world Christians to think about how our lives, livelihoods, and churches support the imperial practices of globalization that threaten the well-being of our sisters and brothers in the developing world.[9] In the context of social justice, we are called to examine how the imperial powers in our contemporary world shape and affect the lives of the "least of these" in our midst. In what ways are usury and taxation being used to exploit the weak and the vulnerable, and to what extent are the profits from these enterprises building up the wealth of the elite and powerful and the systems of wealth that they support? The life-giving word in our texts today gives witness to the possibility for faithful and just leadership and communities of compassion and justice. In a world of stark dichotomies (Democrat/Republican, capitalist/communist, wealth/poverty) we are called, like Jesus, to seek a third way, new pathways that reframe our old assumptions and that hold out the possibility of the transformation of our political and economic structures toward God's vision of justice and peace.

---

8. World Alliance of Reformed Churches, Accra Confession, 2004, paragraph 11.

9. For more detailed information on the Accra Confession, see Rebecca Todd Peters and Elizabeth Hinson-Hasty, *To Do Justice: A Guide for Progressive Christians* (Louisville, KY: Westminster John Knox Press, 2008).

Fourth Sunday in Lent

Randall K. Bush

1 SAMUEL 16:1–13
PSALM 23
EPHESIANS 5:8–14
JOHN 9:1–41

By definition, a dichotomy refers to two mutually exclusive and oppositional reference points. As a society, we are commonly drawn to such polarities, even as we keep wishing that everyone would just learn to get along. The lectionary readings for this Sunday in Lent contain both explicit and implicit dichotomies, such as insiders versus outsiders and light versus dark. But the faith and justice issues in these readings do not lend themselves to tidy either–or answers. What happens when an outsider becomes anointed as a new leader? How do protectors of the status quo react when a change agent appears in their midst and threatens everything they hold dear? Even though a loving shepherd prepares a table for us, how is it possible to enjoy this feast when it is eaten in the presence of enemies? Dichotomies may be part of the rhetoric of Scripture, but the full expression of faith invariably has to move beyond dichotomies to richer, more nuanced understandings of God's activity in our lives and in the world.

1 Samuel 16:1–13

The story of the anointing of David is well crafted and quite descriptive. Samuel is given a risky task to perform, namely, to anoint a new king while an existing king still sits on the throne. The Bethlehem townspeople are deceived about this mission, as is Jesse, who is first invited to a sacrifice but ends up calling his sons together for an unexpected prophetic inspection. In the end, Jesse's youngest son is anointed by Samuel, once again fulfilling the familiar biblical pattern of having a younger sibling take precedence over the elder (e.g., Gen. 25:23; 37:2–4).

153

But from the first verses, a dynamic of anxiety colors the events. Samuel complains to God that to act on this divine mission would be to risk death. City elders rush out to meet the visiting prophet, trembling and fearful that he may be bringing ill tidings. This subtext of nervous anxiety reminds us about the pernicious nature of absolute power, particularly when it slips into patterns that are evil or unjust. Illegitimate power over others undermines trust and causes people to constantly doubt others' motives. This passage also suggests that to counter powers that are evil or unjust, it may be necessary to use methods that are opaque and even duplicitous (such as bringing a heifer to sacrifice when you actually wish to anoint a king). For times like these, it was later spoken that we should "be wise as serpents and innocent as doves" (Matt. 10:16b).

The drama continues to unfold as Jesse's sons parade past the prophet. A key homiletical theme arises in verse 7 with the declaration that we are not to be deceived by outward appearances, since "the LORD looks on the heart." Yet the deeper theological message comes with the reminder that the Lord's choice is often found in outsiders easily overlooked by others. It is the eighth child that Samuel anoints, the boy left behind to watch the sheep. In this story, as in life itself, the one neglected, marginalized, and explicitly forgotten by others is the one on whom God's favor clearly rests. Worldly criteria like age, appearance, wealth, and status are distractions to God's command to judge others based on what virtue and potential lies untapped within them.

It should be noted that prophetic acts are never private acts. Witnesses are necessary when the seeds of change are planted. The examples of David being anointed "in the presence of his brothers," Jesus calling together a group of disciples, and Paul meeting with a few converts in early house churches remind us that real, transformative justice springs forth when a few hearts are united by a fresh vision of God's will for all people.

John 9:1–41

Often in life we reach the wrong answers not from faulty logic, but because we have asked the wrong questions. This happens when people set up a false dichotomy and then insist that the answer must be either A or B. The passage in John 9 contains at least four examples of this flawed reasoning.

First, the disciples ask whose sins caused a man to be born blind—his own or his parents' (v. 2)? Jesus rejects the two choices and offers an answer that has nothing to do with anyone's sin. Second, once the man's eyesight is healed, the Pharisees challenge Jesus' act, arguing that either a person is from God and observes the Sabbath or a person is not from God and breaks the Sabbath laws (v. 16). In Jesus, someone greater than the Sabbath was present among them, so a different option needed to be considered (cf. Mark 2:28).

Third, not happy with the healed man's answers, the Pharisees interrogate him again and tell him he should give glory to God and call Jesus a sinner or risk dishonoring God by vouching for Jesus' righteousness (v. 24). The man refuses to choose between these false choices and instead offers words that have been memorialized in the first verse of "Amazing Grace" (v.25b). Similarly, when the man is urged one last time to choose between following Jesus or Moses (v. 28), his patience comes to an end and he taunts his questioners by stressing the legitimacy of Jesus' divine power.

When situations involving faith and justice are evaluated from the perspective of people with power and authority, the initial responses will often seek to discredit those who threaten the privileges inherent in the status quo. Yet in this passage, a blind beggar stands his ground and speaks truth to power; an outsider and disempowered voice from the margins proclaims that Jesus is from God. His subsequent affirmation, "Lord, I believe," links him with other faithful outsiders in John's Gospel, such as the Samaritan woman (chap. 4) and the paralytic at Beth-zatha (chap. 5).

It should not be overlooked that wherever power imbalances exist in a society, the criminal justice system will be compromised. The interrogation of the healed man led to his being dismissed from the synagogue. It is not clear to what extent this blind beggar possessed any real status within that body; nevertheless, he belonged to its heritage and cultural tradition and he was now being barred from its fellowship. As he was pushed out the door, he taught the so-called wise ones and set the stage for the final verses in which the dialogue comes full circle. Once more the question of sin and blindness is raised, but this time a connection between the two options is acknowledged. Jesus came so that the blind may see and the powerful, sighted ones may become aware of their moral and spiritual blindness (vv. 39–41).

It is easy to let preaching fall into false dichotomies as well. Sermons should not be imbalanced in how they treat politics (e.g., Republicans and Democrats), economics (e.g., 1 percent and 99 percent), criminal justice (e.g., felons and people with no prison record), and nationality (e.g., undocumented workers and natural-born citizens), to cite a few examples. Or, as is the case in John 9, one should not set up Pharisees as Bad Option A with the healed man as Fully Righteous Option B. For Jesus to be the light of the world (v. 5), the gospel message must offer words of grace and glad tidings to all people on both sides of the discussion—A and B.

Ephesians 5:8–14 and Psalm 23

As obvious as the contrast between light and dark may appear, there are gradations inherent in both. Lightbulbs, although bright, come in different wattages; darkness, although opaque and shadowy, is rarely devoid of some illumination. Clearly the writer of Ephesians 5:8–14 is using allegorical language, similar to ideas found in the Gospels (e.g., Luke 11:35; John 1:5). The categories of light and darkness are not precisely defined, except to insist that in Christ we are light and are called to live as children of light. What is also clear is that both light and darkness exist in the world and bear their own fruits. The problem emerges, however, when we set ourselves the task of speaking definitively about what it means to be children of light and children of darkness.

The last half of Ephesians is exhortative, challenging us to lead lives worthy of our calling (Eph. 4:1) and to be imitators of a loving God (5:1). Our lives should be marked by an active intentionality, choosing carefully those with whom we associate. This should not be understood as a strict hierarchy of value, as if those inside our circles of association are intrinsically better than those outside. Rather it should be read pastorally, knowing that our days are short and we should sincerely seek to do what is pleasing to God and caring toward others. An intriguing action verb is found in Ephesians 5:11, where we are urged to "expose" works of darkness. The prophetic role of whistle-blower carries the risk of hardship and alienation. It combines nonparticipation in that which is wrong with the ethical imperative of speaking up either on behalf of others affected by wrongdoing or on behalf of the common good. Recent examples of this include divestment from companies that profit from the machinery of war, boycotting stores with discriminatory hiring practices, public actions blocking oil or natural gas drilling that harms the environment, and protests at state and local government offices that challenge barriers to participation in democratic processes.

The directions given to us are quite general: Do that which is good and right and true (v. 9). We must also ask if the deeds in question are shameful, involve secrecy and forced silence, or if disclosure of them will reduce harm and allow justice to "roll down like waters" (Amos 5:24). Following these injunctions, we step into the light of the Lord and become light ourselves.

In a less direct manner, Psalm 23 also acknowledges the existence of stark opposites in the world, through allegories. We read about green pastures and right paths, as well as dark valleys where evil is near. While a table is prepared with enemies near at hand, the agents of darkness are never ceded ultimate authority. Instead we have a good shepherd and we shall not want; our days will be marked with God-given blessings of goodness and mercy.

The themes of the other three lectionary passages build on the fundamental affirmations contained in Psalm 23. God initiates—as Samuel did in choosing David, not based on appearances but on the heart; as Jesus did in healing the blind man and leading him to true sight and living faith; and in how the

One who is the light of the world shines on us that we may all be children of light. God is the agent for new beginnings, working proactively and calling us to lives of justice and righteousness in a world far too prone to toss off those words as hollow rhetoric rather than embody these virtues in daily practices.

Perhaps the most comforting phrase of this psalm is tucked into verse 3, which offers the assurance that God "restores my soul." Suddenly the same creation that was lovingly formed and called "good" by its Creator is given the gift of restoration. Something broken is healed, both individually and communally. There are no more unmet wants, stormy waters, parched fields, threats of violence or conflict. We are offered idyllic images that touch us at our core, which is why this psalm is one of the few biblical passages with which most people have at least a passing familiarity. Is this vision an absolute, concrete reality in our world today? No. But in this language of anointing, communing, restfulness, and peace, we discover that for which we universally yearn. All of this is wrapped in a promise from a loving God who alone provides for us and, by grace, through us to others.

Oscar Romero of the Americas Day (March 24)

Ada María Isasi-Díaz

NUMBERS 12:4–9
PSALM 94:16–23
2 CORINTHIANS 1:3–6
MARK 8:27–38

Oscar Romero (1917–1980), Roman Catholic archbishop of El Salvador, was a powerful leader in the struggle for human rights, especially among the poor. Romero opposed military regimes and the brutal methods (including torture and assassination) by which dictators maintained power, and he called for economic, social, and legal justice. On March 24, 1980, Romero was assassinated while lifting the consecrated host during Mass. The preacher could join countries in Central and South America in observing Oscar Romero Day on March 24 (or the Sunday nearest that date) as a sign of respect for this martyr and as an act of commitment to continue the struggle for justice. The fate of Oscar Romero gives haunting testimony to the Lenten theme of taking up the cross.

> If they kill me I will rise again in the Salvadoran people. As a pastor I am obligated to give my life to those I love, and that is all Salvadorans. My death, if it is accepted by God, will be the liberation of my people and be like a testimony of hope in the future. A bishop will die but the church of God, that is this people, will never perish.
>
> *Oscar Romero*[1]

The readings for this Holy Day for Justice help us not only to understand how Christians can look up to Oscar Romero as a true Christian witness, but also to grasp the anguish he felt as he lived out his commitment to serve God and to serve the people. The closing words of his last homily, minutes before he

---

1. Miguel Cavada and Marvin Hernandez, eds., *Vida de Óscar Romero, 1917–1980*, 2nd ed. (San Salvador: Equipo Maiz, 2006), 21.

was murdered, were "justice and peace for our people"[2]—a commitment to justice for the poor and the oppressed of El Salvador.

Numbers 12:4–9

The book of Numbers narrates the time that Israel spent in the desert after leaving Egypt and before entering the promised land. It is a time of preparation, a time in which YHWH teaches Israel what it is to be faithful, to be forbearing. These verses in chapter 12 are about YHWH upholding and supporting Moses at a time of crisis, when his leadership was being questioned. What makes Moses special is that YHWH speaks to him face to face. What sustains Moses, at times despite himself, is the intimacy he has with God. It is not that Miriam and Aaron were not right to complain about Moses. It is that in spite of Moses' shortcomings, he is the leader of Israel because God is with him in a very intimate way.

Monseñor Romero recognized his weaknesses: "[I] know my own weaknesses, my own inabilities."[3] He also said, "I recognize my limitations and my miseries, but I cannot renounce the role that Christ has given me."[4] Recognition of his own limitations and weaknesses opened Romero to those around him. He drew his sense of mission and vision not from his own strength but from embracing the needs of the people he had been called to shepherd. Monseñor Romero knew that becoming archbishop meant that he had to lead the church during violent times: "I look at you, dear friends, and I know that my humble ministry is only that of Moses: to transmit the word—'Thus says the Lord.' And what pleasure it gives me when you say in your intimate hearts, or at times in words or in letters I receive, what the people replied to Moses: 'We will do all that Yahweh has ordained.'"[5]

Psalm 94:16–23

What are Christians called to say when society sins? This is the focus of Psalm 94. This psalm, which belongs in book IV of the Psalter, focuses on the terrible events Israel has suffered, including the destruction of the temple and exile. Such reality causes the psalmist to begin by asking YHWH to avenge the oppressed people and to punish the wicked. One can indeed conclude that YHWH alone can change these present evil ways. Then the psalmist speaks

2. My translation. María López Vigil, *Monseñor Romero: Piezas para un retrato* (La Habana: Editorial Caminos, 2002), 317.
3. Ibid., 86.
4. Oscar Romero, *The Violence of Love*, compiled and trans. by James R. Brockman, SJ (Maryknoll, NY: Orbis Books, 2004), 123.
5. Ibid., 152.

to the oppressors about God. Finally, in the section chosen for this feast, the psalmist speaks to YHWH about himself. This section is chosen because the focus of today's celebration is Romero: in these verses, we hear Romero speaking to God about himself. It is a speech of reassurance.

The psalmist, like Romero, seeks to deepen his conviction that YHWH upholds him, comforts him, and that YHWH is his refuge. Such a strong conviction, needed by all those who face evil, is only possible for the pure of heart, for those who are motivated by justice and peace, who are committed to the option for the poor and the oppressed, who are willing to speak truth to power, as Romero did to the very end. Such strong conviction becomes a song of worship shared among God's people who stand with Romero, who are willing to be about justice, no matter what cost.

2 Corinthians 1:3–6

This reading is from the introduction of 2 Corinthians, which most scholars believe is a compilation of letters written by Paul. "False apostles" had come into the community at Corinth, and they questioned Paul's authority. This caused Paul great anxiety and affliction, since he saw himself as an apostle to the Gentiles. For him this mission was part of God's plan, as he proclaims in Romans 1:13–15. The situation in Corinth caused him "many tears" (2 Cor. 2:4). Instead of ignoring the difficulties there and the suffering it caused him, Paul reads his situation of affliction as providing an opportunity for him and others to feel the encouragement of God through Christ's sufferings. Paul does not consider his sufferings as separated from those of the Corinthian community. In 1:5 he clearly indicates that Christ's suffering affects not only him but also the community. This, then, is the basis for believing that the encouragement he receives will also overflow into the community.

Monseñor Romero initially did not have the absolute confidence Paul had when he wrote this letter about his role as an apostle. However, Romero had the wisdom, engendered by humility, to ask for help. Shortly after he became archbishop of San Salvador, his friend Father Rutilio Grande was murdered by the repressive regime for no other reason than defending the impoverished people among whom he worked. On the Sunday following Rutilio's murder, Romero canceled all masses throughout the archdiocese and celebrated one single mass in the cathedral in San Salvador, in which more than 150 priests and more than 100,000 other people joined him. After the mass, while with the priests who had come to Rutilio's memorial, Romero turned to a group of them and said, "Tell me, you tell me what I need to do to be a good bishop."[6] Their advice was simple: listen to the people; be with the people. Romero took their

6. López Vigil, *Monseñor Romero*, 82.

advice to heart. It was the people, their needs and their daily struggles, their faith and how it supported them against all adversities, that radicalized Romero.

Romero's commitment to his work as archbishop was unflinching. The morning of his assassination, one of his coworkers begged him not to go to celebrate mass at a hospital. He responded, "It is my duty . . . we are in God's hands, or, do you not have faith any longer?"[7] He was anguished, not by the daily danger he faced, but by the repression his people suffered. Shortly before he was murdered Romero told a friend, "Yes, the threats have increased, and I take them seriously. . . . I do not want to die. At least, I do not want to die now. I have never loved life more! I tell you honestly, I do not have a martyr's vocation. No. Of course if that is what God asks of me, of course. . . . I only ask God that the circumstances of my death do not call into question what indeed is my vocation: to serve God, to serve the people. But to die now, no; I want a little more time."[8]

Mark 8:27–38

This reading includes what some scholars consider the heart of Mark's Gospel, verses 27–34, where Peter wants to proclaim Jesus as Messiah but is unwilling to embrace the cross. Jesus answers with the harshest words he directs to his disciples: "Get behind me, Satan!" Then Jesus asserts unequivocally the need to take up the cross and follow him.

There are two important considerations regarding these verses. One has to do with the rebuke to Peter. Jesus calls him Satan. In modern times we use "Satan" as if it were the proper name of the devil. The Greek word *satanas* means "adversary." Peter, and by extension all his disciples, are called adversaries of Jesus if they do not follow him. Unless they were willing to follow Jesus, including taking up the cross, the disciples would be adversaries of the kin-dom of God. In order to be able to follow Jesus, the disciples have to have the mind that God has. Verse 33b uses the Greek word *phrōneîs* which refers to practical wisdom, a wisdom that is put into action, into practice. Peter has given the right answer, he has used the right word. However, he does not have the right story, for he is thinking of the messiah, as do others throughout Mark's Gospel, as one related to the Davidic line. Peter and the disciples are told to put on a different mind-set, to look at reality the way that Jesus looks at reality. After two right answers to Jesus' questions—the first one simply asks for information, the second one gives the disciples the opportunity to testify or give voice to what they believe—Peter gives evidence of how super-ficially the disciples understand Jesus and his mission. Jesus uses the event to

7. Ibid., 313.
8. Ibid., 310.

teach the disciples a lesson, to make clear to them that unless they have the wisdom to think the way God does—a wisdom that is incarnated in their lives and that inevitably results in personal sacrifice—they do not really know him and what he is about. If the disciples who are closest to him do not understand what it means to say that Jesus is the Messiah, how can others beyond his closest companions understand? This is why Jesus instructs them not to tell anyone about his being the Messiah.

Romero was also rebuked. He was rebuked by some of the priests and the people when he first became archbishop, for he had been quite conservative. He was not the choice of the priests and the laity of El Salvador who were committed to justice. He was the choice of Rome precisely because he was considered traditional. But Romero was wise. He had common sense or practical wisdom, which means that he was open to changing his mind, to putting on the mind of God. At the mass in memory of Father Rutilio Grande, as he began his homily he was nervous and unsure, "as if wondering whether he should enter or not, through the door that history and God were opening for him. . . . Upon his mentioning the name of Rutilio, there was an explosion of applause. . . . Thousands applauded him and he rose to meet the situation. It was then that he crossed through the door. He entered. For there are baptisms of water and of blood. And there are also are baptisms of the people."[9]

The second important consideration in this text is how terrible are the demands that Jesus makes of his disciples. For Christians, the reference to the cross is positive, for we always connect it with Jesus. To carry one's cross may speak to us of accepting difficulties and struggles, but it rarely conveys the notion of torture and death. But for those living under the Roman Empire, death on the cross (*crux*) was a horror, not only because of the excruciating pain, but also because of the shame and humiliation of being nailed to a cross, naked, where the one crucified could hang for days for all to see. It was indeed terribly difficult for the disciples to have the mind-set required to understand that Jesus the Messiah was teaching and leading them to live in a way that would lead to their confrontation with the authorities, to imprisonment, and death.

For Romero, to take up the cross every day had a meaning closer to the one it had for Jesus and his disciples than it has for most of us. Once Romero threw his lot in with the people, crucifixion was always a possibility. In his speech at the University of Louvain when he was given an honorary degree a month before he was assassinated, Romero said, "The church suffers the fate of the poor, which is persecution. Our church glories that it has mingled the blood of its priests, its catechists, and its communities with that of the massacred people and has continually borne the mark of persecution."[10]

9. Ibid., 86.
10. Romero, *Violence of Love*, 190.

Fifth Sunday in Lent

Lee H. Butler Jr.

EZEKIEL 37:1–14
PSALM 130
ROMANS 8:6–11
JOHN 11:1–45

The texts for the Fifth Sunday in Lent stress the importance of embodiment as the essence of living as human beings. They speak of the vital and necessary integration of our physicality and spirituality. Nobody can exist without the Spirit of God, and God's Spirit must indwell and animate the body for full humanity to be realized. There is an unfortunate tendency to dichotomize human life and judge the parts we want to deemphasize, which ultimately makes us less than human. In order to live as whole and holy beings, we must maintain the divine Spirit as a central component of our embodied existence.

Preaching about the body and encouraging people to live joyous lives as embodied beings is a very difficult task. People too easily accept the history of degrading the body as the pathway to holiness. Our task in preaching these texts is to help people to live faithfully as whole and holy human beings. The proclamation of the Word of God re-creates life's circumstances. Our conditions can be transformed, and we can find new life in this world by the power of God's proclamation. God created humanity, embodied spirit, as good. We must declare the same in our proclamation of new life.

Ezekiel 37:1–14

This familiar and often-preached text identifies the condition of the people and God's ability to restore life. Not unlike the creation narrative, in which God's Spirit was moving across the abyss and God's Word created order out of chaos, God, through commanding the voice of the prophet, transforms desolation into new creation. Also like the creation of humanity who, being made from the dust of the earth, were lifeless until God breathed into them,

163

these fallen soldiers were formed but stood lifeless until God, through the proclamation of the prophet, gave them the breath of life.

Very often we look at a situation and the condition appears to our eyes as this valley full of bones appeared to the eyes of Ezekiel. We see the devastation of blighted communities, and to our eyes, the community seems beyond restoration and hope. Factories that once gave a community its strength, nourished and protected families, are now falling into decay and crumble as a reminder of a prosperous past. But Ezekiel, desiring that his vision would not limit the possibilities, responded to God by saying, "God, you know." Ezekiel understood that his thoughts and his words were not the final thoughts or words in the situation. Also, God did not give Ezekiel a vision of what will be. Instead, God gave Ezekiel a command to speak God's thoughts into being.

Many who have preached this text have focused on putting the bones of the body back together again. Like the children's song "Dry Bones," many preachers describe how one bone connected to another bone: "With the toe bone connected to the foot bone, the foot bone connected to the ankle bone, and the ankle bone connected to the leg bone," and so on. However, the text declares the important lesson that simply putting the pieces together is not enough. Putting the pieces back together without the breath, without God's Spirit, will result in efforts that are not sustainable. An army of political activists who lack spiritual sensitivity and integrity will, like the bones coming together, make lots of noise, but their noise will not bring life. Likewise, throwing money at community problems does not re-create community.

In the end, God interprets what God has done in the valley. God also declares what God will do among the people. God is clear: everything will change, because God is the change agent. Too often, people take credit for simple events that might be described as natural consequences, as signs of a new day. God is the only one who can re-create and restore life.

Psalm 130

The core of one's being is the repository that holds the story of one's whole life. The core, the existential center, contains the joys as well as the banes of one's life. Although we don't always have the words to express what is at the deepest levels of our being, God has access to our stories and is acquainted with every word and feeling. The knowledge that God is able to meet us at our points of need is essential. No matter how deep within our being those points of tumult may be, God is present with us. So often we feel that there is no one to listen to what we want to say. It is therefore extremely important that we believe God is not only capable of listening but also wants to listen to what we have to say, even if we are only able to scream.

The psalmist breathes a sigh of relief that God chooses not to "mark" us for our iniquities. There is, in fact, the strong belief that God forgives us. How unfortunate it is that we unfairly mark one another. Very often marks are made, one against another, to indicate how some people ought to be treated or who should be avoided. We mark children for the purposes of tracking them through the educational system "for the common good." We mark ex-offenders in the name of keeping communities safe. We mark racial and ethnic groups in the name of protecting society. One of the tragic marks that we have accused God of inscribing on humanity is the curse of Ham, which was said to be the mark of blackness. How long will the people of God allow the innocent to be marked by cruel indifference?

The psalmist also reminds us that waiting need not be a passive process of inactivity and stillness. Waiting can be an active process, such as the waiter who serves tables at a restaurant. The psalmist speaks of waiting with hope and hoping with one's entire being. This is an active, rather than passive, anticipation of God's intervention. Stronger and more certain than the anticipation of morning after a long night, our soul waits and watches for indications of God's creative power among us. And because love is the power of God, God chooses to redeem us, removing all marks that identify us as anything less than the children of God.

Romans 8:6–11

The language of the flesh versus the Spirit is a double-edged sword. As an ideology, dualism has split our humanity into flesh and spirit. This ideology keeps us battling within ourselves as one side seeks to dominate the other. We are locked in a constant state of war between good and evil. Dualism not only puts us at odds with God but also creates disruptive tensions within ourselves.

The dualism of humanity has produced a belief system of superior-inferior and dominant-subordinate that has been exploited beneath systems of oppression. It identifies the body as flesh and associates the body with death. Within this understanding, anything having to do with the body is identified as corrupt or evil. Conversely, all that is spiritual is thought to be pure and good. Focusing on the spirit, one creates an alternate reality to escape the body, avoid death, and identify exclusively with the spirit as the only good. Within this construction of reality, oppressed people are encouraged to be otherworldly, to accept their own suffering as the nature of reality, and to seek relief from suffering beyond this life. Dualism, however, refers to two sides. While one is suffering, another is benefiting from imposed suffering. All too often, battered women are encouraged to stay with their battering spouses. She is told her faithfulness may save her husband. On the other side of this dynamic, he benefits and is not held accountable for his wrongful and harmful behavior.

Our constructions of sex and race are also related to the bifurcation of flesh and spirit. "Sex" can identify male and female distinctions as well as refer to lovemaking. When sex refers to male and female, one sex tends to be identified with the spirit and the other with the flesh. When sex refers to sexual intercourse, it tends to be identified as an activity of the flesh that is devoid of the spirit. For centuries, there has been an unreasonable belief that men, who are spiritual, are seduced by women, for women desire the flesh, and lead men away from the spirit. This is further complicated by race often being sexualized. In the same way sex is often dualized into the categories of flesh and spirit, race classifications are often constructed to declare one race as flesh and problematic and another as spiritual and holy. As a result, specific races are regularly described as exotic, erotic, and seductive, making them devoid of the spirit and hostile toward God.

A better way to think about Paul's conversation on the flesh is to make a paradigm shift and see the flesh as selfish concerns and self-centered commitments. Living in the spirit with Christ means living in peace with one's self and others.

John 11:1–45

"Now a certain man was ill." Of all the issues that tend to be gleaned from this text, rarely do we focus on illness, as identified in the opening sentence of the narrative. As a pastoral care issue, should we see the opening verse as an encouragement to equip the laity for ministries of care? How should we respond to a notification of illness? Our tendency is to rush to visit the sick. Jesus' lack of immediate response to Lazarus's condition suggests that we consider other issues associated with physicality as central to this text. This story interweaves issues of body, spirit, mortality, faith, and belief.

Purpose distinguishes the courageous from the foolhardy. Jesus is warned about returning to Judea: his disciples emphasize the fact that the residents of that area had recently attempted to stone him. Their actions were a sign that read, "Stay out!" Social systems regularly offer signs and deterrents to ensure that their community remains unchallenged and unchanged. Struggles for human rights regularly move purposefully despite threats of violence and physical harm. Recognizing Jesus' resolve, his disciples are determined to travel with him and join him, if they must, in death. Facing what they believe to be certain death, they courageously and purposefully journey to Bethany.

Once they arrive in Bethany, Jesus engages in critical conversations about issues of belief and faith with Martha and Mary. The fact that Jesus wept, even as Martha, Mary, and others wept, is an acknowledgment that loss and death are accompanied by deep feelings. Grief is the emotional pain one feels as a result of loss. Because most of us have been socialized to fear death, we see death as a point of no return, as a warning sign that says, "Stay out!" Death is also thought of as an intrusive and powerful enemy. A paradigm shift that declares death a part of the continuity of life can change death from being seen as an enemy to be feared. Jesus attempts to reframe Martha and Mary's understanding of death by describing death as sleep. Although sleep can be experienced as a powerful force, it is not a power that is thought to be final or to bring about the end of life. Sleep tends to be understood as necessary and purposeful and not to be feared. Lazarus has fallen asleep and he can therefore be awakened. It is not the end, but simply a process of rejuvenating the body. By reframing death as sleep, Jesus purposefully shifts their understanding of death and simultaneously their belief in the power of God.

The musical genre of spirituals in the African American religious tradition is a hermeneutical strategy as much as it is a musical expression. There is a spiritual that combines elements of this narrative with elements from the exodus narrative to encourage sufferers to believe in the power of God to deliver us from oppression. The spiritual declares, "Mary don't you weep. Tell Martha not to moan. Pharaoh's army drowned in the Red Sea." It encourages believers not to hold on to suffering and to have faith that God will powerfully deliver us from trouble and restore us to life. Just as Lazarus is awakened and called forth from the tomb by the power of God through Jesus, we also may look to God's power to restore us to newness of life.

César Chávez Day (March 31)

Frederick John Dalton

Job 30:9–31
Psalm 56
Hebrews 10:32–39
Matthew 7:7–12

César Chávez Day, March 31, commemorates the birthday of César Chávez (1927–1993), a Mexican American who was moved by the poor working conditions, exploitative wages, and other injustices against Latino and Latina farm workers in the United States. Chávez organized the United Farm Workers, which led to upgrading the quality of life for such workers. In addition to honoring Chávez, this day calls attention to the solidarity needed to correct injustice, especially when injustice is inflicted upon workers. César Chávez Day further celebrates the ways in which Hispanic peoples enrich and strengthen the larger life of North America.

> When we are really honest with ourselves we must admit that our lives are all that really belong to us. So it is how we use our lives that determines what kind of [people] we are. It is my deepest belief that only by giving our lives do we find life. I am convinced that the truest act of courage, the strongest act of [humanity] is to sacrifice ourselves for others in a totally nonviolent struggle for justice. To be a [human being] is to suffer for others. God help us to be [human].
>
> *César Chávez*[1]

Depending on the kind of physical labor we do to earn a living, life is a hard struggle that may include great suffering. The lectionary readings for this

---

1. Mario T. García, ed., *The Gospel of César Chávez: My Faith in Action* (New York: Sheed & Ward, 2007), 51–52.

day that marks the birth of César Chávez invite us to reflect on the dignity of women and men, boys and girls, who depend on the strength of their muscles and the stamina of their spirits to provide for the needs of those they love as well as themselves. Today's readings reveal that pain and violence, fear and oppression, injustice and affliction are transformed by the grace of God into faith, praise, hope, and salvation.[2] Trusting in God is a hard struggle for all of us. Yet we depend on God for every good gift in life. The life of César Chávez reminds us that we do the will of God when we leave fear behind and choose to struggle for justice with others in order to end the suffering of oppressed workers so that every person may live in dignity as a child of God.

Job 30:9–31

The story of Job is the story of the mystery of human suffering, or perhaps more accurately, the story of human beings resisting and questioning the reality of suffering in the context of their faith in God. Today's reading is part of Job's final, lengthy soliloquy (chaps. 29–31). This speech begins with Job calling to mind his past happiness and culminates with Job announcing his innocence. Job's lament in chapter 30 is structured in three parts. First, Job laments that he is mocked, abhorred, spat upon, and sent sprawling. His prosperity is lost, blown away like a cloud in the wind (v. 15). Job is held in contempt by members of his community, even by those on the lowest rung of the social ladder, the "rabble" who are against him (v. 12). Second, Job laments the physical ailments that afflict him from his skin to his inward parts. His bones ache and incessant pain keeps him from rest (v. 17), his stomach is in turmoil (v. 27), and fever racks his body, burning his bones with heat (v. 30). Job cries out to God, but he hears no response (v. 20) and wonders why God so cruelly persecutes him (v. 21). Third, Job laments that he receives no sympathy from God even though he himself showed sympathy to the needy. He heard the cry of the poor and grieved for their plight (v. 25), a reference which reveals that he is a righteous person. Yet Job finds himself cast into the mire (v. 19) and tossed about by a storm (v. 22), weeping and alone in darkness with no human companionship to ease his plight.

2. In researching the readings for this day I am indebted to the following scholars and their work: R.A.F. Mackenzie and Roland E. Murphy, "Job," in *The New Jerome Biblical Commentary*, ed. Raymond E. Brown, Joseph A. Fitzmyer, and Roland E. Murphy (Englewood Cliffs, NJ: Prentice Hall, 1990); Michael D. Guinan, "Job," in *The Collegeville Bible Commentary*, ed. Dianne Bergant and Robert J. Karris (Collegeville, MN: Liturgical Press, 1989); John S. Kselman and Michael L. Barré, "Psalms," in *New Jerome Biblical Commentary*; Richard A. Clifford, "Psalms," in *Collegeville Bible Commentary*; Benedict T. Viviano, "The Gospel according to Matthew," in *New Jerome Biblical Commentary*; Daniel J. Harrington, "Matthew," in *Collegeville Bible Commentary*; Myles M. Bourke, "The Epistle to the Hebrews," in *New Jerome Biblical Commentary*; George W. MacRae, "Hebrews," in *Collegeville Bible Commentary*.

Young César Chávez first felt the sting of exclusion when he was punished at school for speaking Spanish, the language he spoke at home with his loving family. After César's family lost their small farm in foreclosure during the Great Depression, they packed up their Arizona home and became migrants searching for work in the fields of California. For migrant farm workers like César and his family, life is a hard struggle that includes great suffering of all kinds. Like many migrant workers in the United States today, César's family experienced life on the lowest rung of the social and economic ladder in America. To be a farm worker in America in the second decade of the twenty-first century means low wages at piece rates, harsh and dangerous working conditions, health problems, pesticide risks, substandard housing, exclusion from labor benefits, child labor, and risks and fears related to immigration status. Although the Chávez family, like Job, helped other poor migrant families with kindness and generous support, they remained excluded and poor as they suffered terribly.

Psalm 56

This individual lament is a prayer of need and petition that continues many of the themes found in today's first reading. Weighed down by enemies, oppression, and failure, the psalmist sings of placing one's trust in God even while being afraid (vv. 1–4). The heart of the matter is revealed in verse 5: "their thoughts are against me for evil." The psalmist explains the mystery of evil in terms of foes and enemies who lurk and stir up strife. Hardship and suffering are thus caused by evil that is found in the human heart. However, Psalm 56 turns in another direction when the hymnist affirms that "God is for me" (v. 9). One needs to praise and trust God (vv. 10–11) and be faithful and grateful to God (v. 12), even amid suffering. God's gracious salvation is experienced in the act of hoping in God when all seems lost. Praising and thanking God while things are going wrong is an act of faith that leads from darkness to light. Faith emerges from contexts of uncertainty and doubt, rather than certainty and knowledge.

Although poor, the Chávez family was rich in dignity, love, patience, and generosity. César's parents built their family life on the rock of faith. César learned true wisdom from his parents (who could not read or write) through proverbs, sayings, prayers, and religious devotions. When a parent cannot buy food for the family despite long hours of work, faith is not easy. When a child sees a parent exploited and demeaned, faith is not easy. When a son sees a mother wearing out her body with physical labor in brutal heat and bitter cold, faith is not easy. When a father sees his daughter without shoes and unable to go to school, faith is not easy. Today, Christian faith animates the lives of countless farm workers, and they in turn animate the Christian communities where they worship with gifts of generosity, hospitality, courage, and perseverance. Farm worker families with faith in Jesus Christ have the power to transform a ramshackle dwelling in a farm labor camp into nothing less than a house where God dwells.

Matthew 7:7–12

This passage is part of Jesus' Sermon on the Mount (Matt. 5–7). The final verse is widely considered a one-line summary of Jesus' teaching, the Golden Rule of doing to others "as you would have them do to you." While the Golden Rule is an oft-repeated verse, the key for today's Scripture passage is found in an earlier verse that reveals what our attitude or intentionality in prayer must be if we are to be faithful disciples: "But strive first for the kingdom of God and his righteousness, and all these things will be given to you as well" (6:33). Today's reading is structured around the idea of asking, searching, and receiving, but the most important part is learning to search for what matters most of all: the kingdom of God and God's righteousness and justice. Unless our hearts are searching for God's kingdom of justice and righteousness, we cannot treat others as we would have them treat us, with compassion, mercy, and love. Our searching determines our asking, and that in turn leads to our receiving. Unless our hearts are set on justice, we cannot authentically love others. Living the Golden Rule depends on God's grace, and God's grace is given in abundance to those who strive for the justice of God's reign. When we seek God's kingdom and God's righteousness our prayers will be answered, which means we will be given the good gifts we need to love and care for others in fulfillment of the law and the prophets. We need not seek or ask for anything else.

In 1962 César Chávez quit his white-collar office job as a community organizer to start a farm labor union for migrant and seasonal workers. He was thirty-five years old, married with a large family, and had not worked in the fields for more than ten years. César had left the fields and found a good job, meaningful work, and a steady paycheck. The hard struggle and sufferings of migrant life were memories for him. Yet the injustices remained. Migrant and seasonal farm workers still labored in the fields and still endured hardship and sufferings. The fruit and vegetables on his family's table were planted, nurtured, and harvested by field workers who could not feed their families or afford decent shelter or count on health care in the event of illness or financial security in old age. The truth of injustice remained, even if he had moved up the ladder of success. So César Chávez resigned, moved his family, and began a life of solidarity with the poorest workers in America. César Chávez sought the justice of the kingdom of God above all else. He dedicated the rest of his life, the next thirty-one years (until his death in 1993), to the farm worker struggle for justice—*la causa*, as it is called in Spanish.

Hebrews 10:32–39

The fundamental theological vision of the Letter to the Hebrews is the eternal priesthood of Jesus, whose sacrifice on the cross redeems humanity from sin and establishes a new covenant relationship between God and humanity. The theme of sacrifice is elaborated in chapters 8, 9, and 10. Today's brief reading speaks of "a hard struggle with sufferings" (v. 32) that include abuse, plunder, and imprisonment (vv. 33–35). Yet Christians are called to be compassionate and cheerful in the midst of persecution because the gift of salvation in Christ is greater than anything else in life (v. 34). This letter exhorts Christians to do the will of God and endure in faith for the sake of salvation, no matter the circumstances (v. 36). The final verses of the reading are an exhortation to the community to live in faith and righteousness until Jesus returns "in a very little while."

The struggle for justice requires sacrifice. Multitudes of people around the globe endure poverty-level wages, harsh and unsafe working conditions, inhumane living conditions, hunger, malnutrition, ill health, illiteracy, exclusion or prejudice from surrounding communities, violence, and oppression. The burden of eliminating these conditions must not fall only on those who are oppressed. It belongs to each one of us: we must seek justice above all us so that we may fulfill Jesus' command to do unto others as we would have done to us. As César Chávez said,

> It is possible to become discouraged about the injustice we see everywhere. But God did not promise us that the world would be humane and just. He gives us the gift of life and allows us to choose the way we will use our limited time on this earth. . . . We can choose to use our lives for others to bring about a better and more just world for our children.[3]

In a world where injustice is everywhere, Christian believers have graced opportunities to work for justice, reconciliation, and peace with people of other faith traditions and those who have no religious affiliation. Sacrifice for the sake of justice liberates us for a new life of love as witnesses to God's saving love in Jesus Christ for all people.

3. Frederick John Dalton, *The Moral Vision of César Chávez* (Maryknoll, NY: Orbis Books, 2003), 135.

Sixth Sunday in Lent
(Liturgy of the Palms)

Teresa Lockhart Stricklen

PSALM 118:1–2, 19–29
MATTHEW 21:1–11

The Palm Sunday lections are the same throughout the three-year lectionary cycle, although with a different Gospel text each year. The preacher may want to consult all three years' commentaries in any given year for fuller illumination.

We cannot read everything related to this season on any one Sunday. Chosen lections are excised out of larger contexts, and sometimes these larger contexts are important. Matthew's and Luke's accounts of the triumphal entry include Jesus' cleansing of the temple immediately following his entry into the city, whereas in their Markan source, the cleansing occurs on the next day, sandwiched between two parts of the story about the cursing of the fig tree (Mark 11:12–22). The following comments take the larger context of Matthew and the other Synoptic Gospels into consideration.

Matthew 21:1–11

Matthew's account of Jesus' entry into Jerusalem differs from its Markan source in some important ways. Matthew's triumphal entry looks like a public event that attracted notice. In Mark, the "many people" could be seen simply as Jesus' followers who laud him (Mark 11:1, 7–10), whereas Matthew reports "a very large crowd" (Matt. 21:8). Indeed, there are crowds (plural) both in front of and behind Jesus, and "the whole city was in turmoil" (v. 10), inquiring about Jesus. Whereas Jesus' arrival in Mark looks like the farce of a Roman triumphal entry (see Year B, Liturgy of the Palms, in this series), Matthew's Gospel looks more like a proper triumphal entry according to Roman convention. Jesus is portrayed as the anticipated messiah of Zechariah,[1] hailed as the long-awaited Son of David who will presumably restore the Davidic monarchy. He processes into the temple, as was the customary ending of a triumphal parade; however, the cultic action he performs there is not a sacrifice of thanksgiving but a cleansing of the temple, hearkening back to the action Judas Maccabeus took after rousting the priests whom the Syrian government had hired and installed in Jerusalem (1 Macc. 4:36–59).[2]

After the cleansing of the temple in 165 BCE, Judas Maccabeus rebuilt the altar and restored the temple. Jesus' triumphal entry deliberately alludes to the prophetic expectations of Zechariah 9:9. Also, Jesus' cleansing of the temple (21:12–13), paired with his later assertion that the temple will be torn down and rebuilt in three days (24:1–2), did not win him any friends among the authorities in Jerusalem. From the perspective of the religious leaders who kept Israel's uneasy peace with Rome, Jesus was trouble. No doubt they had the temple's business leaders also breathing down their necks after the money changers' tables went flying about the court of the Gentiles. Even if Jesus' messianic proclamations escaped the notice of Rome, this man from Nazareth (known for being a breeding ground of "hillbilly," hotheaded zealots) had the audacity to flout their authority. What's more, Jesus was backed by the oppressed populace who wanted to bring back the good old days of David. Jesus wasn't just trouble; from their perspective, he was dangerous.

Hailing Jesus as Sovereign troubles the established order. It says to tyrants and their ecclesial collaborators who make the church an arm of the state that Christ alone is head of the church.[3] Confessing Jesus Christ as Sovereign challenges the dominant culture's accepted norms and can result in being included among the names on a state-sanctioned hit list. The power Jesus embodies is that of reliance on God and God's way of sharing beneficent power so that all are included in the divine blessing. He does not execute the expected messianic hopes, although Matthew makes it clear that he had power to call "twelve legions of angels" to fight the Roman soldiers who arrested him (26:53). Instead of the military might of flashing steeds, tanks, or stealth bombers, Christ's rule is inaugurated with an ass and her colt,[4] among the

---

1. See W. D. Davies and Dale C. Allison Jr., *A Critical and Exegetical Commentary on the Gospel according to Saint Matthew*, The International Critical Commentary, ed. J. A. Emerton, C. E. B. Cranfield, and G. N. Stanton (Edinburgh: T & T Clark, 1997), 119.
2. See also Jer. 7:11.
3. See, for example, the 1934 Barmen Declaration (*The Constitution of the Presbyterian Church (U.S.A.), Part I, Book of Confessions*), which was issued against Hitler's appropriation of the church for his own nationalistic ends.
4. Matthew's depiction of Jesus' triumphal entry on a donkey *and* her colt has amused commentators for centuries. With Allison and Davies (122), I am of the opinion that there may be a textual error here that is of little homiletic significance. Jesus did not ride into Jerusalem like a daredevil rodeo rider on two animals.

blind, the lame, and the outcast who receive healing, sight, and care. Christ's followers will not be easy friends with economic leaders or shopkeepers who benefit from bilking the poor or defying the *imago Dei* of people who are sold as objects—either in person or as market share or symbolic notations on a strategic battle plan.

Judgment of injustice is also God's sovereign way, and so we who hail Christ as Sovereign have a mandate to not just make him ruler of our own individual hearts and lives, though this should be true! Christ is Ruler of the whole universe, and so all of creation is to be brought under God's dominion, making us environmental activists, pursuers of human rights, with equality, liberty, and justice for all—not because this is the American way, but because it is God's Sovereign Way. It is established by Christ the King, whose reign has begun and is coming to fruition on a day when all will acknowledge his rule (Phil. 2:10–11). This is why the church involves itself in social issues and politics—not because it is politically correct, but because it is christologically commanded by our confession of faith.

The crowd who hails Jesus, however, functions as a clear reminder of our own sinful desire to sit on the throne of our lives. Yes, "Jesus is king," we shout with the abandon of children (Matt. 21:15) or like stones singing with the music of the universe (see Luke 19:40). But then we make our own plans and ask God to "make it so" for us like a magic genie. This reduces the Master of the universe to the status of our slave, subject to our beck and call. And when God does not perform according to our desires, wishes, and expectations, we dismiss the deity and look for another. The same holds true for holy people who are blessed with access to divine power. When prophets refuse to confer God's sanction for the kings' actions, they are dismissed, banished, or executed, as the story of Elijah exemplifies and Jesus laments: "Jerusalem, Jerusalem, the city that kills the prophets and stones those who are sent to it! How often have I desired to gather your children together as a hen gathers her brood under her wings, and you were not willing!" (Matt. 23:37).

Jesus is clearly the populist leader of a movement that threatens the established order of Jerusalem whose power is centered in the temple. His prophetic and messianic entry into the city, his overturning of the money changers' tables, and his prophecy that the temple would be destroyed and rebuilt in three days resulted in his execution.[5] Based on these actions, his crucifixion could have been easily predicted, given the political arrangements at the time. What is perhaps less predictable is that the populace whom Jesus

---

5. E. P. Sanders, *The Historical Figure of Jesus* (London: Penguin, 1993). Sanders notes that if Rome had suspected the Jesus movement of being significantly militaristic, Jesus wouldn't have been the only one executed by Rome, as his disciples fear.

champions also turns on him. Even his own disciples eventually betray and desert him.

Why? The crowds following Jesus in Matthew's Gospel are very clear about whom they believe him to be when they hail him as the Son of David at his entry into Jerusalem. They expect him to reestablish the Davidic monarchy by routing the Romans and thus fulfilling the ancient promise made to David that his "throne shall be established forever" (2 Sam. 7:16). Although Matthew's genealogy reveals that Jesus is a descendant of David, the Gospel writer also emphasizes that Jesus does not have any military maneuvers up his sleeve. Matthew uses the title "Son of David" elsewhere in the Gospel ironically. The only ones who see Jesus in this way before his triumphal entry are the demon-possessed, the mute, the Syrophoenician woman, blind beggars, and anonymous crowd members who welcome Jesus' miracles as signs from God. Jesus' prophetic action of riding on a donkey, however, fans the embers of the people's perennial messianic expectations, and the Jesus movement becomes the new hot topic for Jerusalem gossip.

Having the marginalized hail Jesus as the Son of David is perhaps a subtle critique against the temple system that denies direct access to God for those who are physically blemished (cf. Lev. 21). In Christ the marginalized are not shunned but are touched by the holy despite their imperfections, and they are ushered into the very presence of God in Jesus. The crowds' cry for the Son of David to "save us now" (the literal meaning of "hosanna") highlights the fact that the blind, the Gentile, the female, the children, the poor who couldn't afford appropriate temple sacrifices (hence Jesus' angry overturning of the money changers' tables)—all of these people cut off from direct access to God had no recourse to hope for anything other than military or divine intervention to restore God's blessings to them. With the exception of the disciples (Matt. 14:33; 16:16), who betray and desert him, and evil or possessed beings (e.g., 4:3, 6; 8:29; 27:40), the people are blind to Jesus' divinity and the fact that in him God is intervening for their salvation. When Jesus does not mount a military campaign because his kingdom is not of this world and because he chooses to use his power to fulfill the promises of God (26:53–54), the crowd turns on him. He does not meet their expectations, so they shout, "Crucify him!" (27:22–23).

Psalm 118:1–2, 19–29

"Save us, we beseech you, O LORD! . . . Give us success!" (v. 25). Note how the cry of the crowd in this psalm is oriented toward a prayer for success. Moreover, it is predominantly a cry for the restoration of Israel's prosperity. Although our notions of success are often measured in dollars, Israel's prosperity was seen in its communal flourishing. In actuality this ideal was probably compromised by corrupt practices and idolatries of wealth and power substituting for true godly prosperity, but the Bible makes it clear that the wealth of God's people is measured by covenantal standards, not money or status. Living in right relationship with the Holy One of Israel is the true measure of success.

The many liturgical uses of this psalm point to its importance during festivals that reiterate and renew Israel's primary covenant with God. (For more on this, see Liturgy of the Palms in Year B of this series.) Replaying David's fortunes, the psalm demonstrates how God saves the beloved. When it is used in a Palm/Passion Sunday service, the preacher could emphasize this irony. Some scholars think the historical Jesus expected divine intervention to save him. Matthew does not show this, however, and emphasizes instead that Jesus willingly chooses to offer himself to God for the fulfillment of the Scriptures when it seems that there is no other way (Matt. 26:53–54). When the crowd turns on him, and Jesus, the Son of David, is brought to death's door, the gates of righteousness are not opened to him; he makes his bed in Sheol after the battle of the cross. Nonetheless, "the right hand of the LORD does valiantly" (Ps. 118:15) and, in anticipation of the events to follow Palm Sunday, resurrection happens. Jesus' faithful trust in the salvation of the Lord (v. 14) enables us to rejoice as Christ becomes the gate of righteousness through which all people may enter into the presence of God—even today.

Martyrs for the faith today bear witness to the truth that those who are rejected by society for standing up for God's Way cannot really be put down. Christianity is flourishing, not dying, in places of martyrdom. God's goodwill ultimately prevails, regardless of attempts to kill or overcome it. This emboldens and strengthens us to persevere when we encounter resistance and oppression while pursuing God's justice among us. "O give thanks to the LORD, who is good; God's steadfast love endures forever" (v. 29).

Sixth Sunday in Lent (Liturgy of the Passion)

Teresa Lockhart Stricklen

ISAIAH 50:4–9A
PSALM 31:9–16
PHILIPPIANS 2:5–11
MATTHEW 26:14–27:66

Passion Sunday ranks in the top three of the most important days in the church year, emphasizing the lengths to which the Holy One will go to be in communion with humanity, the costliness of that commitment, the inhumanity of people bent on their own rule, and the mystery of God at work even amid betrayal, injustice, military and police brutality, and one of the most heinous acts of torture known in history—crucifixion.

The passion narratives are long and powerful when they are presented well orally. The integrity of the whole of this narrative needs to be retained and highlighted on Passion Sunday. It needs no elaborate dramatization, because the story's power comes across in just a simple reading by one person. This is especially true of Matthew's account.

Matthew 26:14–27:66

"When Jesus had finished saying all these things," Matthew writes, transitioning into the passion narrative. It is a common phrase used at the end of all Jesus' major discourses in Matthew, except that now *all* of Jesus' formal teaching, like that of Moses in Deuteronomy 31:1, is at an end. The Word, however, continues to speak, and it comes to pass. Jesus speaks his prediction that he will die on Passover (like the Passover lambs), and the religious authorities begin plotting his death with intensity. He is anointed for his death in an exorbitant act of devotion that ministers to him as he faces death (26:6–13), which contrasts with Judas's betrayal of him for a pittance (26:14–16).

The Anointed One then sits at table with his followers during the Passover meal to announce that one eating with them will betray him, and each of them

178

wonders, "Is it I?" The meal, linked with Jewish covenant meals and the Passover, also alludes to Isaiah 53, with Jesus being "poured out" like the Suffering Servant (Isa. 53:12). Jesus is pouring himself out, indicating he's still firmly in control of the chaos out of which God's promised new creation will emerge through God's forgiveness of sin. Matthew's unique modifications to Mark's account of the Last Supper also have Jesus commanding the disciples to eat and drink, "*all* of you"—not just the good disciples, but Judas, too. Indeed, as Jesus says immediately after the meal, *all* of them will betray him by abandoning him, starting with the kiss of Judas.

The tempo of the narrative picks up like a penny gathering centripetal velocity as it descends into the black hole in the middle of a big circular bank. What had been slowly whirling around in Matthew's passion narrative now begins its descent until it spins with deadly tightness toward the cross. With Judas's betrayal with a kiss, a standard greeting for friends, swords flash. Jesus, however, orders nonviolence. Although he could call 72,000 angels to defend him, he does not, in order that all may be fulfilled. This fulfillment is done by Jesus alone; the disciples flee. Although Peter follows him from a distance, he vehemently denies the Lord thrice, as predicted, before the cock crows. The juxtaposition of Peter's denial and Jesus' "trial" shows Jesus drawing closer to condemnation as Peter further distances himself from the Lord.

Jesus is taken before Caiaphas the high priest, who was charged by the Roman prefect with keeping peace with Rome. Matthew sees Caiaphas as responsible for Jesus' death. At the trial (which is more of an occasion for mockery than a judicial proceding), witnesses cannot agree on their false testimony against him and the charge of destroying the temple finally gets two witnesses. When Caiaphas asks him whether he is the Christ, the Son of God, Jesus says, "You have said so," then Jesus describes the advent of the apocalyptic Son of Man from Daniel 7:13–14 (cf. Ps. 110). The high priest dramatically tears his robe to demonstrate grief for this blasphemy, which, technically, Jesus did not commit. But Caiaphas had already decided that Jesus had to die, and his drama convinces the jury to join in this verdict. The chief priests then spit on Jesus, slap, beat, and mock him, saying, "Prophesy, Christ! Who hit you that time?"

It may be hard for us to imagine this kind of behavior from religious leaders until we remember that members of the Ku Klux Klan are often church leaders. Preachers need to be careful not to perpetuate anti-Jewish attitudes, because even "good people" are not exempt from committing acts of brutality that continue among us today. What makes such things as Jesus' ordeal and the torture at places such as Abu Ghraib especially heinous are the supposedly high ideals of the people behind these acts of violence.

Caiaphas then sends Jesus to Pilate, who in Matthew's account is hesitant to crucify Jesus. This is because the Matthean community was trying to convince the Romans that they were not enemies but friends.[1] Pilate comes off as a better Jew than the chief priests, washing his hands of the murder in accord with Deuteronomy 21:7–8.[2] In actuality, Pilate was known as a capricious despot who was removed from office because he randomly executed too many people, even by Roman standards.[3] Only Rome could execute, but there was cooperation between religious and political leaders that sealed Jesus' fate. Jesus has nothing to say about the charges against him (cf. Isa. 53:7), for Christ does not answer to these authorities, which are both portrayed as corrupt, cruel, and ineffective. Religion and politics must both answer to Christ.

When Judas learns of Jesus' condemnation, he commits suicide, a detail reported in the Gospels only by Matthew,[4] probably because it alludes to Zechariah 11:10–13 (not Jeremiah). Zechariah 9–11 provided an important template for the early Christians to understand Jesus' death, especially for Matthew. Like Peter, Judas knew he had sinned and was remorseful, but unlike Peter, he despaired that he could be forgiven, thereby denying the meaning of Jesus' death.

For more on the crucifixion and burial, see Liturgy of the Passion for Years B and C in this commentary series.[5] The only unique addition of Matthew is the convulsive earthquake that raises the dead at the moment of Jesus' death (27:51b–52). These are apocalyptic signs, indicating that this is the anticipated Day of the Lord. What we seem to have here is "a piece of theology set forth as history,"[6] with allusions to Zechariah 14:5, Ezekiel 37:12–14, Isaiah 26:19, and Daniel 12:2. In the midst of these apocalyptic signs, there is another rending of fabric that provides an ironic counterpoint to Caiaphas's rending of his garment. Jesus' own garment was not ripped, but the veil in the temple's Holy of Holies was completely torn, signifying God's grief at the religious leaders' injustice that resulted in Jesus' crucifixion. With this action, access into the Holy of Holies is now granted through Christ, God's great high priest (cf. Heb. 10:19–20). Even the Gentiles crucifying him may confess, "Truly this man was God's Son!" (Matt. 27:54).

---

1. E. P. Sanders, *The Historical Figure of Jesus* (London: Penguin, 1993), 273.
2. Thomas G. Long, *Matthew*, Westminster Bible Companion (Louisville, KY: Westminster John Knox Press, 1997), 313.
3. Philo, *Embassy to Gaius*, XXXVIII.302, http://www.earlychristianwritings.com/yonge/book 40.html (accessed February 15, 2013).
4. Luke includes this detail later in Acts 1:15–20.
5. See also Raymond Brown, *Death of the Messiah* (New York: Doubleday, 1994).
6. Donald A. Hagner, *Matthew 14–28*, Word Biblical Commentary (Dallas: Word Books, 1995), 851.

Psalm 31:9–16

Psalm 31 is an interesting lection for Passion Sunday because its form is a composite of many different types. It is a lament, but not exclusively, because it is laced with confident trust (vv. 3, 5, 14–15) and thanksgiving (vv. 7–8, 19–20). It sounds as though it would be uttered by a person being martyred—part lament and cry to God for help, as well as speaking with confidence, trust, and thanksgiving for sure deliverance.

Although the lection begins with verse 9, the first part of the psalm is spoken by a person pursued and persecuted by others who have set a trap to capture the psalmist. The psalmist, however, trusts in God, the strong rock, for defense and deliverance. God sees and knows the psalmist's trouble, which elicits joy even in the midst of great fear. Verses 9–16 portray a person whose strength is failing due to grief, perhaps because others have slandered the psalmist, who is considered a reproach and disgrace (v. 13). People dread and flee from the presence of this despised one (v. 11). Nevertheless, the psalmist trusts in God's security and deliverance (vv. 14–15), praying that the divine face will shine upon the psalmist for the sake of God's mercy (v. 16).

There are remarkable similarities between Psalm 31 and Jesus' experiences of rejection, condemnation, death, and promised resurrection. This psalm highlights the cruel nature of human beings and our propensity to destroy goodness. Just as the FBI slandered civil rights leaders in the 1960s, people often seek to ruin those whose goodness threatens their beliefs about how life should be ordered. Jesus' sure faith in God, to whom he commits his spirit (v. 5), threatens the faith and practices that religious leaders had wrought over the years to survive occupation by foreign powers. The Occupy movement across the United States has threatened economic and political power structures and has experienced persecution. Yet it trusts in ultimate justice and vindication, as does Psalm 31.

This psalm also suggests that God's persecuted one expected to be delivered by God from the net of deception. Many scholars think Jesus may have died as a failed eschatological prophet, hence the cry of dereliction. With the resurrection, however, God's face did indeed shine on him. His way of life was vindicated, while the accounts of his crucifixion, usually too shameful to be mentioned, bring the shadowy death-dealing ways of those who counseled against him into the light. We see the ways of sin for what they are and find the Way of God embracing us with God's forgiveness and strength to help us follow his path of confident trust even in the worst possible situations.

Philippians 2:5–11

Jesus and the psalmist use their power in accord with the divine power depicted in the early Christian hymn that Philippians quotes. They do not amass power for their own sakes, but use their agency in service to all of humanity. In the process, they are empowered and exalted by God even if denigrated by others. It is this divine power that flows through them like a waterfall rushing to the lowest place, sustaining them. (See also the comments on Philippians for the Liturgy of the Passion in Years B and C of this series.)

Even the most oppressed people have a God-given power to work for good, though it may result in their deaths. In the book *The Hunger Games*, the protagonist Katniss is a futuristic gladiator who chooses to die rather than kill her friend and opponent in the games. Though virtually enslaved by an imperialistic state, she continually uses her power to choose kindness toward others to defy the powers that be, and in the process she changes the game and the society that demands it.[7] Many who have been raped in war are refusing to hide in shame. Instead, they are using the power of language to tell the truth. Even when others want to spare them shame by hiding their faces from reporters, women like Honorata Kizende respond, "I am not ashamed to show my face and publish my identity. The shame lies with those who broke me open and with the authorities who failed to protect me."[8] We often feel powerless against state-sanctioned violence taking place in other parts of the world. Yet posting reports about these events on social network sites can bring awareness to others. Populist movements uproot tyranny. We can use what agency we have to love God and neighbors and to do what we can as servants of God's realm.

Isaiah 50:4–9a

This is also the attitude of Isaiah's teacher, who bears insult, shame, and reproach, and yet does not hide his face (v. 6). Knowing that God is a constant source of help and strength, he sets his face like flint, certain that he cannot be put to shame, and demands that oppressors be exposed (vv. 7–9). No wonder the early church saw Jesus in this role. He did indeed set his face to go to Jerusalem, even though he knew it would lead to his death (Luke 9:51). In taking on the shame of humanity, however, Jesus puts death-dealing powers to shame. His way is vindicated in the resurrection's new creation that God is bringing to fulfillment among us.

---

7. Suzanne Collins, *The Hunger Games* (New York: Scholastic Press, 2008).
8. Michelle Faul, "Congo Women Fight Back, Speak Out about Rape," msnbc.com, March 16, 2009, www.msnbc.msn.com/id/29719277/ns/world_news-africa/t/congo-women-fight-back -speak-out-about-rape/.

Maundy Thursday

Bob Hunter

Exodus 12:1–4 (5–10), 11–14
Psalm 116:1–2, 12–19
1 Corinthians 11:23–26
John 13:1–17, 31b–35

Maundy Thursday, one of the saddest days in the lectionary calendar, presents us with the challenge of the meaning of sacrifice: Jesus' sacrifice on behalf of the community and the world; Israel's sacrifices as they escape captivity; and our sacrifices as we respond to God's love on behalf of the people of God and the world. The Christian church has long grappled with the meaning of sacrifice, yet we know of its power in our lives as we know experientially the love of God and the love of community, even in the hardest times. We have seen the redemptive power of sacrificial love as people of goodwill throughout history have challenged social ills: Gandhi in India, Bonhoeffer and the resistance to Hitler, Mother Teresa on behalf of the dispossessed, civil rights activists who challenged the conscience of a nation, César Chávez on behalf of farm workers, to name a few. We have a tendency to keep the personal aspect of sacrifice separate from the social enactments of it, and yet they enhance the meaning of one another.

The four passages for Maundy Thursday present the kind of dialectic found in Scripture related to different aspects of sacrifice. We encounter Israel as an oppressed nation escaping the years of torment it has endured and the sacrifices needed to carry off that escape; a sacrifice offered to God in the Psalms because God is a God of mercy who hears the cries of Israel, the oppressed, and all who long for mercy; the preparation of Jesus for a momentous sacrifice at the hands of Israel's Roman oppressors; and Jesus' sacrifice of position and glory to serve those he loves, bidding us to do the same.

Exodus 12:1–4 (5–10), 11–14

Injustice has devastating consequences for the oppressed and the oppressor. Malcolm X found himself in grave trouble for pointing out that violence rooted in the psyche of the United States in the heat of the Vietnam War had come home to roost in the violence that resulted in the death of John F. Kennedy. Perhaps his timing was wrong in making that connection when the nation was mourning its beloved president, but he was right in his assessment that those who live by the sword will often be its victim. Wars often lead a nation to accept violence even within its borders, and certainly other forms of injustice cause a nation, a people, and individuals to become inured to violence.

This Exodus passage has devastation written all over it. We see Israel preparing for a dangerous clandestine escape from years of violent oppression. Their preparation involves packing and a quick meal, with explicit instructions for both. And we see the pending consequence of the years of brutality about to be visited on their oppressors. (The text would seem to indicate this is a direct act of God, though natural consequences of human behavior are often portrayed as divine acts in Scripture.) We are certain that Israel is not bringing the destruction and that their focus is on the reality that God has heard their pleas and answered their cries for freedom. They have cried out for God's hand, and it has finally come! Their cry for freedom has been echoed the world over, but never with more passion than among the writers of the American Negro spirituals:

> When Israel was in Egypt's land;
> Oppressed so hard they could not stand,
> Go down, Moses, 'Way down in Egypt's land.
> Tell old Pharaoh, Let my people go![1]

Nonetheless, the road will be long and the burdens heavy as Israel plods toward the promised land. New occasions for God's intervention will be found and new sacrifices await them.

As we reflect on the momentous events of Passion Week with the promise of Easter, as we face the stripped-down sanctuary and the darkness symbolized by black cloths draped on crosses, we recognize that there are many dark places in our world and in our hearts. We, too, cry out for victory both external and internal. Externally we long to be free as a nation so prone to materialism and focused on things rather than people. Internally we want freedom from our demons of pride and self-doubt. We travel on.

---

1. Traditional spiritual, "Go Down, Moses." See *African American Heritage Hymnal: 575 Hymns, Spirituals, and Gospel Songs* (Chicago: GIA Publications, 2001), #543.

Psalm 116:1–2, 12–19

This psalm picks up the theme of a God who has heard people's cries. The psalmist cries out for mercy and victory over distress, sorrow, and even death itself. The writer has experienced God's victory and offers up a sacrifice of praise. The psalmist's question becomes, what will I give to God in return for the victory that God has given me? And the answer is to fulfill vows made to the Lord by calling on the Lord not just in times of need but in times of victory (vv. 1–2, 12); serving God as a child of the servant girl and all who have sacrificed in the past (v. 16); and joining in communal and public expressions of service to God (vv. 18–19). One of the great themes of Scripture is not just how we handle loss, death, and injustice, but how we handle victory. When Easter arrives, will we gloat that the victory is ours and that we did it ourselves? Or will we still remember the escape from Egypt and the pain of sacrifice that our mothers and fathers had to endure to reach this point? Will we remember God's hand in it all?

This theme is a perennial one as I work with college-age students. Because of the relative ease of their lives today, many students are blind to the sacrifices that were made along the way. But we must not forget what God has done and how victory was brought about through the actions and sacrifices of those who have gone before us. And we must offer a sacrifice of praise, "lest our hearts, drunk with the wine of the world, we forget thee."[2]

Forgetfulness has disastrous consequences for a nation and its people. In the United States, we are forgetting the roles of social movements, unions, and government help in creating a middle class. We are hearing more and more calls to gut those aspects of our social contract. In fact, the very concept of a social contract is disappearing. Rugged individualism is the mantra of the times, implying that we do not need each other or the institutions that bind us together. On this day of symbolic mourning, with so far yet to go, let us remember where we have come from and praise God for all that has been accomplished along the way.

1 Corinthians 11:23–26

Central to remembrance for Christians is remembering the death of Jesus through eating bread and drinking from the cup. This passage bids us to remember Christ's death and institutes the observance that we call Communion. But Communion must be more than symbolic celebration.

---

2. From the third stanza of "Lift Every Voice and Sing," lyrics by James Weldon Johnson, 1899. See *African American Heritage Hymnal*, #540.

I once was a part of a church service where the ministers and deacons (all men) were serving the congregation in a Communion service. The Communion celebration was full of the language of servanthood as the deacons assumed a symbolic service to the church. But this church did not allow for women in the pastorate or as deacons. Being a deacon was not a sacrificial act. It was not an act of service but a position of privilege. Excluding women was predicated on this privilege. One very perceptive woman said to me after the Communion service that the real act of service was not done by the deacons but by the all-women crew who washed the glasses afterward. We so easily make a monument of symbols but fail to get to the heart of the reality behind them.

Jesus' death has taken on meanings that extract it from the historical context that includes Mary singing of God's mercy to Israel through the birth of Jesus. A nation that has known its share of trouble will be remembered and a humble young woman will be exalted because God is not impressed with the self-righteous and the greedy. Such persons will be brought down. The hungry will be fed and the rich will be sent away without (Luke 1:53). Jesus echoed this message when he declared in his inaugural sermon that he had come to set the oppressed free (Luke 4:18).

We also live in a world where greed has been allowed to flourish, and it has resulted in a growing divide between rich and poor, powerful and those without much power. The celebration of Communion must call us back to the full message of Jesus so that we do not succumb to these temptations.

John 13:1–17, 31b–35

This passage begins as Jesus is about to face death. Scripture makes it clear that one of the pains of Jesus' predicament was the betrayal he endured from his followers and friends. In John 13 we see that the betrayal is coming from his innermost circle. But Jesus, knowing the power that he has as one who has come from God and is returning to God, still loves his disciples deeply. So he puts on the garments associated with servants and begins to wash his disciples' feet. Peter is scandalized by this humble behavior coming from one he so reveres. Peter is anticipating the kingdom, and Jesus is not acting like a king.

Peter is not alone. We too are often confused by two elements of Scripture: sacrifice and victory. Sacrifice seems to imply defeat, which is contrary to victory. Like Peter, we recoil at the idea of sacrifice or we embrace a kind of sacrifice that leads back into patterns of repression and oppression. On the one hand, there are people who espouse a prosperity gospel that sells victory without sacrifice. On the other, there are those counseling women to remain in abusive and violent situations or telling people to return to broken and oppressive contexts out of some misguided sense of Christian duty. There are also those who counsel both of these extremes, victory for the powerful and sacrifice for those without power. All the while, many people who have been mistreated spend a lifetime overcoming their misgivings and even self-hatred. Their sacrificial attempts work only to increase their sense of worthlessness.

We must embrace a different kind of sacrifice that always works in the opposite direction of abuse and oppression. Israel's sacrifice is for their escape. David's sacrifice is so that he may remember that escape and what God has done and the mercy God has shown him personally. Our Communion must help us to remember Jesus' sacrifice to break every kind of bondage.

In this passage, Jesus sacrifices for the community on behalf of love. It signals yet another direction for sacrifice: that those who are called to be teachers or who have some measure of mastery within a community must sacrifice on behalf of the community. Without that, every structure soon becomes an oppressive one where some get more and more power and others are reduced to total dependency and self-loathing. We must follow Jesus as leaders, teachers, community workers, and parents who will sacrifice for the community we love, lest we become what we dislike in others.

As we walk into this season of darkness with the promise of Easter before us, may we be armed with a sacrificial love that works against all forms of oppression.

Good Friday

Randall C. Bailey

ISAIAH 52:13–53:12
PSALM 22
HEBREWS 4:14–16; 5:7–9
JOHN 18:1–19:42

Good Friday commemorates the lynching of Jesus by the Romans. They sought his death because of Jesus' revolutionary activities in trying to reclaim the throne in Jerusalem and to liberate his people from Roman oppression. The Romans used crucifixion as a public lynching for runaway slaves, political revolutionaries, and traitors to the state.[1] Since Jesus was not a Roman citizen, he could not have been a traitor to the state. Given his actions presented in the Gospels, he was lynched because he was a revolutionary. The purpose of these lynchings was to terrorize the colonized people so they would not rebel against Rome. While the church has often ignored the political dimensions of Good Friday, the following commentary understands that these are integrally related to Jesus' crucifixion.

Isaiah 52:13–53:12

This is the fourth of the Servant Songs found in Deutero-Isaiah.[2] This unnamed prophet, who speaks to the exiles in Babylon in Isaiah 40–55, tries to help his people deal with their exile and to claim the hope that YHWH will restore their nationhood and homeland. All of these songs speak of the restoration of the nation and the realization of justice, *mishpat*, which the Hebrew prophets understood to be a term of social organization leading to the fair distribution of resources so that all people may reach their maximum potential and the society and nation can thrive.

---

1. Richard A. Horsley, *Jesus and Empire: The Kingdom of God and the New World Disorder* (Minneapolis: Fortress Press, 2003), 29–30.
2. The Servant Songs also include Isa. 42:1–9; 44:1–8; and 49:1–7.

Of particular import for Holy Friday are verses 5 and 12b of Isaiah 53. Both of these verses have been associated with Jesus' crucifixion by Christian believers through the centuries. However, the Hebrew verbs are in the past and present tenses, which means the prophet is describing events that have taken place in the past and that have consequences for his hearers during his lifetime, around 550 BCE.[3] At no point are any future tenses used in this song. Thus to claim that these verses predict Jesus' death and resurrection and bear implications for his followers pushes beyond the purview of Deutero-Isaiah's immediate context. It is more appropriate to say that the events of Jesus' crucifixion were interpreted by his followers in light of Deutero-Isaiah's description of servanthood.

It is also important to recognize that the church has often depoliticized the claims of this text throughout the centuries. According to 52:15 and 53:4–5, the oppression and suffering of the servant is a consequence of his political activity in bringing justice to the people. Similarly, the life and ministry of Jesus may also be interpreted from a revolutionary standpoint, especially as he is called "Son of God," which is a title frequently used to refer to the king in Jerusalem (2 Sam. 7:14), and "Christ," *Christos*, which is the Greek translation of the Hebrew word *mashiah*, the anointed one, another title for kings in ancient Israel (1 Sam. 24:6). The first-century references to Jesus as "Son of God" and "messiah" suggest that he was considered to be a king by his followers—or at least a contender for the throne in Jerusalem.[4] Thus it is ironic that the church often resists political interpretations of his death and its revolutionary implications that are evident in Isaiah 52–53.

Finally, the claim that the Suffering Servant did not speak during his trial has given rise to the words of a spiritual,

> They crucified my savior,
> but he never said a mumbling word.

This portrayal in Isaiah 53:7, which resembles African concepts of martyrdom, speaks more to the experiences of enslaved Africans than the tradition of the "seven last words" of Jesus. Enslaved Africans identified with Jesus as a martyr who was beaten and killed for his activities in trying to free his people, as happened to many of them on plantations. Their singing about him, in songs such as "Ride on, King Jesus" and "Glory to the New Born King,"

---

3. Cf. Makhosazana K. Nzimande, "Isaiah," in *The Africana Bible: Reading Israel's Scripture from Africa and the African Diaspora*, ed. Hugh R. Page Jr. (Minneapolis: Fortress Press, 2010), 138–39, and her discussion of referring to past events in establishing identity for the exiles.

4. Randall C. Bailey, "The Biblical Basis for a Political Theology of Liberation," in *Blow the Trumpet in Zion: Global Vision and Action for the 21st-Century Black Church*, ed. Iva E. Carruthers, Frederick D. Haynes III, and Jeremiah A. Wright Jr. (Minneapolis: Fortress Press, 2005), 91–96.

bespoke their understanding of the crucifixion as the killing of the African revolutionary.

Psalm 22

This psalm is a composite of individual lament (vv. 1–21a) and thanksgiving (vv. 21b–31).[5] It has been chosen for this day because the address to the deity in verse 1a is put into the mouth of Jesus on the cross in Mark 15:34 and Matthew 27:46. In addition, the description of distress (Ps. 22:7) and the reference to casting lots for his clothes (v. 18) are also referenced in other passion narratives (e.g., Luke 23:36; Matt. 27:35).

Psalm 22 appears to have been spoken by one who is experiencing severe social (vv. 6–8) and physical problems (vv. 14–15). While the psalmist begins by accusing God of abandonment, later the statement of assurance (vv. 3–5) and the plea for redemption (vv. 18–21a) speak to a hope that God will intervene on the psalmist's behalf. The stress on the individual and the medical afflictions voiced by the psalmist suggest that something other than revolutionary concerns is present here. The psalmist claims that those who worship God the way the writer does can also be healed (vv. 25–31).

In verse 21b the psalmist suddenly switches to thanking God for having rescued the writer from death. Since the concluding verses do not match Jesus' experiences on Good Friday, it is ironic that the whole psalm is used in the liturgy for this day. The thanksgiving part of the psalm contains exhortation to the congregants that if they pray like the psalmist, they will also be healed. This is contrary to the experience of Jesus on the cross.

Hebrews 4:14–16; 5:7–9

This reading from Hebrews presents Jesus as a "high priest" and intercessor because he has become sinless (4:15b), submissive (5:7), and perfect (5:9) on our behalf. This presentation of Jesus in the priestly role depoliticizes the event of the crucifixion. The claim in this text of his perfection argues for Jesus' divine nature, thereby moving us away from the death of the political revolutionary. While Jesus is described as one who was tested just as we are tested, he passes the test. Again, this reading pushes us away from dealing with the pain of the lynching and the social justice concerns of the event. Its use for this day is part of the church's conscious attempts to deradicalize and domesticate Jesus, so that we will be deradicalized in our practice of the faith

---

5. Peter C. Craigie argues for a third division of a prayer in his *Psalms 1–50*, Word Biblical Commentary (Waco, TX: Word Books, 1983), 197. However, this appears to be part of the thanksgiving.

and not understand "pick up your own cross" to mean that we should get involved in the revolution to free people from oppression in our own time. Thus, the message of this text should be resisted by those engaged in social justice preaching.

John 18:1–19:42

In John's version of the crucifixion of Jesus, a disproportionate amount of guilt appears to be laid on Jewish authorities rather than the Romans. Throughout this narrative, the word "Jews" appears nineteen times, including references to Jewish religious institutions (18:20), religious officials (high/chief priest), and religious customs (18:28, 39; 19:7, 14). John's perspective has often been adopted by the church through the centuries, and it has contributed to the unjust persecution of Jews by Christians.

For example, concurrent with Peter's threefold denial of Jesus (18:17, 25, and 27), the narrator presents Pilate resisting Jesus' crucifixion on three occasions (18:31, 39; 19:6b). Pilate is portrayed as one who is trying to resist the crucifixion of Jesus, while Jesus' disciples are portrayed as complicit in his death and his fellow Jews as proponents and executioners (see 19:16). An analogy could be drawn between this portrayal of Jesus' betrayal by his own people and members of the Black community urging members of the Ku Klux Klan to lynch members of the Black Panther Party. This is the absurdity of the narrative portrayal in this text. This portrayal supports the thinking often expressed in Black preaching that "We are our own worst enemies," which leads to internalized oppression and letting white supremacy off the hook.

In their discussion of the phrase "King of the Jews," Pilate and the religious leaders acknowledge that this crucifixion is indeed a political matter. As king, Jesus fulfills the role of political revolutionary. This claim counteracts the portrayal of the crucifixion as being caused primarily by an internal religious squabble among the Jews. Internal evidence like this makes scholars speculate that the Fourth Gospel was written in the face of rejection of the followers of Jesus by the synagogue and its leaders. The ethnic signifiers and lack of them, however, point to a political sense of exonerating the Romans. Such portrayals are also critical in the casting of the Jews as "Jesus killers" and their subsequent persecutions throughout the Northern Hemisphere.[6]

Three of "the seven last words" are found in this passage. The first, "Woman, here is your son" (19:26), reflects Jesus' concern that his mother be taken care of after his death. However, in 19:25 we are told that Mary is standing with three other females, one of whom is her relative. It appears

6. See Robert P. Carroll, *The Bible as a Problem for Christians* (Philadelphia: Trinity Press International, 1991), 90–116.

that a supportive women's community stayed close to Jesus at the time of his crucifixion when other followers did not. Why would Jesus appear to pull Mary away from this supportive community and toward "the disciple whom he loved"? Oral tradition maintains that Joseph had died and it was the son's responsibility to care for his widowed mother. This tradition is designed to keep us from exploring the lack of honor given to the supportive women's community, just as we have done to the role of the Negro Women's League in the Montgomery boycott and the Mothers' Marches in El Salvador. In other words, this oral tradition uses patriarchy to exonerate the disruption of the women's community. Such interpretations work against social justice preaching.

In 19:28, Jesus is reported as saying, "I am thirsty." In response, "they" give Jesus sour wine (v. 29). While the oral tradition for this statement has often focused on Jesus' humanity and how horrible the respondents are, the lesson of this exchange may be not to expect the oppressor to act other than oppressively. It could also be trying to teach us not to turn to the oppressor to save us from our problems, especially while they are killing us.

In Jesus' final statement, "It is finished" (v. 30), one cannot help but wonder what exactly "it" is. Is Jesus announcing that the revolution is over? Is his job completed? Or has one phase of the struggle come to an end while another will soon follow? The meaning of "it" is not clear, although much triumphalist preaching has asserted that through his crucifixion, Jesus has completed all that he set out to do.

There are many opportunities to address social justice concerns in the texts assigned to Good Friday. In accordance with the Servant Song of Isaiah 53, the Gospel reading describes the courts and governmental authorities as well as religious institutions working against revolutionaries. Amid these torturous circumstances, the Hebrews text attempts to move us away from the horrors of the lynching. These Scripture texts provide opportunities to address themes of betrayal, suffering, and injustice within the context of Jesus' experiences. Like many other martyrs, Jesus experienced not only trials and suffering but also death in pursuit of divine justice. In understanding his death in this way, we are confronted with the question, if I follow Jesus, should I expect that I will also suffer political and social rejection, not only from political institutions but also from religious institutions? "The cross before me," as the spiritual claims, makes us ask, am I willing to make the sacrifices to liberate my people from oppression? Or am I going to romanticize the crucifixion so that I don't have to struggle with understanding that discipleship means putting ourselves, our resources, and our lives on the line for the sake of opposing oppression?

Easter Day (Resurrection of Jesus)

Rhashell Hunter

JEREMIAH 31:1–6
PSALM 118:1–2, 14–24
ACTS 10:34–43
JOHN 20:1–18

This is the day of resurrection, freedom, and empowerment. At Easter, we celebrate Jesus' victory over the powers that enslave us, ushering in a new reign of justice and peace. In the Jeremiah passage, we see that God cares for and comforts those who are exiled. In the Psalter, we learn that one who was once rejected has become the chief cornerstone. In the Acts passage, we are reminded that "God shows no partiality." Arbitrary human categories have no significance in the realm of God. And, in the Gospel of John, the first woman preacher testifies as a witness to the resurrection. Mary Magdalene, told by Jesus to go and tell, shares the good news that Jesus is alive, and she offers her hearers the assurance that God is with them in life and in death.

Easter Sunday is an extraordinary day, even for the most sleep-deprived, overprepared (or underprepared) preacher. We are all together, expectantly waiting to relive, once again, the resurrection story. We come to hear the testimony of witnesses who proclaim that "Christ has risen, indeed." And we are reminded again that we have been given the gift of life eternal from a God whose love never ends.

Jeremiah 31:1–6

In the Jeremiah passage, the call that will bring the exiles back to Jerusalem is affirmed. As God promises to comfort and restore Israel, so God will care for and guide us, even when we are far from home.

Many years ago, I met a woman named Mona whose family fled Palestine during the war of 1948. They rushed out of their home so quickly that they left behind all of their personal effects when they fled to Jordan. When it was

193

safe for them to return, they did so, but there was another family living in their home. They knocked on the front door, and this family invited them inside. Mona saw her mother's tablecloth on the table and many of her family's belongings still in the home. The Jewish family who now inhabited the home said, "The government gave us this home." This family invited the Palestinian family to sit down, and they drank tea together in these bizarre and painful circumstances. One family was made up of refugees who had moved to a new country full of hope, and the other family was exiles who had returned home to find that they no longer had a home.

In Jeremiah 31, God promises restoration to the exiles, and we see themes of homecoming and joy. When people come home from exile and war, it is cause for celebration. But after the parades and parties are over, then the hard work of restoration begins. The second half of verse 13 reads, "I will turn their mourning into joy, I will comfort them, and give them gladness for sorrow." This kind of joy and gladness is felt only after experiencing great pain.

Both of these families experienced hardship and pain in their own ways, yet both were strengthened by their faith in God and the knowledge that God comforts and cares for those who are foreigners in a strange land as well as those who are exiled from the land they know and love. Just as God cared for, guided, and restored God's people many years ago, God will continue to care for refugees, exiles, and immigrants.

Psalm 118:1–2, 14–24

After being rejected, David became king. Likewise, Jesus, the carpenter from Galilee who was regarded by many as a stone that was unfit, became the perfect stone, laid at the corner of the Christian faith. Psalm 118:21–22 reads, "I thank you [God] that you have answered me and have become my salvation. The stone that the builders rejected has become the chief cornerstone."

Some of us know what it feels like to be thrown away. Some of us have felt discounted and have heard "You won't amount to much" or "You won't go very far." And some of us rise above and overcome the low expectations that others set for us. It is amazing when someone who no one thought would amount to much becomes an important part of the human story.

Around 1860, an African American baby in Missouri was kidnapped and sold into slavery when he was only a week old. He was ransomed by a slave owner and returned to Missouri, but he never saw his mother again. He learned to read and write but had difficulty continuing his education because African Americans were not allowed into schools where he lived. He was accepted to college but was later rejected when the school discovered that he was African American. He eventually attended other colleges, received numerous degrees, and became "one of the most thoroughly scientific men of the [African American] race," according to Booker T. Washington.[1]

The little child was George Washington Carver, who became a professor at Tuskegee Institute in Alabama. He established an agricultural school there that was important because many former slaves took up farming as a means of survival. Carver's devotion to God motivated him to use his knowledge to help those who were less fortunate and to feed those who were hungry. He empowered African Americans to become an integral part of the economy and helped Southern farmers to transform the agricultural economy by rotating cotton crops, which depleted the soil if cultivated year after year, with crops such as peanuts, sweet potatoes, and soybeans, helping to restore the soil. Carver discovered hundreds of ways of using peanut plants. His wisdom was sought by leaders in many nations and by people such as Mahatma Gandhi, Thomas Edison, and Henry Ford. Who would have guessed that one who was rejected would become so important?

It amazes us that God often selects those whom we see as inconsequential to lead us to new ways of living. Easter is a day filled with surprises, for it is startling that the One whom the world rejected and saw as useless became the chief cornerstone of our faith. Jesus Christ, seen by some as the stone to be discarded, has become the perfect One to usher in freedom and new life for all of God's people.

Acts 10:34–43

Readers of the Acts passage might imagine themselves in the crowd that day when Peter faced his own fears after being called by God to preach, and not just to his own people but to diverse people, whom God also wanted to hear the good news of the gospel. When Peter arrived in Caesarea, a group of family and friends had assembled at the home of Cornelius and waited to hear what Peter had to say.

The crowd was gathered, and it was time for the sermon to begin. Peter said, "I truly understand that God shows no partiality, but in every nation anyone who fears [God] and does what is right is acceptable to [God]" (vv. 34–35). The *Good News Bible* (TEV) reads, "Whoever fears [God] and does what is right is acceptable to [God], no matter what race [they belong] to" (v. 35). This is Peter preaching for social justice. "God is impartial" is his message, or literally, "God accepts no one's face." In other words, it doesn't matter how you look. Your gender, your social status, your income and assets

---

1. Booker T. Washington, *My Larger Education: Being Chapters from My Experience* (Garden City, NY: Doubleday, Page & Co., 1911), 224. Booker T. Washington was the leader of Tuskegee Institute in Alabama.

do not correlate with your value. Something as arbitrary as hair texture, skin color, or other physical features are not criteria for judging others in the realm of God.

We live our lives, in the North American context, concerned about such things as race and ethnicity, immigration status, political affiliations, economic status, sexual orientation, and physical appearance. But Christ has redeemed us, and we are all sisters and brothers in Christ. Christ's action is the great equalizer. Peter Gomes, the minister of the Harvard Memorial Church, wrote, "Life begins when you realize that by removing the fear of death, Christ has given you, for the first time, full possession of your own life."[2] This is what Easter is about. It is a chance to claim the power of God present in our own lives and to live fully, without blaming others for our circumstances and without living in fear.

John 20:1–18

In the Gospel of John, Mary Magdalene is the first person to see Jesus after he has risen from the dead. Jesus said to her, "Go to my brothers [and sisters] and say to them, 'I am ascending . . . to my God and your God.'" Then "Mary Magdalene went and announced to the disciples, 'I have seen the Lord'; and she told them that he had said these things to her." Jesus issued Mary's call: "Go and tell," he said. "Go and preach!" And the Bible says, "[She] went." So, Mary becomes the apostle to the apostles, as her call is to go and proclaim the resurrection of the Lord to the other disciples. She becomes the first preacher to proclaim the resurrection of Jesus Christ (vv. 17–18).

Unlike the Western church, the Eastern church never erroneously associated Mary with the woman who was a repentant sinner (Luke 7:36–48). Church scholarship has corrected this linkage, as there is no evidence to identify Mary Magdalene with the woman from the city who anointed Jesus' feet. In Eastern Christianity, Mary was never thought to be a prostitute but was considered to be a disciple of Jesus who preached about Jesus' resurrection from the dead. Of course, the resurrection really mattered to those who had lost their friend Jesus Christ. Resurrection was not just an academic question. It was intensely personal. It gave them hope, the promise of eternal life, and the belief that they would see Jesus again.

It is hard to understand how important it is to preach about resurrection at times of death unless you have experienced the death of a dear loved one. I preach better resurrection messages since my father and mother died, because death, new life, and resurrection are now real to me. I am reassured by the fact

---

2. Peter Gomes, *Sermons* (New York: William Morrow, 1998), 76–77.

that my parents put their faith completely in God, who they knew would be with them in life and in death. They put their trust in Jesus, who became one of us, sharing in our sufferings and giving himself for the life of the world. In Christ's death, we recognize that there is nowhere we can go where our faithful protector has not preceded us. In Christ's resurrection we are freed from fear, and we experience the power of God to overcome hatred, injustice, and even death. This is the good news that we proclaim on Easter and every Sunday: not even death separates us from the love of God in Christ Jesus, our Lord.

It is out of the deep reservoir of our faith in Jesus Christ that we experience hope. And, as preachers of God's Word, we proclaim God's transforming justice to those who are rejected or exiled and those who are at the empty tomb this Easter Sunday, looking for Jesus. The effective proclaimer of the Word would do well to dig down deep and share her or his faith this Easter. Why does it matter? It matters because we need to hear the promise, God's promise of an inheritance in the reign of God. And we need to experience God's love, a love that never ends. With God's help, we will celebrate another glorious Easter Sunday, and through the reliving of God's Word, we will be offered a foretaste of the feast to come!

Second Sunday of Easter

Olive Elaine Hinnant

ACTS 2:14A, 22–32
PSALM 16
1 PETER 1:3–9
JOHN 20:19–31

Other than the Sunday after Christmas, the Sunday after Easter reflects the lowest attendance in the church year. Easter—the celebration of the resurrection of Jesus—is over, and along with the drooping lilies and empty chocolate boxes, there are only echoes of alleluias ringing in our ears. Yet the Second Sunday of Easter includes key passages about the meaning of Christ's resurrection for the future. While we spend a lot of effort celebrating the day of resurrection, how often do we consider what it means for our lives and our churches? The Gospel reading from John 20, a Johannine Pentecost, if you will, is included in all three years of the lectionary. In the text, the resurrected Jesus offers his mantle to the gathered disciples who are hiding. A mantle of peace, the Holy Spirit, and forgiveness define his mission and ministry. The disciples, and we, are to go and do likewise. The other three readings for this Sunday stress the importance of Jesus' resurrection and the hope that it engenders in his followers. These particular texts line up in a way that can renew our souls for the work we do in the world.

Acts 2:14a, 22–32

Peter tries to do the impossible. Amid excitement and confusion on the day of Pentecost, he tries to explain the purpose of Jesus' resurrection to a crowd who have just witnessed what seems to some a drunken rendezvous. He draws significantly on what will be familiar to this Jewish audience, the Prophets and Psalms. Just prior to these verses, Peter quotes the prophet Joel, who speaks of God's Spirit being poured out on all flesh, both women and men, both young and old. Beginning in verse 22, Peter reminds those present that

198

they saw and perhaps even experienced the wonders and miracles of Jesus of Nazareth, who came on behalf of God. Although "some of you delivered him unto death," Peter continues, "he did not stay dead." Peter employs Psalm 16, attributing it to David, to convince the hearers that indeed this prayer is meant to foreshadow the "Holy One," Jesus, and that his death and resurrection were prophesied. The purpose of this is to connect his Jewish audience with Jesus the Jewish messiah. For those of us who have never experienced such a transforming event (including many postmodern listeners), this is too pat an answer to the deeper question of who this resurrected Jesus is. We are left to wonder, "What does this mean for us? Who is this God who can raise the dead to life again?"

Peter attempts the impossible by explaining the resurrection. Preachers who follow his lead are likely to spend more time explaining what this means instead of offering something more valuable, such as witnessing to the fullness of life in God's presence. We may not be able to explain the mystery of God's resurrection power, but we can speak of God's power to overcome even death and find meaning in God's life-giving purposes.

Psalm 16

This is a psalm about confidence! Someone in ancient Israel held fast to God and because of this found "fullness of joy" (v. 11). Scholars do not agree on who wrote Psalm 16 or when it was written, but it speaks powerfully to diverse eras and contexts. Whether or not the author was facing imminent death or peril, all of us are familiar with fear and the need for security and protection. Thus it is a prayer that could be spoken by people of different faith traditions in need of safety. Originally, this psalm was not meant to name Jesus as the "Holy One" or the resurrected one. But for the psalmist, living in the presence of God brought meaning to all of life. The author trusts God, whether it is for this life or a future inheritance.

Claiming God as "refuge" does not, in our day, hold the same meaning as for those who heard this prayer in ancient Israel. In their time, a city of refuge was a real place where people could go to be protected from anyone who pursued them, even if they had murdered someone. This place of refuge protected the person until a resolution to the situation could be decided by the community. Everyone had to keep their hands off of the accused or the endangered person until a determination was made and justice could be rendered. By insisting that God is a city of refuge, the psalmist broadens the location and meaning of this concept beyond tribal and regional locations.

Today there are a growing number of refuge communities, as evidenced by four examples. More than twenty years ago in San Francisco, a church called

City of Refuge was created to serve the lesbian, gay, bisexual, transgendered, queer, and questioning community who had not found a welcoming church.[1] A church called Scum of the Earth was formed in downtown Denver by those considered outcasts in society—punks, skaters, homeless people, and drug addicts—who are aware of their need for God.[2] Paul in 1 Corinthians 4:11–13 uses "scum of the earth" to describe those persecuted because of their faith. A mainline denomination, Evangelical Lutheran Church of America, has a new local congregation called A House for All Sinners and Saints. Their description of their endeavor to be the church includes the words "liturgical, Christo-centric, social justice oriented, queer inclusive, incarnational, contemplative, irreverent, ancient."[3] Finally, there is The Unchurch for those who no longer see the traditional church as an option. Formed in 2009, this gathering in Colorado Springs, Colorado, is made up of progressive, postmodern, and emergent Christians grappling with new forms of what it means to be church.[4]

1 Peter 1:3–9

Dated to the latter half of the first century, this epistle written in Peter's name is addressed to the "elect," those chosen or destined by God for salvation. This portion of the letter focuses on the hope that the resurrection brings. It offers assurance that the resurrection provides a reservation for believers in heaven while it also exhorts readers and hearers to rejoice in spite of trials they may be suffering. Exalting genuine faith over precious gold, the author continues to encourage their faith in Jesus Christ, even though they have not seen Jesus themselves. These believers dispersed throughout Asia Minor could have been facing any number of trials—civil pressure for their beliefs, Jewish opposition to the new faith community, scarcity of resources, or internal disputes.

The author of this pastoral letter is determined to comfort those who are suffering when the writer cannot be there in person, sending an uplifting message to as many people as possible in a rather hurried manner.

Communicating comfort and hope to people who are suffering throughout the world can now happen instantly through Internet social sites, e-mails, and text messages. A short message can reach one or even one billion people at a time. We can encourage one another in our faith in God with messages of Christ's resurrection in numerous ways and, like believers scattered

1. http://www.sfrefuge.org.
2. http://www.scumoftheearth.net.
3. http://houseforall.org.
4. http://unchurchcs.com.

throughout Asia Minor, words of encouragement are no doubt reaching people we had never imagined.

One such example of encouraging communication involves a specific population of people. It is a recovery smartphone used by people with drug and alcohol addictions who are hard of hearing or deaf. While cell phones are used in the hearing community for the same purpose, as are twelve-step meetings, people with hearing loss need a specific way to interact with others in recovery. Communication on this device provides quick uplifting messages at times when people in recovery are vulnerable and in need of encouragement. It connects a person directly to a sponsor who can respond by instant messaging. The phone also operates like a GPS device by locating and finding directions for local Alcoholics Anonymous or Narcotics Anonymous meetings. A text message between people in the AA or NA program keeps them focused on the twelve steps when they are tempted to revert to old behaviors.[5]

Imagine the ways we can spread encouragement and hope in the face of suffering throughout our neighborhoods and the world!

John 20:19–31

This section of John's Gospel follows Mary Magdalene's encounter with Jesus in the garden, near the empty tomb. On this resurrection day, Jesus instructs Mary to go tell the disciples that she has seen the Lord and that he has spoken "these things to her" (v. 18). Had the disciples listened to Mary that day, perhaps Jesus would not have had to pay them a visit later when they were hiding behind locked doors. The text says they were living in "fear of the Jews" (v. 19). It seems reasonable that they would be afraid of religious leaders who pursued Jesus' friends and followers. But they must not have taken Mary's message to heart. What did it mean to them to hear that Jesus had come back from the dead, in bodily form? Apparently nothing, until he returned through locked doors and showed them his wounded hands and side and they could see for themselves. Until he says, "Peace be with you," and breathes on them, saying, "Receive the Holy Spirit" (vv. 21–22), they are not confident to return to a world that has killed their friend. Jesus is here to tell them to go back out into the world. He tells them, "If you forgive the sins of any, they are forgiven them, but if you retain the sins of any, they are retained" (v. 23). Is Jesus saying that the central message he brings is one of forgiveness—a place of refuge?

The next scene involves Thomas, the twin. He was not hiding out with the disciples when Jesus came to visit the first time. Does this suggest that he

---

5. Michael Booth, "Smartphone Tackles Addiction," *Denver Post*, December 22, 2011.

was out in the world, unafraid of death? When he is told about Jesus' bodily appearance and his wounds, Thomas wants to see for himself. Just as the disciples had not really believed Mary's report, Thomas wants his own viewing, his own moment with Jesus. The attitude "I am not going to believe it until I see it for myself" seems to be a human trait, fitting for a museum, but not for a movement. The purpose of Jesus' visit is not to gain more visitors for Ripley's Believe It or Not Museum, but to let them experience this resurrection power in their own lives and to know the only place of refuge, of safety, is in God's presence. He wants the disciples to go show this to others.

Remaining in the museum, in hiding, they will only wallow in their fear and lose sight of the purpose of their lives. Surely they are likely to face losses just as Jesus did: losses of family, friends, reputation, peace of mind, physical health, even death. But according to Jesus, his presence among them demonstrates that he not only has faced all of this but also has overcome death itself.

While we are often inclined to focus on Jesus' sacrifice of his life, the resurrection suggests he also sacrificed his death. He did not remain comfortably gone, out of sight or behind stone barriers. His death and resurrection may be understood in a new light:

> Let's face it: death has been done before. Anyone can die. Jesus revolutionized creation because he had the nerve it took not to remain dead. Christ went beyond sacrificing his life. He sacrificed his death. He voluntarily let go of the comfort of death and fought to rise above the grave. The hardest thing we can do is not to die, but to live, and to live abundantly in joy.[6]

Overcoming dead places in our life and society, we can depend on the Holy Spirit to guide us in creating cities of refuge where people can know the presence of God. It time for us to leave our hiding places and return to the world.

---

6. Jack Pantaleo, "The Opened Tomb," *The Other Side* 28, no. 2 (March–April 1992), 8. Pantaleo is a gay man who survived being raped by a stranger. During his recovery, and with the support of friends, he wrote about what it has taken for him not to stay in a "dead place."

Third Sunday of Easter

María Teresa Dávila

Acts 2:14a, 36–41
Psalm 116:1–4, 12–19
1 Peter 1:17–23
Luke 24:13–35

"Were not our hearts burning within us while he was talking to us on the road?" Today's narratives capture our imagination in profound ways. They demand our full attention, drawing from our own experiences of fear and hope, desperation and succor, suffering and reconciliation. They confront believers with the vulnerability of human reason in the face of resurrection. Our deepest desire to believe in the risen Christ and all that this entails for our proclamation of the kingdom is dampened by the frailty of our senses and our personal and social suffering. The readings for this Third Sunday of Easter present the surprising ways in which God's liberation challenges the limitations of our senses to fully understand the new reality of the good news for all proclaimed in the resurrected Christ. With the psalmist we question whether our response adequately witnesses to God's just actions and how these continually transform our reality; with the author of 1 Peter we seek to understand the possibilities of being purified for love of God and each other; with the nascent Christian community we ask for the transforming presence of the Spirit to dwell among us; and with the disciples we excitedly but cautiously whisper to one another, "Are not our hearts burning within us?"

Luke 24:13–35

The story of the disciples walking on the road to Emmaus recalls the story of salvation: it describes how a downtrodden people hoped for a savior and interpreted salvation, and the surprising ways that God delivers salvation and a kingdom in which to live out this new reality. The narrative is intimate. The characters are few but the exchanges are ultimately formative for the church.

Salvation and liberation are presented in a way that touches our own desire for embodied commitment to God's kingdom within history. In the intimate setting of hospitality, storytelling, and a shared meal, we discover the resurrection as true transformation. Through this story our hearts are able to see history as a stage filled with many possibilities in God rather than the battle field of human egoism.

Every effort at liberation and dismantling structures of oppression and injustice may parallel the disciples' sorrow and defeatism as they leave Jerusalem. In verses 13–16 they discuss the events of the past few days, trying to place them in the context of suffering and subjugation at the hands of imperial powers and amid their hopes for a messiah/liberator. Their sense of loss keeps them from seeing that a third person has joined them. Jesus asks, "What are you discussing with each other while you walk along?" (v. 17). Not recognizing him, they describe the important events that have transpired. Theirs is the story of hopes dashed and dreams of liberation torn. They speak of "the things" of Jesus the Nazarene, how they had hoped he would redeem Israel, but he had been sentenced to death and crucified. The story they tell is the story of countless martyrs for justice and liberation. To speak of the things of Gandhi, of Martin Luther King Jr., Dietrich Bonhoeffer, Oscar Romero, Maura Clarke, Ita Ford, and Dorothy Kazel is to speak of the things of Jesus the Nazarene.

The disciples, however, are too overwhelmed to think beyond their pain. The story of the women who went to the tomb earlier that morning, returning with stories of angelic visions and resurrection, does not lift their spirits but adds to their despair (vv. 22–23). Jesus proceeds to interpret the events that have occurred and places them in the context of the story of salvation from Moses and the prophets. However, it is in the intimate act of hospitality and breaking bread together that their eyes are opened to the presence of the risen Christ among them. Formative to many communities' practices of faith, hope, and love is the expression found in verse 35: "Then they told . . . how he had been made known to them in the breaking of the bread." Although Jesus is gone the moment they recognize him (v. 31), they are left with an imprint of the resurrection in their hearts: *"Were not our hearts burning within us while he was talking to us on the road?"* (v. 32). It is this imprint—the experience of the resurrection—that becomes transformational in our lives and the most important tool for our work toward the fulfillment of God's kingdom in history.

This narrative does not have the disciples receiving special powers or performing extraordinary signs. Rather, the pair are transformed in their internal dispositions toward their lived history, a transformation that will move them to witness to the risen Christ in word and deed. The truth of the resurrection empowers the disciples to proclaim the liberation of the spirit, to speak the truth about God's will for life and reconciliation for those who suffer unjustly, for those subjected to unjust execution. A burning heart enlivened by the resurrection, received in the intimacy and hospitality of breaking bread with others, is the gift that awaits us in retelling the stories of martyrs in our time, the bearers of our hope, and our dreams for a kingdom fulfilled.

Acts 2:14a, 36–41

The emerging community, gathered days after the events described in Luke 24, receives the Holy Spirit in a dramatic scene recounted in the first half of Acts 2. In its entirety, Acts records the historical establishment of the church as a community grounded in the resurrected Christ, bonded and empowered by the Spirit, and commissioned to evangelize in God's name. Quoting the prophet Joel, the intervening verses show Peter explaining the role of the Spirit as inspiration, guide, and motivation for the new reality of this emerging community (vv. 17–21). He recounts the life of Jesus in a theological context, how his life and witness were ordained by God from the beginning, his unjust crucifixion, and his defeat of death. Peter carefully relates Jesus in this new context to the religious framework with which the Jerusalem Jews are familiar. Our particular passage has Peter closing his speech in verse 36, asking his listeners to acknowledge their role in the unjust death of him who is "both Lord and Christ." His audience is taken aback by his story and yearns to know what to do. Peter preaches repentance and baptism in the name of Jesus Christ. At the closing of Peter's speech we are presented the wonderful picture of the conversion of everyone present, numbering in the thousands.

This passage includes both a promise and a caution that should ground and shape the work of justice and liberation in our communities. This community that quickly converts thousands lives under the direct effect of the Spirit of God. The drama of Pentecost sets the stage for the growth of the community and the wonderful signs that would accompany the evangelizing mission of the disciples. The promise of the resurrection is that God's Spirit will accompany our efforts to establish the kingdom, our desires to share everything in common just as the early community did, so that everyone's basic needs are met. The caution revealed in this passage gains importance as our efforts to build communities of justice, care, and love of neighbor increasingly cross the boundaries of different faith traditions. The author presents salvation in terms that would make sense to a Jewish audience: repentance of sin and following in God's ways. Peter's speech places the righteousness of the new community in contrast to the sin of those who put Jesus to death on the cross. Those who are not baptized into Christ are therefore judged as complicit in this crime. This temptation to define our righteous cause in terms that negate other groups is ever present in our work for justice. We therefore define the religious "other" as sinners who are unwelcome in the eyes of God. Even the early Christian community, having been blessed with the presence of the Spirit at Pentecost, could not escape our deepest instincts to vilify the other. The consequence of this practice is the justification of further violence. Finally, vilifying the religious other causes Peter to lose sight of the common struggle of the emerging church and the Jewish people, that of fighting the imperial powers of Rome that saw executions of innocent and guilty alike as a way to both maintain order and provide sport.

Psalm 116:1–4, 12–19 and 1 Peter 1:17–23

In the deepest and darkest moments, when death seems to have an unshakable hold on life, the psalmist witnesses to having called on God and being delivered by God's mercy. How does one witness to such an experience of salvation? The psalmist catalogs the suffering endured at the hand of others. The experience of salvation and liberation becomes more pronounced when one is aware of the injustices suffered. This is to be made public, not just in private religious practices, but also in the presence of all people. Like our services to remember victims of domestic violence or a litany of those who have disappeared under a brutal regime, the public proclamation of suffering serves the purpose of proclaiming our deepest desire for and trust in God's liberation. The psalmist acknowledges that our dangerous memories have their place in our religious narratives, including our liturgies and days of remembrances, because these enliven our imagination of God's redemptive activity and our participation in it.

The psalmist speaks of God having loosed his bonds (v. 16b). Is it possible that this represents a person from a lower social status? Someone perhaps outside the circles of religious and political power? Is his witnessing to God's liberation in history going to disturb the religious establishment of the time? Who else will be inspired by this witness to liberation? The Arab Spring of 2011 saw thousands of citizens crying out for the justice that had eluded them through decades of dictatorship, oppression often cloaked in the guise of sacred sanctions. In the fall of 2011, U.S. cities witnessed the outpouring of the 99 percent, demanding that economic justice be measured by how the least among us fare in our society. Our witnessing to the activity of the Spirit for the realization of the kingdom is a dangerous word, so dangerous that our deepest dreams for liberation and transformation, even though repeatedly dashed, rise again by the grace of a liberating and just God. These texts that echo the disciples' sorrow and subsequent surprise at the risen Christ, and the psalmist's witness of the journey from oppression to redemption, keep the paradox of Easter alive in our hearts and imaginations.

In 1 Peter 1: 23 we are told that we have been born anew, "through the living and enduring word of God." This letter addressed to communities suffering distress and persecution for their beliefs reminds the faithful that salvation has come in the form of one who himself suffered great iniquity. The suffering of Christ is placed in the context of God's redemption of all suffering, the consequence of which is that we are remade with a pure heart for sincere and mutual love. In this time of sojourning, when the movement of peoples in the universal quest for life confronts us all with our identity as migrants journeying toward the kingdom of God, it becomes even more important that we witness to the rightful living of those transformed by the death and resurrection of Jesus. Today the violent status quo is often accepted as the way things must be in a fallen creation. However, the author of this letter suggests that we are to live as people who are already members and participants in God's kingdom, regardless of the length or hardship of the journey. Our active quest for justice, truth, peace, and expressions of love witnesses to God's liberating work. It is proclaimed by the psalmist and is the only just response to God's saving activity among us.

Earth Day (April 22)

John Hart

Genesis 1:1–2:4a
Psalm 19:1–6
Romans 8:18–23
Matthew 6:25–34

The Revised Common Lectionary does not contain a season or a Sunday that focuses on the natural world. Earth Day (April 22) can help fill this void. Organizers began Earth Day in 1970 to call attention to the growing ecological crisis, focusing on such things as pollution, using up nonrenewable resources, and creating waste that threatens the survival of the environment. Earth Day gives the minister an opportunity to help the congregation think about a theology of the natural world, about how to become better stewards of the Earth, and about honoring the integrity of all created things.[1] Since Earth Day often takes place in the season of Easter, the preacher could suggest that from the apocalyptic point of view, the resurrection of Jesus points to the regeneration of Earth as well as the whole cosmos.

The Creator put us here to take care of this part of the world. The caribou were created alongside our people; the caribou retain part of the Gwich'in heart, and Gwich'in retain part of the caribou heart. The coastal plain of the Arctic National Wildlife Refuge is where the Porcupine Caribou Herd goes to give birth every spring. . . . We call this area "the sacred place where life began." We won't go there to hunt even if we are starving—some people want to go there for six months' worth of oil.

Sarah James[2]

---

1. Contemporary Christian ecotheology/ethics writers often capitalize "Earth" when referring to the planet. This promotes respect for our planet, aligns capitalization with other planets, and distinguishes planet Earth from earth, the soil of Earth.
2. Sarah James, a leader of the Gwich'in native people, Arctic Village, Alaska (reported from the fieldwork of David Radcliff, director of New Community Project).

In 1970, Earth Day's founders envisioned a day on which, every year, people would be reminded that Earth was experiencing trauma from human actions. Earth needed humankind to respond with efforts to change human consciousness and conduct. People's *consciousness* had to be changed from regarding Earth as merely a source of "resources" available to meet human needs and gratify human wants, to seeing Earth as a sensitive planet to be respected as a provider of natural goods and a nurturer of the living beings who share Earth as their common home. People's *conduct* had to be changed from irresponsible and harmful adaptation of Earth to human wants, to responsible and harmonious adaptation of human individual and community lives to the rhythms of Earth.

Over time, people of faith came to adopt Earth Day as their own, with a new twist: Earth is viewed not as just a planet in the universe, but as a local, revelatory place within God's ongoing, expanding creation. Earth is a sacred or sacramental commons—the locus of divine creativity, permeated by God's immanent, solicitous presence. Earth is to provide natural goods for the sustenance of people and all life. Christians realize that Earth's goods are not "resources," a term that implies they await human extraction and use, but "natural goods" that benefit biota (living creatures) and serve a role where they are in creation. Part of the dynamic geological or evolutionary biological processes of Earth, they may be respectfully taken and responsibly altered by human labor to meet human needs; sufficient goods are to remain in place to provide for other creatures' needs.

Genesis 1:1–2:4a

Consideration of Earth as a divine creation led to reconsideration of and reflection on the implications of biblical teachings related to human-Earth and human-biota relationships. The Genesis 1 creation story (1:1–2:4a) teaches that everything that exists emerges from divine creativity, from which flows the laws inherent in the universe and discovered over centuries by scientists, and in which occur random events that interact with these laws; their encounter produces ever more complex and diverse biotic (living) and abiotic (nonliving) beings. In biblical teachings too, everything that God creates is "very good," and humankind, the "image of God," is to recognize the goodness of all creatures and responsibly ensure that Earth and all biota retain or have restored their "very good" status wherever human conduct has altered it. People should care not only for themselves, but for all life and for Earth.

These themes recur in the flood story in Genesis 6–9. Noah is told by God to save not just his family on the ark, but a reproducing pair of all living creatures; and after the flood, God makes a covenant, signified by the rainbow, not just with people but with every living creature and with Earth.

The teaching that humans as God's "images" should sustain Earth responsibly has profound implications for human life and conduct on Earth Day and throughout the year. When people fulfill creation care as "images of God," they strive to restore creation to the balance and beauty it had naturally by divine command, before humans altered it for better or worse. A beautiful Earth is more transparent to and revelatory of divine love, creativity, and solicitude. Earth that is carefully conserved can be aesthetically pleasing in its own right and recognized as a provider for the needs of all biota. Earth can be, too, a mediation of God's immanence that invites human engagement with divine presence.

Psalm 19:1–6

Psalm 19:1–6 expresses this well. It sings about how the heavens tell of God's glory, a telling not expressed in speech but whose voice and words nevertheless go throughout Earth and are heard by the Creator. It sings, too, of the function of the sun to provide heat and light, beginning when it emerges daily from its divinely created "tent," and as it runs its course from one end of the heavens to the other. Nothing can hide from its heat. The psalmist and all people of faith have been grateful for the life-giving role of the sun as it interacts with all of Earth.

In the last few decades, however, people have become aware of the extent to which human extraction and production processes have changed the life-giving power of the sun into a death-dealing power. Emissions from factories, motor vehicles, and energy plants endanger biota across the planet. Humans have at least exacerbated, if not caused, dramatic increases in the amount of the sun's radiation that reaches Earth and provides heat, to the extent that global warming is occurring at rates not seen before in human, biotic, or geologic history. Global extinctions of species are rapidly accelerating. Drought and forest fires, massive thunderstorms and floods are killing people and other biota, destroying farms and communities, and endangering food production and distribution. Melting ice in Antarctica, the Arctic, and Greenland, and an increased volume of water in seas and oceans because of increased heat (thermal expansion) are causing beaches, homes, farmlands, and even entire communities—as in the Pacific Islands and Alaska—to be washed away. As the United Nations, global scientists, and church bodies including the National Council of Churches, the World Council of Churches, the United States Conference of Catholic Bishops, the Vatican, and the National Association of Evangelicals all have stated, it is the poor of the world who are being and will be most impacted by the effects of global warming. While the psalmist celebrated that nothing can hide from the sun's heat, religious people today are concerned about enhanced solar warmth.

Another form of energy generation, nuclear power plants, has been suggested as a replacement for carbon-emitting coal plants. However, the nuclear option has already contaminated soils, food, and human lungs, as witnessed most dramatically by the disastrous nuclear events at Three Mile Island in Pennsylvania (1979), Chernobyl in the Ukraine (1986), and Fukushima in Japan (2011); nuclear pollution is less apparent and public in the uranium mining practices that pollute groundwater through drilling into Earth. Also, nuclear wastes from power plants have a life of thousands of years and are still in temporary storage sites. Geologically unstable places have been proposed for "permanent" storage, thereby passing nuclear dangers on to future generations.

In order to celebrate the sun's benefits, then, Christians must dedicate themselves to consume less, conserve more, and construct alternative energy-generating facilities. Advances in solar power technologies to provide electricity and heat have been dramatic in recent decades and are now less expensive. States like California, Texas, and Montana now have significant electrical generation of electricity from the sun's light. Use of solar light can become a way to reduce the impact of solar heat. Wind power's promise, too, has dramatically increased. However, the power of the oil corporations has prevented sufficient government support for this budding industry.

Romans 8:18–23

The psalmist's ideas, and Christians' concerns about contemporary events related to them, are complemented by Paul's insights in his Letter to the Romans (8:18–23). After observing that suffering in this life does not compare with the coming glory, Paul notes that creation, too, is suffering. It is awaiting responsible human conduct, since human sinfulness has caused significant problems for the Earth: creation "waits with eager longing" for God's children to be seen; creation is under bondage awaiting its freedom from human harm, and someday "will obtain the freedom of the glory of the children of God"—that is, all creation will be free once more. All creation, in fact, has "been groaning in labor pains until now," trying to give birth to a new creation. Paul declares that not only creation in general, but humanity in particular—"we ourselves, who have the first fruits of the Spirit," also "groan inwardly while we wait for adoption, the redemption of our bodies" (v. 23). In light of the celebration of biotic and abiotic being in Genesis 1 and Psalm 19, and the contrasting impacts of human sinfulness expressed in greed and abuse of Earth's goods, people should become solicitous of the well-being of Earth and all Earth's creatures. We must be faithful to our calling as "images of God": to express respect for all life; to benefit ourselves and our children through our conduct; and to progress toward the coming "glory" Paul envisioned.

Matthew 6:25–34

According to this passage from the Sermon on the Mount, people who trust in God and do God's will need not be fearful: "Do not worry about your life, what you will eat or what you will drink, or about your body, what you will wear" (v. 25). Jesus teaches that just as God provides for the birds of the air and the lilies of the field, God will provide for people, too, if they live responsibly on God's land. Jesus' followers are instructed to strive first for God's kingdom and righteousness, and all these other things will also be given. In relation to considerations raised earlier, this righteousness would include being faithful images of God who care about and for Earth and Earth's creatures, and responsibly use Earth's natural goods to meet everyone's needs. Such careful use of natural goods, and compassionate sharing with neighbors in need, would today and into the future reduce global warming and promote the life-giving properties of unpolluted air, pure water, and productive soil.

People should, as Jesus states in Matthew 6:24, serve God, not Mammon (wealth). In the present age, people demand more and more consumer goods to meet their needs, give them apparent security, and provide them with status symbols of well-being and affluence. However, the greed and heartlessness characteristic of a single-minded focus on acquiring material things reveal life in the service of Mammon, not in the service of God. Christians are called to stop defining themselves by the presence and power of possessions. Rolex watches, diamond rings, and other unnecessary material objects are not just signs of conspicuous consumption; they are also the result of mining practices in the United States, Africa, South America, and other parts of the world, where Earth is polluted, rivers are poisoned, workers are harmed, and native populations are forced from their lands and murdered physically and culturally.

Christians should ask themselves, as they contrast their current consumerist consciousness and conduct with biblical teachings: How many exploited children must die from malnutrition and labor with little or no pay before Christians say "Enough!" and work to help them? How many poor folk will have to continue to buy food that was grown and preserved with harmful chemicals because that is all they can afford before Christian communities intercede to ensure the availability of healthy food? How many oil wells must be drilled on land and in sea before Christians address how coal plants and gas-guzzling cars exacerbate global warming and pollution, threatening life on Earth? Gwich'in leader Sarah James describes above how oil companies, supported by politicians, seek to drill for oil in Alaska's Arctic National Wildlife Refuge, which is not only a refuge for animals, but also a food and cultural resource for the Gwich'in, the "people of the caribou." Drilling in the Porcupine Caribou Herd breeding area would cause extinction of caribou and culture, and dislocation of people whose ancestral artifacts have been dated back more than ten millennia—all for about six months' worth of oil at current consumption rates. In Alaska, the caribou and all biota that would be harmed by drilling and transporting oil, and Earth itself, are groaning now in fear of what human sinfulness—betrayal of the human responsibility to "image" God—will do if drilling is permitted. They are longing, with Paul, for the "freedom of the children of God."

Earth Day—Creation Day—calls for changes in people's consciousness and conduct that will enable us to truly "image" God's solicitous care for God's creation and creatures, and renew the face of God's Earth.

Fourth Sunday of Easter

Scott C. Williamson

ACTS 2:42–47
PSALM 23
1 PETER 2:19–25
JOHN 10:1–10

The lectionary readings for this week describe how the early church interpreted the fellowship that God intends for people of faith. Grounded in God, the community of believers practices right living as they practice public worship, ensuring that each household and every person has the necessary provisions for the day. Giving to each according to need is a measure of right living and the cornerstone of God's economy.[1]

The readings also help us to address some particularly thorny problems of fellowship, discussed below. How does the fellowship evaluate competing standards of justice? How does the fellowship handle social and economic inequality? Further, how does the fellowship of believers adjudicate the contentious disputes that arise over ethnic and cultural differences?

Acts 2:42–47

Communal life for the first converts was a vibrant and tumultuous affair. Peter's vibrant preaching added thousands of new converts in a single day (Acts 2:41). This great evangelistic success supports Luke's claim that the earliest Christians did indeed experience joy-filled fellowship characterized by sharing, generosity, praise, worship, goodwill toward all people, and breaking bread together (vv. 42–47). Communal life also had its share of contention. Take the case of Ananias, who sold a piece of property but failed to share all of the proceeds with the community (5:1–11). Or consider the conflict

---

1. The Greek word *oikos*, translated as "house," is the root of economy. "Economy" refers to God's method of governing the created order.

brewing between Greek-speaking and Aramaic-speaking Jewish Christians over the daily distribution of food to Hellenistic widows (6:1–6). These passages indicate that greed no less than social and cultural difference presented troubling issues that undermined the fellowship from the time of the first converts. Nevertheless, these tensions did not slow the rapid growth of the early Christian community. Both accounts of community—the rapidly growing, joy-filled fellowship and the conflicts of a less-than-perfect fellowship—provide a richer description than either account alone.

The common life of the earliest Christians was formed within a rich matrix of teaching, praying, sharing, and eating together. Doing justice did not require the faithful to perform herculean feats of generosity. Rather, doing justice came through meeting the daily needs of one's neighbors.

The standard of right living in Acts 2:45, "to all, as any had need," squares a contemporary moral norm. A more appropriate standard for today might be "to *some* according to need." This new standard makes the old one largely irrelevant to right living, and sets sharp parameters around charity. Instead of valuing our shared humanity or extending goodwill to all, the new standard esteems rights of individual conscience over the needs of our neighbors.

Recently, a graduate student in counseling at Eastern Michigan University (EMU) was dismissed from her program because she refused to counsel a gay man about his same-sex relationship.[2] The student claimed that she was wrongly expelled by EMU's Department of Counseling and Education because supervisors objected to the Christian beliefs she expressed about the impropriety of homosexuality and same-sex relationships. She asked that the client be referred to another student counselor. EMU argued in court that the student's religious beliefs about homosexuality and same-sex marriage did not trump the ethical obligation of a counselor to not discriminate against clients on the basis of sexual orientation. In March 2010 the federal district court in the Eastern District of Michigan rejected the school's motion to dismiss the case.

The legal matter here concerns constitutional rights to free speech and free exercise of religion. The heart of the moral matter, however, is whether "to all, as any had need" compels Christians to extend neighbor-love too broadly and indiscriminately. If individual conscience dictates the parameters of care and the extent of neighbor-love, then conscience effectively separates the wheat from the chaff, and it is left up to individuals to establish the identity of those beloved persons for whom Jesus died.

2. "Rights of Conscience vs. Civil Rights," Pew Research Center Publications, June 3, 2010.

Psalm 23

The Twenty-third Psalm is a beloved hymn of trust in God's providential care. Followers are as vulnerable to harm as sheep are vulnerable to the attack of predators. Nevertheless the faithful celebrate the goodness and loving-kindness of a God who guards them from harm, guides them to abundant life, sustains them by meeting their daily needs, and comforts them during times of trial. God is the good shepherd. The good shepherd is distinguished from shepherds who have ulterior motives or self-serving agendas that cause them to treat the flock as a commodity for personal gain. These wolves in shepherd's clothing would devour the flock, but the good shepherd is committed to the well-being of the flock.

Two instruments help God to guard and guide the flock. The rod is an instrument, like a club, used to guard the flock by fending off predator attacks. The staff is a long stick that is used to guide the flock by keeping the sheep together.

In light of the lectionary readings for this week, the image of the staff alludes to God's work at holding the church together. The church faces many pressing moral issues and the danger of disunity. Issues around the extent of our obligation to meet our neighbor's needs are generating not only political division within the church but also theological division.

A generation ago, H. Richard Niebuhr warned the church about the danger of henotheism, and we are wise to remember his thought.[3] Henotheism is the worship of a particular deity by a particular family, tribe, or nation. The danger of henotheism is that we locate the value center of our faith in nation, society, or even political party—anything but God.

The Twenty-third Psalm portrays God at work holding the flock together through the dark night of Pharaoh's enslavement, the dark night of unfaithfulness in the Sinai wilderness, and the dark night of contentious dispute over social justice issues such as same-sex marriage, immigration reform, clean energy, and the role of government in civil rights. The political and theological fault lines on these issues are so deep, one wonders if we still worship one God.

Perhaps the psalm reminds us that God did not let the issue of slavery destroy the fellowship. Both slave and slaveholder are guided by God's staff. God did not let the tension between Greek-speaking and Aramaic-speaking Jewish Christians destroy the fellowship. Both are guided to the good life that God intends. God's staff resists our best efforts at henotheism

---

3. H. Richard Niebuhr, *Radical Monotheism and Western Culture* (1960; repr., with a foreword by James M. Gustafson, Louisville, KY: Westminster John Knox Press, 1993).

and the disunity that results as we follow our particular household gods. God is still at work maintaining the integrity of the church, though we render it a caucus.

1 Peter 2:19–25

This passage from the First Letter of Peter is part of a larger address concerning Christian conduct among Gentile unbelievers (2:11–3:12). The larger address presents a number of difficulties for contemporary readers. Instead of condemning the institution of slavery, it urges slaves to endure the unjust suffering meted out by harsh masters. Instead of urging resistance to social injustice, it recommends that the faithful accept the authority of every human institution. Instead of imploring husbands and wives to be partners, it exhorts wives to be subordinate in the home. The address seemingly authorizes a household code that is good news for Gentile converts who are comfortable with these norms, but bad news for powerless slaves and wives. Yet if 1 Peter is read to affirm compliance with injustice as a virtue, then it is misread. The challenge of interpretation is how to reconcile a troubling ethical exhortation to slaves with a call to live as servants of God.

The power of the message is disclosed in a theological paradox. Peter asserts that Christians are servants of God, making them free people (2:16). In their freedom, Christians are to submit to all human authority without becoming conformed to the world (Rom. 12:2). The tension between freedom and submission is the context of God's favor. In submitting to human authority, Christians are submitting themselves to God's will. God develops submission to governing authority and self-sacrifice for the sake of Jesus Christ into "a royal priesthood, a holy nation, God's own people" (1 Pet. 2:9).

Slaves are free in God, though they are enslaved. They too are God's own people. It is not suffering per se that wins God's approval, but rather surrender to God in all things. Those who suffer unjustly yet still manage to sanctify God in their hearts are blessed (1 Pet. 3:13–15). They receive mercy. Peter hopes that even harsh masters might be convicted by the faithfulness of slaves, even if they only see the slaves' endurance and not the underlying faith that makes the endurance both possible and powerful.

A final word on the implications of the text is in order. A thoughtful reader cannot maintain that resistance to injustice is necessarily antithetical to Christian identity or conduct. Rather, the question is whether resistance is practiced in ways that treat adversaries justly or that occasion anarchy by substituting vengeance for law. Those who resist injustice yet still manage to sanctify God in their hearts are also blessed. They receive hope. What matters is that they do justice, love kindness, and walk humbly with God (Mic. 6:8).

Nonviolent direct action is an example of a faithful response to injustice that does not undermine the fellowship of faith or contradict the marks of a Christian (Rom. 12:9–21). During the Civil Rights Movement, Black demonstrators refused to entrust their civil rights to the conscience of a racist nation and championed nonviolent direct action as a way to prick the nation's conscience and change its unjust laws. In choosing nonviolent resistance for the purpose of desegregation, movement leaders rejected the tribal god of white supremacy, a god that revealed its false teaching in the ideology of "separate but equal." Further, movement leaders submitted themselves to the rule of law by filling the jails for justice.

John 10:1–10

In this chapter, John presents Jesus' use of Palestinian sheepherding imagery to distinguish God's sovereignty from the authority of religious leadership.[4] Two images in particular set Jesus apart from the religious authorities. Jesus is the gate to the sheepfold (10:1–10) and the good shepherd (vv. 11–16, 26–27). He calls the sheep from Jewish and non-Jewish communities (4:35–42; 10:16) and unites them into an intimate community of faith. Other shepherds call the sheep as well, but none has the authority of the good shepherd. Though some of these shepherds have served God in the past, like Abraham and Moses, the Gospel of John testifies that some no longer serve God because they are not open to the message that Jesus has brought eternal life into the world. The conflict between the synagogue authorities and the Jewish Christian community sets the context for this text and for the Gospel of John generally.

Jesus calls the authorities thieves and bandits because they claim what does not belong to them. God has given the sheep to Jesus (10:29). Authorities ultimately harm the flock when they serve interests other than the ones that God reveals in Jesus. Unity, mutuality, neighbor-love, justice, and abundant life for all signal the fellowship that God intends for followers.

Contemporary religious authorities may also confuse parochial practices and partisan interests for God's will. They might fight for justice, but they lead the flock astray if they neglect neighbor-love. They might preach unity, but they scatter the flock if they neglect justice. The fellowship that God intends is not fulfilled where any one of these goods is lacking, or where the scope of concern has been narrowed to particular persons.

---

4. Before attending further to the text, it is important that interpreters reject the anti-Semitism that informs some exegesis. The Gospel of John is not a polemic against Judaism or an indictment of the Jewish people. It is an affirmation of the divinity of Jesus by a growing Jewish Christian community.

Holocaust Remembrance Day: Yom haShoah (Early April to Early May)

Clark M. Williamson

Esther 3:8–9
Psalm 137
James 2:8–13
John 8:39–47

Yom haShoah (Heb. for "Day [yom] of Catastrophe [shoah]") is sometimes known colloquially as "the Shoah" or as Holocaust Remembrance Day. According to the Jewish calendar, the date is the 27th of Nisan (a date that varies from early April through early May). Holocaust Remembrance Day could help congregations mourn the murder of six million Jewish people and repent of anti-Judaism and anti-Semitism. While honoring the particularity of the Holocaust, this remembrance can also encourage synagogue and church to join in mutual resistance to all forms of genocide and racial and ethnic oppression.

> The SS seemed more preoccupied, more disturbed than usual. To hang a young boy in front of thousands of spectators was no light matter. . . . For more than half an hour [the child] stayed there, struggling between life and death, dying in slow agony under our eyes. . . . Behind me I heard the same man asking, "Where is God now?" And I heard a voice within me answer, "Here. . . . [God] is hanging here on this gallows."
>
> *Elie Wiesel*[1]

We remember the Holocaust because to be faithful is to remember, to remember is to repent, and to repent is to make possible reconciliation with God and our neighbors. Esther deals with a thwarted attempt at genocide, Psalm 37 with remembrance of oppression, and John 8:39–47 is a passage that

---

1. Elie Wiesel, *Night*, trans. Stella Rodway (New York: Hill & Wang, 1960), 70–71.

was made into a justification of the church's teaching of contempt for Jews and Judaism, of which we need to repent. James provides a bridge between church and synagogue, one which we might cross.

Esther 3:8–9

The book of Esther is pertinent to our contemporary world of empires, genocide, and the Holocaust. Suspicious of empires and realistic about politics, it reflects a time when Jews in the diaspora had to cope with a hostile environment, as they had to do throughout Christendom and in Nazi Germany. The survival of the Jews in Esther depends not on God's deliverance but on human courage, acumen, and commitment to Jewish well-being. Explicitly God is absent from the book of Esther. But that does not mean that God is implicitly absent. Esther's plot turns on an "extraordinary pattern of apparent coincidences."[2] There are several, including the sudden vacancy of the queenship, Esther's becoming queen, Mordecai's detection of the plot of the eunuchs, and the king's insomnia. It may be that "a coincidence is a miracle in which God prefers to remain anonymous."[3]

Today's reading is Haman's genocide proposal to the king. His request is as understated in composition as it is malicious in its objective. It moves from a truth so stated as to make that truth seem sinister to a half-lie and then into complete lies.[4] The truth is that the Jews are "scattered" among the peoples in the kingdom, although Haman does not name the people of whom he speaks and the king is so lacking in curiosity that he does not ask. The partial lie is the claim that their laws are utterly different from those of other people. They are not. The total lie is that Jews did not obey the king's laws. The malicious implication is that therefore the king must issue a decree for their destruction. Then Haman even offers the king a bribe of ten thousand talents to allow him to carry out his genocidal intent.

All of this happened because Haman was infuriated with Mordecai for refusing to bow to him. He turned this personal slight into a plan "to destroy all the Jews" in the kingdom of Ahasuerus. But through Mordecai's urging and Esther's courage, Haman is thwarted and hanged from the gallows he had prepared for Mordecai. Esther is full of irony and the satire of empires.

The explicit purpose of Esther is to inaugurate the feast of Purim, which is observed annually in the synagogue. It is a lively occasion for which

2. Jon D. Levenson, *Esther*, Old Testament Library (Louisville, KY: Westminster John Knox Press, 1997), 18.

3. Ibid., 19.

4. Michael V. Fox, *Character and Ideology in the Book of Esther*, Studies on Personalities of the Old Testament (Columbia: University of South Carolina Press, 1991), 157, cited in Levenson, *Esther*, 70.

participants wear festive clothing and children bring noisemakers for raising a racket every time the name of Haman is mentioned. The best way to understand the book is to visit a synagogue on Purim.

Psalm 137

Being faithful entails remembering. God's faithfulness is expressed by God's promise to remember the covenant. Christians are urged to remember their baptisms. Elie Wiesel has devoted his life to keeping alive the memory of the Holocaust against the people Israel and all other victims of Nazi tyranny. We must also remember slavery, the eradication of Native Americans, and torture that we have inflicted on others. Preachers will propose their own remembrances.

The church has a moral imperative to remember and lament the Holocaust, an obligation that owes much to the prehistory of the Holocaust, in which the church's long teaching and practice of contempt for Jews and Judaism made the Holocaust possible.[5] It is incumbent upon us to remember that during the Holocaust our churches were largely silent, raising no witness of protest. During the Holocaust, Frederick Kershner repeatedly protested against "the indifference of English and American Christians to the extinction of the Jews."[6] Psalm 137 resonates with harsh memory and the intense anguish of exile, of Babylon and Edom. "Edom" in Israel's memory became a symbol for all oppressive empires; in the juxtaposition of today's text and Holocaust Remembrance Day, it symbolizes Nazi Germany. When Jews remember the *Shoah* (the "whirlwind" of destruction), they say "Never again!" never again to any people. To remember is to resist. To forget is to consent.

The promise never to forget Jerusalem refers not only to the place where the Israelites were after the exile. More important is whether God's reign of compassionate justice shapes the life of the people. That is also the question before the church.

The psalm concludes with a plea to God to remember Babylon by visiting destruction upon it, to dash its children upon the rocks. We should not omit these verses from the reading. The psalms are incredibly honest, often expressing the real emotions of the one praying. That we are justified by grace means that we do not have to hide our true feelings from God. And why try to do so anyway? God knows us better than we know ourselves yet somehow

5. See Edward H. Flannery, *The Anguish of the Jews* (New York: Paulist Press, 1985); David A. Rausch, *A Legacy of Hatred* (Chicago: Moody Press, 1984); Clark M. Williamson, *Has God Rejected His People?* (Nashville: Abingdon Press, 1982), 89–122.

6. Cited in the *Encyclopedia of the Stone-Campbell Movement*, ed. Douglas A. Foster, Paul M. Blowers, Anthony L. Dunnavant, and D. Newell Williams (Grand Rapids: Eerdmans, 2004), 428.

manages to love us. What better way is there to deal with such feelings than to work through them in prayer?

John 8:39–47

One cannot but empathize with preachers who have the courage to preach on this passage from John. The impulse to lay it quietly to rest is understandable. Yet not confronting it is to allow its language of vilification to reinforce negative stereotypes of Jews. The most frequently repeated teaching in the Torah (thirty-six times) is: "You shall love the stranger as yourself." A preacher could deal with the question of how Christians today, after two millennia of teaching and practicing contempt for Jews and Judaism, should think and speak of Jews. Urging Christians to love their neighbors is pointless if we allow negative images of those neighbors to go unchecked.

John has been labeled the "father of antisemitism" and his Gospel one of "Christian love and Jew hatred."[7] John uses the term "the Jews" roughly seventy times, more than any other New Testament book except The Acts of the Apostles. This alone does not make John's Gospel anti-Jewish, but that a large majority of John's references are obviously hostile does mean that one of the effects of this Gospel has been that it has been taken as support for teaching contempt for Jews and Judaism.

John's use of "the Jews" is symbolic. It symbolizes those who refuse to believe in Jesus. Preachers should be clear that this passage has nothing to do with the historical Jesus. It comes from John, who puts these words into Jesus' mouth. "The Jews," wherever John uses the term pejoratively, are those whom John distinguishes from his disciples. Hence we will speak of "John's Jesus" to make clear who is speaking in John's Gospel.

The Gospel of John is a highly sectarian book; this Gospel has many enemies. There is "the world," which includes not only "the Jews" but also "the Gentiles." Hostility to Jews dominates John 5–12; antagonism to Gentiles governs John 14–17. Both groups are unbelievers in Jesus and both "hate" Jesus and his disciples (John 15:18–19). There are followers of Jesus who cannot accept his description of the eucharist: "Unless you eat the flesh of the Son of Man and drink his blood, you have no life in you" (6:53). "Many" of Jesus' disciples said: "This teaching is difficult; who can accept it?" (6:60). They "turned back and no longer went about with him" (6:66).

In today's passage, John's Jesus says to "the Jews": "You are from your father the devil, and you choose to do your father's desires. He was a murderer from the beginning and does not stand in the truth, because there is no

---

7. Kaufmann Kohler, "New Testament," in *Jewish Encyclopedia* (New York: Funk & Wagnalls, 1905), 9:251.

truth in him" (8:44). In 8:31 Jesus addresses "the Jews who had believed in him." He says of them that they are Abraham's descendants (8:37), while he denies that same lineage to Jews in today's reading. That John's Jesus is not opposed to the Jewish people per se is cold comfort to Jews who remain faithful to the covenant with the God of Israel.

These are the most negative words spoken of Jews in the entire New Testament. Christians have wrought incredible harm upon Jews by the ways in which they have used them to teach contempt for Jews and Judaism. Medieval images of Jews with horns and tails and in collaboration with the devil abound in Christian art.[8] In the period of witch hunting, the instructional manual drawn up to guide the inquisition associated witches with Jews and the devil in unspeakable atrocities.[9] The long repetition of negative images of Jews and Judaism over the course of two millennia of church history made the Holocaust possible, as it did many an earlier pogrom. Words have consequences, and we are accountable for how we speak of these matters.

Today's passage puts Jews in a bind. They are at fault for failing to believe in Jesus. Yet they are also told that they "cannot accept my word" (8:43b) because their father is the devil. They are held responsible for not doing what they cannot do. Worse, John's Jesus closes the passage with an accusation preceded by a question: "Why do you not believe me?" (8:46). His answer: "You are not from God" (8:47).

John's world is divided between two classes of people: those who are of God and those who are not. We followers of Jesus are the first class. Everybody else is the second class. They are strangers to us and we to them. Unlike John, Paul interpreted the fact that most Jews did not believe in Jesus as happening in the providence of God to enable salvation to come to the Gentiles (Rom. 11:11), and God's ways are inscrutable (Rom. 11:33). Meanwhile, we Gentiles should not forget that we are the wild shoots grafted into the root stock of faith that goes back to Abraham, and, above all, we should not boast over unbelieving Israel, because we stand only upon the unmerited grace of God.

James 2:8–13

James is written to Jesus-followers who are Jewish; it provides knowledge of a community close to the teachings of Jesus, the faith of Israel, and the Sermon on the Mount (Matt. 5–7). James is the only New Testament writer who refers to his community as a synagogue (Jas. 2:2). Not a criticism of

---

8. Heinz Schreckenberg, *The Jews in Christian Art: An Illustrated History* (New York: Continuum, 1996), 241–50. A sixteenth-century painting shows a devil with a "Jewish" nose and pig's ears.

9. An excerpt from the manual "The Hammer Against the Witches" is in Elizabeth Clark and Herbert Richardson, eds., *Women and Religion* (New York: Harper Press, 1977), 116–30.

Paul, it is a connection to an early church that observed the teachings of the Torah. James is a bridge to early Judaism and the teachings of Jesus. Primarily concerned for the well-being of the destitute, it is faithful to Jesus' central mission.

Reading today's passage in light of the paragraph that precedes it contextualizes its concern that the community not show favoritism to the wealthy. It is not possible, apart from hypocrisy, to "believe in our glorious Lord Jesus Christ" (2:1) and at the same time privilege a rich person over one shabbily dressed. God has chosen the destitute to be "heirs of the kingdom" (2:5). James's example reflects the teaching of both Jesus and the Torah: "You shall not be partial to the poor or defer to the great" (Lev. 19:15). A synagogue was a house of worship, of study, a place where the community's resources were used to help the poor, and one where disputes could be settled and justice done. The concern to avoid favoritism would apply in any of these functions of the synagogue.

James is concerned with the whole of the torah, not a single teaching, and keeping it means loving one's neighbor as one's self. His attitude toward the Law (more appropriately, "way") is that of Psalm 119:47: "I find delight in your commandments." Talking is as important as acting: "So speak and so act as those who are to be judged by the law of liberty" (Jas. 2:12). Love is expressed in justice; justice is carried out in love.

Fifth Sunday of Easter

Simone Sunghae Kim

ACTS 7:55–60
PSALM 31:1–5, 15–16
1 PETER 2:2–10
JOHN 14:1–14

The lectionary readings for this week inspire us to steadfastly hold onto our true identity as God's disciples and ambassadors in this adverse world. Both Stephen, the first Christian martyr, and the psalmist assert their utmost confidence in the Lord who is their fortress and refuge in the presence of enemies. Their assurance ultimately hinges on the person of Jesus Christ, through whom every believer's faith, authority, and power are birthed, nourished, and consummated, as demonstrated in the first epistle of the apostle Peter. Jesus Christ is, after all, the epitome and culmination of God's covenantal relationship with us, and his identity as the Son of God (elucidated by the apostle John) presents us with a creative and potent ministerial and eschatological vision. These passages provoke us today to take part in and be the instigators of God's eternal hope and security in Christ's life, death, and resurrection amid this unsettled and fractious global atmosphere.

Acts 7:55–60

This dramatic account of Stephen's martyrdom is preceded by his speech (7:2–53). Ancient religious leaders, like many of us today, not only refused to hear Stephen's message but also became intensely angry and furious at his proclamation of the gospel. There are other parallels between Stephen's story and the account of Jesus' death. The yelling, dragging, and stoning of Stephen (vv. 57–58) resemble the striking, spitting on, and mocking of Jesus as they led him to the cross (Mark 15:19–20). Stephen's prayer, "Lord Jesus, receive my spirit" (Acts 7:59b), echoes that of Jesus on the cross, "Father, into your hands I commend my spirit" (Luke 23:46). Whereas Stephen called on the name of Jesus, Jesus cried out to God, his Father.

In addition, both Stephen (Acts 7:60) and Jesus (Luke 23:34) prayed for forgiveness of their enemies, with Stephen directing his prayer to the "Lord" and Jesus to his heavenly "Father." Stephen's plea for his enemies' forgiveness no doubt contributed to the apostle Paul's conversion and ministry, consequently affecting Christian believers for generations to come. The young man named Saul (who later became Paul) guarded the clothes of Stephen's assailants and watched while they stoned him (Acts 7:58). Paul confessed in 1 Corinthians 15:9–10 that he persecuted the church of God before receiving God's gracious forgiveness.

According to Acts 7:55–56, Stephen received a vision of Jesus standing (Gk. *hestota*) before him rather than sitting, which would have been the expected posture of a teacher and Lord. Could it be that Jesus is standing before Stephen as his advocate rather than sitting as a judge,[1] and is welcoming Stephen into his presence?[2] The spirit of intimacy and care that is shared between Stephen and Jesus must not be overlooked amid this terrible moment of great historical importance for the early church.

This passage offers at least three critical insights related to injustice and oppression. First, our battle against oppressors and persecutors can only be won when we are filled with the Holy Spirit. It begins by saying that Stephen was "filled with the Holy Spirit" (v. 55). It was not necessarily his own human strength but the power of the indwelling Spirit of God that enabled Stephen to die such a death. Only when the Spirit empowers us with the dynamic power (Gk. *dynamin*) mentioned in Acts 1:8 are we able to tackle our enemies.

Second, and closely related to the first insight, is that we must constantly look toward Jesus and him alone for comfort and as a reference point when proclaiming God's reign on earth. Immediately before his death, Stephen consistently focused his eyes and attention on Jesus. He lifted his eyes to see Jesus standing in heaven (7:55–56) and prayed to the Lord to receive his spirit (v. 59) as well as to forgive his enemies (v. 60). Jesus, the Son of God, walked, lived, and died among us. He experienced firsthand what it was like to be mistreated, misunderstood, and betrayed. Without a doubt Jesus is the best and only one to thoroughly understand the pain, suffering, and loneliness of weak and marginalized people. Moreover, Jesus, as our model and Lord, is the

1. John Calvin, *Calvin's Commentaries: The Acts of the Apostles*, trans. John W. Fraser and W. J. G. McDonald, ed. David W. Torrance and Thomas F. Torrance (Grand Rapids: Eerdmans, 1995), 219.

2. G. H. C. MacGregor, "The Acts of the Apostles: Introduction and Exegesis," in *The Interpreter's Bible*, ed. George A. Buttrick et al., vol. 9, *Acts, Romans* (Nashville: Abingdon Press, 1954), 103.

one whom we ought to follow, consult, and imitate amid harsh and adverse circumstances. Many Korean Christian pastors and leaders who were tortured and martyred during the Japanese occupation of Korea (1910–1945) often exhibited love and forgiveness toward the Japanese perpetrators. Unfortunately, most of their persecutors were never brought to justice.

Third, Stephen's prayer to pardon his enemies urges us to exhibit the spirit of forgiveness even amid the worst adversities and circumstances. Following Jesus' example (Luke 23:34), Stephen had the heart to ask the Lord not to charge his murderers' sin against them (Acts 7:60). As Jesus' disciples, we must also learn to forgive the sins of others, even as we confront the evils that are wrongly committed against us and others. In all honesty, I find it extremely difficult to forgive those who intentionally and wickedly abuse the voiceless. For instance, I truly believe that those who physically, verbally, and sexually abuse children as well as physically and mentally challenged people must be dealt with in a more strict and intentional fashion as a way of preventing future criminal acts.

Psalm 31:1–5, 15–16

Psalm 31 echoes much of the same mood and language as Acts 7:55–60. Both texts display the cry of an individual facing opposition and persecution from enemies as well as pleas and petitions to God for protection and deliverance. While the exact source of the psalmist's distress is not known, the text includes many liturgical elements, such as petition, praise, and thanksgiving. It is also important to note that the psalmist is operating under the spirit of his or her covenant relationship with God. The total trust and confidence that the author exhibits rest on the righteousness of God whose love does not fail (vv. 1, 16).

When we consider the tensions we often experience between patterns of injustice that run rampant in our world and our own faith commitments, at least two implications arise out of our encounter with this psalm. First, as an individual lament Psalm 31 suggests that we should not be surprised when storms of opposition come our way and threaten our existence. Such words as "deliver," "rescue," and "redeem" imply that we are surrounded by enemies and attacks are inevitable. For example, church bombings in the United States and other parts of the world, and persecutions against Christians in places such as China, North Korea, Nigeria, and some Middle Eastern countries indicate that Christians are still oppressed in some settings. John 16:33b confirms this by saying, "In this world you will have trouble. But take heart! I have overcome the world" (NIV). While we do not need to lose heart or become pessimistic, it is nevertheless wise for us to know that there are powerful, systemic forces of evil against which we must struggle.

Second, the innocent and marginalized should cling to the covenant God for deliverance and emancipation.[3] The psalmist elucidates that for the sake of God's name the Lord must lead and guide him or her (Ps. 31:3). In addition, it is God's servant on whom God's face should shine (v. 16). The unwavering confidence in God's salvation and redemption that the palmist displays arises out of the fact that God who created the covenant relationship with God's servant is also the agent of final judgment and salvation. This covenant God is faithful and keeps promises as we journey through this unfriendly world of racism, sexism, and classism. This psalm may be a source of encouragement to immigrants, women, and persons who are not Euro-Americans as they encounter prejudice, hardship, and various forms of oppression.

1 Peter 2:2–10

Peter writes this epistle to encourage and admonish believers not to compromise their faith for the sake of worldly values and conduct. He calls them sojourners and pilgrims (2:11), urging them to engage in a holy and godly lifestyle. The analogy of newborn babies craving pure milk (v. 2) echoes Matthew 18:3, where Jesus confirms that only those who are like little children will enter God's kingdom. It is by their innocence and childlike simplicity that believers may embody God's calling.[4] It is critical to this epistle that we cannot fulfill God's calling by our own spiritual sacrifices: only through Jesus Christ can we become "a chosen race, a royal priesthood, a holy nation" (1 Pet. 2:5, 9; cf. Heb. 13:15).

Peter offers a couple of recommendations for today's believers who are facing hardships and sufferings. First, as people belonging to the Lord, the living stone, our prime mission is to be built into one universal temple in this hostile world. Before we are world citizens we are heavenly citizens (Phil. 3:20) who are connected with one another by the Holy Spirit (1 Cor. 12:13). We are to be formed into a "spiritual house, to be a holy priesthood" (1 Pet. 2:5). As believers come together in one accord and live out the life of spiritual sacrifices through Jesus Christ, we will become the light and salt of the world (Matt. 5:13–16). Likewise, transformation and social change begins with the united body of Christ, which will eventually permeate this world of darkness.

Second, having been adopted as God's children, it is only fitting for us to act mercifully and graciously amid even a harsh and apathetic environment. By God's act of choosing us (1 Pet. 2:9) and through the mercy of the Lord

---

3. Peter C. Craigie, *Psalms 1–50*, Word Biblical Commentary 19 (Waco: Word Books, 1983), 260.
4. John Calvin, *Commentaries on the Catholic Epistles*, trans. John Owen (Grand Rapids: Baker Book House, 1999), 61.

(v. 10), we are called righteous (Rom. 4:5–6). Even as we strive for social change, we are advised to follow the footsteps of the Lord by being gracious toward even unlovable enemies. Son Yang-Won (1902–1950), a prominent Korean Christian leader who was martyred by a North Korean soldier during the Korean War (1950–1953), embodied this in a powerful way when he embraced and adopted the killer of his two sons as his own.[5]

John 14:1–14

This Gospel text contains some of the most important Christian doctrines and promises concerning Jesus' identity as well as hope for his disciples. Jesus comforts anxious disciples who are faced with Judas's betrayal, the prediction of Peter's triple denial, and the imminent death of Jesus predicted in the previous chapter (13:21–38). The Greek *kaiean* in verse 3 is to be translated "and if I go" rather than "and when I go," indicating that Jesus would prepare a place for them under the condition that he goes away. Jesus' self-proclamation as "the way, and the truth, and the life" (v. 6) fulfills Stephen's expectation for the Lord to receive his spirit (Acts 7:59) and inspires his disciples with hope that they will be able to do greater things (John 14:12). Jesus is the center and power of the disciples' ministry, their comfort and hope amid times of great uncertainty and hardship.

This potent text nicely sums up this week's lectionary readings concerning the truth about our stance in the world. Our battles against social injustice and evil must be fought from the eternal perspective. Since our everlasting home is in heaven with Christ Jesus (vv. 2–3) and we are just passing through this world as aliens and strangers (1 Pet. 2:11), we must rely on Christ's help as we encounter worldly ills and injustices. No matter how fiercely we work for social justice and peace in the world, our leading focus always should remain Jesus' calling, help, and hope for all creation. Often, what appears to be noble and honorable in human eyes may not coincide with God's grand plan and intentions for the world. Our finite perspective as well as our identity as heavenly citizens constantly remind us of our limitations. But with the Holy Spirit as our guide, Christ's love empowers us to forgive wrongdoing while we work toward its defeat. Christ's love offers us what is best, both personally and collectively as a holy people.

---

5. See Cha Chong-Soon, *Aeyangwon and Martyr of Love, Rev. Son Yang-Won*, trans. Sohn Jae-Kon (Seoul: KIATS Press, 2008).

Sixth Sunday of Easter

Choi Hee An

ACTS 17:22–31
PSALM 66:8–20
1 PETER 3:13–22
JOHN 14:15–21

This week's lectionary readings invite us to follow Jesus' commandments, which are the mission of God's love through the Spirit of truth. The theme flowing through these readings is the manifestation of Jesus' death and resurrection in and to the world through the Spirit. Paul's proclamation of Jesus' resurrection in Acts, suffering for doing what is right in 1 Peter, Jesus' love command in John, and God's salvation after suffering in Psalms 66 show how the death (suffering) and resurrection of Jesus are proclaimed and believed by his disciples, his beloved people, his community, and all the earth. Through Jesus' suffering and resurrection once and for all, these readings teach us about the reality of human suffering in the world and God's righteousness and grace to the world.

John 14:15–21

These verses include a twofold movement in Jesus' message: Jesus promises that the presence of the Spirit of truth is coming to us, and he describes what it means to abide with God. In verse 15, Jesus asserts that if his disciples love him, they will keep his commandments. What does Jesus command? It is clear from the preceding verses that Jesus' command is to "love one another" as he has loved each of us (13:34–35). However, because they abandoned Jesus before and after his crucifixion, it seems impossible for them to practice this love. Jesus knows they cannot love each other and are unable to love as he does. Jesus knows they need his help, and he does not want to leave his people alone. Jesus worries that his departure will lead to despair among his followers who have already experienced his painful departure in death. Therefore, he promises to send the Spirit of truth to them. The *paraklētos*—"Comforter" (KJV), "Advocate" (NRSV), "Counselor" (NIV), "Paraclete" (NJB)—is given to the people and is with them forever after Jesus' departure.[1]

The Spirit comes from God, but once again the world cannot receive the Spirit, just as it did not receive Jesus. Only people who believe in Jesus can know the Spirit. The function of the Spirit of truth is to help the people keep Jesus' love command, because the Spirit will abide with them and be in them. Without the Spirit, people cannot follow him and obey this command. For this reason, the presence of the Spirit assures Jesus' beloved people that they will not be alone until he returns.

When a mother leaves her little children to go to work, she explains to them that her disappearance does not mean she is abandoning them. In order to keep her promise, she leaves her advocate to support her children and tells them where she will be and when she will return. When she reappears, her children know that she kept her promise and they learn to trust her. They know that she will come back to them every day and live with them as she promised.

Before Jesus' departure, Jesus wants to let his disciples know where he will be, when he will come back, and that he will leave his advocate with them (vv. 18–20). He does not want them to believe that he abandons his "little children" (13:33). He makes sure that his disappearance will not be identified with his death but that it holds the promise of his return. To further reassure them, Jesus shares his eschatological secret; he will be in God, and he himself will be in them so that his beloved people are in him and in God. This secret reveals that they are empowered by Christ's presence (the Spirit of truth) to participate in his just and loving reign even as they await his return. We have witnessed this empowerment. People touched by the Spirit of truth, such as Martin Luther King Jr., Mother Teresa, Gandhi, and unknown righteous people, are able to participate in God's justice and gain the ability to fight for justice. Because of the Spirit of truth, people are strengthened in their ability to hold on to hope, to love and live not only for themselves but also for others. The union between God, Jesus, and the people who listen to the voice of the Spirit of truth is now possible among us.

In verse 21, Jesus' relationship with his beloved children, his beloved people, his beloved community, becomes clear. Jesus' repeated promise urges his beloved community to follow his love command. Whoever practices Jesus' commandment, "love one another as I have loved you," will be loved by God and see the revelation of God.

---

1. Gail R. O'Day, "The Gospel of John," in *The New Interpreter's Bible*, ed. Leander Keck et al., vol. 9 (Nashville: Abingdon Press, 1995), 747.

1 Peter 3:13–22

In verses 13–14, it is assumed that people need to pursue doing what is good even if doing good is accompanied by suffering. First Peter takes "do not fear what they fear" from Isaiah 8:12–13 and puts it in the context of the people's experience with Christ. What people need to fear is neither suffering nor persecutors. First Peter warns Christians to fear God, the Lord Christ.

Fear is perhaps the worst feeling we can experience. It is often not based on any real threat but arises when we imagine the worst. It is the feeling by which people are already overwhelmed before they face reality and even after. Fear is often induced by military tactics that seek to control and traumatize people, preventing them from seeing the truth. Not only many combat veterans who experienced war but also people who hear about war live in fear of it long afterward. Fear may overwhelm us to the point that we lose our confidence in God and give up hope. In verse 15, Peter warns about the danger of fear and draws our attention away from unfounded fear, urging us to sanctify our hearts to God. Instead of living in fear, he encourages us to practice the positive activity of working toward sanctification, working toward what is right, justice. To sanctify one's heart with Christ as Lord is an active spiritual practice as surely as seeking justice through our actions. This practice creates hope and can make people unafraid even as they suffer.

These verses teach Christians how to act when they defend their faith and declare their hope in Christ. First Peter suggests that we practice gentleness and reverence in every circumstance, defending ourselves with humble hearts and respecting others when they proclaim their faith in God. When we sanctify Christ as Lord, we must also sanctify others who are members of the one body of Christ. This attitude will keep Christians hopeful rather than fearful.

Verses 18–20 explore Christ's suffering as the basis for understanding all undeserved suffering. Because "Christ suffered for sins," suffering is vital to Christianity. These verses explain that suffering is not from God. It is not God's punishment for our sins, but our sins are sometimes responsible for our own suffering and that of others. Institutional and structural sins such as racism, sexism, classism, colonialism, and all forms of discrimination that we create are responsible for causing and contributing to the suffering of innocent, powerless, and marginalized persons. These sins also cause Jesus to suffer. Christ suffers as the righteous one who brings *you*, all sinners, all believers, all people, and all communities, to God. Christ was put to death in the flesh along with people who are marginalized, poor, powerless, and oppressed. Jesus' suffering and resurrection brings the entire community to God in solidarity with those who are marginalized, poor, powerless, and oppressed. They not only die with Jesus but are resurrected with him. Sometimes to do what is right will create fear and cause innocent suffering and death in our unjust society. However, suffering must not stop us from doing what is right.

Psalm 66:8–20

This passage invites all people to praise God. In the first several verses, God is praised because of God's power and deeds; by the end of the psalm, God's steadfast love is blessed. All people and the entire creation are delivered from rebellious powers by God, whose steadfast love remains with us always.

Here again, suffering occurs in God's creation. However, there is hope in the way God listens to those who suffer and saves them amid their suffering. "If I had cherished iniquity in my heart, the Lord would not have listened" (v. 18). This suggests that because I did what is right, God will answer me. Suffering does not just occur as a form of divine punishment in this passage. It understands suffering as God's test (vv. 10–12a) as well as a pathway to God's salvation (vv. 12b, 17–19). God's power, deeds, and love come from divine salvation amid suffering. Indeed, suffering is overcome by God's power and love. As people put their faith in God to save them, they joyfully anticipate God's saving action on their behalf. People with faith trust God, who will not reject their prayer. Suffering cannot stop people from trusting God. It cannot prevent people from praising God. It is possible to believe in God despite suffering. To do so, we must learn to trust God beyond suffering and to anticipate God's help to come.

Acts 17:22–31

Paul arrived in Athens and debated with some Epicurean and Stoic philosophers about the good news of Jesus' resurrection (17:18b). They soon brought him to the Areopagus and asked him to explain this foreign divinity and new religion. As a Christian missionary, Paul becomes a model for proclaiming the Christian God in a foreign land.

Paul observed their worship and culture and learned that the people of Athens were very religious "in every way" (17:22). The Areopagus was located in the midst of a multicultural and multireligious city. The Athenians and many foreigners lived there together and were interested in everything new. Because of their curiosity and open minds, they were eager to hear Paul speak about his religion.

In verses 23–31, Paul observes their culture, finds evidence of an "unknown god," and refers to this in his teaching. He does not speak of a foreign God, but introduces his God in the guise of their familiar but not well understood "unknown god." Paul uses the cultural and religious concepts familiar to the

Athenians as he offers his teaching in a new place, incorporating his careful observations about the people he encounters. As a Christian missionary, he did not fear what he had to say about his God and religion to this new city, but he also showed respect for the culture, the people, and their religions. He hybridized his Christian beliefs into their own cultural poets and tried to make a bridge between his religion and theirs with "gentleness and reverence" (1 Pet. 3:16). At the same time, he proclaimed Jesus' resurrection and God's justice to the world without "fear" (1 Pet. 3:14).

All four of this week's passages ask us to consider how we may practice God's commandments with gentleness and respect to each other, beyond our fears and suffering. Loving one another is not a conditional practice, but an unconditional one that we need to keep doing. It does not make exceptions because of differences in race, sexual orientation, gender, social class, or economic standing. Loving one another needs to be embraced in our multireligious, multicultural society today more than ever. Our differences should not be the cause of unjust treatment of others. Instead, these differences provide new opportunities for us to practice God's love command. Loving each other means doing good for others, on behalf of others. It is what we do even if it incurs suffering in an unjust society. We must not stop our outreach on behalf of others because it brings suffering on us. Just as Jesus overcame death on our behalf, we must, by the power of Christ's Spirit, overcome the unjust suffering of others with him every day of our lives.

Peace in the Home: Shalom Bayit (Second Sunday in May)

Marie M. Fortune

LEVITICUS 18:1–18
PSALM 91
2 CORINTHIANS 4:16–5:11
MATTHEW 8:18–22

The new Peace in the Home: Shalom Bayit replaces Mother's Day and Father's Day, which often tend to sentimentality, can promote stereotypes of women and men, sometimes idealize family relationships, and exclude persons who are not parents. The purpose of preaching on Peace in the Home is to call the congregation to help all people live in settings of security, love, and justice. It affirms the diversity of family lifestyles common in our churches and cultures, including traditional households, the single life, gay and lesbian families, and biologically unrelated people who live as family. The preacher can also make connections to Sexual Assault and Abuse Awareness Month (April) and Domestic Violence Awareness Month (October).

Getting the "overview" of Jesus' and Paul's perception of the family enables you and me to see to it that the component parts of the whole human community as a living system of face-to-face relationships are mobilized around the nurture and the enlargement of children's life. They are not shut up to the suffocation of an unventilated nuclear family. God has other faces and forms in addition to those of mother, father, brother and sister. Basic sources of hope are not shut up to these significant persons alone.

Wayne E. Oates[1]

---

1. Wayne E. Oates, "The Extended Family," in *When Children Suffer: A Sourcebook for Ministry with Children in Crisis*, ed. Andrew D. Lester (Philadelphia: Westminster Press, 1987), 195.

In Judaism, *shalom bayit* (peace in the home) is a highly valued expectation for every Jewish family. It is the essence of family values—the assumption that family members will live together in peace, respect, and harmony.

One of the contradictions of the practice of *shalom bayit* is its misuse to mean silence about what goes on in the home to the outside world. It may also be assumed by some that the peace of the home is solely the woman's responsibility and if everything is not fine, it must be her fault when things go awry. For a battered woman, this misinterpretation can render her silent and lead her to blame herself for the abuse she and her children may be experiencing. These two assumptions make it unlikely that a woman will seek help for herself and her children.

The same is true for Christian women in the church. It is the facade of a happy family that is important, the appearance in church on Sunday morning even if her makeup is unusually heavy. What goes on behind closed doors is private and not to be discussed, because that would be to air the dirty laundry.

Peace in the home, rightly understood and practiced, lifts up the essential value of the worth and dignity of each family member; the home should be a place of safety and respect for each one and especially of protection for the most vulnerable.

When I train or consult with clergy, I still on occasion hear, "But no one ever comes to me with domestic violence or sexual assault." To which I have to ask, "Why are your people not coming to you with something that is so common in their lives and families?" Pastors would like to conclude that "we don't have these problems here in our congregation." But this is not statistically possible. People in all of our churches carry memories, scars, or open wounds. But we will not *hear* about their pain if we do not *speak* about it. This is why it is so important that we preach about family relationships and the possibility of abuse to give people permission to come forward and seek help. "Peace in the Home" is a theme in which we can explore these issues proactively.

At first reading, this series of passages may be confusing, especially to women and children who, under normal circumstances, have the least power in the family structure—then and now.

In my comments about preaching on peace in the home, I will frequently remind the reader that you are preaching to victims, survivors, and perpetrators of abuse within the family every Sunday. One in three people (at least) sitting in the pews has had personal experience themselves or with someone in their immediate family of physical, verbal, or sexual violence. They are listening very carefully for any word that speaks to them and to their memories or current experiences.

You are also preaching to the bystanders, those who surround victims, survivors, and perpetrators, who see and hear the abuse but do not want to get involved. However, the bystander may be an enormous resource in this situation.

For better or worse, religious teachings, doctrines, and sacred texts are always relevant for Christians facing sexual or domestic violence. Too often in the past (and present) teachings, doctrines, and texts have been roadblocks to ending the abuse and bringing healing and safety. For example, "Wives, be subject to your husbands" or "God hates divorce" can easily be misinterpreted to silence victims of abuse and justify the actions of abusers.

But teachings, doctrines, and texts may also serve as powerful resources. Especially in Scripture, the Prophets, Psalms, and Gospels speak to the experiences of the vulnerable and oppressed and call the powerful to account.

This needed approach requires a critique (or deconstruction) of the roadblocks that can be created by patriarchal interpretations of religious teachings and a development (or reconstruction) of useful resources that empower victims and survivors to address their experiences.

- Victims need to be heard and believed, to be protected from further harm, and to find justice.
- Abusers need to be held accountable for their abuse and called to repentance.
- Bystanders need to provide for both.

In other words, it is the work of the faith community, as bystanders, to do whatever we can to provide resources to those struggling with abuse. This is the lesson of the Good Samaritan (Luke 10:29–37). Of all the bystanders, he was the one who stopped and cared for the victim, providing safe shelter and ongoing support.

So I will be cautioning the reader regularly to carefully remember who is listening to your preaching. There will be those who are only allowed out of their homes to come to church, who as adults remember clearly the abuse of one parent by the other, who as teens may be in an abusive dating relationship, who as children were sexually abused by an adult or teen. There will also be those who have abused or are currently abusing a family member, some of whom are struggling with guilt and shame but don't know where to turn.

As a preacher and pastor, you are a generalist and not a specialist. You do not have to have all the answers. But you can be a resource rather than a roadblock and begin by opening the door and giving your congregation permission to come to you. Then you will have the opportunity to connect an individual or family to the community resource they need while continuing to walk with them pastorally.

Leviticus 18:1–18

In the Leviticus passage, which focuses on sexual relationships, there are two points to be made. First, the purpose of the purity laws regarding sexual relations was to set the Jews apart from the Egyptians and Canaanites. And second, the prohibitions here against "uncovering the nakedness" of another person refer to not having sexual contact with that person.

These rules, addressed to the male head of household, specify every possible permutation of relationship for the man—except one. The prohibition against sex with one's daughter or son does not appear.[2] Scholars disagree about whether this means that father-daughter incest was practiced, but they do suggest that the assumption was that the reproductive function of the daughter (along with that of other females in the household) was owned by the father. A violation of these prohibitions involving another man's kin listed here was viewed as theft.[3]

The ethical teaching in this passage that is relevant to our contemporary reading is the prohibition of sexual contact with family members other than one's adult intimate partner. Incestuous abuse, which is usually inflicted on children or teens, is damaging to that individual, but it is also devastating to the family structure, which should be a place of safety and protection for its most vulnerable members.

Psalm 91

This is one of the more reassuring psalms, and its primary image is of shelter and refuge. It offers support to a battered woman and her children as they seek safe shelter (v. 4a): "[God] will cover you with his pinions, and under his wings you will find shelter." (See also Ps. 55:8.) The psalmist promises that she will be protected and that she need not fear. But God's protection does not come to us while we are passive. It comes when we seek out the resources God provides for us.

In other words, the caution here is that this psalm should never be preached to a battered woman in order to advise, "Have faith, pray harder, and God will take care of you." Rather, this psalm calls to mind the story of the man on his

2. I will never forget the call I received from the Child Protective Service worker who was interviewing an eight-year-old girl who had been raped by her father. She told the worker that her father said that the Bible said it was acceptable for him to have sex with her. They called me to ask where to find that in the Bible. The issue of misuse of Scripture is extremely important in addressing abuse in the family. For further discussion of this passage, see Marie M. Fortune, *Sexual Violence: The Sin Revisited* (Cleveland: Pilgrim Press, 2005).

3. Judith Romney Wegner, "Leviticus," in *The Women's Bible Commentary*, ed. Carol Newsom and Sharon Ringe (Louisville, KY: Westminster John Knox Press, 1992), 40–41.

roof in the midst of a raging flood. First a neighbor came by in a canoe, but he refused a ride. "God will take care of me," he said. Then a firefighter came by in a boat, but he refused a ride. "God will take care of me," he said. Then a helicopter hovered overhead and dropped him a line, but he refused the line. "God will take care of me," he said. So he kept praying to God and finally asked, "When will you save me, O God?" God replied, "I sent you a canoe, and a boat, and a helicopter. What more do you want?"

God does not promise that there will be no trouble, but rather, "I will be with them in trouble" (v. 15). God will give you the strength and courage to seek safety and help.

Matthew 8:18–22

In contrast to the images in Psalm 91 of shelter and refuge, Matthew has Jesus saying to a follower that he has no place, no shelter. When another asks Jesus to wait until he can go and bury his father, Jesus seems somewhat cavalier in saying, "Let the dead bury their own dead."

Perhaps Jesus is simply naming the transient nature of his ministry here. He established no church, built no buildings, and did not settle in one place. He is on the move and invites his people to follow. Literally this is a challenge to families, because families in all their multiple manifestations need some stability in order to thrive. They need the shelter promised in Psalm 91 in order to raise children and attend to the elders.

Jesus rejects a literal shelter, yet he is sheltered by many as he travels and preaches. But he affirms the spiritual shelter of God. For a battered woman on the run, this may be all that she has. But she also needs a literal safe place to take her children where she will be protected from her abuser.

2 Corinthians 4:16–5:11

In Paul's Second Letter to the Corinthians, he is in conflict with that church and his authority is being challenged; he has been called weak by church leaders. He has suffered "deadly peril" in Asia (1:10). Amid his trials and tribulations, in this passage Paul looks to a larger context, reminding us that the experiences of this world are not the whole story. Instead, that which comes from God is eternal. "So we do not lose heart. . . . for we walk by faith" (4:16; 5:7). We may not have an earthly tent, but we have God's house. This imagery echoes Jesus in the preceding passage.

Again Paul reassures us of God's presence even in the worst of times. But a word of caution: as communities of faith, we are called to make God's presence manifest for a victim of abuse. This means we must not pass by on the other side, but stop, listen, and provide what we can for safety and healing.

Many victims of abuse feel abandoned by God, often because no one wants to stop and get involved. A battered woman with whom I spoke talked about feeling abandoned by God because she couldn't get away from her abuser. Later, after she escaped and was free from the abuse, she looked back and remembered the prayer about the footsteps in the sand. A person walking on the beach usually saw two sets of footsteps, her own and God's. But suddenly in crisis, she looked down and saw only one set, and assumed that God had abandoned her. Only later did she realize that the single set of footsteps belonged to God, who was carrying her through the crisis. This woman realized then that God had been there helping her and her children to survive the life-threatening violence of her husband.

To reassure a victim of abuse that God is present should not be a challenge to her faith: "*If* you are a good Christian, *if* your faith is strong, you will know God's presence." That just makes her feel guilty. But rather to reassure her means to *be* God's presence to her and, at some point when she can reflect, to help her realize God's role in her journey.

Ascension of Jesus

R. Mark Giuliano

PSALM 47
EPHESIANS 1:15–23
ACTS 1:1–11
LUKE 24:44–53

With the ascension, the Jesus story turns away from Jesus and his power toward the early church and its empowerment. Jesus' disciples organize and wait with expectation for the promised Helper who is coming. For followers who are anxious about Jesus' leaving, today's readings call disciples to engage in the countercultural act of praising God during hard times while equipping them with gifts and tools for carrying out the difficult and unique mission of God's transforming justice in the world.

Psalm 47

Those who are in search of quiet or contemplative worship today should not look for it in Psalm 47. This psalm, likely originating in the time of Solomon or David, directs music leaders to call worshipers' whole selves into the praise of God—heart, body, and soul. With singing (v. 6), hand clapping, and even shouts with loud songs (v. 1), the congregation is led to joyful acclamation. God's royal enthronement is highlighted with blowing the shofar, the ram's horn widely used in religious ceremonies and to announce holy days. For children of the 1960s and '70s, this kind of celebration may invoke a spirit similar to a stadium rock concert.

While some readers may find appealing this image of the faith community cutting loose with exuberant expressions of praise, others, such as we Presbyterians who like to do everything decently and in order, may be somewhat challenged by an invitation to wild and unabashed celebration of God's crowning reign over all the earth. But even Presbyterians should take heart:

Psalm 47 offers direction for organized praise, led by the chief musician or music leader.

Nonetheless, preachers of Psalm 47, perhaps in partnership with congregational music leaders, will not want to miss the opportunity to move the congregation carefully to holistic and visceral expressions of praise. Simply using the text as an opportunity to discuss the appropriateness of clapping hands in worship may miss the point; Psalm 47 calls us not to *talk about* praise, but actively to *engage in* celebration.

One of the most countercultural acts the church can do during times of economic anxiety, social discouragement, conflict, and war is to lift up praise to God with joy, playfulness, and humor. Consider delighting worshipers and God by having the choir hold up "applause" signs or "shout amen" placards every time your sermon says something marvelous about our God who not only watches from God's heavenly throne but engages and sustains the community in its works of mission and justice.

Ephesians 1:15–23

The Epistle to the Ephesians lifts up important themes that both inform and empower the emerging church at Ephesus as well as the contemporary church. Faith communities who feel lonely in their labor of justice or stressed under the weight of growing economic and social disorder may find in this text spiritual sustenance and empowerment to continue their important mission.

In the first chapter, the writer of Ephesians, pseudo-Paul, exhorts the community by sharing a personal prayer for new Gentile Christians. Adapted for preaching, the prayer is an easy mark for a three-point sermon. It encourages us to experience three things in Christ: hope (Gk. *elpis*), the riches of the inheritance of the faith community (*hagiois*, saints), and the power (*dunameos*) of faith in Jesus (1:18–19). These are distinctive gifts given to the church to help it persist in its mission of transformation and justice. When one of our city councillors and some of the Occupy Cleveland group joined us in the city's center for Sunday morning worship, I reminded them that "the Old Stone Church has been occupying Public Square for over 190 years" and that we had been waiting for them to join us in our mission; we had gifts to share. It was a good reminder to the occupiers and to the rest of the gathered community that in the vocational struggle for justice, we are gifted by God with hope, the blessings of life in the body of Christ, and strength in Jesus as we occupy the broken places of our world, confront corrupt powers and principalities, and work to transform unjust systems and social structures. These revolutionary tools of change are available not only to the church, but to all who join in its work.

Luke 24:44–53

A few years ago our congregation gathered for a discussion about our mission to and future in our urban neighborhood. Members who were concerned about shrinking budgets and the growing needs of the community explored a move to the fertile grounds of the suburbs. One member, a survivor of the Sierra Leonean civil war, delivered a passionate plea to keep the church planted in the economically arid soil of our struggling neighborhood: "If the church abandons the neighborhood, people will lose hope; the neighborhood will die."

His voice echoed the anxiety Jesus' disciples experienced when they learned that Jesus would leave them. In John's Gospel, for example, Jesus promises his disciples that he will not leave them orphaned (John 14:18a) and comforts their sorrow-filled hearts (16:4b). From the beginning, the disciples appear to be a somewhat jittery bunch who, when it comes to the absence of Jesus, suffer from separation anxiety (Mark 1:36).

In more recent times, we hear anxious protests from Jesus' followers when new bishops shut down long-standing urban parishes and presbyteries hammer plywood over stained-glass windows and oak doors of financially strapped congregations who can no longer foot the bill of being God's people amid neighborhoods in transition or decay.

Following the crucifixion and resurrection, however, much has changed for Jesus' followers; anxiety gives way to hope. The disciples are on the move, back from Bethany to Jerusalem, readying themselves to meet the Helper whom Jesus would send in his absence. The mood of Ascension Sunday is one of joyful expectation, empowerment, and hope within the present and ever-emerging church.

For Luke, the ascension (Gk. *anephereto*, being carried up) of Jesus signals both his lordship through the fulfillment of everything that was written about him "in the law of Moses, the prophets, and the psalms" (24:44b) as well as the new chapter soon to be penned in the life and mission of the apostles, their companions, and followers. As in the other Synoptic Gospels (Matt. 28:18–20; Mark 16:15–16), Jesus' mission for the church in Luke 24:47 is clear: in the name of Jesus, the apostles are to proclaim the message of repentance and forgiveness of sins to all peoples (Gk. *ta ethnē*, nations). Along with their commission, the apostles are sent to Jerusalem, where the new Jesus movement will have its birth (Acts 2).

Luke's text provides an opportunity for preachers to lift up the important theme of corporate empowerment in a culture of isolated and disempowered individualism. Lest we twist Luke's ascension account into a sermon that pats individuals on the back in our peculiar era of personal and privatized religion, let us remember that here and throughout the Gospels, Luke's Jesus speaks in the plural. He addresses not only individuals, but a people, his followers as a whole—apostles, companions, an Emmaus road couple (24:33).

While preachers will address personal concerns with their congregations, they ought to avoid reducing Luke's message to private experiences of Jesus. Luke provides the opportunity to embolden individuals by calling them out of the lonely futility and meaninglessness of isolation and into the corporate mission of the church and the presence of the Holy Spirit that empowers it. Of course, personal prayer and individual action are parts of our daily walk, but our disciplines find strength and joy in their connectedness to the body as a whole. Jesus' mission is not simply for you or me; it is a mission for you *and* me and many others.

As individuals, we may be pebbles who create infinite ripples of untold effect on the pond of life, but as a collective, we are the dam that abates the tide of injustice, we are the breaker wall that diffuses the powerful thrust of self-serving political agendas and corporate sprawl, and we are the turbine drawing ultimate power from the mysterious river called "Holy Spirit." As individuals, we may murmur truth to power, but as the body of Christ we roar.

Congregations in urban contexts are often burdened with an overwhelming sense of discouragement and powerlessness fueled by the relentless, outstretched hand of poverty, growing drug trade, increasing gang populations, senseless acts of violence and killing, corporate abandonment and joblessness, transiency, and dwindling resources for public education or programs of opportunity for neighborhood renewal. As individuals, our hearts can harden as hope dwindles. Pastors and other leaders, often overwhelmed by the imbalance between the heartache and joy of urban ministry, admit to being accosted by a seductive and incessant voice that whispers: "Leave the city; move away."

As participants in the church and its mission, however, we are often empowered by restorative worship, prayer, and study. We have the advantages of collective imagination, spiritual nurture, and mutual encouragement in our common work for the welfare of the city. We find solidarity with like-minded and similarly spirited friends who engage the city and confront its challenges. Within the body corporate, God's word of hope is spoken and becomes flesh in our lives; God's Spirit, as if giving mouth-to-mouth resuscitation to those who are drowning, revives us. Within the community of faith, we are reminded of who we are and to whom we belong.

Recently, our stewardship committee invited church members to write about what our downtown Cleveland church meant to them. One person wrote that the church "provides opportunities to serve as Jesus would have us do, something that is extremely difficult to do outside of the church." As Christ ascends, he has a mission for his church; it is a mission impossible for individuals locked in isolation, but it finds completion in the corporate life of the community of faith.

Acts 1:1–11

Reading the first verses of Acts, we might imagine the opening crawl text to George Lucas's *Star Wars* or the review of "last week's episode" on a television drama. Luke's first words, addressed to his old friend and patron mentioned in Luke 1:3 and simply identified as "Theophilus" (Acts 1:1), are a summary of the events and meaning of Jesus' story so far.

However, while Luke's précis is a reminder of where we have been in the story, it is also the backstory for that which is about to come. The backdrop is "all that Jesus did and taught from the beginning until the day when he was taken up to heaven, after giving instructions through the Holy Spirit to the apostles whom he had chosen" (1:1–2). What he offers are the coming empowerment of the Holy Spirit, the birth of the church in Jerusalem, and the acts of the apostles in the world (or, as William Willimon in his commentary on the book of Acts prefers to call them, "the acts of the Holy Spirit").[1]

Here, Luke's text provides preachers an opportunity to locate the congregation's story within the larger historic narrative of the Jesus movement. It may also be an occasion to explore a more recent or immediate backdrop to the life and work of the congregation. Preachers may use this time to lift up the stories of local saints whose faithful acts, which may perhaps reflect "suffering" in ways similar to Jesus (1:3), bear witness to the work of social justice and transformation, or to the mission and justice of God that inform our identity, reveal the presence of God, and point to that which is still to come.

The ascension opens a new chapter in the Jesus story: Jesus has now been enthroned at the right hand of God; the first ones who follow him in faith provide the backstory to the sequel in which we now participate.

---

1. William H. Willimon, *Acts*, Interpretation series (Atlanta: John Knox Press, 1988), 8.

Seventh Sunday of Easter

Luke A. Powery

ACTS 1:6–14
PSALM 68:1–10, 32–35
1 PETER 4:12–14; 5:6–11
JOHN 17:1–11

Every passage for this Sunday reveals that creative tensions exist in the life of faith. These tensions show that the Christian life is neither absent of pain nor comfortable. The Acts reading demonstrates that a community gathers to be scattered out of its comfort zones across different borders. In the psalm, God is high but stoops low and wages war to protect the needy. First Peter teaches that Christians will suffer, and in John's Gospel Jesus prays for the disciples who remain in a hostile world while he prepares to depart from it.

Acts 1:6–14

In the context of the promise to be baptized with the Holy Spirit (1:4–5), the disciples "come together" (v. 6; cf. 2:1), but their gathering is for the ultimate purpose of scattering across various boundaries. They come together to eventually leave. When they gather, Jesus is "lifted up" (v. 9) and departs. Before that, he reveals that being with him is not the purpose of discipleship. That would be too comfortable. The "power" of the Spirit that they will receive is for becoming "witnesses . . . to the ends of the earth" (v. 8). The disciples gather around Jesus to be sent out into the world in the power of the Spirit, transgressing geographical, ethnic, and even gender boundaries. Their experience of God in Christ "demands a witness."[1]

The Spirit thrusts the disciples into world mission. They are not to be "gazing up" (v. 10), so heavenly minded that they neglect doing earthly good. This is not surprising in light of "the Spirit of God Without-Within,"[2] who

---

1. William H. Willimon, *Acts*, Interpretation series (Atlanta: John Knox Press, 1988), 20.
2. Howard Thurman, *The Centering Moment* (New York: Harper & Bros., 1969), 21.

works across personal, communal, and social realms. "Heaven" is repeated four times in this passage (vv. 10–11), but after Jesus ascends, the "two men in white robes" (v. 10) ask a much-needed question, "Why do you stand looking up toward heaven?"(v. 11). The disciples are being called back to earth, "to the ends of the earth" (v. 8), rather than singing "I'll Fly Away" repeatedly. They are not to be escapist, daydreaming about the pearly-gates pie-in-the-sky to come, but are to go and "be . . . witnesses" in the whole world (v. 8). They set their gaze back on earth, return to the city of Jerusalem, going down "from the mount called Olivet" (v. 12). They were up on a spiritual, heavenly high, but the Spirit would soon immerse them in an earthly mission to lift others up.

After Jesus' disciples came down the mountain, they went to a "room *up*stairs" where "all" (1:8, 14; 2:1, 4, 12, 17, emphasis added) prayed constantly. Their first response to the call to mission was prayer, revealing the interrelationship between prayer and prayerful action, which was also evident during the Civil Rights Movement. Furthermore, the inclusive nature of Christianity is noteworthy with the incorporation of "certain women" (1:14) as equal participants.

Women in that day were considered to be of lower status than men. But Luke goes so far as to name "Mary the mother of Jesus" (v. 14) as a disciple. Up to this point, there have only been references to men. Mary is put on par with the male disciples. This is significant today, also, when ordained ministry is often denied to women and especially when preaching is still viewed primarily as a "male art."[3] Thus to know that "Mary the mother of Jesus" was present and named among his disciples is no small matter. Even the women are gathered to be scattered, to be baptized in the Spirit, to be witnesses and to prophesy (2:18). The gospel is far-reaching as it stretches across gender and ethnic boundaries. No segregated enclaves are allowed, making many people uncomfortable. The gospel propels Christ's disciples out of narcissism into mission and engagement with others in untraveled territory.

Psalm 68:1–10, 32–35

The creative tension within the Christian life continues in this psalm. The tension is not reduced simply because this is a song. God is high and mighty, riding on the clouds, transcendent, abiding in the heavens (vv. 4, 33–34). Yet God also proves to be immanent, working on earth, caring for orphans, widows, prisoners, the desolate and needy (vv. 5–6, 10). This God of majestic

---

3. Roxanne Mountford, *The Gendered Pulpit: Preaching in American Spaces* (Carbondale: Southern Illinois University Press, 2003), 102.

wonder is a god for the weak and worn. Thus the members of this God's kingdom should be down-to-earth and not lost amid heavenly clouds. God is earthy and earth-shaking (v. 8). No wonder the psalmist exhorts the audience to "sing" (vv. 4, 32) so many times. Mere prose is insufficient for praise of God. The "kingdoms of the earth" (v. 32) are exhorted to sing and lift their voices to this "awesome" God (v. 35) who possesses "a mighty voice" (v. 33). However, not everyone sings when meeting God, especially God's enemies (vv. 1–2). The righteous are glad (v. 3) but the wicked will melt away (v. 2). The God of wonder, worthy of musical praise, is also a God of war.

The presence of a warrior God in this passage may also explain why not everyone greets God with a happy song. The opening lines, "Let God rise up, let his enemies be scattered" (v. 1), are a part of an ancient song of war describing when the Lord was enthroned on the ark, leading people into war (cf. Num 10:35). God is even painted as a stormy god (Ps. 68:7–10). God is palpably present in the air and land and moves the universe. The "clouds" (v. 4) indicate God's presence and the "presence of God" shakes heaven and earth in the wilderness (v. 8), echoing the theophany at Mount Sinai (Exod. 19). This present and powerful God fights and always wins. God is victorious, establishing God's reign. A warlike god may make us uncomfortable in an age when many claim that their earthly battles are endorsed by God, suggesting that killing one of God's creatures is God's will. This is a part of the tension within Christianity in which many still sing "Onward, Christian Soldiers" alongside "Dona Nobis Pacem."

But the psalmist makes plain on whose behalf God fights—the orphans, widows, prisoners, and needy. Martin Luther King Jr. died fighting on behalf of sanitation workers in Memphis, Tennessee. Others continue to battle for the rights of poor farmers and the lives of innocent children. God does not delight in war but fights to save those ravaged by death-wielding powers (Ps. 68:30). The psalmist does not celebrate war and death, but the reign and presence of God who fights to save the oppressed because "God is a God of salvation" (v. 20). Although God is high in the heavens, God rides the clouds, and as long as God rides, we know that (in the words of the spiritual), "no [one] can a-hinder me."

1 Peter 4:12–14; 5:6–11

The writer of 1 Peter also reveals that the Christian life is not cozy but is lived in tension amid demanding circumstances. Echoing earlier themes (cf. 1:6–8; 3:13–17), chapters 4 and 5 speak of a "fiery ordeal" (4:12) and "a roaring lion . . . looking for someone to devour" (5:8; cf. Ps. 22:13). But it is not "strange" (1 Pet. 4:12) that this should happen, because in this setting many Gentiles were converting to Christianity, a despised foreign religion. Fellow believers "in all the world [were] undergoing the same kinds of suffering" (5:9). In addition, 1 Peter asserts, if you are reviled for Christ, "you are blessed, because the spirit of glory, which is the Spirit of God, is resting on you" (4:14). There appears to be a blessing for those who suffer, because the Spirit rests on those who suffer for Christ's sake.

There is a tension represented here in this teaching about rejoicing in suffering, blessing because of suffering, and (the spirit of) glory in suffering. Of course, the Spirit does not make Jesus a "superman,"[4] and even he must endure suffering on the cross. His fate suggests that suffering cannot be avoided for his disciples. This provides an antidote to those who view life in the Spirit as a pain-free prosperity jackpot. However, this idea of glory or rejoicing in suffering can also be dangerous. Some may interpret this as suggesting that all suffering is redemptive, and consequently subject themselves to unjust suffering as an avenue to union with Christ. On the other hand, those in power, maintaining the status quo that benefits them, could use this teaching as a way to encourage and justify the unnecessary suffering of millions of hungry persons as a sign of the Spirit's presence in their lives. Were those who were beaten, bruised, battered, and lynched through the storms of the Civil Rights Movement wrong if they did not rejoice in their unjust suffering? When teenagers or children are bullied because they are different in some way, and bullying leads to suicide, where is the glory in that? Is suffering always redemptive?

There are life lessons learned through pain, yet those in pain need to be ministered to and not left to drown in despair. Pain is not to be prayed for in order to reach the height of some spiritual nirvana. The verdict is still out about redemptive suffering, but the writer in 1 Peter seems to point in this direction: following Jesus is not for those who want to live their lives on easy street. Discipleship includes suffering, but also consolation that God will eventually exalt Christians (5:6), "restore, support, strengthen, and establish" them because God cares (5:10, 7).

John 17:1–11

Tensions within the Christian life are also evident in John's Gospel. As Jesus offers his final prayer to the Father before his crucifixion, the disciples are about to be "scattered" (16:32). It is bad enough that they are going to depart from one another, but Jesus adds that they "face persecution" (16:33) in the

---

4. Jürgen Moltmann, *The Spirit of Life: A Universal Affirmation*, trans. Margaret Kohl (Minneapolis: Fortress, 1994), 93.

world. He wants them to know that following him entails suffering. Jesus has to endure it because "the hour has come" (17:1), the hour when he will leave the world through death (16:28). But the disciples must remain in the world. For Jesus, it is an hour of glory (17:1, 4, 5), although it will not be easy. His glory will be gory. But this is the paradox of the Christian life—to live in glory one must die, and the death itself is part of the glory. This is why Jesus prays for his disciples.

Jesus knows that they will need all the prayer they can get. His focus is on them, not on the world (17:9). Jesus appears to be a bit exclusive here, even careless toward "the world," a world that God so loved (3:16). He prays for the disciples' protection "so that they may be one, as we are one" (17:11, 21–23). Their unity is crucial in a hostile world. He wants them to come together and be distinct, set apart from the world (vv. 14–16). Perhaps Jesus prays in this way because he is set on leaving at the appropriate "hour." He says, "I am no longer in the world, but they are in the world" (v. 11a). What does it mean for a Christian to be in the world but not of it? How does one live in this tension—loving a world of which one is not supposed to be a part? Does this mean we should be modern-day puritanical isolationists, turning our backs on "the things of the world," a world God came to save? What does Christian witness look like in this scenario, a world of great divides—Muslim versus Christian, Republican versus Democrat, citizen versus "illegal alien"? There are no simple answers to bridging the divides between "the world" and "us." Even Jesus, in this passage, does not seem to be much help. However, he does show us that even during difficult times, amid obvious tensions, one can pray. Finishing his work (v. 4) was not painless for Jesus, and doing his work today is no different. But if discipleship means anything, it means that one can do as Jesus did, look up to heaven (v. 1) and pray to the One who, in the words of the spiritual, can "guide [our] feet while [we] run this race."

Day of Pentecost

John S. McClure

NUMBERS 11:24–30
PSALM 104:24–34
1 CORINTHIANS 12:3B–13
JOHN 20:19–23

Pentecost shatters our usual understanding of how life is to be lived and organized, from the perspective of God's reign of justice. This Sunday's texts highlight several aspects of this larger theme. Numbers 11:24–30 shows us a God whose Spirit operates beyond the boundaries of "the camp" and cannot be contained in the usual places we expect. Psalm 104:24–34 celebrates God's creative "wisdom," which has ordered the created world in ways that provoke amazement and wonder. First Corinthians 12:3b–13 shows how this same divine wisdom has also established and ordered a new creation, the body of Christ, which is organized, not according to human wisdom, but according to the gifting of the Holy Spirit. John 20:19–23 encourages us to overcome fears that would constrict the reconciling mission of God's Spirit in the new creation.

Numbers 11:24–30

The book of Numbers focuses attention on the question of who will be numbered among God's people. Chapter 1 lists the twelve tribes who, having escaped from Egypt, are now in the process of nation building. The book as a whole poses the question of how Israel is to respond to other peoples: Moabites, Midianites, Amorites, Caananites, and so on.

In Numbers 11:24–30, the Spirit of God comes down in the cloud, speaks to Moses in the tent of meeting, and then rests on the seventy elders. What is most noticeable is that this tent is *outside* the camp. God's Spirit is manifest in a place other than the gathering of the people of God, and the people argue

251

against Eldad and Medad when a portion of God's Spirit comes to rest on them within the camp.

The opposite is usually the case in congregations today. We often assume that God's Spirit will manifest itself within our "camp" first of all. The ground outside the camp is identified as "the world," or "mission territory," the place where "others" live. As Moses clarifies, however, God will be manifest wherever God desires. The problem lies in limiting God's Spirit to one location or another, or assuming that our usual patterns of practicing the presence of God preclude God's presence beyond those boundaries.

It is always tempting for a nation, when obsessed with counting its numbers and deciding who is in and who is out, to locate God in one place instead of another. The result is a theology of scarcity and a God only large enough to belong to one people, one land, one temple, one religion, or even one sect. This tension between drawing or expanding boundaries is at the very heart of the entire book of Numbers, even as it is at the heart of our contemporary experiences of terrorism, immigration, and religious pluralism. Where is God? Upon whom will God's Spirit come to rest? Where will these Spirit-filled people reside?

If we answer on the side of scarcity and exclusion, we lend support to the kind of violence that leads terrorists to fly airplanes into buildings, or angry people to spray words of hate on the walls of mosques and synagogues. In these instances, one is tempted to say: "Your God is too small."

This text, however, points in the opposite direction and bears witness to the same Spirit found at Pentecost in the book of Acts, a Spirit who does not discriminate based on the usual boundaries drawn by those concerned to protect "the camp." Instead, the Spirit uses God's criteria, seeking out those whom God is claiming, whether inside or outside our usual boundaries and expectations.

Psalm 104:24–34

Given the other lectionary texts for this Sunday, the most important theme to note in these verses is the amazement expressed by the psalmist at what God, in God's wisdom, has made. This is clearly a God whose wisdom defies human understanding, whose wonders far exceed human categories and constrictions. The hymn "All Things Bright and Beautiful" repeats the psalmist's refrain of amazement: "The Lord God made them all!" (cf. v. 24). These verses also extol the entire creation's dependence on God. It is by virtue of God's handiwork that all things exist. God provides with generous abundance for all living things, not merely for one particular group or nation. The picture of abundance painted so beautifully here stands in stark contrast to a theology or economics of scarcity. Although we in our nation and our community depend on God, God has provided "manifold works" (v. 24), filling the earth with food and provisions for *all* living things. Remembering that all things come from God challenges human tendencies to act as if one group can or should claim ownership of these things and hoard them at the expense of others. Instead, the psalmist's vision encourages an attitude of thanksgiving and a generosity that is similar to that shown to us by God. God is thanked over and over again for lavish generosity, and this thanksgiving reminds us of our own identity as those who can follow in God's footsteps.

This text also points forward to the epistle reading for this week. Although Psalm 104 focuses on God's amazing wisdom in the first creation—God's creation of the natural beauty and order of the world—Paul, in 1 Corinthians 12, picks up this same theme and applies it to the new creation and the way things are ordered within the body of Christ. Once again, the abundance of God's provision remains central.

1 Corinthians 12:3b–13

"United we stand, divided we fall!" These words could easily be etched over this lectionary text. Paul is speaking to a congregation whose unity is seriously threatened, not so much by forces without as by forces within. The Corinthians have fallen prey to competing loyalties and ideologies. Infighting has distracted the young church from its divine purpose. As the body of Christ, the church is God's new creation on earth, a community of love, justice, and reconciliation in the world. In 1 Corinthians 1:18–25, Paul has made it clear that this community embodies the "wisdom of God," which is foolishness by the standards of most human organizations. This wisdom constitutes a reversal in the way that communities are organized. Within the body of Christ, hierarchy and one-upmanship give way to participatory, shared leadership. Life in Christ is life in which pecking orders disappear and spiritual giftedness takes over.

Instead of organizing the church around status, class, privilege, education, or gender roles, Paul urges the community to organize itself according to the many ways the Holy Spirit empowers each member for the "common good" (v. 7). In other words, spiritual gifts do not exist to support yet another hierarchy of individuals, but to build up the community for its mission.

When preaching for justice and transformation, the preacher can help the congregation to catch a glimpse of what community looks like within the new creation. Instead of a society in which many are marginalized as underprivileged and have-nots while others boast multiple privileges and powers, Paul imagines a community in which all are gifted with apportionments of God's

Spirit. Instead of a spiritual economy of scarcity, we again see what we saw in Numbers 11 and Psalm 104: a world of plentitude in which God desires to pour out spiritual gifts on many, beyond our usual expectations.

Paul realizes, however, that even spiritual gifts can be subdivided and shaped into a hierarchy. He reminds the Corinthian congregation that this is only possible if they lose sight of the fact that they only have these gifts by virtue of their status as "members of the body," which, as Paul points out throughout chapter 12, is the body of Christ, the new creation, the eschatological presence of the reign of God on earth. Within the body of Christ, spiritual gifts are always focused on the common good, from Jews or Greeks, slaves or free (v. 13). All of the usual ways in which people are organized by class, ethnicity, gender, social status, or education are irrelevant within this new creation. All that is relevant is the way that God's gifts empower each for the common welfare of the whole.

What ideologies are competing for our attention today, inside and outside our churches? What pecking orders have we established within our congregations that subtly or not so subtly divide us? In what ways are we making some spiritual gifts more important than others, elevating one part of the body of Christ to a status above others? How can we, as a community, recapture Paul's vision of a Spirit-gifted, participatory community "baptized into one body . . . made to drink of one Spirit" (v. 13)?

John 20:19–23

A group of Jesus' faithful followers were huddled together in a house with the door locked out of fear of those who represented the religious and political status quo of their day. Although the analogy is not perfect, this portrait of a group of people cowering before the religious and political authorities reflects some of the fear experienced today by those concerned with social justice, in the face of religious and secular authorities. This is especially true in light of the growing union between fundamentalist religion and powerful political authorities in our day. Harry Emerson Fosdick, in the 1920s, preached a sermon titled "Shall the Fundamentalists Win?" One could easily argue that fundamentalism is, indeed, winning, when one looks at much of the American and global scene.

We hear in John's fearful attitude to "the Jews" a fear of the then-majority interpreters of their religion by a frightened minority. In our context, of course, Judaism no longer represents religious hegemony, and any sermon on this text would need to handle an analogy between first-century Judaism and American religious fundamentalism very carefully to clarify these differences in historical context. But the analogy is not unfounded. Whether warranted or not, *fear* of religious authorities in high places is easily spawned among marginal groups or movements. Many of us who share a vision of society marginalized by American neoconservatives and apocalypticists know what it is like having one eye glued to the peephole of the locked door as we preach, prepare church budgets, write e-mails and letters, decide on church mission statements, and make decisions regarding where we will stand on difficult social issues. Sometimes we even worry for our safety and survival.

In this context, John's story provides us with at least three insights. First, we notice that Jesus doesn't seem to be surprised that his followers have gone into fearful retreat, and he works immediately to counteract their fear. The text says that Jesus "came and stood among them" and said, "Peace be with you" (v. 19). Although we may think we have no chance against what we perceive to be gathering forces outside the door, there is reason to take heart and not let our fears destroy our witness for justice.

Second, Jesus encourages the disciples to participate with him in "sentness," to stay focused on their mission and overcome their fears. "As the Father has sent me, so I send you" (v. 21): not to sit around and think of ways to keep out of trouble; not to avoid conflicts; not to sit for hours on end, fearfully weighing each word in an e-mail or sermon in order to stay out of church (or civil) courts; not to spend our lives debating and second-guessing ourselves so that we never make a decision about real issues in which people's lives and health are at stake. If we give in to fear and commit ourselves only to lukewarm strategies of self-preservation, then we can't help but wonder if we are really being the church that Christ sends to embody Christ's peace and justice in the world.

Third, the story tells us that Jesus "breathed on them and said to them, "Receive the Holy Spirit. If you forgive the sins of any, they are forgiven them; if you retain the sins of any, they are retained" (vv. 22–23). The disciples are given a new commission, to look for ways to breathe the Spirit's freedom, openness, and love into the lives of others. In short, we, like the disciples, are told to become the inhalation and exhalation of God's Spirit, the Spirit of forgiveness, of release from the powers of sin, evil, and death, in a world that knows only the retaining and recycling of human sin and evil.

First Sunday after Pentecost (Trinity Sunday)

Kee Boem So

GENESIS 1:1–2:4A
PSALM 8
2 CORINTHIANS 13:11–13
MATTHEW 28:16–20

Trinity Sunday invites us to reflect on the mystery of the Trinity and its implications for Christian faith and life. The Trinity has practical implications for Christian spirituality and social justice. This week's readings gather important passages related to the Trinity in the context of creation and God's invitation to human beings to continue the creation as God's coworkers. As we explore the readings with regard to the life of the Trinity, two themes emerge: God's invitation to relationships with God and others (humans and creatures), and our partnership with God as coworkers. These themes will demonstrate how spirituality and social justice are interrelated as we reflect on the Trinitarian relationship at the heart of Christian life.

Genesis 1:1–2:4a

The first reading concerns how the world came into existence. The creation described in the first chapter of Genesis reflects Trinitarian activity. As God the Creator initiates all acts of creation, the Spirit who is hinted at in the description of "a wind from God" (1:2) accompanies the Creator. We might think that we will not be able to find a locus for the second person of the Trinity in this story. However, we are reminded by one of the Christian communities of the first century that the second person of the Trinity was with God during creation: according to John 1:1, "In the beginning was the Word, and the Word was with God, and the Word was God."[1] God created the world

1. The association of Genesis 1:1–2:4a with John 1:1–18 is well argued in Mary L. Coloe, *God Dwells with Us: Temple Symbolism in the Fourth Gospel* (Collegeville, MN: Liturgical Press, 2001), 21–23.

256

out of God's words, and the Christ as the Word participated in the creation, while the Spirit accompanied this whole process.

This feature of the Trinitarian activity is hinted at in Genesis 1:26 when God says, "Let us make humankind in our image, according to our likeness." Although it is believed that the plural refers to "the divine council or heavenly court," the plural reference may also be suggestive of the triune God who participates in the work of creation relationally in God's own being. The creation in general and the creation of humankind in particular originate from "a dialogical act rather than a monological act" of God.[2] God works in relationship with Godself to bring about creation.

The story of the creation continues to focus on relationships as it unfolds. At the heart of the creation lies God's act of naming what God creates (1:5, 8, 10). This is the way in which God continues to interact with creatures. God does not stop interacting with creatures after completing the creation. God still communicates, sustains, and responds to them, seeking an ongoing relationship with them.

This activity of God's naming creatures has a parallel, that is, the naming by human beings in Genesis 2:19–20. In this second account of creation, human naming is an act of participation in the act of the creation indicating that God has invited humans to sustain and respond to the creatures as divine coworkers. The human responsibility as God's coworkers in the creation story is clearly stated: "God blessed them [humankind], and God said to them, 'Be fruitful and multiply, and fill the earth and subdue it; and have dominion over the fish of the sea and over the birds of the air and over every living thing that moves upon the earth'" (1:28). "Dominion" here is not an invitation to exploitation, but implies care giving. God wants us to relate to creatures as God relates to them in caring ways.

The main reason that humankind can participate in the act of God's continuing creation is that we are created in the image of God (1:26). The context in which this statement is posed is one of relationship (as the divine council may signify the members of the Trinity): "Then God said, 'Let us make humankind in our image, according to our likeness'" (1:26a). As the three persons of the Trinity relate with one another, humankind has been endowed with the ability to relate to others as persons created in the image of God. It is the image of God within us that is the basis of the power to relate to God and others.

Thus, the creation story is permeated with caring relationships of all kinds as God creates out of the divine Trinitarian relationship. Humankind is invited to live out this life of relationships with God and also with God's

2. Terence E. Fretheim, "Genesis," in *The New Interpreter's Bible*, vol. 1 (Nashville: Abingdon Press, 1996), 345.

creatures as divine coworkers. This first reading provides a framework for understanding the next readings. With Genesis in mind, we will pay attention in the next readings to the implications of the Trinitarian relationship for Christian spirituality and social justice.

Psalm 8

This psalm demonstrates the artistic technique of inclusio as it places praising God's sovereignty at the beginning as well as the end of the psalm: "O Lord, our Sovereign, how majestic is your name in all the earth!" (vv. 1, 9). God is exalted as the creator of the universe, which is distinguished from the human sovereignty explored in the remainder of the psalm. This structure (enhanced by the use of inclusio) indicates that human sovereignty or partnership in the world should be placed in service to God's sovereignty and our praising of it. After all, we are coworkers, and God provides the originating power and imaginative source of all creation.

Between the first and last verses are several thematic parallels to the story of creation in the previous passage from Genesis. Following the general allusion to creation in verses 1b and 3, the theme of relationship becomes prominent. The psalmist points to God's care giving that has been provided to creatures, especially to human beings: "What are human beings that you are mindful of them, mortals that you care for them?" (v. 4). God does not leave human beings alone, but is mindful of us and cares for us. In other words, God wants to be in relationship with humans. God's passionate desire to have relationships with us persists.[3] Spirituality is not simply about practices, visions, and ecstatic experiences, but about having relationships with God and imitating the divine Trinitarian relationship in our own Christian lives, which includes just and loving relationships with all creation.

The image of God is also present here: "Yet you have made them a little lower than God, and crowned them with glory and honor" (v. 5). Human beings share something with God although they are "a little lower than God." This something shared with God (the image of God) enables them not only to have a relationship with God, but also to have relationships with other human beings and creatures. The psalmist says, "You [God] have given them [humankind] dominion over the works of your hands" (v. 6). Once again, dominion means care giving. As God cares for human beings, God wants us to offer Godlike care to other creatures and all creation. This is God's vital invitation to human participation in the continuation of creation as God's

---

3. This is the main thrust of prayer emphasized by a well-known spiritual director in the United States. See William Barry, *God's Passionate Desire* (Chicago: Loyola University Press, 2009).

responsible coworkers. Today the world suffers from environmental problems such as pollution, global warming, climate change, species extinction, and landfills. The whole creation groans and waits for "the revealing of the children of God" (Rom. 8:19). We are the responsible coworkers of God who continue to sustain the creation that arises out of Trinitarian relationality.

2 Corinthians 13:11–13

It is not uncommon for Paul to close his letters with admonitions concerning his "sense of what is most needed in the community."[4] The final greeting that he offers in his Second Letter to the Corinthians is no exception. Paul exhorts the community in Corinth to engage in caring, respectful relationships with one another. The heart of this passage clearly focuses on the Trinitarian relationship: "The grace of the Lord Jesus Christ, the love of God, and the communion of the Holy Spirit be with all of you" (v. 13). This model benediction suggests that believers should place their lives in the care of the Trinitarian relationship. The Christian life is about experiencing the Trinitarian relationship at work in our lives, enjoying it, and living up to God's relationship with us through our relationships with others.

It seems that Paul wants to point out the practical implications of the Trinitarian relationship as they are related to human relationships. Before he explicitly introduces the members of the Trinity in his benediction, he argues first that right human relationships must be practiced: "Put things in order, listen to my appeal, agree with one another, live in peace; and the God of love and peace will be with you" (v. 11). The movement suggested here is from love and peace in human relationships to those with God in the Trinitarian relationship. Our relationships with others and our relationship with God are interrelated. If one is distorted, the other experiences the same fate. As we embody loving and just relationships with others, we will more fully experience our relationship with God, whose nature is one of mutuality and care within the fullness of the Trinity.

Liberation theologians and Christian social activists know well the vital and necessary ways that human and divine relationships affect one another. We embody the Trinitarian relationship in our caring relationships with other human beings, while God's relationship with us provides the source and strength of our work for social transformation. Accordingly, prophets and mystics share the same source of their ministries. We pray in order to transform the world, while we engage in the concerns of social justice in order to deepen our relationship with God. This mutuality of relationship with God

4. J. Paul Sampley, "Second Corinthians," in *The New Interpreter's Bible*, ed. Leander Keck et al., vol. 11 (Nashville: Abingdon Press, 1996), 178.

and others is the essence of Christian spirituality as well as the work of liberation and social justice.

Matthew 28:16–20

Here we find another reference to the Trinity. This time it is within Jesus' call to make disciples of all nations, baptizing persons in the name of the triune God. This Great Commission takes place on a mountain, where the disciples meet the risen Lord as he shares with them his final teaching. The mountain setting reminds us of another mountain where Jesus taught his followers about discipleship in the Sermon on the Mount (chaps. 5–7). Jesus' final words in 28:19–20a are also about discipleship: he urges them to make disciples of all people, baptizing them into a new community of faith that is predicated on the relationships within the Trinity and teaching its members everything that Jesus has taught his earliest followers about discipleship.

What is "everything" that Jesus has taught them about discipleship? James Robinson argues out of his lifelong quest for the historical Jesus that everything Jesus taught can be summarized, "Trust God to care for you, and hear God calling on you to care for your neighbor!"[5] Disciples are therefore taught to trust the Trinitarian relationship at work in their lives and to manifest this in relationships with neighbors as well.

Dietrich Bonhoeffer vehemently opposed the Nazi regime as German national identity became the ruling ideology, and he chose instead to teach about Christ's way of discipleship.[6] It was Bonhoeffer's conviction that our relationship with the Trinity should be enacted in our relationship with neighbors, because we see "a physical sign of the gracious presence of the triune God" in our neighbors.[7] Social justice emerges out of this gracious relationship with God as Christians manifest divine care in our relationships with others as Jesus' disciples.

As we reflect on the readings for Trinity Sunday, God invites us to live in ways that embody the Trinitarian relationship every day. Whether we are working toward environmental justice, economic distributive justice, equality between women and men, or human rights for LGBTQ persons, it is our responsibility as God's coworkers to embody a life of loving relationships with others as the Creator, Christ, and Spirit relate to one another and all of creation.

5. James M. Robinson, *The Gospel of Jesus: In Search of the Original Good News* (New York: HarperSanFrancisco, 2005), xi. He also makes reference to Matt. 28:16–20 in a line of argument similar to mine.

6. See Dietrich Bonhoefffer, *The Cost of Discipleship* (New York: Simon & Schuster, 1995).

7. Dietrich Bonhoeffer, *Life Together* (New York: Harper & Brothers, 1954), 20.

Proper 3

Safiyah Fosua

ISAIAH 49:8–16A
PSALM 131
1 CORINTHIANS 4:1–5
MATTHEW 6:24–34

The emphasis for this day arises out of the Gospel text: "Seek first the kingdom of God and its righteousness and all other things will find their rightful place" (Matt. 6:33, my trans.). Sadly, we often lose sight of God's priorities and turn our attention to *those other things*. We are not immune to becoming divisive and prideful like the believers in Corinth, instead of meek and trusting like the writer of Psalm 131. Whenever we forget that God loves *all* of us and has made provision for *all* of us, we tend to fight over resources. The readings this week encourage us to remember that God is mindful of our needs and cares about all of us. We have no need to divide into camps and wage wars for resources, to form hierarchical relationships, or even to worry obsessively about everyday things. We are beloved and our names are carved on the palms of God's hands (Isa. 49:16a).

Isaiah 49:8–16a

Isaiah 40–55, also known as Second Isaiah, is believed to have been written during the final days of the Babylonian exile. This passage, which follows the second Servant Song (Isa. 49:1–6), is an elaboration on the mission and ministry of the coming Servant, with a description of the kind of deliverance the people of Israel should expect. The speaker is God and the people being discussed are the exiled Israelites.

God paints a word picture of a return quite different from that which they experienced during the time of their wilderness wanderings in Egypt. This time, when they return from Babylon, they will not hunger or thirst (v. 10). Instead of the unforgiving desert they will travel along a good road (v. 11).

261

The songs of the mountains, earth, and heaven will celebrate God's compassion on the suffering people. The once-scattered Israelites will be gathered from the north, the west, and from faraway Syene in southern Egypt.

The passage ends with the promise that God could no more forget the exiled people of Israel than a pregnant woman could forget that she is pregnant or a nursing mother could forget about her infant child. And even if they could, God could not forget Israel, for Israel is carved on the palms of God's hands.

In reading these words, I hear distant echoes of the sermonic refrain of generations of dark ancestors who dared to insist that "trouble don't last always," as a preface to the message of hope that they knew would stand in stark contrast to the incredible cruelty and adversity they faced as slaves, and the unbelievable post-slavery contradictions that persist into this century. I experience even this memory as a contradiction, because today bold words of comfort and hope are often handed sheepishly to sufferers on fancy note cards, whispered into weary ears, or given as a secret prescription to the hopeless. Who will now dare to sing the Song of the Servant aloud or to echo God's promises from the housetops? Do we have the courage to preach such hope—or are our sermons chained to easy answers and polite certitudes? Do some of us hesitate to proclaim things that we cannot personally guarantee, lest we be found guilty of peddling false hope (or sued for spiritual malpractice)?

Scholars seem to be in agreement about the speaker, God, and the subject of the discourse, Israel, but to whom else is God speaking? We have dealt with the particularity of so many of the messages from the prophets that we often forget that the God who spoke long ago continues to speak to us today through ancient words of prophecy. If Isaiah 49:8–16a is only a description of the work of the Servant, we can all sit back, study these texts at arm's length, and wait for the Servant to come and set things right. If, however, these words extend to all God's faithful, if we are God's present-day agents of deliverance, the implications are different.

There are several points of comparison between this passage and Luke 4:18–19, which describes the mission of Jesus. As followers of Christ, we are also charged to do things that society considers outrageous—such as preaching freedom to twenty-first-century prisoners. We are charged to lift forgotten people out of darkness and to take the lead in teaching disadvantaged populations how to make sufficient food and clean water available to their communities. In an era when many lands have fallen into exploitive hands, we are charged to join ongoing work toward a just future for desolate people, both at home and abroad. A number of secular organizations have already undertaken this work, work that Christians were charged to do. What, however, transforms secular works of charity into the work of

God? What kind of people must we become in order to do this work in the *name of God?*

Psalm 131

Psalm 131 gives us a welcome rest from the heaviness of Isaiah 49 with its exiles and captives, the contentiousness of yet another letter from Paul to the Corinthians, and the human preoccupation with money, details, and material things in this week's passage from the Sermon on the Mount. Psalm 131 is the twelfth of the Songs of Ascent, a collection of fifteen psalms within the book of Psalms. These songs were sung by travelers on their way *up* to Jerusalem for feast days. As a group, the songs reflect the pietistic concerns of pilgrims. Psalm 131, which speaks of humility and childlike trust, concludes with an exhortation to hope in the Lord.

The psalmist uses comparisons and contrasts that remind us of other passages in Wisdom literature. Haughtiness and self-importance in verse 1 are contrasted with the psalmist's humility and simplicity. The simplicity of the psalm is deceptive; it deals with a weighty spiritual issue. In Proverbs 6:16–19, haughty eyes top the list of seven things that God hates, and "haughty eyes and a proud heart" are called sin in Proverbs 21:4.

The psalmist's use of the phrase "like a weaned child with its mother" has led some to speculate that the psalmist was a woman.[1] As long as this young child is near a parent, the child's soul is calmed and quieted. The image of a very young child hidden in her mother's skirts or clinging to one leg of her jeans paints a familiar picture of trust and reliance. Verse 2 recalls Jesus' encouragement to be humble like children (Matt. 18:4). The last verse of this short psalm exhorts Israel to hope in God.

If the troubling question of Isaiah 49:8–16a is, "Who has the courage to preach hope in an age of easy certitudes?" the equally troubling question for Psalm 131 is, "Who is virtuous enough to sing this song on the way to church?" In a cultural environment that confuses self-importance with confidence, who, with integrity, is able to speak about humility? Are we humble enough to join the scarcely noticed movement of young people who are trading the affluence of the suburbs for the poverty of several troubled inner-city communities to *live* the gospel among their neighbors? Who, today, will risk résumé or reputation to side with the poor, the persecuted, or the immigrant? In a politically correct environment—where empowerment and assertiveness are the orders of the day—how many Christians can we name who model the

---

1. Most Bibles attribute this psalm to David. For more about the gender of the psalmist, see J. Clinton McCann Jr., "The Book of Psalms," in *The New Interpreter's Bible*, vol. 4 (Nashville: Abingdon Press, 1996), 1208.

humility spoken of in Psalm 131 that is necessary in order to work with others toward fulfilling God's just purposes?

1 Corinthians 4:1–5

Paul's first letter to the Christians in Corinth reflects the myriad challenges that he faced in reorienting this predominantly Gentile faith community to the unique ethos of first-century Christianity. The letter, which was written to address concerns that had been brought to Paul, reveals that the Corinthians had problems abandoning sexual immorality, putting their previous religious practices into proper perspective (as seen in the discourse about meat offered to idols), and understanding how to relate to the leaders of the Christian movement. The Corinthians were ensnared by age-old "who is the greatest" arguments and had divided into factions: "'I belong to Paul,' or 'I belong to Apollos,' or 'I belong to Cephas,' or 'I belong to Christ'" (1 Cor. 1:12b). Indirect speech about this problem is sprinkled throughout the first three chapters of 1 Corinthians. However, in chapter 4, Paul speaks directly to the issue.

Perhaps it is fortunate that the Revised Common Lectionary provides only a small portion of this confrontational but didactic speech, because we are often confused by the unfamiliar style of argument that Paul employs. From the vantage point of twenty-first-century niceness, it looks as though Paul runs the risk of being guilty of the same kind of boasting that he condemns in the Corinthians. The point of his argument is that even highly respected church leaders like Paul, Apollos, and Cephas were merely servants of Christ and *oikonomous mustêriôn theou*, house or estate managers of the mysteries of God (4:1). The statement flies in the face of hierarchical thinking everywhere! There are no greater or lesser apostles; all are servants of Christ and under the judgment of Christ. All of the apostles are on equal footing; they are colleagues and not part of a hierarchy. All are employed by Christ, so there is no room for comparisons or boasting or factions. "Under these terms, Paul can say that his stewardship is not under the judgment of the Corinthians, but only under God who approves and disapproves his stewardship (4:4–5)."[2]

If Psalm 131 is an endearing picture of humility, clearly 1 Corinthians 4:1–5 is a troubling snapshot of the flip side of humility—pride. Paul's words continue to indict us. Our myriad divisions distract us from our real mission, which is to be present, as people of God, in a troubled world.

---

2. Boykin Sanders, "1 Corinthians," in *True to Our Native Land: An African American New Testament Commentary*, ed. Brian K. Blount et al. (Minneapolis: Fortress Press, 2007), 284.

Matthew 6:24–34

"No one can serve two masters." Jesus clearly describes another significant stumbling block: confused priorities. A key to interpreting Matthew 6:24–34 is found in Jesus' statements contrasting God and wealth ("mammon," KJV). While *mammon* is simply the Aramaic word for money or possessions,[3] it has come to be identified with idolatry to wealth and possessions.

The passage, which comes from the Sermon on the Mount, is part of a larger section (6:19–34) that deals with the right use of money and wealth. Jesus uses a series of metaphors to raise questions: What are your life's priorities? Whom do you serve? The rich have already been addressed in verses 19–21 in the conversation about treasures in heaven. Matthew 6:25 is directed to ordinary people. Any visitor to the countries of the two-thirds world will quickly conclude that much of the energy of daily life is directed toward making sure that there is enough. Enough food. Enough water. Enough clothing. The majority of the world's people are striving for the basic necessities of life. Jesus' followers were not being encouraged to abandon self-care, but to abandon the human preoccupation with having more "stuff," even if we must exploit others to have it.

We see this tension today in skewed perceptions about scarcity and wealth that frequently lead to hoarding and violence. Wars have been waged over the *illusion* of garnering enough—enough water, enough fertile farmland, enough oil, enough . . . Entire groups of people have been marginalized or demonized over the very thought that their having any part of the pie would mean less for another group. Overfilled *closets* and overfilled *bellies* both betray subconscious concerns about having enough.

To this, Jesus says ENOUGH! Stop worrying about food or drink or clothing and redirect your attention to the things of God. No more storing stuff in barns and storage pods. No more redefining boundaries and borders to make sure that we have enough natural resources to satisfy our greed. No more pushing people out of the line for a larger share. The righteousness of God and the realm of God are our ultimate priorities.

---

3. Douglas R. A. Hare, *Matthew*, Interpretation series (Louisville, KY: John Knox Press, 1993), 73.

Proper 4

Diane G. Chen

GENESIS 6:9–22; 7:24; 8:14–19   DEUTERONOMY 11:18–21, 26–28
PSALM 46   PSALM 31:1–5, 19–24
ROMANS 1:16–17; 3:22B–28 (29–31)
MATTHEW 7:21–29

This week's commentary approaches the issue of social justice indirectly, focusing on the formation of God's people. In order to do God's work of justice and mercy in this world with effectiveness and integrity, we must be grounded in two foundational convictions. First, we must acknowledge God's authority. Only God has the power to save and to judge, in God's way and according to God's timing. Second, we must commit ourselves by faith to God's saving agenda. There is nothing ambiguous about God's expectations. Obedience leads to life, while rebellion leads to death. The choice is ours. So are the consequences.

Psalm 46 and Genesis 6:9–22; 7:24; 8:14–19

"Be still, and know that I am God!" (Ps. 46:10). What images come to mind? Do we hum the slow, steady melody of the popular hymn by the same name and see ourselves sitting quietly to hear God's still, small voice? Reading this verse in isolation, we may assume being still means calming our restless hearts. In context, however, stillness is an imperative. We are "commanded to stillness" before God's awe-inspiring power.

Confidently, the Israelites assert that YHWH is *their* God: "The LORD of hosts is with *us*; the God *of Jacob* is *our* refuge" (Ps. 46:7, 11; emphasis added). Immeasurably powerful, YHWH is committed to Israel and has chosen this people from among the nations. Like a massive fortress encasing everything within its walls, God is Israel's "refuge and strength" (vv. 1–2). God has delivered Israel time and again. Those who sing this psalm need not be afraid when they are in trouble, for surely YHWH will help those who belong to God.

266

What kinds of trouble are in view here? The psalmist pictures cataclysmic ones—trembling mountains, roaring waters, and warring nations, troubles that threaten to destroy lives, instill fear, and cause despair. Intimidating though these natural and human powers may seem, as soon as YHWH intervenes, the divine word overwhelms chaos and restores order. In sharp contrast to raging floods and terrifying earthquakes, God's presence is like a river of gladness traversing God's secure and immovable city (vv. 4–5). To curb human aggression, God "breaks the bow, shatters the spear, [and] burns the shields." Disarmed, soldiers stop fighting (v. 9). When God subdues chaos and imposes peace, "kingdoms totter, . . . [and] the earth melts" (v. 6). It is in this context that YHWH commands everything to be still. Because YHWH is God, YHWH is exalted above all (v. 10).

In the story of the flood, Noah's stillness resides in his obedience. In Genesis 6, God is about to destroy the earth in response to widespread sin and violence practiced on earth. In Hebrew, the same root verb, *shachath*, is used twice: because the whole earth *ruined* itself, God *will ruin* it. *Shachath* appears four times in rapid succession, emphasizing the seriousness of the offense that warrants God's sweeping punishment (Gen. 6:11–13). Rhetorically, using the same verb for both God and humankind suggests a bidirectional relationship between creator and creation. God not only creates but also responds to that which God created. Had the earth not been corrupt, God would not have sent the flood. Had Noah not been righteous, God would not have saved him and his family. God's actions—the annihilation of a corrupt earth and the preservation of a righteous remnant—are direct responses to human attitudes toward the divine. Rebellion results in destruction, but obedience leads to life.

Throughout this story, God alone speaks. This way of storytelling highlights God's authority from beginning to end. God explains to Noah the divine plan and establishes a covenant with him ahead of time. God gives instructions for building the ark and tells Noah when to enter and when to leave. Although Noah is silent, his actions speak volumes about his complete submission. The author writes: "Noah did this; he did all that God commanded him" (6:22). Again, after the flood, it was only after God had given the cue to disembark that "Noah went out with his sons and his wife and his sons' wives" (8:18). Not a word of question, doubt, or protest is attributed to this "righteous man, [who is] blameless in his generation" (6:9).

Noah's stillness before God means neither indifference nor inaction. Because Noah acts, he and his family are spared. We too live in a corrupt generation where exploitations are commonplace, from human trafficking to ignoring the environment. Will we stand up as the Noahs of our generation because we know that YHWH is God? Will we demonstrate our faithfulness with concrete action, even if it invites ridicule and opposition?

Deuteronomy 11:18–21, 26–28 and Psalm 31:1–5, 19–24

The alternate Old Testament readings echo the theme already found in Psalm 46 and the story of Noah, that those who trust and obey God will receive abundant blessings, but those who rebel will suffer judgment and widespread failure. These two alternatives are clearly presented in the terms of the covenant between YHWH and Israel.

Deuteronomy 11:18–21 is almost a restatement of Deuteronomy 6:6–9. Both passages instruct Israel on what to do with the Law. They are like bookends of an inclusio, between which Moses recounts how the generation that came out of Egypt failed to trust God. Now a new generation stands at the edge of the Jordan, within sight of the promised land. Israel must once again decide whether to follow YHWH.

What does YHWH require of Israel? Because God loves Israel, God gives them the law, teaching them how to live as God's covenantal people. In response, Israel's love for God is expressed in faithful obedience to the law. Through constant recitation and praxis, it is internalized into the people's hearts, minds, and souls, yielding proper behavior before God and others, both at home and in the community, from one generation to another (11:18–21).

The terms of the covenant are clear. Fidelity to YHWH and obedience to the divine commandments will bring prosperity, peace, and longevity in the land for generations to come. Disobedience and following pagan gods will lead to destruction and abandonment (vv. 26–28). Once the Israelites come into contact with the Canaanites and see their military prowess, economic resources, and religious practices, the temptation to assimilate will be strong. Of these two ways, which one will Israel choose?

While the Old Testament is replete with accounts of Israel chasing after the Asherahs and the Baals, there are some who remain faithful. In Psalm 31, the psalmist is determined to choose YHWH for salvation and life even as danger and death loom large.

"Into your hands I commit my spirit" (Ps. 31:5). With these same words, Jesus breathed his last (Luke 23:46). Whereas Jesus surrenders his life to his Father while hanging on the cross, the psalmist's situation is more difficult to identify. Nevertheless, it sounds grim. The psalmist's enemies are like poachers, setting traps to hunt him down like an animal (Ps. 31:4). They are like invading armies putting a city under siege (v. 21).

Although despairing of life itself, the psalmist, like Jesus, has not lost faith. Instead of letting fear distort his perception of reality (v. 22), the writer affirms what he knows about God. First, YHWH has the power to save. God is a bastion of strength, a rock, and a fortress, behind which the fugitive seeks refuge (vv. 1–3). Despite the hidden snares around him, the psalmist finds safety hiding "in the shelter of [God's] presence," beyond the reach of "human plots" and "contentious tongues" (vv. 19–20). Second, YHWH has the obligation to save because of the divine covenant with Israel. When the psalmist says, "You have redeemed me, O YHWH, faithful God" (v. 5), the writer is invoking the image of redemption. As Israel's owner, it is God's responsibility and prerogative to buy back those who belong to him. If God did so at the exodus event, why not save the psalmist now? Third, YHWH must maintain divine integrity. God's righteousness demands that goodness be extended to those who fear God and wait for divine deliverance. It also requires that God repay the proud in equal measure (vv. 1, 19, 23–24). Knowing where she or he stands before God, the psalmist prays for God to intervene. Courage and patience are called for until salvation comes.

Our world, too, is plagued with violence and corruption. Crimes are rampant and resources are scarce. One person's gain is another's loss. It may feel to many of us as if there is not enough to go around. We feel oppressed, exploited, and unsafe. In turn we become selfish and protect our own interests. The temptation is to take justice into our own hands. We want to fight back, prove ourselves to be in the right, vindicate our name, and destroy the wicked. To justify our actions, do we sometimes confuse our self-righteous motivations with God's guidance? Do we usurp God's prerogative by trying to save ourselves and punish others?

These Old Testament texts remind us to trust that God will right the wrongs of this world. The psalmist takes refuge in God, and lets God be deliverer and warrior, both for the nation (Ps. 46) and for the psalmist (Ps. 31). Noah walks with God and lets God be judge over sin and violence. Any activism on our part must be fueled, first and foremost, by God's vision and not our ambitions or indignation. It is YHWH, not us, who orchestrates judgment and salvation. Our task is to respond faithfully and obediently at all times, always guarding against misguided fervor that may derail the very works of justice and mercy that God has called us to do.

Romans 1:16–17; 3:22b–28 (29–31)

Not only is Romans 1:16–17 a fitting introduction to Paul's explication of the gospel, it also summarizes what is said about divine action and human response discussed above. God exercises divine power to save those who trust that God is faithful, just, and merciful. Those who are in right relationship with God will receive the full benefit of God's justifying ("righteousizing") action; namely, the gospel of salvation.

God's saving power, demonstrated in Jesus' resurrection, completely overturns the shame of Israel's messiah dying on a Roman cross. Paul writes: "I am not shamed by [or of] the gospel" (1:16). That which is folly to the Greeks and a stumbling block to the Jews, Paul views as the revelation of God's righteousness and the good news of the crucified Christ (cf. 1 Cor. 1:18–24; 2:2).

In Romans 3, Paul explains why God has only one plan of salvation for all peoples, whether Jew or Gentile (3:29–30). "All have sinned and fall short of the glory of God" (3:23). This is the human predicament: without deliverance, all will face God's judgment of eternal death. In Romans 1–2 Paul explains how Gentiles sin by ignoring God, whereas Jews sin by breaking God's law. Without Christ, Jews and Gentiles are equally culpable before a holy God. Human beings are helplessly trapped under the power of sin. Only a greater power than sin—the power of God—can save us.

Two images in 3:24–25 explain the effects of the gospel. First, justification is "through the redemption that is in Christ Jesus." Redemption is a commercial image that refers to buying back slaves. In the backdrop is God's redemption of Israel from slavery in Egypt. Now Jesus delivers believers from bondage under sin to freedom in the Spirit (see Rom. 6). Second, God offers Jesus as *hilastērion*, the mercy seat that covers the ark. The ritual on the Day of Atonement is in view here. The high priest enters the Holy of Holies, offers a sacrifice to atone for Israel's sins, and sprinkles the blood of the animal on the mercy seat (Lev. 16:3–34). Once and for all, Jesus' death atones for the sins of those who trust in its efficacy, allowing them to be justified ("righteousized") before God.

The righteousness of God requires that both justice and mercy be upheld. As noted in Deuteronomy 11, obedience yields blessing and disobedience, curses. God is just and does not allow sins to go unpunished. Yet God is also merciful and offers God's Son to die on behalf of sinful humanity, so that those who accept this gift of grace by faith will be spared. Salvation is no longer based on one's ancestry, but is received through faith in Jesus Christ as Messiah of Israel and Savior of the world.

Since all persons sin and need salvation, the dividing wall between Jews and Gentiles is demolished by the gospel (Rom. 3:27–30; cf. Gal. 3:28; Eph. 2:1–22). Must not all other dividing walls we erect come down as well? If salvation is by grace through faith, the rich cannot say to the poor, or the learned to the uneducated, or men to women, or the powerful to the powerless, or the ethnic majority to the ethnic minority, that the latter are unworthy of salvation or somehow lesser in God's sight. If God shows no partiality, how can we, the redeemed of the Lord, make judgments on who is worthy and who is not?

Matthew 7:21–29

This passage reiterates the choice between these two ways and warns against self-deception. Located at the end of the Sermon on the Mount, the parable of the Wise and Foolish Builders parallels other contrasts that Jesus has already made between bearing good and bad fruit, between entering through the wide and narrow gates, and between giving lip service and obeying with concrete action.

In Wisdom literature, building analogies are used to describe life before God: "Like a house in ruins is wisdom to a fool" (Sir. 21:18). "A wooden beam firmly bonded into a building is not loosened by an earthquake; so the mind firmly resolved after due reflection will not be afraid in a crisis" (Sir. 22:16). Jesus' point is similar. Building a solid house means not only hearing Jesus' teachings, but also living according to them. In good weather, houses look identical above the foundation. But when a storm hits, the integrity of the builders' work will surely be tested. Needless to say, it is better to be a wise builder than a foolish one, and the choice is ours.

Wisdom and folly are not measured by intelligence, but by one's ability to discern God's ways. The wise trust and obey God, but fools deceive themselves. In Matthew 7:21–23, Jesus issues strong warnings against those who practice spectacular deeds of power, prophecy, and exorcism, lest they end up being rejected and cast out as evildoers. Jesus does not elaborate why, but from their showy religiosity, one may surmise that these false prophets are more interested in self-aggrandizement than in glorifying God.

Self-deception is especially dangerous among believers. We can convince ourselves that we are doing the right thing in Jesus' name, yet remain oblivious to our insatiable appetite for honor and recognition. The more successful we are in doing God's work, the more susceptible we are to self-deception if we are not careful. The line between gratitude and self-satisfaction is fine: "Thank God for the size of this congregation that I have built!" "Thank God for the large sums I have raised for this missions cause!" "Thank God for the transformation of this neighborhood with these community projects!" Very soon, we put a possessive pronoun before that which rightly belongs to God. We refer to God's gifts as *"my* church," *"my* donations," and *"my* programs." Like a house built on sand, our achievements look sturdy from a distance yet collapse under the "storm" of God's final judgment. Only the spiritual house, built on the rock and grounded in practiced obedience to Jesus and humble acknowledgment of God's empowerment, will stand firm into eternity.

Proper 5

Song Bok Jon

GENESIS 12:1–9   HOSEA 5:15–6:6
PSALM 33:1–12   PSALM 50:7–15
                                                  ROMANS 4:13–25
                                    MATTHEW 9:9–13, 18–26

The texts for Proper 5 call for spiritual and liturgical renewal accompanied by repentance and reorientation toward God. Genesis 12:1–9 recounts the faith of Abraham, who obeyed God's command to live as an immigrant in a foreign land. Psalm 33:1–12, Hosea 5:15–6:6, and Psalm 50:7–15 address the human folly of depending on human counsel rather than God's. Thus they urge us to repent and worship God with all of our hearts, minds, and spirits. Romans 4:13–25 addresses the division among the Roman church and urges the believers to turn to God, who justifies God's children through faith. Finally, Matthew 9:9–13 and 18–26 describe Jesus as he crosses the boundaries of human customs, calling believers to invite outsiders into the circle.

Genesis 12:1–9

The story of Abram begins with God's command to leave his country, kindred, and father's house (v. 1). God commands him to become an immigrant and to abandon the family business that Terah, his father, had long established in Haran. God demands that Abram give up his prosperity, social status, and friends, and does not even tell Abram where he is going, except to say that it is "the land that I will show you" (v. 1). Abram's only motivation to leave his hometown appears to be God's promises: "I will make of you a great nation, and I will bless you, and make your name great, so that you will be a blessing" (v. 2). The command of God for Abram to live as an immigrant and the promises God gives him may also be what motivates contemporary immigrants to leave their families, businesses, and homes. While many immigrants are often stereotyped as "illegal aliens," the story of Abram invites us to consider them as more than mere cheap laborers, but as those who respond to their divine calling. The immigrant journey does not always include the fulfillment of promises for a better future; many immigrants endure discrimination due to differences in ethnicity, language, culture, and nationality.

Despite the perils and challenges on his immigrant journey, Abram follows God's command, taking along his wife Sarai, nephew Lot, and all of his possessions. When they arrive at Shechem, God appears to Abram and promises, "To your offspring I will give this land" (v. 7). Here a serious problem arises. The land was already occupied by the Canaanites (v. 6). Does this mean that God would eradicate the Canaanites so the offspring of Abram could settle there? This promise of God has been the driving force of enmity between Palestinians and Israelites for centuries; the latter claim that God has given the land to them and the former have long occupied the same land. Does God endorse the massacre of people as a way to fulfill the divine promise? Walter Brueggemann suggests that there is no evidence that Abram was called to conflict with the Canaanites. Rather, he was called to live harmoniously with them and believe in the promise of God by "permitting the reality of blessing to be at work."[1] Brueggemann does not associate the promise of God with violent intentions for the fulfillment of this promise.

The story of Abram as a sojourner challenges the United States today as it also struggles with influxes of immigrants. While society labels them "illegal" or "undocumented," one must always remember that the history of the United States also begins with immigrants who came as pilgrims. Unfortunately, the pilgrims found the occupation of Native Americans a hindrance to their settlement. While the United States celebrates its achievements, justice, and freedom, we must not forget the bloody massacre of the "Canaanites" in this land, including many Native Americans who first welcomed the European aliens with hospitality.

Psalm 33:1–12

The psalmist invites people to sing "a new song" with shouts and with musical instruments such as the lyre, harp, and strings (vv. 1–3). God deserves praise because God "loves righteousness and justice" (v. 5). One should notice the inseparability between worship and ethics. Churches often consider worship to be an inward activity that cares for the souls of their members and social activism on behalf of the less fortunate as an outward ethical activity. However, according to Psalm 33, this dualistic notion of worship and ethics is not supported. One who praises and worships God must sing of God's justice

---

1. Walter Brueggemann, *Genesis*, Interpretation series (Atlanta: John Knox Press, 1982), 124.

and righteousness, vindicating the oppressed and marginalized. We who confess the righteousness of God truly worship God by acknowledging that our ethical disposition and behavior are nurtured through prayer, Scripture study, singing, and serving in community.

In verses 6 through 9, the psalmist praises God who created the world by divine word and breath. Here we encounter a problem for those who have experienced natural disasters such as Hurricane Katrina and the earthquake in Haiti. How can one sing "the steadfast love of the LORD" (v. 5) while suffering from natural disasters? Although we may question the justice of God in allowing such catastrophes to befall God's children, the Rev. Enso Sylvert, pastor of the Evangelical Church of Grace in Haiti, comments, "In moments like this, with destruction all around, with electoral crisis in the air, with cholera in the water, people have only God. God is Haiti's only uncorrupted leader."[2] One who witnessed the collapse of his church building and the death of his neighbors still sings to God, who he believes will bring justice and righteousness to Haiti.

In verse 10, the psalmist urges the people not to trust "the counsel of the nations" and "the plans of the peoples." While many nations justify their unjust behavior, their actions often result in violence and destruction in order to gain oil, territory, money, and control over others. Facing the destruction of his nation and the corruption of his government, the Rev. Sylvert's cry resembles the psalmist's: "In times such as this, we must not give up our God who loves justice and righteousness." As we witness natural disasters, wars, and national conflicts, Psalm 33 challenges us to consider anew where we will find hope for justice and righteousness, and where we will give our allegiance. Do we seek human counsel or God's?

Hosea 5:15–6:6

This passage alternates between the voices of God's people (6:1–3) and God (5:15; 6:4–6), with the former urging us to return to the latter. For which sins did God indict the people? How did they break their covenant? Both external and internal causes led to God's wrath. First, both Israel and Judah sought alliance not with God but with foreign countries. King Pekah of Israel forged an alliance with Syria in defiance of Assyria. Both Syria and Israel urged Judah to join in their alliance and threatened war against King Ahaz, who then allied with Assyria. Consequently, in 733 BCE Assyria invaded both Syria and Israel, making the former its vassal and deporting many people from

---

2. Deborah Sontag, "A Year Later, Haunted but Hopeful, Haiti Struggles Back," *New York Times*, January 4, 2011.

Israel.[3] The people did not seek God in times of distress, but depended on human counsel instead. Their love for God vanished like a "morning cloud" and the dew in the early morning (6:4). Second, God accuses Israel: "There is no faithfulness or loyalty, and no knowledge of God in the land" (4:1). While swearing, lying, murder, stealing, and adultery pervaded their society, the religious leaders—prophets and priests—did not alert their people or urge them to repent.

The conflict between Israel and Judah reminds us of the tension in the Korean peninsula. On November 23, 2010, North Korea fired dozens of artillery shells at Yeonpyeong Island in South Korea, killing two South Korean marines. The attack shocked many people around the world and elevated tensions between the two Koreas. Lee Myung Pak, the president of South Korea, ordered the military to retaliate fourfold for any attack by North Korea. Most churches in South Korea supported their government's policy of violent retaliation. The Christian Council of Korea gathered for a prayer meeting for the nation on November 26, 2010, and declared that the South Korean army should increase its forces along the border and retaliate if attacked by North Korea. Two days later, South Korea and the United States began allied military training in the west sea of South Korea. North Korea strongly opposed this training because the U.S. aircraft carrier involved posed a significant threat to its nation.

Hosea speaks to this and other conflicts: "Come, let us return to the Lord" (6:1). He proclaims that it is not human counsel or allied force but God "who will revive us" and "raise us up" (6:2). When people are killed, distressed, and lost, what must religious leaders do? Churches must realize that our dependence on weapons, allies, and treaties will not lead us to unity, peace, and reconciliation. It is only by seeking the knowledge of God who redeems all of creation by grace that both Koreas and all nations can sit at the same table. Churches in the United States should also question U.S. foreign policies that favor certain countries while attacking others. Are there not similarities between the United States, ancient Syria, and Assyria? Hosea prophesies about the unhappy destinies of countries that ignore God's counsel.

Psalm 50:7–15

Psalm 50 calls for liturgical renewal among believers in God. God is described as a judge who summons God's people to court. God tells them that God would not accept "a bull from your house, or goats from your folds" (v. 9). However, it is not the sacrifices themselves that pose the problem. James Luther Mays

---

3. Daniel J. Simundson, *Hosea, Joel, Amos, Obadiah, Jonah, Micah*, Abingdon Old Testament Commentaries (Nashville: Abingdon Press, 2005), 6.

points out that it is a huge misunderstanding if "a sacrifice is brought as a gift to God from 'your house' and 'your folds' and offered as something transferred from their ownership to God's possession."[4] There can be no transferring of possessions, because everything that is created by God belongs to God. God declares as God's own "every wild animal of the forest . . . , the cattle on a thousand hills, . . . all the birds of the air, and all that moves in the field" (vv. 10–11). Therefore the message of Psalm 50 criticizes a prosperity gospel that transfers one's possessions to God in expectation of a reward.

Psalm 50 also supports prophetic preaching that invites people to both repentance and love of God. Prophetic preaching is often misunderstood as indicting the accused for his or her wrongdoings. However, addressing the people's sins is not the purpose of Psalm 50. Rather, God urges people to sincerely repent of their sins because they are God's people whom God wants to deliver "in the day of trouble" in order to show divine salvation (v. 15). Therefore preachers must understand that the purpose of preaching is to eventually restore the relationship between God and God's people, as the psalmist proclaims in Psalm 50.

Romans 4:13–25

In this text, Paul argues, "For the promise that he would inherit the world did not come to Abraham or to his descendants through the law but through the righteousness of faith" (v. 13). Paul's statement refers to Genesis 15, in which God promises Abraham that his offspring will be as numerous as the stars in heaven (Gen. 15:5). It is then said, "He believed the LORD; and the LORD reckoned it to him as righteousness" (Gen. 15:6). Paul describes how Abraham "did not weaken in faith" (Rom. 4:19) when the reality of his and Sarah's old age defied God's promises. Paul firmly argues that there was no distrust in Abraham but he "grew strong in his faith" (v. 20). Here one encounters a conflicted report about Abraham; when God promised Abraham that Sarah would bear a son, he "fell on his face and laughed, and said to himself, 'Can a child be born to a man who is a hundred years old? Can Sarah, who is ninety years old, bear a child?' " (Gen. 17:17).

Paul, however, does not mention the laughter of Abraham. Leander Keck insists that Paul is either ignoring it or considers Abraham's laughter evidence of "distrust" because "this laughter actually underscores the radical otherness of God's promised action."[5] Traditionally, the church has understood

---

4. James Luther Mays, *Psalms*, Interpretation series (Louisville, KY: John Knox Press, 1994), 196.
5. Leander E. Keck, *Romans*, Abingdon New Testament Commentaries (Nashville: Abingdon Press, 2005), 130.

Abraham to be an exemplar of faith, a model for Christians in Paul's time as well as our own. However, Paul's report of Abraham could hinder us from viewing Abraham as a human being who suffered from the barrenness of his wife and laughed at God's joke of promising children in their old age. In contrast to Paul's report, Abraham was a vulnerable man who lied to Pharaoh, telling him that Sarah was his sister so that Pharaoh would spare his life. He also participated in "human counsel" with Sarah to maintain his patriarchy through Hagar's baby.

Therefore, preaching from Romans 4 must not bypass the gap between Paul's report and Genesis's description of Abraham. It is not that Paul is blindly praising Abraham as the prototype of faith for all Christians; he is trying to reconcile Jewish and Gentile Christians in the Roman church. However, Paul's interpretation of Abraham does present a problem for contemporary Christians who struggle with their own frailties and weaknesses. Preaching this text with honesty in pointing out the different accounts of Abraham may help us to better appreciate that God's grace overcomes our failures and embraces us because we are considered righteous through our faith in God, who is full of mercy and love for all God's creation.

Matthew 9:9–13, 18–26

After Jesus proclaimed, "Repent, for the kingdom of heaven has come near" at the beginning of his ministry (Matt. 4:17), he taught, healed, and drove out demons. Jesus crossed boundaries between the healthy and sick, pure and unclean, and life and death. Most Jews regarded tax collectors as traitors who allied with the Roman government and exploited their own people. However, Jesus crossed that boundary by calling Matthew to be his disciple and sitting with other tax collectors and sinners for dinner. Jesus also crossed gender boundaries. While a leper came directly to Jesus and begged for healing (8:1–4) and a leader of the synagogue personally asked for the resurrection of his daughter (9:18), the woman suffering from hemorrhages for twelve years approached him from behind, daring only to touch his garment. Douglas Hare argues that her timidity reflects her following prescribed gender roles.[6] Like Jesus, she is also willing to cross boundaries of gender expectations. The need for healing prompted her to seek divine help.

Robert E. Luccock, in agreeing with Floyd Filson that this text addresses Jesus' refusal to quarantine himself from sinners, asks the provocative question, "When the church retires within a safe enclave, keeping itself away from

---

6. Douglas R. A. Hare, *Matthew*, Interpretation series (Louisville, KY: John Knox Press, 1993), 106.

a suffering world, do we not put Jesus in quarantine?"[7] While working as a Methodist minister in New Hampshire in 2010, I invited a person walking downtown to the church dinner. My guest said, "Can I bring my friend with me? She is decent enough to enter church." His words still linger in my head as I reflect on this text. While the church opens its door only to such "decent persons," Jesus called the tax collector, had meals with sinners, healed the woman in pain, and raised a young girl from the dead. While Jesus refused to be "quarantined," is the church, which is his body, quarantining itself from God's children?

7. Robert E. Luccock, *Preaching through Matthew: Expository Reflections on the Gospel of Matthew* (Nashville: Abingdon Press, 1980), 86.

Proper 6

Carolynne Hitter Brown

GENESIS 18:1–15 (21:1–7)   EXODUS 19:2–8A
PSALM 116:1–2, 12–19   PSALM 100
                                                            ROMANS 5:1–8
                                      MATTHEW 9:35–10:8 (9–23)

A full understanding of social evil and God's plan for social justice demands a hard look at illness and violence against the body. In any given congregation, it is certain that all but the very young have been affected by sickness or death, either for themselves or through a loved one. Cancer, AIDS, diabetes, infertility, anorexia, multiple sclerosis, kidney failure, mental illness, paralysis, heart disease, depression, miscarriage, and a host of other bodily troubles wage war against all kinds of people. This is to say nothing of the hunger, starvation, and poverty-related diseases rampant in many places around the world. Accidents, war, and abuse present still more types of physical harm. Body disablement is a true leveler of people; sickness and death show no partiality to the rich or poor, black or white, male or female, even if certain types of diseases or conditions affect some groups more than others. All people are vulnerable to one form or another of physical illness or harm, and ultimately, the end of life. Most physical suffering seems meaningless, and those who are afflicted are often left asking, "Why has this happened?"

The readings for today are foundational for preaching social justice. Themes of suffering, waiting, and injustice permeate them and are given dignity. These Scriptures teach a liberating mind-set, one focused on the sovereignty of God, trust, gratitude, hope, and certainty that God's goodness will be displayed. The seeming injustice of bodily suffering and the imminence of death can be universally understood. Used as a metaphor, it serves as a springboard for considering other types of injustice. No human can control the eventual decay of the body, even less the ravaging effects of serious illness. In God's great wisdom, God uses the body to teach spiritual truth. Is it any wonder that God became flesh in the form of Jesus Christ in order to reach out to humankind, or that the ordinances of baptism and Communion involve washing and breaking the body? The spiritual truths that apply to physical suffering apply to all forms of suffering, and these Scriptures offer liberating insights for dealing with injustice.

Genesis 18:1–15 (21:1–7)

Genesis 18:1–15 reflects the effect that long-term suffering can have on people, particularly bodily suffering. When God informed Abraham that the time had come to fulfill God's promise of making Sarah a mother of "nations" (Gen. 17:16), Sarah laughed. She laughed at the irony of God fulfilling something she had long stopped hoping for. Sarah and Abraham had both grieved over not having a child, and given the culture of her day, Sarah undoubtedly suffered much shame because of it. Her sense of loss and her desire for control over her own circumstances drove her to tell her husband to sleep with her servant so that they could have a baby. And Abraham was willing to do it. After years of waiting, a disastrous affair, and menopause, Sarah found it funny that God would now show interest. Her words, "After I have grown old, and my husband is old, shall I have pleasure?" indicate her profound belief that "pleasure," or good things, were not meant for her. When Sarah denies laughing, it is because she is finally seeing the power of God—she fears God.

Genesis 21:1–7 is key to understanding how Sarah's (and Abraham's) suffering relates to social justice. Seminal to the text is the simple but life-giving statement, "the LORD did for Sarah as he had promised." A woman who had given up hoping for God's promise at last saw it fulfilled. A crucial component of God's justice is God's timing. Referring to the "day of judgment and destruction of the godless," 2 Peter 3:8 reminds believers, "With the Lord one day is like a thousand years, and a thousand years are like one day." In Sarah's mind, time had run out for her to have the child from whom a nation would descend. Yet God was still working. Preachers can use this biblical text to remind those who are working and waiting for God's justice to hope in God and trust in God's power. God will fulfill God's purposes and bring promised blessings to fruition.

Exodus 19:2–8a

These verses speak powerfully of the covenantal relationship between God and the Israelites. God makes a contract with them. God initiates the contract by declaring justice for the Israelites and by delivering them from physical bondage. Now God claims, "If you obey my voice and keep my covenant, you shall be my treasured possession out of all the peoples" (v. 5). This covenant between God and the Israelites is at the heart of Christian belief and Christian social justice. When the Israelites are unable to keep their part of the deal, Jesus Christ comes as "the mediator of a new covenant, so that those who are called may receive the promised eternal inheritance, because a death has occurred that redeems them from the transgressions under the first covenant" (Heb. 9:15). The physical oppression the Israelites faced in Egypt directly parallels the emotional and spiritual suffering people face when they are unable to live up to the expectations demanded by God's holiness. Through the work of Jesus Christ on the cross (i.e., his physical death and bodily resurrection), all people can access freedom from pain and suffering. Again, God allows physical suffering to demonstrate eternal spiritual truths.

This passage also demonstrates God's willingness to work on behalf of groups of people. God claims the "house of Jacob," the Israelites, as a "priestly kingdom and a holy nation" (Exod. 19:6). This powerful spiritual concept awakened the religious imaginations of African American slaves who likened themselves to the Israelites and created an entire theology of liberation around the belief that if God freed the Israelites from physical bondage, God would free them also. They sang and danced these truths deep into their hearts when they created spirituals like "Go Down, Moses":

> No more shall they in bondage toil,
> Let my people go,
> Let them come out with Egypt's spoil,
> Let my people go.
>
> Go down, Moses,
> Way down in Egypt's Land.
> Tell ol' Pharoah,
> Let my people go.
>
> O let us all from bondage flee,
> Let my people go,
> And let us all in Christ be free,
> Let my people go.
>
> Go down, Moses,
> Way down in Egypt's Land.
> Tell ol' Pharoah,
> Let my people go.

We need not always weep and mourn,
Let my people go,
And wear these slavery chains forlorn,
Let my people go.[1]

In a world full of oppression, Exodus 19:2–8a and its spiritual truths are life giving and offer hope for social change.

One of the most liberating truths of this passage is that God brings freedom from suffering in order to draw people to God's self. God uses power to display love and to captivate people with divine glory. God says through God's powerful work, I "brought you to myself" (Exod. 19:4). To preach social justice is to preach God's amazing love and desire for people, as well as God's purposeful acts on behalf of their well-being.

Psalm 116:1–2, 12–19

Like Sarah after Isaac's birth, the psalmist in Psalm 116 declares God's work in bringing about justice. The psalmist sings of love for God, saying that God hears, God listens. Although it is not included in the readings for today, the middle of the psalm speaks of the author's pain and physical suffering. Death was so close that the psalmist beseeched the Lord, "Save my life!" (v. 4b). Key to the writer's experience was his or her own agency in pursuing healing and freedom—actively calling on God and petitioning God with specific requests for help and well-being. The psalmist played an important role in accomplishing recovery, asking God over and over again to bring about a miraculous change. Healing faith believes in a God who listens and responds. The psalmist understands God as One who values human life and pain, especially pain that results in death. The author acknowledges God is compassionate even when God does not bring an end to physical pain: "Precious in the sight of the LORD is the death of his faithful ones" (v. 15). God hurts when God's people hurt.

After being restored to health, the psalmist accepts responsibility for proclaiming God's work in the community. Just as Sarah said, "Everyone who hears will laugh with me" (Gen. 21:6), the psalmist twice acknowledges a duty to "pay my vows to the LORD in the presence of all his people" (Ps. 116:14, 18). A socially just world is created when works of God are shared for the benefit of others. An act of personal healing demonstrates God's glory and goodness and stands as a proclamation of freedom, particularly to those within "the courts of the house of the LORD" (v. 19).

---

1. For more on African American theology in the spirituals, see James H. Cone, *The Spirituals and the Blues* (New York: Seabury Press, 1972; repr., Maryknoll, NY: Orbis Books, 1991), 28.

Believers seeking social change can pursue the liberating steps laid out by the psalmist. First, the psalmist asks God for change (v. 4). Literally, the writer offers supplication, humble entreaties to One of power. Second, the psalmist waits (vv. 10–11). In waiting, the psalmist is faithful and hopeful and continues to ask for justice. Even while suffering, the psalmist calls on God and specifically requests healing and freedom (vv. 3–4). Next, God answers and brings about a powerful work (vv. 6, 8). The psalmist declares, "You have loosed my bonds" (v. 16). Finally, the psalmist responds with public gratitude and personal obedience (vv. 13–14, 17–19). The writer offers to be God's servant, fulfills vows to God, makes thanksgiving sacrifices, and does all of this in the presence of the community. Ultimately, all glory for change goes to God. God is gratified by the loving, grateful response of the one healed.

Psalm 100

This text builds on the final step of the social justice model set forth in Psalm 116. A psalm of thanksgiving, it demonstrates a way of being for those committed to lasting social change. A posture of gratitude is the precondition for approaching the all-powerful Maker—the ultimate Source who made all things from nothing. All beings belong to the Creator. Therefore, "all the earth" is admonished to "worship the LORD with gladness" (vv. 1–2). This worship involves the body, as expressed in Romans 12:1: "Present your bodies as a living sacrifice, holy and acceptable to God, which is your spiritual worship." The pivotal point is found in the final two verses of Psalm 100. Verse 4 repeatedly underlines the need to approach God with thankfulness and praise, while verse 5 emphasizes the character of God: God is good, and God's love and faithfulness endure "to all generations." People are to be as unwavering in their thankfulness as God is in divine love and goodness.

In today's society, lust for material things, recognition, luxury, comfort, and constant stimulation leave many in a state of discontent. To be grateful at all times is countercultural. When God's people are deeply committed to gratitude and fully believe in God's desire to work for their good generation after generation, transformative work is done. The psalmist wants the reader and hearer of this song to believe that change begins in the heart of each individual person when we are thankful, joyful, and know that "the LORD is God" (Ps. 100:3).

Romans 5:1–8

Perhaps the most critical assertion of the apostle's text here is that even in suffering, he has abiding peace with God. This peace stems from the knowledge that Paul will one day share in the glory of God. As all the texts for today have demonstrated, God works in the world and in the lives of God's people to bring glory to God's self. Paul's deep understanding of God's ultimate purpose for creation, a social and natural world functioning together in covenantal harmony, produces a hope that "does not disappoint" (v. 5). Paul's hope, wrought through suffering, endurance, and character building, is possible through the transforming infusion of God's love into his soul by the Holy Spirit. He knows this transfusion of love can transform wicked hearts and the systemic evil thwarting God's world order, a point he makes plain by saying, "While we were still weak, at the right time Christ died for the ungodly" (v. 6). If the love of Christ can change our hearts, then it can change the heart of every evildoer. From here springs hope. God is at work in the lives of people. In fact, "God proves his love" (v. 8). In the face of suffering, God is not still. God is actively changing hearts through the power of Christ. As believers face evil and hope for transformation, they are called to remember that "we have obtained access to this grace" only through Christ. Christians must extend grace to those who have not yet experienced the love of God.

Matthew 9:35–10:8 (9–23)

When Jesus came proclaiming the new kingdom, he accompanied his teaching with miraculous bodily healings. He appointed his disciples to go to the Israelites preaching the good news of the kingdom and commanded them to perform all types of healing miracles as part of this mission. Healing of the body is a sign of God's movement in the world, and in this case, the future realm of Christ is foreshadowed by miraculous wonders involving physical bodies. This concept is key to a theology of social justice: healing and restoration are evidence of God's work in fulfilling God's covenantal plan for all creation, including God's people.

As God, Jesus had compassion on the people he met because they were "harassed and helpless," with no shepherd to guide them (9:36). Their social sphere was dismally distorted and no longer reflected God's intended purposes. Christians are called to proclaim restoration of God's world through the new covenant in Christ and to labor in the world to bring about God's design for nature and humankind. As workers, we are to go out and "harvest" the fruit already ripened by God, who always works ahead of us. As shepherds, Christ's disciples seek to bring healing to the "lost sheep" and must "give without payment" (10:8). The way of Christ, and the way of social justice, is to shepherd, love, and seek the restoration of God's world with no thought of personal recompense.

Jesus cautions that in commissioning this work, "I am sending you out like sheep into the midst of wolves" (10:16a). The work he calls us to fulfill is one of risk, perhaps even bodily injury or death. The kingdom of God requires loving and choosing God's social order over personal gain and even, if need be, our own lives. This does not mean that God's workers blithely make themselves a target for persecution. Rather, they are to be "wise as serpents and innocent as doves" (10:16b), using every opportunity for the glory of God. Jesus says, "You will be dragged before governors and kings because of me" (10:18), but he then promises to give his disciples everything they need to make the most of such circumstances. In these most difficult moments, "the Spirit of your Father" will speak through Christ's servant (10:20). Those who seek justice and peace as part of God's plan for the world can be certain that God will sustain and reward them (10:22).

Juneteenth: Let Freedom Ring (June 19)

James Henry Harris

Isaiah 61
Psalm 34:11–22
2 Corinthians 6:1–10
Mark 5:1–20

Slavery was abolished in most of the United States at the conclusion of fighting between the Union and Confederate armies in April and May of 1865. However, slavery continued in Texas until June 19, 1865, when a Union army arrived in Galveston and announced freedom for slaves. That date (Juneteenth) celebrates the actual end of slavery and sometimes includes the reading of the Emancipation Proclamation and an abundant outdoor meal. A Juneteenth sermon might reflect critically on the degree to which people of color in the United States are still in need of emancipation from racism and other systems of injustice.

> Neither slavery nor involuntary servitude, except as a punishment for crime whereof the party shall have been duly convicted, shall exist within the United States, or any place subject to their jurisdiction.
>
> *Thirteenth Amendment to the U.S. Constitution, 1865*

These texts proclaim the good news of freedom and liberty to those who suffer oppression and unfreedom. My mother used to say that "God don't like ugly," and this dislike manifests itself in miraculous deliverance from torment and bondage. Juneteenth celebrates these redemptive acts of God experienced by Blacks as freedom and liberation from American chattel slavery. We can discern from these texts that freedom, salvation, and liberation can be experienced in spite of suffering and evil. God is a righteous deliverer from all forms of bondage, and Blacks can now celebrate their deliverance from the evils of slavery.

Isaiah 61

The language of the sixty-first chapter of Isaiah is descriptive of the prophet's mission and message: to proclaim good news to the poor and oppressed and to proclaim the year of jubilee. In the words of the Negro spiritual, "I got shoes in that kingdom—ain't that good news?"

The realm of God in the Isaiah text and in the spiritual song is a "now" kingdom rather than an eschatological one. The demands of the kingdom are such that a confrontation with the powers about poverty, justice, fairness, and the liberation of the oppressed is an urgent enterprise that calls for a new "nowness," an immediacy that cannot be postponed. The preacher, the servant, and the community of faith are called to the task of bringing about the kingdom of God, now. Social justice as a theory and practice is a holy phenomenon grounded in the word of the Lord and the Spirit's anointing. The language of the prophet in Isaiah 61 is so integral to the nature and will of God that the writer of the Gospel of Luke places these prophetic words on the lips of Jesus as a testimony to his self-understanding.[1] The servant's mission is to announce and effect social justice and transformation in the church and world. This is what it means for the individual and the community to be holy, anointed, and spiritual. The servant of the Lord is called to understand her identity as a preacher and human being to be ineluctably related to the poor and oppressed. This is the antithesis of what we often hear preachers espousing on radio and television today.

This text is about freedom and proclaiming the year of jubilee or release from slavery. That is why this Scripture resonates in the hearts and minds of African Americans. Like the Israelites in Egypt, Africans in North America were slaves for 250 years. After the Emancipation Proclamation of 1865, de facto slavery continued in the United States as Jim Crow laws and segregation practices prevailed for another hundred years. Those who have been poor and oppressed, chattel slaves, are now free to rejoice and to "display [God's] glory" (v. 3b). The glory of the Lord has been expressed in Black church life from the brush-harbor days of slavery to present-day storefronts and mega-churches. There is no shortage of glorifying the Lord because our memory is not obviated by suffering but is infused with both suffering and hope because we too are now ministers and "priests of the LORD" (v. 6).

Both like and unlike exilic Israel, African Americans nearly lost everything that created familiarity: their homes, their families, their land, their names,

---

1. Luke 4:18–19. See also Rowan Williams, *Resurrection: Interpreting the Easter Gospel* (Cleveland: Pilgrim Press, 1982).

their language, and, to some extent, their memory.[2] There was a deliberate and systematic attempt to erase from Black consciousness any connection with their African past by separating members of the same tribe and placing slaves from different tribes together to ensure a lack of communication among them. The interstate selling of slaves via the auction block was one of the most cruel and debasing elements in the system of slavocracy.

The words of the prophet Isaiah redirect us to the real reason for our existence: to bring good news, bind up the broken, and proclaim release, jubilee, and comfort (vv. 1–2). These words outline the mission of all God's people—servants, preachers, prophets, of the synagogue, mosque, and church.

Psalm 34:11–22

Psalm 34 moves in a linear progression from perpetual praise to the sage advice and wisdom of the elder: "Come, O children, listen to me; I will teach you the fear of the LORD" (v. 11). It mimics the spirit of Proverbs 1:7, "The fear of the LORD is the beginning of knowledge; fools despise wisdom and instruction."

There seems to be a growing number of parishioners and students who indeed shun wisdom and instruction. The Sunday schools and Bible academies are sparsely attended, and many seminary students are more interested in obtaining a degree than studying and developing the discipline required to be considered wise. There seems to be no fear of the Lord, thus no vector to direct their knowledge or wisdom. Without this, there is little chance that ministers will be prepared to "do good; seek peace, and pursue it" (Ps. 34:14). White-collar crime and the vulgar capitalists who oppress the poor; violence; and Black-on-Black crime reflected in the violent lyrics of musical geniuses like Lil' Kim, Lil Wayne, 50 Cent, and the messiah of rap music, Tupac Shakur, have not contributed to peace or positive instruction for the youth of our society.

If we look closely at some of history's greatest villains, we come to the realization that much of their temporary greatness is forgotten and has since been filed away as awful examples. What do we want our greatness to be? We should be building a legacy of depositing positive values in the lives of God's people. As the psalmist writes, "Keep your tongue from evil, and your lips from speaking deceit. Depart from evil, and do good; seek peace, and pursue it" (vv. 13–14).

---

2. My reference here is informed by Jacques Derrida, *Monolingualism of the Other, or The Prosthesis of Origin (Cultural Memory in the Present)*, trans. Patrick Mensah (Stanford, CA: Stanford University Press, 1998), and his dictum "I only have one language and that language is not mine" (p. 1).

In answering to the question, "Why do we do these things?" we must recognize that "God is a God who empathizes and sides with the poor and the oppressed."[3] God rewards all of us for obeying God's commands and encouraging those who are disheartened and brokenhearted in the midst of tribulation. No one who takes refuge in God will be doomed. As worry, hassle, and danger seem to us unconquerable, God's mercy and grace are able to conquer all that and more. This is good news indeed. And we are the ones to share it.

Mark 5:1–20

We first encounter the Gerasene demoniac living among tombs, confined to caves outside his hometown, and possessed by evil spirits. His pathos and pain are palpable, indicting the church today whenever it turns away from those who suffer.

The man's townsfolk had abandoned him, and although no person could hold him down, he chose to remain among the tombs night and day, where "he was always howling and bruising himself with stones" (v. 5). A person whose body is in pain naturally cries out as a response to the pain![4] The victim is the demon, the spirit of suffering, and Jesus' ability to transform this demoniac's torment into tranquility is a testimony to the nowness of the kingdom. This man's pain cannot wait to be addressed in the "sweet by-and-by."

The whole experience of chattel slavery was masterminded by those who Frederick Douglass felt were demon possessed. In his autobiography *My Bondage and My Freedom*, Douglass describes symptoms of "possession" exhibited by the slave master:

> His strange moments excited my curiosity, and compassion. He seldom walked alone without muttering to himself; and he occasionally stormed about, as if defying an army of angry invisible foes. . . . Most of his leisure was spent in walking, cursing and gesticulating like one possessed by a demon. Most evidently, he was a wretched man, at war with his own soul and the world around him.[5]

From slavery to the present, there has been torment and torture of African Americans: beatings, hangings, long prison sentences, violations of human and civil rights, and so on. For some, this torment, pain, anguish, agitation,

---

3. Cf. James H. Cone, *God of the Oppressed* (Maryknoll, NY: Orbis Books, 2003).

4. James H. Harris, *Preaching Liberation* (Minneapolis: Fortress Press, 1996), and idem, *Pastoral Theology: A Black Church Perspective* (Minneapolis: Fortress Press, 1995).

5. Frederick Douglass, *My Bondage and My Freedom* (New York: Miller, Orton, Miller & Mulligan, 1855), available from Project Gutenberg at www.gutenberg.org/files/202/202 -h/202-h.htm.

and evil is experienced as a demonic, bruising force, making them cry out for help and healing.

In spite of torment due to systemic evils such as racism and sexism, or personal failures such as drug addiction, or mental or physical illness, there is a ray of hope. Whatever demon causes you to cry out night and day, to bruise yourself, to scream for help, to wander among the tombs, these demons are not all-powerful, and your torment, torture, anguish, and pain are not everlasting. We can move beyond torment to tranquility and, like the man in the text after encountering Jesus, we may be "clothed and in [our] right mind."

Before Jesus steps into the picture to provide this man with hope and healing, his expectations of Jesus are consistent with his expectations of those with whom he had previously dealt. He expected Jesus to harm him in some way, and he begged Jesus not to add to the torment that he had already experienced.

After his encounter with Jesus, the man who had been naked, disoriented, ruffled, and ragged is now the essence of tranquility, the quintessence of control, the paragon of polite society. This man is living testimony to the power of God, embodying a metamorphosis greater than that of Gregor Samsa in Franz Kafka's *Metamorphosis*.[6] This tormented man, who could not sit or keep still because of what postmodern medicine may attribute to attention deficit hyperactive disorder (ADHD), multiple personality disorder, or compulsive behavior; this man, who roamed and wandered aimlessly among the dead, is now sitting calmly. No chains. No leg irons. No straps. No fetters. He can move his hands and feet; he can shout without harming himself. He is sitting peacefully, "clothed," dressed up. He has been utterly transformed.

Today, no one comes to places of worship without problems and issues that need to be addressed. Of course, there is tremendous difficulty in "delivering" people from some situations, and we find it easier to push difficult problems and people to the margins by employing a modus operandi that says, "Out of sight, out of mind." But banishment does not end pain. Jesus shows us how to step towards those who are suffering and the evil forces overpowering them. By God's power, we may join with him in confronting evil among us.

2 Corinthians 6:1–10

Near the beginning of this passage, Paul quotes Isaiah: "At an acceptable time I have listened to you, and on a day of salvation I have helped you" (Isa. 49:8). He goes on to insist, "See, now is the acceptable time; see, now is the day of salvation!" (2 Cor. 6:2b).

---

6. For an excellent definition of transformation, see Hans Gadamer, *Truth and Method* (London and New York: Continuum, 1975). See also Franz Kafka, *Metamorphosis and Other Stories* (New York: Dover Publications, 1996).

Whether we realize it or not, the world in which we live thrives on dysfunction and disease. What would happen to hospitals and the economy if there were no disease, no HIV/AIDS, no cancer? What would happen if there were no wars to spark national pride and investment in domestic goods? The economic infrastructure would implode.

Paul simply and succinctly states that we—as the body of Christ and God's people—should fully embrace the fact that we are God's agents of change. We need to comprehend God's purpose, see God's will, and obey the tasks to which we are called. The church has a responsibility to work itself out of the business of placating the poor with a salve rather than providing a real change of conditions. Jesus comes to the side of the oppressed and marginalized. We should do the same. When there are no more oppressed or oppressors, victims or villains, rich or poor, and so on, then the church's mission will have been completed and restoration and transformation will be made manifest in our world. This is what Paul Tillich may have meant by "the eternal now"[7] and what Jesus meant in saying to Mary and Martha regarding their brother Lazarus's death: "I am the resurrection and the life—now." Resurrection-like freedom and justice is not on the horizon of distant vistas. It is not a proleptic vision to be realized in the eschaton, but it is a present phenomenon. "See, now is the day of salvation" (2 Cor. 6:2).

---

7. Paul Tillich, *The Eternal Now* (New York: Charles Scribner's Sons, 1963), 122–32.

Proper 7

Edward L. Wheeler

GENESIS 21:8–21
PSALM 86:1–10, 16–17

JEREMIAH 20:7–13
PSALM 69:7–10 (11–15), 16–18
ROMANS 6:1B–11
MATTHEW 10:24–39

This week's lectionary readings focus on the unjust sufferings that faithful persons experience. The Romans 6 passage is an exception to the week's general pattern; in it, Paul responds to a particular critique of his argument for the primacy of grace and faith over the law. However, all these texts share a common theme of God's redemptive re-creative activity in the face of unjust, oppressive, and life-denying situations.

Genesis 21:8–21

This text continues the story of Hagar and Ishmael begun in chapter 16. This disturbing passage raises troubling questions about the treatment Hagar and Ishmael receive at the hands of Sarah and Abraham.

The tension that likely existed in Abraham's household once Sarah gave birth to Isaac is easily imagined. Unable to conceive, Sarah had encouraged Abraham to have a child by Hagar. Now Sarah sees as a threat the child born of that relationship. Ishmael's mocking of Isaac is the pretext for eliminating the problem, but the real reason for the expulsion is revealed in Sarah's conversation with Abraham: "Get rid of that slave woman and her son, for that slave woman's son will never share in the inheritance with my son Isaac" (21:10; all Scripture quotations in this essay are from NIV). Sarah never even acknowledges that the "slave woman's son" is also Abraham's firstborn son.

The text paints Abraham in a more positive light, describing him as being "troubled" because he seems to appreciate the injustice of Sarah's request and recognizes Ishmael as his son. However, God calms Abraham's fears by reminding him of the divine promise made in 17:20. "I will make the son of

292

the maidservant into a nation also, because he is your offspring" (21:13). God recognizes Ishmael as Abraham's son even though Ishmael's conception was Sarah's plan, not God's.

With God's reassurance, Abraham follows his wife's instructions, provides food and water, and sends Hagar and the newly weaned Ishmael into the desert of Beer-sheba. This is an unjust situation that is painful to imagine.

The situation becomes even more compelling when the water runs out and Hagar believes her son will die. Leaving the weakened boy under a bush, Hagar cries, and the magnitude of the injustice done to them bears down on the reader. The slave woman who became a surrogate for Sarah now finds herself alone in the desert with no water, and her son is dying.

In the midst of a seemingly hopeless situation, the text makes a transformational statement. "God heard the boy crying, and the angel of God called to Hagar from heaven" (v. 17a). At the point of despair, God steps in. Through an angelic messenger, God calms Hagar's fears and affirms the promise made earlier to Abraham concerning Ishmael. "Then God opened her eyes and she saw a well of water" (v. 19). The text strongly suggests that the well had always been there but Hagar, consumed with grief and anxiety, had not seen it. God helps Hagar see the well and reminds her of God's promise.

In the midst of life's injustices it is easy to lose sight of God's promises. The stress and strain of our predicaments can blind us to the deliverance that is available. Sometimes it takes an intervention from God to help us recognize the salvation at hand. As we continue to wrestle with deep distrust among Abraham's heirs and violent power struggles in the Middle East, we must remember that both Jews and Muslims are God's children. Injustice perpetuated against one by the other robs both of an awareness of God's promises to all. Just as Isaac is heir to God's promise, so is Ishmael blessed by God through his relationship to Abraham. The outcast is blessed by the same God who will protect and provide for all children.

Psalm 86:1–10, 16–17

We are unsure of the exact circumstances that inspired the composition of this psalm of David. However, it is clear that the psalmist is in a perplexing situation. Classified as one of the individual laments that may refer to personal distress or speak symbolically on behalf of the nation, this psalm has the characteristics of a personal lament. It is characterized by petitions to God interspersed with proclamations of the psalmist's righteous behavior and celebrations of God's character and nature.

The rhythm of the psalm is established early. Beginning with a plea for help and a description of the psalmist's humble status (v. 1), the writer requests that God "preserve my life" and declares his or her devotion to God (v. 2). While demanding no special treatment because of personal faithfulness, the psalmist speaks clearly of his or her positive relationship with God. Therefore, the psalmist approaches God with what might be described as "holy boldness" (vv. 2–4).

The psalm continues in verses 5–7 with an important modification. Here the focus shifts away from self-justification to praise for who God is. It is God's very nature that provides the basis of the psalmist's hope, culminating in the statement of faith, "In the day of my trouble I will call to you, for you will answer me" (v. 7).

While maintaining the character of an individual lament, verses 8–10 break from the earlier pattern the psalmist had established. Here the motif is one of identifying and celebrating the greatness of God. That greatness is recognizable by all nations, not just Israel. The God of Israel is far more than the tribal God of this once-nomadic people. Psalm 86 proclaims the universality of God's majesty and the reverence due to God.

The closing verses return to the traditional pattern of lament. The psalmist is facing enemies and pleads for God to give "a sign of your goodness, that my enemies may see it and be put to shame" (v. 17). Finally, the psalmist closes by proclaiming trust in God, remembering that "You, O LORD, have helped me and comforted me."

It is easy to be discouraged when you find yourself unemployed because of the closing of the plant where you have worked for ten years, the stack of unpaid bills is mounting, and the health insurance has been canceled. As difficult as it may be, during these times we must trust in God who is just and will not abandon us. That trust sustains us in the struggle for justice.

Jeremiah 20:7–13

This dynamic pericope reveals the prophet's personality, his convictions regarding his prophetic call, and his ultimate trust in God. However, it also begins with an uncompromising critique of God. Jeremiah accuses God of having deceived and enticed him: "You overpowered me and prevailed" (v. 7). This reaction stems from the persistent mistreatment Jeremiah has received as a consequence of his faithfulness to God. Jeremiah's complaint suggests that he believed his criticism of the nation would be accepted and would contribute to the transformation of the nation. Instead, the nation rejected him and God's message.

Jeremiah's critique seems reasonable at first glance, but further examination reveals God had not promised Jeremiah that his message would be accepted. Rather, the call passage in 1:4–19 suggests otherwise. In particular,

1:8, 19 assume that Jeremiah would face opposition. Rather than God having deceived Jeremiah, had Jeremiah deceived himself as to what he could expect from his proclamation on God's behalf?

Whatever the case, Jeremiah decides that he will no longer speak God's word. However, in words that transcend time and communicate God's call to us in the twenty-first century, Jeremiah announces that he cannot abandon his call to proclaim the word of God because the word of the Lord "is in my heart like a fire, a fire shut up in my bones. I am weary of holding it in; indeed, I cannot" (20:9).

In verse 10, Jeremiah continues his lament by describing the mistreatment he has received from his friends. They wait for him to make a reportable mistake so they can exact their revenge for his judgments against them. The dubiousness of Jeremiah's friends contrasts sharply with God, whom the prophet announces will protect and vindicate him (vv. 11, 12). Jeremiah's confidence in God expressed in verse 13 is the complete opposite of where he began in verse 7. Jeremiah proclaims, "Sing to the LORD! Give praise to the LORD! He rescues the life of the needy from the hands of the wicked." Jeremiah's profound humanity allows him to express his honest dissatisfaction with God and to trust in God to rescue him.

The Rev. Dr. Jeremiah Wright had long been an advocate for the poor and the marginalized, including years of ministry in Chicago. He dared speak a word of judgment on unjust systems and challenged his community and the United States to live up to their highest moral aspirations. However, rather than receiving praise, his words in one sermon were taken out of context and he was condemned during the 2008 presidential campaign along with those who were associated with him. Those who proclaim a prophetic word of justice on behalf of the oppressed and the marginalized must not expect the praise and celebration of the status quo. Nevertheless, may God's prophetic message be like "fire" shut up in our bones so that we speak and believe that God will not abandon faithful messengers.

Psalm 69:7–10 (11–15), 16–18

This Davidic psalm reminds the reader of Jeremiah 20:7–13. The theme of being unjustly disgraced is repeated in verses 7–10. Strangers and family members ridicule the psalmist as a result of the psalmist's zeal for the Lord. The psalmist appears to blame the Lord for this mistreatment. "For zeal for your house consumes me, and the insults of those who insult you fall on me" (v. 9).

While an element of despair is clearly evident in the opening verses, the prayer found in verses 13–18 reflects a mixture of faith and doubt. The fact that the psalmist dares to call on the Lord during a time of need is a sign of faith and an indication that the psalmist believes God is able to do what is being asked of God. Yet the prayer does not convey the absolute certainty of deliverance that either Jeremiah 20 or Psalm 86 articulate. The author of Psalm 69 prays without identifying what God will do.

The key to the psalmist's implied faith that God will respond is embedded in two verses. Verse 13 begins, "But I pray to you, O LORD, in the time of your favor; in your great love . . ." The psalmist's faith is predicated on the conviction that God's very nature is constituted by love and that divine love will manifest itself as mercy for the psalmist (v. 16). Both Psalms 69 and 86 claim that their hope for deliverance is dependent on God's goodness and love. That reality can be trusted even amid the trials both writers face. It is that reality that helped keep Martin Luther King Jr. steady and faithful in the face of strong opposition to his critique of the Vietnam War and the military-industrial complex that was leveled against him even by powerful voices in the African American community.

Romans 6:1b–11

In this pericope, Paul refutes detractors who argue that his abandonment of the law invites lawlessness and a lack of morality. He opens his defense with the question, "Shall we go on sinning so that grace may increase?" He emphatically answers, "By no means!" (vv. 1b–2a). Paul then seeks to connect Christian baptism with the ethical and moral life that is expected of the person "who has died with Christ."

Paul argues that those who are baptized "into Christ" are baptized into Christ's death (v. 3) so that just as Christ has been raised, they too will be "raised from the dead" and "through the glory of the Father, we too may live a new life" (v. 4). This "new life" means that those who are in Christ are no longer slaves to sin, because just as Christ died to break the yoke of sin, those who die in Christ through baptism have been set free from sin's control. Therefore, though Christians are free from having to justify themselves through obedience to the law, the new life in Christ leads one to live a moral and ethical life. If sin is characterized by broken relationships between God and humanity and within the human family, then the absence of sin is characterized by reconciled relationships and the peace, justice, and love that is inherent in such relationships. Justice is possible when reconciliation takes place and Christ becomes the new model for relationships.

A man was an active church member, but he came to the office of the editor of a denominational magazine in the early 1970s intent on doing bodily harm to him because of the articles he had written opposing racism and calling for repentance and reconciliation.[1] The editor calmed the situation by citing Scripture and inviting the visitor to return for further Bible study. Over the next year they met several times. At the last meeting the visitor gave the editor a substantial check to support his "cutting-edge" ministry, but before he left he asked the editor why his pastor had not preached about the need for racial reconciliation. The courage of the editor to be prophetic had helped change this man's attitude about race and his faith in a profound way. The new life in Christ leads to moral and ethical behavior, a life that models God's justice.

Matthew 10:24–39

This passage focuses on the cost of discipleship. Verses 24 and 25 make it clear that Jesus is master and teacher. Those who follow him are students whose goal is to be like the teacher. However, here and in our other texts for today, it is assumed that those who are faithful to God can expect to be misunderstood and criticized, just as Jesus was.

Verses 26–31 inform those who follow Christ that they ought not fear those whose power is limited to the corporal world. "Rather, be afraid of the One who can destroy both soul and body in hell" (v. 28b). Jesus assures his listeners that the One who has the power to destroy body and soul is concerned about them. This God knows when sparrows fall as well as the number of hairs on our heads.

Verses 32–39 substantiate that discipleship has a cost far beyond name calling (v. 25). The gospel forces persons to make choices that disrupt our most significant relationships. Much like the prophet Jeremiah's predicament, the faithful followers of Jesus will find that the gospel may sever parental ties and disrupt familial connections of all kinds. Christ requires a radical loyalty that ultimately claims all of one's life. However, in a paradoxical conclusion, Jesus assures us that "whoever loses his life for my sake will find it" (v. 39b).

This text challenges us to seriously consider the cost involved in following Christ. Are injustices against gay, lesbian, transgender, and bisexual persons, unfair lending practices against Blacks and Hispanics, unequal pay for women, and inadequate health care for the poor concerns for which you would risk your reputation and social status? What injustices are you willing to accept to ensure your own comfort? Have those of us who ought to be risking our lives on behalf of Christ lost our lives, reputations, relationships, or financial security while attempting to save them?

---

1. Story received by the author in private conversation while working for the Home Mission Board of the Southern Baptist Convention, 1974.

Gifts of Sexuality and Gender (June 29)

Valerie Bridgeman

LEVITICUS 19:15–18
PSALM 139:13–18
MARK 12:28–34
1 CORINTHIANS 12:12–26

This new feast, Gifts of Sexuality and Gender, envisioned for late June, assumes that sexuality and gender are gifts of God through which people embody covenantal relationship. While the church has often held that relationships between people of different genders are the norm, many people believe that sexuality can be expressed in other modes, including relationships between people of the same gender, as well as those with multiple sexual identities and those who are asexual and questioning. In connection with this feast, the preacher could help the congregation explore ways that it could deepen its understanding of sexual identity and expression.

As religious leaders, we affirm sexual and gender diversity as gifts people offer to their congregations and communities. . . . While most of us may be accustomed to categorizing people as male or female, heterosexual or homosexual, binary thinking fails to reflect the full diversity of human experience and the richness of creation. The courageous witness of lesbian, gay, bisexual and transgender people (LGBT), along with a growing body of social and scientific research, inspire us to affirm sexual and gender diversity as a blessed part of life.[1]

What a remarkable collection of texts to reflect on "gifts of sexuality and gender." While the phrase "sexuality and gender" often becomes code for

1. Religious Institute on Sexual Morality, Justice, and Healing, "An Open Letter to Religious Leaders on Sexual and Gender Diversity," 2007. See www.religiousinstitute.org/sites /default/files/open_letters/diversityopenletter_0.pdf.

"homosexuality" and "women," these texts offer us an opportunity to think about our embodied living as people of God. We are reminded that we are God's own, created wonderfully and woven together into a web of mutuality and relationship. In my own thinking, "sexuality" and "gender" are both complex terms that sometimes get reduced to manageable language or imagery, which then render them inaccurate. We are complicated beings, called into community with the Three-in-One and with one another. Negotiating these relationships not only is an intellectual, emotional, and spiritual task, but it involves our bodies as well. These texts call us to manage our lives with these relationships in mind, no matter how we experience our sexuality or our gender.

Leviticus 19:15–18

The church father Origen once wondered whether Leviticus, a book full of priestly codes and prohibitions, could offer anything of reward to its readers. Centuries later, today's believers might also ask which Levitical laws, with their odd requirements covering everything from mold to facial blemishes to sexual behavior, apply to our distinct historic location and which we may designate as examples of what it meant to previous generations to be uniquely God's people. The lead-in to this text is a variation of the Decalogue (cf. 19:3, 11–14; Exod. 20:2–17; and Deut. 5:6–21). Part of the priestly Holiness Code, Leviticus 19 is a statement about living as the people of God. These rules are designed to make them different and set apart, easily recognizable as God's chosen ones. The passage lifted out for our discussion is expressly about human community.

How do you want to be loved? For who you are? For what you have done? For your history? Leviticus 19:18 declares that we should love neighbors as ourselves. Does that mean that I should love the next person as if she were I? Does it mean that I cannot possibly love another person if I do not love myself? Perhaps the writer intends both of these questions to be answered affirmatively. Certainly verses 15–17 indicate a kind of mutual justice. Judge rightly. Don't slander. Don't profit off your neighbor's death or blood. Don't hate any of your kin in your heart. Don't take revenge or bear a grudge. My mother's way of making such declarations would be summed up in one sentence: treat people the way you want to be treated.

I wonder what would happen in our societies if we saw others as we would want to be seen by them, or if we treated persons whose sexual orientation or sexual expressions are different from ours as if we ourselves were differently oriented. Would the news outlets profit off the stories of the deaths of LGBTIQ[2] people if we refused to turn a voyeuristic eye toward their broadcasts?

---

2. LGBTIQ signifies persons who are lesbian, gay, bisexual, transgender, inquiring, intersex, queer, or questioning.

What would happen if we who claim this distinct relationship with a holy God would resist hateful and vengeful words and actions toward those who don't look like us or love like us? These words from Leviticus beckon us to a daily holiness of love and of kindness that is grounded in God's commitment to our humanity and loving relationships with one another.

Psalm 139:13–18

A young man I know—I will call him John—hates this text. John does not experience his life as wonderful because he is black, gay, male, and creative. He laments his existence more than he celebrates it. When I asked him why he could not see his life as part of God's "wonderful works," he answered that the church has made it clear to him that he is a "mistake," a "monstrosity" of creation. I pushed him as we read this text together. He believes he has been homosexual from birth. He tells story after story of how he knew. And still, he cannot see himself as a person who is "formed" by God.

This psalm, as John's story attests, may be a blessing or a curse to those who are not a part of the dominant vision of "acceptable" sexual orientations or gender expressions. And yet the psalmist proclaims that we are uniquely and intentionally knitted together by a deity who knows us intimately well before we are birthed from our mothers' wombs. We learn that God beheld us before we took form. Scientists are discovering that sexual orientation and gender identification may be as much "nature" as "nurture." People may resist these findings, preferring instead to quote certain biblical texts as "proof" that God detests and hates same-gender loving people. But for people who have both female and male organs, and people concerned that they may be trapped in a body unsuited to their self-identity, these verses hallow our having been purposefully created by God, whose intentions for us are indeed wonderful and blessed (v. 14). This psalm attests to an intimate creative process, one in which God involves the divine being and *thinks* of us. That truly is a weighty thought. We are known and beloved of God.

Mark 12:28–34

Squabbles and arguments seem to be the way religious conversations are remembered. No surprise, then, that the question of the greatest or primary commandment arose in the midst of an argument. The answer is revealing: love God with your entire self and love your neighbor as if the neighbor were you. It is, according to Jesus, the wisest answer to this very important religious dispute. Love is the ultimate defining answer to all religious squabbles. That sounds clear and easy enough, doesn't it? But how hard it seems for us to give people space to express love-in-being, including the expression of love through their sexuality or individual understandings of gender. In fact, we have so divorced loving God from our physical bodies that the primary commandment itself may seem foreign. "Love God with all your strength" commands the bodily love for God. It is expressly physical; it is connected to our human bodily existence. For people who do not share the dominant culture's experience of bodily existence (e.g., differently abled people or sexual minorities), this physicality often is deemed aberrant at best and abhorrent at worst. We who still squabble over, ignore, or misunderstand the primary commandment need to struggle through what it means in the face of diverse sexualities and gender expressions. Would we find in these commandments a way to accept people who declare their love for God but do not express their faithful living in the same ways that we do?

There are undoubtedly people in our own congregations (and people intimately related to our congregants) who wonder about God's love and our love for them. This passage reminds us that we must respond with integrity—that is, with our whole bodies, souls, understandings, and hearts—to speak and live on behalf of those who are despised and hated by others for who God has created them to be.

1 Corinthians 12:12–26

The body is one. There are not several bodies of Christ, but only one. This may seem obvious, but we would be hard pressed to believe it if we paid attention to the divisions and dissensions in the church today.

Paul makes a case for plurality and difference as gifts from God. He argues for diversity in unity. The body is indeed intact. But this same body requires various members to function, as only they are able. What if men, women, and transgender people bring unique gifts to the body? What if heterosexual, homosexual, bisexual, transgender, and intersex people are necessary for a full picture of the Christ and in order for the church to be the vicar of Christ on earth? What if . . .

This text also teaches us that God has arranged the members of Christ's body. It admonishes each of us to value our place in the body. We cannot say, "I am not a hand, I do not belong to the body," or any other such comparative statement. The body is not a "single member." Perhaps the most intriguing statement in this treatise on the body concerns the role of the "weaker" or "less honorable" parts of the body. For years of Christian history and theologizing, women have been considered and treated as being among the less honorable members of Christ's body. And yet this text declares that those "parts" are "indispensable." The same might be said to the church about LGBTIQ

Christians in the midst of our congregations. Such friends have been marginalized and in some places rejected, and yet they are present in and around our congregations as indispensable to our relationships with one another and God. Many have been brutalized by cruel words and deeds and have suffered at the hand of church teachings and policies. Yet many stay and claim their rightful places as members of this one baptized and confirmed body. Together, all of us are the body of Christ.

What all these texts have in common is the assurance that we are connected not only to God, but also to one another. We are not disembodied spirits floating through this world. God created us with bodies and we are wonderfully made. We are created to be in community with one another, to love others as we love ourselves. This commandment, taken seriously, forces us to remember that people are not theoretical creatures—people come with bodies that love, long, feel, and want the fullness of life that God intends for them. Whatever arguments arise over gender and sexuality in the church and society, we must remember that we are all complex people, created and loved by a complex God.

Proper 8

Pablo A. Jiménez

GENESIS 22:1–14   PSALM 13
JEREMIAH 28:5–9   PSALM 89:1–4, 15–18
                                       ROMANS 6:12–23
                                   MATTHEW 10:40–42

The readings for this Sunday suggest a common theological theme: the choices we make may reveal God's will or resist God's purposes. Faithful Christians must take sides: Are we for or against God's project for humanity and the world? We can be obedient or disobedient (Gen. 22); truthful or deceiving (Jer. 28); slaves of sin or slaves of life (Rom. 6); faithful or unfaithful (Matt. 40).

Genesis 22:1–14

The story of Abraham and Isaac is both inspiring and troubling. On the one hand, it highlights Abraham's devotion to God. On the other, it appears to validate child abuse and human sacrifice.

Notice that I said "appears," because this first impression is deceiving. The intention of the text is precisely to disavow human sacrifices. The key verse in this section is verse 12, in which God stops the impending sacrifice. One of the many aims of this text is to teach Abraham and his descendants that the God of Israel does not approve of, need, or accept human sacrifices.

This text lends itself to a narrative treatment. The preacher may design a narrative sermon with a plot twist: God seeks not only to test the patriarch's faith but also to teach him a lesson. God is not like the other Canaanite divinities, which crave human blood.

This text presents several ethical and moral dilemmas when we read it from our postmodern standpoint. First, testing the faith of a human being in such a radical way seems cruel. Is it fair to play with people's feelings in such a sordid way? Why did God ask Abraham to perform such an abhorrent task?

Second, although Isaac did not die, an animal died in his place. What does this text suggest to us about animal rights and God's relationship to animals? And third, might Abraham's cruel treatment of his son be considered justification for the abusive treatment of children?

Thus Genesis 22:1–12 presents profound theological and ethical dilemmas that ministers should engage both in the classroom and in the pulpit. Children's rights and animal rights are vitally important topics. Child abuse is a horrific crime that goes largely unnoticed by most of our society. Similarly, animal abuse is inexcusable and often hidden from view. People may justify cruelty to others in the name of God; religion may be used (or misused) to justify abuse and exploitation if the perpetrators claim that God directed them to act that way.

To be sure, human sacrifice is an inhumane practice that was prevalent in ancient societies. Today, our society sacrifices people in different ways. The most dangerous false god that threatens our world today is the market, which is the driving force behind many personal, corporate, and political decisions. In the name of economic security and prosperity, nations plant one crop to the exclusion of others (ceasing crop rotation) and exhaust the soil of its nutrients. People are summarily hired or fired according to profit margins with little thought of the human and social value of their labor. Health care is often denied to those who need it most. Sacrificing people is seen as part of the social cost of keeping the economy afloat. Genesis 22:1–12 reminds us that human sacrifice—on any altar—is simply wrong.

Jeremiah 28:5–9

The narrative of Hananiah's clash with Jeremiah is riveting. We learn from chapter 27 that God commands Jeremiah to make a yoke and put it on his neck. This prophetic act symbolizes God's judgment against Israel, which had been "given" by God to the Babylonians (27:6–7).

In his prophecy, Jeremiah stresses that God will punish whoever opposes Babylonian rule (27:8). Jeremiah also warns against the "*shalom*-prophets," the seers supported by the king who usually validated any plan the king proposed (27:9). The *shalom*-prophets assured Judah of divine intervention on their behalf.

Jeremiah, still wearing his yoke, prophesies to the king and priests (27:12–22). However, this select crowd is not receptive to the prophet's oracles. They are convinced that Jerusalem cannot fall at the hands of its enemies, and they assume Jerusalem is divinely protected (see also Pss. 48 and 125).

In Jeremiah 28 we see the clash between Jeremiah and Hananiah, a prophet who was a friend of the king's court. This *shalom*-prophet affirms that God will completely restore Judah in two years and will bring back King Jeconiah and the exiles from Babylon (28:1–4).

Initially, Jeremiah proclaims his hope for the returned exiles and Judah's independence (v. 6). However, the prophet's tone quickly changes and he offers a solemn warning (v. 7). Both Hananiah and Jeremiah belong to a long line of prophets, many of whom had seen their share of calamities (v. 8). This text also suggests that many false prophets had raised false expectations for peace, and God's way of determining if a prophet's words are true or false is to wait and see if the prophecy is fulfilled (v. 9). This is most clearly the case for those who prophesy peace: only if peace prevails will the people know that the prophet had been sent by God.

Next, Hananiah takes center stage, choosing to ignore Jeremiah's words. He breaks Jeremiah's yoke as a sign of what God will do to the Babylonians on Judah's behalf (vv. 10–11a). Jeremiah responds quietly. Rather than confront Hananiah, the prophet walks away (v. 11b). Later, the Bible tells us that God instructs Jeremiah to prophesy an oracle of judgment against Hananiah (vv. 12–16). He unmasks Hananiah as a false prophet, insisting that God had not sent him (v. 15). As punishment for his sin, Hananiah dies that year (v. 17).

This text invites us to consider how we will recognize divine truth and what it means to tell the truth in God's name. It also raises three distinct challenges. First, because many postmodern people believe that truth is relative and that each person knows only his or her own version of truth, how do we reconcile this fragmented vision of truth with what is often presented in the Bible as a univocal view of truth (that is, a kind of ultimate truth or faith claim)? Second, many people today do not believe that God speaks to us in an audible voice. In the absence of such a voice, how do we receive prophetic counsel and divine oracles, guidance, and correction? Third, this passage challenges us to address the possibility of divine punishment rendered by God against God's enemies. How do we reconcile such a view with a forgiving, merciful God? It is no doubt best for preachers to address such questions directly by naming one or more of them. For example, when considering claims of divine truth the preacher may point out that "relative" truth is not nonexistent truth. While avoiding harsh dogmatism, we may weigh the long-term veracity of various claims, seeking God's wisdom to discern what is consistent with God's way of caring for exiled and oppressed persons. Just as the prophets analyzed social and political developments, we too must assess the times and the governments we support. We must be willing to address hard questions, take a long view of history as the arena of divine actions, and seek guidance that will benefit all people.

Psalm 13

Psalm 13 is a brief psalm of individual lament. The psalmist presents a case before God, asking for divine intervention and favor.

The opening phrase is mesmerizing: "How long, O LORD?" Anyone who has ever suffered can relate to this expression of desperation and exasperation. The psalmist feels forgotten by God. He or she complains to God, "How long will you hide your face from me?" (v. 1b). The complaint extends to verse 2, where the psalmist asks how long he or she must bear psychological and spiritual pain. Toward the end of this verse, we find the reason the psalmist is suffering so much: an unnamed "enemy" is attacking.

Next, the psalmist asks for divine intervention (v. 3). The writer fears death (v. 3b), which is the ultimate goal of the enemy (v. 4).

As do most psalms of lament, this one ends with a vow of praise (vv. 5–6). In a sudden reversal, the psalmist affirms faith in God's steadfast love, even in the midst of pain.

This psalm offers hope to all who suffer, particularly those who suffer oppression and persecution. The psalmist depends solely on God, who is the writer's only hope. The testimony of the psalmist encourages us also to seek God's help amid the struggle for social justice, especially as we face adversity and resistance. This was certainly the experience of the church in Central America during the 1980s, which remained faithful to God in the midst of civil wars that rocked the subcontinent. With God's help, we may experience emotional and spiritual health as we remember God's steadfast love and sing our praises to God for whatever good gifts we may have.

Psalm 89:1–4, 15–18

Psalm 89 is the final psalm of the third book of the Psalter (Pss. 73–89). In structural terms, this psalm blends two literary forms: a psalm of praise (vv. 1–18) and a psalm of lament (vv. 38–51). The verses selected for today's lectionary reading belong to the first form.

The opening two verses of Psalm 89 praise God for steadfast love shown to Israel. This complex theological concept is based on the Hebrew word *hesed*, which describes divine love. It can also be translated as covenant love, mercy, grace, and solidarity. *Hesed* is love that God grants on the basis of the divine covenant uniting God and humanity. *Hesed* is divine love at its best.

The connection between divine love and the covenant is clearly stated in verses 3 and 4, where the psalm celebrates the promises made to King David. Here, David personifies Israel as a whole. The psalm therefore affirms the divine love for all the people of God.

This is made explicit in verses 15–18. In verse 15 we find a blessing on the people of God, particularly those who remain faithful to the covenant. Obedience produces joy, which leads the people to praise God (v. 16). God is the "glory of their strength" (v. 17), a phrase that affirms the power of divine love.

Verse 18 poses a challenge. The first part affirms that God protects Israel as a warrior God. However, the second part is ambiguous: it is not clear whether the psalmist is affirming God alone as the king of Israel or King David whom God uses as a shield. These two interpretations are irreconcilable. Either God alone is king or David is not only king but also God's preferred instrument for the protection of Israel. If God is the true king and our only sovereign ruler, then all other rulers and governments must stand subject to God and remember that no state is ultimately supreme. God thus stands as judge to indict unjust laws and earthly rulers who do not have ultimate control. However, if we believe that our king is God's gift to us, then we must be careful not to legitimize any government, ruler, or military establishment as divinely instituted.

After the sad events of September 11, 2011, many churches and church leaders in the United States developed a nationalistic theology summarized by the phrase "God bless America." This "USA theology" tended to legitimize military interventions in Iraq and Afghanistan. While we certainly love our country, would it not be more theologically correct to call on America to bless God?

We must be clear from whom we derive our authority and to whom we are accountable—both as citizens and as advocates for God's just and loving purposes.

Romans 6:12–23

The Bible presents sin as a negative spiritual force, not as the mere transgression of laws and regulations. Accordingly, Romans 6 describes sin as a slave owner that oppresses and exploits those who are held captive under its demonic rule (v. 16) and compares those who sin with slaves who voluntarily surrender their freedom. Just as surprising, the text expands the metaphor to suggest that people must choose between two kinds of slavery. One may be a slave of sin or a slave of righteousness. This section ends by comparing the "wages" paid by these masters. Sin pays with death, while righteousness pays with life. Sin kills those who are under its rule, while the slaves of Christ will enjoy everlasting life.

From the standpoint of peace and justice, using slavery as a theological image is troubling. As I write this from the Spanish-speaking Caribbean, I remember the devastating consequences of slavery. As a descendant of former slaves, I find the image offensive, even in its positive mode (slaves of righteousness). Sermons on this topic should not treat slavery lightly and should not ignore the egregious violence used to enforce a slave-based economic system. Forgetting the pain caused by this system would be immoral.

Today we face new forms of bondage. For example, the United States consumes enormous quantities of illegal drugs, mainly produced in and imported from Latin America. While users in the first world defend their right to use these drugs, the production and trade of such substances has devastating effects south of the border. It is estimated that more than 25,000 persons have died in recent years due to the wars between the drug cartels in northern Mexico.

Nevertheless, the message of the text is clear. Paul urges us to choose between two spiritual paths: a negative life that leads people to death because it separates people from God and a positive one that leads to abundant life because it draws people closer to God.

Matthew 10:40–42

The Gospel of Matthew includes five discourses or sermons that summarize Jesus' teachings. Matthew 10:40–42 forms the conclusion of Jesus' second discourse (chap. 10), called "the missionary discourse" because it describes the mission that Jesus gave to his twelve disciples.

A troubling aspect of this text is Jesus' instruction to "go nowhere among the Gentiles, and enter no town of the Samaritans, but go rather to the lost sheep of the house of Israel" (10:5–6). This chapter presents a very narrow view of Christian mission. However, the Gospel corrects this exclusive understanding with the story of the Canaanite woman's faith in Matthew 15:21–28. Also, Matthew ends with an inclusive understanding of mission: "Go therefore and make disciples of all nations" (28:19). These wider understandings of mission offer a different perspective for understanding Jesus' missionary instructions in 10:40–42.

In these verses, Jesus challenges us as Paul did in Romans 6: we must choose whom to serve. Those who receive Jesus' teachings receive God (Matt. 10:40). Those who receive Jesus' emissaries receive Jesus and, therefore, God (v. 41). And those who show mercy to evangelists will be properly rewarded (v. 42).

Once again, the language of the Gospel reading is alien and archaic. Postmodern people do not think in such either–or categories. In many parts of our society, exclusion is frowned upon and inclusion is seen as a virtue.

Yet Matthew 10:40–42 challenges us to be deliberate in the choices we make. The image of giving a cup of cold water to "one of these little ones" is very powerful. The identity of the "little ones" is debated; scholars identify them with the disciples, Gentiles who had come to faith, or Christians expulsed from the synagogues. In any case, today the text challenges the church to receive the excluded with love and to offer hospitality to "the other."

Fourth of July: Seeking Liberty and Justice for All

Ronald J. Allen

1 SAMUEL 8:19–22
PSALM 72:1–7
1 PETER 2:11–17
MATTHEW 14:1–12

Many churches join the larger culture in the United States by celebrating the Fourth of July as Independence Day.[1] However, reflective Christians note that independence from Great Britain in 1776 did not bring freedom to slaves. Moreover, people at Fourth of July events sometimes uncritically wave the flag and celebrate the nation (including national policies that deny God's purposes). However, the preacher can take advantage of the interest in public life generated by the Fourth of July to help the Christian community think critically about the degree to which the United States (or any nation) is truly an environment of liberty and justice for all. What needs to happen for all people in this nation to live in liberty and justice?

What, to the American slave, is your Fourth of July? I answer; a day that reveals to [us] more than all other days in the year, the gross injustice and cruelty to which [we are] the constant victim. [To us], your celebration is a sham. . . . This Fourth of July is yours, not mine. You may rejoice, I must mourn. To drag a [people] in fetters into the grand illuminated temple of liberty, and call upon [them] to join you in joyous anthems, were inhuman mockery and sacrilegious irony.

Frederick Douglass[2]

1. While these comments focus on the Fourth of July as Independence Day in the United States, they could be adopted for similar days in other nations. Canada, for instance, celebrates July 1 as Canada Day in honor of Canada being officially united as a single country on July 1, 1867.

2. Frederick Douglass first delivered this address in 1852. See "The Meaning of July Fourth for the Negro," in *The Life and Writings of Frederick Douglass*, ed. Philip S. Foner (New York: International Publishers, 1950), 2:192.

The passages for today focus on leadership and justice. Israel seeks a monarch (1 Samuel). Psalm 72 sets out the purpose of monarchical rule. Herod and Jesus point to two different purposes of leadership (Matt. 14). To what degree is a population obligated to obey the leaders and laws of the state (1 Peter)? Using the perspective of Frederick Douglass (from the quote above), the preacher can use these texts to explore the degree to which the United States is a community of liberty and justice for all. How can the church take a lead in calling for liberty and justice for those to whom they are denied?

1 Samuel 8:19–22

According to the Deuteronomic theologians (who edited the books of Samuel), the tribes of Israel were a loosely knit confederacy into the time of Samuel. Each tribe had its own land, its members living in covenant with one another and with other tribes. When they were confronted with challenges, God used charismatic leaders (judges) to mobilize the tribes in cooperative response. By contrast, the countries around Israel were ruled by monarchs with strong central governments who sought to control their own populations and to conquer other populations.

Samuel was a faithful judge. However, wanting to be like other nations, the elders of Israel asked Samuel to anoint a monarch over them. Samuel warned them against this choice. Instead of living in covenant with one another, Samuel said, they would serve the ruler as soldiers, servants, and farmers, and would place their land and animals at the monarch's disposal. Nevertheless, the people insisted that Samuel anoint such a ruler.

The Deuteronomic writers justify Samuel's wisdom and critique the notion of monarchy by chronicling how Samuel's prophecy came true in the reigns of Saul, David, and Solomon. The troubles of imperial rule were magnified when the nation split into two countries, Judah and Israel. Moreover, many of the rulers were unfaithful, eventuating in national defeat and Babylonian exile.

On the Fourth of July, this story warns churches and nations not to be mesmerized into wanting to operate like other institutions whose goal is to control others. Rulers and nations who follow this path can expect a fate similar to the one that befell the divided monarchy: eventual defeat and exile.

Without idealizing, the preacher can call attention to the tribal confederacy as a model for the church and for other communities (including government). Decision making was close to the people so that members of the community felt ownership and responsibility. Both leaders and people could adapt quickly to changing circumstances. Resources were near at hand and the members of the tribes were responsible for using them. Such communities seek not to consolidate their own power but to serve the purposes of covenantal blessing for all.

Psalm 72:1–7

The notion of covenantal community is in the background of Psalm 72. God desires for all members to live in *shalom*—a life with meaningful work, food, shelter, clothing, and other forms of security. According to Psalm 72, the monarch in Israel is responsible for seeing that the community embodies this quality of life. The ruler is to see that all members of the community live in justice and righteousness (vv. 1–2). Indeed, the psalm emphasizes that the ruler is to give special attention to the poor and the needy (vv. 4, 12–14) and to take actions that disempower those who crush the needy (vv. 4, 14).

Relatively few nations have monarchs today. Queens and kings are largely symbolic figures in many countries that continue to maintain these offices. Nevertheless, the preacher can regard the monarch in Psalm 72 as representative of the purposes of leadership in government. Presidents, prime ministers, members of Congress and Parliament, and all other leaders are to see that *all* in the community live in *shalom*.

The Fourth of July is an ideal occasion for the preacher to reflect with the congregation on the degree to which leaders in all spheres of life enact justice and righteousness. The preacher can reinforce efforts that flow toward *shalom*. But the preacher must call leaders to account when their policies and behaviors work against covenantal blessing for all.

Matthew 14:1–12

Clark Williamson, who taught systematic theology at Christian Theological Seminary, points out that this text and the next (the feeding of the five thousand, Matt. 14:13–21) contrast two approaches to leadership.[3] Herod represents the present evil age, and Jesus points to the present and coming realm of God.

Matthew 14:1–12 describes Herod as a tetrarch, that is, a ruler appointed by Rome over the regions of Galilee and Perea (an area just east of the Jordan River). After she divorced her husband Philip, Herodias had married Herod. However, since Philip was Herod's half brother, Herod violated Jewish law by marrying a close relative (Lev. 18:6–16; 20:21). John the Baptist, acting as a prophet, called Herod to account, but Herod imprisoned the Baptist. The

---

3. Clark M. Williamson and Ronald J. Allen, *Preaching the Gospels without Blaming the Jews: A Lectionary Commentary* (Louisville, KY: Westminster John Knox Press, 2004), 137–38.

daughter of Herodias asked Herod to behead John, and Herod granted her request. Herod's behavior thus typifies the death-dealing present evil age and its leadership, especially the Roman Empire.

By contrast, in Matthew 14:13–21, Jesus feeds a hungry crowd in the wilderness. Herod has access to the vast resources of the Roman Empire, and his banquet ends in death. By contrast, Jesus, empowered by compassion, feeds the crowd with the meager resources of five loaves and two fish. The realm of God does not take life but sustains it.

On a day intended to remind the nation to seek liberty and justice for all, this text pushes the preacher to ask, "Which people, policies, and circles of opinion in our national life lean in the direction of Herod, and which ones lean in the direction of the realm of God?" For example, the national healthcare reform that began in the United States in 2009 will make it possible for more people than ever to receive health care. However, the debate that followed revealed that some leaders are quite willing to let uninsured people die on the streets. The latter is the spirit of Herod. A realm approach asks, "How can we turn our limited resources into maximum care for all?"

1 Peter 2:11–17

Christians sometimes cite this text (and others like it) to flatly suggest that people should obey the laws of the state and do what its leaders say. However, the writer of 1 Peter (whom I call "Peter," although this letter is likely pseudonymous) intended not to set forth a general principle valid in every time and place but to propose a strategy for witness in the time and place of the congregation to whom this letter was addressed

Scholars agree that unconverted Gentiles outside the congregation to which Peter wrote maligned the congregation as evildoers (v. 12). Outsiders looked down on the congregation and would not take its witness seriously. According to verses 11–12, a major purpose of the letter is to encourage the congregation to live in ways that would persuade their opponents not to fear the congregation. First Peter 2:13–17 is part of that strategy.

Gentiles sought an orderly social world and feared chaos. At the time of 1 Peter, many Gentiles, especially Romans, believed that the gods had ordained a highly stratified society to maintain the stability of the community, with people in the lower strata subservient to those who were "above" them. The emperor and the Roman government were at the peak of the social pyramid. Peter urges readers to accept the authority of the emperor and other authorities because God can work through those offices to maintain a peaceful and orderly world.

Government is intended to reinforce those who do right (those who build up community) and punish those who do wrong (those who break down peace and order; see vv. 13–14). If the members of the church live peacefully, they will "silence the ignorance of the foolish" Gentiles who mistakenly perceive the church as a threat to the well-being of the social world (v. 15). Since the congregation serves the living God (and not idols), Christians are free, that is, their identity and worth are not determined by their place in the existing social pyramid but by God's grace and call (v. 16).

On the Fourth of July, the preacher may join Christians across the centuries who have struggled with the relationship of the church to the laws and leaders of the state. What should the church do when the government does wrong? What should Christians do when the government punishes those who do right? Indeed, what should the church do when the government itself becomes a source of chaos and injustice?

In 1963, Martin Luther King Jr. was jailed in Birmingham, Alabama, for violating statutes that enforced segregation. Some clergy criticized him for breaking the law. Dr. King addressed these critics and in so doing articulated a persuasive understanding of the relationship between the church and obedience to the state.

> You express a great deal of anxiety over our willingness to break laws. This is certainly a legitimate concern. Since we so diligently urge people to obey the Supreme Court's decision of 1954 outlawing segregation in the public schools, it is rather strange and paradoxical to find us consciously breaking laws. One may well ask, "How can you advocate breaking some laws and obeying others?" The answer is found in the fact that there are two types of laws: there are just and unjust laws. I would agree with St. Augustine that "An unjust law is no law at all."[4]

The preacher's call is to help the congregation think critically about particular laws and the degree to which they are just or unjust.

Ironically, the church that obeys unjust laws and leaders contributes to the long-term instability of the social world. Injustice creates conditions that ultimately diminish a community. The church that engages in civil disobedience as a means to rectify injustice contributes to the long-term security of the social world.

---

4. Martin Luther King Jr., "Letter from Birmingham City Jail," in *A Testament of Hope: The Essential Writings and Speeches of Martin Luther King, Jr.*, ed. James M. Washington (San Francisco: HarperSanFrancisco, 1986), 293. John Calvin articulated a similar point in his *Institutes of the Christian Religion*, ed. John T. McNeill, trans. Ford Lewis Battles, Library of Christian Classics (Philadelphia: Westminster Press, 1960), 4.20.32, p. 1520; cf. 2.8.38, pp. 403–4.

Proper 9

Marjorie Hewitt Suchocki

GENESIS 24:34–38, 42–49, 58–67   ZECHARIAH 9:9–12
PSALM 45:10–17   PSALM 145:8–14
                                        ROMANS 7:15–25A
                                        MATTHEW 11:16–19, 25–30

The lectionary texts for this day hold intimations and potential judgments for us. Are we hospitable to the stranger? Do we offer water to those who thirst—not allegorically, but actually, in the deserts peopled by migrants seeking work to support their families? Do we work for peace, or do we merely mouth the phrases of peace? Are we concerned for those in prison, and do we actively support prison reform? What about our hospitality and concern for those who are homosexual? Do we force exclusion on them, demanding that they deny their bodies? These texts challenge us to consider whether our hospitality toward others will include our caring acceptance of them.

Genesis 24:34–38, 42–49, 58–67

Abraham sends his servant to Nahor to find a wife for Isaac. Arriving in the city of Nahor, the servant meets a young woman who has just drawn water from a well. The servant determines that if she shares the water with him, and also draws water for his camels, it will be a sign that she is the chosen wife for Isaac. The issue is not incidental, for hospitality is a high mark of righteousness. Rebekah not only gives water to the stranger, but she gives water to his camels as well, drawing many jars of water to slake the thirst of ten camels. When she brings the stranger to her brother's house, the law of hospitality requires that Laban extend food and lodging, and so he does. Following these signs of righteousness, the marriage is agreed upon, and the story concludes with Rebekah meeting Isaac in the field, going with him to his mother's tent.

Today we do not decide whether a marriage is desirable according to whether or not the chosen one draws water for us and our camels! But the issue of hospitality and its connection with righteousness should not be lost. The theme is repeated throughout Scripture, often imaged as a gift of water to the stranger in that dry, thirsty land.

There are images in print and on video of persons crossing the borders and deserts of the southwestern United States, driven by poverty in their own land—a poverty to which we in America have certainly contributed with our cocaine and heroin addictions, and with market policies that drive down the economic stability of previously sustainable farming communities. As persons leave devastated economies in search of work that will enable them to send money back to their families, they dare to cross the great deserts of the Southwest. Some churches leave water at designated places in the desert, hoping to sustain the migrants on their harsh way. But how do the rest of us exercise hospitality to the stranger? Do we offer water; do we draw from our lavish wells? Do we seek to address the conditions that make for thirst? Are we righteous?

In this text, hospitality to the stranger results in marriage and blessing. If and when we offer water to the strangers in our midst, what joining together of cultures and peoples will follow? In such mixtures, there is the promise of blessing.

Psalm 45:10–17

The Genesis text this week bespeaks hospitality and marriage; these verses from Psalm 45 offer us a marriage rich in all the trappings of royalty, celebrating the marriage of the king. The paean of praise celebrates the wealth and status of the king as well as the virtues of the bride. The bride, herself a king's daughter, wears clothing "interwoven with gold" (v. 13 NASB). There are gifts, an ivory palace, many companions, and general rejoicing. The movement of the psalm follows the movement of ceremony. The bride leaves her father's house, moving in celebration and ceremony towards the king, finally entering his palace. The final blessing is, "In the place of ancestors you, O king, shall have sons; you will make them princes in all the earth" (v. 16). Thus the movement of this psalm is not only ceremonial in the journey toward marriage; it is also a woman's journey from father to husband to sons.

The journey might give pause to contemporary women, who could well ask about the mothers and sisters and daughters, and whether or not, after all, a woman's life is really so determined and defined by her relation to men. But the text is not about contemporary women, nor does it raise such questions. Rather, it celebrates the passage of the generations in the context of a wedding for the king (who, according to 2 Sam. 5:13, had many wives and concubines).

The prelude to the lectionary text praises the king by speaking of his glories in battle and of the righteousness that merited his being anointed. It is good for the king to be reminded in the midst of his merriment about righteousness and justice; it would be quite a long time before these qualities and privileges were extended to women as well as men.

Zechariah 9:9–12

People who know Handel's *Messiah* cannot help but hear it in these passages. The text takes us to precursors of Palm Sunday: the king is "humble and riding on a donkey, on a colt, the foal of a donkey." Bathed in these familiarities, how do we hear the text? We do so by looking beyond its familiarities into its deepest call: peace with justice. Peace is attained by cutting off the weapons of war, and speaking "peace to the nations." This dominion of peace finds its deepest evidence in the release of prisoners, made "free from the waterless pit," and given hope.

Our own nation must bow down before this text, for release of the prisoners is hardly our agenda, whether these prisoners are political or civil. As for "waterless pits," our own political prisons have included waterboard pits, and release is hard to come by. How do we speak "peace to the nations" when our own policies require regular increases in military spending and the enormous difficulty of undoing our decisions to imprison and torture those we consider our enemies?

Ample justification for military policies is always offered, with all the logic of military tacticians. And many of these justifications create the very conditions that make for war. The politics of war feed on themselves, creating the conditions they must fight. Peaceful alternatives are hard to come by. Indeed, when they are tried, such as in the building of schools, the schools are often destroyed by those we name as our enemies, and whom we then attack. And so the alternative of war asserts and reasserts itself, swallowing as many people as possible in its maw of death and destruction. Over against such cycles of human destructiveness, the text cries out for destruction not of one another but of our weapons, that we might live in a context of peace.

The truth of the commitment to peace is proven by how we treat those we have imprisoned. The issue is wider than that raised by military prisons; it calls attention to civil prisons as well. How is it a witness to peace when we turn prisons into a profit-making industry that benefits by keeping persons who have broken our laws imprisoned as long as possible? How is it a commitment to peace when the best we can do in response to killing is to kill the killer?

Christians call Jesus the Prince of Peace. This ancient text from Zechariah asks us to measure the meaning of such a title. Do we follow the Prince of Peace who once entered the city in humility? Our attitudes and actions toward war and toward prisons will tell us the answer.

Psalm 145:8–14

The wonder of this psalm as a whole is that it not only sings of the power of God, but it carefully defines God's power. We are accustomed to images of God that use metaphors such as king, warrior, and rock, or that equate God's power with the uncontrollable strength of natural storms. This psalm draws us away from such images, redefining power so that it undercuts—and perhaps even destroys—these images. After beginning the psalm with expressions of praise at the unsearchable greatness of God and the power of God's awesome acts, the psalmist says just what this greatness and these awesome acts are. They are grace, mercy, loving-kindness, and goodness to all. The glory of God is the goodness of God, and the majesty of God is the mercy of God. The final definition of divine power is this: the Lord sustains all who fall, raises up all who are bowed down, and nourishes us all.

Over against such a definition, some might cry out that far too often, those who fall are crushed, those who are bowed down are utterly destroyed, and the nourishment promised is but dust in the mouth of those suffering in famines caused by drought or war. Where is the truth of God's power over against such evils? Answers to such questions abound in theological tomes filled with complex and sophisticated arguments. Perhaps the best way for us to deal with these questions is to ask ourselves which of the two sets of power images best fits the understanding of God that we see in Jesus Christ. Which definition of power draws the best model to live by? If it is the model of goodness and mercy, then we will seek to live by such a model. By definition, this means that we will be drawn to address the problems of the fallen, the bowed down, the hungry, and all that these images represent. We will seek to enact a world where goodness and mercy trump the forces of destruction. As we do, will it not be the power of God that drives and calls us to such actions? Is God not working through us? Therefore "my mouth will speak the praise of the Lord, and all flesh will bless [God's] holy name forever and ever" (v. 21).

Romans 7:15–25a

Was Paul married? Why do we know nothing of his personal life? We know that Aquila and Priscilla, husband and wife, traveled together on their missionary journeys, and that Paul called his fellow prisoners Junia and Andronicus (presumably wife and husband) outstanding among the apostles. There was certainly precedent for Paul to marry and continue his calling, had he been so inclined. Why does it seem that Paul was not married?

Romans 7 offers a speculative suggestion. Bearing in mind that "member of the flesh" is usually a euphemism for the male sexual organ, read the text as if you were a homosexual, struggling against your homosexuality under the conviction that it is wrong. There is no question but that Paul considered homosexuality "unnatural." In this same letter, he speaks of men who "abandoned the natural function of the woman and burned in their desire toward one another" (1:27 NASB).

"For what I am doing," writes Paul, "I do not understand; for I am not practicing what I *would* like to *do*, but I am doing the very thing I hate" (7:15 NASB). He "agrees with the Law" that this is wrong, and that the law is good. And then we have a peculiar dissociation, where Paul separates himself from his body. His agreement with the law is an identity with the law (this from the great apostle of freedom from the law in Galatians!), so that his body's desires are not really Paul's, but just belong to his body, an alien thing. "I practice the very evil that I do not wish," he says, and then disavows it: "but if I am doing the very thing I do not want, I am no longer the one doing it, but sin which dwells in me" (v. 20 NASB). What kind of reasoning is this, from the man who begged Christ three times to remove a thorn in his flesh over which he seemed to have no power?

Anyone involved in pastoral care with persons tormented by a sexuality they hate may recognize the feelings expressed by Paul in this text. If one is convinced that homosexuality is condemned by God, then the inability to rid oneself of the hated orientation is an agony. But most often sexual orientation is a given, present from conception, and sexual desire will direct itself accordingly whether one wishes it or not. Wretched man that he is, Paul's way out seems to be disavowal of the body and condemnation of the separated body as sin.

Which of us would so counsel a gay or lesbian person? In Paul's day a dissociation of mind from body may have been culturally acceptable, but we would hardly advocate such dualism today. Perhaps we might note that our Scriptures were written more than two thousand years ago. In ancient Judaism, all practices that endangered the continued propagation of Israel were condemned. Incest threatened the viability of the child; masturbation "wasted" the seed, as did homosexual practices. In the New Testament, homosexuality was identified with Greek culture, and the power of Greek culture threatened to absorb subordinate cultures such as Judaism within its ethos, for Greek culture flourished in the Roman Empire.

But what if the need to propagate through childbirth is no longer so pressing—on the contrary, what if we have already so populated the earth that humans are a threat to other species? And what if homosexuality is not a mark of an alien culture, but instead is known to be a genetic orientation? What then? Shall we still counsel the person to follow a Pauline prescription, and dissociate from one's body, consigning it to "sin?" Or shall we rather revert to the Paul of Galatians, claiming freedom from laws that foster self-hatred?

Paul may or may not have been homosexual. In 1 Corinthians 7, he argues that the urgency of the gospel recommends that persons remain single if possible, so as to avoid the competing cares of a household. But in this day and age, amid so much homophobia and heterosexism, the text of Romans 7:15–25 surely should give us pause. We must seek more responsible ways of understanding sexuality while affirming loving relationships that nourish the whole person.

Matthew 11:16–19, 25–30

"Wisdom is vindicated by her deeds." Jesus shares this parable of the inexplicable unresponsiveness of people to the cry of the children: the children give beauty, but there is no responsive dance of acclamation; the children lament piteously, but no one cares. Likewise, when prophecy is given—whether the prophecy is the dire warning from John the Baptist or the prophecy of joyous grace from Jesus—the response is dismissive. The Baptist is dismissed as crazy; Jesus is dismissed as irresponsible. If wisdom is vindicated by her deeds, then such dismissals of John and Jesus show the responders to be fools.

The writer of Matthew ends chapter 11 by citing a prayer of Jesus, thanking God that although the so-called wise ones of his day had not accepted him or his message, the "infants," the lowly, heard and accepted. Then follow the beautiful words, "Come to me, all who are weary and heavy-laden, and I will give you rest. . . . For my yoke is easy, and my burden is light" (vv. 28, 30 NASB). Christ urges us to take his yoke upon us. Live the peace of God, and through such living, "wisdom is vindicated by her deeds." Through such living, the peace of God will come.

Proper 10

Cláudio Carvalhaes

GENESIS 25:19–34
ISAIAH 55:10–13

PSALM 119:105–112
PSALM 65:(1–8) 9–13
ROMANS 8:1–11
MATTHEW 13:1–9, 18–23

We are living in what the Christian liturgical calendar calls Ordinary Time. What does "ordinary time" mean? I propose reading each text assigned for Proper 10 with a specific community of people in mind. (The community will vary from year to year; see my comments for Proper 10 in years B and C of this series.) Based on what liberation theologians in Latin America still practice among base communities, we will explore how a particular community interprets the Bible from its lived realities, akin to what German theologians call the *Sitz im Leben*, or "the setting of life." That means that I will draw understandings of the text from the voices of people who are reading these texts from their contexts and giving input from their current religious, social, political, and economic situations, which are quite different from those of mainline faith communities in the United States. This exercise in interpretation can aid the pastor's listening by attending to the specific ways each community understands these texts and how people's insights shed light on what the preacher needs to say. My hope is that this approach will inspire you to read these texts with members of your own community of faith and that your community may learn something from the perspectives of the community I represent here.

The texts for Year A will be read from the perspective of a pastor who is living in a community of small farmers on the outskirts of Sao Paulo, Brazil. This community, called Santa Fe, is part of a social movement in Brazil called Landless Worker's Movement (in Portuguese, Movimento dos Trabalhadores Rurais Sem Terra, or MST), the largest social movement in Latin America, with an estimated 1.5 million landless members. The MST carries out long-overdue land reform in a country marred by brutal, unjust land distribution.

320

In Brazil, 1.6 percent of the landowners control nearly half (46.8 percent) of the land on which crops can be grown. The MST has obtained land titles for more than 350,000 families in 2,000 settlements as a result of its actions, and 180,000 encamped families currently await government recognition.

The people of Santa Fe have already received their land and are beginning the process of developing a cooperative to plant, harvest, and sell their produce. They gather on Wednesday nights for a *mistica*, a time when people encourage each other, bring important symbols to the celebration, read the Bible, sing, and talk about life, faith, the movement, and their work on the land.

The pastor says to the gathering of twenty people, "Friends, we are here to read the Bible and figure out what these texts have to do with our community in Santa Fe. What is God telling us to consider, to do, to change, to engage, to transform here today?

"We are also in the midst of celebrating a liturgical period called Ordinary Time, which is the daily stuff of life fueled with extraordinary encounters with God. At this crossroads between the ordinary and extraordinary lies what we might believe about God's presence, God's miraculous works, and our (extra) ordinary lives. It is a time between the seasons of Pentecost and Advent, that is, between the time when the Holy Spirit descended on the disciples to begin the church of Christ and the advent of God's coming in Jesus to live among us as 'Emmanuel.' What are we to do with these biblical texts during this time?"

The numbers in parentheses below indicate statements that different participants made in the conversation about the text.

Genesis 25:19–34

As people read this story, they offer varied responses. (1) I don't understand what you are saying about "ordinary/extraordinary" but I know one thing: something is happening to Rebekah, a barren woman now pregnant with twins! I think God is always showing us something and we must pay attention. (2) God is exaggerated. This is the love of God, always too much, beyond any reason, calculation, or proper affection. See what happened to us! We had nothing, we were lying on the streets. That boy over there was living under a bridge, and look now where he is! He is in school! Look where we are, in our own houses! It seems exaggerated but it is not! It is fair! God's exaggeration is justice, but when people have too much, this exaggeration is sin!

(3) Twins out of an impossible pregnancy sounds like a joke! Some of the holiest things are laughable, ridiculous, incomprehensible according to any reasonable account of the world. Look at us: we were excluded from the economic system, from any form of access, and because we organized ourselves,

God gave us victory! The powerful don't want to see us organized. They say God is just, but only according to their own laws of preserving their rights and land! (5) That's right. What is not right is Rebekah liking one son more than the other.

(6) Jacob was not fair either. Why does he charge his brother Esau his birthright for a pot of food? Where did he learn that? That is what the big landowners do, they take the land, call it private property, but it benefits very few people. (7) The lentil soup is like the land, it should be given to anyone who is hungry. (8) Jacob abused Esau, but Esau didn't take care of his own rights either. It is like us, if we don't pay attention to our rights and organize and fight for them, we are going to be abused by others. We must care for what God has given to us and give to others what is right. Without abuse!

Isaiah 55:10–13

(1) God's word is like the movements of nature; it has seasons and purposes. The rain comes to water the earth and give it life. I've never seen this snow. (2) It is ice from the sky. Thank God we don't have it here. (3) There is a cycle in nature and a cycle in the word of God. But today the climate is messed up and the word of God is also messed up, with people making it whatever they want. (4) Everything is messed up.

(5) The word of God is like a seed that needs to be planted in good soil so that it can grow and live. Every time we meet to decide the future of our community, like today, we must hear the word of God for the goodness of our community. (6) And we need to hear what is important for our people. (7) The text is saying that the word that goes out of our mouths should be careful so as to fulfill God's mission. (8) That's why we speak the truth to the government! Why has our country never had agrarian reform? Where is the word of God that claims justice? It is one of the prophets who says "Do justice, love mercy, and walk humbly with God." Don't you see some people going to church to succeed only for themselves? We must succeed with each other; that is the only way we can succeed, when we are together in the fight, and then people get scared and call us communists. (9) Wasn't Jesus a communist? Is it because he wanted everybody to have a just life, that made him a communist? (10) What we have to know is this: you are either in favor of or against the common good for all; you cannot be neutral! (11) Every neutrality is false! (12) Exactly!

Psalm 119:105–112

(1) Again, the word of God is here; now it is like a lamp. It took a while to get electricity here, but now we have it. We can live without electric light,

but we can't live without the word of God! (2) We all know what it is to be afflicted, to not have enough to eat, to go from one place to another, losing our belongings, our bearings. If it was not for our *companheiros*, we would not have it, and we would be afflicted forever. (3) The word of God is like the joy that Rebekah felt! (4) I know what it feels to be afflicted all the time, and not have a chance to rest. . . . My sons are on the streets and not able to go to school. (5) I always have a candle burning near my Bible at home, I light a candle every night and say a prayer, be it an ordinary or extraordinary day, as you said before. Every day is a struggle, every day!

(7) Let us not forget that this psalm is a song, and we know the power of singing. (8) Sometimes singing is all we have left. . . . Singing is more than making a nice melody: it is about going beyond what we see, it is about surviving! When we sing we keep the breath of life moving in and out, and the movement of desire and faith alive. (9) Did you watch that documentary that said singing was key for the fight against apartheid in South Africa?[1] Without songs and singing there wouldn't be any revolution; without songs and singing they would have not prevailed in their struggle. So friends, let us do like the psalmist and the people of South Africa: Let us sing to the Lord for a new land and a new world!

Psalm 65:(1–8) 9–13

(1) This is so beautiful! And this is exactly what is going to happen here. Our fields will be filled and plentiful! God provides the grain and the water. (2) Well, not necessarily! The water is provided by God, but the grain belongs to the rich. They have the seeds, and those who have the seeds have the richness of the earth. We can't buy the seeds; they are too expensive, and that is why we are having so many problems planting our crop this year. Besides, we didn't have enough rain last year and we lost almost everything that we had. And this year we are having too much water and we run the risk of losing it again. We are destroying God's nature and we are suffering from the changes of nature. (3) Remember our brothers in the United States when our *companheiro* came to talk to us? He said that there, people cut the top of the mountains with explosions to get coal, and these explosions destroy the whole environment. (4) But here we are seeing Brazil's largest river, Sao Francisco, being artificially transplanted to another place, a movement that will kill the river in many places and destroy entire communities who live off of it. (5) If we don't protect our rivers, these companies from the north will dump their

---

1. *Amandla! A Revolution in Four-Part Harmony*, directed by Lee Hirsch, released in the United States in 2002. This documentary tells the story of Black South Africans through the eyes of white prison guards and executioners, Black activists and musicians.

waste in our waters. We cannot let it happen! We must do something! We cannot wait and expect somebody else to do it for us, like we did to get our land. (6) But we must talk to the people who live near that company to pressure them! There are people who work in that company and they are afraid of losing their jobs. (7) But we must work with them and see how we can fight for clean water for all of us! Otherwise what the Bible says here will only be poetry, nice words. (8) We need to organize and trust the blessing of the Holy Spirit to be with us again, as when God came at Pentecost and when we got our land. God can do it again!

Romans 8:1–11

(1) Because of Christ's righteousness, the Spirit is with us. When we fight the good fight, the Spirit of righteousness is with us. (2) The very Spirit of Jesus! (3) Away from Jesus we lose our sense of justice, we live in the flesh of our sins, start to accept injustice as normal and think we don't need to help others. Life comes in the struggle! We had nothing and now we have a house! We were like dead people. Now, we have our land to produce and we will eat out of our own work! Now we have the Spirit of life living in us! Alleluia! This is the extraordinary in our everyday experiences, the life of the Spirit of Jesus Christ in our lives. (4) But we have to be vigilant! (5) Yes, we do, but we also have to remember that the agrarian system in Brazil still relies on the hands of 1 percent of the population. (6) This is the spirit of death! (7) Yes, it is! (8) Now that we have schools for our kids it is easier to see life happening in the flesh of our sons and daughters, our own flesh. We need to teach them to fight for their rights!

(9) The same Spirit that prepares the earth, the same Spirit that inhabited the womb of Rebekah, is the Spirit who lives in us today. (10) Yes! The living Spirit in our bodies today is the same Spirit that raised Jesus, and this is what is called *grace*! Grace is the life of God in our bodies. Grace is the Spirit of life in the midst of death helping us to choose life. (11) Yes! (12) Alleluia! That is how I feel it: this exaggerated grace is the capacity to continue in the fight when everything is against us.

Matthew 13:1–9, 18–23

(1) Before we think about this method of plantation we must ask: To whom does this soil belong? Is the sower working for a big landowner? Or is he sowing his own land? This is important to ask because of resources and understanding the consequences of what happens. This sower seems to not know his soil very well, otherwise he would not waste his seeds in these three parts

of the terrain. He lost too much and I don't know if he can afford a new crop. (2) Well, see the text, he didn't throw the seed but they fell from his sack. Perhaps he needs to be more careful and attentive to his sack, to the birds, to the soil. He should study better his soil so that he will avoid waste. (3) But then the text says that the seed is the word of the kingdom and how people react to it. (4) If that is right, then we must be careful with the words of the kingdom of God the same way that we must be careful with the seeds we have. (5) But we must let God give the growth both of the soil and of people's hearts. (6) I wish we could have our harvest the way it is described at the end, with fruits in one case a hundredfold, in another sixty, and in another thirty. (7) We cannot afford to lose three-quarters of our plantation, otherwise we go hungry and are in debt. (8) We should rely on the Holy Spirit. (9) Yes, but if you are a big landowner "the spirit (of the money) will help you more." (10) That is true. (11) In everything the presence of the Spirit guides us, in our losses and our gains. (13) For the sake of our communities and not for ourselves. Hopefully.

Proper 11

Joni S. Sancken

GENESIS 28:10–19A   PSALM 139:1–12, 23–24
ISAIAH 44:6–8   PSALM 86:11–17
                         ROMANS 8:12–25
          MATTHEW 13:24–30, 36–43

In this week's lectionary texts, the biblical authors bear witness to God's empowering and faithful presence even when trouble and deep trauma threaten life and a meaningful future. From Jacob's first encounter with God at Bethel while traveling away from family and home (due in part to Jacob's own scheming), to God's promised redemption of exiled Israel in Isaiah 44 and the presence of weeds amid the wheat in Matthew's parable, all creation longs to be set free from bondage and decay (Rom. 8:21–23) and to live into God's future. The God who knows us intimately rebuilds us from the rubble of broken trust and ruptured relationships, granting us abundant blessing and a new identity as God's witnesses in the world.

Genesis 28:10–19a

Genesis 28:10 picks up in the middle of Jacob's saga, which began with last week's text (25:19) and proceeds through chapter 36. Approaching this passage from an angle of justice for all God's people shines a light on themes of scarcity and abundance. Jacob journeys away from his mother's love and comfortable life as a tent dweller in Beer-sheba towards his family's homeland to find a wife among Rebekah's kin. The circumstances surrounding Jacob's departure are rife with family conflict over limited family gifts and resources, with Isaac and Rebekah each favoring a different son. After securing his brother Esau's birthright in exchange for a simple meal, with Rebekah's help Jacob goes on to impersonate his twin in order to receive Isaac's blessing (27:5–29).

Esau's bitter cry, "Bless me, me also, father! . . . Have you not reserved a blessing for me?" (27:34, 36), is the cry of those whose need is not met, often the working poor who live with day-to-day scarcity, making a choice between paying rent and buying groceries. The fear of scarcity is deeply ingrained in human nature and has contributed to the unequal distribution of resources locally and globally, serving as an underlying cause of war and violence where those in power strive to keep control in order to feed their longing for abundance. Learning of Jacob's treachery, Esau hates Jacob and plots to kill him (27:41). Thus Jacob sets out alone with his stolen blessing into an unknown future.

But Jacob is not alone. He stops for the night, using a stone for a pillow, and meets the Lord in a revelatory dream (28:11–13). God reveals God's presence to Jacob as the God of his ancestors and extends to him the same promise of land and progeny made to his father and grandfather. The allusion to descendants as abundant as "the dust of the earth" (v. 14) is an allusion to God's promise to Abraham of offspring as numerous as stars and sand (15:5; 22:17). In contrast to Isaac's limited blessing, for which Esau begs, God's blessing for Jacob is abundant; "all the families of the earth shall be blessed in you and in your offspring" (28:14). God's blessing stands as a challenge to us today as we seek to use the earth's resources wisely. God has provided enough for all creation.

Jacob awakens from his dream, surprised to have met the Lord in an unexpected place. He proclaims the campsite holy, "the house of God," "Bethel," anoints his stone pillow with oil, and sets it up as a pillar. In the verses immediately following this selection, Jacob vows to let the Lord be God to him in exchange for assuring material well-being and safety (28:20–21). Even in this instance of divine revelation and promise of abundance, Jacob strives to secure resources for himself by bargaining with God.

Jacob's encounter with God at Bethel would become a touchstone for him during times of fear and disorientation. Years later, God speaks to Jacob, reminding him, "I am the God of Bethel, where you anointed a pillar and made a vow to me" (31:13), and later God calls on Jacob to settle in Bethel and uphold his vow (35:1–15).

The symmetry and repetition within Jacob's story highlight the differences. Jacob has another life-changing encounter with God at night. This time rather than traveling alone, he is accompanied by a vast company displaying his material prosperity: flocks, wives, children, oxen, donkeys, slaves. On the eve of reuniting with Esau, Jacob wrestles with God at the ford of the Jabbok and receives a limp and a new name, Israel, "the one who strives with God" or "God strives" (32:22–31).

Isaiah 44:6–8; Psalm 139:1–12, 23–24; Psalm 86:11–17

Read in light of the trauma experienced on a social level by Israel during the sixth-century BCE Babylonian exile, Isaiah 44:6–8 reveals points of contact between God's redemptive purposes and abiding presence and the ways communities experience trauma today. Trauma is caused by an act of violence that produces lasting physical and psychological effects. Cathy Caruth discusses trauma as a pattern of "forgetting and return" or "oscillation between a *crisis of death* and the correlative *crisis of life*" so that life itself becomes defined by the repetition of prior threat.[1] Trauma can lead to losing the sense of time, disorientation, and difficulty with discerning identity. People and communities who experience trauma usually feel deeply unsafe. While we often explore trauma as an individual concern, trauma in one community member's life affects the whole community, and sometimes a whole community can experience trauma but manifest the symptoms of trauma among its members in different ways.

The author of what is often referred to as Second Isaiah (chaps. 40–55) addresses the concerns of a traumatized community with God's words of comfort and promises of restoration. In the verses immediately preceding today's reading, God reaffirms Israel's chosen status and identity as belonging to God. The experience of exile may have called into question the power of God in the face of Babylon and Babylon's god, but these verses attest to God's holy power and singularity. Verse 6 names God as "King of Israel," ruling in the political sphere, as well as "Redeemer," which implies a more intimate connection, such as the redemption offered by kin to one who has fallen into slavery (Lev. 25:47–49.) The exiled community of Israel can find refuge and healing in God and can trust that God alone is in charge: "I am the first and I am the last; besides me there is no god. Who is like me?" (Isa. 44:6–7). Freed by God from fear and trauma, the community is given identity and purpose in the task of witnessing, a task that provides continuity throughout salvation history, connecting with the identity and purpose of Christian communities today.

Similarly, Psalms 139 and 86 bear witness to the presence of God in both intimate and grand settings, during times of great uncertainty and peril. The psalms are meaningful for individual devotion and study, but these prayers offer a glimpse of witness in the practice of public worship as a corporate event. In *Body Politics*, John Howard Yoder writes about the practices of the church as events of witness performed "before the watching world" as a way

---

1. Cathy Caruth, *Unclaimed Experience: Trauma, Narrative, and History* (Baltimore: Johns Hopkins University Press, 1996), 7, 15, 63. Emphasis is Caruth's.

to connect Christian communal acts, like worship, with God's good intentions for the world.[2]

Like the verses from Isaiah 44, Psalm 139 attests to God's singularity and all-knowing (1–6), all-encompassing (7–12), powerful presence. Verses 19–22, which precede the second part of the selection, are sharp in tone, as the psalmist expresses hatred and calls for violence against those who oppose God. Verses 23–24 reflect a defensive posture, contrasting the psalmist and those who are set against God. These two verses express a desire for God to search the inner disposition of the psalmist for wickedness, and profess openness and trust in God along with a desire to live according to "the way everlasting." The violence in verses 19–22 stands in contrast to God's "way" as later expressed by Jesus (Matt. 5:44).

Psalm 86, read from the standpoint of threatened people, becomes a creed-like witness to God, who is "merciful and gracious, slow to anger and abounding in steadfast love and faithfulness" (v. 15). Verses 16–17 call on God to preserve God's "servant" (86:16). God's favorable action toward Israel will further bear witness to the power of God (v. 17).

This desire to serve as a faithful witness to God continues to inspire the church community today. These passages offer varied views of what the faithful path of witnessing entails while attesting to God's sovereignty in the midst of trauma, challenge, or threat.

In the midst of Liberia's civil war, Nobel laureate Leymah Gbowee moved from trauma victim to survivor, organizing the Women of Liberia Mass Action for Peace, an interfaith movement involving public prayer and nonviolent actions such as sit-ins, and demonstrating with signs, dance, and singing near a road traveled by then-president Charles Taylor and during peace talks with warlords.[3] God's Spirit empowered the women of Liberia to pray and act to bring about peace and change, including successful peace talks and the fair election of the first woman president of Liberia.

Matthew 13:24–30, 36–43

This parable and its explanation, which occur only in Matthew, fall within a series of parables about the realm of heaven offered by Jesus in chapter 13. The parables themselves are told to the crowd, but (as in Mark 4:34), the explanation for the parable of the Weeds in the Wheat in Matthew 13:36–43 is told afterward to the disciples alone. The parables here are a means

---

2. John Howard Yoder, *Body Politics: Five Practices of the Christian Community before the Watching World* (Nashville: Discipleship Resources, 1997), vi–ix.

3. Leymah Gbowee, *Mighty Be Our Powers: How Sisterhood, Prayer, and Sex Changed a Nation at War* (New York: Beast, 2011).

of confounding the crowd, told in such a way that they will not understand (13:10–17, 34), while an explanation is offered to the disciples.

The parable uses an agrarian context like the parable of the Sower that precedes it, beginning with good seed sowed in a field only to have an enemy come and purposely sow weeds among the wheat. Both wheat and weeds are allowed to grow up together and are separated at the harvest, the weeds to be burned in bundles and the wheat stored in the master's barn. Jesus' later explanation to the disciples casts the setting and characters allegorically to provide a cosmic sense of God's eschatological action in relation to creation. Jesus' explanation points out that the field in the parable is the whole world, not just the church. Good and evil are allowed to coexist in the world, and the kingdom of heaven is manifest in the mixed context of good and evil until "the end of the age." Matthew uses this phrase twice in this selection (vv. 39, 40) and in several other places, including the final words of the book (13:49; 24:3; 28:20). "The end of the age" is broadly eschatological, a general way of describing the simultaneous end of the way things are now and the fulfillment of God's intentions for the world.

Creation is affirmed in that the seed that was sown by the Son of Man is good seed and produces harvest (vv. 24, 30). Further, neither the master nor the Son of Man is willing to risk harming the wheat by removing the insidious weeds, whose roots have likely become entangled with the wheat (v. 29). From a standpoint of those who feel called to work for justice in the field of the world amid both wheat and weeds, the parable teaches that the presence of weeds is not a cause for inactivity. God calls workers to continue to care for the field as a whole until the time of harvest, later explained eschatologically as "the end of the age" (v. 39). Communities can bear witness to the presence of the kingdom of heaven even when weeds are visible. When a suburban congregation's fair-trade store was robbed and members of the congregation seriously injured, the pastor thought that particular ministry was finished. However, the congregation pulled together to repair the damages and rebuild, gathering in the store one year later for a worship service of remembrance and hope. The presence of weeds does not destroy the wheat, and the presence of evil will never thwart God's good intentions.

Nevertheless, the mixed state does not continue forever, and the parable illustrates God's ultimate intention of destroying the weeds that threaten the wheat and the evil that threatens abundant life. What are the weeds that threaten a harvest of abundant life in our world? Systemic evils such as racism, sexism, and prejudices of all kinds are weeds that entangle the roots of every human institution. The presence and the promise of ultimate eradication of these weeds are not signals for us to be inactive, although the parable does caution us to take great care so that in trying to pull out weeds we do not harm the wheat.

Rather than attempting self-righteous weed pulling, we can engage in what Walter Wink refers to as "naming," "unmasking," and "engaging" the "powers that be"; that is, the systems, institutions, and structures that can take on a life of their own and display the same mix of wheat and weeds that pervades all of creation.[4] Unveiling the powers highlights the presence of weeds in the systems that run our world and God's redemptive action toward the world that will ultimately redeem even the powers. Belief that God is redeeming the powers frees us to engage them with a spirit of love and accountability rather than judgment, trusting that God will ultimately bring the harvest and burn away every trace of the weeds.[5]

Romans 8:12–25

Romans is a letter with the personal, relational, and situational particularities that accompany that mode of communication. Paul did not found or visit the church at Rome, yet he cares deeply about this congregation and desires to engage in "mutual encouragement" in the faith (1:8–13). These verses from Romans 8 reflect some of the themes found in our other passages. Like Matthew's parable, for Paul God is active in a world where suffering is present and for which Christ died. Like the Psalms and Isaiah, Paul also places his eschatological hope in God, believing that all of creation will ultimately be freed from bondage, connecting the suffering of the present age with Christ's suffering so that creation may also be glorified in and through Christ (vv. 17–23).

Paul describes those who live according to the Spirit as children of God. Verses 19–21 offer empowerment to those who live according to the Spirit; the glorious freedom they enjoy will one day be enjoyed by all of creation. Verse 20 is rhetorically difficult. However, if we follow the line of Paul's argument, it is human will exercised according to the flesh that subjected creation to futility, not God's will.[6] God's will is that creation will experience the same Spirit-led glory offered through Christ to children of God. Paul's imagery of creation "groaning in labor pains" is evocative and appropriate as it attends to both present suffering and future hope (vv. 22–23).

Emerging in the aftermath of the terrorist attacks on September 11, 2001, the STAR (Strategies for Trauma Awareness and Resilience) program has brought tools for healing and restoration to diverse contexts, from veterans suffering with post-traumatic stress disorder to families struggling to rebuild

---

4. Walter Wink, *The Powers That Be: Theology for a New Millennium* (New York: Doubleday, 1998), 34–35.
5. Ibid., 34.
6. Luke Timothy Johnson, *Reading Romans: A Literary and Theological Commentary* (New York: Crossroad, 1997), 128.

their homes after the 2010 earthquake in Haiti. Participants often emerge as leaders within their communities. While not negating suffering, programs such as STAR bear witness to the truth that suffering and death do not have the final say. In a sense, suffering is limited by being situated in Christ and the sure future glory guaranteed by Christ.[7]

7. Ann Jervis, *At the Heart of the Gospel: Suffering in the Earliest Christian Message* (Grand Rapids: Eerdmans, 2007), 106.

Proper 12

Wilma Ann Bailey

GENESIS 29:15–28   1 KINGS 3:5–12
PSALM 105:1–11, 45B   PSALM 119:129–136
                                          ROMANS 8:26–39
                              MATTHEW 13:31–33, 44–52

The story of ancient Israel is a story of alienation and a search for a place to call home. The Israelites formed as a people in the wilderness, a liminal space between slavery and freedom. They were not Egyptians, not Canaanites, and not Mesopotamians, although their roots include all of these peoples and cultures. They were a new idea of a people whose identity, destiny, and dignity were shaped and formed by their allegiance to YHWH, a God who traveled with them to the depths of their misery and the heights of their joy. That allegiance was formalized in a series of covenants.

Their earliest memories of being aliens and immigrants caused them to understand the vulnerability felt by those who longed for the security of place. Their laws and customs taught them to be kind to aliens and strangers, remembering that they were once aliens and strangers in foreign lands. Throughout history, people have been driven from home by war, famine, drought, lack of jobs, desire for education, health-care needs, and lack of opportunities to grow and achieve their potential. It is hard to be in a new place where it is difficult to make yourself understood because the language is different and where people take advantage of your ignorance of the local laws and customs. The model of ancient Israel is one with which we can all identify if we reach deep enough into our memories, because all of us are immigrants from somewhere. The call of these lectionary texts is to be just and kind and walk humbly with God, knowing that whoever you are, you and your people were once aliens in a strange land.

Genesis 29:15–28

After deceiving his father and obtaining a blessing intended for his older brother, Jacob flees to Haran, where he is taken in by his mother's relatives. As an outsider and runaway, Jacob is in a vulnerable position. He enters into an agreement to work seven years for his uncle Laban to earn the hand of Laban's younger daughter, Rachel. Laban then tricks Jacob into marrying his older daughter, Leah. If it were true that the custom was to marry the older daughter first, Laban could have informed Jacob of this before they entered into their original agreement. Jacob protests, but there is little that he can do. He is in Laban's house and Laban's country. Whatever they may be, the laws and customs favor Laban. When Laban requires Jacob to work another seven years for his younger daughter, he ends up working a total of fourteen years. The first seven years were for Rachel, and the second seven years were also for Rachel.

Immigrants and aliens of all lands are often cheated in the workplace because they do not know their rights or the customs and laws of a new place. Sometimes they are afraid to stand up for themselves out of fear of deportation or abuse. Although Jacob has a bag of tricks of his own, we sympathize with him because he is vulnerable. He is the alien. Laban should have been kind and generous rather than take advantage of his kinsman.

1 Kings 3:5–12

Solomon starts out his career as a coregent with his father, David. At his father's instructions (1 Kgs. 2:5–9), after David dies Solomon ruthlessly murders those who were loyal to his father because their positions and the respect granted to them by the community are a threat to him. Solomon feared that they might undermine him.

Solomon is clever. For his first public act of worship he chooses a high place in Gibeon, the home of Saul, the first king of Israel and David's nemesis. High places were local places of worship favored by ordinary people, as opposed to the major shrine in Jerusalem that was closely associated with the king and the priestly elite. This was a political move on Solomon's part, a way of signaling his desire to keep the kingdom united.

Solomon's prayer for an understanding heart takes place at Gibeon in the context of a dream. The text clearly states twice that it was a dream (3:5, 15). In the Bible, dreams are a means of conveying the divine will, but there was also skepticism about dreams (Eccl. 5:3, 7). God, after all, spoke to Moses "face to face" and not through dreams (Deut. 5:4; 34:10). Solomon's dream serves the function of legitimizing his reign. Unlike his father, David, and the first king of Israel, Saul, Solomon never proved his leadership abilities by leading

Israel in battle. Unlike his predecessor, he was not chosen by both the people and God. According to 1 Kings 1–2, Solomon came to the throne through the political manipulations of his mother, Bathsheba, and the prophet Nathan.

Solomon begins his prayer by connecting himself to David, whose attributes he lists. Notice that he does not speak about his own devotion to God, but David's. He then says that God caused him to reign in place of David although he is only a child who does not yet know "how to go out or come in." His exaggerated humility (Solomon had been ruling with David for some time) is consistent with ancient Near Eastern custom. Solomon then asks for "a heart that listens for justice" (author's trans.) so that he may discern between what is good and bad (3:9). Solomon knows that the people over whom he has been placed as king are God's people, not his own. He is a caretaker, not the ultimate sovereign. Noting that Solomon did not ask for long life, riches, or the life of his enemies, God grants Solomon's wish in the dream. God also promises him everything else that he has not asked. The dream dialogue suggests that the function of government is to provide justice. Protecting the empire, acquiring wealth, and having a long reign are by-products, not the main business of government.

The Arab Spring of 2011 was a series of uprisings by discontented people against leaders who have used their offices to enrich and privilege themselves and their families at the expense of poor and middle-class people who are struggling to make ends meet and to use the education and skills they have acquired. Those who find themselves in leadership at any level must acknowledge that they were not placed in these positions for their own benefit but to serve the people in their charge.

Psalm 105:1–11, 45b and Psalm 119:129–136

Psalm 105 begins with a ringing call to thank and praise God. Humans are reminded that they stand before one who is greater than they and to whom they owe their very existence. Israel's relationship to God is described as a covenant in Psalm 105. In Psalm 119, one of the stipulations of the covenant, keeping the commandments, is a central theme.

Outside of Israel, covenants were agreements between parties. In the ancient Near East, kingdoms sometimes constructed their relationships with other kingdoms in the form of covenants, with each side having specific obligations to fulfill.

Several covenants mentioned in the Bible are associated with key people: Noah, Abraham, and Moses. Each covenant involved particular, designated parties and specific stipulations. For example, a seminal covenant was made between God and Abraham. God promises Abraham land and descendants.

In return, Abraham must circumcise all the male children of his household (whether they were born into it or purchased as slaves). Abraham interprets the promise of land as a direction to buy land (Gen. 23). It is not to be taken by military force. In the case of Noah, the covenant is between God and all living things. It is unilateral: God promises to never again destroy human and animal life with a flood. Under the covenant of Moses, the people of Israel are expected to follow the instructions that God gave at Sinai. Those instructions are received as a blessing because they spell out how the Israelites are to live with God, their neighbors, and each other.

Thanksgiving and praise are appropriate responses to God's promises. The frequent calls in the Bible to remember what God had done help to link the present with the past. God had already fulfilled one part of the agreement. Israel must now keep its part.

Psalm 119 is the longest psalm in the Protestant canon. It is structured as an eight-fold acrostic, with each letter of the Hebrew alphabet repeated eight consecutive times. The portion designated for this week uses the sixteenth letter of the alphabet, *pe* (similar to the English letter *p*). The words that appear at the beginning of each verse of this text in Hebrew are "wonderful," "opening up," "mouth," "turn," "steps," "redeem," "face," and "channels." The following phrases directed to God appear in several verses: "turn to me, be gracious to me" (v. 132), "redeem me" (v. 134), "let your face shine on your servant" (v. 135; author's trans. et al.). This portion of the psalm asks God to redeem the people from oppression and reminds them that only a free people can fully keep divine precepts. A slave is not free to keep the Sabbath; one cannot obey God's instructions when the slave master is giving opposing instructions. The slaves want to positively respond to divine instructions but cannot do so until God intervenes in earthly matters and sets them free.

The psalm reminds the reader that justice and worship are parts of the same whole. When members of the Occupy movement, protesting corporate greed and inequality in society, camped outside St. Paul's Cathedral in London, the congregation was forced to deal with the relationship between justice and worship. Some congregants thought that this justice movement had no place in sacred space. The church, they said, is not a business or a bank. Others welcomed Occupiers, arguing that this is exactly what the church ought to be about. Talking about justice and worship in an abstract way is easy. Living with it is more difficult, but necessary if we are to be faithful to the teachings of Jesus.

Romans 8:26–39

The confession that "we do not know how to pray" is followed by the reassuring thought that the Holy Spirit intercedes with groans that are deeper than we are able to express. We do the best that we can. God knows our limitations and searches our hearts. A well-known phrase in verse 28 can be translated at least three different ways, each with a slightly different meaning: "We know that all things work together for good for those who love God, who are called according to his purpose" or "God makes all things work together for good" or "in all things God works for good" (see the NRSV notes).[1] The first suggests that for those called to fulfill God's purposes, all things work together for good. In other words, the whole is good even if not all of the parts appear to be good. The second phrase suggests that all things may not naturally work together for good, but God can make them work for the good. The last suggests that God is working for the good in all things, although presumably not all things turn out well. Each expresses a different notion of how God works. While some people would like to interpret this phrase as saying that Christians will always experience good, that is not quite what any of the variants suggest. What is good may not always be what is painless, easy, or respectable. The text does not address the question "Good for whom?" For the called ones themselves? For the purposes of God?

The theological issue of predestination has been debated for centuries. This text does not ask us to decide who is predestined or even exactly what it means to be predestined. It clearly states that only God justifies and no human has a right to condemn anyone. The text describes the advantages of being predestined but does not speak of those who are not predestined. It is speaking to a suffering community to encourage its members and has nothing to say about those who are deemed "not predestined." Does being "not predestined" mean that one has no access to God? Does this text leave room for those who were not predestined but found their way to God nevertheless? Whatever the answers to these questions may be, we must not lose sight of the fact that the purpose of this passage is to comfort those who have cast their lot with Christ. It does not condemn those who are otherwise inclined. Recently, Muslims have experienced prejudicial treatment and condemnation because of the actions of extremists who are unrelated to them either culturally or theologically. Christians are not encouraged to judge and condemn others but to welcome and love them, even as they are encouraged to share their faith with others. The well-known phrase promising us that nothing can separate the faithful from the love of God assures those whose lives and faith are under duress that God's presence and powerful love are with us always.

---

1. *The Holy Bible: New Revised Standard Version* (Nashville: Thomas Nelson Publishers, 1990), note for Rom. 8:28a.

Matthew 13:31–33, 44–52

These excerpts from Matthew's Gospel contain four statements about the realm of God. The realm is like something that starts out small and insignificant (a seed, yeast), then grows into something large and useful for animals and humans. The kingdom of heaven is also like something that is hidden (a treasure, pearl) and then found. Someone recognizes its value and sells everything to purchase it. In the first four parables, there is something of great value that is initially not appreciated because it is small or hidden. The seed, the yeast, the hidden treasure, and the pearl may be compared to the poor, the young, the alien, and the disenfranchised. There is something valuable in these that, if given the opportunity, will prove to be useful to the world. These parables offer images of encouraging possibilities that arise as we recognize and participate in God's transformative work of welcoming persons who are differently abled, come from other countries, have few resources, or are disregarded and overlooked.

The fifth parable is different from the other four and has no counterpart in Mark or Luke. The kingdom of heaven is like a net that initially contains all kinds of fish, but eventually the good are put into baskets and the bad are discarded. According to this image, the angels separate evil people from righteous ones at the end of the age.

The final parable does not indicate what the kingdom of heaven is like; rather it compares the scribes of the kingdom of heaven to a householder who "brings out of his treasure what is new and what is old." Today, when the old is quickly discarded and replaced by what is new—whether people, ideas, or objects—this parable reminds us that both what is old and what is new have their place among us.

Many people are insignificant in the eyes of the world. They do not win prizes or gain recognition, but God knows and values them. If the world were wise enough to help them use their talents, we would all be better off. It is not for us to separate the good from the bad. Our knowledge of the whole of individuals is limited. Such separation is to be done at the end of the age, and not by us. In this text, that responsibility is left to the angels.

Proper 13

Grace Ji-Sun Kim

GENESIS 32:22–31   PSALM 17:1–7, 15
ISAIAH 55:1–5   PSALM 145:8–9, 14–21
            ROMANS 9:1–5
           MATTHEW 14:13–21

This week's readings speak to us of struggles, aspirations, and the difficult work of moving into God's intended future. In Genesis, we encounter Jacob the trickster who is redeemed by God. Isaiah reminds us to seek grace in unexpected places, calling us to break bread with those who are different from us, for it is God who restores and provides help for all people. Both of the psalms and the reading from Romans encourage us to seek justice and dismantle our ill-formed prejudices. Lastly, the Gospel lesson reminds us to bring whatever small gifts we have to Jesus, who will multiply what we offer for our sake and the well-being of others.

Genesis 32:22–31

The history of families in Genesis reveals dysfunction, deceit, jealousy, and violence. "Jacob" means the "grabber"—the one who tries to supplant the place of another, more legitimate holder of authority. At birth, Jacob tried to pull Esau back into the womb so that he would be the firstborn inheritor. Failing that, he took advantage of hapless and famished Esau to claim the family inheritance. In return, Esau vowed to kill Jacob. During his fear-filled flight to Uncle Laban's home, Jacob had a vision of a heavenly ladder at Bethel. Years pass; Esau hears that Jacob is returning, and this is where we find ourselves in the passage.

It is time for Jacob to accept responsibility for his conniving ways. But he stalls, hoping to placate Esau with gifts and groveling. He arranges his flocks, wives, and children as shields to precede his encounter with Esau. Sending

339

them across the river Jabbok ahead of him, Jacob rests alone and waits for dawn, knowing that he will face Esau in the morning.

Jacob is deeply troubled. His past is catching up with him, and he wrestles with anxiety and uncertainty. Suddenly he finds himself in what seems like a real wrestling match. But whom is he wrestling? Is it his own guilt and shame for having used and abused others? Is it YHWH? The account of the struggle ends with the author saying that Jacob struggled with God and prevailed. He did not give in to despair or fear. He hung on, but Jacob does not walk away unchanged; he has a new name and he limps into the future, scarred by the struggle.

The women, wives, maids, and children are silent. They are simply pawns to be manipulated and exploited, as Jacob has placed them in a potentially dangerous situation that could lead to enslavement and even death in order to buy his own safety. This passage challenges us to reflect on what we must wrestle with, our lack of concern for the well-being of others, and even our willingness to make others pay for our wrongdoing and selfishness. Without a thought, we exploit others who are weaker than ourselves, purchasing clothes made by child laborers or others who do not receive a living wage, exploiting and devaluing others for the sake of our own desires. Can there be redemption for our disgrace as the rich and powerful dominate and oppress those who are weak, poor, and marginalized? This story provides good news; Jacob the oppressor is redeemed. God keeps the promise made at Bethel. If God can use Jacob to build a nation, then we also have reason to hope that God will redeem and use us in spite of our greedy, exploitative, and self-centered behavior. This will not happen without struggle, but genuine change is possible.

Isaiah 55:1–5

This passage offers encouragement to discouraged and exiled Jews in Babylonia as the Babylonians are about to be defeated by the Persians. The prevailing assumption was that the Jews were defeated and exiled because of their parents' and grandparents' sins. How can they possibly be restored? Will they ever return home?

Isaiah offers words of hope and acceptance. God forgives us even when we do not deserve it. As God promised David, God made an everlasting covenant and is faithful no matter what the ancestors did. However, even though a new day and a new life are being offered here, a few conditions are implicit in these verses. The passage says, "Seek the Lord, listen to God." To accept nourishment from God means that one must accept responsibility for faithfully doing God's will. This is not a free pass to do whatever one may want to do—the returnees risk repeating the same greedy, unjust, and idolatrous behaviors that disgraced their ancestors. Instead, faithfulness includes stewardship. There will be a time when all who are thirsty can come to the waters and be satisfied. However, as our society continues to exploit the earth and consume more than our basic needs, we take more than our share of resources or pollute resources that may provide sustenance for others. In order to build a just world where all have enough to drink and eat, the rich have to learn to live with less and governments must not allow politics or power plays to take precedence over the needs of their citizens.

Furthermore, a risk is posed in this passage. Because God will restore Israel and all nations will see it, others will come to the newly restored covenant community. The risk is what happens next. Will the forgiven and restored people dominate the newcomers (Gentiles) and make them servants and second-class citizens of the new community? The question is posed to all of us: What do you do when "others" come? Will you share your food, resources, and employment opportunities with them?

There are serious implications here for Christian congregations who face "others" coming to their local congregations and the larger communities in which they live. Many of us and our churches are xenophobic. When we fear scarcity of goods or opportunities, we tend to demonize newcomers and strangers. But Isaiah urges us to break bread with those who are different from us. We must work toward building a just society where no one will be thirsty or hungry and where all will be satisfied regardless of their ethnicity, sexual orientation, or religion.

Psalm 17:1–7, 15

The psalmist is a righteous person who demands God's help. He or she prays for guidance and insight, assuming God will grant these because God is faithful. The psalmist prays for deliverance from wicked, hostile adversaries, in a prayer composed of petitions for deliverance, a plea of innocence, a petition for the adversaries' defeat, and a conclusion that asserts trust in God.

While it would be easy to identify with the psalmist who seeks God's justice, it might be more interesting to think about those who are marginalized speaking in the psalmist's voice for deliverance from us; that is, seeking justice from all who are privileged and hold social, economic, political, gender-related, and religious privileges and power over others. When we view ourselves as someone's adversaries, it informs our sense of justice as we ask whom we are taking advantage of or ignoring. We may also catch a glimpse of what restoration and "communion" would look like if we were to include those on the periphery, such as LGBTQ persons, the poor, social outcasts.

Having a meaningful relationship with God includes having healthy relationships with others.

Two images in this text are compelling—God as judge and God as protector. They temper one another: God as judge seeks to protect and provide refuge for us, and God as protector issues just and fair decrees. Acceptance facilitates righteousness, and we need to practice both in our relationships with others. As we read this psalm from the underside of history, from the perspective of people who are disenfranchised, dominated, and exploited, we need to recognize our own culpability. As we acknowledge and confess our sins, we may join the psalmist in calling on God to "hear a just cause" (v. 1).

Psalm 145:8–9, 14–21

In the spirit of Isaiah 55, this psalm also describes YHWH as one who feeds the hungry and fulfills the needs of all who call on the Lord. We find here a God who is powerful and compassionate and has concern for all creation (v. 9).

People desire and seek power in all aspects of life. People with power often try to exhibit their power by exerting their will on those who are subordinate to them. In many instances, the powerful exert more power than is necessary to keep people "in their place" and to maintain the status quo. Colonialism is an example of exerting power in overt and covert ways so that the colonized will remain powerless, subordinate, and voiceless. We still feel its repercussions today.

In contrast to humanity's power, God's power is shown in love. God is "gracious and merciful, slow to anger and abounding in steadfast love" (v. 8). God is good to all, and not just to the rich and powerful. God is righteous and "upholds all who are falling, and raises up all who are bowed down" (v. 14). Those who turn to God can take comfort in knowing that God is near (v. 18). God answers the prayers of those who turn to God (v. 19). God who is powerful will empower those who are powerless. The wicked who reject and despise what God offers cannot live forever, but God's unfailing care is shown toward those who seek to serve God (v. 20).[1] God shows compassion and care to those living on the margins of society: the poor, the powerless, the homeless, the colonized, the voiceless, and the subaltern. Ultimately the powerless will be empowered.

As we witness God's power at work in the world, the social implications quickly become evident. We need to do what God has done for humanity: to work for social justice and to raise those who are downtrodden by political, religious, and social corruption. We need to empower the powerless, listen to and acknowledge the oppressed, and help the voiceless to speak.

---

1. Cyril Okorocha, "Psalms," in *Africa Bible Commentary*, ed. Tokunboh Adeyema (Grand Rapids: Zondervan, 2006), 743.

God "is near to all who call on" God (v. 18). In the midst of whatever problem we find ourselves, we are to call on God, and God will listen and heed our calls. This is good news to those who have lost all hope in humanity. We require God's strength and wisdom to fight against evil constructs, ideologies, understandings, and beliefs that this world continues to perpetuate and disseminate. God is at work among us and within us to bring about new patterns of relationship and the well-being of creation.

Romans 9:1–5

Paul is writing to expatriates from Palestine, Asia Minor, Syria, and other regions, including many members of the original Christian community in Rome who were probably Jewish. For them, Jesus was the long-awaited messiah of Israel, and they saw themselves as his followers. Evidently, strong tensions existed between Jewish and Gentile believers. In this passage, Paul speaks boldly of what he perceives to be the problem of Israel's unbelief in Jesus, while strongly affirming God's everlasting covenant with the people of Israel.

In the early to mid 40s CE, the emperor Claudius expelled all Jews from Rome because of alleged disorder in the Jewish section of the city; thereafter, it is likely that the Roman Christian communities were led by Gentile Christians. However, Nero (54–68) allowed the Jews to return, contributing to a power struggle between Jewish and Gentile Christians. In this brief passage from Romans 9, Paul struggles with the reality that most Jews had not accepted Jesus as the messiah.

One danger of this passage is to conclude that Jews are damned and Christians today should set out to convert them. The history of such efforts is grim. In Romans 11, Paul anticipates that God is faithful to God's covenant with Israel; somehow, before the end of the age, God will bring Israel to faith (that is, will save all Israel; 11:26). Paul's intention here is not to see God's people "cut off" from the olive tree, but to recognize God's gracious purposes at work even amid Israel's rejection of Jesus. While some of these branches have "broken off" and other Gentiles have been grafted onto the tree (11:17), Paul insists that God intends to bring mercy to all people, both Jews and Gentiles (11:32).

This epistle addresses clear ethnic divisions in the congregation. Election was so deeply entrenched in Jewish identity that perhaps it was a stumbling block to belief in Jesus. This stumbling block is evident among Christians today. There is a tendency for humans to think in terms of "us" and "them," and this disrupts an ecclesiology that is not based on our ideas of what is acceptable but on God's gracious will to redeem all people. We cannot imagine that people who are different from us religiously, socially, ethnically, and by sexual orientation would experience God's salvation. Rather than maintaining segregation, this passage prompts us to open the doors and embrace newcomers into the covenant community. In later passages in Romans, the newcomers are fully welcomed. God remains in control and will accomplish God's redemptive purposes. The missional life of Christians is expressed by how we live, share, and work for justice with others who are also God's people.

Matthew 14:13–21

In Matthew, Jesus is the new Moses. Jesus goes across a body of water, initiating a new exodus, and feeds a crowd in the wilderness. He is weary and pressured and needs time alone. Still, those who are curious and needy come to him. They perceive that Jesus, not Herod, has the power and authority to restore life and give both spiritual and physical sustenance to those who follow him.

Jesus tells the disciples to feed the people, but they can only see what is before their eyes: nothing. They want the crowd to go elsewhere. However, Jesus insists that the disciples feed them, and they scrounge for whatever they can find. It seems very little, but in the hands of Jesus, little becomes much, and it is distributed by the disciples. Afterward, the disciples still do not understand what has happened, but they keep on giving to the hungry people what Jesus gives to them.

We have a tendency to live with a mind-set of fear and scarcity; we fear that we do not have enough to feed the poor or care for the sick. This passage gives us hope, whether we are individuals or small and struggling congregations: we have the means to do more than we think we can for God's suffering people. Jesus offers a vision of the abundant life, the kingdom of sharing God's resources here and now. This passage urges us to bring any small gifts that we have—money, talent, and time—to dedicate them to Jesus, because he will multiply what we have as we give it to others.

In this passage there is a sense of urgency to share with others. In Korea, it is common to greet a person by asking, "Have you eaten?" If neither person has eaten, the next phrase will be, "Let's go share a meal together." In a society that values community, it is very rare to eat alone. Even something basic like rice is eaten together with family and friends. Likewise, it is not really a community of faith when some have more than enough food and others have very little or none. This passage commands us to share whatever we have so that we can eat with one another. Scripture speaks of the kingdom of heaven as a banquet where we sit down in a celebration of community, rejoicing and sharing our bread with one another. Bread shared is the most delicious bread of all. Bread shared with those in need or those who are "other" than the people we usually eat with is the most satisfying meal of all.

Proper 14

Arthur Van Seters

GENESIS 37:1–4, 12–28 1 KINGS 19:9–18
PSALM 105:1–6, 16–22, 45B PSALM 85:8–13
ROMANS 10:5–15
MATTHEW 14:22–33

How do we understand the providence of God? Joseph's journey through the lens of Psalm 105, the disciples' venture on a stormy sea, Paul's attempt to grapple with preaching to Gentiles, and Elijah's questioning of his prophetic commission invite us to ponder our assumptions about God. When theological reflection on God's relationship to the realities of our broken humanity opens itself to these texts, there may be some surprises. God's ways may be different from what we expect. Therein lies a challenge for our ethics.

Genesis 37:1–4, 12–28 and Psalm 105:1–6, 16–22, 45b

Jacob's family is clearly dysfunctional. Joseph, born to his father's favorite wife, Rachel, is disliked. The gift of a robe with long sleeves (following the Hebrew text rather than the Septuagint's "coat of many colors") is a sign of special status, as was Tamar's garment in 2 Samuel 13:18. When Joseph shares his princely dreams in which his brothers and the rest of the family are depicted as subservient to him, even his father rebukes his grandiose imagination, and his jealous brothers come to hate him.

Naively, Jacob sends Joseph to report back on the welfare of his shepherding brothers. They want to silence the despised tattletale for good. But Reuben, the eldest and the one who would be held responsible, plans surreptitiously to rescue him. Judah hatches the idea of selling Joseph to a caravan of traders bound for Egypt, which the brothers believe will surely result in his death. However, both Reuben and Judah know that bloodguilt is an awesome power. The detestable robe is dipped in goat's blood to deceive their father, who is shattered by sorrow.

The microcosm of this family portrait captures the larger tensions of the nation and raises deep questions about fairness, justice, guilt, and deceit. Theology is largely hidden, although acute human failure is everywhere evident. Where is God in all of this? In the intervention of Judah? Via passing traders? In the subsequent unfolding of events, Joseph (who continues to dream in prison) rises from the depths to become the prime minister of Egypt. In that position his youthful dreams appear to be prescient when his impoverished brothers, devastated by famine, eventually stand before him to beg for food.

While the lectionary for the following Sunday picks up at Genesis 45 to articulate Joseph's (and the narrator's) theology of providence, the accompanying Psalm 105 anticipates that response. The psalm praises the wonder-working activities of God throughout the history of Israel, and the story of Joseph is a shining example. It was *God* who summoned Joseph even though he was sold as a slave. God was preparing for the time when a famine in Canaan would threaten his family's future. Their salvation, and by implication the destiny of God's chosen people, would be dependent on that young Hebrew slave. God kept testing Joseph through Egyptian imprisonment until the vital moment when Pharaoh needed his wisdom, a divine ability to see how the future would unfold.

Psalm 105 is entirely positive (unlike the following psalm, in which human failures are exposed). Genesis 37 and Psalm 105 are intended to be read side by side. But the reference to human failure in the case of the Joseph story is absent in the latter text, which begins instead with recollections of God's covenant with Israel and the exodus. In light of these juxtapositions, the reader might miss a central justice question raised by the larger story of Joseph and leave the sermon at the level of moral reflections on the breakdown of a family. However, the crucial context for interpreting Genesis 37 alongside Psalm 105 is Genesis 47 (which does not make it into the lectionary). Here the stunning results of Joseph's economic policies as prime minister are made apparent. In the midst of famine, "Joseph bought all the land of Egypt for Pharaoh" and, the narrator adds, "As for the people, he [Pharaoh] made slaves of them" (vv. 20–21). Ultimately, his policy of enslavement would also include Joseph's own people many years later.

This disastrous result forces us to look beyond Joseph's theological explanation lest appeals to God's providence lead to justification for the subjugation of people and entire communities. The New England Puritans used a similar sense of providence to justify exterminating the local indigenous people. The Joseph story, therefore, has to be viewed through the lens of the prophetic vision of Isaiah 61:1 ("liberty to the captives") and the bold witness of Jesus (Luke 4:16–19). When weakness is poured out in unquenchable love,

the barriers of broken families, potential fratricide, and degrading enslavement are transcended and justice emerges as universal *shalom.*

Matthew 14:22–33

The evolution of genuine discipleship is very important as Matthew seeks to
help a church facing severe persecution. When Jesus *pressures* (a good translation for the Greek verb, *distazo*) his followers to cross the Sea of Galilee
without him, one senses a kind of test. What would it be like for the disciples
to venture out *on their own?*

These disciples have previously been described as people who have given
up virtually everything to follow Jesus (4:18–20). They have become Jesus'
own family, seeking to do the will of God (12:49–50), and have been given
special instruction to understand the stories of God's new order (13:10–16).
All of this happened while Jesus was with them. Now he sends them off alone
while he stays to pray.

Soon the disciples are shrouded in darkness and their boat (a metaphor for
the church) is tossed about like a cork. The hours pass ever so slowly until
finally Jesus arrives mysteriously and unexpectedly. His disoriented followers
regard him as a ghost and are filled with terror. Jesus allays their fear and tells
them, "It's me." The Greek uses the "I am" formula, echoing the words of
God to Moses, "I AM WHO I AM" (Exod. 3:14). Readers are reminded that Jesus
is the very presence of God, Emmanuel (Matt. 1:23). The Creator who stilled
the waters of chaos at the very beginning is still able to make a path "through
the mighty waters" (Ps. 77:19; Isa. 43:16).

At this point Peter (as representative disciple) asks if he too can venture out
to "walk on water." Is Peter implying, "Can you extend this nature-defying
act to me?" As Jesus gives him permission, Peter steps out of the boat but,
alas, is distracted by the chaotic storm. Crying out for help, he is rescued.
Exercising faith is more challenging than he realized! Here Matthew may
also be indicating that faith is not about doing the impossible but trusting that
God is still accessible when the church is faced with the impossible.

In the end, when Jesus is in the boat and the storm abates, Matthew adds
an important detail. The disciples worship Jesus with the words, "Truly you
are the Son of God." In Mark's parallel account, the disciples appear to be
"utterly astounded" (6:51). Matthew, however, reminds the church that in
worship, faith evolves toward maturity.

In our own time, the church has often found itself under threat. During
the long conflict in southern Sudan, church communities knew that faith
depended on trusting the presence of God amid violence and the chaos of
injustice. In Kenya a number of years ago, a local pastor, Timothy Njoya, was

asked about his years of struggle against the corrupt Moi government. His theological response was arresting. He said, "I live in the present as though the reality of what will ultimately be already is."

In Western secular society, the church needs a spirituality that is not escapist but that discerns a fundamental connection with its social order. The sea that is churning here can be seen in massive inequities through economic manipulation, monopolistic interests that thwart adequate health care, and the powerful influence of militarism. Faith needs to counter these realities. We are not called to "walk on water" but to trust the presence of the Spirit to give us discernment, courage, and help as we seek to work toward God's alternative order.

Romans 10:5–15

Reflection on the task of preaching in Romans 10:5–15 could well start with the apostle's words, "I am not ashamed of the gospel" (1:16). Paul is not speaking about having courage to preach an unpalatable message. Rather, he is recognizing what God has been doing in the world to set things right (the meaning of Paul's phrase "the righteousness of God"). As a result, he sees no shame, as a Jew, in preaching to Gentiles. He is convinced that out of faithfulness God ultimately sets things right for Israel as promised, but implicit in that faithfulness, God's goodness is so overflowing that it sets things right for all humankind, and indeed for creation itself. This is what frames the whole of this carefully argued letter.[1]

Chapters 9–11 address the refusal of the Jewish community to recognize Jesus as the messiah. Paul agonizes over this response. The Hebrew prophets had already grasped that the messiah would not only establish a new covenant with Israel, but also would embrace the Gentiles (Isa. 11:10). In Christ, as Paul argues elsewhere, the wall between Jew and non-Jew has been demolished (e.g., Gal. 3:28).

In Romans 10:5–15 Paul connects doing the law with living (quoting Lev. 18:5) and faith (Deut. 30:12–14). He argues that the Torah is manifest in Jesus of Nazareth, who came to us incarnate, especially in the cross, and ascended from the depths when he was resurrected from the dead (echoing Ps. 107:26). The very essence of faith is confessing Jesus Christ as Lord (an early baptismal formula) and believing that God raised him from the dead. God is affirmed as a God of life, a God of salvation.

Paul then reaches back to the universal vision of the ancient prophets, echoing Isaiah 28:16 by writing that "No one who believes . . . will be put to

---

1. See Thomas G. Long, "Preaching Romans Today," *Interpretation* 5 (2004): 270–75.

shame" and Joel 2:23 with "Everyone who calls on the name of the Lord will be saved." In light of these themes, "there is no distinction between Jew and Greek." The message is clear but needs to be proclaimed. Preaching requires a preacher, but a preacher for such a message has to be called. The sequence of rhetorical questions that lays out all of this ends with an affirmation from Isaiah 52:7, "How beautiful are the feet of those who bring good news!" This last passage is a prelude to the final Isaianic Servant Song. It touches on what is a stumbling block for many Jews: a suffering messiah, which is just as problematic as convincing them that their messiah would be equally accessible to non-Jews. In fact, Paul discovered that a suffering messiah was increasingly accepted by outsiders who were often on the margins. Grace surprised and attracted them! No wonder preaching such a message requires a power from beyond oneself, an inner call of the Spirit.

Paul apparently believed that the response of the Gentiles to Christ would eventually convince his fellow Jews that, in line with the testimony of the prophets, God was indeed setting things right for his people Israel. This is why he ends this section of his letter with a doxology: "O the depth of the riches and wisdom and knowledge of God!" followed by "For from him and through him and to him are all things. To him be the glory forever. Amen" (11: 33, 36).

With Tom Long, one must emphasize that this passage is not about the superiority of Christianity over Judaism. It is about God setting things right for everyone, regardless of geography, ethnicity, or any other identity that divides human communities.[2] In a world where the struggle for peace in the Middle East has been so dominant over the last half century, this lection from Paul, read in context, points to a gospel that transcends boundaries through the sheer goodness of God. *Shalom* is a gift of grace, not a settlement imposed through military intervention and violence.

1 Kings 19:9–18 and Psalm 85:8–13

The church is often pulled between two opposing forces: pressure to conform to its surrounding culture and the prompting of the Spirit to be faithful to its calling as a community of faith. Israel under King Ahab was seriously challenged by the fertility cult of Baal worship and its orgiastic rituals. Ahab's Phoenician consort, Queen Jezebel, aggressively promoted idolatrous religious behavior and slaughtered many of Israel's prophets. Often injustices emerge when those in authority (like the malleable Ahab) fail to give wise leadership. The role of the prophet was to challenge false allegiance, call the

2. Ibid.

faithful back to their covenant with God, and clarify the ethical implications of Torah.

In I Kings 18 Elijah confronts King Ahab at Mount Carmel. The result is overwhelming victory for the Lord: the prophets of Baal are exposed as impotent and destroyed. But in chapter 19 Elijah is on the run. Jezebel has threatened to kill him. He flees south, first into the wilderness and then to Mount Horeb (another name for Mount Sinai). There he hides in a cave. Utterly depressed, he pours out his complaint to the Lord and yearns for death. He has lost his sense of call. In his jeremiad he fails to acknowledge that the prophet Obadiah has saved a hundred fellow prophets (18:13). He feels totally alone. Depression has a way of distorting reality.

God responds to Elijah in theophanies: torrential wind, powerful earthquake, and raging fire. But Elijah does not sense God in any of these. Then there is "the sound of silence" (the literal translation of the Hebrew text), that awesome stillness after the storm. At this point Elijah becomes aware of God's presence but still protests his commission and repeats his complaint word for word (vv. 10 and 14). He remains in the depths of despair.

What is God to do? God neither argues with him nor sets the facts straight. Rather, God reconfirms him by giving him a new mission. Elijah is to anoint others who will continue the struggle on behalf of Israel. God also promises that in the end seven thousand will remain faithful. God's ways are mysterious and unexpected. The pyrotechnics of theophany are replaced by serene stillness. The prophet goes into receptive mode and is reoriented to journey on in faith. The ministry of prophets is not based on strong personalities and is not a license for individual self-assertion. True ethical engagement arises from the God who enables all people to fulfill their divine commission. Prophecy is enacted when God's servants yield to the prompting of the Spirit.

The juxtaposition of this passage with Psalm 85 is extraordinarily helpful. The psalm opens with a fervent cry to God for social restoration and spiritual revival rooted in God's *hesed*, God's unconditional love. Verse 8 then reveals the psalmist praying for the ability to hear God speak. The writer seeks the grace and generosity of God on behalf of God's people. The attention is supremely on God as a faithful covenant-keeper who establishes righteousness and peace. The future for this people and their land is bound up with the character of YHWH, Lord of the covenant. Even the event of the exile cannot dislodge the determination of God to establish *shalom*. Elijah (like Moses in Exod. 33) is deeply aware of human frailty, and the narrator uses God's encounter with him to point to a gospel of persistent grace. The prophet could well have sung Psalm 85 to celebrate the character of God as the fundamental basis for prophetic ministry.

Sojourner Truth Day (August 18)

JoAnne Marie Terrell

ISAIAH 59
PSALM 107:1–9
1 JOHN 1:4–2:6
MATTHEW 19:26–30

Born into slavery about 1797 in Ulster County, New York, Isabella Baumfree experienced a religious conversion and call to public ministry in 1843.[1] New York, like other northern states, had "gradual" emancipation laws, but Isabella knew in her heart that God had already set her free. So she "told Jesus it would be all right if he changed [her] name" because when she left the state of bondage she wanted "nothin' of Egypt" left on her account. According to her story, the name Sojourner was given to her in a vision, for she understood that she was to walk about the country preaching and doing God's will. To this name she added Truth, becoming a great advocate in the cause of freedom from oppression for African Americans and women.

An extraordinary orator, Sojourner followed her call to lecture and preach for the rights of women and the abolition of slavery. Her work included advocating for black soldiers during the Civil War, opposing the death penalty, and calling for other civic liberties. Her speech "Ain't I a Woman?" addressed to the Ohio Women's Rights Convention in 1851, is among the most persuasive, moving, and timeless testimonies to the God-given rights of women. On this Holy Day for Justice, when we celebrate women's suffrage in the United States, we remember Sojourner Truth's powerful and enduring civil rights ministry on behalf of women, African Americans, and all God's people.

This morning I was out walking. I saw the wheat holding up its head. I went up an' took hold of it. And there was no wheat there!

1. Since the birth date of Sojourner Truth is not known, we observe Sojourner Truth Day on the anniversary of an event that fulfilled a deep desire of her heart—the ratification of the Nineteenth Amendment in the United States (August 18, 1920) granting women the right to vote.

351

[Due to a weevil infestation!] I said, "God, what is the matter with this wheat?" And [God] said to me, "Sojourner, there is a weevil in it." Now I hear talking about the Constitution and the rights of man. I come up and take hold of this Constitution. It looks mighty big, and I feel for my rights, but there ain't any there! Then I say, "God, what ails this Constitution?" [God] says to me, "Sojourner, there is a little weevil in it."

Sojourner Truth[2]

"We the People of the United States, in Order to form a more perfect Union, establish Justice, insure domestic Tranquility, provide for the common defence, promote the general Welfare, and secure the Blessings of Liberty to ourselves and our Posterity, do ordain and establish this Constitution for the United States of America." America's sacred documents—the Declaration of Independence, the Articles of Confederation, and the Constitution—are the intellectual expressions of a motley people's quest for nationhood. The Constitution specifically outlines the terms of the social compact made not only *between* them, but *for* them as well, through representative government. Its preamble, quoted here, provides an elegant, persuasive tone for the body of the work. The enumerated and personified ideals are lofty, standing out like a head or a sheaf of wheat, reaped and bound, ready rhetoric to be dispensed as sacred words to a newly devised nation.

Sojourner Truth's experience contradicted this unfolding metanarrative about liberty, as she was born into slavery and suffered as a slave. Her rhetoric may not have been as elegant or intellectually phrased, but she is an articulate mystic and wise prophet in the quest for true liberty. She refused to equivocate her absolute right to be free as an African American and a woman, unlike the "three-fifths compromise" (1787), the Fugitive Slave Act (1793), and provisions in the Constitution that defined her as inferior and rendered her defenseless before she was even born. Her words and actions are in stark opposition to the Missouri Compromise (1820) and a second Fugitive Slave Act (1850) that signaled the intention of keeping her and her people as chattel in perpetuity. Eighty years after her death in 1883, another African American mystic and prophet, Martin Luther King Jr., spoke as an intellectual would to the emptiness of America's sacred rhetoric, describing an unfulfilled "promissory note"[3] that, according to Alabama's governor, "[dripped] with words

---

2. Sojourner Truth, *The Narrative of Sojourner Truth* (1859; repr., New York: Arno Press, 1968), 147.

3. Martin Luther King Jr., "I Have a Dream," speech given at the Lincoln Memorial in Washington, D.C., in August 1963, in *A Testament of Hope: The Essential Writings and Speeches of Martin Luther King, Jr.*, ed. James Melvin Washington (San Francisco: HarperCollins, 1991), 217.

of interposition and nullification" of the rights of black men and women.[4] Sojourner Truth's homespun and powerful example of the "weevil infestation" continues to speak to the plagues of racism, sexism, classism, homophobia, and xenophobia in public discourse and how these policies belie the nation's stated creeds.

As we remember her words and work, Sojourner Truth stands as an exemplar of God's justice amid the terrors of slavery and the ensuing evils that have long plagued America. The Scripture texts for this Holy Day for Justice illuminate the age-old question of theodicy[5] (from the Greek, *theos* = God; *dicke* = justice), typically formulated in this way: if God is all-good and all-powerful, why is there evil and suffering in the world? Rather than wrestle with the question of whether God is just, the biblical authors locate the problem of evil in human systems and conduct, naming these as root causes of the alienation that humans perceive between themselves and God, and between one human community and another (or others). Together, these texts certify that divine power, goodness, and the divine intention of justice are inviolate and arise from God's steadfast love and ceaseless provision for humanity.

Isaiah 59

This chapter of the book of Isaiah is part of what is often referred to as Second Isaiah (chaps. 40–66, dating immediately before and just after the fall of Babylon in 539 BCE) or Third Isaiah (chaps. 56–66). Chapter 59 opens with a vigorous assertion of God's power and compassion (v. 1). The verses that follow reframe the question of theodicy as a lament over the alienated social, political, and spiritual condition of Judah, a remnant of the people Zion, whose sacred rhetoric holds that God chose to covenant with them as their divine provider and protector. The Babylonians had taken Judah's ruling class into exile in 587 BCE. During the last days of captivity, Isaiah regards Judah not merely as a victim of injustice but as complicit in the lawlessness of their leaderless nation (vv. 2–8). The elucidation of Judah's confession is a reflection of its theological heritage. This passage intimates the sacred memory of a people who understand themselves to be in a covenant relationship with God (vv. 2, 13, 18) and value truth, peace, justice, and public accountability (vv. 4, 6–8, 12–15); confirms the Deuteronomic interpretation of their fate (vv. 12, 13, 15b); and reaffirms the coming of God, both as an avenger against their adversaries (vv. 16–19) and as redeemer of a repentant nation (vv. 20–21). It

---

4. Ibid., 219.

5. For a discussion of theodicy as the source and governing norm of black liberation theology (and by extension, other theologies of liberation), see William R. Jones, "Theodicy: The Controlling Category for Black Theology," *Journal of Religious Thought* 30, no. 1 (Spring–Summer 1973): 28–38.

may be said that we are living in lamentable times, and that while we who preach social justice are committed to naming oppression and its sources, we also confess that we ourselves have played a part in our alienated conditions.

The contemporary preacher may use this passage heuristically to help the congregation revive a sense of its identity as a people who live in covenantal relationship with God. Amid the cycle of cruelty inflicted on African Americans, God has promised to be with us and for us as surely as God acted on behalf of God's people throughout the narratives of Scripture to bring about the redemption of both the oppressed and their oppressors. Or the preacher may speak of our own complicity in the degradation of our communities, helping us to reprioritize the core values of truth, peace, justice, and mutual accountability that are essential not only to Christians but to all human beings who live in communities of various kinds around the world. Yet another option is to help the congregation evaluate its own theological heritage, embracing that which empowers ministries of justice, love, and compassion, as well as identifying and rooting out that which denies these life-giving gifts to others. Finally, we must reaffirm the active presence and empowerment of a liberating, redeeming God. The avenging God was certainly not the God of Sojourner Truth, Martin Luther King Jr., or the masses of Black people who, following Christ Jesus, embraced principles of nonviolent resistance while working to fulfill God's purposes among us.

Psalm 107:1–9

These verses acknowledge the truth of suffering in human life as well as the spiritual and sociopolitical afflictions we experience both individually and collectively. Yet they steadfastly refuse to implicate God in our suffering. Instead, this psalm of thanksgiving was likely sung by those on pilgrimage to Jerusalem to celebrate a cultic feast day or perhaps as the people returned from Babylonian exile (v. 3).[6] It offers up praise to God for steadfast love (vv. 1, 8), for miraculous provisions (vv. 4–6, 8–9), for "making a way out of no way" through "dangers seen and unseen" (vv. 4–7)[7] until they reached "a city to dwell in" (v. 7).[8] We may readily discover parallels here between the ancient Hebrews and

---

6. Herbert May and Bruce Metzger, eds., *The Oxford Annotated Revised Standard Version of the Bible*, commentary on Ps. 107 (New York: Oxford University Press, 1977), 740.

7. These utterances are commonly confessed in the Black church across its several denominations (and in Black congregations within white denominations) and are vested with sacred authority. They are one of the means by which the Black church sustains its identity as such without a centralized community from which to receive directives. For a discussion of what constitutes the Black church, see C. Eric Lincoln and Lawrence Mamiya, *The Black Church in the African American Experience* (Durham, NC: Duke University Press, 1990).

8. See Heb. 11:10: "For [Abraham] looked forward to the city that has foundations, whose architect and builder is God."

those who endured displacement from their homeland, domination, debilitating separations from family, brutality, and even death during American slavocracy. For those born into slavery, the experience of having "no city to dwell in"—no place in Africa or America that could truly be called "home"—surely would have made the promises voiced in America's sacred rhetoric appealing to African Americans on visceral as well as intellectual levels.

Through the sacred rhetoric of Psalm 107, the preacher concerned with social justice may be able to help a contemporary congregation accurately name the sources of oppression in their midst and also inspire direct action on behalf of immigrants, those enslaved by traffickers in the sex industry, and persons displaced by drought, famine, earthquakes, war, and other disasters. For those born into and experiencing oppression today, the acquired practice of naming oppression ought never to negate the need to praise God for accompanying us through suffering, for empowering us to endure and overcome oppression, and for promising us a "city that has foundations, whose architect and builder is God" (Heb. 11:10).

Matthew 19:26–30

Peter longs to know what he may receive for having lost home, kin, and all of his possessions as he pursued a life of faithfulness to Christ. Would he be compensated? If so, when and how? What might Christ's response to Peter suggest to people who suffer today because of injustices rendered against them as they seek to be faithful amid trying or desperate circumstances? Belief in divine reward for persons who suffer unjustly has been criticized as greatly contributing to the passivity that plagues oppressed people in the face of their great struggles for liberation. Yet it is no light thing either to want or need to know of God's ultimate sovereignty and power amid the suffering and deprivations one experiences, whether those deprivations are as substantial as losing a loved one or job, or as frustrating as losing time and energy in pursuing a just cause. These experiences also challenge a sense of "somebodiness."[9]

Ironically, this story is prefaced by a concern for the eternal fate of the rich, who do not suffer in ways that poor people do, for example, for want of food, adequate housing, and medical care. Although we cannot claim to understand it fully, the good news for the rich is that eternal life is possible.[10] The good news for those who are oppressed and who turn to Christ for understanding and help is that eternal life—life which is given to us *now*—is

---

9. Cf. James H. Cone, *God of the Oppressed* (San Francisco: Harper & Row, 1975).

10. The Matthean text uses *zoen aionion*, or "age-lasting life," apropos of its time and theological development of the concept of eternal life. Later texts such as 1 Tim. 6 use *tes ontos zoes*, "the life which is life indeed," which is a qualitative description rather than a quantitative, temporal understanding of the life Christ Jesus gives to those who believe in him. Nevertheless, both

guaranteed. In the early nineteenth century, Sojourner Truth and other African Americans, male and female, enslaved and free, found agency and voice
in the Christianity of an America that was in the ecstatic throes of its Second
Great Awakening. The religion of Jesus bestowed on them "somebodiness"
that the Constitution denied them and that heretofore they could not claim
on any grounds. Thus, it is quite possible that they viewed eternal life not
merely as a compensatory reward to be granted after death, but as that which
dispelled their passivity and empowered their witness during their lifetimes
on earth. We who are their biological and spiritual descendants should not do
less with this great promise and gift of God.

1 John 1:4–2:6

Christianity holds within it, like the Constitution and the United States' other
sacred documents, the promises of life, liberty, and blessedness. When the
slaveholders extended this beacon of hope to the slaves through Christian
evangelism, they did so with the caveats that the slaves' lives were to remain
dependent on their owners' rule and whims, no matter how cruel; that the
liberty granted in Christ was spiritual and not temporal; and that the blessedness they could anticipate would come from the slaveholders' benevolence.

The "weevil infestation" in slaveholding Christianity continues to have
ramifications for those for whom the full measure of Christianity's promise is
still withheld because they are poor, black, brown, red, sexually marginalized,
disabled, young, elderly, and/or female. Consonant with an understanding of
blessing as organic and coming from a God fully vested in our joy (v. 4)[11] and
sin as corporate (and even personal sin as having corporate implications),[12] this
passage from John's epistle speaks to the need for entire peoples' redemption from the vicious cycle of sin that is imposed from without by others
and internalized and revisited on the generations that follow us (vv. 6–8). It
calls for confession of our personal sins and of our complicity in maintaining
systems of oppression (vv. 9–10). It also signals God's willingness to cleanse
and remove the stigma of sin through our advocate, "Jesus Christ the righteous" who "is the *expiation* for our sins" (2:1–2 RSV).[13] The thoroughgo-

phrases share something of the same reassuring power to those who are already blessed enough
to believe, both in the promise of eternal life and in its giver and guarantor.

11. Cf. John Armstrong, *The Idea of Holiness and the Humane Response* (Boston: Unwin
Hyman, 1981).

12. Cf. Olin Moyd, *Redemption in Black Theology* (Valley Forge, PA: Judson Press, 1979).

13. The Greek word *hilasterion* may be translated as "propitiation," but that word (which
is associated with appeasement) denotes an objective theory of atonement in which God is the
acted-upon object who is appeased by sacrifice and changes divine disposition toward loathsome
humankind. This atonement theory is amenable to focusing on individual, private sin. It does
not align with Hebraic understandings of communal or shared sin. In this subjective atonement

ing nature of God's investment in us contrasts sharply with the devaluing of whole segments of humanity by dominant and oppressive cultures and people. As Sojourner Truth taught through her example of the "weevil" within, the task of the prophetic Christian preacher is both to celebrate the self-giving, loving, and just God and to expose every lie concerning those whom God creates and loves.

theory, God is the acting subject who provides the system of sacrifice, in this case, God's own Son, Jesus, to remove the sources of alienation among and within the covenanted people. See JoAnne Marie Terrell, *Power in the Blood? The Cross in the African American Experience* (Eugene, OR: Wipf & Stock, 2005).

Proper 15

Sunggu Yang

GENESIS 45:1–15
ISAIAH 56:1, 6–8

PSALM 133
PSALM 67
ROMANS 11:1–2A, 29–32
MATTHEW 15:(10–20) 21–28

The lectionary readings for this week provide a critical theological lens through which we may examine immigrant issues currently confronting the United States. Who are the foreigners and immigrants who have come to share and enjoy the abundance, either material or spiritual, of this "God-blessed America"? What should be the social attitude of previous residents in America toward these late arrivals? What relationship does God desire to create among people who have begun to mix in with the rest of society? The Genesis reading advises, "Welcome immigrants who bring many blessings of God," while Isaiah says, "Worship together in joyful unity." In a similar vein, the psalms praise the joyfulness of all kindred living together in sacred unity (133:1) and God's saving power among all nations and people (67:2–3), while the evangelist Matthew and the apostle Paul uphold the mercy of God abundantly given to Jews and Gentiles; that is, upon all races, nationalities, cultures, social classes, and genders, without discrimination.

Genesis 45:1–15 and Isaiah 56:1, 6–8

According to Terence E. Fretheim, in Genesis 45 we encounter a significant theological claim beyond the literary account of a tearful reunion between Joseph and his brothers. God, through the lips of Joseph, appears as the real subject or master planner of Joseph's migrant story.[1] In particular, two important verbs alert us to God's guiding role in these events, and they are

---

1. For the following exegetical observations on the Genesis reading, I am indebted to Terence E. Fretheim, "The Book of Genesis," in *The New Interpreter's Bible*, ed. Leander E. Keck et al., vol. 1 (Nashville: Abingdon, 1996), 641–47.

both spoken by Joseph: "God sent me" (Heb. *salah*, "send"; vv. 5, 7, 8) and "God has made me" (Heb. *sim*, "make"; vv. 8, 9). God is the prominent subject who does great things for Joseph and his family.

God brought Joseph, a foreigner and forced immigrant, to the land of Egypt not only to preserve his life and eventually his family's well-being, but also to save Egypt and all other nations surrounding it during years of severe famine. What is notable here is that God does this through the hands of an immigrant, Joseph. Egypt and the world around it are preserved and blessed by the presence and wisdom of this foreigner.

As we consider our own treatment of legal and illegal immigrants in the United States, have we embraced foreigners and strangers as if they are "Josephs" who have come to America by the grand plan of God to save their families and possibly this American nation? Or have we confronted them as potential criminals and social pariahs to be subject to tough immigrant identification laws and unmerciful deportation? Do some of us, even Christians, simply want to avoid immigration issues because we think that they do not directly relate to our everyday lives? When the state of Arizona supported a controversial new immigration law in 2010, most Christians in Arizona and throughout the United States remained indifferent about what was happening, except a handful of courageous clergy members and laity. Even now when other states are considering similar controversial laws, few voices from the church offer alternative visions and resolutions. We keep silent. We want to stay away. We just do not want to talk about those other Josephs or "potential criminals."

Third Isaiah (chaps. 56–66), speaking to a community that has returned from exile during the reign of King Cyrus of Persia, prophesies that welcoming and embracing "foreigners" is what God will soon carry out in the land of Israel, where the Israelites are commanded to "maintain justice, and do what is right" (Isa. 56:1, 6). God will bring these foreign settlers to a blessed, promised land and make them joyful in God's house of prayer along with others.[2] It is significant that this prophecy is given to the returning exiles who themselves lived in a foreign land as strangers. Living in a foreign land as marginalized aliens, the Israelite exiles no doubt experienced injustice, social marginalization, and political oppression. To the returning "once-foreigners" of Israel, God adamantly says regarding their relationships with the foreign settlers among them, "Maintain justice, and do what is right." When this happens, God's house (or perhaps the whole land of Israel) will be called "a

---

2. When the exiles returned, there were a considerable number of Edomites, Arabs, Phoenicians, Arameans, and other foreign nationals living in Israelite territories. See Bernard Gosse, "Sabbath, Identity and Universalism Go Together after the Return from Exile," *Journal for the Study of the Old Testament* 29, no. 3 (2005): 369–70.

house of prayer for all peoples" (v. 7). This is nothing less than a great vision of the blessed land of God where true unity and harmony among all nations is achieved! Undoubtedly, Isaiah's vision of embracing foreigners in our midst and welcoming them with blessings and joyfulness is analogous to our present circumstances, because God continues to ask us to trust and believe not only that foreigners and strangers need us but also that we need one another to fully realize God's intentions and blessings among us.

Joseph's immigrant story subtly and vitally informs us that when God brings foreigners to a God-blessed land, God does so not only to prevent them from suffering through perilous circumstances in their homelands, but also to protect, bless, and prosper the land and people who warmly embrace those in need. Obviously, God has blessed America in many ways, and immigrants from many countries still come to America to be part of the blessings we enjoy and often take for granted. Isaiah adamantly asks if we are ready to participate in these grand divine plans by which God wants to make the blessed land of God a house for all nations and peoples. More than anything, Isaiah asks if we can maintain justice and do what is right in embracing immigrants as necessary partners in God's blessings. However complex the questions and issues surrounding immigration may be for us today, we know that Scripture offers us an invaluable perspective as we seek to fulfill God's just and loving purposes among us.

Psalm 67 and Psalm 133

Psalm 67 is a communal song of thanksgiving that was probably intended for a harvest festival (v. 6). It strongly affirms God's rule and sovereignty over all peoples and nations; indeed, in just seven short, poetic verses, the psalm repeats the words "peoples/nations" eight times (vv. 2, 3, 4, 5) and "earth" four times (vv. 2, 4, 6, 7). Most importantly, the psalmist wants to stress that God demonstrates this universal sovereignty by executing justice on the earth "with equity" for all the peoples (v. 4). Literarily, the psalmist achieves this by a typical chiastic structure:

> A vv. 1–2 Blessings and God's saving power among all nations
> B v. 3 Refrain
> C v. 4 Key profession of God's sovereignty through justice
> B' v. 5 Refrain
> A' vv. 6–7 Blessings and God's reign on the earth

What could it mean that God executes justice for and among all peoples and nations? As Cain Hope Felder puts it, texts like Psalm 67, among myriad other lessons, may teach us to "engage the new challenge to recapture the ancient biblical vision of racial and ethnic pluralism as shaped by the Bible's own universalism."[3] In other words, in this particular sense of universalism, the text solemnly asks us if we are now joyfully and *rightfully* joining God's vision for great harmony among all racial and ethnic groups. In the current context of American immigration concerns, the psalmist seems to suggest that it is only when we include persons who are marginalized and oppressed that God's justice is achieved among different people who live together. As we join in a communal song of thanksgiving, we celebrate the abundance of what we have to share because of God's gracious gifts to all of us.

Psalm 133 is a truly joyful song, a vivid vision of the same grand harmony poetically pictured in Psalm 67. Regarding that grand harmony among peoples, the psalmist exclaims, "How very good and pleasant it is when kindred live together in unity!" (v. 1). Furthermore, the psalmist wants to accentuate the joyfulness, sacredness, and breadth of that unity by using gorgeous similes of "the precious oil" and "the dew of Hermon" (vv. 2–3). Throughout the Psalms (e.g., 23:5; 92:10; 141:5), the pouring of oil demonstrates hospitality, jubilation, and blessed relationships, while the abundant dew coming down even to Zion from Hermon (located about 200 kilometers north of Jerusalem) symbolizes the rich extent of God's ever-flowing blessing.[4] Of course, Psalm 133 itself does not seem to address any racial or ethnic harmony but rather the national unity of ancient Judah and Israel, the southern and northern kingdoms. Yet the traditional association of Psalm 133 with the Lord's Supper reflects the Christian church's broader vision of unity emerging out of this text. As at the Communion table, there is to be no distinction or oppression between high and low, privileged and underprivileged, rich and poor, developed and underdeveloped, white and black, educated and uneducated, abled and disabled, multiple-generation residents and recent immigrants. God desires that all varieties of people live together in justice, unity, and peace.

Romans 11:1–2a, 29–32

In these verses the apostle Paul offers a strong apologetic against those who say that the gospel of Christ now belongs only to believing Gentiles, and not to the Jews who initially rejected the message of Jesus. Paul knows and insists that the gospel of Christ is not under the dualistic rule of either–or, but in support of the symbiotic relation between all parties involved in faith, especially, in this case, Jews and Gentiles. For Paul, there is a symbiotic relationship

3. Cain Hope Felder, preface to *Stony the Road We Trod: African American Biblical Interpretation*, ed. Cain Hope Felder (Minneapolis: Fortress, 1991), ix.

4. J. Clinton McCann Jr., "The Book of Psalms," in *The New Interpreter's Bible*, ed. Leander E. Keck et al., vol. 4 (Nashville: Abingdon, 1996), 1214.

between the Christian faith of Gentiles and that of Jews. God's love and "election" of Israel never end, Paul insists (v. 28). These are irrevocable gifts. Just as Jews have received mercy yet many have rejected the gospel of Christ, so do Gentiles receive God's mercy through Christ's gospel.

These verses are of seminal importance for Jewish-Christian relations today. Because of the harsh history of Christians persecuting Jews, it is urgent for us to realize that we have often misconstrued Christ's grace as if it is a right given to some people rather than a blessing intended for all. Each group's obedience or disobedience to God can function positively in its effects on others. For instance, while many Jews did not follow the way of Christ, many Gentiles received the gospel of Christ, seeing the recoil of the former as a *mauvais exemple*. Yet Jews may turn to faith in Christ when they see the faithful life of Gentiles who once were unfaithful.

Those whom we may consider "Gentiles" in America today, especially immigrants from various non-European countries, may well find themselves in a similar relationship to Euro-American Christians in at least two ways. First, fast-growing (evangelical) churches among immigrant groups challenge decreasing attendance among Euro-American mainline churches throughout the modern and postmodern eras. Enthusiasm for the Christian faith and faithful ways of life among recent immigrants of all faith traditions often trigger the envy of mainline, Euro-American Christians. Second, and perhaps more importantly, immigrants' very presence and the way we treat them provide a critical reflection of what American Christianity truly believes, including its terribly compromised social conscience. Have we been willing to welcome immigrant residents to our neighborhood? Are we ready to enjoy worshiping together in the same building, at the same hour? Have we not rejected the pastoral applications of immigrant pastoral candidates? Do we pay immigrants equally for their work? Are we prepared, when necessary, to put aside our own social and political privilege for the sake of immigrants, as Christ humbled himself in his own way and descended from heaven in human flesh? Immigrants may be among us today to test and refine our faith and Christian social consciousness as we embrace, deny, or resist their presence.

Matthew 15:(10–20) 21–28

At first glimpse, Jesus' words and actions are scandalous. "Always-must-be-merciful" Jesus snaps at a pitiful Canaanite woman and wants to turn her away. Further, he seems to say, "I will love and thus save *only* my own people." However, Jesus' harsh words and actions are but a subtle, subversive tactic that ultimately points toward a greater ethic of faithfulness and opens the way to a broader salvific vision.

What Jesus finally tells the Canaanite woman and how he reacts to her recall the words of Paul and Barnabas in the book of Acts: "It was necessary that the word of God should be spoken first to you [the people of Israel]. Since you reject it and judge yourselves to be unworthy of eternal life, we are now turning to the Gentiles" (Acts 13:46). Jesus says that his most urgent mission is to save the lost people of Israel. Yet his mission changed, as did that of Paul, because a Gentile, a foreigner, an outcast, the "unclean" Canaanite woman comes in faith to Jesus seeking his grace and mercy, while others, like some Pharisees, "the Israelites of Israelites," chosen ones of God, reject him. As the previous verses indicate, Jesus is suspicious of those whose words and actions betray what is in their hearts; namely "evil intentions, murder, adultery, fornication, theft, false witness, slander" (v. 19). In light of this, Jesus chose to broaden his mission.

Two critical lessons for social justice are revealed in Jesus' words and behavior. First, God is the God of salvation for all; there is no distinction before God with respect to race, nationality, culture, social class, and gender. Second, God rejects believers who, while still believing, like to continue in their social evils and live deceptively and harmfully toward others.

As we focus on justice for immigrants today, these two lessons of Jesus apply directly to our Christian consciences and even to the national conscience of "God-blessed America." Above all, we have forgotten that God's salvation is for all, and we often blame and reject those who come to America from other racial, cultural, and social backgrounds seeking religious freedom, daily bread, equal social treatment, better education, and political liberty. Why do we blame and reject them? What do we fear? Do we think that immigrants may take away "our" blessings, either spiritual or material, and that God has a limited number of blessings to share with us? Once again, let us remember Jesus' teaching: God is the God of all and offers salvation for all people. God also invites us to share and enjoy with others what we are granted freely and abundantly by God. But we must also remember that God will reject and harshly judge us if we continue to pursue our selfish interests and treat underprivileged and undocumented immigrants cruelly. How long will we pay them less than minimum wage in order for businesses to maximize their profits and ensure cheap purchases for ourselves?

Jesus himself wants to broaden his mission horizon and to offer great compassion toward all others, including this Gentile, foreign, outcast, underprivileged, and "alien" woman living outside of his "God-blessed" society. This same Jesus calls us to minister as he ministers and for the same purposes. Now is the time to follow the ways of Jesus Christ.

Proper 16

Mary Alice Mulligan

EXODUS 1:8–2:10

PSALM 124

ISAIAH 51:1–6

PSALM 138

ROMANS 12:1–8

MATTHEW 16:13–20

Like a clarion call, Matthew's Peter declares the Christ. But then Jesus orders the disciples into silence. Like them, we must take time to struggle with the fullness of the Christian message. Today's Scriptures remind us of the embodiment of faithful witness and the necessity of corporate ministry. We may note the focus as "embodying justice communally." Shiphrah and Puah act together; as a nation, Israel is to take justice to the peoples; we present our bodies together as sacrifices. Only together are we the body of Christ. Like an ember separated from the fire, those who attempt to respond to the gospel alone will burn and go out. Our interconnectedness as a people is crucial, but these passages also remind us we are part of God's interconnected creation. What damages the earth hurts each and all of us.

Exodus 1:8–2:10

People easily zoom through this passage, skimming the midwife section, eager to get to Moses. But these early verses, focusing on Shiphrah and Puah, need attention, for they stretch us toward a proper response to oppression and the need for courage to do justice and bring about transformation, regardless of one's position. If we focus on the first fourteen verses of the lection, we see that a courageous response to oppression depends on our openness to YHWH.

Although Pharaoh is Egypt's most powerful person, the enslaved Israelites frighten him. His reaction is to oppress them by exerting power over them, what has been called "power as control."[1] Pharaoh commands over-

1. Sally Purvis, *The Power of the Cross: Foundations for a Christian Feminist Ethic of Community* (Nashville: Abingdon, 1993), chaps. 1 and 2.

seers to burden the Israelites with forced labor and ruthless demands. They comply. Something sounds quite familiar: the powerless workers groaning under double shifts with no overtime pay or benefits, the increases in rent and food costs, as well as the taskmasters' increasing heartlessness. The overseers would probably say they are just following orders, just doing their job, which involves collaborating with an oppressive political system.

An opposite reaction comes from the seemingly powerless midwives, Shiphrah and Puah. When directed to kill Hebrew boys at birth, the women conspire to save them, following what they believe God requires. Purvis calls this participating in "power as life." In refusing to collaborate, the midwives defy Pharaoh, thus demonstrating justice in action. Literary analysis reveals the narrative appears intentionally constructed to show an ironic contrast between collaboration with and defiance of the power demands of the social order.

But take note: we listeners have been set up. The section ends with Pharaoh's repetition of the oppressive command: kill the Hebrew boys. Hearers must now choose to collaborate or defy injustice. Although our congregations are not commanded to kill Hebrew babies, powers are expecting us to remain silent (i.e., collaborate) as schools receive massive budget cuts, as young people find it easier to acquire guns and drugs than jobs, and as children wander streets after school. Communities of faith that fear YHWH need to figure out new midwifery schemes to become physically involved in saving our children. Preaching might remind the congregation that anytime even the most powerless and vulnerable defy unjust powers, God's divine intentions for the earth are advanced.

The remainder of the passage, describing the rescue of Moses, is not unimportant, for we know his role in the Hebrew exodus. But the midwives' actions set the stage for his rescue. They are models, challenging us to defy forces that threaten our children and to become involved in literally saving the lives of our children.

Psalm 124

This amazing psalm fits into the category of songs of reversal. Sung by people following the cessation of some crushing circumstance, these effervescent words credit YHWH with their survival, indicating that divine intervention has saved them. It mentions enemies and threats of drowning, but no historical event we can pinpoint. Not mentioning the specifics is common to psalms. Psalmists express fear, anger, guilt, joy, relief, doubt, and numerous other emotions without mentioning the historical details. Perhaps this is why words of the psalms resonate with myriad experiences through the millennia.

How do people who live with oppression keep getting up in the morning? How does the person who works two jobs but still has to rob Peter (the cookie jar with the rent in it) to pay Paul (the monthly bus pass to get to work) keep getting out of bed and going to work? When some disaster is momentarily averted, how do they rejoice so vigorously? Listen to the ones who sing this psalm. They have trust in YHWH, stronger than anything many of the rest of us have ever known. What can we learn from them if we listen? And how do those who live in relative comfort (knowing they can pay for both a surprise car repair and the mortgage) ignore those who struggle every day, allowing them to keep struggling, as if we have no mutual responsibility?

When we who live fairly comfortably hear such psalms, in addition to being baffled at how some people continue to function, we should be overcome with shame. Almost every week in worship, someone makes the claim that we are God's hands and feet. Does the congregation believe what they are saying? If we participate in faith communities whose theological sophistication rejects the possibility of divine intervention in any supernatural way, how are such psalms to be sung today, unless we get busy breaking the stranglehold that oppression and poverty have on our sisters and brothers who are looking to God for salvation from the torrent of overwhelming odds threatening to drown them?

Isaiah 51:1–6

How easy it is to immerse ourselves in scholarship focusing on the three "books" of Isaiah, each springing from different historical periods. Juliana Claassens reminds us that "scholars now tend to read Isaiah as a whole, being sensitive to the way in which images and themes reverberate throughout the whole book."[2] One of the themes she emphasizes is how the text assists our "imagining an alternative world."[3] Not only in relation to exile, but throughout history, humans and all creation have suffered from tragedies, exploitations, violence, and threats of extinction. "At certain key moments throughout Isaiah, the prophets dare to dream of a world that is different, offering a powerful reminder that the current reality is not all there is, that another world may be possible."[4]

This little passage from Isaiah 51 directs God's people, in anticipation of divine judgment, to pursue righteousness, to share the ways of YHWH beyond the Israelites, for the apocalypse envisioned here involves the whole

---

2. L. Juliana Claassens, "Isaiah," in *Theological Bible Commentary*, ed. Gail O'Day and David Petersen (Louisville, KY: Westminster John Knox Press, 2009), 209.

3. Cf. the idea of "alternative community" in Walter Brueggemann, *The Prophetic Imagination* (Philadelphia: Fortress Press, 1978), 25.

4. Claassens, "Isaiah," 217.

earth and all of its inhabitants. Only God's protection allows survival; security is in YHWH's eternal salvation.

The warning that "earth will wear out like a garment, and those who live on it will die like gnats" (v. 6b) sounds ominously familiar. This text opens wide the possibility of preaching a solid ecotheological sermon, for humanity *is* wearing out the earth, emptying our terrestrial home of resources, and driving species to extinction. As desertification spreads and sea levels rise, humans and all other life forms on earth are threatened. Already, drought-induced starvation leaves millions vulnerable to dying "like gnats" on sun-scorched earth.

YHWH's protection may be depicted by Isaiah as divine apocalyptic deliverance, but there is also the instruction for listeners to heed and to teach in order that justice may shine like a light to all peoples. Appropriately we leave divine work to God, but humanity may share living in ways that go with the grain of God's salvation. In considering ecological disasters already upon us, calling congregations into conscientious life choices that honor creation is pastorally responsible. Humans are divinely called to live into the pattern of God's deliverance. In discussing the evolutionary struggle of creation and the coming new creation, Christopher Southgate offers the idea that "human beings can be—if not the midwives of the new creation—then at least among those that attend the birth, hold creation by the hand, and boil water as needed."[5] Such figurative instructions assist us in figuring out how to live in a world of goodness *and* injustice, living confidently toward God's purposes now and eternally.

Psalm 138

As many psalms do, Psalm 138 vacillates between certainty and insecurity. Kathleen Farmer explains, "Assurance and doubt can wash back and forth over the faithful. Comfort and anguish can intermingle within the same psalm as within the same speaker. The transition from anxiety to assurance in the psalms, as in human life, is not always neatly or permanently made."[6] This psalm confidently recalls reasons to trust YHWH's commitment to protect the lowly; yet resembling our own uncertainty, the psalmist concludes with supplication.

The singer bursts with praise for God's faithfulness, listing not specific events but reminders of the value of worship and God's consistent presence.

5. Christopher Southgate, *The Groaning of Creation: God, Evolution, and the Problem of Evil* (Louisville, KY: Westminster John Knox Press, 2008), 95. Southgate connects science and theology, articulating humanity's ecological responsibilities for God's ambiguous world.
6. Kathleen Farmer, "Psalms," in *Women's Bible Commentary*, expanded ed., ed. Carol Newsom and Sharon Ringe (Louisville, KY: Westminster John Knox Press, 1998), 150.

How like our own need for reminders of divine justice that triumphed in the past. Contemporary congregations may profit from remembering where and how YHWH's justice has succeeded in transforming church and society. For instance, we can thank God for women's winning the right to vote, for child labor laws, for an end to legal segregation, for some states' recognizing marriages regardless of gender, for continuing efforts to end poverty, for churches' welcoming previously excluded persons into leadership. Such reminders strengthen our resolve for future endeavors.

But even when the psalmist has recounted God's companionship through trials, she reveals uncertainty, too. Hear the curious, very human, language of reversal at the conclusion. Remembering that forces of injustice are real and powerful, the psalmist acknowledges that people "walk in the midst of trouble" (v. 7). No wonder the psalmist firmly asserts that YHWH will protect us. We also may affirm God's protection. We can list biblical accounts of God's mighty acts; we say God has been our shield and defender throughout our lives. But in the end, we still feel the need to send YHWH a memo—Don't forget us, OK?

Romans 12:1–8

Paul calls us to total commitment—to offer our lives as "living sacrifices," not dying to please God, but turning ourselves over to God's purposes so we become fully alive: this is our spiritual worship. Chapter 12 brings a sharp correction to congregations where people seem split between the "camps" of justice or spirituality rather than claiming the interconnectedness of our physical activities of service and our spiritual lives. Spirituality and justice making are mutually dependent; each is essential. Joyce Hollyday goes so far as to claim: "Doing justice is a spiritual discipline; social witness is as fundamental as prayer in a believer's life. . . . I believe that we deepen our knowledge of Christ and our need for prayer as we engage in the world's suffering."[7] Romans 12 also calls us to understand who we are communally (and organically). We must live in ways that build up and honor the body of Christ, since we are members of one another. But pushing the organic metaphor further, we might easily recognize we are also parts of the universe. All creation is interconnected, and how we live affects others. Congregational decisions should all be grounded in considerations of God's intentions for the whole world.

Decades ago, George Forell claimed bluntly that Paul taught that "[faith] takes [one] out of . . . isolation and incorporates the individual into the body

7. Joyce Hollyday, *Then Shall Your Light Rise: Spiritual Formation and Social Witness* (Nashville: Upper Room Books, 1997), 14.

of Christ. As members of this body, Christians are responsible for the church and the world. . . . Christians as members of the body of Christ are servants of mankind."[8] The gifts each person possesses serve to make the body of Christ functional. We need each other to survive, although survival is not the goal. The body exists to be in service to the world God loves.

Romans 12 invites us to consider not only the interconnectedness within the congregation and our interconnectedness with the world, but also the connection between responsibility to care for the earth and our own health. Such ideas make easy links back to Isaiah, where ecological matters have theological import. Our futures are tied to our attending to God's purposes for a healthy planet. We depend on the well-being of each other.

Matthew 16:13–20

Some people love to preach this passage; others avoid it. It almost seems as if those who love to preach it do so because they believe they have all the answers, while those who dread it fear they can be certain of almost nothing about Christ. We could learn from one another.

In each of the Synoptic Gospels, this encounter between Jesus and his disciples reflects a decisive turning point. One phase of Jesus' life is over. "From that time on," verse 21 explains, Jesus taught about his suffering and death in earnest. This is the only time in Matthew when Jesus asks his followers to identify who he is. In this, we might hear a word of caution about evangelism that hurries people into confessing faith in Christ when they have walked with Jesus only briefly. True faith cannot be rushed. Peter's declaration of Jesus as the Christ, the son of the living God, comes only after several years of discipleship. Jesus' response to Peter pointedly reminds us that faith is a divine gift; we cannot gain it for ourselves or demand it from others. In addition, Jesus claims that he builds the church. The church does not exist by our efforts.

Certainly these brief verses guide us to consider what it means to proclaim Jesus as Messiah. Every congregation needs to spend time reflecting on possible christological interpretations. How are we to understand this fundamental faith claim? After we spend sufficient time on christological issues, we appropriately turn to the community of faith. If faith is a gift of God and if Jesus builds the church, what are our responsibilities?

Although the evangelist's main focus seems to be identifying the Christ, Matthew's Jesus gives his followers the task of binding and loosing. This direction has been interpreted in various ways through the centuries, but we can agree that the church is instructed to make active choices. Holy power

---

8. George Wolfgang Forell, *The Christian Lifestyle: Reflections on Romans 12–15* (Philadelphia: Fortress Press, 1975), 9. I leave most gender-specific references as published.

is invested in the church, allowing us to guide correction of one another's behaviors, to offer forgiveness of one another's sins, and apparently even to exert authority over the presence of evil among us. The church is responsible for taking moral action against social wrongs. We are called to get involved with people who need to be loosed (e.g., children who are trafficked, persons who are addicted). We are empowered to work to set them free. And the church is given the power to become involved with those who need binding (e.g., people who are beating spouses, corporations involved in ecological destruction, those profiting from the international drug trade). Because we believe in Jesus as Christ, the church is directed to take up his ministry in the world.

Jesus' final comment ordering the disciples into silence makes sense in light of their ignorance of his future. People were expecting a messiah of power, but Jesus exhibits seeming powerlessness. He claims the necessity of his execution. Until the passion and resurrection, the disciples are unable to articulate what it means to be the Christ. We, however, preach on this side of the cross and empty tomb, so we appropriately give effort (admitting our limitations) to assisting the congregation's understanding of who Jesus is and what it means that he is the Messiah of God.

Proper 17

David J. Frenchak

Exodus 3:1–15
Psalm 26:1–8

Jeremiah 15:15–21
Psalm 105:1–6, 23–26, 45c
Romans 12:9–21
Matthew 16:21–28

Domination is the use of power by one group of people to suppress the freedom and human rights of another group of people. It is essential that we understand social justice as it relates to whole groups of people rather than individuals. The individual must ask questions that have to do with the larger dynamics of principalities and powers. Central to our reflection on these texts is the question of how we understand and address power when it has become apparent that there is injustice between groups of people.

Matthew 16:21–28

Cultural values dominate more of our lives than we realize, and it is therefore critical that we understand the dominant culture in which we live. In North America, much of our culture worships success, and even casual observers can recognize the value we place on winning. For example, the victory cup, not the cross, is raised at many sporting events. Ritually honoring accomplishments with a victory cup can be seen in other contexts as well, including those that honor the theater, films, music, business, and even educational accomplishments. Most of us have witnessed a victory celebration following a contest or battle between combatants where the victor, holding the cup high, parades through the stadium.

While victory may be an identifying characteristic of our dominant and "dominating" culture, and the winner's cup may be the dominant symbol for our worship of winners, victory and winning are powerfully evident as they provide the motivational energy of principalities and powers throughout history. This text from Matthew 16 brings us face to face with the clash of values

371

between a dominating culture and a culture based on the spiritual values of the Christian tradition. The clash is evident in the contrast of symbols for the two cultures: the victory cup and the cross.

Peter experienced a distinct clash of cultures when he heard Jesus announce his impending suffering and death. Peter had just made a great confession of faith in Jesus: "You are the Anointed One, the son of the Living God" (Matt. 16:16), a confession that earned him the great accolade of being named "the rock" on which Jesus would erect his church and which the forces of evil would not be able to destroy. Peter no doubt developed his expectations of Jesus' lordship according to what he had learned from his faith tradition and experiences as a Jew. He could not comprehend that Jesus' reign would not guarantee triumph and lead to victory over their oppressors, the Romans. According to ancient Jewish understandings of the royal title "Son of God," David had received a promise that his son would rule after him and that God would ensure a royal house from his lineage. "I will be a father to him, and he shall be a son to me" (2 Sam. 7:14). Zechariah also looked for the victory of the king who would rescue Jerusalem: "Lo, your king comes to you; triumphant and victorious is he, humble and riding on a donkey" (Zech. 9:9). According to Peter's understanding of Jewish tradition, history, and Scripture, the messiah did not come to accept defeat and death at the hands of the Romans. Thus he refused to accept Jesus' prediction of his passion. The implanted image of success, as well as the place of honor that victory would afford him, was preventing Peter from hearing Jesus' teaching about the way of the cross.

Jesus, however, was focused on living out his calling as a prophet, and he had a clear understanding of what that meant. It meant going to the city of Jerusalem and confronting the principalities and powers he found there. Cities are often thought of as dangerous places, places not amenable to or even compatible with the pastoral images of Christ. They are often seen as dark places of injustice rather than justice. Cities, however, are an ideal place to study and see the principalities and powers at work, and essential places for the church to fulfill its calling to take up the cross and follow Christ. As social, economic, and intercultural centers of American life, cities are ripe with potential for conversation and commerce among artists and businesspeople, immigrants and long-term residents, neighborhoods and urban planners. Amid the conflicts and challenges are opportunities for new ways of learning and living together.

By going to the city of Jerusalem when public humiliation and execution were highly probable, Jesus was expressing his willingness to accept the dangers that awaited him there. He also knew that his followers would face similar risks and hardships. Jesus proclaimed a new understanding of what it means to "save" one's life for the sake of others, rather than lose oneself in the hope of gaining worldly success and accomplishments (Matt. 16:24–26). In these verses, Jesus offers us a new understanding of the dynamics of winning and losing and the consequences of choosing the wrong value system. In the spiritual value system advocated by Christ, the winner (previously thought to be the dominating power) is the loser and the loser is the winner. If we choose to honor domination and value winning at any cost, we do so at the peril of losing our souls. Those who do not take up their own calling, symbolized by the cross, face the perils and dangers of being enemies to the cause of justice. Those who choose to live according to the values of the dominant system, claiming victory or superiority over others, and holding high the cup of victory over their heads, lose their souls.

There is no way anyone committed to social justice can avoid conflict and confrontation with the principalities and powers. It is part of the cross we must bear. The invitation to follow Jesus sets us on a path that leads to cities where the principalities and powers of destruction are lodged. This is the prophetic alternative to the mainstream culture that worships victory.

Romans 12:9–21

This reading clearly spells out the radical difference between those who take up their cross and follow Christ and those who are ruled by the dominant culture. Paul outlines the values and virtues, not of the dominant way of structuring the social order, but of a new spiritual perspective that redefines what winning looks like. It is, however, not merely an alternative to the dominant culture but a way of understanding good and evil, a concern that runs throughout this text. Those who take up the cross are to "hate what is evil, hold fast to what is good" (v. 9). At the end of the text, Paul again admonishes, "Do not be overcome by evil, but overcome evil with good" (v. 21). His words help us to appreciate that the spiritual way of looking at the social order turns the values of the dominant culture on its head: instead of being governed by greed, pride, or success, love urges us toward all that is good and in the best interests of our neighbors.

When we show love toward someone, we are moving them toward God's goodness. To love someone is not simply to cater to the specific likes and dislikes of that person. It is rather to act toward that person in ways that help them experience more of God's goodness. Genuine love permeates this chapter of Romans, offering us no fewer than twenty-four clear declarations of what love looks like in our relations with others, among persons who are more often focused on success and gaining advantage rather than on relating fairly and lovingly to others.

Exodus 3:1–15

There may not be a better biblical story to relate and highlight the political, social, and economic dynamics of domination than the story of the exodus. God is faithful to God's people, including those who are aliens, immigrants, and oppressed, because God's justice will not be denied. Nor is there a better story about what it means to deny oneself and take on God's call to give up one's personal comfort and security for the sake of serving others than the story of Moses, a reluctant prophet who had a physical encounter with God at Mount Horeb.

A one-sentence sermon based on this text could be "God's faithfulness to justice will not be denied." This passage gives a clear picture of God's faithfulness to an alien, immigrant, and oppressed people. As an instrument of divine justice and freedom, Moses receives a dramatic call from God. His story also reflects a common human response to God's call to be an instrument of social change: he does not believe he is worthy or able to fulfill God's call. It is helpful to remember that Moses appeared to be happily employed by his father-in-law. However, the divine call to prophetic witness was not given to Moses' father-in-law, a priest, but to a layperson. The text gives the preacher an opportunity to address the fact that God, in the pursuit of justice, often calls laypeople to be instruments of justice.

God's faithfulness is historical. The God of Abraham, Isaac, and Jacob moves backward and forward through history, insisting that God's just and loving intentions for creation will be fulfilled from generation to generation. There is no leaving the neighborhood or abandoning cities for the sake of greater opportunities elsewhere: God is faithful to regenerating and loving the people through all times and places, all tragedies and crises.

Jeremiah 15:15–21

Here we meet face to face with the weeping prophet of social justice. Jeremiah has taken up God's costly call, and we can hear his tormented voice in the middle of his lament. Jeremiah is beset by persecutors (v. 15) but insists that he has been faithful to God (vv. 16–17). He has ingested God's Word and avoided unsavory conduct. Because of this, Jeremiah is isolated and persecuted. He pleads to God, from whom he expects acknowledgment and understanding. Jeremiah's experiences offer a poignant reminder that following God's will does not make for an easy journey. In facing the principalities and powers of our own communities, we are likely to encounter not only resistance but rejection, persecution, and defiance from the very people who surround us as we pursue God's justice.

While Jeremiah initially experienced "joy" and "delight" in taking up his prophetic vocation (v. 16), he now describes his pain and wounds as "unceasing" and "incurable" (v. 18). "Joy" and "delight" also appear to have characterized the life that Israel expected for itself and that God intended for Israel; but now, in the latter days of Israel's nationhood, joy and delight are to be cut off (see also 7:34; 16:9; 25:10).

In the lectionary text for today, Jeremiah does not experience restoration. He has yet to complete his part in bringing divine judgment on Israel. Verse 19 introduces conditional language into his description of their dilemma. "If" Israel had acted otherwise, things would be different, but according to earlier verses Israel repeatedly defied God's will with a firm declaration, "we will not" (6:16–17). The return that Jeremiah calls for here is not the same as earlier demands that were made of Israel (e.g., 3:12, 14; 4:1–2). Jeremiah returns to his original commission, and many of the ideas and images found in 1:18–19 are repeated here.

But more is said in chapter 15 than in chapter 1. In 15:21, Jeremiah extends the reference to opponents who are called "wicked" and "ruthless." The extension hints at some concession to Jeremiah's characterization of what he is enduring ("on your account I suffer insult," 15:15). Yes, return is always appropriate, but God's call to Jeremiah was finally not contingent upon it.

Lurking within the individual assurance given to Jeremiah is hope for Israel. When in exile, Israel wonders if the wicked and the cruel permanently control its future. In the singular "you" of verse 21 resides the possibility of a plural "you." In the midst of judgment, that shift is Israel's hope. Rachel/Israel will be comforted as Jeremiah was supported against its opposition. Israel, in exile, recognized that in Jeremiah's vocation its own destiny was mirrored. The one appointed to be against them was supported by the God who is their hope.

Psalm 26:1–8 and Psalm 105

Work for social justice is often accompanied by public misrepresentations of one's motives, actions, and faith, often resulting in public questions regarding the character of the prophet. The leader of social change and justice must be spiritually centered and have an abiding faith in the faithfulness of God that is worthy of celebration.

Psalm 26 is frequently likened to the story of Job, but the circumstances of this psalm may or may not resemble his. This psalm and the two following it probably arise out of the context of captivity, because they contain prayers, supplications, complaints, and resolutions of the Israelites in words that resonate with the period of the Babylonian exile. This lament is not unlike

Jeremiah's lament. Like the prophet, the psalmist knows how painful it is to be falsely accused. For those who have chosen to follow the way of prophetic ministry and have taken up their cross in faithfulness to Christ, it is understandable to want naysayers silenced and false accusers vanquished. When moving against the tide of dominant cultural expectations and values, prophetic witnesses expect God's vindication and the fulfillment of divine justice.

Psalm 105 identifies no fewer than six reasons to celebrate God's faithfulness in the midst of false accusation: God's deeds, works, strength, presence, miracles, and judgments are all sources of hope and empowerment as we seek to participate in God's compassionate and just work. Repeatedly biblical and contemporary prophets reflect on their tradition and history, identifying God's steadfast presence and faithfulness. Such reflection is an essential act of worship that provides strength and support for our public actions. We have in this psalm a model for how people from any tradition may gain strength for the work of social justice by looking back on their history and identifying the deeds, works, strength, presence, miracles, and judgment of God at work in the world. These may be recounted by local faith communities and by entire denominations and nations. It requires reading history from God's perspective rather than accepting events at face value, so that we may begin to recognize where God is present among us, actively supporting and encouraging new ways of relating to other people, cultures, and nations.

Proper 18

Barbara K. Lundblad

EXODUS 12:1–14
PSALM 149

EZEKIEL 33:7–11
PSALM 119:33–40
ROMANS 13:8–14
MATTHEW 18:15–20

The semicontinuous reading cycle focuses on the Passover story, a story central to liberation struggles over many centuries. The preacher may well decide to stay with the Exodus text, celebrating that story in worship with the myriad musical instruments of Psalm 149. Ezekiel and Psalm 119 complement Matthew's Gospel. Are these texts primarily about judgment and guilt or repentance and restoration? The Romans text, with Paul's call to love one another, may hold the clue to that question.

Matthew 18:15–20

This section of Matthew's Gospel is often called "the church discipline manual." Others call these verses "the church reconciliation manual." The difference between those two titles can lead to very different implications and actions. Is the goal to exclude those who have sinned against us or to do everything possible to restore sinners to our communal life? The answer to that question may come from Jesus' parable of the Shepherd Seeking for One Lost Sheep, which precedes this text: "So it is not the will of your Father in heaven that one of these little ones should be lost" (18:14). Today's Gospel lays out what shepherding means after Jesus has gone away. It seems clear that these verses come from Matthew's community rather than Jesus' own teachings. There was no "church" during Jesus' lifetime, and Matthew is the only Gospel writer to use this word. He has already used it once before when Jesus is talking to Simon Peter: "And I tell you, you are Peter, and on this rock I will build my church [*ekklesia*]" (16:18a). If Peter is the rock on which the church is built, the rock seems to be cracking two chapters later.

377

"If another member of the church sins against you," the manual begins (18:15a). The NRSV translation has replaced "brother" with "another member of the church." This translation makes some things clearer: this isn't your blood brother but your adopted brother, as part of the church. This translation is also more inclusive: the other member might be a woman. However, the NRSV loses the strong relational word. This person isn't simply on the membership rolls or in the church directory; this person is your relative.

The goal of today's Gospel is a family reunion—the title might well be "How to Get the Family Together Again." First, go to your brother or sister while the two of you are alone. The goal isn't embarrassment but restoration. If you are not heard, don't give up: take one or two others as witnesses. If that still doesn't work, "tell it to the church; and if the offender refuses to listen even to the church, let such a one be to you as a Gentile and a tax collector." That punishment is ironic since Matthew—by tradition the author—was a tax collector. He is now part of the very church addressed by these verses! Jesus has already reached out to the Gentiles in healing the centurion's servant, the Gadarene demoniac, and the daughter of a Canaanite woman. Being treated as a tax collector or Gentile doesn't seem so bad! The goal is still to bring these estranged relatives back into the community—even as Matthew the tax collector was invited and the Canaanite woman received more than crumbs from Jesus.

This process depends on knowing that someone has sinned, which leads to the discussion of binding and loosing. "Truly I tell you," said Jesus, "whatever you bind on earth will be bound in heaven, and whatever you loose on earth will be loosed in heaven" (v. 18). Jesus had said the same thing to Peter in chapter 16. Now Jesus extends that authority to the disciples.

Binding and loosing are rabbinic terms defined as the authority to declare something forbidden or allowed. " 'Binding and loosing on earth as in heaven' means interpreting former expressions of God's will . . . so as to show 'what is fitting for now' in a specific situation of the church's experience."[1] Jesus gives examples of binding and loosing in the Sermon on the Mount. "You have heard that it was said . . . but I say to you." Sometimes Jesus binds the text more deeply; sometimes he looses a text or replaces it with something new. Now Jesus calls the disciples and, by extension, the church to this task of testing texts and traditions.

Church history is marked by controversies over binding and loosing. Should women in difficult labor be given anesthesia even though God decreed pain in childbirth (Gen. 3:16)? Should slaves obey their masters, as Ephesians 6:5 insists? Should women be ordained when they are commanded to keep silence and never teach men (1 Cor. 14:34–35)? Should clergy preside at weddings

1. Daniel Patte, *The Gospel according to Matthew: A Structural Commentary on Matthew's Faith* (Philadelphia: Fortress Press, 1987), 233.

of divorced people when Jesus says such marriages break the commandments (Mark 10:11)? The church has been engaged in the task of binding and loosing for centuries. Now the fiercest battles are over homosexuality. Are the biblical texts binding or are there faithful reasons to loose the texts that have been interpreted to condemn gay people? Faithful people fear that the church is abandoning Scripture by calling for new interpretations of these texts.

Preachers can help people see that Jesus called his followers to this task of interpretation long ago. This is not a matter of watering down the Bible but of discerning what remains binding and what should be loosed because it has become hurtful or even deadly. Such discernment can only be done faithfully in community and in the presence of Jesus. One person alone cannot discern such important matters of life and faith. The community is essential, which is why reconciliation is so important. "Where two or three are gathered in my name, I am there among them" (Matt. 18:20).

Romans 13:8–14

This portion of Paul's Letter to the Romans can be helpful for discerning whether to bind a teaching or set it loose. Paul claims that all the commandments "are summed up in this word, 'Love your neighbor as yourself.'" This was one of the texts that moved doctors to give anesthesia to women suffering deadly pain: how could they refuse if they loved her as their neighbor? This admonition to love one another comes immediately after Paul's call to obey the governing authorities because they have been "instituted by God" (v. 1). Did he think it was time for a kinder, gentler word? Or was he saying that obeying the authorities is subject to this call to love the neighbor? The first seven verses of Romans 13 could not stand up to the light of neighbor love in South Africa during the days of apartheid.

In many ways these verses about love are a brief summary of Paul's love chapter in 1 Corinthians 13—a chapter often read at weddings, but not written for a bride and groom. Paul was writing about love within the divided Corinthian Christian community. That chapter has a surprise ending, according to Krister Stendahl: "[Paul] ends by saying, so there remains those three: faith, hope, and love, and the greatest of these is faith. Well, that's what he should have said, according to his own thinking. The basic line: He is the apostle of faith, everything depends on faith. But here, suddenly, there is a breakthrough in his thinking, and he says: And the greatest of these is love, *agape*, esteem of the other."[2] This deep love for the other, especially for the one who disagrees

2. Krister Stendahl, "Why I Love the Bible," *Harvard Divinity School Bulletin* 35, no. 1 (2007). Available at https://www.hds.harvard.edu/news/bulletin_mag/articles/35-1_stendahl .html (accessed June 5, 2010).

or is different, is the motivation for reconciling a brother or sister in Matthew 18. This neighbor love is also the word that tempers absolute loyalty to governing authorities. Paul's own appeal to obey the government came from his sense that the time was very short—the night was far gone and the day was near. Believers are subject to the timeline of Christ's return, and that return was imminent. Yet between the call to obey and the appeal to "make no provision for the flesh" comes Paul's strong word, "Love does no wrong to a neighbor; therefore, love is the fulfilling of the law" (Rom. 13:10).

Ezekiel 33:7–11 and Psalm 119:33–40

In Ezekiel we hear the themes that centuries later become the heart of Jesus' teaching about reconciliation. What sounds so threatening is in essence God's call for sinners to return. The key to this chapter comes in verse 11: "Say to them, As I live, says the Lord GOD, I have no pleasure in the death of the wicked, but that the wicked turn from their ways and live." The first ten verses of this chapter speak of a sentinel or sentry chosen by the people themselves. If this sentinel sees trouble coming and blows the trumpet and the people receive the warning, they will be saved. If not, they will perish. But if the sentinel sees trouble and fails to warn the people, their destruction will be on his head. At verse 7 there is a shift. God speaks directly to Ezekiel: "So you, mortal, I have made a sentinel for the house of Israel." This echoes God's earlier call to the prophet: "Mortal, I am sending you to the people of Israel. . . . Whether they hear or refuse to hear (for they are a rebellious house), they shall know that there has been a prophet among them" (Ezek. 2:3, 5).

That call sounds as though Ezekiel is completely alone (and often this seems to be the case). Sometimes when preachers face opposition to sermons calling for justice, the defensive response can be, "At least they know there has been a prophet among them." While this may be reassuring, God's words to Ezekiel in chapter 33 are almost identical to the words spoken to the sentry chosen by the people. We do not need to see this sentry as president of the church board to lift up the importance of people in a congregation taking responsibility for one another in the life of faith. The sentry's goal is God's goal—not punishment and death, but repentance and life. Preachers are reminded that sentries may be laypeople who are advocating for justice in their daily work, pushing the congregation to remember the poor, and even urging the minister to speak more boldly. When the sentry sees wickedness, the alarm must be sounded. For the prophets, wickedness usually meant greed, neglect of the poor, unfair dealings in the marketplace, and idolatry. Do we see any of these things happening in our community and our country? If so, the sentries in the pulpit and in the pews dare not keep silence.

The sentry's task isn't to scare people to death, but to turn them toward life. In his book *The Prophets*, Abraham Joshua Heschel writes,

> The prophets communicated God's anger over the sins of the covenant community. However, what God intends is not that his anger should be executed, but that it should be annulled by the people's repentance. In the final analysis, it is hope and deliverance, not death and destruction that are the ultimate objectives of prophetic preaching.[3]

Or as Krister Stendahl once told a group of pastors in Manhattan, "The true prophet of doom prays like hell that he or she will be proved wrong."

Psalm 119 is a fitting partner to Ezekiel 33. Turn to almost any verse of this long psalm and you will hear words of praise and thanksgiving for the law of God. The whole psalm is shouting, "*L'Chaim*"—to life! This is far different from the sense of the law as a body of rules. Joseph Sittler lamented that Christians often miss the life-giving aspects of the law:

> The rhetoric of praise, of adoration, of appreciation, of the blessedness of the law in the Old Testament remains simply incomprehensible under our conventional Christian understanding. . . . We've got to come under the amplitude of Jewish testimony to the meaning of the law and the moral vivacity, instruction and ordering function of the law in the structure of human life and religious obedience to God.[4]

What glorious words—amplitude and vivacity! Psalm 119 spills over with synonyms for the law, as though one word isn't adequate—law, decrees, statutes, ordinances, commandments, precepts, ways, word—all of them leading to life. *L'Chaim*!

Exodus 12:1–14 and Psalm 149

After the call of Moses in last Sunday's lectionary, the text moves to chapter 12 and the heart of the exodus story. The chapters in between describe the confrontations between Moses and the pharaoh, each contest ending in one more plague on the land. Still Pharaoh would not let the people go. God tells Moses about the last deadly plague in chapter 11; in chapter 12, all that God foretold takes place. But chapter 12 doesn't begin with the leave-taking or the plague of death. Rather, this chapter begins with liturgical rubrics laid out in great detail. This section comes from the Priestly writer intent on setting out

---

3. Abraham Joshua Heschel, *The Prophets* (New York: Harper & Row, 1962), 224–25.
4. Joseph Sittler, *Gravity and Grace: Reflections and Provocations*, ed. Linda-Marie Delloff (Minneapolis: Augsburg, 1986), 104, 105.

instructions in good order—the date exact, the preparations clear, the lamb without blemish. Everything is in order: provision for small households to join together, instructions for roasting the lamb, and warning to burn whatever remains before morning. One instruction has nothing to do with eating: take some of the blood and put it on the doorposts of the house. "The blood shall be a sign for you on the houses where you live: when I see the blood, I will pass over you, and no plague shall destroy you" (v. 13). This meal and this sign of life-saving blood are the roots of Passover. "No ceremony was more important in ancient Israel or early Judaism than Passover. To participate in the ritual was to remember and become a part of the story it celebrated."[5] At the Passover Seder, a child asks the question, "Why is this night different from all other nights?" The question is in the present tense.

Exodus is a story of reversals, of slaves set free and the powerful thrown down. This story has sustained Jewish people through pogroms and holocaust. This story became the freedom song of African American slaves in America. But there is a shadow side to the story: the firstborn of the Egyptians are slaughtered, both children and animals. Can there be freedom for some without destroying others? There is another story about a blood-red sign that could be a conversation partner with this passage. Joshua 2 tells the story of Rahab, the prostitute who saved the Hebrew spies sent on reconnaissance in Jericho. Before she let them down through her window in the wall, Rahab asked for a sign that her family would be spared. "Tie a crimson cord in your window," they said. "Gather all your family inside your house and you will be spared." The blood-red sign saved Rahab and her family, even though others in Jericho were destroyed. What would be changed if communities and nations saw the blood-red sign on the homes of all people?

Psalm 149 is a joyous celebration of victory reminiscent of Miriam's song at the sea (Exod. 15:20–21). Echoes of exodus reversals are heard as God "adorns the humble with victory" (Ps. 149:4). The psalmist invites the faithful to "sing for joy on their couches." Perhaps they are reclining for the Passover meal. Verses 6–8 celebrate vengeance, and this presses preachers and hearers to ask the question raised about the Egyptian deaths: can there be freedom for some without destroying others? That question is not only an ancient one. Perhaps Rahab could join Miriam to lead the dancing and singing, the two of them and the congregation finding new ways to celebrate without destroying one another.

5. Fred B. Craddock, John H. Hayes, Carl R. Holladay, and Gene M. Tucker, *Preaching Through the Christian Year: Year A* (Philadelphia: Trinity Press International, 1992), 429.

Simchat Torah: Joy of the Torah
(Mid-September to Early October)

Esther J. Hamori

DEUTERONOMY 33:1–5
GENESIS 1:1–5
JOSHUA 24:14–18
PSALM 119:57–64

Simchat Torah (pronounced sim-khat tor-ah) is a Jewish holiday celebrating the joy that comes with the gift of the Torah (the five books of Moses). In the synagogue, the Torah scrolls are taken from the ark into the congregation, often accompanied by dancing. Simchat Torah comes after Sukkot in the month of Tishrei (between mid-September and early October). The lectionary readings listed below reflect the practice of reading from Deuteronomy and Genesis in succession, honoring the Jewish practice of turning from the end of the Torah to its beginning. These readings (along with readings from the rabbinic tradition) remind us that interpretation involves ongoing conversation with the fullness of Scripture's many visions.

> Ben Bag-Bag used to say of the Torah: Turn it and turn it again, for everything is in it. Pore over it, and wax gray and old over it. Stir not from it for you can have no better rule than it. Ben Heh-Heh used to say: According to the effort is the reward.
>
> *Pirkei Avot*[1]

These texts highlight God's gift of the Torah and the choice we make—continually, repeatedly—to observe it and celebrate it. In the passage from Deuteronomy 33, we see Moses' final blessing of the Israelites, remembering the gift on Sinai; we then turn anew to the beginning of creation in Genesis 1. The passage from Joshua 24 tells of Joshua's charge to the Israelites to choose for themselves whom they will serve, and of the difficult commitment they

---

1. *Pirkei Avot* 5:25, 26.

choose. Psalm 119 expresses such a commitment individually. As we read the end of the story and the beginning again each year, we see both creation and the Torah itself afresh. We can take Simchat Torah as an invitation to renew our commitment, and as we read about God's *hesed*—God's love, justice, and mercy—filling the earth, we may consider anew how we can put into practice our love of what is just.

Deuteronomy 33:1–5

These are Moses' famous last words. The passage begins: "This is the blessing with which Moses, the man of God, blessed the Israelites before his death." Here, for the first time in the book of Deuteronomy, Moses is called a "man of God." This is not a generic term for a person of faith in the Hebrew Bible—it refers to a type of prophet. The main Hebrew word for "prophet" (*navi'*) is also used of Moses (e.g., Deut. 34:10). There is nothing in Moses' last words, however, that would provide a reason to give him this title only now. He is a prophet because of what he had already done before this time. For many people, the primary picture of a biblical prophet is that of a man rebuking the unfaithful and calling out for justice in the public square, or of someone encouraging the downtrodden through beautiful poetry about hope in God. Moses does not fit these pictures. So what exactly was his prophetic legacy?

It was, of course, the Torah. In verse 4, we hear Israel's voice celebrating their prophet: "Moses charged us with the law, as a possession for the assembly of Jacob." Another way to translate this would be, "Moses commanded for us the Torah, the heritage of the congregation of Jacob." This is what Simchat Torah celebrates: Moses gave us the Torah (which means "teaching," rather than "law"), and it is the heritage of the congregated peoples.

The Torah has not always fared well in Christian history. Anti-Judaism has taken different forms at different times: in some periods, Christians destroyed and burned Torahs and other Jewish books, and even today, it is common to hear the poisonous idea that Judaism is legalistic or spiritually dead. In addition to being offensive to Jews and Judaism, this is simply inaccurate. The practice of any religion can become rote, and it is always easier to see this in a tradition other than one's own.

The Torah is largely a laying out of ideas related to justice and instruction in social ethics. God commands us to take care of widows and orphans, not to abuse the poor, and so on—in short, to treat one another ethically. Throughout the history of Judaism, the heart of rabbinic commentary has been ongoing discussion about how to understand and apply the ancient teachings, always reevaluating and reinterpreting these for new contexts. (As a first-century Jew, Jesus participated in this tradition from within Judaism, just as other early Jewish teachers did.) Promulgating the negative views of the Torah mentioned above is not just a Christian theological perspective, though this has been the common rationale; it is a damaging mischaracterization of Jews and Judaism.

During the first century BCE in Jerusalem, Rabbi Hillel was asked how to summarize the Torah while standing on one foot. He responded, "That which you hate, do not do to others. That is the entire Torah; the rest is commentary. Go and learn it."[2] In other words, the core of the Torah is to love your neighbor as yourself. Note that the rest of the Torah is not excess material, however: it is commentary, explaining how to treat others with love and justice. This is why Hillel adds, "Go and learn it."

When the biblical prophets demand righteousness from the people and justice for the oppressed, they are basing this on the Torah. The famous demands for social justice in Micah 6 and Isaiah 51, for example, are both surrounded by the prophets' references to God's Torah (usually translated "instruction," "teaching," or "law"). This is the Teaching of justice that brings life, and we celebrate the chance to study it anew each year.

Genesis 1:1–5

On Simchat Torah, we finish reading Deuteronomy and immediately begin the annual cycle of weekly Torah readings again with Genesis 1, reminding us that the Torah is a never-ending story. This great celebration includes singing and dancing, and processing around the synagogue, sometimes spilling outdoors as well.

"In the beginning." What sense does it make to start reading here in the middle of Simchat Torah services, after having just read the end of Deuteronomy? Shouldn't this text be read at the beginning of something? The earth was formless and void, no? So why contemplate this right after the death of Moses, well into the story of the people of Israel?

The playwright Jon Adam Ross has developed a show that explores the cyclical relationship between Moses' last breath and Adam's first breath as read on Simchat Torah. Ross used an African folktale to illustrate this idea: There was once an old man and a baby yet to be born, crossing on a path. The old man said, "What's troubling you, young one?" The baby responded, "I'm scared; what's it like where I'm going?" The old man responded, "Oh, it's an amazing place. You'll live and laugh and celebrate." The baby seemed relieved, but then asked the old man, "Thanks! But what's troubling *you*, old man?" The old man said, "I, too, am scared. What's it like where *I'm* going?"

2. *Shabbat* 31a.

The baby responded. "Oh, it's an amazing place. You'll live and laugh and celebrate." In Ross's show, Moses and Adam crossed each other on the stage as they entered and exited the story, while the rabbi and a young child read this folktale.[3]

Simchat Torah brings together the end and the beginning, and we may see each story in a different light when reading them side by side. In Genesis 1, the idea of the earth being formless and void, with darkness over the face of the deep, might sit reasonably well with us. But what about after the death of Moses? The prophet and leader of the people has died, and now once again the darkness is over the face of the deep. The darkness is somehow darker this time around, reflecting the loss and trauma of human experience.

Similarly, reading only Genesis 1, it seems natural that at the creation of the world, God was there. Reading from the end of the Torah, we see that people have filled the earth, cities have flourished; we have lived, strived, and died, and darkness is once again over the face of the deep. But even now, God is present to start something new.

Gradually, we see the beginning of creation again. God speaks things into being, separates, organizes, and names. Reading this each year on Simchat Torah, instead of thinking, "Oh yes, the story of creation, I know this one," we may notice more the intricacy and diversity of God's creation. In verse 5, for instance, God calls the light Day and the darkness Night; "and there was evening and there was morning, the first day." This is not merely a separation of binary poles; note the multitude of names in this one verse! Light, day, morning, darkness, night, evening! God creates every different time of day: twilight, afternoon, midnight, dawn, dusk ... Reading this story after the death of Moses and the return of darkness, and after we have lived through the cycle of another year, we know each of these more intimately.

Joshua 24:14–18

It is all well and good to rejoice in the Torah: upon recognizing that this was God's gift of ethics, of instruction regarding how to treat others with justice and kindness, who wouldn't celebrate? We see over and over again in Scripture, however, that it is deeply embedded in human nature to know what is right, and to do otherwise.

Joshua charges the people to make a commitment: "Choose this day whom you will serve" (v. 15). The people respond quickly that of course they will serve the Lord, who freed them from slavery and protected them along the

3. Jon Adam Ross developed this show while working as artist in residence at Anshe Emet Synagogue in Chicago, 2005. Folktale and performance as summarized by Jon Adam Ross, private correspondence with author, February 15, 2010.

way as they passed through dangerous territory. If we stop reading here, the people's decision may appear easy enough. The continuation of the story, however, indicates that their choice was a little more complicated. Joshua is not satisfied by the people's initial statement, and he answers them, "You cannot serve the LORD!" (v. 19). This is a surprising response. But the people insist, and Joshua tells them that they are witnesses against themselves that they have chosen God. In other words, it is a serious commitment they are making, and they will need to live up to it. The people commit, and Joshua makes a covenant with them. The text tells us that Joshua "wrote these words in the book of the law of God" (v. 26) and initiated a ceremony of renewal.

There are many things we know to be right, to be just. However, knowing is not enough. Stating our position is not enough. It is dangerous to have high ideals: we will almost certainly not live up to them. Joshua's tough words remind us that it is not sufficient to say the right things; we are accountable for actually doing what is right, working for what is just. It is easy to say, "Racism is bad; anti-Judaism is bad; domestic violence and pornographic demeaning of women are bad," and so on. It can be harder to act accordingly—for example, in not tolerating injustice where we see it. As Joshua told the people, their choice is harder than making a simple statement. We might use Simchat Torah as an opportunity to renew our commitment to the Torah's emphasis on justice, and challenge ourselves to consider where we need to take just action.

Psalm 119:57–64

The whole of Psalm 119 is a celebration of Torah, and a declaration of passion to study and observe it. This is not just a matter of *feeling*, of loving God, and loving the ideas of mercy or justice. The psalmist is also utterly dedicated to *doing* what is right. As we saw in the previous text, in which Joshua emphasizes that claiming the Torah is not enough and claiming to be the people of God is not enough, we see here too that the psalmist's emphasis is on action. The poet says in verse 57, "I promise to *keep* your words," not just to read them or think about them. Verse 59 continues, "When I think of your ways, I turn my feet to your decrees." It will be encouraging to readers who are aware of their own imperfections to know that the word for "turn" here also frequently means "turn back." Perhaps at one point this person of faith did stray, but now, the psalmist's determination for justice is unyielding.

The poet celebrates that the earth is full of God's *hesed*. This Hebrew word has no English equivalent. It is often translated "loving-kindness," and it refers to love, justice, and mercy all wrapped together. This is what the Torah is. It instructs us in how to do *hesed*, and for this reason, on Simchat Torah we celebrate the gift of the Torah anew every year.

Proper 19

Carlos F. Cardoza-Orlandi

EXODUS 14:19–31
PSALM 114

GENESIS 50:15–21
PSALM 103:(1–7) 8–13
ROMANS 14:1–12
MATTHEW 18:21–35

Miracles abound in today's Scripture readings; however, they do not reflect popular ideas of supernatural miracles. Instead the miracles in these texts point to concrete experiences of liberation: they speak of God's justice and reconciliation embodied in forgiving one's enemies and caring for others.

Exodus 14:19–31 and Psalm 114

This is a miracle story of liberation. It is a miracle in the middle of a war based on vengeance and pride—notice that the Exodus text refers to the "army of Israel." Egypt and Pharaoh, after dramatic divine intervention, had no other choice but to comply with Moses' demand on behalf of God: "Let my people go." And so they did . . . apparently. The intervention of God in these liberation narratives points to the asymmetrical encounter and relationships between Pharaoh and his military regime and the recently but loosely organized army of liberated slaves. The most powerful military force of the region is pursuing a group of slaves who have been given a promise of land and stability. The asymmetry is abysmal, difficult to see and understand.

A couple of examples may help us "see" the asymmetry and, consequently, the danger that accompanies such a disproportionate encounter. One example is the Iberian-Amerindian encounter in the Americas during the era of *La Conquista*. Under the claim of Christian evangelization, the exploitation of Amerindians by *conquistadores* and *encomenderos* (those who were given a piece of land to evangelize the native people and keep them as slaves) ultimately generated a genocide, particularly in the Caribbean. Paradoxically, in the story of *La Conquista*, Iberian Christians may be compared to Pharaoh and the "heathen" Amerindians may be associated with the Israelites.

Another example, closer to our own historical time, is the persecution and death of Amerindian groups in Guatemala and other regions of Central America who suffered at the hand of self-identified *dictadores evangélicos* (evangelical dictators) and their military regimes during the civil unrest and wars of the 1970s to 1990s. Even some of the most conservative missionary groups from the United States working among Guatemalan Amerindians cautiously raised their voices to name the abuses to Amerindian *evangélicos* simply because they were Amerindian.[1]

In this text God intervenes to bring balance to an asymmetrical encounter. First, the reader finds the pillars of cloud and fire to keep a distance between the armies. The pillars provide time and space for Israel's withdrawal. Second, despite this intervention from God, the Egyptian army continues to pursue the Israelites and a second intervention occurs: God "clogged their chariot wheels so that they turned with difficulty." At this point the Egyptian army seems to recognize that the asymmetry of power which gave them a significant advantage and the promise of domination is divinely obliterated. They say, "Let us flee from the Israelites, for the LORD is fighting for them against Egypt."

The final verses (26–31) present problems for many of us. God violently wipes out the Egyptian army after they had decided to turn back. Consequently "the people feared the LORD and believed in the LORD and in his servant Moses" (v. 31). God's annihilation of their enemies becomes the foundation of their faith in God. This is a troublesome yet realistic position to take.

God's miraculous intervention balances the encounter, creating a level plain. But God takes it further; the oppressor is eliminated. Does this suggest that oppressors have no opportunity of being liberated except by their death? Does the death of the Egyptian army suggest that powers of domination and oppression need to be not only eradicated but also annihilated? The text shows the intention of the Egyptian army to reconquer and destroy the Israelites for the sake of asserting their power and restoring their pride. Was the Israelites' attempt to flee a temporary strategy? Did God see in the Egyptian army the absolute impossibility of redemption, and therefore death becomes the equalizer?

---

1. For more information on these historical events, see Luis Rivera-Pagán, *A Violent Evangelism: The Political and Religious Conquest of the Americas* (Louisville, KY: Westminster/ John Knox Press, 1992), and Carlos F. Cardoza-Orlandi, "Is There Morning without Joy? The Religious Experience of the Guatemalan Amerindians under Fire," *Koinonia* 1 (Spring 1993): 70–84.

If we discover that our Christian communities exercise asymmetrical power over others in ways that resemble the Egyptian army, what can we do? What kind of miracle would we need to bring about new life rather than seek the eradication of others by God? If our Christian communities resemble the Israelites, do we seek faith that is nourished by the death of others? What kind of miracle do we need to transform our memories, experiences, and expectations so that war and death are not the foundation of our faith and relationships with others?

Genesis 50:15–21

This final story in the lengthy saga of Joseph and his brothers adds another level of complexity to our understanding of relationships and the kind of miracles that generate faith, life, and peace. The level of complexity this text offers is fear of retaliation, particularly when asymmetrical relationships shift: here the oppressed person (Joseph) could become the oppressor and those who oppressed him (his brothers) could now become the oppressed.

During the difficult dialogue regarding apartheid in South Africa, many Dutch Reformed Christians prophetically spoke against apartheid. Yet they were cautious when imagining the future. In theological dialogues, particularly among Christian communities in the Reformed family, it was common for many Western Reformed theologians and Christian leaders to raise the theological principle of "total depravity" as a subtle and cautious argument against change. The question was: could the oppressed become the new oppressor? It was a valid concern that has taken many years to address as indigenous persons who were oppressed have sought truth and reconciliation with their white oppressors.

I love my mother tongue, Spanish. When I meet people who speak my mother tongue, I immediately shift to Spanish. Yet I have to do more than change languages. I have to modify my Spanish if I am speaking to a Mexican, Nicaraguan, Argentinean, or Spaniard. We all have different nuances of language, but we can still communicate. However, during more than twenty years of living in the United States it never fails that, in my place of work, when I am speaking with someone in my mother tongue, others around us say, "You two are dangerous. What are you plotting?" At the beginning I did not know what to answer. I was too perplexed. Later, I began to reply with some level of retaliation, "Yes, we are planning a coup d'état and you are on the list for eradication." More recently, I remain silent and saddened. I have come to the conclusion that we think about retaliation because of who we think we are (the focus of others' agendas), what we have done (now it is the other person's turn to retaliate), and who we have become (the oppressed person become the oppressor).

The miracle of this text—and the insight offered in it—is that Joseph does not retaliate, but rather forgives and reconciles with those who have hurt him. Joseph does not become an oppressor, as his brothers expected!

It is interesting how different languages suggest differences in interpretation. In the Spanish Bible *Dios Habla Hoy*, Joseph's brothers send a messenger who appeals to Joseph based on the request of Joseph's father. Joseph is moved, and then his brothers enter the scene and humble themselves before Joseph (vv. 16–19).[2] According to the New Revised Standard Version, Joseph's brothers "approached" or "commanded" Joseph based on the fictitious appeal of their father. Both Joseph and his brothers weep at the encounter. In the former version, a mediator is present. In the latter, the encounter seems to be more direct. Cultures do have codes of interaction in times when retaliation is expected. Yet the miracle emerges in Joseph's theological reflection—his *testimonio*—of his life journey: "Do not be afraid! Am I in the place of God?" (v. 19). God intended Joseph's journey to be for the good . . . of Joseph alone? No. For the "good, in order to preserve a numerous people, as he is doing today" (v. 20).

Joseph's reinterpretation of his journey, his *testimonio*, is the miracle that transforms the possibility of retaliation into renewed relationships and reconciliation. Joseph embodies the biblical hope that the oppressed do not have to become the oppressor. It is possible for change to occur without retaliation!

Psalm 103:(1–7) 8–13

This text challenges the image that we might get from the narrative of Exodus, and yet it points to Joseph's words and actions in Genesis. Only God may vindicate the oppressed. Both Joseph and the psalmist know God's place and asymmetrical power. Joseph is not God, and the psalmist knows that humans are not to vindicate anyone. God's asymmetrical relationship with creation locates God's activity in a different sphere.

"The LORD is merciful and gracious, slow to anger and abounding in steadfast love" (v. 8). The character of God is not to "deal with us according to our sins, nor repay us according to our iniquities" (v. 10). God's character is paradigmatic: God's asymmetrical power in relation to us is grounded in steadfast love for us, and this love is the source of our salvation. Paradoxically, the power asymmetry is to our advantage!

One of the most demanding crosscultural mission experiences is to live on other people's terms. There is no equality of terms when we engage with others according to their customs and practices. This is also true in the

2. *La Biblia de Estudio: Dios Habla Hoy* (Puerto Rico: Sociedades Bíblicas Unidas, 1994).

human-creation encounter. We never interact and relate with one another under the same terms or conditions. Our personal and collective histories, our class and economic circumstances, gender and sexual orientation, and our ethnicity or race shape the encounters and dynamics we experience and may frustrate our expectations. For example, a group of dedicated Anglo American Christians may be eager to begin a Hispanic/Latino/a ministry only to discover that the Hispanic/Latino/a community is cautious, perhaps even resistant to the hospitality offered to them. The Anglo American group may wonder why they are resistant, and may be oblivious to how the media portray Anglo American opinions of Hispanics/Latinos/as. Paradoxically, the power asymmetry—namely, Anglo American power over Hispanics/Latinos/as—is not beneficial to the latter group. This differential in power is far from gracious and redemptive. What kind of miracle is possible in this situation? Might the miracle be an inversion of power or the paradoxical use of power by those who are willing to give over their power to others and receive the God-given gifts and empowerment of those they seek to serve? Are we called to imitate God through the power of the Holy Spirit?

Romans 14:1–12

Paul immediately addresses this same point. Asymmetrical power is rigid if we live only for ourselves! Consequently war, death, retaliation, vindication, and a culture that seeks pleasure and redemption at the expense, and even death of others, are justified.

The text begins with an appeal to break asymmetrical relationships: "welcome those who are weak in faith, but not for the purpose of quarreling over opinions" (v. 1). To welcome and accept the weak as a source for vindication and retaliation is sinful. Paul strongly suggests breaking the asymmetry by granting the weak equality before God: "we will all stand before the judgment seat of God" (v. 10b). Paul's unique equalizer belongs to the eschatological realm. Regretfully, many Christians, particularly in the West, dismiss the eschaton as a real historical event. Many Christians in Africa, Asia, and Latin America think about the eschaton as the point where eternal life or eternal damnation is determined. Few Christians see the eschaton as an equalizer with current consequences—what we do today determines how our future is shaped.

However, Paul is stubbornly clear for whom Christians are to live: "We do not live to ourselves, and we do not die to ourselves. If we live, we live to the Lord, and if we die, we die to the Lord" (vv. 7–8a). Consequently, asymmetrical power dynamics find an equalizer in the fact that we live on the Lord's terms.

Matthew 18:21–35

This text is incredibly powerful and challenging. The asymmetry of power is clearly demonstrated in this text. Power is first used to claim payment of debt. Not paying the debt would result in further exploitation. The king wanted what belonged to him. Yet the text provides a dialogue: the slave implores mercy and the king is moved to forgiveness. A miracle happens. Power is used to forgive. Forgiveness is the key to understanding the way asymmetrical power is to be transformed. Power is ultimately intended for liberation and reconciliation.

Nevertheless, it seems that the text also raises and answers our previous question: could the oppressed become oppressors? For Matthew it seems that the answer is yes. The forgiven slave becomes oppressor of another slave. Yet the ultimate source of power in the parable, the king, uses his power to raise a question to the forgiven slave: "I forgave you all that debt because you pleaded with me. Should you not have had mercy on your fellow slave, as I had mercy on you?" (vv. 32b–33). Should mercy generate mercy? Should forgiveness generate forgiveness? Should liberation generate liberation? Should reconciliation generate reconciliation? Yes, they should!

But the starting point is one of radical, unconditional forgiveness. The story does not tell us whether the king had previously been forgiven. Forgiveness emerges out of the goodness of the king. Forgiveness emerges, according to the NRSV, "out of pity" for the slave. I do not like the popular understanding of "pity." It might suggest a kind of cheap grace. However, "out of pity" might also suggest "out of shame." But whose shame? Shame for the slave? Shame of the king who, despite his wealth and power, continues to demand more—and from a slave?

The King James Version offers the word "compassion" instead: the king forgave the slave "out of compassion." The Spanish Bible *Dios Habla Hoy* also suggests compassion, "el rey tuvo compasión" (the king had compassion). The *Reina Valera* version takes it to another level, "movido a compasión" (moved to compassion) or "movido a misericordia" (moved to mercy).[3] What moves the king to forgiveness generates many interesting perspectives about a first step toward using asymmetrical power for the benefit of others. But two things are critical: first, there needs to be a turning point of discontinuity in the way asymmetrical power is conceived and used in our communities. Second, such turning points of discontinuity, in the power of the Holy Spirit,

---

3. *La Biblia de Jerusalén*, 1989, www.bibliacatolica.com.br/la-biblia-de-Jerusalen/mateo/18, and *La Santa Biblia*, versión Reina Valera, 1960, http://www.biblegateway.com/passage/?search =Matthew%2018:21-35&version=RVR1960 and http://www.biblegateway.com/passage/?search =Matthew%2018:21-35&version=RVR19771960.

break the power *continuum* of asymmetrical relationships by offering a different way of using and distributing power: with kind acts of reciprocity.

Consequently, the miracle spoken of here has to do with the character
of the Christian community—a community that thrives not simply in the
changing of structures for justice, but in the peaceful acts of offering what we
have been given by God: a memory of liberation, an experience of justice and
reconciliation, and an expectation of living in a community that engenders
peace and communion with each other and creation. This is the miracle the
world needs today!

International Day of Prayer and Witness for Peace (September 21)

Willard Swartley

MICAH 4:1–5
PSALM 67
EPHESIANS 2:11–22
MATTHEW 26:47–56

In 1981, the United Nations established Peace Day for individuals and communities to take practical steps for peace, such as lighting candles, organizing public events, observing a Day of Ceasefire, and making peace in personal and political relationships. In 2002, the UN set September 21 as the permanent Peace Day. In 2004, the World Council of Churches designated September 21 (or the closest Sunday) as International Day of Prayer for Peace. We enlarge the title to International Day of Prayer and Witness for Peace to encourage churches to repent of our complicity in violence, to pray for peace, and to take other actions that witness to God's will for all peoples to live together in *shalom*.

> Christians love their enemies because God does so, and commands his followers to do so. . . . Human wrath does not accomplish the justice of God. . . . When the Christian whom God has disarmed lays aside carnal weapons it is not, in the last analysis, because those weapons are too strong, but because they are too weak. [We direct our lives] toward the day when all creation will praise not kings and chancellors but the Lamb that was slain as worthy to receive blessing and honor and glory and power (Revelation 5:12–13).
>
> *John Howard Yoder*[1]

1. John Howard Yoder, *He Came Preaching Peace* (Scottdale, PA: Herald Press, 1985), 20–29.

These four texts consist of visions of and witness to God's peace incarnated among humans and nations. The Hebrew Bible texts were penned by the prophet Micah and the psalmist against the context of many wars and impending exile because of Israel's rebellion against God's moral prescriptions for community life (Exod. 20:1–17). Israel's idolatries, Sabbath desecrations, and killing in wars brought judgment. The vision for peace is eschatological. The Gospel and Epistle texts voice the reality of a new creation, birthed by the incarnate Word, Jesus Christ, who in the Matthew text renounced violence in the face of impending arrest and crucifixion. Set against the *Pax Romana* of the time—a tenuous peace of violence, subjugation, and oppression—the Ephesians text celebrates peace achieved: former enemies become fellow pilgrims in one new body of Christ. Jesus is the peacemaker, and his body of peace, the church, witnesses to peace before a watching world, where wars and rumors of war continue.

Micah 4:1–5

"In days to come . . ." What a way to begin the vision for peace and security. Is it always in the future? Micah's visionary text of beating "swords into plowshares" parallels Isaiah's (2:1–4). When two of Israel's great prophets stir the hopes of the people in this way, history had better listen to prophecy. The shape of the future will differ from the past.

Many nations will stream to Jerusalem, for from its symbolic center of divine presence, Zion, instruction will go forth; indeed, "the word of the LORD" will sound out across the mountains and valleys (Mic. 4:2b). Many nations will hear and come to receive it as well as their judgment. Who will "beat their swords into plowshares, and their spears into pruning hooks" (v. 3b)? The nations will. Indeed, "nation shall not lift up sword against nation, neither shall they learn war any more" (v. 3c). What a vision! When will it come to pass?

Israel secured its borders and refused the words of the prophets. Instead of fulfilling God's promise to Abraham to be a blessing to the nations, Israel wielded weapons to destroy their adversaries. Sometimes northern Israel and southern Judah fought internally (2 Chr. 25:17–24; Judah provoked the war, but Israel won). Micah's vision judged Israel for its warring ways and instilled hope that the future would be better. Who then will take the lead? The Israel of today, with its arsenal of weapons, is certainly not doing it. Nor is the United States, with its 800 military bases around the world. Nations seek security by stockpiling weapons. Where does hope for the fulfillment of this prophecy lie?

Beyond the cessation of war, a vision of security emerges: they shall all sit under their own vines and under their own fig trees. In Palestinian culture this is a powerful image, since Palestinians now are losing their fig trees daily. They are losing their symbol of security, of being at peace and not afraid. They are also losing a source of nourishment and livelihood. They are losing their houses as well. "Sitting under the fig tree" connotes both safety from threat of war and violence and freedom to meditate on God's word, the instruction of the Lord going out to the nations (4:2c; cf. guileless Nathaniel in John 1:47–48). And no one shall make them afraid. Fear eats the soul, constructs enemies, and dehumanizes the "other." Witness the result of 9/11 in the American psyche and the consequent war and devastation in Iraq and Afghanistan. Is prophetic vision real, or only a dreamer's mirage?

The final phrase of verse 4, "for the mouth of the LORD of hosts has spoken," parallels the end of verse 2, "the word of the LORD [goes out] from Jerusalem." A key point of this text is the power of the Lord's word. What Israel lacked then, and nations lack today, is trust in the Lord and the prophetic word. This was Isaiah's reprimand to King Ahaz when he was mustering troops for war. Bernhard Anderson suggests we translate Isaiah 7:9b, "If your faith is not sure, you will not be secure."[2] Herein lay the downfall of the nations. They stockpile weapons but do not do what prophetic Scripture teaches. Whence comes fulfillment?

Micah 4:5 answers when and how this prophetic word is fulfilled: when the peoples of the earth have freedom to walk (live), "each in the name of its god," and those of us who claim this text as Scripture truly "walk in the name of the LORD our God forever and ever."

Psalm 67

Psalm 67 represents an authentic word of praise. It reflects the same themes as Micah's prophecy—"that your way may be known upon earth, your saving power among all nations" (v. 2)—grounded in God's graciousness, blessing, and face shining upon us. The call to worship is to all the peoples (v. 5). This is not a provincial comfort for my, or even our, soul, but a social, political reality that embraces the peoples of the earth. Indeed, "Let the nations be glad and sing for joy, for you judge the peoples with equity and guide the nations upon earth. *Selah*" (v. 4). I take that *Selah* to be an ancient version of Jesus' "Truly, truly, I say . . ." It is the clap of joy, the "Amen" of African American worship. The praise and blessing resounds again, and again, until "all the ends of the earth revere him" (v. 7b).

---

2. Anderson shared his translation of this text with an OT biblical theology class at Princeton Theological Seminary in 1969–1970.

Matthew 26:47–56

The Gospel and Epistle texts point the way. In Matthew 26:47–56, Jesus refuses to repay in kind. When swords flash at his arrest by the religious authorities who are colluding with the Roman political power, Jesus halts the natural human response when one of his disciples draws his sword and lops off the ear of the high priest's servant—a fortunate amateur's aim. Jesus' memorable words ring down the nations' defense corridors of the ages: "Put your sword back into its place; for all who take the sword will perish by the sword" (v. 52). This reality is evident throughout history. History books are often structured around wars fought, won, or lost. The stories of peacemaking are often neglected.[3]

We cannot say that Jesus was nonresistant only because he had no power to do otherwise. Jesus disabuses us of this way of thinking: "Do you think that I cannot appeal to my Father, and he will at once send me more than twelve legions of angels?" (v. 53). With faith like Elisha's (2 Kgs. 6) or Hezekiah's (2 Kgs. 18–19), Jesus could have miraculously blinded or thrown into confusion the "large crowd with swords and clubs" who came to arrest him (v. 47).

But Jesus did not do it. Instead, he broke the cycle of violence, taking it into himself, exposing the violence in his suffering. As John Howard Yoder, responding to Girard's thesis on violence as endemic in human history, puts it,

> If the phenomenon of violence is not rational in its causes, its functions, its objectives, neither will its cure be rational. The cure will have to be something as primitive, as elemental, as the evil. It will have to act upon the deep levels of meaning and motivation, deeper than mental self-definition and self-control. It will have to be sacrifice. There will have to be innocent suffering. . . .
>
> The response that is needed is then not a new way to think about it—what we might properly call a "theological critique"—but something to be done about it. The response is divine judgment, not an explanation, not an evaluation, but an intervention.
>
> The name of that intervention is Jesus.[4]

With Jesus as "intervention," a new way of thinking, acting, and living opens. Those who enter the kin(g)dom beat "swords into plowshares." Jesus introduces a new politics and a new model for imitating (*mimēsis*) the One whose *desire* does not generate violence. Jesus frees us from the reflexive

---

3. James Juhnke and Carol M. Hunter, *The Missing Peace: The Search for Nonviolent Alternatives in United States History* (Scottdale, PA: Herald Press, 2001). See also Willard M. Swartley, *Covenant of Peace: The Missing Peace in New Testament Theology and Ethics* (Grand Rapids: Eerdmans, 2006), 431–71.
4. John Howard Yoder, "Theological Critique of Violence," *New Conversations* 16, no. 3 (Fall 1994): 3–4, 5.

response of repaying sword with sword. "Love of enemy" smites the sword, the violence, and opens a new reality.

Ephesians 2:11–22

Ephesians 2:11–22 tells this story. Former enemies, alienated from God, become one through Christ whom God sent into human history and culture as the peacemaker to create a new human reality. The alienated and uncircumcised Gentiles enter the remnant household of God (vv. 11–12). The biggest "but" in the Bible marks the end of that alien existence: "But now in Christ Jesus you who once were far off have been brought near by the blood of Christ. For he is our peace; in his flesh he has made both groups into one and has broken down the dividing wall, that is, the hostility between us" (vv. 13–14).

Paul's peacemaking manifesto marks the end of ethnic rivalry, hatred, violence, and war. "This passage, which posits enmity and peace to be antithetical, marks the crucifixion of Christ as a turning point. It declares Christ to be the bringer of peace, the one providing access to God as well as creating a new unity for those once separated in this world and living as enemies, objectively speaking."[5]

Those "far off" in verse 17 are here not diaspora Jews, as in Isaiah 57:19, but enemy Gentiles who are now brought near. Christ's peacemaking "has broken down the dividing wall, that is, the hostility between us" (v. 14b). How did this happen? It happened by Jesus refusing to repay in kind but rather making peace between the warring parties so that he "might reconcile both groups to God in one body through the cross, thus putting to death that hostility through it" (v. 16). The Greek literally says killing the hostility in him, or, by the cross. The cross plucks out the roots of rivalry, hatred, violence, and war. Jesus Christ becomes our peacemaking, redemption, truth, righteousness, wisdom, and love. We celebrate new life because we

- have access in one Spirit to the Father;
- are no longer strangers and aliens, but citizens with the saints;
- are also members of the household of God, with Christ Jesus himself as the cornerstone. In him the whole structure is joined together and grows into a holy temple in the Lord; in whom we also
- are built together spiritually into a dwelling place for God.

5. Erich Dinkler, "*Eirēnē*—The Early Christian Concept of Peace," in *The Meaning of Peace*, ed. Perry B. Yoder and Willard M. Swartley, rev. ed. (Elkhart, IN: Institute of Mennonite Studies, 2001), 95–96.

The first and last of these blessings in Christ signify vertical relationships. We each and together have access to God and God dwells with all of us in Christ. The old temple with "fences" that limit access is gone. In Christ Jesus, we are all holy to God (echoing Ps. 99).

This marvelous text mentions "peace" four times and "both one" four times. It is a good baptismal or confirmation text for every candidate to memorize. Such a word, recited before the congregation, sears peace and peacemaking into the soul, welcoming peacemaking to its rightful place in Christian living, Christian ethics, and Christian theology.

How then are we to live this peace today? And who are the "we"? It is Jesus-people, who seek to live the vision. It follows that we are the ones needed to witness to the earthly nations, just as Micah and the psalmist did, to stir and guide the conscience of the nation toward peace, breaking down barriers of enmity, renouncing violence, and seeking friendship with the opposition, at home and abroad. With "middle axioms"[6] we connect Jesus' model of love and justice to the nations of this world.

---

6. John Howard Yoder (*The Christian Witness to the State* [Newton, KS: Faith and Life Press, 1964; 2nd ed., Scottdale, PA: Herald Press, 2002]) uses "middle axioms" to describe the church's witness to the state. Such witness advocates moral values that stand in continuity with the church's ethic, but recognizes that government at its best only approximates Jesus' ethic. The goal of this witness is to assist the state to be more moral than it is, to choose the better of several alternatives. The church speaks from Jesus' moral standard of God's will for human life to "the state" but uses a middle language. To illustrate, rather than counsel the state to love its enemy, the church advocates a course of action that most reduces enmity and that is most likely to develop friendly relations.

Proper 20

Catherine Gunsalus González and Justo L. González

EXODUS 16:2–15
PSALM 105:1–6, 37–45

JONAH 3:10–4:11
PSALM 145:1–8
PHILIPPIANS 1:21–30
MATTHEW 20:1–16

In these passages, everyone seems to be laboring. The parable of the Workers in the Vineyard speaks of those who seek work and find it at different times of the day. In his Letter to the Philippians, Paul prefers staying in this life because of the work he can do, and he calls on the Philippians to join in that work. In Jonah, the work of creation is God's labor. Both psalms speak of the great works that God has accomplished. Only the Exodus passage does not deal with this theme. However, closely related to labor is the theme of food. For most of us, our labor, our employment, is a means of providing money for the necessities of life. The workers in the vineyard need to work in order to eat, and there is desperation in the voices of those who have waited all day and still have no work. In the verses from Exodus the Israelites are afraid they will not have enough food, and they remember with fondness the meals they had in Egypt. Even slavery was better than their new freedom without food! Both of these themes—work and food—are of major importance for justice. Injustices that restrict access to either of these leads to stunted lives and death. For the preacher who seeks to emphasize justice, these passages provide ample opportunity to do so.

Matthew 20:1–16

This Gospel passage is probably familiar to most Christians. The owner of a vineyard seeks workers throughout the day. To the first group he offers "the usual daily wage," and he promises to pay the others "whatever is right" (v. 4). At the end, each receives a full day's wage, and the early workers complain that they have been treated unfairly. If we understand that the employer is

401

God, and the wage is eternal life with God, then it makes perfect sense that even those who come to faith late in their lives receive the same eternal life with God. Surely those who have lived with the knowledge and experience of God's love and mercy for fifty years should not complain about those who come to such knowledge only a few weeks before they die! Rather, those early believers should rejoice that they lived with such joy and grace so many years.

However, were we to transfer the parable to a work situation in our society, it would look quite different. There seems to be a great injustice here. And yet the workers who came late had spent the whole day seeking to be hired. They lived with the possibility that they would receive no wage and their family would go hungry.

It is quite easy to move from the parable to the current situation of day laborers waiting for someone in a truck to drive by and call for a few of them to come and work. Justice looks different to those who are employed than to those who seek work and do not find it. Whose perspective are we to take in our search for justice? In many of these situations, even those who work all day are denied a good wage. Especially if those hired are immigrants—and particularly if they are immigrants without papers—employers may feel free to deny them any wage at all when they have labored all day. The desperation is there in almost all day-labor pools: no work, no food. No human being should live in such desperation. Those who live with the security of employment need to feel the fear of those who lack such security. In a bad economy, even those who once felt secure may begin to feel sympathy for those who have lived year after year with such fear. The end of the parable shows an employer who holds each worker as deserving of a wage that supports life. Even the time they spent waiting for work was in itself work.

The church must be on the side of those who search for work and do not find it until the last hour. The church has every reason to work against the exploitation of workers who have no recourse against employers who defraud them—in wages or in safe working conditions.

The question may still be raised, is it not an injustice that those who were hired later received the same wage as those who worked all day? Is it not an injustice to seek work and not find it? The justice of God is gracious, and is concerned for both those who have work and those who do not.

Philippians 1:21–30

Paul is not saying that this life—life in the flesh—is a bad thing. Rather, his desire to be with Christ is so strong that he would prefer to be with Christ in the life beyond death than in this life. However, since Christ has work for him to do in this world, he will gladly remain. Some Christians are so concerned about the life to come that they have little interest in this world. That is not Paul's message here, but it could be so misconstrued if care is not taken.

Paul is not afraid of joining those who are suffering. He plans to visit them again, and gives them directions for living faithfully in the present time. Both Paul's actions in preferring to be with those who suffer rather than to seek his own happiness, and his words to the Philippians, are important for us. His choice of solidarity with the Philippians is modeled on the work of Christ, who chose to be with humanity, oppressed by the forces of sin and evil, rather than remain in the glory of God. In fact, Paul's words here are a prelude to the hymn in Philippians 2:1–11 that immediately follows today's passage. Paul has the "mind . . . [that] was in Christ" and he makes the same choice that Christ made (v. 5). Paul calls on the Philippians to follow this model as well.

Paul urges the Philippians to live a life "worthy of the gospel." He makes the same call to us. Most of us are in a different situation than the ancient Christians in Philippi. They were being oppressed by those who found the gospel repulsive and sought to turn Christians from their faith. In general, we live in a society that does not directly oppose the gospel. Perhaps if we were truly faithful, if our lives were lived in love for the poor, in opposition to the forces that like to keep things as they are, we too would experience greater oppression. In many ways, our society gives lip service to the gospel but supports structures and policies that deny the love of neighbor that the gospel proclaims.

Paul knew in his own experience the suffering that faithfulness brings, and he urges the Philippians not to be afraid of that suffering. He calls us to live in that fashion as well, and to take the side of those whose faithful lives bring them the hostile response that Christ, Paul, and the Philippians willingly endured.

Jonah 3:10–4:11

Jonah is a very reluctant prophet. He does not want to urge the people of Nineveh to repent, because they are the great enemies of Israel. He would prefer to see them destroyed by God. He finally does obey and is quite successful! They repent, and the passage for today picks up at that point. Because of the people's repentance, God decides not to destroy the city. For this reason, Jonah is angry with God, sits down, and pouts. Even more, he decides life is not worth living, because his enemies have been saved from God's wrath.

Christians are not exempt from such feelings. The nation's enemies are ours as well, and to seek their good is viewed as traitorous. The first casualty of war is the truth about the enemy. Dehumanizing those we oppose is the first step in propaganda. They now are seen as evil incarnate, and any sympathy for them is unpatriotic. Jonah was caught in this bind: he was successful as a prophet but he felt that as a loyal Israelite, he had failed.

The rest of the story pits God's attitude toward Nineveh against Jonah's. Jonah has forgotten that God is not only the God of Israel but also the true God of the Ninevites, even though they do not know it. God is the creator of all nations. Israel is given this knowledge and therefore has the task of proclaiming it to all. God not only created the Ninevites but also labored to allow Nineveh to become a great city.

God creates a plant to shade Jonah from the sun, and Jonah is pleased. Then God destroys the plant, and Jonah again is angry. God's major point is that Jonah is sad because the plant is destroyed, and yet he did not labor in its creation. God created the Ninevites and their great city, and shouldn't God be angry if it has to be destroyed? At the end of this book, God says that there were a hundred and twenty thousand children in Nineveh and also many animals. All were created by God and deserved to be saved. This is an important passage as we consider ecological concerns. God is the creator of the whole world, and even animals and plants are loved by God. Justice is due to them also. Our concern for God's justice encompasses not only the enemies of our nation—or our social group—but the whole of creation as well.

Psalm 145:1–8

The psalm selected to go with the Jonah passage emphasizes God's mercy and love for all, because God's wondrous works include all of creation. The company of the faithful praises the characteristics of God that Jonah particularly disliked in his encounter with Nineveh! God is praised for showing goodness and righteousness, and God's goodness is seen in mercy and forgiveness. Human goodness is often defined as hatred for the enemies of society. Our understanding of goodness should be based on the character of God, not on the attitudes of a fallen world. Verse 8 in particular points to God's great mercy and slowness to anger.

If the emphasis in the Jonah passage is on God's love for all of creation, including the animals, then it would be very helpful to include verse 9 of this psalm, since that verse echoes the message of Jonah, that God who created all things loves all that has been created and seeks its welfare.

Jonah was aware of the character of God revealed in this psalm. He knew that God seeks the redemption of all. He also knew that he did not like these divine characteristics, yet he did not hide the fact that God is indeed merciful.

It is helpful to remember that the psalms were used in Israel's worship. They were major instruments in shaping the faith of the people. If a congregation constantly sings hymns that speak of God's love for all that has been created, then the message of the need to be concerned for all creation is easier to proclaim. Pastors should be involved in the selection of hymns that are sung by the congregation, aware that these may have a greater impact on the people's faith than the sermon itself. What we sing and what we pray in our worship has an enormous impact on what we believe.

Exodus 16:2–15; Psalm 105:1–6, 37–45

The exodus had barely begun. The people had seen the great power of God in forcing the Egyptians to let them leave. In fact, the Egyptians were so afraid that they did not stop the Hebrews from taking silver and gold with them. The mighty hand of God was seen in the deliverance of the Hebrews and in their progress across the sea. However, the people were now afraid that they would not have enough to eat in the desert. When they were slaves in Egypt, they had a diet that now seemed wonderful. The passage from Exodus includes their complaints, although the psalm only mentions the gracious response of God.

In the Exodus passage it is clear that if there is enough food, even oppression may be preferable to the specter of starvation. It does not seem that hunger had become extreme—it was still quite early in the journey—and yet the fear of starvation made them wish for a return to Egypt, even with its oppression. We should not be surprised that many in our own day prefer the oppression under which they live to an unknown future that can kill in its own way. The battered wife or the alien who works for very little money in harsh conditions may fear that freedom could be worse than their present circumstances if there is no guarantee of food. While the Israelites were being directly led by God, the battered wife or alien may have to survive at the mercy of a society that has often been hostile or uncaring toward them. We once heard a Central American say that it would be a privilege to be exploited: that would at least mean that they were employed! Does the church have a role in providing security for the future of those who are fearful of leaving their oppressive situation?

God promises the people food, but says that this is a test. Will they be obedient if they have food? Those of us who are not afraid of hunger in the foreseeable future have little excuse not to be obedient. The Israelites are to gather only enough for the one day, with the exception of the day before the Sabbath. As we know from the rest of the story, they did not obey. Many collected more manna than they should have, trying to hoard it—and God undid their injustice!

Psalm 105 begins with praise for God's faithfulness to the covenant. The people are to remember all of God's marvelous works on their behalf, obviously including what happened in the exodus. The latter part of the psalm speaks of the security the people now have. Christians of the two-thirds world have remarked to those of us in the one-third world that it is easier to be a Christian when you are poor and live in a poor country than when you are rich and have power. Those of us who have the security of food and other necessities have no excuse for disobedience, but it appears that the more security God gives us, the less we trust in God. Instead, we constantly search for more and more security. To be secure in this world's goods should be seen as a test. Will we be faithful? Will we use what we have for God's purposes or hoard it for ourselves, always afraid of not having enough? The purpose of security is to be free to follow God's will. The poor person must seek the necessities of life—and trust in God's justice. The person who already has enough must help provide what others need—and also trust in God's justice. Both must remember the lesson of the exodus: the security of sufficient resources is for the sake of obedience, not an end in itself.

Proper 21

Noelle Damico

EXODUS 17:1–7   PSALM 78:1–4, 12–16
EZEKIEL 18:1–4, 25–32   PSALM 25:1–9
                                    PHILIPPIANS 2:1–13
                                    MATTHEW 21:23–32

"Is the LORD among us or not?" ask the newly liberated Israelites as they search for water in the wilderness. The texts for Proper 21 explore the ambiguity of God's presence and action in our world and the challenge of remaining faithful. Exodus recounts the people's anxiety and vulnerability as they wonder whether God is with them in the wilderness. In Ezekiel, God speaks to the Judean leaders exiled in Babylon. God reproves them for blaming their ancestors for their current trials and challenges their understanding of divine judgment. In Psalm 78, the psalmist extols God's presence with the Hebrew people, enumerating God's wrath and compassion since the exodus. In Psalm 25, the psalmist petitions God amid difficulty, seeking to know God's ways. Writing from jail, Paul reminds the Philippian assembly that faithfulness to Christ makes its own trouble in a world dominated by Rome. And in Matthew, Jesus is confronted by priests and scribes who challenge his authority to instruct and heal.

Exodus 17:1–7 and Ezekiel 18:1–4, 25–32

In our passages from Exodus and Ezekiel, the Hebrew people are living contingently in wilderness and exile. These passages explore the human tendency to doubt God and blame others during hard times. In Exodus, God provides food and water to the freed slaves, encouraging their trust. In Ezekiel, God instructs the exiles in Babylon to begin taking responsibility for their own lives and choices.

No sooner has Miriam finished her exultant victory song than the book of Exodus recounts three stories that reveal the Hebrew people's need and

407

anxiety. First the water at Marah is bitter and they fear they will die of thirst. God sweetens the water so they can drink (15:23–25). When they are in the wilderness of Sin, the people fear they will die of hunger. God provides manna from heaven, daily nourishment, equitably distributed to all (16:1–16). As their journey continues, the people reach Rephidim. Again they find no water and again the people are fearful. Despite God's act of liberation and concrete responses to their worries about sustenance, they do not yet trust that God will make a way for them.

God provided yesterday, but will God again provide for us today? In fear and frustration they turn on Moses, "Why did you bring us out of Egypt, to kill us and our children and livestock with thirst?" (17:3b). Yet again God provides water, instructing Moses to go ahead of the people and strike the rock at Horeb. The writer of Exodus explains that Moses then names that place where water poured forth "Test" and "Quarrel" because the Israelites challenged, "Is the LORD among us or not?" (17:7).

Despite Moses' frustration, the questions, uncertainty, and impatience of the people reflect the frightening contingency of their situation. Yes, God freed them dramatically from bondage in Egypt, but now they are in the wilderness. How can they be assured of God's continued presence when the resources for life are not apparent? It is a legitimate question. When they were slaves they lived and died, worked and ate at the hands of their overlords. Slavery had a certain security when it came to food and housing and schedules. Now freed, this community of vulnerable people must figure out how to survive. They are frightened by the possibility of God's abandonment. They are not yet able or ready to trust God or themselves.

Similar disorientation and anxiety is frequently experienced by men and women who are released from prison after serving many years. They are thrust back into the world with little to no resources, fewer connections, and a rap sheet. It is not easy to start anew, and nearly impossible to do so without a decent job and a community of support. Desperate, many people turn to crime to survive or, overwhelmed, take their own lives.[1]

While Moses is impatient with the people, God is patient. God continues to demonstrate that "God will provide" for them as they walk into a new and uncertain life together.

---

1. People have endeavored to address these problems for many years. See a 1916 article from the *New York Times* about a former offender who founded The Prisoners' Relief Society in Huntington, West Virginia, at http://query.nytimes.com/gst/abstract.html?res=F50B15FE 355B17738DDDAA0894DF405B868DF1D3 (accessed October 1, 2010). In our own day the movement for restorative justice advocates repairing the harm caused by crime by bringing together victims, offenders, and community members; see www.restorativejustice.org.

The book of Ezekiel was written from exile in Babylon by a single author, likely a priest who probably participated in the first deportation in 597 BCE. It is filled with vivid oracles of judgment, doom, and restoration. In this passage, God challenges the despondent exiles.

Without power or the perceptible possibility of changing their circumstances, the exiles blame their forebears for the suffering they are experiencing, repeating a proverb to the effect that children bear the consequences of their parents' sins. They charge, "the way of the Lord is unfair." Through Ezekiel, God addresses the exiles, insisting that all lives belong to God and that the proverb is nonsense. God enjoins them from even repeating it and calls the people to look carefully at their own lives. "I will judge you, O house of Israel, all of you according to your ways," promises God (Ezek. 18:30), demanding that they repent and live.

Exile is no time to abandon the covenant and blame others. Times of difficulty are precisely the moment for careful observance of the law. But there were real questions about how to do this. The temple had been destroyed: how could they offer sacrifices? They were in a foreign land and some were compelled to serve their captors: how could they live as "the house of Israel" in another's house? When does compromise constitute transgression? Is it better to do something rather than nothing? Or is doing something far worse? Answers are not forthcoming from this text. Instead God insists that they take responsibility for discerning how to live rightly. As we seek to live justly during difficult times in a complex, global world, we wonder about such questions also. But God did not relieve the exiles of hard decisions and does not relieve us either. God simply exhorts, "Turn, then, and live" (v. 32b).

Psalm 78:1–4, 12–16 and Psalm 25:1–9

In Psalm 78, the psalmist ominously urges listeners to "give ear" to "dark sayings from of old" (vv. 1, 2). This foreshadowing barely prepares us for what will come: a harrowing recitation of the Hebrew people's transgressions and the outpouring of God's compassion and wrath. The verses that are a part of our lection tell us that God liberated the people from slavery in Egypt. But the verses beyond the lection recall God killing the people for their disobedience and the people returning as fearful sycophants; God extending compassion, and the people acting provocatively; God destroying the land, sending fire and plague and allowing the people to be slashed to pieces in battle, and then choosing to guide only the tribe of Judah into the future. The NRSV's editors have given a perfunctory subtitle to this psalm, "God's Goodness and Israel's Ingratitude." But readers are left breathless by the violence of God and the suffering of this admittedly disobedient people.

In verse 4 the psalmist affirms, "We will tell to the coming generation the glorious deeds of the LORD, and his might." This psalm is designed to teach. But to teach what, we wonder uncomfortably?

Whether or not we agree with the psalmist's theological conclusions about God's character, the writer provides us with an important paradigm for learning: telling the whole story. This psalm describes the relationship between Israel and God in brutal detail. Such honesty is necessary for true learning; we must tell of suffering as well as triumph, of wrongdoing as well as righteousness.

Too often in our world, we tell a truncated or sanitized version of history that avoids accounts of domination and suffering, masks real injustices whose repercussions continue in the present day, and provides trivial moral instruction for life together. Consider how we teach the story of Thanksgiving to our children. We explain how Squanto and other Native "Americans" helped the pilgrims survive that first year in the "New World." At the supposed first Thanksgiving, the two communities amicably enjoyed a feast and gave thanks (to a Christian God).[2] With an "all's well that ends well" flourish, we discuss multiculturalism or the importance of family and home. But we fail to say how John Winthrop, governor of the Massachusetts Bay Colony, later declared the land a legal "vacuum" because the native peoples had not subdued it; or how the Puritans appealed to the Bible to justify their use of force to take the land; or how the colonists went on to brutally slaughter hundreds of Pequots, in massacres that were aided and abetted by Cotton Mather.[3] Our official Thanksgiving story truncates this tale of domination and gives us, instead, an easy image of bicultural friendship.

As uncomfortable as the full text of Psalm 78 is, we would do well to read and wrestle with this account of failure and salvation. In so doing we may be better able to name the complexities and culpabilities of our own personal, ecclesial, and national stories and create a common history that learns from past transgressions.

In Psalm 25 the petitioner's claim is staked on God's steadfast love and succor despite trouble all around. The psalmist reminds God of God's mercy and confesses past sins. The psalmist prays, "Make me to know your ways, O LORD." What did the psalmist learn while pursuing God's ways? Does the writer come to a new understanding of opponents by following God's ways?

---

2. While the Wampanoag and colonists celebrated the harvest together, according to historical sources from the 1620s, there was no common event of giving thanks, but rather separate traditions of giving thanks for each people. See Plimoth Plantation, Wampanoag Homesite Frequently Asked Questions, www.plimoth.org/features/faqs/homesite-faq.php#18 (accessed October 1, 2010).

3. Howard Zinn, *A People's History of the United States* (New York: HarperCollins, 1980), 13–15.

Do enemies stay enemies from which the psalmist must be rescued? We do not know how God responded to the particular petitioner of Psalm 25, but this song's refrain, "make me to know your ways," is a model prayer for us as we endeavor to live justly and be receptive to God's leading.

Philippians 2:1–13

Paul writes to the assembly at Philippi, "Let the same mind be in you that was in Christ Jesus" (v. 5). He cites an early hymn describing how Christ Jesus set aside his equality with God to become incarnate and how he was obedient to the point of death on a cross. Remembering that crucifixion was the Roman Empire's punishment for sedition, the closing lines of the hymn are provocative and political: every knee shall bow, in heaven and on earth, and every tongue shall "confess that Jesus Christ is Lord." Paul then urges, "Therefore, my beloved, just as you have always obeyed me, not only in my presence, but much more now in my absence, work out your own salvation with fear and trembling" (v. 12).

The word that solicits our attention in the Christ hymn and Paul's appeal is "obedience." When Paul uses the word "obedience," he does *not* mean submission to authority or the order of the world. Nor does Paul suggest that the assembly in Philippi submit themselves to *Paul* and his teaching. Rather, Paul uses the word "obedience" to mean allegiance to Jesus and his vision of God's realm. This is a dangerous loyalty that dares to go up against the authorities of this world in the name of fidelity to God. Its sure product is salvation, but it is salvation born from "fear and trembling." As he was writing from jail, the assembly knew these were not mere metaphors.

While in our prior texts people cry to God from the midst of trouble, in this epistle, Paul makes clear that obedience to Christ brings on trouble; it brought Jesus to the cross and landed Paul in jail. Where is God in the midst of trouble? God in Christ Jesus is the troublemaker, the instigator, propelling us through word and action to defy dominating powers and principalities of our day in order to be faithful citizens of God's dawning realm.

Matthew 21:23–32

Our Gospel passage takes place the day after Jesus has ridden into Jerusalem to the crowd's chants of "Hosanna" (literally, "save us now"; 21:9b). With the whole city "in turmoil" (21:10), he storms the temple, overturning the tables of the money changers and healing the blind and lame. With dramatic direct action, Jesus indicts the twin and oft-collaborating authorities that regulated life for Jews in first-century Palestine: the Roman Empire and the temple.

Not surprisingly, as soon as he sets foot in the temple the next day, Jesus is confronted by the priests and scribes. They demand to know "by what authority" Jesus is doing these things and who gave him that authority.

Appeals to authority presume the legitimacy of existing systems and leaders. Such appeals have been used for millennia to silence, in particular, the voices of people who are not beneficiaries of established practice or policies.

Jesus is never one to pale before authority. In reply, he poses a political and theological conundrum about the provenance of John's baptism. Experienced politicians, the priests and scribes refuse to answer. Jesus matches their nonstatement with his own refusal, suggesting that his authority has no worse grounding than their authority. We infer (because he has bested them in argument) that Jesus is more of an expert than they on these matters.

According to the Gospels, Jesus dared to interpret and follow the Torah in new and challenging ways that called into question some of the practices of the temple, which was then the guarantor of Jewish religious practice. For example, his healings were without the imprimatur of the priests and occurred outside the sacrificial system. He ensured justice and wholeness for the poor and vulnerable first, and measured interpretations of the law and religious practice by whether they upheld this commitment. In doing so, Jesus mirrors God who "executes justice for the oppressed" (Ps. 146:7) so as to repair covenant relationships that the privileged have broken due to their own design or carelessness. If religious practice and scriptural interpretation do not serve to heal and restore people to right relationships with one another, Jesus abandons them.

Matthew portrays the religious leaders as blinded by questions of authority. They are unable to see the shortcomings in their own institutional practices and scriptural interpretations. Only two chapters later, Jesus shouts, "Woe to you, scribes and Pharisees, hypocrites! For you tithe mint, dill and cummin, and have neglected the weightier matters of the law: justice and mercy and faith. It is these you ought to have practiced without neglecting the others. You blind guides! You strain out a gnat but swallow a camel!" (Matt. 23:23–24).

Within the Christian tradition, churches and individuals differ greatly in our approaches to and interpretations of Scripture, as well as in governance, worship, practices, and witness. Buffeted by competing claims, we can become disoriented like the recently freed Israelites and cry out, "Is the LORD among us or not?" And in our desire to be faithful to tradition we can mistakenly appeal to authority, as the priests and scribes did. Jesus invites us instead to evaluate our commitments in terms of whether they ensure justice and well-being for those who are oppressed.

Peoples Native to the Americas Day (Fourth Friday in September)

Martin Brokenleg

2 KINGS 8:1–6
PSALM 57
ROMANS 2:1–11
LUKE 13:31–35

Native American Day is often observed on the fourth Friday of September in the United States and National Aboriginal Day on June 21 in Canada. Peoples native to North America celebrate their identities, histories, and cultures, and also demonstrate for justice. The preacher could help Eurocentric communities repent of the atrocities they have perpetrated against Native Americans and First Nations or First Peoples (as they are known in Canada) and could also help the congregation become more informed about the culture, practices, and religious beliefs and practices of indigenous communities, especially those shared by original inhabitants and later comers.

It is curious that Christians are led logically to believe that "God," until the birth of Jesus, cared only for one small people on the face of the earth, leaving all others to ignorance, "sin," idolatry, self-destruction, and eternal damnation. For Indian peoples, the message only becomes more difficult because it is conveyed through the clear inference that "God's" love (in the Jesus event) was denied Indian peoples until God, in God's graciousness, sent White people to kill us, lie to us, steal our land, and proclaim the saving gospel to us.

George E. "Tink" Tinker [1]

---

1. George E. "Tink" Tinker, *American Indian Liberation: A Theology of Sovereignty* (Maryknoll, NY: Orbis Books, 2008), 132.

All of the readings appointed for today raise the issue of justice at its most fundamental level, including concerns about Native people's rights to own and live on land that rightfully belongs to them. The Shunammite woman's land was returned to her by royal decree, but the psalmist bemoans the fate of people who have been trampled by evildoers; Paul warns the Romans that God will judge their behavior, regardless of who they are; and Jesus laments the wrongful slaying of prophets. In light of unresolved moral issues related to Native land claims, these texts remind us of God's intention to restore what has wrongfully been taken away from Native people and to issue judgment against those who ignore divine justice.

2 Kings 8:1–6

Israel is about to endure a famine. Elisha tells the Shunammite woman, whose son he had restored to life, to travel to a foreign land and become a resident foreigner among the Philistines. She listens to the voice of God's prophet, and returns to her homeland only when the famine ends. The crown appropriates her land in her absence. When the king asks Elisha's servant to tell him what Elisha has done, Gehazi says that Elisha resurrected the woman's son. The woman then asks the king for the rightful return of her land, and the king complies. An official is appointed to see that the woman's land is restored to her.

Native people are intensely related to the land. The Hebrew Scriptures identify indigenous populations as "the people of the land." A survey of names in the Hebrew Bible reveals a single term used for a people, their geographic location, and their governance system, that is, Moab, Philistia, Shunem, Edom. Native North Americans understand that they are in a relationship with a specific geography as a living being. When the earth is spoken of as "mother," this is not a poetic nicety but rather the most accurate expression of the people's relationship with the land. Non-Native governments conceptualize the earth as a commodity and not as a living being. Even contemporary environmentalists often refer to the earth as a commodity. This attitude is profoundly different from Native Americans' experience of the land as a living mother. A Native American who hears about the Shunammite woman being a foreigner in a land not her own understands deeply the dislocation that she must have experienced. Being away from one's land disorients an indigenous person spiritually, socially, and psychologically in a way difficult for nonindigenous people to conceptualize.

The Shunammite woman saw Elisha doing miraculous things with God's power. She knows that his prayer raised her son from the dead. Elisha directed her to survive the seven-year-long famine that struck Israel. Elisha's servant Gehazi opened the way for the woman to ask the king for the return of her land. Once more, the Shunammite woman saw a miracle when the king returned her land to her. For Native North Americans who have centuries-long land claims with governments, the return of the woman's land seems like a profound miracle.

Psalm 57

This psalm exalts God for protecting one who is under assault. The psalmist appeals to God to shame those who trample on others and speaks very specifically of a net being set and a pit being dug to entrap the psalmist.

This lament is familiar to Native American peoples who have experienced terrible and purposeful entrapment at the hands of European conquerors. When European explorers first arrived at lands occupied by First Nations, they declared these lands open and free for them to claim. They believed it was fair for them to do so because these lands were not owned by Christians but occupied by "heathens" who had no right to claim the land. According to the "doctrine of discovery," only Christians could own land: this understanding dates back to the 1400s when King Henry VII granted a charter to John Cabot. Cabot was instructed to declare any lands in the Americas not owned by Christians to be available for occupation and ownership by European conquerors. This understanding has been asserted as legal precedent in more recent centuries, including U.S. Supreme Court decisions (e.g., *Johnson v. McIntosh*, 1823), and decisions of the Supreme Court of Canada (e.g., Gitksan land claims in British Columbia).

What is the true title of lands currently occupied by Christian dioceses and judicatories today? What right does a congregation have to the land occupied by its church building if that land is not legally cleared of other owners or titles? More to the point, what moral right does any Christian body have to land that belongs to Native peoples?

This psalm also speaks of God's enduring love awakening the soul of the psalmist, who gives thanks for God's justice and faithfulness (vv. 8–10). It is this hope that strengthens us to continue working for God's just and loving ways among us.

Native North American communities have song traditions that are mainly dictations from the spirit world. Most of these songs are wordless and convey deep emotion or spiritual states. This differs from the psalm tradition that either reveals the psalmist's inner world or reports the soul's dialogue with God. Native song expresses loss of persons to death but almost never laments the loss of status or the loss of anything other than human life. Even so, Native people can emotionally identify with the psalmist who is trampled by others. Much of recent First Nations history includes being overcome by foreign armies, institutions, and cultural ways.

Romans 2:1–11

Paul writes to the Romans about the judgment of God. He says that God's silence should not be interpreted as indifference and that God judges communities and persons on the basis of their behavior. Wrath and fury will come to those who are doing bad things, but honor and immortality will come to those who do good things.

This section of Paul's letter focuses on God's judgment. Paul understands that no one can come to salvation without God's help, and he specifically targets members of his own religious community who opposed him and acted self-righteously. He also points to God who impartially judges the actions of every individual and community, no matter what their ancestry. Paul insists that God's judgment is based on criteria of justice and good behavior. What does this text mean in light of the history of how Euro-Americans have treated Native peoples? In what ways have dominant people in the Americas demonstrated self-righteousness at the expense of First Nation peoples? What attitudes does the dominant culture have toward other peoples in the world?

Historians and legal experts attest that neither the United States nor Canada observes the hundreds of treaties that already exist between these countries and the Native peoples among them. Western legal systems define a treaty as an agreement between two sovereign nations, and international law treaties have international status. If, therefore, the United States does not keep the terms of its treaties with Native Americans, its status in the international community is suspect. How can any nation in the world trust a country that has a long history of violating its own agreements, including violations against both the economic and moral rights of indigenous peoples? Can such a nation claim to be just in any way? Because of their considerable economic and military power, North American countries often feel entitled to criticize other nations, sometimes telling them what to do. Paul reminds his readers that their self-righteousness condemns them. Their actions condemn or acquit them.

Luke 13:31–35

Well-intentioned Pharisees come to warn Jesus about Herod. Jesus says that Jerusalem has a reputation for killing prophets, and that is why that city will be destroyed. Although he teaches in many locations, Jesus speaks with great concern and tenderness for Jerusalem and its people. His deep love for the people is reflected in his desire to gather the people under his wing, like a mother hen. In these verses, Jesus prophesies his own future even as he speaks lovingly of God's people and their rejection and murder of prophets.

Prophets have appeared in the history of Native peoples also. Those who were given special knowledge have guided indigenous communities to right understandings and good behavior. Listening to "revealers" requires an open heart as well as a desire to make positive use of sacred ways. There is no memory of a sacred prophet being killed for the message that was taught among Native American peoples. Most Native communities welcomed new teachings even if they were not clearly understood.

Native North Americans have lived successfully in the Americas for more than 500,000 years, and Native land claims existed long before the current governments of North America existed. Popular opinion assumes that a treaty "gives" something to Native peoples, and treaties specify what the Native nation is "giving" to the contemporary government: in other words, treaties state what compensation the contemporary government is giving the Native people as payment for the surrendered land. Native people surrendered large tracts of North America in return for food, clothing, education, and services that were promised in perpetuity. None of those payments were made in full and none lasted more than a few years, yet Canada and the United States still claim title to those lands.

The very existence of Native American peoples stands as a judgment against the "Christian countries" that make up the Americas. First Nations do not need to instigate court cases to raise questions about property rights and environmental concerns. History and the principles of law raise questions about injustices rendered against Native peoples and their land claims. The moral integrity of Christians is challenged as long as treaties are not observed, Native land claims are not satisfied, and the historic wrongs are not repented of. It is not the responsibility of Native peoples to fulfill these treaties, because this is fundamental to the very identity and integrity of all Christians in the Americas.

A primary justice issue for Christians in the Americas involves satisfying the land claims of all Native peoples. Without this, no Christian can speak with any degree of moral authority. Moreover, ignoring this fundamental injustice has resulted in innumerable grievances, economic hardship, the devastation of Native cultures, religions, and peoples. Ignoring these claims not only results in untold hardship to people and nature, but denies God's justice and leaves Christians vulnerable to divine judgment and condemnation.

Proper 22

Amy E. Steele

Exodus 20:1–4, 7–9, 12–20   Psalm 19
Isaiah 5:1–7   Psalm 80:7–15
                                   Philippians 3:4b–14
                                   Matthew 21:33–46

This week's lectionary readings are related to the ancient covenant God made with humanity through the children of Israel. Exodus 20 outlines God's expectations. Isaiah reflects on humanity's failure to remember those expectations. Psalm 80 laments a communal need for restoration, and Psalm 19 concludes that prior to, parallel with, and in spite of human frailty the cosmos remains a faithful witness to the glory of God and God's ancient covenant. Jesus' parable in Matthew 21 recalls Isaiah's vineyard to describe the consequences of human disobedience to the covenant. Finally, Philippians reminds us of Psalm 19, that a righteousness witness is a faithful witness. It also suggests that religious consciousness is shaped by and through determined faithfulness.

Exodus 20:1–4, 7–9, 12–20

The Ten Commandments consist of pronouncements and principles given by God to Israel. They solidify Israel's relationship with God and seal their identity as God's people. The first three commands provide the foundation for Israel's monotheistic faith and serve as reminders of their relationship with God during their wilderness wanderings and beyond. The fourth command establishes a day of rest and recalls the rhythm of God's work and rest in creation. Mark Searle argues that this rhythm "both hallows or glorifies God and sanctifies people through their imitation of God."[1] In other words, when the people of God perform their work and enjoy their rest, they glorify both

---

1. Mark Searle, "Sunday: The Heart of the Liturgical Year," in *Between Memory and Hope: Readings on the Liturgical Year*, ed. Maxwell E. Johnson (Collegeville, MN: Liturgical Press, 2000), 62.

God and humanity and the covenant that drew them together. Finally, the last set of laws focuses on the people's relationship with others, demanding that Israel refrain from the violence perpetuated by dishonoring parents, marriage partners, and neighbors.

The references to women in verse 17 are problematic. In ancient societies, women (both wives and slaves) were considered property, much like oxen. The directive to refrain from "coveting" wives as well as female and male slaves assumes the privileges of a patriarchal system supported by a slave-based economy. Despite these problems, Moses projects a new vision of communal relationships that is based on Israel's unique relationship to the Lord God who has freed them from slavery. Israel is simultaneously asked to remember the good works of God and to imitate them. According to Searle, "Imitation of God is also involved in the liberation motif: freedom is a supreme value, the foundational gift of God to Israel, to be enjoyed not only by those who have the wealth to enjoy the luxury of leisure but also by those who work for them."[2]

Through their liberative actions, the people of God are called to critique oppressive political and economic systems that promote unfair wages, unsafe working conditions, child slave labor, and sex trafficking. The people of God are called to listen to the cries of the oppressed and support campaigns for a living wage and safe working conditions in developing countries. We must collectively ask questions about the manufacturing of our beloved technological devices, clothing, and shoes. When we do not raise critical questions, we perpetuate the very systems of poverty we hope to eradicate and fail to fully honor the covenant God made with God's people.

Isaiah 5:1–7

In the fifth chapter of Isaiah, the prophet uses poetry and metaphor to convey a spirited message. Isaiah's beloved is God and God's vineyard is Judah. The vinedresser invests himself in a portion of land, digging and planting at will. He even builds a watchtower and a wine vat in expectation of its productivity. The vintner's work was a "pleasant planting" (v. 7), but the results were terribly disappointing. The vineyard fails to produce a harvest, and he allows it to be overrun by briers, thorns, and wild creatures. God provides a detailed list of grievances against the inhabitants of the southern kingdom that includes greed, excessive drunkenness, bribery, and the perversion of justice (vv. 8–23). God will judge them accordingly and no longer ensure their survival.

This text reminds people of faith to remain committed to God's call to act justly toward all people. It also cautions us against assuming postures of

2. Ibid.

privilege, as if our way of life or worship will somehow guarantee our safety and well-being. When we are tempted to become complacent and assume that our own, homogenous worldview is best, Isaiah warns us that we are subject to God's standards of justice. Isaiah's warning is especially poignant given the debates in the United States about building mosques amid dominant Christian and secular cultures. These legal battles and the willful destruction of property by zealous Christian groups reflect an arrogant and homogenous worldview that often confuses patriotism with unquestioned loyalty to a particular set of religious beliefs and practices. Isaiah depicts God's sorrow over human unrighteousness and urges us toward God's life-giving purposes for all creation. Without these, life will be as desolate as God's vineyard (vv. 9–10).

Psalm 19

According to this psalm, nature is familiar with God's glory (vv. 1–6) while humanity has to be tutored by the laws, precepts, and ordinances of the Lord in order to testify to divine glory (vv. 7–10). Instruction in religious truth, suggests the psalmist, is more valuable than gold and sweeter than the "drippings of the honeycomb" (v. 10), and people are dependent on it to learn how to fully articulate the glory of God.

From this psalm we may infer two things. First, familiarity with Scripture enlarges our memory about who God is and who God has been. That God has been intrinsically and characteristically concerned about the poor is not a novel idea to those familiar with the biblical record. That God holds God's people accountable for the treatment of the poor is not news to those familiar with Scripture. Thus advocating for the rights of the poor is aligned with the work of God. Second, Psalm 19 ends in prayer and encourages us to turn regularly to God in prayer. Because humanity is subject to failure even with all of our acquired wisdom and knowledge, the psalmist's prayer suggests that humility is a commendable human quality, enabling us to acknowledge that God's thoughts and ways are always superior to ours.

Psalm 19 illustrates nature's witness to God's glory and invites us to be shaped by its praise of God. Just as we are transformed by the biblical witness, we are also reconstituted by the mystery of nature's glorious witness to divine transcendence. If humans fail to recognize God's glory, the natural world will always assume its place in the cosmic choir.

Psalm 80:7–15

Psalm 80 begins with a cry for restoration and help. The psalmist petitions God on behalf of the community to remember God's original gracious acts, to remember the origins of the covenant that God made to God's people, to remember what "your right hand planted" (v. 15). Throughout these petitions are regular cries, "Restore us, O God of hosts" (vv. 3, 7, 19).

A familiar analogy to nature is also present in this psalm. Israel is the vine brought out of Egypt, and God is responsible for driving out the nations and planting Israel in a new land (v. 8). A reading of these conquests could wrongfully lead to a justification of holy war, colonialism, or imperialist sensibilities where people conquer one another in the name of God. Governments should refrain from justifying their military strategy based on a religious-political logic like this. Nevertheless, the psalm paints a picture of the people of God deeply rooted in the land. Scholars believe that this vine is a metaphor for the reach of the Davidic kingdom that extends from the base of mountains and valleys to the sea (vv. 10–11). The message the psalmist conveys is that God's good planting produced fruit, but for reasons unidentified, God had ceased cultivating the vineyard. Despite the ravages from wild animals, the psalmist depicts hope. The last two verses of our reading (vv. 14–15) summon God to remember the vine, "the stock that your right hand planted."

This new millennium has suffered natural disasters including tsunamis, earthquakes, floods, tornadoes, and massive fires. Each event in its own right has been devastating. We have also witnessed the tragedies of war, racial profiling, discriminatory practices against the LGBTQ community, and willful predatory lending. However, Psalm 80 reminds the people of God that hope resides in prayer. Hope is a theological value that we must always remember. When the church has failed itself and others, hope is the seed that springs forth with new life-giving possibilities. In our most difficult situations, our greatest hope is that God will remember creation, and we will not be abandoned to our own devices. Hurricane Katrina does not offer the final word to the residents of New Orleans. Neither will the residents of Joplin, Missouri, define themselves by the tornado of 2011. Hope is the foundations upon which both communities are rebuilding themselves.

Philippians 3:4b–14

According to the first chapter of Philippians, Paul wrote this letter from prison to the church he founded in Philippi during his second missionary journey. Today's passage begins with Paul's recognition that by traditional standards, he has every reason to boast about his position before God (3:4b–6). His description of what he has lost and gained in Christ reveals that these standards have been completely overturned: he no longer values his lineage, educational training, status, or zeal. Paul describes these aspects of his life as "rubbish" in comparison to "the surpassing value of knowing Christ Jesus my Lord" (v. 8). But Paul fails to recognize Jesus' Jewishness, his lineage, his lack of formal training, his occupation. In other words, Paul fails to recognize Jesus' *life*. Instead, it is Jesus' sufferings (on the cross), his death, and his resurrection that Paul wants to know and value. However, when Paul forgets Jesus' life, he forgets at least two aspects of Jesus' ministry.

First, he forgets that Jesus radically confronted prevailing notions of righteousness. According to Jesus' words and deeds, righteousness is understood as ministry to the poor, the parentless, the prisoner, and all who are broken (see Luke 4:18–19). Second, Jesus is critical of the Pharisees, but he nevertheless uses them as standards for what is important when he says that your righteousness must exceed that of the Pharisees (Matt. 5:20). This lectionary reading substantiates an argument made by Obery Hendricks, who contends that underestimating the life of Christ, and the religious and social critique in which he engaged, results in political docetism that denies Christ's full humanity and public mission. The result is an overemphasis on spiritual values like personal piety while Jesus' prophetic teachings are disregarded.[3]

Scholars have been critical of the inability or unwillingness of the church to articulate arguments against the enemies of human dignity. Immigration policy is one example. Public sentiment decries the ineffectiveness of governmental authorities to prevent "illegal immigrants" from entering the United States, insisting on tougher laws for those found guilty of violating immigration law and tighter security as a preventative measure for the future. In adapting the language of Paul, clergy might say that we must no longer argue over notions of who is and is not a legal resident: instead, we may identify "illegal immigrants" as our neighbors, literally our geographic neighbors to the south, and our universal neighbors whom Jesus invites us to love and help.

Matthew 21:33–46

Verse 33 of Jesus' parable echoes the imagery of Isaiah 5:1–2. A landowner plants a vineyard, places a fence around it, digs a wine press, and builds a watchtower. What is unique to Matthew's parable is the middleman. The landowner hires tenants to tend the vines and oversee the production of the wine. However, the tenants are intent on securing their own gain, and the parable ends with a question to Jesus' disciples: "Now when the owner of the vineyard comes, what will he do to those tenants?" Jesus concludes that the reign of God will change hands. It will be given to people who produce the fruit of the kingdom, from the landowner to the tenants.

3. Obery M. Hendricks Jr., *The Politics of Jesus: Rediscovering the True Revolutionary Nature of the Teachings of Jesus and How They Have Been Corrupted* (New York: Doubleday, 2006), 76–80.

In *Parables as Subversive Speech*, William Herzog II provides several important clues to a prophetic understanding of this parable.[4] Herzog notes that
it was not uncommon for wealthy landowners to secure land from the fore-
closed loans of an underclass of landowners who suffered from meager har-
vests. For the wealthy, Herzog argues, this meant solidifying wealth, class,
and social position. However, for the peasant, losing land meant losing economic security and status among peers because the landless person was not
able to contribute material goods or other resources to the local community.

Historical research on vineyards suggests that it often took five years to
develop a good harvest. Although the time from planting to harvesting is not
given here, we may speculate that this land had been previously owned by someone other than the wealthy landowner who dominates the parable. Has this
wealthy landowner hired the previous owner as a tenant farmer? The violence
in the parable reflects class warfare between the owner and the tenants as the
peasant farmer revolts against an unjust system that favors the wealthy. Finally,
Herzog suggests that since the telling of the parable is an allusion to the text in
Isaiah 5, the "punch line" in Isaiah helps us to understand the underlying meaning of Jesus' parable. The parable is meant to convict the "acquisitive greed of
the ruling class of Judah."[5] Verse 45 concludes, "When the chief priests and the
Pharisees heard his parables, they realized that he was speaking about them."

It is estimated that the American foreclosure crisis that was precipitated by
the housing boom of the 1990s and early 2000s saw more than four million
families lose their homes between 2007 and early 2012. The rapid increase in
the number of foreclosures in the United States may make some Americans
more sensitive to the context of Jesus' parables of the vineyard. The people
of God have a responsibility to practice economic justice and to hold institutions accountable when they willfully seduce home buyers into purchases and
agreements beyond their means without carefully attending to the terms of
their repayment. Predatory lending in housing and financial services (e.g.,
payday loans) takes advantage of persons who are vulnerable to financial fraud.

This parable draws our attention to the consequences of greed and suggests that greed often results in violence. The expectation is that those who
associate themselves with the reign of God will advocate for justice on behalf
of the poor and will not take advantage of unfortunate circumstances to secure
their own financial gain. From the perspective of those who are economically
vulnerable, the parable of the Vineyard does not seem to pass judgment on
the violent tenants, but rather on those who have usurped their land and taken
their means of livelihood.

---

4. William R. Herzog II, *Parables as Subversive Speech: Jesus as Pedagogue of the Oppressed*
(Louisville, KY: Westminster John Knox Press, 1994), 98–113.
5. Ibid., 104.

World Communion Sunday
(First Sunday in October)

Joseph R. Jeter Jr.

ISAIAH 25:6–8
PSALM 75
1 CORINTHIANS 10:14–22
MATTHEW 26:26–30

On World Communion Sunday (the first Sunday in October), congregations across the world partake of Communion. Someone has described the sacred table on this day as 25,000 miles long. In our fragmented world, in which groups often relate with suspicion and violence and even try to destroy one another, the churches of the world coming together to break the loaf and drink the cup is a sign of God's intention for all peoples to live together in love, peace, and justice. The sermon might help the congregation confess ways that it contributes to the fragmentation of the world and to resolve to witness to love, peace, and justice.

The Eucharist should build community; but world relations are destroying persons and peoples. The Eucharist is universalist, the world is racist. The power of the Eucharist tends towards an egalitarian society; but the world powers are hegemonistic. Whereas the Eucharist motivates humble service, arrogant domination prevails on the international scene. The eucharistic bread is a common meal for all; but bread in the world is a commodity for trade. In the Eucharistic ideal, land is for common use; in the present system of nation-states, land is for the successful conquerors.
Tissa Balasuriya[1]

---

1. Tissa Balasuriya, *The Eucharist and Human Liberation* (Maryknoll, NY: Orbis Books, 1979), 141–42.

Isaiah 25:6–8

At the beginning of Isaiah 25, there is a mixture of wonderful things and disaster, but verses 6–8 tell of God's grace for the people who have been impoverished. No longer will the people lack good food and become unknown and disgraced. Isaiah can be bewildering at times. In chapter 24, God is angry with you and, apparently, everybody. People try to praise God, but to no avail. There is nothing but terror, devastation, punishment, and the pit. Nevertheless, please keep reading! The storm clouds break and the sun shines through. Isaiah 25:6–8 cannot be read without gratitude. In difficult times for a person, family, church, country, or the world, there is wonderful news here that God really does care for *all* peoples, including you and me, them and us. God's mercy is overwhelming. In spite of every fear and desperation, hope *is* here.

Time and again in this text the setting is "this mountain," surely Mount Zion, symbolizing Jerusalem. In verse 6 God prepares on the mountain a rich feast of food and wine for *all* peoples. In verse 7 God "will destroy on this mountain the shroud that is cast over *all* peoples, the sheet that is spread over *all* nations; God will swallow up death forever." The words in verse 8 are touching, for "the Lord GOD will wipe away the tears from *all* faces and the disgrace of his people he will take away from *all* the earth."

This text is "an announcement of salvation with eschatological overtones,"[2] and one that we find reiterated in 1 Corinthians 15 and Revelation 21. Death is swallowed up and is no more. The shroud has been removed. Vivid metaphors. There are two contemporary manifestations of the strong images in this text appropriate to World Communion Sunday. The first is of God's feast of rich food and wine for all peoples on the mountain. Many people today would find such a feast revolting, thousands of calories as opposed to the all but zero calories from a bit of cracker and a tiny cup of juice.

This comes from our living in a fat-rich land.[3] If we lived in a harsh place where the land was not so fat (as billions do), we might look at it differently. Hungry people are thus closer to the classical—and the biblical—understanding of fat, "the richest and most nourishing part of anything, the choicest produce of the earth."[4]

God did not intend the rich feast to fatten those already well fed, but to bring good food to *all* the people, most of whom were seriously underfed.

2. Gene M. Tucker, "Isaiah 1–39," in *The New Interpreter's Bible*, vol. 6 (Nashville: Abingdon, 2001), 216.
3. Adapted from Joseph R. Jeter Jr., *Re/Membering: Meditations and Sermons for the Table of Jesus Christ* (St. Louis: Chalice, 1996), 170.
4. Definition 2c, *Oxford English Dictionary*, vol. 4 (Oxford: Clarendon Press, 1961), s.v. "fat."

Isaiah gives us a strong reminder that the bread and the cup are not really prepared in the kitchen, but in the heart of God. And God prepares it for *all*. It is up to us to serve that food to *all*.

The second image is of God destroying "the shroud that is cast over all peoples, the sheet that is spread over all nations; he will swallow up death forever." In the first episode of the television show *The Paper Chase*,[5] the professor stands over a first-year law student who is not prepared for class. Professor Kingsfield raises his arms as though he is draping something over the student: "This is a shroud, Mr. Hart. You are dead." Kingsfield ignores him after that. Then one day Hart comes to class with a sheet over him and stands there. Kingsfield, quite perturbed, moves to Hart and rips off the sheet, and Hart immediately answers the question Kingsfield had asked. I thought a theological point had just been made clear. The only one who can remove the shroud is the one who put it there. Scripture suggests in Genesis 3 that after Adam and Eve sinned, God told them what they would do "all the days of their lives," not unlimited days. On that day God shrouded both of them. But in this text God rips the shroud off of them and swallows up death forever in the gift of eternal life.

Psalm 75

The main theme of this psalm is that God will judge and punish the boastful wicked. This can refer to both individuals and nations.[6] But appropriate to World Communion Sunday, there is a colorful metaphor for the administration of the punishment. We in our time see the eucharistic symbols as lovely, moving, and polysemous. We come to the table in remembrance and gratitude for the sacrifice of Jesus that effects the redemption of all.

There is, however, another side to this. In several centuries BCE, the lees or dregs of wine were symbols of punishment. Prophets frequently used this symbol (e.g., Isa. 51:17; Jer. 25:15; Zeph. 1:12; Ps. 75:8).[7]

Perhaps it is appropriate on World Communion Sunday to think of Jesus' sacrifice and also of others whom Jesus loved and for whom he died, those whom we may have ignored, individually, as a church, as a country. Maybe the wine or juice should on this day not be sweet but sour. Perhaps it is appropriate to think of the sacrifice of people like Stephen (ca. 34–35 CE) and Dietrich Bonhoeffer (April 9, 1945) and others who died for Jesus. As a reminder,

5. The television program (CBS, 1978–1986) was based on a motion picture by the same name (20th Century Fox, 1973), and the film was based on a book by the same name by John Jay Osborn Jr. (Boston: Houghton-Mifflin, 1971).
6. See J. Clinton McCann, "Psalms," in *The New Interpreter's Bible*, vol. 4 (Nashville: Abingdon, 1996), 978.
7. See Jeter, *Re/Membering*, 24.

take the cup of blessing and punishment, and drink it . . . from the bottom. Forgiveness comes.

Matthew 26:26–30

This text, along with Mark 14:22–26, Luke 22:14–23, and 1 Corinthians 11:23–26, frames the institution of the Eucharist. Each of the four texts is a little different, with Matthew most closely following Mark. If we ponder it, we realize the Eucharist (Holy Communion, Lord's Supper, or Last Supper) was instituted with very few words. A multitude of tomes about the Eucharist have been written: *The Shape of the Liturgy* by Dom Gregory Dix and *Eucharist and Eschatology* by Geoffrey Wainwright, for example.[8] Even this short commentary is more than three times the length of Matthew's text.

Moses and seventy-three other Israelites ate a meal and saw God (Exod. 24:9–11); so did Jesus' disciples (Luke 24:28–31). As on several other occasions in Scripture, holy moments broke in to a meal: on a mountain, in an upper room, in a garden, at sea (Gen. 2:15–16; Isa. 55:1–5; Acts 27:33–38).[9] Luke has Jesus establishing the Eucharist before the meal begins, but Mark and Matthew have Jesus interrupting the meal twice. First, "while they were eating," he broke in to say, "one of you will betray me," which surely subdued whatever pleasantry there was in the room (Matt. 26:21). Sometime later, "while they were eating," Jesus took bread and cup, blessed and broke the bread, and gave thanks for the cup (vv. 26–27).[10] Speaking metaphorically, Jesus said the bread represented his body and the wine in the cup represented his blood.[11]

It may come as a surprise that neither Matthew nor Mark speak of Jesus asking his disciples to "do this in remembrance of me." Churches everywhere tend to have some form of that phrase carved into Communion tables, but those words come from Paul (1 Cor. 11:23–36) and Luke (22:19b). Remembrance is a critical part of the Eucharist for people, but its antipode is just as important: anticipation and participation. Stanley Hauerwas offers this brilliant insight:

---

8. Dom Gregory Dix, *The Shape of the Liturgy*, 2nd ed. (London: A & C Black, 2000); Geoffrey Wainwright, *Eucharist and Eschatology* (Nashville: Order of St. Luke, 2002).

9. See commentary on Exodus 24:9–11 for World Communion Sunday in Year C of this series.

10. The awkward terms "cup" and "fruit of the vine" instead of "wine" were probably chosen, according to M. Eugene Boring, "to maintain the connotations of Passover, which had several references to 'the cup'" ("Matthew," in *The New Interpreter's Bible*, vol. 8 [Nashville: Abingdon, 1995], 471). Whether or not this is the reason for Matthew and Mark's choice of "cup," it does make it easier for twenty-first-century Christians at the table who find the words "wine" (poison to recovering alcoholics) and "juice" (lacking sacred dignity) troublesome.

11. Those whose faith includes transubstantiation or consubstantiation accept literally Matthew's words: "This is my body" and "This is my blood."

The church does not just remember Jesus when we do what he commanded we do, but in fact we become Jesus' memory for the world so that the world might be reconciled. We do not remind the world of Jesus as if he is dead and our memory keeps him alive. The exact opposite is true; because Jesus lives we can be made participants in his time. The Eucharist is the feast that makes Christ's time the time in which his people live. . . . This meal, therefore, becomes the meal of unity binding Christians through time and space to be one body, one Christ for the world. That we have been made one makes it impossible, therefore, for Christians to contemplate killing other Christians with whom we share this meal. Such killing is not murder . . . it is suicide.[12]

In Matthew 26:29, Jesus says that this really is his last supper and that he will not drink wine again until he drinks it again with his disciples in the realm of God. When Jesus was offered wine at the cross, he declined. He indicated that his death established a new covenant between God and God's people, and that this covenant will be manifested by the forgiveness of sins and the coming of God's reign. Forgiven by Jesus and on the cusp of this new kin-dom, we are living, in one body, together, in Jesus' time. This is very exciting.

Moreover, according to biblical scholar Warren Carter, the word *aphesis*, generally translated as "forgiveness," can also mean "release" or "jubilee." He writes:

Jesus' death, like the exodus from Egypt, the return from exile in Babylon, and the year of jubilee, effects release from, a transformation of, sinful imperial structures, which oppress God's people, contrary to God's will. His death establishes God's justice or empire, including release from Rome's power. Release from sins, then, has personal and sociopolitical and cosmic, present and future dimensions.[13]

Here we are in Matthew's future and God's presence. The arms of the cross reach out to us. Our future, then, depends on the death of Jesus and our covenant with God. I believe that forgiveness can mean jubilee. I also believe resurrection can mean justice.

1 Corinthians 10:14–22

Paul, answering questions from Corinth, wrote two separate pieces about eating meat that had been offered to idols, 8:1–13 and 10:14–11:1. Worried that eating such meat might result in the worship of idols by those weak in the faith, Paul encouraged the knowledgeable faithful to avoid eating idol-tainted

12. Stanley Hauerwas, *Matthew* (Grand Rapids: Brazos Press, 2006), 219.
13. Warren Carter, *Matthew and the Margins* (Maryknoll, NY: Orbis Books, 2000), 507.

meat. I am not aware of Christians today having this problem. But the question always arises: What do Christians resist in today's world that may be comparable to what ancient Christians resisted? Alcohol or drug consumption? Do we push away from our Communion tables and worship services persons with HIV/AIDS just as the ancients avoided lepers? Leprosy then; HIV/AIDS now. Shorter life spans then; Alzheimer's disease now. There will always be new challenges and concerns to consider. But we must remember that faith in God brings both freedom and the responsibility to determine what is Christlike in our relationships with others.

Paul then wrote: "The cup of blessing that we bless, is it not a sharing in the blood of Christ? The bread that we break, is it not a sharing in the body of Christ? Because there is one bread, we who are many are one body, for we all partake of the one bread" (10:16–17). As I write this on the eve of World Communion Sunday, it is the 200th anniversary of the birth of an American religious movement which unfortunately would later splinter into three groups.[14] Today hundreds of people from each of the three churches gathered for what we called the Great Communion. Representatives from each church led the different parts of the service, and the differences among the churches seemed to slip away when *all* of us worshiped as one body and shared in the Lord's Supper together. It was a moving experience that holds wonderful possibilities for the days ahead.

14. The Christian Church (Disciples of Christ), 1832; Churches of Christ, 1906; and Christian Churches/Church of Christ, 1968.

Proper 23

Miguel A. De La Torre

Exodus 32:1–14	Psalm 106:1–6, 19–23
Isaiah 25:1–9	Psalm 23
	Philippians 4:1–9
	Matthew 22:1–14

Waiting for God is never easy. The wait can be discouraging, disappointing, and disheartening. From the margins of our world, the dispossessed and disenfranchised have been waiting for such a long time, crying out for succor. The plight of the world's wretched is compounded by what seems at times to be a god that cannot hear their cries. Is God deaf or dead? Or worse, does God not care enough to save those who suffer? Each day we read in our morning newspaper of people who die because of hunger, preventable diseases, or natural disasters. When we consider these senseless deaths, it seems to deny more than confirm the paternal love of God. Is it possible to convince of God's love the father who lost his daughter to starvation because world economies and political systems are structured to use the bulk of their resources to shower a few people with unimaginable wealth while many others starve? How do we explain to a mother that God cares as she comforts her son who was raped by soldiers charged with maintaining the world's imbalance of resources? One is forced to ask, where is this God whose mercies endure forever? Some of us shake our fists toward a vacant heaven, wondering where the giver of life has gone. Others who are tired of waiting for justice fashion their own gods, as did the children of Israel. Some choose to place their trust in what they themselves can create rather than the Creator.

Exodus 32:1–14

This passage tells of a time when the people became anxious because they tired of waiting for a word from the One who liberated them from bondage in Egypt. Camped at the foot of Mount Horeb, landless and with few prospects

430

for meeting their daily needs, they began to wonder if this God of life was going to accompany them on their long journey through the valley of death. Would you have acted any differently? Would you have also taken the gold rings out of the ears of your spouses, your sons, and your daughters and presented them to Aaron? Is it not easier to have a more tangible god—one that can be seen, touched, created after one's own image (in this case, a golden calf)? Would we not be more secure if we were to rely on a god made of gold or, in reality, on gold alone?

But gods of gold make poor substitutes. And those who link their future to such gods are in peril of facing a fate similar to that of the golden calf: destruction. The stiff-necked people who choose mammon over God risk being consumed by their own greed. Fortunately, God raises up prophetic voices like Moses who hold God to God's promises.

Psalm 106:1–6, 19–23

The psalmist reminds us that the people forgot the God who saved them by performing great feats in Egypt on their behalf (v. 21). It is always easier to see God and remember God's calling in the light of day than in the darkness of night. Yes, we can begin our songs with the psalmist and give thanks to God who is good, whose love is everlasting (v. 1), but when the pressures and burdens of reality weigh us down and darken our perspectives, when God seems silent during our trials and tribulations, what becomes of our praise and worship? How much easier it is to be cynical and to trust in the gods of our own making! We look to power, privilege, and possessions as our saviors, our rescuers. If truth be known, those who rely on power, privilege, and possessions seem to do well in the eyes of the world, if not better, than those at Horeb waiting for a word from the Creator of all. The rich seem to die at peace in their satin-sheeted beds, while the homeless die whimpering in the gutters. We have fashioned our prayers to call those who have power, privilege, and possessions blessed, and those without these things cursed—secretly wishing that we, too, were blessed. We have associated success in this world with finding God's pleasure for us. What we lack, we can name and claim. In fact, if we are truly honest with ourselves, the bulk of our prayers are for these not-so-foreign golden gods.

Perhaps our prayers are more closely related to our personal expectations than we realize, and perhaps we are expecting something of God that is not right. When our expectations are not met, or when we are not pleased with the response we get, we quickly turn to making our own gods, trusting that they can be more easily controlled. However, the psalmist reminds us that we find happiness and fulfillment when we observe justice (v. 3). Unfortunately, the meaning of "justice" is usually lost in the ambiguous English word "righteous," used in most English biblical translations. When Euro-Americans read "righteous" in their Bibles, Hispanics read the word *justicia*, which is translated as "justice." For most English speakers, "righteous" means morally right or justifiable, acting in an upright, moral way. This definition implies an action that may be performed privately. Justice, on the other hand, based on the concept of *justicia*, can only occur within community, manifesting itself in relation to others. Communalism rather than individualism is privileged when the words *justo* and *justicia* are read in the Bible. Stranded on a desert island, an individual can be righteous by remaining conscientious and God-fearing in thought. But justice can never be practiced in isolation; by its very nature, it needs others to whom justice can be administered and with whom justice is practiced. In short: no community, no justice. Justice cannot be reduced to a private expression of faith; it is a public action that necessarily involves others.

We are called to do justice, regardless of whether God responds to our cries. Rather than waiting for God to meet our needs, we are called to do justice to the disenfranchised among us, to meet the needs of others. Rather than waiting for a miracle from God, we are called to be the miracle for which others have been praying. When we feed the hungry, provide drink to the thirsty, and clothe the naked, we become God's answer to those who are crying out for grace and mercy. But simply offering handouts from our excess possessions is never enough. The true praxis, the true act of justice, occurs when we begin to ask why so many in our world go without having their basic needs met. No doubt asking such questions invites persecution, fear, and outrage from those who have more than they need. As Brazilian Archbishop Dom Helder Camara says, "When I give food to the poor they call me a saint. When I ask why they are poor, have no food, they call me a communist."[1]

Philippians 4:1–9

Paul writes to the Philippians that we are not to give way, but are to "stand firm" and remain faithful in the Lord (v. 1). The church of Philippi, started by a woman, Lydia, was facing a schism. Just as the children of Israel placed their trust in their own creations, this early church was placing its trust in individuals rather than the community as a whole. There appeared to be two camps within the church, one led by Euodia and the other by Syntyche (v. 2). All too often, Eurocentric churches stress the salvation of the individual, as in Jesus being *my* personal Savior. Yet for many churches from the margins

---

1. Darryl Trimiew, "H. Richard Niebuhr on Responsibility," in *Beyond the Pale: Reading Ethics from the Margins,* ed. Stacey M. Floyd-Thomas and Miguel A. De La Torre (Louisville, KY: Westminster John Knox Press, 2011), 135.

of the dominant culture, the emphasis seems to be more on the community. The concern is for communal salvation, and it is not oriented just toward the next life, but to this one as well. It is never the individual's betterment (physical or spiritual) that takes priority, but the sustainability of the community and the quality of people's lives (temporal and eternal) that are most important. A commitment to justice provides the basis for critical reflection on the experiences of disenfranchised communities that are emboldened to struggle for social change. The attempt to hear what appears to be a silent God stems from a need to articulate liberative responses to everyday circumstances faced by communities that could be significant in bringing about a more just social order.

Paul encourages these church leaders not to place their trust in individuals, but to move toward a communal approach to faith. They, and we, are to put aside differences and, for the sake of the gospel, come together. Tolerance is encouraged because, after all, the Lord is near. Prayers are to be offered if there is a need for anything. But Paul falls short of assuring us that God will provide whatever is asked. Instead, the only answer to our prayers that we can expect from God is the peace of God, a peace that "surpasses all understanding" (v. 7). Amid our hunger, thirst, and nakedness (both physical and spiritual), we are called to pray. We can pray to God, but there is no guarantee that God will meet our immediate needs. When our prayers do not seem to go higher than our bedroom ceiling, we are left with several choices: we may follow the example of the church at Philippi that trusted individuals; or we may follow the example of God's people at Horeb who trusted in their own creations; or we may follow the advice of the psalmist who assures us that happiness and fulfillment is found when we exercise justice (Ps. 106:3). If we keep doing all the things we are taught, specifically seeking God's justice before all else, then the promise Paul made to Euodia and Syntyche, that the God of peace will be with them, is also given to us. Prayers may not be answered in accordance with our expectations, but amid our struggles we are promised God's peace.

Isaiah 25:1–9

What about those who prefer to place their trust in power, privilege, and possessions? Are these fortifications sufficient or simply illusions? Will such securities be enough to protect and rescue us in times of crisis? These may provide temporal reassurance, but they lack eternal substance.

The prophet Isaiah shows us heaps of stones that were once fortified cities, citadels of the proud that no longer exist and will never be rebuilt (v. 2). These constructions were built to keep people safe and secure, but they failed to accomplish their task. The privileged may have walls to hide behind, but these are temporary, whereas Isaiah's God is a refuge for the poor, a refuge for the needy and all who experience distress (v. 4). The God of life chooses not to play the part of a magician or benevolent genie who at the utterance of a command from the poor turns their dispossession into riches and wealth. Those who lack material well-being and remain faithful to God's call for justice are promised peace from God, who shelters them from the storm and shades them from the heat (v. 4).

Yes, calves of gold such as hedge funds, retirement funds, and gated communities may provide the means to build structures that safeguard our power, privilege, and possessions, but the foundations of such fortifications are often rooted in shifting sand, and with time these buildings collapse, leaving nothing but a pile of rubble as testimony to the inability to establish one's own security.

Matthew 22:1–14

Amid life's uncertainties, we are given God's peace, a peace embedded in a messianic vision of the Lord of hosts preparing a banquet for all people, a banquet where the finest wines and richest foods are served. On that day, mourning will end, death will be vanquished, and every tear will be wiped away by the very hand of God. Hope in God will not be in vain, for salvation will come from God's outstretched arm (Isa. 25:6–9). However, while all are invited to this feast, not everyone will choose to come.

God's reign, according to Jesus' parable in Matthew 22, is like a king who prepared a feast for his son's wedding. The invitations were sent, but no one bothered to come. Because a sermon on this passage may unwittingly contribute to anti-Judaism if the preacher casually relates these characters to institutional Judaism, it is wise to acknowledge that many Christians have disregarded or disparaged God's gracious invitation to join the divine feast through the centuries. Indeed, the church continues to safeguard admission to God's Communion table, often refusing to welcome immigrants and minorities who await our welcome. In the parable, when the king sends his servants to discover the reason for the people's absence, they provide flimsy excuses. Some even mistreat and kill the king's messengers. Furious, the king brings destruction upon those who refuse to join in the banquet and partake of the hope and promises of the king (vv. 1–7).

As the story continues, the wedding is ready, but there are still no guests. So the king sends his servants to the crossroads and byways to invite everyone, both the deserving and the unworthy, to the banquet. The house is filled, but not everyone chose to be "changed" by the invitation. One individual did not bother to put on the proper attire and chose not to change his clothes to be in the presence of the king. This individual, like some of us, trusted his old rags, his former self, and refused to be renewed by the Creator of all. He trusted the darkness of his life prior to receiving God's invitation, rather than the promise of a banquet where all are now welcomed. To trust in one's former self, a self that refuses to be changed by God's invitation, results in being cast out into the darkness where there is much weeping and grinding of teeth (vv. 8–14).

Psalm 23

Some people place their trust in gods of their own making; others trust individuals rather than communities; still others construct fortifications, believing they will provide security against outside threats; and there are those who trust in themselves, in the rags they wore prior to God's invitation. All of these end badly. But blessed are they who trust in God amid darkness. They may declare with the psalmist, "The LORD is my shepherd, I shall not want" (v. 1). Even when they walk through the valley of the shadow of death, there is no evil that need be feared (v. 4). While waiting by the side of a mountain for a word from God, or seeking an elusive peace in a church rocked by dissension, when the walls of our security are reduced to a pile of rubble, or the feast presided over by the King of kings requires us to put aside our former selves to become a new creation, we can persevere if we first and foremost allow the Shepherd to lead us on the path of justice for the sake of God's name (v. 3). In following the gospel and doing God's will, we discover that regardless of the circumstances of our lives, the depths of our despair, or even the silence of God, goodness and loving-kindness will follow us all the days of our lives. This passage offers us God's great promise that ultimately and always we shall live in the house of the Lord forever, and ever, and ever (v. 6).

Night of Power (27th Night of Ramadan)

John Kaltner

Genesis 21:8–21
Psalm 100
1 John 2:7–11
Matthew 15:21–28

The Night of Power (*Laylat al-Qadr*) is important to the Islamic community because, according to Islamic tradition, that is the night that God revealed the Qur'an in its entirety to the prophet Muhammad through the angel Gabriel (Jibril). The Night of Power is observed on the 27th of Ramadan. Since Islam follows the lunar calendar (which is shorter than the solar calendar), it eventually occurs in all of the months of the solar calendar followed by Christians.[1] Given the tensions between some Christian and Islamic communities, the preacher could use the occasion of the Night of Power to consider relationships between these groups. What do we have in common? Where do we differ? How can Christians encourage respect between the two communities?

We [God] have indeed revealed the (Message) in the Night of Power. And what will explain to thee what the Night of Power is? The Night of Power is better than ten thousand Months. Therein come down the angels and the Spirit by God's permission, on every errand: Peace! This until the rise of Morn!

Surah 97[2]

The readings for this Holy Day for Justice challenge us to embrace the diversity that exists in the world and invite us to celebrate it as a gift from God.

---

1. From 2011 through 2020 the date of the Night of Power moves from September to August, July, June, May, and April.
2. Surah 97, describing *Laylat al-Qadr*, Night of Power, in Abdullah Yusef Ali, *The Meaning of the Holy Qur'an*, 9th ed., Arabic and English Texts (Brentwood, MD: Amana Corporation, 1997), 1676

The differences between us do not have to lead to divisions. They can be an opportunity to experience the boundless love and care of our Creator, who nourishes and sustains all people. We see this played out in the lives of two women who were outsiders, foreigners whom some deemed unfit to be part of their community or worthy to sit at their table. Their stories force us to ask ourselves some tough questions. How do I marginalize and exclude people? Who are they? Why do I do this? How can I be more tolerant?

Genesis 21:8–21

It is tough being an older brother in the Hebrew Bible. Scripture contains many stories that speak of firstborn males who are rejected or passed over in favor of their younger siblings. The theme is so common that many scholars believe it might be an intentional device that is meant to reflect some of the historical experiences of the Israelites, who were a relatively small and vulnerable group. The younger brother—the undersized runt of the litter—represents Israel, who is favored by God despite being puny and insignificant.

A similar symbolic reading is commonly applied to stories about Ishmael and Isaac, the sons of Abraham who are central to this passage. It is often claimed that they represent two sets of people who share roots in a common source. Ishmael is considered to be the ancestor of Arabs or Muslims, and Isaac is the forefather of the Jewish and Christian communities. There is nothing in the Bible to support this idea, which is too simplistic a way of understanding the origins of these groups. But it does highlight an undeniable fact: there are many points of contact among the three monotheistic faiths.

Despite those similarities, we often tend to focus on the differences in ways that privilege one side over the other. Members of Isaac's branch of the family tree are sometimes quick to point out that he was the child of the promise, the one chosen by God to pass on the covenant. As a result, Ishmael and his descendants are marginalized and belittled as unworthy or inferior distant relatives who were rejected by God.

Anyone who believes that has not read carefully this passage from Genesis. Like many families, this one experiences tension and division. Irreconcilable differences lead to a split. Child custody is worked out, and each party goes its separate way. But God does not play favorites in this breakup by privileging one side while ignoring the other. The future of each is secured as God explains what awaits them. Isaac will have many children and continue Abraham's line, but Ishmael, too, will prosper. In fact, the passage says twice that Ishmael will have so many offspring they will become a great nation (vv. 13, 18).

God speaks to Hagar, the Egyptian who is not one of the "chosen people," and reassures her that her son will survive and thrive. God also opens her eyes so she can see the water source she and her son desperately need. This is a God who responds to persons in need, regardless of who they are or where they are from. God's concern for Ishmael is expressed in a subtle but powerful way in the story. Immediately after Hagar lifts up her voice and weeps (v. 16), it is stated that God heard the boy's voice. Not the mother's, the boy's. It is Ishmael, the older brother who many think was rejected by God, who gets God's attention.

This story is not found in the Qur'an, and Hagar is not present at all in Islam's sacred text. In fact, the only woman ever mentioned by name in the Qur'an is Mary, the mother of Jesus. Even though it is not in Islamic scripture, other Muslim sources include the tradition about Ishmael and Hagar that is preserved in Genesis 21. The events that are portrayed there are far more significant for Muslims than they are for Jews or Christians because they play a central role in the annual pilgrimage to Mecca, one of the five pillars of Islam. Muslims reenact Hagar's frantic search for water by walking back and forth seven times between two points named Safa and Marwa in a ritual called the sa`i. It is meant to acknowledge humanity's dependence on God, and every year the millions of Muslims who participate in it are a reminder of the "great nation" that Ishmael has become.

Matthew 15:21–28

Today's Gospel reading presents another story about a mother who is concerned about the welfare of her child. Like Hagar, the Canaanite woman is a non-Israelite. And like Ishmael, the daughter in this story is rescued from harm. But the reason for that happy outcome is different this time, and it adds an interesting twist to the story that raises some significant questions.

In the Genesis text, Ishmael's survival is a result of divine intervention. In the midst of a bleak situation he and his mother cry out in desperation, and God steps in to save them. Hagar has lost all hope and is convinced that her son will die, so she gives up and sits down some distance away so she won't have to witness his death.

That is not the way the Canaanite woman responds to her circumstances. She takes the initiative by coming to Jesus and shouting at him, begging for his assistance. At first Jesus doesn't respond, and when he finally does it appears he has heeded his disciples' request to send the woman on her way. But she does not give up, and just when Jesus thinks that he has had the last word, she delivers what might be the best comeback line in the Bible (v. 27).

Jesus acknowledges that it is the woman's faith that heals her daughter. He is not responsible for it, like God in the story from Genesis. It is her doing. And what kind of faith does she have? It is Canaanite faith, non-Israelite faith, foreign faith. Jesus calls attention to this when he says she is a dog rather than a sheep. But the woman does an amazing thing when she is called a dog. She does not deny it or say that she wants to become a sheep. She embraces it and says, "Yes, I am a dog. But that does not mean I do not deserve your care and help." Jesus' response shows he values the faith of a dog as much as the faith of a sheep.

Some Christians believe that the world would be a better place if everyone adopted Christianity. They think Islam is a misguided faith and Muslims need to convert to Christianity in order to be saved. But to think that is to ignore the lesson behind this story, that it is the quality of one's faith, rather than the specific form it takes, that is important. Conviction, not conversion, is what is needed.

Like his disciples, the Canaanite woman was a follower of Jesus, but she expressed her faith in him in a different way than they did. When she called Jesus "Son of David," she was using a special title that recognizes him as the Messiah. Christians are sometimes surprised to learn that Muslims, too, are followers of Jesus. He is a venerated figure in Islam—a prophet to whom God spoke, who was virginally conceived, and who is called the Messiah in the Qur'an. Muslims do not agree with Christians on all matters regarding Jesus, and some of those differences have profound theological implications. Nonetheless, like the Canaanite woman, Islam shows that belief in Jesus can take many forms.

Psalm 100

This psalm strikes the same note of universalism that is found in the two previous readings. It invites "all the earth" (v. 1) to join in a celebration of creation. In this poem we are all God's people and, in an echo of the Gospel story, we are the sheep of God's pasture. The psalm is full of language and imagery that express the pure joy that will result when divisions and differences are overcome. The anxious cries of Hagar, Ishmael, and the Canaanite woman will be replaced with joyful noise, gladness, singing, praise, blessing, and thanksgiving.

Drawing on common human experience, the psalm refers to God in several ways that people can relate to: as creator, shepherd, and king (vv. 3–4). This is reminiscent of the Muslim practice of reciting the ninety-nine names of God. In several places the Qur'an refers to God's names. "There is no god but God, and to God belong the most beautiful names" (Qur'an 20:8). This led to a tradition that God has ninety-nine names, each of which identifies some aspect or quality of the divine nature. Like the images in the psalm, many of the names call attention to God's relationship with creation, like "the king," "the creator," "the protector," and "the loving one."

1 John 2:7–11

The Night of Power that is recalled on this Holy Day for Justice refers to an evening toward the end of the month of Ramadan in the year 610 CE when the prophet Muhammad first began to receive the revelations that would eventually comprise the Qur'an. This reading from 1 John begins with a sentence that succinctly describes how Muslims understand the relationship between their sacred text and the Bible. "Beloved, I am writing you no new commandment, but an old commandment that you have had from the beginning; the old commandment is the word that you have heard."

Islam teaches that throughout history, God has spoken to humanity through prophets, and many of their names are familiar to Bible readers. Among them are Noah, Abraham, Moses, David, Jonah, and Jesus. The message that these prophets delivered to their people was the same in every case: there is only one God to whose will all human beings must submit. According to Muslim belief, this message was sometimes distorted by the followers of the prophets, and that necessitated the sending of a final prophet, Muhammad, whose Qur'an accurately communicated God's will.

The Qur'an is therefore not a "new commandment," to use the language of 1 John, but is the same message that has been delivered to humanity throughout history. This means that Muslims believe the Qur'an and the Bible have the same divine source, just as the offspring of Isaac and Ishmael trace their roots to the same figure, Abraham. The Bible and the Qur'an might be thought of as books that preserve the family history as told from two different perspectives. They are different not because one is right and the other is wrong, as some on each side mistakenly assume. The differences are due to the unique contexts and issues that shaped each side of the family tree. That is what enables the message to be "old" and "new" at the same time.

The author of 1 John uses the image of light frequently in this reading. Who is the brother or sister one must love in order to live in the light? Perhaps this is an invitation to those on the Isaac side of the family to reach across to those on the Ishmael side. If they do so, they might discover that, as both the Qur'an and Bible teach, God is present in the light.

> God is the light of heaven and earth. God's light is like a niche in which is a lamp. The lamp is inside a glass like a shining star with oil from a blessed olive tree from neither the east nor the west. The oil practically gives light even when it is not lit—light upon light. God guides to the light whomever God will. God gives such examples for people and knows everything. (Qur'an 24:35)

Proper 24

Henry H. Mitchell

ISAIAH 45:1–7   EXODUS 33:12–23
PSALM 96:1–9 (10–13)   PSALM 99
                                          1 THESSALONIANS 1:1–10
                                               MATTHEW 22:15–22

Modern technology's conveniences can make us less aware of the Creator's purposes, as we live more in response to ads and trends in the mass media than to God. Common thought holds that if there is any divine purpose, it is overly idealistic and demanding. Some prefer self-centered goals to the inconvenience of following divine goals. Among Christians, there is widespread failure to follow God's will in all of life's decisions. "Christ's lordship" seems only a pious phrase.

An intellectual basis for resistance to traditional beliefs and values is often sought in the theological problems of theodicy: How could an omnipotent, gracious, and loving God permit creation to contain so much evil and suffering? Freedom of moral choice may explain some catastrophes, but catastrophes such as tsunamis, in which thousands lose their lives, seem to some to invalidate any belief in God's grace and justice. The readings for this week present a wide range of historic doctrines, along with solid apologetics supporting reasonable belief and gut-level trust in the God of creation, grace, providence, and justice—One who is the ultimate ruler and Lord of human history.

Isaiah 45:1–7

Through Isaiah, God says that the mighty King Cyrus of the great Persian Empire is serving at the pleasure of Jehovah, Lord of the Israelites. Cyrus is God's "right hand." God has worked through unbelievers time after time and is Lord over *all* human history. We have free moral choice in many lesser decisions, but the major *ends* of history ultimately fulfill the will of God.

441

This is in spite of the sinfulness of God's instruments, and not *because of* any ethical goodness they may have. World history abounds with examples of victory for lesser powers whose cause was just—victories by the hand of God. For instance, slavery might still exist if it were left up to most North-erners. New Yorkers sympathetic to slavery participated in anti-draft riots and burned the homes of and murdered many African Americans. Lincoln's Emancipation Proclamation freed none of the slaves in the states that had not seceded from the Union. Furthermore, he resisted enlisting African Ameri-cans until compelled to do so by military necessity, offering them only half the regular pay. White Union officers brutally exposed African American troops, intentionally dropping howitzer shells on them in what is now called "friendly fire." Finally, the political influence of the abolitionists was negli-gible. Thus, credit for the emancipation of our grandparents belongs only to the Lord of History.

The newly freed slaves first proclaimed the Lord of History as the one who freed them. Uneducated ex-slaves were heard to declare, "Marse Lincum sign de paper, but Gawd de one what sot us free."[1] Another instant theologian in this matter was President Lincoln. Upon signing the terms of surrender, he mounted the Capitol steps and declared, "In reference to you, colored people, let me say God has made you free."[2]

God rules the ends of history, but many people still question the good-ness and power of God, who permits the unspeakable suffering of tsunamis and other natural disasters. But a larger consideration of scientific insights may afford us a new perspective. In a twelfth-grade physics class, I remember "Professor" Bailey asking what would happen if frozen water did not expand into ice. There was silence. He asked whether it would make a difference if, instead of expanding and floating, the ice sank to the bottom, like everything else. Again, silence. He jovially pointed out that heat exchange between sur-face and underground water would be cut off by the heavier hunks of sunken ice, and the earth would get too hot during summer and too cold during winter for human life to survive. With a tear in his eye, Mr. B commented that this was a public school, and he could not say more. He clearly wanted to tell us about God who was able to arrange creation in ways that allowed humankind to live on earth.

Mr. B would have loved a comment from the article "Why We Need Earthquakes." The article explained, "Without plate tectonics, earth's land

---

1. Folk saying recalled by author.
2. Isaac J. Hill, *A Sketch of the 29th Regiment of Connecticut Colored Troops* (Baltimore: Daughtery, Maguire & Co., 1867), 26, 27, quoted in W. E. B. DuBois, *Black Reconstruction in America: 1860–1880* (1935; repr., New York: Free Press, 1998), 112.

would be submerged to a depth of several thousand feet."[3] These earth-shifting masses cause quakes and tsunamis, but without them there would not be higher ground for humans and other creatures to occupy. To be sure, we must learn to understand God's purpose for us—and we must also work to develop buildings that will absorb the power of these natural disasters, as we did in the aftermath of earthquakes in San Francisco and Los Angeles. We must educate ourselves and others on heeding the signs of impending natural disasters and do all that we can to prevent global warming and its terrible consequences. Or perhaps we may join other creatures who know how to flee to safety when they sense God's signals of impending danger. Ideally, we will cease questioning the purposes of the Lord of History and seek to find our own place and purpose in God's creation.

Our role is to seek all possible knowledge of the universe and then to be content within our limitations, with the hope that, in the afterlife with God, "We will understand it better by and by."

Psalm 99

God's lordship over the earth and its history is to be held in awe, not feared. In joyful response to divine sovereignty, we must stand in awe of God's greatness and support justice that reflects divine mercy and forgiveness.

Do we, as Americans, fully understand and seek justice in this great democracy? Do we consider our justice constitutionally guaranteed or do we recognize, rejoice, and tremble when we consider God's rule and reign over us, as does the psalmist?

The answer is a resounding No; we seek a majority vote as the guarantor of justice, mistaking political power for righteousness. As an example of this, we have only to consider the report of a jury trial where the wisdom of the minority was overruled by the wrongheadedness of the majority: a veteran African American court reporter, seated as a juror with two other African Americans (both with legal experience) and nine whites, heard evidence against a Black male accused of assaulting a white female.[4] The defendant faced a jail term of fifty-two years. Despite nonexistent injuries, the jurors voted nine to three for a guilty verdict. The white jurors deeply resented the legal insights of the three Black jurors and never once dealt with their objections. The accused was saved by a hung jury (with no retrial) from what would have been an unjust prison term, based on a majority vote of presumably fair-minded citizen-jurors. We shudder to think how many others have received

3. Dinesh D'Souza, "Why We Need Earthquakes," *Christianity Today* 53, no. 5 (May 2009): 58.
4. Personal communication to the author from an anonymous source.

unjust verdicts and have served undeserved sentences due to the prejudices of unjust power-holders. A jury that does not celebrate and pursue God's justice is an instrument of injustice and oppression, no matter how skillfully masked their patriotic jury duty may be. Our God quite literally loves justice, equity, and righteousness.

The psalmist portrays God as holy and transcendent, as well as loving and intimate. God's justice is more than a cold, abstract concept that focuses on a distant, retributive ideal: it is practiced in the specific instances of daily life, by the loving and forgiving Lord of History. To seriously seek justice is as deeply spiritual and pleasing to God as prayer and generosity to the poor. It is surely as pious, "religious," and spiritual as worship.

The quest for justice may lead one into politics, which is often believed to be too "dirty" for believers. The Rev. James Poindexter, a native of Richmond, Virginia, and pastor of the Second Baptist Church of Columbus, Ohio, gained insight and oratorical skill by listening to the conversations of legislators in the state capital's barbershop while they had their hair cut and faces shaved. He responded in later years to those who criticized his prophetic leadership as "dirty politics" and inappropriate for a gospel preacher by citing examples of Jesus and the Hebrew prophets: "Wherever there is a sin to be rebuked, no matter by whom committed, and ill to be averted or good to be achieved by our country or mankind, there is a place for the pulpit to make itself felt and heard . . . the task requires all available hands to secure the ends for which governments are formed."[5]

Psalm 96:1–9 (10–13)

Here again we find the theme of praising God who is the creator of all the earth, its people, creatures, and nature. The psalmist's strong emphasis on God's salvation, glory, splendor, strength, and power is finally supplemented with praise of God's holiness and the righteousness and equity of divine judgment.

The psalmist insists that God is worthy of all this praise. In fact, the psalmist's praise picks up on the waves radiating from plants and rocks, converting them into what could be sounds of praise. Could this be what Jesus was referring to when he spoke of the rocks crying out (Luke 19:40)?

Teaching and preaching from this psalm must emphasize equally rejoicing in God and in God's justice and righteousness. Praise is empty when it does not include a balanced and holistic celebration of *all* of God's being and purposes.

---

5. Carter G. Woodson, *The History of the Negro Church* (Washington, D.C.: Associated Publishers, 1972), 202.

Not that God needs our praise, since rocks cry out on God's behalf. But to neglect our praise of God or the practice and praise of divine justice and righteousness misrepresents God's intentions for our lives. The entirety of God's purposes demands both praise of God and righteous living. We have misunderstood worship if we think we can worship God while choosing our own unhealthy lifestyles or immoral practices. Indeed, all creation is called to celebrate God and God's justice; after all, the psalmist concludes this song of praise with a vision of trees rejoicing over God's righteous judgment of the earth.

1 Thessalonians 1:1–10

The apostle Paul is often heard defending himself against false charges, especially in 2 Corinthians. We hear this underlying his First Letter to the Thessalonians also as he takes pride in furthering the witness of the Thessalonian Christians. As former idol worshipers, the Thessalonians provide an impressive example of how God used Paul's ministry to convert and reorient people's lives. In verse 9, he takes special pride in the fact that they had completely turned away from idols, with their own witness now becoming effective as the gospel was spread as far away as Greece and Macedonia.

This reminds me of the unlikely witness and ministry of a popular musician. Someone was used by God (as was Paul) to win Bono to Christ. He in turn (like the Thessalonians) has influenced innumerable other unlikely musicians to be used by God in healing ministries in Africa. They still sing praises to earn a living, as it were, but their music helps bring divine justice and mercy to places otherwise neglected by the world. An article titled "Songs of Justice, Missions of Mercy" describes this as "the Bono Factor," and describes the process: "Musician-led activism crossed a threshold in December 2002 when Bono traveled to Nashville, a stop on his AIDS-awareness Heart of America tour, to meet with Christian bands and artists."[6] God's great and glorious deeds find their way to the ends of the earth not only by God's power but also by our participation in the gospel's outreach to others.

The day is over when Christians need to feel compelled to choose between worshiping God and doing acts of justice and merciful concern for others. Neither is complete and authentic without the other. Only the combination of these is acceptable to the living and true God who desires the well-being of all creation.

---

6. Mark Moring, "Songs of Justice, Missions of Mercy," *Christianity Today* 53, no. 11 (November 2009): 30–32.

Matthew 22:15–22

This story is often seen as a tribute to the clever thinking of Jesus, and it is certainly right to recognize Christ's wisdom as he encountered adversarial situations. However, this incident may also be of great practical help and importance in serving as a model for our ministry to strangers and enemies. Two aspects of Jesus' strategy come to mind.

First, Jesus entered the culture of the Pharisees. He used words and images out of their language and experience. In continuing to address their question about taxes and using the image of the coin, Jesus was able to stay within their frame of reference and to avoid fruitless conflict. To stay in their world was to allow communication within their value system. One cannot argue effectively about values to people who are unfamiliar with them. One argues *within* the assumed value system of the opponent, as if it were common ground. This is not a matter of conceding to strange or adverse values, but rather of using them as a beginning point from which to reach for higher purposes.

The Pharisees' failure to draw Jesus into a debate was sufficient evidence of their defeat. However, the second strategic decision that Jesus made offered them the opportunity to leave without further insult or injury: he refrained from declaring himself right and offered instead a wise saying at the conclusion of his discourse (v. 21b). This may well have contributed not only to their amazement but also to an openness to listen again to this new teacher from Galilee. Without violence to his enemies, episodes such as this establish Jesus' lordship in history.

Exodus 33:12–23

It is best to read this passage with a sense of humor. Moses has experienced enough of God's personal election to feel his oats spiritually. He craves even more of God's glory, which, of course, would strengthen his leadership. Incidentally, the evidence of God's glory given to Moses (through his radiant countenance) would have also incurred great respect and glory for Moses. However, he makes the mistake of setting terms and conditions on God. How else will the people be assured of God's presence in all that is happening, unless it is evident to him and all others?

Moses' questions and arguments exert pressure. It is comparable to saying, "If I am to continue to lead God's people, here is what God needs to do." Imagine Moses' nerve!

And imagine God's patience in devising a plan to satisfy Moses' request without burning him to a crisp. Moses apparently had no idea how utterly presumptuous it was for him to suggest an eye-to-eye conference with God.

Give him a bit of spiritual insight and authority, and Moses is suddenly aspiring to commune with God on equal terms.

Moses is not the only one to do this. If God does not reveal answers to our questions, we are likely to deny God's very existence.

Theologically, it appears that the wisdom of knowing our limitations and praising the One who sets them is at least as old as Exodus. God alone is omniscient. Human beings who seek to share that attribute know not the awesome error of their efforts to be self-appointed judges and rulers of the universe.

World Food Day (October 16)

James L. McDonald

Deuteronomy 24:19–21
Psalm 113
Acts 6:1–6
Mark 8:1–10

World Food Day, which was first observed in 1981, takes place on October 16 in recognition of the founding of the United Nations Food and Agriculture Organization. The purpose of World Food Day is to arouse action against world hunger. From the perspective of World Food Day, the preacher can encourage the congregation to engage in comprehensive efforts to end hunger by directly providing food for hungry people, by pressing for patterns of growing and using food that benefit local communities, by taking action designed to change systems of food production and distribution, and by advocating healthy and responsible eating.

> You and I are walking along the downtown canal and see a toddler fall into the water. The canal is only a few feet deep, but the child goes under. We watch her struggle. I decide that I can't risk ruining my new shoes and pants by getting them wet. You determine that you can't afford the time it would take to get the child out. . . . We turn away, leaving the child to die. We would never do that, would we? We already do. Nearly a billion people go to bed hungry every night.
>
> *Fran Quigley*[1]

The relationship between food and faith is strong. The Bible is full of stories of hunger, bread, and feeding. From manna in the wilderness to the Lord's Prayer, from the Last Supper to John's revelation that God will culminate

---

1. Fran Quigley, "Save Kids Drowning in Poverty," *Indianapolis Star*, February 23, 2009.

salvation history with a moment when humankind will "hunger no more" (Rev. 7:16), the importance of food in the practice of our faith cannot be underestimated. Each of the passages appointed for World Food Day emphasizes this critical relationship. Bread and hunger are central themes in Jesus' earthly ministry. You will find the story of the feeding of the multitudes in all four Gospels, and twice in Matthew and Mark. This is an opportunity for the preacher to move the congregation to accept that addressing hunger—physical hunger, not just spiritual hunger—is an integral part of Christian faith. Gandhi is widely credited in the popular press, scholarly literature, and elsewhere with saying, "There are so many hungry people that God cannot appear to them except in the form of bread."

Deuteronomy 24:19–21 and Psalm 113

In Deuteronomy and throughout the Bible, God's intention for humanity is abundantly clear: the most vulnerable must be protected and cared for. The verses here are pointed and specific: no one should go hungry. Share the food you have with those who do not have enough.

As Psalm 113 reminds us, God's intentions reflect God's very nature. God is exalted above every other god in every time and place. Yet God's first concern is for the poor and needy, whose misfortune God seeks to reverse. We give glory to God when we seek to reflect God's nature in our own actions.

Many of the laws in Deuteronomy no longer seem applicable in the twenty-first century. But their underlying principle remains valid even today. Citizenship brings responsibility, personal and shared, for our common life. As Christians, we are not only citizens of a country; we are citizens of the world.

Deuteronomy should not be read simply as a recitation of Jewish law without acknowledging the context. Context is half the message here. The last book of the Torah, Deuteronomy interrupts the flow of salvation history to remind the people of Israel what their journey to the promised land is all about.

Once you were slaves; now you are free.

Once you were no people; now you are God's people.

Once you lived by human rule; now you live by God's rule.

Apart from its specific laws, Deuteronomy says this: Don't forget whose you are, people of Israel. The God who created the world brought you here, to this time and place. And God saved you for a purpose. God blessed you so that you would be a blessing to others. Remember that, O Israel, as you enter the promised land.

In the twenty-first century, the contextual equivalent of entering the promised land may be a global economic recovery from the Great Recession. If we Christians measure the economic recovery only by the return of profits to business and rising investments on Wall Street, without thought for the well-being of the hundreds of millions who were driven deeper into hunger and poverty, we have forgotten who we are as God's people. Our economic recovery in the United States will be neither just nor sustainable if prosperity and economic stability continue to elude the majority of the world's people.

A return to the "business as usual" that got us into the economic mess would be the equivalent of the Israelites' return to the slavery they knew in Egypt. Before Israel crossed the Jordan, God asked them to adopt a new set of laws and establish a new set of social relationships. Today, God asks the same thing of us as we think about the future of the economy, globally and in the United States. The laws of Deuteronomy are not about personal holiness so much as they are a prescription for social relationships: "Here is how I want you to live together, O Israel. Here is what it means to be God's people."

Mark 8:1–10

The story of the feeding of the four thousand in Mark highlights a conflict between Jesus' desire to feed the crowd and the disciples' protest that there is not enough food to give them. This is the issue Fran Quigley raises in the quotation above, and it is what one often hears from Christians and other people of goodwill when confronted with the problem of hunger. "Nice idea, pastor, but the problem of hunger is too big to solve." The compassion of do-gooders is trumped by the realism of good but worldly-wise people.

The shocking reality is that in a world where more than one billion people go to bed hungry every night, enough food is being produced to feed everyone. This has led some to assume that the real problem is food distribution, that is, we just need to figure out how to get food to people who need it. But getting wheat grown in Montana to hungry people in Mexico, Mozambique, or Myanmar is not a solution.

The shameful reality is that the majority of the more than one billion hungry people around the world are themselves farmers—smallholder farmers in poor countries. Nearly 70 percent of chronically hungry people live in rural areas. They work hard, day in, day out, year-round to produce food, but they cannot feed themselves or their families. The main cause of hunger in the world is not poor food distribution; it is the lack of resources available to poor people themselves because they are poor.

Until recently, the world had been making progress against hunger. In 1970, one in three people around the world went to bed hungry. By 2000, the number of hungry people was one in six. Over those three decades the number of hungry people in the world had been reduced in absolute terms, from 970 million to 800 million, even as the world's population was rising. In places like China, Chile, Ghana, Vietnam, Brazil, Bangladesh, and Thailand, significant numbers of people have been moving out of poverty, and chronic hunger has decreased. This great exodus from poverty is the experience of God's liberation in our time. Ending hunger is not an impossible dream.

The world knows a lot about what it takes to end hunger. The main ingredient is political will, something that ebbs and flows. It takes the engagement of the whole society—government, the private sector, nongovernmental organizations, religious leaders, and ordinary citizens—to make an economy work for everyone, including the most vulnerable. But political leadership is a key element, and people of faith, using the power of their moral voice, can catalyze and motivate that political leadership to step up and do something about hunger.

With so many hungry people living in rural areas and relying on farming for their livelihoods, it makes sense for public policy to concentrate on improvements in agriculture, especially smallholder agriculture. After years of neglect, there is fresh interest in agriculture and an emerging global effort to reform and revitalize agricultural systems to address the resurgence of hunger and food insecurity across the globe. As Christians, we can let our political leaders know that hunger is an important issue we want them to address and encourage them to devote more resources to supporting smallholder farmers, most of whom are women.

When Jesus saw that the crowd was hungry, he asked his disciples to figure out how to feed them. His sense of compassion meant that he was truly interested in their well-being, not just in an individual sense, but in a collective sense as well. More than simply providing each person with some bread, he was trying to organize a common meal, a supper shared in the Spirit. The disciples looked at the solution in terms of food. Jesus asked them to look for a solution based on the people themselves.

The disciples thought the problem was too big, their resources too meager. But Jesus saw something they could not see: the possibility of human community, the satisfaction that comes when people work together to solve problems, the joy of human solidarity. Jesus' leadership transformed a disparate group of hungry people into a community of compassion and justice.

God was present when four thousand people broke bread and gave it to each other. The miracle was that so many strangers were willing to share what they had with one another. All were filled; there was more than enough. It was a moment not of transaction but of transformation.

Acts 6:1–6

This passage reminds us that in every community, Christian or not, there is unjust discrimination. In the early Christian community a problem arose because Greek-speaking widows were being ignored in the daily distribution of food. A group of people was being treated differently for no good reason, based on the language spoken, and probably their (low) social status as well.

One of the root causes of hunger continues to be unjust discrimination, including racism. One tribe prevents another from receiving what rightly belongs to all. This occurs within communities, within countries, and internationally. Despite its proscription in international law, hunger is often used as a weapon of war and oppression. How can such discrimination ever be justified? How can such actions and tactics ever be permitted?

The early apostles reacted to public criticism of their program and established a diaconate to change the way they carried out their responsibilities to hungry people and ensure fairness. The Greek *diakonia* is translated as "service." But service as it is used here means more than feeding hungry people. It means doing justice. Here, a wrong is addressed; an act of unjust discrimination is redressed; a breach of community is healed.

Doing justice means transformation. Everything is changed: the people, the circumstances, and the relationships. Justice is the act of establishing or restoring broken relationships that respect the dignity and honor the worth of each person. Justice involves a new partnership between the parties involved. Each comes to the table as an equal in God's eyes. Each brings something to the table. The solution to the problem is negotiated, and each must change to accommodate the new relationship. In doing justice there is a new creation.

At the core of the Christian life is the sacrament of the Lord's Supper, when all who trust Jesus as Lord and Savior gather at table to share bread broken and cup poured out. In so doing, Christians unite themselves with Christ in order to be his body in service to a broken, hungry, and hurting world. In that act, food and faith are inextricably bound together, just as they were for the early church.

Each of the Scripture readings emphasizes the way in which a community figured out a new way to help those who were hungry. Compassionate laws, better public policies, and moral leadership—each of these is needed to address hunger in this country and around the world.

Proper 25

Angela Cowser

DEUTERONOMY 34:1–12	PSALM 1
LEVITICUS 19:1–2, 15–18	PSALM 90:1–6, 13–17
	1 THESSALONIANS 2:1–8
	MATTHEW 22:34–46

This week's lectionary readings call for God's people to live obedient, holy lives. A holy person's first loyalty should be to God, which means love of God and neighbor without manipulation, limits, or conditions, and obedience to justice, peacemaking, and righteous living.

Deuteronomy 34:1–12

Deuteronomy is a book of stories from Israel's past told to shape identity and form behavior. The covenant between Israel and God is framed by exclusive loyalty and fidelity to each other; God will assure the well-being of Israel, and Israel will live by trust in and obedience to God.

With the exodus and events at Sinai and the wilderness behind him, Moses speaks at length to the people. His death is imminent, and the people are gathered on the edge of the promised land. Israel stands at a turning point; obedience means life and prosperity, and disobedience will yield death and destruction. Moses' concern is that Israel remember to be faithful to its covenant with God, the tenets of which should be decisive and obeyed in every aspect of Israel's public. Just and compassionate relations with neighbors, near and far, will provide important marks of faithfulness.

In God's social order, people will love God with their whole selves. God's principles for holy living and proper worship include the following lessons: God's teachers will instruct everyone, especially children, to observe God's commands and decrees (Deut. 6:7). One-tenth of all that the fields produce will be set aside for God (14:22). Every seventh year, all debts and loans will be canceled (15:1). Judges will be impartial, serving "justice, and only justice"

453

(16:18–20). Perfect obedience will yield a society without poverty (28:1–14), whereas disobedience will yield social injustice and destruction of the nation (28:15–68).

When claimants other than God receive our highest loyalty, the poor are not justly treated. Instead, wealth concentrates in the hands of a few, while oppression and injustice toward the oppressed increase. In our day, many small business owners cannot obtain the credit needed to expand their businesses. Many middle-class families are sliding into poverty. Visits to food banks are at record levels. Many will justify, individualize, or spiritualize these conditions, but institutions and individuals must find ways to address these injustices. Oh, how I long to live in a community where debts are forgiven, children are taught to do justice when they rise and when they lie down at night, and the truth is told. That is a place where the Lord really is our life!

Leviticus 19:1–2, 15–18

Leviticus is a book of instructions for holiness. The first half teaches the faithful how to worship God; the second half outlines rules and standards for holy living. After delivering detailed guidelines pertaining to sexual conduct, in chapter 19 God reminds the people that holy living includes keeping the commandments, cultivating a loving attitude toward family members and neighbors alike, and being good stewards of the land and its yield by protecting and honoring workers, poor people, and foreigners.

Holding to prescribed sexual boundaries is an important signifier of holiness; however, equally important to God are the ways we appropriate land, harvest, and money with respect to the poor. God is generous to us; why then should we not be generous to others, especially foreigners and people encountering financial hardship? I think one answer relates to how we think about poverty. Do we assume that people are pathologically poor because of cultural deviance and unhealthy psychosocial characteristics, or do we believe that poverty may be explained by structural forces, including racism? Similarly, do we consider people to be pathologically rich because of cultural deviance and unhealthy psychosocial characteristics, or is excessive wealth explained by structural forces that privilege those in power? Good people disagree about the reasons for economic hardship or success, but both poor and wealthy in the Bible are shown a way through calamity and exploitation.

Just, fair, and impartial judgments are also important. In Leviticus 19:15–18, people are unjustly accused due to partiality, discrimination, lying, envy, jealousy, and hatred shown toward them. Today many people are falsely accused and imprisoned for crimes they did not commit. Most emerge from jail poorer than when they entered. According to the Innocence Project, a national litigation and public policy organization dedicated to exonerating wrongfully convicted people through DNA testing, the average length of time served by people who were exonerated was thirteen years.[1] Their average age at the time of their wrongful convictions was twenty-seven. Only half of the 280 persons exonerated through DNA testing have been financially compensated for their incarceration. Seventy-five percent of wrongful convictions occur through eyewitness misidentification, 50 percent through improper forensic science, 25 percent through false confessions and incriminating statements, and 19 percent through the word of informants. People whose slander and lies cause others to suffer are enemies of God. However, God offers us a way out of this morass by remembering that we can and should treat others the way we want to be treated. Vengeance is best left to God, who is slow to anger and great in power. God will not leave the guilty unpunished.

Psalm 1

Covenant theology between Israel and God means exclusive loyalty and fidelity to each other. God assures the well-being of God's people, and the people are to live with trust in and obedience to God. However, God's people do not remain faithful. In both Deuteronomy and Leviticus, Moses exhorts Israel—and all peoples and all nations, for all time—to form their identity and behavior according to divinely ordained ways of justice, peace, and righteousness.

Book 1 of the Psalms (Pss. 1–41) presents humans as blessed, fallen, and redeemed by God. The writer of Psalm 1 echoes Moses' words in Leviticus by saying that blessed people are those who delight in the law of the Lord and meditate on it day and night. The "happy" are God-centered people whose faithfulness to God is their highest loyalty. Conversely, the wicked are sinners who choose the wrong way; mockers are the overconfident who arrogantly refuse to accept instruction and correction. The wicked trust in their wealth and in the abundance of their riches; visibly, they prosper. Conversely, godly prosperity means being connected to and in communion with the Lord. For those with eyes to see, the prosperity of the righteous is real and is visible to those who are being saved. But for those who are perishing, the prosperity of the righteous is hidden. At all costs, the ways of the wicked, sinners, and mockers are to be avoided.

This text recalls a day in March 1965 at the Edmund Pettus Bridge in Selma, Alabama, where peaceful civil rights marchers were attacked and beaten by sneering segregationists and anxious policemen in a paroxysm of

---

1. http://www.innocenceproject.org (accessed December 7, 2011). Since the organization's founding in 1992, more than 250 people have been exonerated through DNA testing in the United States, including 17 who were at one time sentenced to death.

hate and violence. The wicked were confounded and confused; the peacemakers were those who heard the word of God and obeyed it at great personal cost, even unto death.

The eschatological perspective that the psalmist provides proclaims that God's reign is both a present and a future reality. Helping believers frame their understanding of prosperity in biblical terms confirms for new and mature believers alike that happiness is hearing the Word of God and doing it. I worked with a group of happy people in 2010, the Shack Dwellers of Namibia, which includes 22,000 poor families who have banded together to fight poverty and homelessness by leaving their shacks and building their own modest homes. They have given their whole selves over to God and community, and in doing so are changing their families, communities, and nation. They have said no to individualism, and yes to an abundance of riches gained through sharing resources one with another. Brick by brick, house by house, the Shack Dwellers say yes to life. Happy are those who delight in the teaching of the Lord and doing God's will.

Psalm 90:1–6, 13–17

Psalm 90, one of the oldest psalms, affirms the eternal nature of God, creator of all worlds. The first two verses speak of God's time and eternal sovereignty, omnipotence, and power. This psalm is to be read in the context of Moses reminding us to be faithful and obedient to God, our Alpha and Omega, the First and the Last, the Beginning and the End.

For many postmodern Americans, it is the market, not God, that rules. Remarkably, what matters is not good parenting or faithful citizenship, but rather one's individual brand, one's market position or market share. In this scheme, God is irrelevant and people who believe in God are considered quaint and often pitied.

In many quarters, there is indifference, ignorance, even embarrassment about God and belief in God. According to Eric Weiner, "In my secular, urban and urbane world, God is rarely spoken of, except in mocking, derisive tones. It is acceptable to cite the latest academic study on, say, happiness or, even better, whip out a brain scan, but God? He is for suckers, and Republicans."[2]

We believe fervently in ourselves. We build up our self-esteem, improve our self-worth, and labor to increase our net worth; we are self-centered, self-absorbed, self-directed, and self-ruled. But is our security and salvation really to be found in ourselves and the marketplace? By no means! It is God and

2. Eric Weiner, "Americans: Undecided About God?" *New York Times*, December 11, 2011.

only God who has been our "dwelling place" from generation to generation. To the quaint who revere and obey God, the Potentate of Time will remain our "dwelling place" from everlasting to everlasting. Likewise, our prosperity and security are found in doing the work that God teaches us to do, for "God, who has been our help in ages past and our hope for years to come, will be our guard while life shall last, and our eternal home."[3]

The Psalter tells us that the nature of God is revealed in divine *hesed*—compassion, grace, and steadfast love—offered to all people. But God also punishes the guilty: the arrogant and autonomous, those who are willfully dismissive of and refuse to relate to God. Verses 13–17 plead for God to forgive the sinfulness that alienates us from God, creation, and each other. If we repent, God will relent. Because God is eternal and faithful and eternally faithful in turning toward humanity, our time on earth can become more meaningful, purposeful, and enduring as we enter into justice and caring relationships with others.

Happiness is delight in the teaching of the Lord and in doing God's will. Even as I tremble and weep, I am happy when standing in the pulpit, preaching a Holy Spirit–inspired sermon to the humble, or distributing Communion elements to the heavy-laden. Blessed are those who hear the word of God and obey it. Just as Moses called the people of Israel, we should also live faithfully and gratefully drink in the Word of God, meditating on it day and night, with gratitude.

1 Thessalonians 2:1–8

First Thessalonians is the earliest of Paul's extant letters, which makes it the earliest Christian document in the New Testament. Thessalonian Christians were faithful people who responded to Paul's gospel by forming a new community of persevering believers who were learning to lead lives worthy of God, in mutual love and trust. Repentance from the old practices and acceptance of the new, even unto death, were powerful markers of membership. But saying yes to the gospel often meant conflict and alienation, persecution, and even death. To people who were giving up everything, Paul was encouraging steadfastness and persistence until the Day of the Lord. Then as now, people must choose and continue to choose whom they will serve.

Prior to his first trip to Thessalonica, Paul had been imprisoned, yet he continued to preach—not for money, fame, or popularity, but to save souls and to build up the body of Christ in mutual love and trust. Then as now, we contend with a plethora of preachers who speak with competing motives and

---

3. Adapted from verse 1 of "O God, Our Help in Ages Past," in *African American Heritage Hymnal* (Chicago: GIA Publications, 2001), #170.

offer (mis)interpretations of the gospel. In Paul's time and ours, much that passes for "gospel preaching" is nothing more than silky words crafted to please mortals and not God, who tests our hearts.

It is difficult to preach the gospel so that it pleases God, even in a nation that views itself as Christian, for there are so many other commitments, issues, and little gods that compete for our souls. For example, how do I preach against racism when most of the churches in America are still the standard-bearers for racially segregated worship? How do I preach about justice when so many fellowships are content to offer only minor tokens of charity, or worse, nothing at all to help the poor? There is apathy and opposition to the gospel from within and without. Still, God's reign, in which the happy find refuge and life, is both a present and a future reality. The call is to lead a life worthy of God. In my experience, this includes participating in Bible studies that are loving and relational, challenging norms, assumptions, and prejudices that blight our Christian witness. It also means working with community organizations that help shape a more just social, political, and economic order for *all* people, especially the poor and oppressed whom God loves.

Matthew 22:34–46

Matthew 22:34–46 comes near the end of the Gospel, which begins with Jesus' birth and moves into the Sermon on the Mount, the performance of many miracles, and Jesus' proclamation of God's reign. Here Jesus is contending with differing reactions to his teaching and ministry. For example, he confronts different Jewish groups about disputes over which laws and traditions will govern Israel. In this pericope, Jesus fields a third hostile question from a Pharisee about which commandment is the greatest. Jesus responds with two answers: to love God with all of our heart, soul, and mind (cf. Deut. 6:5) and to love our neighbor as we love ourselves (cf. Lev. 19:18). Here, Jesus expands the definition of neighbor to include one's enemies. The kind of love Jesus speaks of is an unmanipulative, unlimited, unconditional love, based on commitment and demonstrated through right action. After he delivers his answer, the religious leaders are silent and refrain from asking Jesus any more questions.

Why were so many so angry about Jesus' teaching? Jesus' parables and exchanges identify him as the Son of God. Jesus denounces the religious leaders for failing to understand and do the will of God. Jesus anticipates an expansion of God's reign that includes not only Jews but also Gentiles who follow God's will. In our day, where can we learn how to produce the fruit of God's reign? Peacemakers can learn how to resolve violent international conflicts nonviolently at the U.S. Institute of Peace. Seminarians can learn about nonviolence, conflict mediation, and peacemaking at several seminaries in the United States, and laypeople interested in reconciliation and compassion in the service of nonviolent social action can find kindred spirits in the Fellowship of Reconciliation. There are many ways to learn the ways of "happiness," please Jesus, silence Satan, and cause the angels in heaven to dance with joyous abandon. May it be so.

Children's Sabbaths
(Third Weekend in October)

Shannon Daley-Harris

2 KINGS 4:1–7
PSALM 127
EPHESIANS 6:1–4
LUKE 2:41–52

The National Observance of Children's Sabbaths® weekend was founded by the Children's Defense Fund in 1992 to encourage religious communities to honor children as sacred gifts and to nurture, protect, and advocate on behalf of children. Congregations focus worship, education programs, and activities on the urgent needs of children in our nation and on God's call to respond with justice and compassion. This event is designated for the third weekend of October. The sermon is a vital opportunity to give voice to the crises facing our nation's children—such as poverty, violence, lack of health care, abuse, and neglect—as well as opportunities for us to respond with justice and mercy to increase the quality of life for children in the local community and throughout our nation.

> The Bible is replete with the images and power of small things which achieve great ends when they are grounded in faith: a mustard seed, a jawbone, a stick, a slingshot, a widow's mite. We must not, in trying to think about how we can make a difference, ignore the small daily differences we can make which, over time, add up to big differences that we often cannot foresee.
> *Marian Wright Edelman*[1]

The first pair of texts, from the Hebrew Scriptures, offer a glimpse of how our efforts along with God's inspiration and guidance can provide for the needs of families. The two passages from the Gospel and Epistle speak to the complex

---

1. Marian Wright Edelman, *Families in Peril* (Cambridge, MA: Harvard University Press, 1987), 107.

dynamics in parent-child relationships and remind us that our family relationships lie within the broader embrace and context of God's love and claim on our hearts, minds, and lives. All of the texts invite us to be aware that in every aspect of our lives—in our working, parenting, learning, and loving—God is at the center.

2 Kings 4:1–7

The story of Elisha and the widow's oil is the first of several stories in which Elisha might be called a community organizer or multi-issue child and family advocate. After this story, he goes on to tackle the health and healing of a child, feeding the hungry, and more. This prophet who has counseled political leaders and been involved in affairs of state is also engaged at the most immediate, personal level with the poorest and least powerful members of the community.

Like widows of her day (and sometimes in ours), the mother in this passage has become financially vulnerable and is in debt to a creditor. Legally, the creditor has the right to take her children (see also Exod. 21:7). Although in desperate circumstances, she is not a passive victim: she appeals to the prophet for help. The prophet does three key things. First, he listens to her description of the problem. Second, he asks her what she thinks he should do. Third, he asks her what resources she has to bring to the solution.[2] Building on the widow's own, if meager, resources—just a vial of oil—the prophet outlines a plan that includes borrowing empty vessels. Note that the prophet does not tell the mother to go to her relatives, closest friend, or nearest neighbor: he tells her to "borrow vessels from *all* your neighbors" (v. 3, emphasis mine). The children also get involved, collecting the vessels.

This story offers timeless insights. First, it affirms the strength of the mother who took the initiative in seeking help. Second, Elisha models how God's people can respond to parents by asking how we may best be of help (rather than guessing or assuming we know best), asking what resources parents and other caregivers have to offer, and knowing that God will use all of our efforts and contributions to be of help to others. Third, all of the family members were involved in helping to improve their circumstances. In this case, the children also served as participants and advocates to ensure their own freedom and future. Finally, the entire community shared their resources to aid their neighbors, as we may expect that our communities and nation may respond to the needs of desperate families and contribute to their well-being.

---

2. In *Helpmates, Harlots, and Heroes: Women's Stories in the Hebrew Bible*, 2nd ed. (Louisville, KY: Westminster John Knox Press, 2007), Alice Ogden Bellis builds on Johanna van Wijk-Bos's insights into this story, including these vital elements of Elisha's response.

We catch glimpses of this prophetic approach in the global movement for microcredit loans (i.e., small loans to very poor people, especially women, who seek financial security through self-employment) and in the "family preservation" approach to child welfare (i.e., seeking when appropriate and possible to build on the best in fragile families to strengthen them rather than removing their children). Those who work with and on behalf of children will hear vital insights in this passage that will help guide them on this Holy Day for Justice on behalf of children.

Psalm 127

This Song of Ascent is associated with pilgrimages to Jerusalem and is a companion to Psalm 128 (see commentary for Children's Sabbaths in Year C of this series). We who are on a journey toward justice might keep a version of this song on our lips.

The first verse contains two sayings that emphasize the importance of understanding that our personal peace and security are dependent on God's involvement in our lives. In verses 3–5, the focus shifts from our work to a description of families whose children are believed to be a blessing from God (the NRSV translates the Hebrew word *banim* as "sons," but the RSV, KJV, and JPS use the more inclusive and equally valid translation "children"). The "heritage" spoken of in verse 3 may also refer to the Davidic dynasty or the family lineage of each pilgrim. It is interesting to note that a possible link arises between the first two and the last three verses because the Hebrew word for build (*bana*) used in verse 1 begins with the same letters as the Hebrew for children (*banim*.)

On Children's Sabbaths, we celebrate children as a source of joy, strength, and honor. We affirm our calling to build a world that is safe for children, in which *every* child knows love and security, happiness and faith, justice and joy. Whether we are working to build the movement to assure justice for children, to build up our communities so that they are safe, supportive places for all children, or to build our own strong families, we are reminded that God is the architect and we must rely on God's guidance in our efforts. Similarly, whether we are working to end the violence and abuse that take the lives of children every day in our nation; to protect our communities from the dangers of drugs and alcohol, bullets, and bullies; or simply to keep the children in our families safe, we are reminded that our security ultimately rests in God's hands and we can seek strength from God for the work we do. To keep those who love, serve, and advocate on behalf of vulnerable children from exhaustion or burnout, we must encourage and remind one another that God's power is at work among us and beyond us and will continue to work on behalf of all our children.

Luke 2:41–52

Luke gives us Scripture's only glimpse of Jesus after infancy and before adulthood. It is bracketed by verses reminding us that these years were pivotal for Jesus as he "grew and became strong" (v. 40), gaining wisdom and divine favor (v. 52).

Like the stories that precede it, this Lukan passage portrays Jesus being raised in the context of his faith, his community, and his family. He was raised as an observant Jew, traveling to Jerusalem with his family each year to participate in the festival of Passover. We get a feel for the close-knit community in which Jesus was raised, suggested by Mary and Joseph's initial lack of concern for their child's whereabouts for an entire day when they assumed he was safe with other travelers.

We also encounter an emotion familiar to many parents: Mary and Joseph were "astonished" when they found Jesus at the temple. However, we do not know if they were surprised by where they found him (at the temple) or what he was doing (teaching the rabbis). Jesus asks, "Why were you searching for me? Did you not know that I must be in my Father's house?" (v. 49). He must have known that his parents would miss him, but he may have been surprised that they did not know where to find him.

Thereafter we read that Jesus returned home and "was obedient" to his parents (v. 51). Fred Craddock and Eugene Boring offer this insight into the primacy of obedience to God which supersedes obedience to anyone or anything else:

> Just as the adult Jesus will make one trip to Jerusalem (in the Lukan narrative) to encounter the teachers in the temple and finally give his life in obedience to the Father's will, so the boy Jesus makes one trip to the temple (in Luke's account), encounters the teachers in the temple, and knows that doing the Father's will is supremely more important than family connections (14:25–33, esp. 14:26!).[3]

What are the implications of this passage for Children's Sabbaths? First, it encourages our efforts to ensure that all children, like Jesus, are embraced by the vital combination of family, faith, and community. Second, while Jesus was still a child, there was much for the adults to learn from him, much that "amazed" the religious leaders, much that puzzled but later became clear to his parents. We must take time to listen to and learn from our children. Third, we must provide all children with the basic needs of sound nutrition, good schools, prenatal care and health care, adequate family income, safe

---

3. M. Eugene Boring and Fred B. Craddock, *The People's New Testament Commentary* (Louisville, KY: Westminster John Knox Press, 2004), 184.

Preaching God's Transforming Justice, Year A

neighborhoods, and strong families so that they may increase in wisdom and in years. We must assure children that they are loved by God and us, so that they may recognize and joyfully receive "divine and human favor."

Ephesians 6:1–4

This passage bears many similarities to Colossians 3:18–22, another household code that includes material that is problematic or offensive to modern ears. Both include directions to fathers or husbands who are assumed to be the head of the household, and include instructions for slaves to obey their masters. How is it possible to hear God's liberating call for justice in this text?

Children are directly addressed in verses 1–3, as if the author expects them to hear its contents directly, not mediated by a parent or religious leader. The Greek word for children, *teknos*, "simply denotes a physical descendant and is not age-specific; it can refer to adult children as well as small or young children, depending on the context."[4] Obeying parents is assumed to be the ethical norm, and the author quotes the commandment to honor father and mother (Deut. 5:16; Exod. 20:12). However, many scholars think the commandment in the context of the Hebrew Bible was directed to *adult* children about caring for, and not abusing, elderly parents (see Exod. 21:15, 17; Sir. 3:1–16). The author of Ephesians points out that fulfilling the commandment to honor one's parents comes with the promise of one's own well-being, not harm, and one's own secure old age.

Verse 4 directly addresses fathers. At best, this verse suggests that the child-parent relationship is not a one-way street but is a relationship of mutual accountability to each other as well as to God. Restraints are established for fathers: "do not provoke your children to anger." In a context where fathers had virtually unbridled authority over their children, this verse represents an improvement in caring for children's well-being.[5] Fathers are urged to raise their children with what appears to be compassionate "discipline and instruction of the Lord."[6]

---

4. Judith M. Gundry-Volf, "The Least and the Greatest: Children in the New Testament," in *The Child in Christian Thought*, ed. Marcia J. Bunge (Grand Rapids: Eerdmans, 2001), 48.

5. "While Roman law granted fathers almost absolute authority over their children, the abuse of paternal authority brought forth pleas for moderation by Roman and Jewish writers alike" (Gundry-Volf, "Least and Greatest," 54).

6. The term for discipline that is used in v. 4, *paideia*, "spans the range between appropriate discipline for young children to the philosophical instruction of the older adolescent. (Sir. 1:27 connects 'fear of the Lord' *paideia*, and wisdom)" and the term for instruction, *nouthesia*, "refers to verbal correction or education" (See Pheme Perkins, *The New Interpreter's Bible*, vol. 11 [Nashville: Abingdon, 2000], 453).

As we interpret these household codes for our own time, we affirm the important role that parents are to play in the nurture, guidance, instruction, and spiritual formation of children. But surely when two parents are in the home, we affirm *both* adults as equal partners in sharing the responsibility for raising children. We also recognize that in many one-parent families, it is often the mother who shoulders this responsibility alone.

All parents may hear in this passage a word of caution because our actions greatly impact our children's hearts and minds. This passage does not promote the use of corporal punishment in disciplining children, but it points the way to parental responsibility for instructing children about Christ's life and teachings. All adults in our churches may act in ways that lift children's spirits or crush them, plant hope or destroy it, nurture confidence and godly wisdom or stifle it. Together, we are called to guide children as disciples of the Christ who gathered children into his arms and blessed them.

All Saints' Day

Gennifer Benjamin Brooks

REVELATION 7:9–17
PSALM 34:1–10, 22
1 JOHN 3:1–3
MATTHEW 5:1–12

The connection of All Saints' Day with the celebration of the martyrs of the church comes alive in John's vision. Throughout the readings for this feast of the church one can see a picture of deliverance and triumph over injustice that calls forth exuberant praise. The realm of God has come in all its fullness, and the people of God cannot but rejoice in the majesty of God's love. Deliverance in its ultimate form comes through the construction of a community in which the children of God have come into their own. "Free at last, free at last, thank God almighty, we are free at last."[1] The martyrs are vindicated, the oppressed are delivered, as all claim their inheritance as beloved children of God. The people who have been outside of social power are on the inside; they are redeemed. The realm of God has become a reality, and peace and justice reign.

Revelation 7:9–17

John's apocalyptic vision of the redeemed multitude is presented as a contrast to an earlier picture of a fractured human family. This numberless group, shrouded in the coded mystery of John's vision, are the martyrs who have been steadfast in their worship and victorious in life and death. They are dressed in white, signifying their martyrdom, and they carry the symbols of their commitment, affiliation, and reverence for their divine Shepherd. These

---

1. These words are taken from the traditional spiritual "Free at Last" as quoted in the "I Have a Dream" speech delivered by Martin Luther King Jr. on August 23, 1963, at the Lincoln Memorial in Washington, D.C. See James M. Washington, ed., *A Testament of Hope: The Essential Writings and Speeches of Martin Luther King, Jr.* (San Francisco: HarperCollins, 1991), 216.

are the ones who have survived the injustice and oppression of their time and have the assurance of ultimate victory because of the Shepherd's continued guidance.

As the gathered community, the church triumphant, they offer a picture of divine love worthy of praise. The Lamb that was slain is their redeemer. The multitude consists of those who have been downtrodden, afflicted, hungry, thirsty, oppressed, and despised for being strangers in a strange land. Yet under the leadership of the Lamb, in a manner reminiscent of Jesus' triumphal entry into Jerusalem, they offer extravagant praise to God for their experience of divine presence and saving grace. John's vision takes flesh in the pictures of children who have been abducted, abused, and killed. The martyrs in our day include the innocent ones who are stolen and sacrificed to the gods of power, privilege, and indulgence as sex slaves and child laborers. These have hope of ultimate redemption through the Lamb even as other faithful persons labor for their release.

Their presence with the Lamb is testimony of their redeemed status and of the universality of the beloved community where there is no discrimination based on language, race, color, tribe, national origin, or any other social marker. The great ordeal through which they have come, unspecified in John's vision, is nevertheless representative of systemic oppression and injustice. Whether or not we consider these verses as prescient of John's impending martyrdom, they recall for us the continual worsening of racism, militarism, neocolonialism, warmongering, and ever-escalating violence to individuals, communities, and nations globally.

The multitude offers its song of praise to God, and the angels join them because salvation comes only from God. It is the song of slaves, torn from distant homelands, who survived the Middle Passage only to suffer ever-worsening abuse at the hands of cruel, death-dealing masters. Amid unnamed and perhaps unimaginable oppression comes a vision of redemption and release, of retribution and reparation. It is salvation from God. John offers a testimonial to the redemptive love of God through the Lamb. Freedom is coming; vindication is a sure promise; God will deliver. No more does blood signify the trials and tribulations of their experience, of the violence and pain that heralded martyrdom. The blood of the Lamb is the source of their cleansing and newness.

The Lamb ushers in a new age and a new vision of life. Those who have experienced the pains of enslavement and abuse, of emptiness and insecurity, of hopelessness and loss, cry out no longer, because the Lamb is the Shepherd who will lead all those who suffer to fullness of life. They have been made pure not by the whiteness of human identity but with the purity of divine light that strips away the clouds and darkness that accompany oppression and injustice in any age and gives clarity of sight, purpose, and being. It is Christ with us in glorious array, and all heaven and earth are one in praise of God.

Psalm 34:1–10, 22

In this song of praise, the psalmist invites the hearers to participate in the celebration that comes because of divine deliverance. The psalm is presented as an individual's response of thanksgiving to God, but it also invites others to join in offering praise for God's redeeming love. It is at once a testimonial, a word of counsel, and an invitation to worship, praise, trust, and keep faith in God. Yet the very words of assurance that seem to trip so easily off the tongue of the psalmist present a theological challenge that cannot be avoided. The psalmist seems to suggest that God's grace is selective, that God is present with and delivers only those who fear God and live a life of holiness and righteousness (vv. 7–8).

So how does the poor soul who has lived righteously and cried to God yet was not saved from trouble hear these words? There is no song in the throat of the one for whom deliverance never seems to come. What is the song of the homeless and the lost; of those who are caught in economic, ecological, or emotional nightmares; of the poor mother, once rich in children, who sees each child lost to the violence of the streets, or incarcerated by an unjust penal system? For those who fear the arrival home of their once-beloved helpmeet who now is abusive, who looked to the systems designed to help the needy and from whom even more was stolen—including their dignity, pride, and self-actualization—what is the source of their praise or their boasting?

The psalmist has confidence in the efficacy of the divine-human relationship and offers the assurance of God's deliverance from trouble to those who follow a way of life that is holy and righteous. This psalm does not offer unrealized hope, but a living witness to God's presence in times of need, to God's saving power in times of distress. It is cause for joy and a call to faith that is worthy of praise at all times and seasons. It is a living testimony of praise to God.

1 John 3:1–3

These verses from John's letter claim for his hearers the identity of children of God in the present day. We hear a tension between the now and not yet presence of God's realm. However, John gives us the assurance of divine presence and approbation both in the immediate, present moment and in an eternal future, and his words call us to faithful living. Only the one, the Holy One, the Creator who makes all things new, knows the shape, form, and purpose of this new thing that we will become. John assures us that it is enough to solidify the hope that we have, to cleanse the mind of doubt, to purify the spirit from fear of the unknown, and to cause those who know Christ to pursue Christlike purity of will, purpose, and son-ship. It is hope for the future that John offers us, an apocalyptic hope in the promise of future revelation.

This apocalyptic hope says we will be something more, like Christ, like God. Our present reality as children of God offers a foundation for future hope. But what does this text mean for those whose hope has been whittled away by systemic derision and the degradation of their ethnic or gender identity? One's identity is a precious gift of God for God's glory. It is a matter of great frustration to those who have little in the way of material possessions that their circumstances often empower others to deny their identity. What hope is there for those on the margins who remain unrecognized by society, who do not see themselves nor are seen as children of God, people who consider themselves or are considered children of no one? And what of those poor souls whose cries have not been heard and whose invisibility has little or nothing to do with their connection to an unknown Christ but to their circumstances as nameless, faceless strangers?

John's message calls believers to live in the reality of their citizenship in Christ that comes with Christian baptism. The nomenclature "children of God" applies to those whom society has shunted to the sidelines or discarded completely and encourages us to imagine possibilities for their renewal and acceptance. As renewed children of God, not only is hope possible, but it assures all of us of our rightful place in the family of God.

Matthew 5:1–12

In these verses, Jesus provides instruction for all disciples of every era. His words catch us unaware because they call for a response that is contrary to that which would be expected of rabbinic teaching. It reverses the established order of society and challenges the hierarchy of both Roman and Jewish culture. The rabbi knows the law but this teacher changes the rules, turning the world upside down. Matthew expands the notion of the poor beyond material ownership to the spiritual realm. Blessedness is not simply happiness; it is peace and contentment. Poverty saps the spirit in much the same way as it diminishes the body, and peace and contentment in the midst of such terrible circumstances seem unrealizable dreams compared to the harsh realities of grief and mourning, hunger and thirst, war and violence, oppression and injustice. Jesus' teaching seems to fit only with an eschatological hope. It falls far short of the reality of normal living and calls into question the disciples' ability to meet its requirements.

Millions of poor people in the world often do not feel blessed, nor do they experience happiness in their situation. Yet in many places around the world, many others who are also beset by poverty face the hardships of their life with songs of praise and thanksgiving to God. This perspective is generally unfathomable to middle-class society in the United States, where wealth is often considered synonymous with happiness. Corrupt social and economic systems result in abuse of the poor; there is little comfort for those who mourn the loss of hopes and dreams; the meek are stepped on; mercy is in short supply; and those who work for peace are ridiculed. These problems reflect the corruption of God's creation and require the creation of a new world. Christ gives a vision of this new world order, to be inhabited in the present under his authority and power. It is a vision of the realm of God that Christian believers are called to fulfill now as surely as the saints of God receive these blessings in the world to come.

The message of the coming realm is clear. It is a new creation of renewal and restoration, calling the hearers beyond the immediate moment into God's intended future. It calls and invites all disciples into a new way of being, a new community, a beloved community where individualism is subject to the unity of purpose, mission, and communal life in Christ. It is a view of success and community approbation that is contrary to society's criteria. Jesus speaks of a coming realm where those who are downtrodden will be lifted to new heights. Oppressive systems in which hunger and poverty and grief are the results of power and privilege will be overthrown; the persecution and violence of the present time will give way to peace and justice. The invitation to rejoice directs the hearers beyond their present situation, to a hope that is based on faith in the one who delivers this vision of God's realm among us. The eschatological hope is of a coming realm, God's new creation that will restore the children of God to their rightful places. Christ will reign supreme and deliverance will be celebrated in the beloved community.

Proper 26

Elizabeth J. A. Siwo-Okundi

JOSHUA 3:7–17
PSALM 107:1–7, 33–37

MICAH 3:5–12
PSALM 43
1 THESSALONIANS 2:9–13
MATTHEW 23:1–12

Whenever election time nears, leaders come forward and search for ways to attract attention and gain votes. Leaders once applauded and viewed as saviors have undoubtedly failed to fulfill their promises. They insist that if they had just one more term, they could continue doing what they said they would do. Other leaders have held their positions for the greater part of their lives and are so confident of their chances for success that their campaign efforts are minimal. Still others try to prove that they deserve an opportunity to serve. Some people become leaders simply because the community calls them to leadership: they have charisma and are able to understand the needs of the people and the politics of change, especially during political movements, uprisings, and community crises. Yet other groups of leaders appoint themselves to positions, force people to vote for them, or bring about enough fear that the masses are afraid to seek other options. Whether elected, called by the community, or self-appointed, leaders do not exist without followers and supporters. Our lectionary readings examine the complexity and impact of various styles of leadership and caution us in selecting, following, and being leaders.

Joshua 3:7–17

After the death of Moses (Deut. 34: 5–8), a young man named Joshua is selected to lead the people of God into the new land and to ensure the safe transport of the sacred ark of the covenant. The ark contains the Ten Commandments and represents God's presence and covenant with the people. Joshua carefully and boldly addresses the people and prepares them for their future. He directs them to "select twelve men from the tribes of Israel, one from each tribe" (Josh. 3:12). Although Joshua does not yet specify the role of the twelve, it is clear that they are to serve in some capacity as leaders.

Joshua's statement is important for two reasons. First, it shows that he is not selecting the leaders himself but is telling the people that it is *their* duty to shape their future by choosing their own leaders. He could have easily scanned the crowd, quietly chosen his favorite people to fill positions, and then announced his decision to an unsuspecting crowd—a tactic used by leaders worldwide. But Joshua is more concerned with the people than he is with the possibility that someone will take his position. He recognizes that he cannot lead the people on his own and that it is important for the next generation of leaders to start preparing early. Joshua does not involve himself in the selection process or try to sway the decision. Many leaders today become so involved in the decision-making process for new leaders that the results are essentially of their making. But Joshua simply makes the announcement and lets the people decide how they will proceed.

Second, Joshua's statement highlights the importance of diversity in leadership. It is critical that all the tribes of Israel—not just two or three—are represented. No one voice is more important than another. During elections and political movements, we often select people only from our own group, without meaningful consideration of others. Nations that are new to independence can attest to this strategy. When first gaining independence from colonial rulers and dictators, leaders are quick to appoint leaders only from their own representative group. At first, such strategies make sense, ensure loyalty, and reward those who have faithfully sought independence. But in the long term, nations become divided, and schools, land, property, and other important interests become noticeably well developed in the lands of the leaders but embarrassingly underdeveloped elsewhere. Well-established nations can also attest to this self-preserving strategy and have witnessed similar results. Similarly, when a political party announces its candidate, very often all members of that party vote for the candidate, regardless of the individual's qualities, ideas, or preparation. Flaws are excused and faults are hidden. In these situations, people begin to recognize the downside of electing and appointing people strictly according to party affiliations.

Joshua challenges us to consider leaders from diverse backgrounds, allowing for a breadth of accountability among diverse leadership, and hoping to diminish people's fears that any one group would be ignored or privileged over others. It must also be noted that Joshua's directive to select "twelve men" need not be a reason to disregard women as potential leaders. Although Joshua (living in the second century BCE) may have indeed intended that only men should be selected, the more important point for us today is that our leadership should be diverse; men, women, immigrants, citizens, poor, wealthy, young, old, and others should be eligible for consideration.

After making his statement, Joshua continues his mission. In addition to the twelve leaders that the people select, the religious and spiritual leaders—the priests—are the ones to lead *all* of the people: "When the people set out from their tents to cross over the Jordan, the priests bearing the ark of the covenant were in front of the people" (v. 14). The religious leaders are not in the background but are visible and prominent in the movement forward. They are the first ones whose feet touch the waters of the Jordan, and when they do so, the waters are held back, creating a safe surface for the people to cross (vv. 15–16). It is thus the priests who test the dangerous waters. When the passageway is safe, then the people begin crossing the Jordan (v. 16). The religious leaders remain in their position "until the entire nation finished crossing over the Jordan" (v. 17). This passage reminds religious and spiritual leaders that we have a special role in leading people. Ours is not to risk lives but to ensure safety in crossing new territory, developing new strategies, changing plans, implementing ideas, or rallying for a cause. We are "in front of the people." What we do and do not do is visible to all. Certainly, we will make mistakes, but our mistakes are before us. We must not forget that not only our successes but also the mistakes, sins, and scandals we commit will impact the people we serve.

Micah 3:5–12

Micah speaks against leaders and, in particular, prophets who wrongfully use their positions of authority over others. Too often, we make excuses for leaders (as well as ourselves) when we behave wrongly. But according to Micah, we must not deny the wrongful behaviors of bad and dangerous leaders. They can be identified by at least four characteristics. First, they lie and lead people astray by telling them that all is peaceful and well with their nation just as long as they have plenty of food and resources, regardless of how hungry others may be (v. 5). In other words, they make life more difficult for those who are hungry. Second, they "abhor justice and pervert all equity" (v. 9). That is, they hate, detest, despise, and loathe justice, and work to alter or modify equity among others so as to benefit themselves. Altering *all* equity means that even the slightest appearance of fairness and justice does not have a chance to survive. To abhor justice and to pervert all equity, one must know what *is* just and equitable! Micah alerts us that bad leaders do indeed know what is just and equitable but have chosen to ensure that these ideals never survive. Third, they build their cities and nations with the blood, sweat, and tears of the people they claim to lead (v. 10). In particular, bad leaders use money wrongfully to control people and manipulate situations (v. 11). The rulers, for example, give judgments for a bribe! Undoubtedly, equity and justice are perverted when judgments favor the highest bidder instead of those who are right.

The fourth sign of bad leaders is their claim that in all they do, "surely the LORD is with us!" (v. 11b). To do evil and claim that God is part of it is a tactic that is used to confuse and control people. People who suspect that a leader is misusing or abusing leadership may hesitate or even stop their investigation if they are led to believe that God is on the side of the leader. Many leaders have lied, made terrible decisions, killed, or declared war with the certainty that "surely the LORD is with us!" As person after person is hurt or killed, the leaders insist, "No harm shall come upon us!" (v. 11). Or, in today's terms: "We are fine! There are no problems here." They declare victory in the midst of lost jobs, stolen retirements, orphaned children, shattered communities, widowed women, and dead or violated bodies. Anytime leaders claim that God is with them even as they are doing something evil, people will indeed be led astray.

In essence, each of these four acts or signs is inextricably bound to the others. If ever we doubt our leaders (and ourselves as leaders), we need only test them (and ourselves) against the description offered by Micah. This kind of leadership is shameful and results in the ruin of the nation (v. 12).

Psalm 107:1–7, 33–37 and Psalm 43

But how should we lead? In Psalm 107, the psalmist shares glimpses of God's leadership. We learn that God is good (v. 1), offering help to people from all lands—east, west, north, and south (v. 3). When the people cried to God for help in their trouble and distress, the psalmist tells us that God "led them by a straight way" (vv. 6–7). God's ways are straight, while the ways of the leaders described by Micah (and many leaders today) are distorted. They pervert equity, whereas God is fair and serves people everywhere. While the leaders in Micah are content to eat and stuff themselves with food as their nation goes hungry, God is concerned with the hunger of the people. According to the psalmist and those whom God has redeemed, God "satisfies the thirsty, and the hungry" and "lets the hungry live" (vv. 9, 36). The result of God's leadership is that the people are able to establish a place to live, grow their own food, and produce enough to sustain themselves (vv. 36–37). The people "sow fields," unlike Micah's description of Zion needing to be plowed (Mic. 3:12). God's leadership results in safety, security, and sustainability for everyone.

Our people depend on our leadership for their very survival. When we fail to be true and good leaders, our people suffer. They lean on God for support, for they know and trust that God's leadership is just. In Psalm 43, the psalmist begs God for deliverance from those who are "deceitful and unjust" (v. 1). Tired of oppression, the psalmist pleads to God, "O send out your light and your truth; let them lead me" (vv. 2, 3). Let *them* lead me? The psalmist's plea indicates that the psalmist is tired of being led by lies and deceit. Let them (i.e., God's light and truth) lead me, rather than the tangled lies of the leaders before me.

Many voices today cry alongside the voice of the psalmist. These voices are tired of the greed, abuse, and lies of leaders. They cry to God, "Defend my cause against an ungodly people" (v. 1). The ways of leaders are so wicked and crooked that they are considered ungodly. It is because of such leaders that the very soul of the psalmist is restless and hopes in God alone (v. 5). Together, Psalms 107 and 43 point us to God's way of leadership and urge us to listen to the cries of the people we claim to serve. Their cries may never make it to the headlines because they have been stifled by fear, bribes, and threats. But voices of justice and hope are ever present because we know that God will vindicate all who are oppressed.

1 Thessalonians 2:9–13 and Matthew 23:1–12

When we lead in God's light and truth and are mindful of the voices of God's people, then our focus becomes clearer and our determination to serve God's people increases. In the opening verses of 1 Thessalonians 2, Paul and his colleagues in ministry share how they have served without greed, flattery, deceit, or impure motives (vv. 1–8). This lectionary text continues by discussing their leadership style. As leaders, they "labor and toil," working "night and day" while sharing God's love (v. 9). But their work is not for the sake of themselves or for show. They conduct themselves in ways that are "pure, upright, and blameless," such that God and the people serve as their "witnesses" (v. 10). Their conduct makes it possible for them to urge, encourage, and plead with others to also lead lives that are pleasing to God (v. 12). They ask of others what they themselves are already doing. They also thank the people and "constantly" thank God for the way in which the Thessalonians have received them (v. 13). Too often, leaders forget to thank the people they serve. But Paul and his colleagues—despite whatever problems may be found and debated concerning their leadership and ideas—remember to thank the people. Doing so is especially important because the Thessalonians, like the people we serve today, face many social pressures and need encouragement.

Our people need encouragement when they vote for leaders who are not wealthy but are selfless and honest in their efforts to strengthen the community; when they risk their jobs and even their lives so that others can have safe communities, health care, education, and employment opportunities; and when they confront bullies at school, in the church, at work, and in the government. Going against the pressures of society can be lonely, discouraging, and frustrating, but reassurance from good leaders can help keep the needs of the people in the forefront of our concerns.

When leaders are removed from the needs of the people they serve, it is easy for them to forget why people need them. Leaders can easily become entangled in self-promotion and feelings of grandeur. Such is the case with some of the religious leaders of Jesus' time as well as Christian, religious, and other leaders in our own time. Jesus warns the crowds and disciples that regardless of what the scribes and Pharisees say, "do not do as they do" (Matt. 23:3). The leaders whom Jesus indicts are trying to appear pious and powerful. They wear nice clothes, have the best seats in the synagogues, are given special treatment at parties and functions, are greeted with respect, and are given special names and titles (vv. 5–7). Their lifestyle seems luxurious and fun. We often pay attention to leaders who are wealthy and receive high praise from others. Some would argue that material goods and high praise are signs of being a true leader. Jesus warns that such outward signs are merely for show so they may be noticed by other people, but true leadership entails service and humility (vv. 5, 11–12). According to Jesus, "The greatest among you will be your servant" (v. 11).

Each of us is a leader in one way or another. In our homes, schools, universities, churches, communities, and world, we are leaders. Our responsibilities change from one situation to the next, but what remains constant is that we are accountable to the people we serve and to God. Our children and families, students, parishioners, friends, and neighbors rely on us to be leaders who carry the love of God in our hearts and lead in ways that are humble, encouraging, just, good, and true.

Proper 27

Bob Ekblad

JOSHUA 24:1–3A, 14–25 PSALM 78:1–7
AMOS 5:18–24 PSALM 70
1 THESSALONIANS 4:13–18
MATTHEW 25:1–13

All of the texts for this Sunday call for our undivided loyalty to God and ask us to remember God's purposes as we remain vigilant in acting justly toward God and others. Joshua calls the people to serve the Lord "in sincerity and in faithfulness." Amos lambasts religious practices that are devoid of justice and righteousness. The psalms call people to teach their children about God's acts of liberation, to put full confidence in God, not forgetting God's works but observing divine commandments even as we plea for deliverance from enemies. The Epistle and Gospel readings remind us of Jesus' second, unpredictable coming. Jesus' parable calls believers to be ready and attentive so that we may have enough oil to see and enter the celebration of his return.

Joshua 24:1–3a, 14–25

Joshua gathers all the tribes of Israel before God and calls them to leave their idols and pledge total allegiance to the Lord. In God's presence, Joshua reminds them of what God has done to bring them to this place and time, and his comments elicit a hasty response from people who have not yet counted the cost of total faithfulness.

Joshua emphasizes that Abraham's father, Terah, and brother Nahor served other gods "beyond the Euphrates"—offering information about the patriarch's relatives' idolatrous practices in Ur and Haran not mentioned in Genesis 11:26–32. By exposing their ancestors' idolatry and unworthiness and proclaiming God's deliverance of Abraham and his offspring from false beliefs, Joshua admonishes the people to avoid their ancestors' failing.

477

Joshua emphasizes four key actions that the Lord (YHWH) has done on behalf of their forefather Abraham that sets Israel's God apart from other gods. First, Joshua emphasizes the Lord's "taking" Abraham from beyond the river (stressing God's action in Gen. 12:1–4). In taking Abraham away from homeland, relatives, and his father's house (Gen. 12:1), including idolatrous cultural and religious practices, God's actions anticipate Jesus' later call to "hate" father, mother, and all other family ties (Luke 14:26), and to accept the sword that cuts people free from attachments and allegiances that impede them from being wholly given to him (see Luke 12:51–53).

Three other verbs command our attention. Joshua portrays God as acting to save the people by having *led* Abraham, *multiplied* his descendants, and *given* him Isaac. God's grace and saving initiative subverts all notions of relying on ancient Near Eastern religious practices that emphasize deity-appeasing sacrifice. Joshua's theology removes the need for child sacrifice to attain prosperity and security—which continues today as young men and women are sent to die in combat, and children are aborted or neglected in the interest of careers or addictions.

What are some of the belief systems, attachments, and allegiances we have inherited that compromise our full allegiance to God and the divine realm? Have we too readily believed our ancestors' stories that attribute success to hard work, human intelligence, capital, ethnic or national superiority? Have we inherited a tendency to place our confidence in human accomplishments more than in God's actions on our behalf? Do we laud military or national leaders and place our trust in political parties as sources of security and protection, rather than in God? How does idolatry manifest itself today? It is important that we identify and question anything that pulls our attention away from God.

Joshua urges the people, "Choose this day whom you will serve" (Josh. 24:15). The people respond with the right answer (vv. 16–18). They have good intentions and voice the right theology but appear to be overconfident in their ability to follow the Lord. They take comfort in their election, in the Lord who "drove out before us all the peoples . . . who lived in the land" (v. 18). The Septuagint uses the Greek verb *ekballo* (cast out, drove out) here, which may remind us of Jesus' ministry of casting out invisible spiritual intruders that occupy religious insiders—as in his first miracle of casting out an unclean spirit from a synagogue attendee (Mark 1:21–28). Jail inmates in my weekly Bible studies regularly identify being preyed on by and susceptible to powers such as anger, addictions, discrimination, pride, lust, legalism, and jealousy. The legal system is incapable of remedying these maladies by sentencing people to prison or demanding that they pay fines. They also recognize that when their lives spin out of control and they are forced to face the consequences of their behavior, they are more open to surrendering their lives to God with all their hearts. Joshua warns the people that God is not tame and cannot be controlled. He calls them to commit 100 percent of their hearts to acting decisively against evil, lest God "turn and do you harm, and consume you, after having done you good" (Josh. 24:20).

The people must go beyond mere lip service and "put away" the false gods, giving their hearts to the Lord (v. 23). Once again, the people say what sounds right and respectable: "The LORD our God we will serve, and him we will obey" (v. 24), but we do not know if their hearts are fully given to God. What might it look like to truly give your heart to God and put away all other "gods" in your personal life, family, and congregation?

Amos 5:18–24

Amos addresses religious and ethnic insiders in Israel who appear to assume that God is on their side. Presumption, entitlement, and overfamiliarity with God arise when God's favor is accepted as an endorsement of one's practices and mind-set.

Earlier, in Amos 1:3–2:3, the prophet's oracles of judgment against Israel's neighbors may have given him credibility among his own people, something akin to the way many Americans welcome tirades against Iran, al-Qaida, the Taliban, and North Korea. In subsequent chapters we hear God taking Israel by surprise with prophetic critiques against their rejection of Torah, oppression of the poor, and general immorality (2:4–8; 3:9–10; 4:1–5; 5:10–11). Which practices and mind-sets might God's prophets focus on in your community?

In response to the people's eager anticipation of the Lord's return, the prophet warns: "Alas for you who desire the day of the LORD! Why do you want the day of the LORD? It is darkness, not light; as if someone fled from a lion, and was met by a bear" (5:18–19a).

In speaking to his staunchly religious compatriots, Amos clearly articulates that sacrifices and worship, without justice for the poor and vulnerable, are repugnant to God (vv. 21–23). Why does he offer such a strong critique? Amos was in touch with vulnerable people living at the margins whom others overlooked or exploited. Today, we may consider immigrant farm laborers, gang members, and others whom we consider members of the underclass and are disproportionately numbered among jail and prison inmates, unable to afford good legal help or to find release from a penal system that demands fines and requires restitution from people nearly unemployable because they have been labeled illegal residents, felons, or sex offenders.

The prophet reveals God's heart for justice and righteousness. "Let justice roll down like waters, and righteousness like an ever-flowing stream" (v. 24).

What would a river of abundant justice and righteousness look like if it were to flow through your community?

Psalm 78:1–7 and Psalm 70

In order to remember God's miraculous interventions in the lives of our forebears, we must deliberately pass on their stories to new generations (78:4). The psalmist reminds people to tell their children about God's interventions in history (that is, to share testimonies) and to teach them the lessons of Israel's Torah so that future generations will "set their hope in God, and not forget the works of God, but keep his commandments" (v. 7). Without this conscious effort to pass along faith from generation to generation, people will pay attention to other stories, putting their trust in other competing interests and powers that will function as false gods and become the dominant influences of their lives and memories.

National and racial or ethnic superiority are nourished by stories about founding fathers and veterans. Stories about sports heroes and the rich and famous make idols of celebrities and nurture illusions of extravagant lifestyles that disrupt healthy priorities and degrade community values. What stories of God's interventions can you remember and amass into a "faith bank" that people can access to inspire their trust in God?

In Psalm 70, the psalmist models trust in God and crying out to the Lord for deliverance and help. "Be pleased, O God, to deliver me. O LORD, make haste to help me!" (v. 1). In contrast to Psalm 78, which was prepared for use at public festivals, Psalm 70 is a personal lament that gives voice to the agony of one who has been wrongfully accused and mistreated. Instead of experiencing unending shame and humiliation, the psalmist pleads for relief from those who have dishonored and harmed him or her. Like an abused child fleeing to a beloved teacher, or a battered wife who shows up at someone's doorstep, the psalmist expects help. God's greatness is the source of the psalmist's hope and salvation (v. 4). God responds to those who are "poor and needy" (v. 5). Will we?

1 Thessalonians 4:13–18

Paul offers comfort to the believers in Thessalonica. These early Christians were so eager for Jesus to return in their lifetimes that they grieved when their believing family and community members died, fearing they would miss out on his imminent return. Paul comforts them with several insights that he no doubt received through divine revelation.

First, he encourages believers not to grieve as if they were unbelievers (i.e., those "who have no hope," v. 13). Because of Jesus' death and resurrection— the core affirmation of faith and the source of their hope—they are assured of victory over death. Jesus' resurrection includes all believers because "God will bring with him those who have died" (v. 14). Second, Paul states that people who are still alive at Jesus' coming will not have an advantage over those who die before he returns. To the contrary, those who are "dead in Christ will rise first" (v. 16b). Finally, everyone who is in Christ "will be caught up in the clouds together . . . to meet the Lord in the air; and so we will be with the Lord forever" (v. 17).

Paul closes this chapter by admonishing people to "encourage one another with these words" (v. 18). Would Paul's words comfort you and your contemporaries today? If not, why not? In what ways might people find Paul's insights comforting today? Paul's audience is a persecuted minority, not at home in this world, but very conscious of their need for and longing to be with Jesus. While this attitude could look like escapism, Jesus-style discomfort with this world puts people in a place of greater willingness to live as agents of God's justice and righteousness, despite the cost or consequences of their actions.

Matthew 25:1–13

Jesus' parable of the Ten Virgins who went out to meet the bridegroom invites rapprochement with the church as a bride waiting the imminent return of Jesus, the bridegroom (see 2 Cor. 11:2; Eph. 5:25–32; John 3:29; Rev. 19:7; 21:2, 9; 22:17.) The number of virgins and the differentiation between "wise" and "foolish" has always unsettled me, suggesting that individual attitudes and practices ultimately determine what will happen to us, and that some people will be separated from others on the basis of their actions. Jesus intends to put people into crisis mode, inspiring them (and us) to be ready for his return, the subject of the preceding chapter (Matt. 24:42–51). Jesus means to provoke us into asking, "Am I one of the wise or foolish maidens, and what is the difference?" The reader instinctively wants to know more of what distinguishes those who are prepared from those who risk missing out. What might this parable mean for us today?

Both the five wise and the five foolish women are labeled virgins, an idealized state likely identifying them as religious insiders. And yet all ten virgins fall asleep while waiting for the delayed bridegroom. All wake up at the midnight shout: "Look! Here is the bridegroom! Come out to meet him" (v. 6b; the same term, "to meet," is used in 1 Thess. 4:17). Each of them takes her lamp and goes out to meet the groom.

Whether they have oil to keep their lamps burning so they can be fully present at the bridegroom's advent is what distinguishes the wise virgins from the foolish. The wise virgins have enough for themselves, but not enough to share. They tell the foolish virgins to go and buy oil from the dealers, and while they are away, the bridegroom arrives and enters the wedding feast with the five wise virgins, and the doors are shut. Later the other virgins return, saying, "Lord, lord, open to us." But he refuses their entry. Why? Surely, these later bridesmaids are not guilty of incorrectly asking for admission; their words are reminiscent of Jesus' teaching in the Sermon on the Mount when he reminds his disciples that not everyone who cries, "Lord, Lord" will enter the kingdom of heaven, but only those who do God's will (7:21). Jesus values very highly doing God's will and fulfilling God's just purposes.

It is also important to note that in the Septuagint the same Greek word for lamp that is used here (*lampas*) is related directly to the presence of God (see Gen. 15:17; Exod. 20:18; Ezek. 1:13; Dan. 10:6). This is also true of the oil (Gk. *elaion*) that was used to keep the lamps in the tabernacle and temple (which uses a different word, *laxnos*) continually lit, signifying God's ongoing presence in their midst (Exod. 27:20; Lev. 24:2; Num. 4:9, 16). The word "oil" (*elaion*) is used extensively in the Septuagint when speaking of offerings and the anointing of people—another sign of God's presence that consecrates and empowers (Exod. 29:2, 7, 21; 30:24; Lev. 8:10–12). Matthew's Jewish readers and hearers would have been aware of these references. They would have recognized in Jesus' parable a call for each individual to be filled with the Holy Spirit, a comforting sign of intimate communion with Jesus that is needed for endurance and to recognize and be recognized by him when Christ returns.

To know and be known by Jesus through the anointing of his Spirit is no doubt more attractive and possible for people who are poor, marginalized, and oppressed than it is for them to comply with rigorous religious practices or social activism. That is the work of those who have spiritual, economic, and social resources to address systemic ills by shining lights on dark places of injustice. But for anyone enduring hardship, being filled with the Spirit is critical to keeping faith while coping with homelessness, imprisonment, illness, or family conflicts. We need the Spirit of Christ to anoint and empower us both for enduring what is wrong and for helping to create what is right. The wise maidens teach us that we must keep our eyes fixed on the one who baptizes with "the Holy Spirit and fire" (Matt. 3:11)—the coming bridegroom, Jesus himself.

Proper 28

L. Susan Bond

JUDGES 4:1–7
PSALM 123

ZEPHANIAH 1:7, 12–18
PSALM 90:1–8 (9–11), 12
1 THESSALONIANS 5:1–11
MATTHEW 25:14–30

This series of readings comes toward the end of the church year, right before Advent and themes of anticipation. The readings should be particularly engaging and perhaps troubling, since they survey themes of divine anger, retribution, and ultimate, eschatological judgment. The Judges text claims that God punishes Israel by selling them to the Canaanites, Psalm 123 begs for divine mercy, and Psalm 90 claims to be overwhelmed by God's wrath. God speaks in Zephaniah, telling the people to be silent in the face of the coming distress, while the Matthean text sounds its familiar wailing and teeth gnashing. The Thessalonian text alone offers a sliver of hope, making the opposite argument: God has not destined us for wrath.

1 Thessalonians 5:1–11

First Thessalonians is widely considered to be the oldest existing Christian document and among the undisputed Pauline letters. This pericope addresses the question of preparation for Christ's return and how believers will be able to predict it. We know that Christian communities across the centuries have attempted to predict the second coming. What we may overlook is that the American character, with its covenantal language and historical notions of manifest destiny and imperial power (and to a large extent, the character of Eurocentric civilization), has been particularly susceptible to apocalyptic and millenarian rhetoric, conflating biblical notions of church into national notions of world domination.

Paul begins his comments with a gentle chiding: "For you yourselves know very well that the day of the Lord will come like a thief in the night."

You cannot plan for it. Besides the surprise and stealth involved in a midnight theft, we should remember that thieves steal away something we would rather protect. With the use of one image, Paul sets the rhetorical stage for deconstructing and unmasking human attempts at calculation. The image of Christ as a thief, while disturbing, is consistent with an early Christian theology of Jesus as a trickster who robs Satan of his victory by rising from the dead.

Paul's images and apocalyptic theology recognize only two worlds, two ways of being, two generations, and two fathers. The basic structure of Paul's apocalyptic thought is grounded in the idea that the world is constantly in danger of temptation and corruption by the powers and principalities that hold communities together in corrupt systems of domination, seductively blinding people and binding them in captivity. The old age, or "this generation," is dominated by the powers and principalities. "The System deludes people into thinking not only that they deserve their positions [of privilege or powerlessness] but that this social order is the only one possible."[1]

Part of the prophetic task of the religious leader, what Walter Brueggemann calls "the prophetic imagination," is to name the powers and their operation, and to point to an alternative vision of God's hope for the world.[2] The proclamation of God's future was a fundamental challenge to hierarchies based on merit, social status, national power, imperial hopes, or any other kind of human construct. As Christiaan Beker puts it, the motifs of dualism (old/new, blind/sight, dark/light, captivity/freedom) emphasize "that God's plan *for* the world engages the Christians in a battle *against* the present structures of the world."[3]

The battle is rhetorical and spiritual, and not sociopolitical warfare against those who defy us. Paul says that we will not be equipped with traditional military weapons, because our battle is not literal; it is one of ideas and commitments. Surprise again! "Forget about your hardened armor," says Paul. "Forget about Kevlar and night scopes. You don't belong to the night anymore. You belong to the day, to the resurrection. I am arming you with unconventional weapons."

In a lovely parabolic reversal, Paul's apocalyptic comments shift from focusing on a specific end time to focusing on a specific way of being in the world in the present. He subverts conventional warfare language and unmasks

---

1. Charles L. Campbell, *The Word before the Powers: An Ethic of Preaching* (Louisville, KY: Westminster John Knox Press, 2002), 27.
2. See Walter Brueggemann, *The Prophetic Imagination* (Philadelphia: Fortress Press, 1978).
3. J. Christiaan Beker, *Paul's Apocalyptic Gospel: The Coming Triumph of God* (Philadelphia: Fortress Press, 1982), 44.

conventional interpretations that abuse the warfare language to support armed aggression and physical violence against other nations and religions.

Matthew 25:14–30

Matthew's parable of the Talents is a continuation of the reflections about how the church deals with the absence of Jesus and its survival amid imperial rule. Chapters 24–25 declare eschatological judgment on Rome's world as God's purposes are established. Eschatological judgment does not require an apocalyptic end time.

In the parable, a rich man not only leaves his estate to his "slaves," he "delivers over" (Gk. *paradidomai*) his treasures. The same word will later be used to describe the "delivering over" of Jesus to the authorities. The word used for "possessions" (*hyparxonta*) includes not only material goods but one's entire substance and life. The man makes a sacrificial gift of epic proportions to his slaves, and then he leaves.

He has divided up the sacrificial gifts according to each slave's *dynamis* or power. The first two invest and double their gifts, and the third saves or hides it under a metaphorical bushel, the recommended treatment for unsavory salt (5:13–16).

So far, the story and all of its financial wheeling and dealing has taken place in *chronos* time (that is, regular chronological time). But after the master appears, breaking into regular time, he takes up "a word" with his slaves. This word or *logon* was familiar to the early church as Christ the Word, the gospel. In other words, the first thing the Lord does when he comes is to gather his slaves around "a word," the gospel. Preachers, take note. We gather folks around the inbreaking and present Word to hear what the Lord will do *now*.

Remarkably, the master begins his critique not against the empire, and not against unbelievers, but against his own too-timid slave. As the slave makes excuses, he appears to call his lord a thief (vv. 24–25; cf. 1 Thess. 5:2). The response is swift and definitive: "You thought you could protect my sacrificial gift? You weren't willing to take any risks? Surprise!" Jesus comes to steal it away. The final image of a slave cast into the darkness, wailing and gnashing his teeth (Matt. 25:30), is not an image of afterlife punishment but of what happens now, in ordinary time, when the *logon* breaks in and steals our sense of safety and security.

Like the Pauline text, this parable contrasts two ways of being the church in the world. It is not a call to individual piety or tithing, but a call to social protest and a way of living that contrasts with the ways of the empire. Even in the absence of Jesus Christ, churches can be faithful and continue the risky business of resisting the ways of the empire, or we can hoard and protect our own institutional and personal interests, which will leave us miserable and far from God's purposes.

Zephaniah 1:7, 12–18

Zephaniah was a seventh-century prophet who preached during the divided kingdom, predicting that Judah and Israel would be punished by God on the coming Day of the Lord. According to the prophet, God's judgment would be harsh for their sins of idolatrous worship and their failure to turn toward God and seek divine guidance. This text continues the themes of the day, announcing doom that borders on the catastrophic.

At the beginning of the text, the prophet commands the people to silence, a silence of terror where the gathered people begin to realize that they are the victims and not the victors. The enemies within Zephaniah's world are not outside but inside the faith community; those who are cynical and have low expectations, thinking that the Lord will do nothing, either good or bad. In verses not included in this passage, he urges them to humility and solemnity in their public gatherings. The imagery is military, evoking the war trumpet and battle cry, claiming that even the mighty warrior will cry out (v. 14). The imagery also invokes the flood, claiming that God will sweep everything from the face of the earth.

Preachers will want to be careful not to reinscribe images of a bloodthirsty warrior God that run through both Testaments, parallel to a God of mercy and forgiveness. Instead, justice concerns that can be lifted from this reading include notions that God *does* judge the way God's people live and worship, the ways that communities of believers are tempted by worldly dominations and national pride. There is a strong critique in these verses of the complacency that comes with silver and gold and the way political and economic powers conspire to eclipse the purposes of God; some will find here a legitimate critique of the popular prosperity gospel. This is a reminder that we serve a passionate God who demands faithfulness and integrity; there is an implicit critique of both agnosticism and atheism. Beyond the violent imagery, we are reminded that our God is involved in history and that we can neither ignore nor underestimate the radical claims of God on our communities. We are not allowed to be complacent, but are called to humility and spiritual honesty.

Judges 4:1–7

This text follows a familiar pattern: Israel has sinned and God either did or will punish them. When the people repent or cry out to God, God offers some hope for deliverance.

The story of Deborah is one of the few story cycles in the Bible where deliverance comes through female agency. The story is dramatic and bloody, full of the kind of deception and intrigue we find in contemporary action films. As the only female judge mentioned in the book of Judges, Deborah wages a successful counterattack on Jabin, the king of Canaan and an enemy of Israel. Closely paired with this narrative is the story of Jael, who murders Jabin's general, Sisera (4:17–21). Taken together, the stories of Deborah and Jael provide one of the rare Hebrew Bible explorations of women who behave as heroes for Israel in ways that are not stereotypically feminine. Generally in both Testaments, women are defined by their sexuality and reproductive status; they are virgins, harlots, barren or pregnant. In the stories of Deborah and Jael we have two female lead characters who act like male warriors in the conquest of Canaan. The stories do, however, bear a heavy theological burden, since we want to be cautious about promoting violence or deception, whether the protagonists are male or female.

Justice concerns can be addressed by attending to the textual claims that God does indeed raise up ordinary leaders for extraordinary times, even among the least expected populations. In this regard, God is not sexist about fully invested female leadership. God is no "respecter of persons." In a time when the church still struggles with women in leadership roles, a sermon about Deborah could be crafted to promote the divine mandate for equality without regard to gender and without reducing women to their sexuality or reproductive states. Indeed, some scholars argue that Deborah was middle-aged at the time of her victory over Jabin, and that she continued to be a judge until her death at the age of seventy-plus years. How empowering Deborah is for second-career women in ministry or for senior women in leadership roles![4]

Psalm 90:1–8 (9–11), 12

What a discouraging word this psalm brings to us! The psalmist sings of mortality and human insignificance, using images of death, dust, withering grass, and being swept away. Scholars remind us that this is the only psalm associated with Moses and suggest that this connection affirms the psalm's wisdom themes related to God, humanity, and time.

The psalm raises the theological question of how we can find significance and hope in our human endeavors. It could tempt believers to despair and

---

4. For a fuller exploration of women warrior types, women warriors in ancient Israel, and Deborah and Jael as female warriors in the Hebrew Bible, see Gale A. Yee, "By the Hand of a Woman: The Metaphor of the Woman Warrior in Judges 4," *Semeia* 61 (1993): 99–132. Yee also addresses issues of male surrogacy/imitation, the "pushy broad," and questions of violence and gender transgression.

inactivity. There is a "woe is me" or "woe are we" tenor to the poetry, with the text's final plea, "Teach us to count our days that we may gain a wise heart."

However, the words of verse 12 also provide clarity. If our time is so brief compared to the infinite stretch of divine time, the words of the psalm stand as a kind of reality check for us to set priorities and focus on what is most important. "Teach us to count our days" is a way of asking for the wisdom and discernment to know which things are valuable and which are not. Given the broad scope of history contained in the psalm (some argue that it spans precreation to eternity), human life and the work of our hands can only be significant insofar as they contribute to God's purposes. Even if we do not share the psalmist's theology about living under the wrath of God, we can agree with the moral mandate to spend our days wisely, since we never know when they will end.

From a social justice perspective, it reminds us that the time for justice is always now, and not in some delayed future. The psalm assumes the narrative voice of Moses, who never made it to the promised land. His farewell address to the Israelites is echoed in the words of Martin Luther King Jr., "I've seen the promised land. I may not get there with you." King's famous lines were prefaced by a commentary on longevity: "Like anybody, I would like to live a long life. Longevity has its place. But I'm not concerned about that now. I just want to do God's will."[5]

Those of use involved in social justice initiatives are prone to two opposite and equally problematic orientations. On the one hand, we're tempted to think that our immediate project or goal is more critical than it is. On the other hand, we are tempted to despair. The psalmist reminds us that the entire drama unfolds not on our timetable, but in God's eternity. At the same time, since we only have a brief "watch in the night," we need to use our time as if every moment were the last.

Psalm 123

This reading is part of the Psalms of Ascents cycle (Pss. 120–124) and probably comes from a festival pilgrimage (ascending) to Zion/Jerusalem for worship. Since this cycle addresses the theological issues of exile and pleas for divine help, preachers need to identify the community's own exiles and those who have contempt for them. The primary images are those of sight and vision as the community looks toward God for help and begs God to turn divine eyes toward their struggle and the scorn they suffer at the hands of

5. Martin Luther King Jr., "I See the Promised Land," in *A Testament of Hope: The Essential Writings and Speeches of Martin Luther King, Jr.*, ed. James Melvin Washington (New York: HarperCollins, 1991), 286.

"those who are at ease." Unlike other Psalms of Ascent, Psalm 123 shifts the gaze from Zion and its earthly geography toward the throne room of heaven, where God reigns supreme. The imagery of the psalm also includes the language of complete dependency. A servant looks to the master for help, and a maid looks to the mistress for rescue. The petition for mercy occurs twice in this short psalm. The pilgrim community seeks a word of mercy and grace, a word that is absent from their current world.

Preaching peace, justice, tolerance, and global human rights puts many contemporary congregations in a position of marginalization, not only within the contemporary culture, but within the Christian mainstream. This psalm could provide an excellent petitionary prayer for social justice congregations or events. Preachers might also turn our attention to individuals and groups of people who suffer social prejudices and economic inequality, such as women, various racial and ethnic groups, and children. Whereas other psalms in the cycle use imagery of climbing the temple steps, this psalm imagines steps to heaven. It is analogous to the imagery of Jacob's ladder and the lyrics of the spiritual "We are Climbing Jacob's Ladder," where the "least of these" anticipate an audience with God.

Proper 29 (Reign of Christ)

Jennifer L. Lord

EZEKIEL 34:11–16, 20–24   PSALM 100
PSALM 95:1–7A   EPHESIANS 1:15–23
MATTHEW 25:31–46

There is no way around it today: the gospel pronounces judgment. On this Reign of Christ Sunday we read this apocalyptic account of the sheep and the goats. It is a story about judgment from the Gospel according to Matthew so we know that Jesus is interpreting and holding to the spirit of the Law of God. In Ezekiel this judgment happens between sheep and sheep, and the good sheep are given safe pasture. Both psalms sing about God as the good shepherd providing this safe pasture. Finally, the Letter to the Ephesians confirms Christ as the ruler of all things. On this Reign of Christ Sunday we hear about Christ who holds all power and who will judge all the people of the world.

Matthew 25:31–46

Matthew uses "realm" language in a theological sense and uses this language more than any other New Testament writer. It is assumed, then, that Matthew's hearers knew this terminology and that it was not foreign to them, as it is to most of us in American church contexts. Part of our parsing of the term is to understand that God's kingdom is not about a place but about the nature of the realm of God. God's realm includes not only those who are members of Christ's church but all who subject themselves to God's reign. This Gospel recognizes competing kingdoms until the end times, when ultimately God's reign will be the only ruling authority.

All of this serves as background to the drama of the sheep and the goats. These words are Jesus' last discourse before the final days of his earthly life. The parables leading up to this section warn about being prepared for the coming of the Son of Man. But in this account, "When the Son of Man comes in his glory, and all the angels with him, then he will sit on the throne of his glory" (v. 31). The text indicates that all the people of the world will gather (as individuals), and they will be judged. The judgment divides them into two groups: those who are blessed because they cared for the "least of these," and those who are cursed because they offered no care for the needy ones. None of this is news in Matthew's Gospel. Loving God and loving others as oneself is set forth as the linchpin for life in God (22:37–39).

Again, the kingdom of God is not a location or a state of emotion or even a social service activity. The kingdom is life in God that plays out as love of the needy ones. The kingdom is manifest when we, out of conviction of our life in God, visit someone hospitalized and share in their agonized journey through medical procedures and predictions. The kingdom is manifest by the church group who visits the imprisoned and does not shun them if and when they are released. The kingdom is manifest by educators who teach life skills to those with cognitive disabilities and support their education and vocational training. The kingdom is manifest in students who staff meal service trucks for the homeless. The kingdom is manifest as we constantly keep vigilant awareness for those who are in any sort of need and find ways to act in crisis and effect change for chronic systemic injustices.

This passage still carries shock value. For some, the shock is the assertion that we see the Son of Man when we see the neediest among us. For some, it is that these ethical actions are indivisible from a pronouncement of judgment and its cosmic repercussions. The preacher may focus on either of these but will be well served to keep them in tension: participation in the kingdom of God is not reduced to good social ethics, nor is it possible for us to claim kingdom lives without love of the least of these. When we overemphasize the first, we can become smug in our humanitarian efforts. When we overemphasize the second, we miss the heart of the gospel as Matthew presents it to us.

This account will not let us cut mission money from our church budgets in these lean economic years. This account says that all week long, even in our individual lives, we must be on the watch for the least of these and be prepared to feed, shelter, visit, clothe, welcome, and care for the sick and imprisoned. This account asserts that God's judgment about these actions is upon us all our lives long. It holds us accountable to challenge sociopolitical systems that perpetuate the oppression of all who are in need of food, shelter, clothing, health care, and other basic necessities. This account says that this is what life in Christ, life in God's reign, looks like.

Ezekiel 34:11–16, 20–24

Ezekiel writes about judgment also. In the verses preceding our passage, God judges the shepherds of Israel for not feeding their sheep (v. 2). Then, in this day's reading, Ezekiel sets out good news for the sheep of Israel: the Lord God will search out sheep as a good shepherd would. Ezekiel heaps image upon image and makes all of us want to be the sheep who are brought in, gathered, and fed on the mountains and by the watercourses. According to Ezekiel, these sheep will be fed with good pasture in the mountain heights, they will "lie down in good grazing land," they will "feed on rich pasture" (vv. 13–15). That is not all: the passage announces that the Lord God will search out the lost, the strayed, the injured, the weak, and put them aright.

This shepherd also protects sheep from one another. The verses that follow issue a warning to all sheep, because everyone is subject to judgment in this mixed fold (vv. 17–22). Who among us has not experienced the sheep who push "with flank and shoulder," who butt the weak ones with their horns and scatter them (vv. 20–21)? Woe to those who do this. Woe to us if we are the ones who push and butt and scatter. Here the judgment is clear: it is not just judgment on the shepherds but even on the sheep that calls for our attention. As quickly as we want to blame leaders, large systems, and faceless bureaucrats for life's ills, we cannot point only at the rich and powerful, according to these verses. Even sheep are judged. Even we who are not always the leaders or the bureaucrats are judged. If we push and butt and scatter, we are judged and separated from the flock. If we, as members of the sheepfold, act selfishly and push others out of our way for a better position in life, we find ourselves judged, according to this text. If we belittle a peer out of resentment, if we gossip about a colleague out of jealousy, if we withhold a well-deserved compliment of a friend because of envy, we are the very ones who push and butt and scatter. In this sheepfold both followers and leaders are judged for actions that do not contribute to the strength and well-being of the group.

Ezekiel writes in times of corrupt leadership. He writes at a time when the exiled people are deeply acquainted with disruption and fear. Perhaps sheep brutalizing other sheep is human nature during times of duress. Perhaps it is also what happens when the pressures from bad leaders and fearful existence cause us to turn on one another. It is good news, then, that Ezekiel's words announce God's judgment in the midst of the fold. This judgment is good news, because it is God's condemnation of brutal leaders who hurt their sheep and of the sheep that ignore and injure their fellow sheep. God is keeping watch over the powerful and the less powerful and will judge any actions that harm the sheep.

Psalm 100 and Psalm 95:1–7a

These are psalms appointed to be sung after the Ezekiel reading. They beg us to join in singing: "O come, let us sing to the LORD; let us make a joyful noise to the rock of our salvation!" (95:1). And "Make a joyful noise to the LORD, all the earth. Worship the LORD with gladness; come into his presence with singing" (100:1–2). They continue the good news we find in Ezekiel's announcement that God is a shepherding God. God is an ingathering God. God is the giver of food and safety. God provides good pastureland for our sustenance and our rest. It is God's pasture (95:7). Indeed God is pasture; God is our pasture. This God, according to the words of these psalms, holds the mountains and the seas in hand, the depths and the heights (95:4). The God who gives pastureland, who is our pasture, is the one who sets all creation in its courses and keeps watchful care. This creating God is not absent, but is present as shepherd to the sheep. These psalms held alongside Ezekiel let us know that the judging God is the one with vast perspective (holding seas and mountains!) but is also the one who pays attention to the injured, the lost, the strayed, and the weak. The judgments have a purpose: to protect the goodness of the pastureland and the safety and well-being of the sheep.

Perhaps we all saw this in the reports of aid workers in Haiti in the aftermath of the earthquake in 2010. We saw sheep butting and pushing and scattering. Perhaps we also saw those with the very mind and hands of God protecting the orphans, judging the sheep, and working to give good pasture by establishing local clinics and health care, helping to build homes and schools.

Ephesians 1:15–23

As in Matthew, we find here an image of Christ enthroned. There is no judgment in this passage, but there is power. God has put Christ at the high place—at the right hand of God. Christ is all-powerful over all time, all space, and "fills all in all" (1:23). Again, there is no judgment in this passage. But it is implied: Jesus Christ is the one who reigns over every dominion, and this reign includes passing judgment on what he sees and hears. This is a hopeful claim. It is a difficult claim to believe, because we see so much news that counters this claim: large companies have resources to find legal loopholes that permit continued injury to the lands and waters in the name of progress and economy; children, elderly people, and other dependents suffer due to restrictions in health-care coverage; incessant barriers keep the poor from education and vocational advancement. The good news is that Jesus Christ, the one who reigns over every dominion, is watchful of every dominion: church, state, corporate, individual, local, and global. Everything is under his scrutiny. And he is exalted above all powers that would hurt or destroy. Even though we don't always see this, we live into this hope. Our watchfulness is shaped by the very One who has perspective from the high place; our vision is to be transformed by the One who sees all.

This passage of thanksgiving (v. 16) and prayer (v. 17) is part of the larger context that includes the entire Letter to the Ephesians and its numerous references to demonic powers (e.g., 2:2; 5:11; 6:12). It is important to see that this passage asserts Christ's exaltation (enthronement) above all powers, including those that threaten the order of things divine or human. In other words, this passage implies judgment of all powers that rebel against Christ. The end of time is even invoked: "not only in this age but also in the age to come" (1:21). The risen and exalted Christ is now ruling over all things and will at the end time rule over all things, including any hostile powers. This is what the church experiences: the exalted One who rules over all things.

The church encounters this claim in the language of songs and hymns and prayers and Scripture readings week after week. We say and sing and pray and hear these claims. And sometimes we see this ruling power of Christ with our own eyes. In one congregation it is the return of people who have been shamed and hurt by the church: they are welcomed back by someone they trust, and they return, ready to turn their pain toward intentional welcome of others who have likewise been hurt. The powers that would keep the injured ones away are thwarted, and a new beginning occurs. We encounter the ruling power of Christ in the aid poured out for Haiti and Chile, acts that happen over against bureaucratic red tape; we see it in the challenges made against unfair immigration laws, in an educational venture in Harlem. The ruling power of Christ is made manifest in those who see the world as God wills it to be and then act on that vision. The hostile powers are put down. We get glimpses of this truth. It is the work of the church to see these things "with the eyes of the heart enlightened" (v. 18) so that we may see and proclaim the ways in which hostile powers are put down.

Ephesians proclaims the power and the life of Christ our God who "fills all in all" (v, 22). Set alongside Matthew's account, this Christ is not only the One we seek to serve as we encounter the neediest ones among us and beyond us. This Christ is the One whose life enables our "love toward all the saints" (v. 15). Matthew would have us know that the saints include the most wretched ones, whether or not they are Christians. Ephesians keeps our eyes on the largest picture of all: Christ "who fills all in all." With the "eyes of the heart enlightened" we live out here and now the reign of Christ, offering right care to all the needy whom we meet. Ezekiel, aided by the Psalms, does not let us overlook how we treat those closest to us, sheep of our own fold, nor does he allow us to easily trust all leaders with their earthly power. With the eyes of our hearts enlightened we live according to God's realm.

Thanksgiving Day

Traci C. West

DEUTERONOMY 8:7–18
PSALM 65
2 CORINTHIANS 9:6–15
LUKE 17:11–19

Giving God thanks should be a countercultural activity. These Scripture passages provide guideposts for leading a faithful Christian life that challenges U.S. cultural norms of individualism, selfishness, and greed. From Deuteronomy we learn that remembering to give thanks to God counters the contemporary cultural ideal of boasting about having achieved complete economic self-sufficiency. Psalm 65 joyfully acknowledges the abundance of natural resources God has created for all people, not exclusively for our own families, neighborhoods, or nation. Popular wisdom claims that God blesses "the child who has his [or her] own." But in 2 Corinthians 9, it is not accumulation of one's own possessions but generous, communal sharing that demonstrates a Christian commitment to give thanks to God. Finally, in Luke 17, "a foreigner" who has just been healed in his encounter with Jesus is identified as a model of faith-filled thanksgiving. All of these texts startle us with their suggestions about the society-altering morality of thanksgiving.

Deuteronomy 8:7–18

This passage from Deuteronomy teaches us that the practice of giving thanks for material dimensions of our shared lives is fundamentally about remembering. When you give thanks to God for the goods you possess and have easy access to, which aspects of your routine material existence do you choose to acknowledge? Which seem too minor to include? These prayer choices reveal the depth of our awareness of what we have. A prayer of thanksgiving creates a narrative for the moral history of our economic lives. The specific elements to remember include the land beneath our feet (vv. 7–9), the water that we must drink to stay alive (v. 7), the precious minerals buried in the ground that are mined to create material comforts and possessions (v. 9), and the core ingredients of food that we rely on for nourishment (v. 8). But we are to remember that God is the source; it is God who has provided for us, not the power of our own hands (v. 17). In the idolization of economic independence in U.S. culture, one of the most virtuous declarations an individual can make is "I own my house because I worked hard to earn it." But according to Deuteronomy, any claim about attaining what we possess exclusively through our own efforts is a God-denying act or one that forgets about God (v. 14).

The political implications of giving thanks also require our scrutiny. When thanking God for clothes or food or church communities, what exactly are we attributing to God? Are we thanking God for the conditions of grossly underpaid workers who toil for inhumanely long hours to produce our clothes and shoes? Are we thanking God for allowing our fruits and vegetables to be picked by laborers who may have been forcibly exposed to toxic pesticides and housed in unsanitary, desolate barracks? When remembering to give thanks to God for our houses of worship, do we also name the historic "removal" of Indians who were probably the first occupants of "our" property? Does our narrative of gratitude for the land God has given to us for our churches and homes indicate agreement with our national leaders who believed that the hand of Providence guided the hand of the "American race"?[1] As President Andrew Jackson declared in 1830, "What good man would prefer a country covered with forests and ranged by a few thousand savages to our extensive Republic, studded with cities, towns, and prosperous farms?"[2]

Globally, too many human lives and homes have been destroyed in the name of historic claims that God has given natural resources to specific cultural groups. A sermon on this text must not become yet another occasion for theologically supported racist and ethnocentric claims that fuel such conflicts. Neither should it reinforce giving thanks for the land, water, food, or wealth that we possess because God has given it to "us," a supposed "American" race, a term that has historically referred to white U.S. Christians. Instead, this text should inspire us to repentantly name the heinous developments that have so often followed when we take possession of the natural material resources we are grateful to God for having created.

---

1. Reginald Horsman, *Race and Manifest Destiny: The Origins of American Anglo-Saxonism* (Cambridge, MA: Harvard University Press, 1981), 202.
2. Ibid.

Psalm 65

Psalm 65 offers thanksgiving by proclaiming the bounty of God's creation and celebrating its abundance. God answers our prayers (v. 2), forgives our wickedness (v. 3), and delivers the gift of salvation to us with awe-inspiring deeds in nature and human society (vv. 5–7). The resulting bounty from God's creative activity is for everyone in the world. It is intended to incite joy. This psalm reminds us that God's abundance is not solely for Christians, heterosexuals, white people, or U.S. citizens and immigrants with green cards. Evidence of God's amazing presence and generosity extends to all the earth, even parts that seem farthest away (vv. 5b, 8a). In response, God is due praise (v. 1), and not solemn, dour-faced, whispered thanks.

Psalm 65 emphasizes the capacity for happiness and joy with which all creation is endowed and which it exuberantly expresses in response to God (vv. 4, 8, 12, 13). Even "the gateways of the morning and the evening shout for joy" (v. 8b). The emphasis on universal joy provides a benchmark for recognizing authentic, justice-filled thanksgiving to God. In accord with this psalm, praising God in church fails dismally whenever we persecute, reject, or marginalize LGBTQ Christians called by God to ordained ministry as well as those asking their churches to bless their committed relationships with the same pastoral care and wedding celebrations that heterosexual members receive. It is the gravest offense to God when we express thanks for all of creation while simultaneously robbing some of God's people of the happiness and joy of fulfilling their Christian vocations and honoring their Christian covenantal relationships. Instead, Psalm 65 calls us to offer affirmative and raucous celebrations of God's vast, diverse, and generous creative activity (vv. 9–13).

2 Corinthians 9:6–15

This passage reminds us of the countercultural economic relationships of the earliest Christian communities. Voluntary sharing of one's resources for the good of the community was understood to be an expression of giving thanks to God (vv. 11, 12). Whereas Deuteronomy emphasized the need to take account of our dependence on material goods and recognize God's role as Creator, this pastoral epistle commends the act of *sharing* material goods. It offers a specific scriptural mandate from Isaiah 55:10 for Christian communities to share with the poor (2 Cor. 9:8–9).

This message from 2 Corinthians diverges from contemporary understandings of many Christians who want to share their goods only with those who are "deserving." Christian gay rights activists, for example, too often focus mainly on gaining rights that financially benefit middle-class gay, lesbian, bisexual, and transgendered persons. Unfortunately, most Christians do not feel an obligation to share resources with members of our communities who are poor and may be chronically unemployed, homeless, or formerly incarcerated. In particular, economically poor women of color who depend on public assistance to support their families are frequently subjected to shaming attitudes and controlling regulations. However, in its injunction about sharing, 2 Corinthians 9 does not include paternalistic distinctions between those who are "deserving" and "undeserving." When this passage emphasizes support for ministry as a means of giving thanks to God, it disrupts patterns of paternalism and social hierarchy. In the ancient context of this passage, "the basis of the patronage system was power and authority, so that the patron might stand to gain power and position. . . . The client became bonded to the patron out of a sense of gratitude, and the patron maintained power through further giving."[3] Therefore, in 2 Corinthians, Paul can be understood as circumventing this patronage system by making it clear that the point of giving to Christian ministry—to "the needs of the saints" (v. 12)—is to express thankfulness to God. In his multicultural work with varied Christian communities, Paul stresses a countercultural form of humility. By focusing on giving thanks to God, Paul deflates the power, status, and ambitions of the giver.

This emphasis on humility and voluntary giving (v. 8) differs from most contemporary Christian stewardship strategies. Today we are influenced by ever-present advertisements that use subtle forms of psychological coercion to convince us to give our resources to obtain products that we do not need and cannot afford and, in some cases, that harm our health. Designed by commercial marketing firms, these messages also overwhelm any sense of having "enough of everything" (v. 8). Radically departing from this kind of coercive, capitalist marketing framework (which Christian groups often mimic when fund-raising), this Scripture text commends generous communal sharing of resources without compulsion (v. 8). There is no promise of prosperity in return for sharing or any kind of special recognition as a reward, not even the publication of the giver's name on a donor list.

Luke 17:11–19

In this passage the expression of thanks for divine healing draws attention to bodily health as well as the cultural labels we attach to human bodies to justify valuing some people more than others. Jesus miraculously heals ten human beings (bodies) at once (v. 14). In recent years, there have been public debates

---

3. Sze-kar Wan, "Collection for the Saints as an Anticolonial Act: Implications of Paul's Ethnic Reconstruction," in *Paul and Politics: Ekklesia, Israel, Imperium, Interpretation*, ed. Richard A. Horsley (Harrisburg: Trinity Press International, 2000), 214.

about the right to health-care benefits for unionized state workers, company retirees, as well as the elderly who are ill and all others who depend on Medicaid programs. Many politicians, lobbyists, company executives, and segments of American voters have pushed hard for cutbacks of such health-care coverage. In contrast, the healing miracles in the Gospels demonstrate the sacred priority of healing those who are ill. In this story, the ten lepers, including a Samaritan "foreigner," are immediately healed, without regard for their cultural identity. This Gospel standard for health care directly contradicts the 2010 Patient Protection and Affordable Care Act signed into law by President Barack Obama, which denies health insurance to foreign-born members of our communities who are labeled "illegal aliens."

Giving thanks to God is an occasion for addressing the conflicts that exist between peoples with differing cultural backgrounds. Jesus was on his way to the holy city of Jerusalem when this healing miracle occurred (v. 11). He seized the thankful response of the healed Samaritan as an opportunity to compare him to others who were ungrateful and, apparently, Judean (the likely audience of Jesus). The Samaritans were an ethnoreligious community that did not believe Jerusalem was the holy place to worship God. In accord with their Samaritan traditions, they chose to worship at the foot of Mount Gerizim.

As Jesus points out, "this foreigner" was the only one "to return and give praise to God" (v. 18). The tension between the two communities is a palpable concern in this Gospel scene. Since Jesus seems to suggest that the correct place to glorify God is at his feet, this comment addresses the heart of the dispute between the two groups over the proper place to worship God. Christians today can easily celebrate the glorification of God by individuals as a means of ignoring or silencing racial and ethnic group conflicts and racist injustices in which those individuals are implicated. For instance, in the United States, when a Euro-American and a Latino jointly proclaim their individual salvation by Jesus Christ, some view this as an achievement of Christian harmony and unity as long as current racist attitudes and policies that privilege whites over stigmatized Latinos/as are not mentioned. But it is a false harmony. The surprising commendation of the Samaritan by Jesus demonstrates that individual praise and thanks of God are authentically worshipful precisely when we engage the ethnocentric tensions and racist practices that persist in our communities.

Contributors

Ronald J. Allen, *Christian Theological Seminary*

Dale P. Andrews, *The Divinity School, Vanderbilt University*

Randall C. Bailey, *Interdenominational Theological Center*

Wilma Ann Bailey, *Christian Theological Seminary*

Dianne Bergant, CSA, *Catholic Theological Union*

L. Susan Bond, *Lane College*

Alejandro F. Botta, *Boston University School of Theology*

Valerie Bridgeman, *Lancaster Theological Seminary*

Martin Brokenleg, *Vancouver School of Theology (Emeritus)*

Gennifer Benjamin Brooks, *Garrett-Evangelical Theological Seminary*

Carolynne Hitter Brown, *Southern Baptist Church, Cambridge, Massachusetts*

John M. Buchanan, *The Christian Century*

Randall K. Bush, *East Liberty Presbyterian Church, Pittsburgh, Pennsylvania*

Lee H. Butler Jr., *Chicago Theological Seminary*

Terriel R. Byrd, *School of Ministry, Palm Beach Atlantic University*

Charles L. Campbell, *The Divinity School, Duke University*

Carlos F. Cardoza-Orlandi, *Perkins School of Theology, Southern Methodist University*

Cláudio Carvalhaes, *Lutheran Theological Seminary at Philadelphia*

Diane G. Chen, *Palmer Theological Seminary, Eastern University*

Choi Hee An, *Boston University School of Theology*

Monica A. Coleman, *Claremont School of Theology*

Elizabeth Conde-Frazier, *Esperanza College, Eastern University*

Angela Cowser, *Garrett-Evangelical Theological Seminary*

Shannon Daley-Harris, *Children's Defense Fund, Washington, D.C.*

Frederick John Dalton, *Bellarmine College Preparatory School, San Jose, California*

Noelle Damico, *Presbyterian Hunger Program, Presbyterian Church (U.S.A.)*

María Teresa Dávila, *Andover Newton Theological School*

Miguel A. De La Torre, *Iliff School of Theology*

Bob Ekblad, *Tierra Nueva and The People's Seminary, Burlington, Washington*

Joseph Evans, *Mt. Carmel Baptist Church, Washington, D.C.*

Marie M. Fortune, *FaithTrust Institute, Seattle, Washington*

Safiyah Fosua, *Wesley Seminary at Indiana Wesleyan University*

David J. Frenchak, *Seminary Consortium for Urban Pastoral Education (SCUPE) (Emeritus)*

Lincoln E. Galloway, *Claremont School of Theology*

Kenyatta R. Gilbert, *The Divinity School, Howard University*

R. Mark Giuliano, *Old Stone Church, Cleveland, Ohio*

Chris Glaser, *Metropolitan Community Church, Atlanta, Georgia*

Catherine Gunsalus González, *Columbia Theological Seminary (Emerita)*

Justo L. González, *Asociación para la Educación Teológica Hispana (AETH), United Methodist Church (Retired)*

Esther J. Hamori, *Union Theological Seminary, New York*

James Henry Harris, *Samuel Dewitt Proctor School of Theology, Virginia Union University, and Second Baptist Church, Richmond, Virginia*

John Hart, *Boston University School of Theology*

Olive Elaine Hinnant, *United Church of Christ, Denver, Colorado*

Ruthanna B. Hooke, *Virginia Theological Seminary*

Bob Hunter, *Diversity Specialist, InterVarsity Christian Fellowship*

Rhashell Hunter, *Racial and Ethnic Women's Ministries, Presbyterian Church (U.S.A.)*

†Ada María Isasi-Díaz, *The Theological School, Drew University (Emerita)*

Joseph R. Jeter Jr., *Brite Divinity School (Emeritus)*

Pablo A. Jiménez, *Vega Alta Christian Church, Vega Alta, Puerto Rico, and Chalice Press*

Nicole L. Johnson, *University of Mount Union*

Song Bok Jon, *Boston University School of Theology*

Nyasha Junior, *Howard University School of Divinity*

John Kaltner, *Rhodes College*

Grace Ji-Sun Kim, *Moravian Theological Seminary*

Simone Sunghae Kim, *Yonsei University, South Korea*

Jennifer L. Lord, *Austin Presbyterian Theological Seminary*

Barbara K. Lundblad, *Union Theological Seminary, New York*

Fumitaka Matsuoka, *Pacific School of Religion (Emeritus)*

John S. McClure, *The Divinity School, Vanderbilt University*

James L. McDonald, *San Francisco Theological Seminary*

Alyce M. McKenzie, *Perkins School of Theology, Southern Methodist University*

Marvin A. McMickle, *Colgate Rochester Crozer Divinity School*

Henry H. Mitchell, *Interdenominational Theological Center (Emeritus)*

Mary Alice Mulligan, *Christian Theological Seminary*

Ched Myers, *Bartimaeus Cooperative Ministries, Oak View, California*

Dawn Ottoni-Wilhelm, *Bethany Theological Seminary*

Peter J. Paris, *Princeton Theological Seminary (Emeritus)*

Rebecca Todd Peters, *Elon University*

Luke A. Powery, *Duke University*

Melinda A. Quivik, *Liturgical Scholar, Houghton, Michigan*

Stephen G. Ray Jr., *Garrett-Evangelical Theological Seminary*

Sharon H. Ringe, *Wesley Theological Seminary*

Joni S. Sancken, *Eastern Mennonite Seminary, Eastern Mennonite University*

Elizabeth J. A. Siwo-Okundi, *Boston University School of Theology*

Chandra Taylor Smith, *The Pell Institute, Washington, D.C.*

Christine Marie Smith, *United Theological Seminary of the Twin Cities*

Kee Boem So, *New York Presbyterian Theological Seminary (Korean Presbyterian Church Abroad)*

Amy E. Steele, *The Divinity School, Vanderbilt University*

Teresa Lockhart Stricklen, *Office of Theology and Worship, Presbyterian Church (U.S.A.)*

Marjorie Hewitt Suchocki, *Claremont School of Theology (Emerita)*

Willard Swartley, *Associated Mennonite Biblical Seminary (Emeritus)*

JoAnne Marie Terrell, *Chicago Theological Seminary*

Leonora Tubbs Tisdale, *The Divinity School, Yale University*

Jeffery L. Tribble Sr., *Columbia Theological Seminary*

†Arthur Van Seters, *Knox College (Emeritus)*

Traci C. West, *The Theological School, Drew University*

Edward L. Wheeler, *Christian Theological Seminary (Emeritus)*

Clark M. Williamson, *Christian Theological Seminary (Emeritus)*

Scott C. Williamson, *Louisville Presbyterian Theological Seminary*

Sunggu Yang, *The Divinity School, Vanderbilt University*

Scripture Index

505